# MANAGEMENT AND ORGANIZATIONAL BEHAVIOR CLASSICS

# MANAGEMENT AND ORGANIZATIONAL BEHAVIOR CLASSICS

*Fourth Edition*

*Edited by*

## MICHAEL T. MATTESON
*Professor of Organizational Behavior and Management*
*University of Houston*

## JOHN M. IVANCEVICH
*Cullen Chair*
*and*
*Professor of Organizational Behavior and Management*
*University of Houston*

1989

Homewood, Illinois 60430

**Cover design:** Interface Studio

The previous editions of this book were published under the title *Management Classics.*

**Sponsoring editor:** William R. Bayer
**Project editor:** Ethel Shiell
**Production manager:** Bette Ittersagen
**Compositor:** Carlisle Communications, Ltd.
**Typeface:** 10/12 Century Schoolbook
**Printer:** Malloy Lithographing, Inc.

**LIBRARY OF CONGRESS**
**Library of Congress Cataloging-in-Publication Data**

Management and organizational behavior classics / edited by Michael T.
   Matteson, John M. Ivancevich. —4th ed.
      p.   cm.
   Rev. ed. of: Management classics. 3rd ed. 1986.
   Includes bibliographies and index.
   ISBN 0-256-06895-X (pbk.)
   1. Management.  2. Industrial management.  3. Organizational
behavior.  I. Matteson, Michael T.  II. Ivancevich, John M.
III.  Management classics.
HD31.M2917 1989
658—dc19                                                      88—6403
                                                                CIP

*Printed in the United States of America*

   5 6 7 8 9 0 ML 5 4 3 2 1

# Preface

The practice of management is as old as humankind. Throughout time, people have joined with others to accomplish goals, first in families, later in tribes, and still later in more sophisticated political and organizational units. Ancient peoples transported entire nations across great distances; pyramids, temples, shrines, ships, and cities were constructed; systems of government, farming, and commerce were created; wars were waged against other tribes and nation-states. These elaborate social endeavors were undertaken through the use of management techniques and processes. Despite the use of management procedures by our forebears, virtually no attempts were made to accumulate and synthesize knowledge of management practice. What knowledge that did exist was passed along between tribal leaders or parents and offspring or was learned through experience.

The principal objective of the three previous editions of this book of readings was to provide the reader with what the editors believed were classics in the field of management—writings that have had a demonstrated and continuing impact on the development of management thought and practice. In this, the fourth edition, we have expanded that focus beyond the classical management processes, which provided the framework for the earlier editions, and included organizational behavior topics as well. It is becoming increasingly difficult (if not impossible) to separate the topics of *management* and *organizational behavior*, whether one is a practitioner, student, or teacher.

Thus, the primary objective of this fourth edition is to make available to the reader the outstanding contributions to the management *and* organizational behavior literature. Attainment of this objective is facilitated by three major subgoals of the book. First, an anthology of management and organizational behavior must *include the works of recognized, respected, and pioneer scholars in the field.* The list of contributors is a veritable who's who of management and organizational behavior. Second, the readings should *broaden the understanding of management and organizational behavior* that the reader receives from studying textbooks in the field. A guide to using this book as a supplement in both management and organizational behavior courses is presented in the Cross-Reference Guide beginning on page xi. Indexed by topic, this guide presents a readings selection for virtually all major topic areas typically covered in either management or organizational behavior courses. Finally, the readings, many written years ago, need to *have relevance for contemporary managers and students* who spend much of their time working in, learning about, coping with, and shaping organizations.

The importance and diversity of management and organizational behavior as fields of inquiry necessitates a book of readings such as this. The complexity and dynamic nature of these fields stems in part from the variety of disciplines from which they borrow principles, procedures, and models; economics, sociology, statistics, mathematics, engineering, and psychology are several of the contributing disciplines. Not surprisingly, this diversity of background produces different interpretations of organizations and employee dimensions with which managers must deal daily. The practicing manager is consequently faced with sorting out these differences and, hopefully, reaching some point where enlightened and successful practice can be initiated.

Some readers, understandably, might ask why a book composed of "classics" needs to undergo periodic revision. There are a number of reasons. In every edition, we have been forced to make choices among many excellent articles. Not every article meeting the criteria of being a classic could be included in previous editions. In this edition we have included several articles which, were it not for space limitations, would have appeared in earlier editions.

Second, it has been a dozen years since the first edition of *Management Classics*. In the intervening time, the range of selections that could be considered "classic" has increased.

Finally, and perhaps most importantly, feedback from users of previous editions has played a significant role in shaping this edition. It was this kind of feedback that played a major role in the decision to include organizational behavior topics in this edition. The ultimate test of any book is how useful it is. Using your feedback, we have revised this edition to make it an even more effective and useful tool.

This edition is organized into five sections, with editorial comments for each section. We have prepared these comments so the section is clearly introduced and the reader understands the management process or organizational behavior topic that will be covered. Additional comments introduce each reading selection and provide an introduction to that selection. Part One includes six articles that discuss traditional, behavioral, and systems approaches to understanding management and organizational behavior. Part Two contains nine articles that address three classical management processes: planning, organizing, and controlling. In Part Three, four articles focus on individual behavior, while in Part Four the same number of readings emphasize group behavior topics. Finally, Part Five contains 16 articles on managing organizational behavior; these are evenly divided between the topics of leadership, motivation, decision making, and organizational development.

This edition of *Management and Organizational Behavior Classics* could not have been compiled without the contribution of the writers of the articles to the fields of management and organizational behavior. To each of these writers, and to their publishers, we extend sincere thanks for permission to publish the articles in this book anthology. Finally, we wish to thank all the users of the three previous editions who gave us the benefit of their experiences. We hope you find this edition continues and improves upon the usefulness of the earlier volumes.

*Michael T. Matteson*
*John M. Ivancevich*

## CONTRIBUTORS

Robert C. Albrook
Chris Argyris
C. West Churchman
L. L. Cummings
Peter F. Drucker
Amitai Etzioni
Henri Fayol
Daniel C. Feldman
Fred E. Fiedler
Mary Parker Follett
Wendell French
John W. Gardner
Frank B. Gilbreth
Lillian M. Gilbreth
J. Richard Hackman
Frederick Herzberg
George C. Homans
Irving Janis
Robert Janson
Robert L. Kahn
Fremont E. Kast
Steven Kerr
Harold Koontz

Edward E. Lawler III
Rensis Likert
David C. McClelland
Douglas M. McGregor
Norman R. F. Maier
Abraham H. Maslow
Fred Massarik
Henry Mintzberg
Greg Oldham
C. Northcote Parkinson
Jeffrey Pfeffer
Kenneth Purdy
James E. Rosenzweig
Harold Rush
Warren H. Schmidt
William G. Scott
Stanley E. Seashore
Herbert A. Simon
George A. Steiner
Robert Tannenbaum
Frederick W. Taylor
Max Weber

# Contents

Kathy
Bob
Ellen
Carol
11/7/92
10-12

# Cross-Reference Guide

The purpose of this cross-reference guide is to match a variety of topical areas in management and organizational behavior with the articles in this text. Since the content of the articles makes them suitable for use in principles of management courses, as well as in organizational behavior courses, articles have been cross-referenced with topics typically found in both courses. Reference to this guide should greatly facilitate course and reading assignment planning.

# PART ONE

# Foundations for Understanding Management and Organizational Behavior

There is continued debate about whether management and organizational behavior theories are or are not useful. First, it is difficult to isolate any particular set of principles or models in "pure" form from various modifications and efforts to translate those principles into practice. Second, particular principles of management and organizational behavior are interpreted differently by various individuals, and the result is often confusion and misunderstanding. Third, the major schools of thought in management and organizational behavior house people with differing backgrounds, values, and experiences. These differences create some conflict among the disciples of management and organizational behavior theory, which is manifested by their turning a deaf ear on ideas, propositions, and principles proposed by individuals outside their particular orientation. The classicist ignores the behavioralist, the field researcher ignores the laboratory researcher, and the academic ignores the practitioner. All of which delays our efforts to understand what is going on in organizations and what we can do to improve organizational efficiency and effectiveness.

Each of the major schools of management thought, along with the contributions made by organizational behavior research, has provided the following positive contributions:

- Knowledge that can be used by practicing managers.
- The translation of knowledge so it can be used by managers.
- Propositions and hypotheses that can be used scientifically to research managerial and organizational behavior processes, functions, and theories.
- Adding to the already existing theories, models, and techniques that serve as the foundation for theorists, researchers, and managers.

- Terminology that has been used to understand what managers do.

These positive contributions should suggest that a variety of approaches need to be thoroughly examined when attempting to comprehend the workings of living human organizations.

The pioneers of management thought and organizational behavior, such as Fayol, Follet, Taylor, Homans, Likert, and Argyris, intended their ideas about the processes of management to be a cumulative body of knowledge. For example, Fayol argued that, because of their widespread value and applicability, management concepts should be taught in universities. The long-range goal of a cumulative body of knowledge in management and organizational behavior has not yet been achieved. Instead, what we find are different approaches, principles, models, and theories. In this first section of *Management and Organizational Behavior Classics* we have purposely included articles of such pioneers as Taylor and Follet, as well as more contemporary contributors. In this and later sections we will include articles that are associated with a variety of orientations to management and organizational behavior. As you will see, these different orientations are seldom mutually exclusive; rather, in many ways they draw from and build upon one another, with each contributing to the goal of a meaningful cumulative body of knowledge.

# 1

# What Is Scientific Management?

*Frederick W. Taylor*

*In this excerpt from Congressional testimony, the "Father of Scientific Management" explains the true nature of scientific management and the mental revolution it involves. From this selection we see it is far more than a simple efficiency process or time saving device; rather it is a mental attitude which must permeate an organization.—Eds.*

Scientific management is not any efficiency device, not a device of any kind for securing efficiency; nor is any bunch or group of efficiency devices. It is not a new system of figuring costs; it is not a new scheme of paying men; it is not a piecework system; it is not a bonus system; it is not a premium system; it is no scheme for paying men; it is not holding a stop watch on a man and writing things down about him; it is not time study; it is not motion study nor an analysis of the movements of men; it is not the printing and ruling and unloading of a ton or two of blanks on a set of men and saying, "Here's your system; go use it." It is not divided foremanship or functional foremanship; it is not any of the devices which the average man calls to mind when scientific management is spoken of. The average man thinks of one or more of these things when he hears the words "scientific management" mentioned, but scientific management is not any of these devices. I am not sneering at cost-keeping systems, at time study, at functional foremanship, nor at any new and improved scheme of paying men, nor at any efficiency devices, if they are really devices that make for efficiency. I believe in them; but what I am emphasizing is that these devices in

SOURCE: Excerpt from testimony of Frederick W. Taylor at hearings before the Special Committee of the House of Representatives to Investigate Taylor and Other Systems of Shop Management, January 25, 1912, pp. 1387–89.

whole or in part are not scientific management; they are useful adjuncts to scientific management, so are they also useful adjuncts of other systems of management.

Now, in its essence, scientific management involves a complete mental revolution on the part of the workingman engaged in any particular establishment or industry—a complete mental revolution on the part of these men as to their duties toward their work, toward their fellow men, and toward their employees. And it involves the equally complete mental revolution on the part of those on the management's side—the foreman, the superintendent, the owner of the business, the board of directors—a complete mental revolution on their part as to their duties toward their fellow workers in the management, toward their workmen, and toward all of their daily problems. And without this complete mental revolution on both sides scientific management does not exist.

That is the essence of scientific management, this great mental revolution. Now, later on, I want to show you more clearly what I mean by this great mental revolution. I know that it perhaps sounds to you like nothing but bluff—like buncombe—but I am going to try and make clear to you just what this great mental revolution involves, for it does involve an immense change in the minds and attitude of both sides, and the greater part of what I shall say today has relation to the bringing about of this great mental revolution. So that whether the details may be interesting or uninteresting, what I hope you will see is that this great change in attitude and viewpoint must produce results which are magnificent for both sides, just as fine for one as for the other. Now, perhaps I can make clear to you at once one of the very great changes in outlook which come to the workmen, on the one hand, and to those in the management on the other hand.

I think it is safe to say that in the past a great part of the thought and interest both of the men, on the side of the management, and of those on the side of the workmen in manufacturing establishments has been centered upon what may be called the proper division of the surplus resulting from their joint efforts, between the management on the one hand, and the workmen on the other hand. The management have been looking for as large a profit as possible for themselves, and the workmen have been looking for as large wages as possible for themselves, and that is what I mean by the division of the surplus. Now, this question of the division of the surplus is a very plain and simple one (for I am announcing no great fact in political economy or anything of that sort). Each article produced in the establishment has its definite selling price. Into the manufacture of this article have gone certain expenses, namely, the cost of materials, the expenses connected with selling it, and certain indirect expenses, such as the rent of the building, taxes, insurance, light and power, maintenance of machinery, interest on the plant, etc. Now, if we deduct these several expenses from the selling price, what is left over may be called the surplus. And out of this surplus comes the profit to the manufacturer on the one hand, and the wages of the workmen on the other hand. And it is largely upon the division of this surplus that the attention of the workmen and of the management has been centered in the past. Each side has had its eye upon this surplus, the working man wanting as large a share in the form of wages as he could get, and the management wanting as large a share in the form of profits as it could get; I think I am safe in saying that in the past it has been in the division of this surplus that the great labor troubles have come between employers and employees.

Frequently, when the management have found the selling price going down they have turned toward a cut in the wages—toward reducing the workman's share of the surplus—as their way of getting out whole, of preserving their profits intact. While the workman (and you can hardly blame him) rarely feels willing to relinquish a dollar of his wages, even in dull times, he wants to keep all that he has had in the past, and when busy times come again very naturally he wants to get more. Thus it is over this division of the surplus that most of the troubles have arisen; in the extreme cases this has been the cause of serious disagreements and strikes. Gradually the two sides have come to look upon one another as antagonists, and at times even as enemies—pulling apart and matching the strength of the one against the strength of the other.

The great revolution that takes place in the mental attitude of the two parties under scientific management is that both sides take their eyes off of the division of the surplus as the all-important matter, and together turn their attention toward increasing the size of the surplus until this surplus becomes so large that it is unnecessary to quarrel over how it shall be divided. They come to see that when they stop pulling against one another, and instead both turn and push shoulder to shoulder in the same direction, the size of the surplus created by their joint efforts is truly astounding. They both realize that when they substitute friendly cooperation and mutual helpfulness for antagonism and strife they are together able to make this surplus so enormously greater than it was in the past that there is ample room for a large increase in wages for the workmen and an equally great increase in profits for the manufacturer. This, gentlemen, is the beginning of the great mental revolution which constitutes the first step toward scientific management. It is along this line of complete change in the mental attitude of both sides; of the substitution of peace for war; the substitution of hearty brotherly cooperation for contention and strife;

of both pulling hard in the same direction instead of pulling apart; of replacing suspicious watchfulness with mutual confidence; of becoming friends instead of enemies; it is along this line, I say, that scientific management must be developed.

The substitution of this new outlook—this new viewpoint—is of the very essence of scientific management, and scientific management exists nowhere until after this has become the central idea of both sides; until this new idea of cooperation and peace has been substituted for the old idea of discord and war.

This change in the mental attitude of both sides toward the "surplus" is only a part of the great mental revolution which occurs under scientific management. I will later point out other elements of this mental revolution. There is, however, one more change in viewpoint which is absolutely essential to the existence of scientific management. Both sides must recognize as essential the substitution of exact scientific investigation and knowledge for the old individual judgment or opinion, either of the workman or the boss, in all matters relating to the work done in the establishment. And this applies both as to the methods to be employed in doing the work and the time in which each job should be done.

Scientific management cannot be said to exist, then, in any establishment until after this change has taken place in the mental attitude of both the management and the men, both as to their duty to cooperate in producing the largest possible surplus and as to the necessity for substituting exact scientific knowledge for opinions or the old rule of thumb or individual knowledge.

These are the two absolutely essential elements of scientific management.

# 2

# Management as a Profession

*Mary Parker Follett*

*In this article, Mary Follett, whose philosophy was that any productive organization must give recognition to the human element, argues for the professionalism of management and for the need for managers to prepare themselves as seriously for the profession of management as for any other. Written over 60 years ago, its contents are as timely today as if they were written yesterday.*—Eds.

The word "profession" connotes for most people a foundation of *science* and a motive of *service*. That is, a profession is said to rest on the basis of a proved body of knowledge, and such knowledge is supposed to be used in the service of others rather than merely for one's own purposes. Let us tonight ask ourselves two questions: (1) How far does business management rest on scientific foundations? (2) What are the next steps to be taken in order that business management shall become more scientific?

## PRESENT SIGNS OF A SCIENTIFIC BASIS FOR BUSINESS MANAGEMENT

We have many indications that scientific method is being more and more applied to business management. First, of course, is the development of so-called "scientific management" which, after its early stages, began to concern itself with the technique of management as well as with the technique of operating.

Secondly, there is the increasing tendency toward specialized, or what is being called functionalized, management. Functionalized man-

SOURCE: Reprinted from Chapter IV of *Business Management as a Profession,* edited by Henry C. Metcalf (Chicago: A. W. Shaw Company, 1927), pp. 73–87, by permission of McGraw-Hill Book Company.

agement has, indeed, not yet been carried far. In some cases the only sign we see of it, beyond the recognition that different departments require different kinds of knowledge, different kinds of ability, is the employing of experts for special problems. In other cases a further step is taken and a planning department is created; but the powers given to planning departments vary greatly from plant to plant—some take up only occasional problems as they are asked, some are only advisory bodies. Yet in most plants the functionalization of management is a process which in one way or another has gained a good deal of ground recently. That is, the fact is very generally accepted that different types of problems require different bodies of knowledge.

In the third place, arbitrary authority is diminishing, surely an indication that more value is being put on scientific method. The tendency today is to vest authority in the person who has most knowledge of the matter in question and most skill in applying that knowledge. Hiring, for instance, is now based on certain principles and special knowledge. The job of hiring is given to those who have that knowledge. It is not assumed by someone by virtue of a certain position.

Perhaps nowhere do we see more clearly the advance of business management toward becoming a profession than in our conception of the requirements of the administrative head. It would be interesting to take some firm and note how one duty after another has in recent years passed from the president to various experts, down to that most recent addition to many businesses, the economic adviser. One president, of whom I inquired what he thought exactly his job to be, said to me: "I can't define my job in terms of specific duties because I can't tell what special duty which I have today may be given at any moment to someone better able than I to handle it." One of the interesting things about that remark (there are several) is that he recognized that someone might handle some of his duties better than he could; and yet he is an exceedingly able man. He saw that some particular task might develop a special technique and that men might be trained as experts in that technique.

The stereotype of the successful businessman is indeed changing. The image of the masterful man carrying all before him by the sheer force of his personality has largely disappeared. One good result of this is that we now consider that executive leadership can in part (remember, I say only "in part") be learned. Sheldon calls executive leadership "an intangible capacity." I do not wholly agree. Someone else says it is "beyond human calculation." There are many things, we hope, which have not yet been calculated which are not beyond calculation. I think that one of the hopes for business management lies in the fact that executive leadership is capable of analysis and that men can be trained to occupy such positions. I do not, of course, mean every man; but not every man can become a doctor or an architect. I mean that for business management, exactly as for other professions, training is gaining in importance over mere personality. I know a man who told me 10 or 15 years ago that he relied on his personality in business dealings. He has not made a success of his business. It was once thought that the executive's work rested largely on "hunch," and his subordinates' on obeying—no science in either case. The administrative head who relies first on the magic shortcut of "hunch," and secondly on his adroitness or masterfulness in getting others to accept his "hunch," is, I believe, about to be superseded by a man of different type.

Can you not remember the picture we used to have of the man in the swivel chair? A trembling subordinate enters, states his problem; snap goes the decision from the chair. This man disappears only for another to enter. And so it goes. The massive brain in the swivel chair all day communicates to his followers his special knowledge. An excellent plan if—there seem to be too many if's in the way! And so we resort to the humbler method of scientific research, the method of all the professions.

But with this agreed to, there is another misconception in regard to the administrative head. Many writers speak as if he were only the glue to hold together all these departments and functions of our big modern plants. As the need of coordination is daily and hourly felt in these vast, complex organizations, it is said that the president must do the coordinating. True; but I think that coordination is very different from matching up the pieces of a picture puzzle, to change our metaphor. Later, I am going to say just what I think it is; but let me say now that those of us who think of the administrative head as more than a mere coordinator and those of us who think that administrative decisions should rest on more than "hunch" (although "hunch," too, is important) are thinking of scientific foundations for business management.

A significant indication of the different type of management required today is the fact that managers are somewhat less inclined to justify their behavior by a claim of abstract "rights." An employer used to say, "I have a right to treat my men so and so." Or, "My behavior in this matter is perfectly reasonable." Today there are many who are more inclined to say: "If I treat my men so and so, how will they behave? *Why* will they behave in that way?" It takes far more science to understand human beings—and their "rights"—than to proclaim loudly our own rights and reasonableness.

We have a very interesting indication of the new demand made upon management in the fact that the idea, which is everywhere gaining ground, that we may have greater conscious control of our lives is seen in the business world most significantly. For example, those fatalistic rhythms, business cycles, are now considered susceptible to study, not as mysteries wholly beyond the comprehension of man. Again, take unemployment. Consider the steel industry. There you have an imperishable commodity. Moreover, you can calculate pretty well the demand. And you have rather permanently located firms and mills. There seems no reason, therefore, why the steel industry should not eventually be stabilized. Every time we take a problem out of the unsolvable class and put it into the solvable, and work at it as such, we are helping to put business management on a scientific basis. Mr. John Maynard Keynes, in an address last summer, spoke of the three great epochs of history described by Dr. John R. Commons,[1] and stated his belief that we are on the threshold of the third of those epochs. The first of these was the era of scarcity, which came to an end in about the fifteenth century. Next came the era of abundance, the dominating idea of which was the doctrine of laissez faire. Finally, there has come the era of stabilization upon which we are now entering and in which the doctrine of laissez faire must be abandoned in favor of deliberate, conscious control of economic forces for the sake of the general social good.

Many people today think of business not as a game of chance, not as a speculative enterprise depending on rising and falling markets, but as largely controllable. The mysteriousness of business is in fact disappearing as knowledge in regard to business methods steadily increases.

This is seen in the increased sense of responsibility for failure. You know the old excuses if a business failed or was not getting on well: the hard terms of bankers, the unscrupulousness of competitors, the abominable behavior of trade unions. I think that today there is less inclination to take refuge in such excuses; that there is a tendency to seek the difficulty in the running of the business. There is greater frankness in facing difficulties and a keener zest in overcoming them. You know, perhaps, the story of little Mary who was naughty and was told by her mother to go into the next room and ask God to forgive her. When she came back her mother said, "Did you do what I told you to?" And received the reply, "Yes, I did; and God said, 'Mercy me, little Mary, I know heaps worse'n you.'" Many an employer takes this attitude, but their numbers are diminishing.

Moreover, many of the points disputed with trade unions, many points which both sides have thought to be legitimate fighting issues, are now considered problems which we should try to solve. To increase wages without increasing price is sometimes a solvable problem. Wherever thinking takes the place of fighting, we have a striking indication that management is coming to rest on scientific foundations. In international relations—but I have only to mention that term for you to see the analogy, for you to see the barbarous stage we are yet in, in international relations. Businessmen have the chance to lead the world in substituting thinking for fighting. And businessmen are thinking. One of the things I have been most struck with in the last four or five years has been the vitality of the thinking of businessmen. I said last winter to a professor of philosophy, "Do you realize that you philosophers have got to look to your laurels, that businessmen are doing some very valuable thinking and may get ahead of you?" And he acknowledged this fully and generously, which I thought was a significant concession.

Finally, management, not bankers nor stockholders, is now seen to be the fundamental element in industry. It is good management that draws credit, that draws workers, that draws customers. Moreover, whatever changes come, whether industry is owned by individual capitalists or by the state or by the workers, it will always have to be managed. Management is a permanent function of business.

There are many circumstances, let us note in concluding the first part of this talk, which are impelling us toward a truly scientific management: (1) efficient management has to take the place of that exploitation of our natural resources whose day is now nearly over; (2) keener competition; (3) scarcity of labor; (4) a broader conception of the ethics of human relations; (5) the growing idea of business as a public service which carries with it a sense of responsibility for its efficient conduct.

## WHAT ARE THE NEXT STEPS TOWARD MAKING BUSINESS MANAGEMENT MORE SCIENTIFIC?

Recognizing that business management is every day coming more and more to rest on scientific foundations, what has it yet to do? First, the scientific standard must be applied to the whole of business management; it is now often applied to only one part. Business management includes: (1) on the technical side, as it is usually called, a knowledge of production and distribution, and (2) on the personnel side, a knowledge of how to deal fairly and fruitfully with one's fellows. While the first has been recognized as a matter capable of being taught, the latter has been often thought to be a gift which some men possess and some do not. That is, one part of business management rested on science; the other part, it was thought, never could. Oliver Sheldon says: "Broadly, management is concerned with two primary elements—things and men. The former element is susceptible to scientific treatment, the latter is not."[2] And again: "Where human beings are concerned, scientific principles may be so much waste paper."[3] If we believed that, we should not be here tonight in a Bureau of Personnel Administration.

Let us take that statement—that human relations are not susceptible of scientific treatment—and ask what scientific treatment is. Science has been defined as "knowledge gained by systematic observation, experiment, and reasoning; knowledge coordinated, arranged, and systematized." Can we not accumulate in regard to human relations knowledge gained by systematic observation, experiment, and reasoning? Can we not coordinate, arrange, and systematize that knowledge? I think we can.

Sheldon says further: "There may be a science of costing, of transportation, of operation, but there can be no science of cooperation."[4] The reason we are here studying human relations in industry is that we believe there can be a science of cooperation. By this I mean that cooperation is not, and this I insist on, merely a matter of good intentions, of kindly feeling. It must be based on these, but you cannot have successful cooperation until you have worked out the methods of cooperation—by experiment after experiment, by a comparing of experiments, by a pooling of results. . . . It is my plea above everything else that we learn *how* to cooperate. Of course, one may have a special aptitude for dealing with men as others may have for dealing with machines, but there is as much to learn in the one case as in the other.

In all our study of personnel work, however, we should remember that we can never wholly separate the human and the mechanical problem. This would seem too obvious to mention if we did not so often see that separation made. Go back to that sentence of Sheldon's: "There may be a science of costing, of transportation, of operation, but there can be no science of cooperation." But take Sheldon's own illustration, that of transportation. The engineering part of transportation is not the larger part. Please note that I do not say it is a small part. It is a large part, and it is the dramatic part, and it is the part we have done well, and yet the chief part of transportation is the personal thing. Everyone knows that the main difficulty about transportation is that there have not always been sensible working arrangements between the men concerned. But you all see every day that the study of human relations in business and the study of technique of operating are bound up together. You know that the way the worker is treated affects output. You know that the routing of materials and the maintenance of machines is a matter partly of human relations. You know, I hope, that there is danger in "putting in" personnel work if it is superadded instead of being woven through the plant. You remember the man who wanted to know something about Chinese metaphysics and so looked up China in the encyclopedia and then metaphysics, and put them together. We shall not have much better success if we try merely to add personnel work. Even although there is, as I certainly believe there should be, a special personnel department run by a trained expert, yet it seems to me that every executive should make some study of personnel work a part of that broad foundation which is today increasingly felt to be necessary for the businessman.

If, then, one of the first things to be done to make business management more scientific is to apply scientific methods to those problems of management which involve human relations, another requirement is that we should make an analysis of managers' jobs somewhat corresponding to the analysis of workers' jobs in the Taylor system. We need to get away from tradition, prejudice, stereotypes, guesswork, and find the factual basis for managerial jobs. We know, for instance, what has been accomplished in elimination of waste by scientific methods of research and experiment applied to operating, to probable demand for commodities, and so on. I believe that this has to be carried further, and that managerial waste, administrative waste, should be given the same research and experiment. How this can be done, I shall take up later.

The next step business management should take is to organize the body of knowledge on which it should rest. We have defined science as an organized body of exact knowledge. That is, scientific method consists of two parts: (1) research, and (2) the organization of the knowledge obtained by research. The importance of research, of continued research, receives every year fuller and fuller appreciation from businessmen; but methods of organizing the results of such research have not kept pace with this appreciation. While business management is collecting more and more exact knowledge, while it is observing more keenly, experimenting more widely, it has not yet gone far in organizing this knowledge. We have drawn a good many conclusions, have thought out certain principles, but have not always seen the relation between these conclusions or these principles.

I have not time to speak here of more than one way of organizing in industrial plants our accumulating knowledge in regard to executive technique. There should be, I think, in every plant, an official, one of whose duties should be to classify and interpret managerial experience with the aid of the carefully kept records which should be required of every executive. From such classification and interpretation of experience—this experience which in essentials repeats itself so often from time to time, from department to department, from plant to plant—it would be possible to draw useful conclusions. The importance of this procedure becomes more obvious when we remember that having experience and profiting by experience are two different matters. Experience may leave us with mistaken notions, with prejudice or suspicion.

A serious drawback to a fuller understanding of and utilization of executive experience is that we have at present (1) no systematic follow-up of decisions, of new methods, of experiments in managing;

and (2) no carefully worked out system of recording. Poorly kept records, or the absence of any systematic recording, are partly responsible for what seems in some plants like a stagnant management, and in all plants for certain leaks in management. For instance, the fact that we have no follow-up for executive decisions with a comparing of results—a procedure necessary before business management can be considered fully on a scientific basis—is partly a deficiency in recording. The fact that an executive, if he wishes to introduce a certain method (not in operating but in management itself), cannot find in any records whether that method has been tried before or anything like it, and what the results have been, is a serious deficiency in recording. If an executive is facing a certain problem, he should be able to find out: (1) whether other executives have had to meet similar problems, (2) how they met them, (3) what the results were. It seems to me very unfortunate that it is possible for one man to say to another, as I heard someone say at the suggestion of a new method, "I believe our department tried that a few years ago, but I've forgotten what we thought of it."

I have heard it said that the Harvard football team was put on its feet when Percy Haughton introduced the system of recording football experience. After that, if someone thought he had a brilliant idea that such and such a play could be tried on Yale, the first thing done was to examine the records; and it might be found that that play had been tried two years before and failed. It might even be discovered why it had failed. This system of recording—I believe it already existed at Yale—was Mr. Haughton's great contribution to Harvard football. Because of it, the team could not, at any rate, go on making the *same* mistakes.

The recording of executive experiences, which will probably need a technique somewhat different from that used for the rest of business recording, should have, I think, our immediate attention. The system of both recording and reporting should be such that records and reports can be quickly mastered, and thus be practically useful to all, instead of buried underneath their own verbiage, length, and lack of systematization. And there should be required, from every executive, training in the technique of keeping records and making reports.

But we need more than records. We need a new journal, or a new department in some present journal; we need sifted bibliographies of reports; ways of getting information from other parts of the country, from other countries; above all, we need executive conferences with carefully worked out methods for comparing experience which has been scientifically recorded, analyzed, and organized. When many different plants are willing to share with one another the results of their experience, then we shall have business policies based on wider data than those of the present.

The Graduate School of Business Administration and the Bureau of Business Research of Harvard University are now collecting cases of business policy, thus opening the way for classifying and cross-indexing. Harvard has, of course, been able to get hold of a very small number of cases, but this seems to be a valuable and significant undertaking.

I have been interested also in what a certain recent committee, with representatives from various firms, deliberately stated as its object: "the comparison of experience." I should like to know how frank and full their exchange of experience was; but any attempt of this kind is interesting, indicating, as it does, the attitude on the part of those participating that they expect to gain more by working together than they will lose (the old idea) by allowing other firms to gain any intimate knowledge of their affairs.

Moreover, not only should we analyze and compare our experience, but we should deliberately experiment. We should make experiments, observe experiments, compare and discuss these with each other, and see what consensus we can come to in our conclusions. For this we should be wholly frank with one another. If we have the scientific attitude toward our work, we shall be willing to tell our failures. I heard of a man who made an ice machine which did not work, and the following conversation took place between him and a friend he met:

*Friend:*

   I was sorry to hear your experiment was a failure!

*Man:*

   Who told you it was a failure?

*Friend:*

   Why, I heard your ice machine wouldn't work.

*Man:*

   Oh, that was true enough, but it was a great success as an experiment. You can learn as much from your failures as from your successes.

From such experimenting and from the comparison of experience, I think certain standards would emerge. But we should remember that, as no Taylorite thinks there is anything final in "standardization," so we should not aim at a static standardization of managerial method, executive technique. We should make use of all available present experience, knowing that experience and our learning from it should be equally continuous matters.

If science gives us research and experimentation as its two chief methods, it at the same time shows us that nothing is too small to claim our attention. There is nothing unimportant in business procedure. For instance, I spoke above of record keeping. I know a firm where they tell me that they are not getting nearly so much advantage as they should from their records because they have not yet worked out a system of cross-indexing. Yet to some, cross-indexing may not seem to be of great importance. I know a man who says frequently about this detail or that, "Oh, that doesn't matter." Everything matters to the scientist. The following incident seems to me to have some significance. I told a man that I was working at the technique of the business interview, at which he seemed rather amused and said, "I guess most businessmen know how to conduct interviews." It was evident that he thought he did—but he is a man who has never risen above a small position. Later, I said the same thing to a clever man in a good position, a New York man, by the way. I said it a little hesitatingly, for I thought he too might consider it beneath his notice, but he was much interested and asked if he might see my paper when finished.

I have spoken of the classification of experience, the organizing of knowledge, as one of the necessary preliminaries to putting business management on a scientific basis. This organized body of knowledge tends at first to remain in the hands of a few. Measures should be taken to make it accessible to the whole managerial force. There should be opportunities for the training of executives through talks, suggested readings (including journals on management), through wisely led discussion groups and conferences, through managers' associations, foremen's associations, and the like. The organized knowledge of managerial methods which many of the higher officials possess should spread to the lower executives. In some cases, the higher official does not even think of this as part of his responsibility. He will say to a subordinate, "Here is what I want done; I don't care how you do it, that's up to you." Indeed, many an official has prided himself on this way of dealing with subordinates. But this is changing. It is part of the Taylor system that standards and methods for each worker's job are made accessible to the worker; also knowledge of the quality of work expected, which is shown him by specifications or drawings. Some such system should be developed for management. To develop it might be made part of that analysis of managerial jobs which I spoke of a few moments ago. Indeed, more and more of the higher executives are seeing now that managers' jobs as well as workers' jobs are capable of carrying with them accepted standards and methods.

Of course, it is recognized that many of these standards and methods need the sanction of custom rather than of authority, that they should be indicated rather than prescribed, also that much more elasticity should be allowed than in the detailed instructions of the Taylor system—but this is all part of that large subject, the method of training executives. Possibly in time, as business organization develops, we shall have an official for executives corresponding to the functional foreman who is sometimes known as the "methods instructor," an official whose duty it will be to see that certain managerial methods are understood and followed, as it is the duty of the functional foreman to see that certain operating methods are understood and followed. But I should not advocate this unless the executives were allowed fullest opportunity for contributing to such prescribed methods. The development of managerial technique has been thought by some to involve the risk of crushing originality, the danger of taking away initiative. I think that, rightly managed, it should give executives increased opportunity for the fruitful exercise of initiative and originality, for it is they themselves who must develop this technique even if helped by experts. The choice here presented is not that between originality and a mechanical system, but between a haphazard, hit-or-miss way of performing executive duties and a scientifically determined procedure.

Yet when business management has gained something of an accepted technique, there still remains, as part of the training of executives, the acquiring of skill in its application. Managerial skill cannot be painted on the outside of executives; it has to go deeper than that. Like manual workers, managerial workers have to acquire certain habits and attitudes. And just as in the case of manual workers, for the acquisition of these habits and attitudes three conditions must be given: (1) detailed information in regard to a new method; (2) the stimulus to adopt this method: and (3) the opportunity to practice it so that it may become a habit.

A businessman tells me that I should emphasize the last point particularly. He says that his firm has been weak just here; that they have done more preaching than giving opportunity for practice. He says: "We've given them a lecture on piano playing and then put them on the concert stage. This winter we are going to try to invent ways of giving real practice to foremen so that a set of habits can be formed." No subject is more important than the training of executives, but as it is a subject which would require an evening for the most superficial consideration, we cannot speak further of it tonight. Let me just say, however, as a hint of what I shall elaborate later, that if you wish to train yourself for higher executive positions, the first thing for you to decide is what you are training for. Ability to dominate or manipulate others? That ought to be easy enough, since most of the magazines advertise sure ways of developing something they call "personality."

But I am convinced that the first essential of business success is the capacity for organized thinking.

In conclusion: What does all this imply in regard to the profession of business management? It means that men must prepare themselves as seriously for this profession as for any other. They must realize that they, as all professional men, are assuming grave responsibilities, that they are to take a creative part in one of the large functions of society, a part which, I believe, only trained and disciplined men can in the future hope to take with success.

## NOTES AND REFERENCES

1. John Rogers Commons, 1862–1945. American economist, educator, and author. Also had considerable influence in labor legislation.—Editor
2. Oliver Sheldon, *Bulletin of Taylor Society* 8, no. 6 (December 1913), p. 211.
3. Oliver Sheldon, *The Philosophy of Management* (London: Sir Isaac Pitman & Sons, Ltd., 1923), p. 36.
4. Ibid., p. 35.

# 3

# The Management Theory Jungle

*Harold Koontz*

*A true modern-day classic, this selection is perhaps the most frequently reprinted article in the management literature. In it, Koontz classifies the major schools of management theory into six main groups which, he argues, have resulted in a "semantics jungle." The article describes the need to disentangle the resulting confusion and integrate management and other disciplines.—Eds.*

Although students of management would readily agree that there have been problems of management since the dawn of organized life, most would also agree that systematic examination of management, with few exceptions, is the product of the present century and more especially of the past two decades. Moreover, until recent years almost all of those who have attempted to analyze the management process and look for some theoretical underpinnings to help improve research, teaching, and practice were alert and perceptive practitioners of the art who reflected on many years of experience. Thus, at least in looking at *general* management as an intellectually based art, the earliest meaningful writing came from such experienced practitioners as Fayol, Mooney, Alvin Brown, Sheldon, Barnard, and Urwick. Certainly not even the most academic worshipper of empirical research can overlook the empiricism involved in distilling fundamentals from decades of experience by such discerning practitioners as these. Admittedly done without questionnaires, controlled interviews, or mathematics, observations by such men can hardly be accurately regarded as a priori or "armchair."

SOURCE: Reprinted by permission of the author and publisher from "The Management Theory Jungle," *The Academy of Management Journal*, December 1961, pp. 174–88.

The noteworthy absence of academic writing and research in the formative years of modern management theory is now more than atoned for by a deluge of research and writing from the academic halls. What is interesting and perhaps nothing more than a sign of the unsophisticated adolescence of management theory is how the current flood has brought with it a wave of great differences and apparent confusion. From the orderly analysis of management at the shop-room level by Frederick Taylor and the reflective distillation of experience from the general management point of view by Henri Fayol, we now see these and other early beginnings overgrown and entangled by a jungle of approaches and approachers to management theory.

There are the behavioralists, born of the Hawthorne experiments and the awakened interest in human relations during the 1930s and 1940s, who see management as a complex of interpersonal relationships and the basis of management theory the tentative tenets of the new and undeveloped science of psychology. There are also those who see management theory as simply a manifestation of the institutional and cultural aspects of sociology. Still others, observing that the central core of management is decision making, branch in all directions from this core to encompass everything in organization life. Then, there are mathematicians who think of management primarily as an exercise in logical relationships expressed in symbols and the omnipresent and ever revered model. But the entanglement of growth reaches its ultimate when the study of management is regarded as a study of one of a number of systems and subsystems, with an understandable tendency for the researcher to be dissatisfied until he has encompassed the entire physical and cultural universe as a management system.

With the recent discovery of an ages old problem area by social, physical, and biological scientists, and with the supersonic increase in interest by all types of enterprise managers, the apparent impenetrability of the present thicket which we call management theory is not difficult to comprehend. One can hardly be surprised that psychologists, sociologists, anthropologists, sociometricists, economists, mathematicians, physicists, biologists, political scientists, business administration scholars, and even practicing managers, should hop on this interesting, challenging, and profitable band wagon.

This welling of interest from every academic and practicing corner should not upset anyone concerned with seeing the frontiers of knowledge pushed back and the intellectual base of practice broadened. But what is rather upsetting to the practitioner and the observer, who sees great social potential from improved management, is that the variety of approaches to management theory has led to a kind of confused and destructive jungle warfare. Particularly among academic disciplines and their disciples, the primary interests of many would-be cult leaders seem to be to carve out a distinct (and hence "original") approach to management. And to defend this originality, and thereby gain a place in posterity (or at least to gain a publication which will justify academic status or promotion), it seems to have become too much the current style to downgrade, and sometimes misrepresent, what anyone else has said, or thought, or done.

In order to cut through this jungle and bring to light some of the issues and problems involved in the present management theory area so that the tremendous interest, intelligence, and research results may become more meaningful, it is my purpose here to classify the various "schools" of management theory, to identify briefly what I believe to be the major source of differences, and to offer some suggestions for disentangling the jungle. It is hoped that a movement for clarification can be started so at least we in the field will not be a group of blind men identifying the same elephant with our widely varying and sometimes viciously argumentative theses.

## THE MAJOR "SCHOOLS" OF MANAGEMENT THEORY

In attempting to classify the major schools of management theory into six main groups, I am aware that I may overlook certain approaches and cannot deal with all the nuances of each approach. But it does seem that most of the approaches to management theory can be classified in one of these so-called schools.

### The Management Process School

This approach to management theory perceives management as a process of getting things done through and with people operating in organized groups. It aims to analyze the process, to establish a conceptual framework for it, to identify principles underlying it, and to build up a theory of management from them. It regards management as a universal process, regardless of the type of enterprise, or the level in a given enterprise, although recognizing, obviously, that the environment of management differs widely between enterprises and levels. It looks upon management theory as a way of organizing experience so that practice can be improved through research, empirical testing of principles, and teaching of fundamentals involved in the management process.[1]

Often referred to, especially by its critics, as the "traditional" or "universalist" school, this school can be said to have been fathered by Henri Fayol, although many of his offspring did not know of their parent, since Fayol's work was eclipsed by the bright light of his contemporary, Frederick Taylor, and clouded by the lack of a widely available English translation until 1949. Other than Fayol, most of the early contributors to this school dealt only with the organization portion of the management process, largely because of their greater experience with this facet of management and the simple fact that planning and control, as well as the function of staffing, were given little attention by managers before 1940.

This school bases its approach to management theory on several fundamental beliefs:

(1) that managing is a process and can best be dissected intellectually by analyzing the functions of the manager;

(2) that long experience with management in a variety of enterprise situations can be grounds for distillation of certain fundamental truths or generalizations—usually referred to as principles—which have a clarifying and predictive value in the understanding and improvement of managing;

(3) that these fundamental truths can become focal points for useful research both to ascertain their validity and to improve their meaning and applicability in practice;

(4) that such truths can furnish elements, at least until disproved, and certainly until sharpened, of a useful theory of management;

(5) that managing is an art, but one like medicine or engineering, which can be improved by reliance on the light and understanding of principles;

(6) that principles in management, like principles in the biological and physical sciences, are nonetheless true even if a prescribed treatment or design by a practitioner in a given case situation chooses to ignore a principle and the costs involved, or attempts to do something else to offset the costs incurred (this is, of course, not new in medicine, engineering, or any other art, for art is the creative task of compromising fundamentals to attain a desired result); and

(7) that, while the totality of culture and of the physical and biological universe have varying effects on the manager's environment and subjects, as indeed they do in every other field of science and art, the theory of management does not need to encompass the field of all knowledge in order for it to serve as a scientific or theoretical foundation.

The basic approach of this school, then, is to look, first, to the functions of managers. As a second step in this approach, many of us have taken the functions of managers and further dissected them by distilling what we see as fundamental truths in the understandably complicated practice of management. I have found it useful to classify my analysis of these functions around the essentials involved in the following questions:

(1) What is the nature of the function?
(2) What is the purpose of the function?
(3) What explains the structure of the function?
(4) What explains the process of the function?

Perhaps there are other more useful approaches, but I have found that I can place everything pertaining to management (even some of the rather remote research and concepts) in this framework.

Also, purely to make the area of management theory intellectually manageable, those who subscribe to this school do not usually attempt to include in the theory the entire areas of sociology, economics, biology, psychology, physics, chemistry, or others. This is done not because these other areas of knowledge are unimportant and have no bearing on management, but merely because no real progress has ever been made in science or art without significant partitioning of knowledge. Yet, anyone would be foolish not to realize that a function which deals with people in their various activities of producing and marketing anything from money to religion and education is not completely independent of the physical, biological, and cultural universe in which we live. And, are there not such relationships in other "compartments" of knowledge and theory?

### The Empirical School

A second approach to management I refer to as the "empirical" school. In this, I include those scholars who identify management as a study of experience, sometimes with intent to draw generalizations but usually merely as a means of teaching experience and transferring it to the practitioner or student. Typical of this school are those who see management or "policy" as the study and analysis of cases and those with such approaches as Ernest Dale's "comparative approach."[2]

This approach seems to be based upon the premise that, if we study the experience of successful managers, or the mistakes made in management, or if we attempt to solve management problems, we will somehow understand and learn to apply the most effective kinds of management techniques. This approach, as often applied, assumes that, by finding out what worked or did not work in individual circumstances, the student or the practitioner will be able to do the same in comparable situations.

No one can deny the importance of studying experience through such study, or of analyzing the "how-it-was-done" of management. But management, unlike law, is not a science based on precedent, and situations in the future exactly comparable to the past are exceedingly unlikely to occur. Indeed, there is a positive danger of relying too much on past experience and on undistilled history of managerial problem solving for the simple reason that a technique or approach found "right" in the past may not fit a situation of the future.

Those advocating the empirical approach are likely to say that what they really do in analyzing cases or history is to draw from certain generalizations which can be applied as useful guides to thought or action in future case situations. As a matter of fact, Ernest Dale, after claiming to find "so little practical value" from the principles enunciated by the "universalists," curiously drew certain "generalizations" or "criteria" from his valuable study of a number of great practitioners of management.[3] There is some question as to whether Dale's "comparative" approach is not really the same as the "universalist" approach he decries, except with a different distiller of basic truths.

By the emphasis of the empirical school on study of experience, it does appear that the research and thought so engendered may assist in hastening the day for verification of principles. It is also possible that the proponents of this school may come up with a more useful framework of principles than that of the management process school. But, to the extent that the empirical school draws generalizations from its research, and it would seem to be a necessity to do so unless its members are satisfied to exchange meaningless and structureless experience, this approach tends to be and do the same as the management process school.

### The Human Behavior School

This approach to the analysis of management is based on the central thesis that, since managing involves getting things done with and through people, the study of management must be centered on interpersonal relations. Variously called the "human relations," "leadership," or "behavioral sciences" approach, this school brings to bear "existing and newly developed theories, methods, and techniques of the relevant social sciences upon the study of inter- and intrapersonal phenomena, ranging fully from the personality dynamics of individuals at one extreme to the relations of cultures at the other."[4] In other words, this school concentrates on the "people" part of management and rests on the principle that, where people work together as groups in order to accomplish objectives, "people should understand people."

The scholars in this school have a heavy orientation to psychology and social psychology. Their primary focus is the individual as a socio-psychological being and what motivates him. The members of this school vary from those who see it as a portion of the manager's job, a tool to help him understand and get the best from people by meeting their needs and responding to their motivations, to those who see the psychological behavior of individuals and groups as the total of management.

In this school are those who emphasize human relations as an art that the manager should advantageously understand and practice. There are those who focus attention on the manager as a leader and some-times equate management to leadership, thus, in effect, tending to treat all group activities as "managed" situations. There are those who see the study of group dynamics and interpersonal relationships as simply a study of socio-psychological relationships and seem, therefore, merely to be attaching the term "management" to the field of social psychology.

That management must deal with human behavior can hardly be denied. That the study of human interactions, whether in the environment of management or in unmanaged situations, is important and useful one could not dispute. And it would be a serious mistake to regard good leadership as unimportant to good managership. But whether the field of human behavior is the equivalent of the field of management is quite another thing. Perhaps it is like calling the study of the human body the field of cardiology.

## The Social System School

Closely related to the human behavior school and often confused or intertwined with it is one which might be labeled the social system school. This includes those researchers who look upon management as a social system, that is, a system of cultural interrelationships. Some-times, as in the case of March and Simon,[5] the system is limited to formal organizations, using the term "organization" as equivalent to enterprise, rather than the authority-activity concept used most often in management. In other cases, the approach is not to distinguish the formal organization, but rather to encompass any kind of system of human relationships.

Heavily sociological in flavor, this approach to management does essentially what any study of sociology does. It identifies the nature of the cultural relationships of various social groups and attempts to show these as a related, and usually an integrated, system.

Perhaps the spiritual father of this ardent and vocal school of management theorists is Chester Barnard.[6] In searching for an answer to fundamental explanations underlying the managing process, this thoughtful business executive developed a theory of cooperation grounded in the needs of the individual to solve, through cooperation, the biological, physical, and social limitations of himself and his environment. Barnard then carved from the total of cooperative systems so engendered one set of interrelationships which he defines as "formal organization." His formal organization concept, quite unlike that usually held by management practitioners, is any cooperative system in which there are persons able to communicate with each other and who are willing to contribute action toward a conscious common purpose.

The Barnard concept of cooperative system pervades the work of many contributors to the social system school of management. For example, Herbert Simon at one time defined the subject of organization theory and the nature of human organizations as "systems of interdependent activity, encompassing at least several primary groups and usually characterized, at the level of consciousness of participants, by a high degree of rational direction of behavior toward ends that are objects of common knowledge."[7] Simon and others have subsequently seemed to have expanded this concept of social systems to include any cooperative and purposeful group interrelationship or behavior.

This school has made many noteworthy contributions to management. The recognition of organized enterprise as a social organism, subject to all the pressures and conflicts of the cultural environment, has been helpful to the management theorist and the practitioner alike. Among some of the more helpful aspects are the awareness of the institutional foundations of organization authority, the influence of informal organization, and such social factors as those Wight Bakke has called the "bonds of organization."[8] Likewise, many of Barnard's helpful insights, such as his economy of incentives and his theory of opportunism, have brought the power of sociological understanding into the realm of management practice.

Basic sociology, analysis of concepts of social behavior, and the study of group behavior in the framework of social systems do have great value in the field of management. But one may well ask the question whether this *is* management. Is the field of management coterminous with the field of sociology? Or is sociology an important underpinning like language, psychology, physiology, mathematics, and other fields of knowledge? Must management be defined in terms of the universe of knowledge?

## The Decision Theory School

Another approach to management theory, undertaken by a growing and scholarly group, might be referred to as the decision theory school. This group concentrates on rational approach to decision—the selection from among possible alternatives of a course of action or of an idea. The approach of this school may be to deal with the decision itself, or with the persons or organizational group making the decision, or with an analysis of the decision process. Some limit themselves fairly much to the economic rationale of the decision, while others regard anything which happens in an enterprise the subject of their analysis, and still others expand decision theory to cover the psychological and sociological aspect and environment of decisions and decision makers.

The decision-making school is apparently an outgrowth of the theory of consumer's choice with which economists have been concerned since the days of Jeremy Bentham early in the nineteenth century. It has arisen out of such economic problems and analyses as utility maximization, indifference curves, marginal utility, and economic behavior under risks and uncertainties. It is, therefore, no surprise that one finds most of the members of this school to be economic theorists. It is likewise no surprise to find the content of this school to be heavily oriented to model construction and mathematics.

The decision theory school has tended to expand its horizon considerably beyond the process of evaluating alternatives. That point has become for many only a springboard for examination of the entire sphere of human activity, including the nature of the organization structure, psychological and social reactions of individuals and groups, the development of basic information for decisions, an analysis of values and particularly value considerations with respect to goals, communications networks, and incentives. As one would expect, when the decision theorists study the small, but central, area of decision *making,* they are led by this keyhole look at management to consider the entire field of enterprise operation and its environment. The result is that decision theory becomes no longer a neat and narrow concentration on decision, but rather a broad view of the enterprise as a social system.

There are those who believe that, since management is characterized by its concentration on decisions, the future development of management theory will tend to use the decision as its central focus and the rest of management theory will be hung on this structural center. This may occur and certainly the study of the decision, the decision process, and the decision maker can be extended to cover the entire field of management as anyone might conceive it. Nevertheless, one wonders whether this focus cannot also be used to build around it the entire area of human knowledge. For, as most decision theorists recognize, the problem of choice is individual, as well as organizational, and most of what has been said that is pure decision theory can be applied to the existence and thinking of a Robinson Crusoe.

## The Mathematical School

Although mathematical methods can be used by any school of management theory, and have been, I have chosen to group under a school those theorists who see management as a system of mathematical models and processes. Perhaps the most widely known group I arbitrarily so lump are the operations researchers or operations analysts, who have sometimes anointed themselves with the rather pretentious name of "management scientists." The abiding belief of this group is that, if management, or organization, or planning, or decision making is a logical process, it can be expressed in terms of mathematical symbols and relationships. The central approach of this school is the model, for it is through these devices that the problem is expressed in its basic relationships and in terms of selected goals or objectives.

There can be no doubt of the great usefulness of mathematical approaches to any field of inquiry. It forces upon the researcher the definition of a problem or problem area, it conveniently allows the insertion of symbols for unknown data, and its logical methodology, developed by years of scientific application and abstraction, furnishes a powerful tool for solving or simplifying complex phenomena.

But it is hard to see mathematics as a truly separate school of management theory, any more than it is a separate "school" in physics, chemistry, engineering, or medicine. I only deal with it here as such because there has appeared to have developed a kind of cult around mathematical analysts who have subsumed to themselves the area of management.

In pointing out that mathematics is a tool, rather than a school, it is not my intention to underestimate the impact of mathematics on the science and practice of management. By bringing to this immensely important and complex field the tools and techniques of the physical sciences, the mathematicians have already made an immense contribution to orderly thinking. They have forced on people in management the means and desirability of seeing many problems more clearly, they have pressed on scholars and practitioners the need for establishing goals and measures of effectiveness, they have been extremely helpful in getting the management area seen as a logical system of relationships, and they have caused people in management to review and occasionally reorganize information sources and systems so that mathematics can be given sensible quantitative meaning. But with all this meaningful contribution and the greater sharpness and sophistication of planning which is resulting, I cannot see that mathematics is management theory any more than it is astronomy.

## THE MAJOR SOURCES OF MENTAL ENTANGLEMENT IN THE JUNGLE

In outlining the various schools, or approaches, of management theory, it becomes clear that these intellectual cults are not drawing greatly different inferences from the physical and cultural environment surrounding us. Why, then, have there been so many differences between them and why such a struggle, particularly among our academic brethren, to obtain a place in the sun by denying the approaches of others? Like the widely differing and often contentious denominations of the Christian religion, all have essentially the same goals and deal with essentially the same world.

While there are many sources of the mental entanglement in the management theory jungle, the major ones are the following:

### The Semantics Jungle

As is so often true when intelligent men argue about basic problems, some of the trouble lies in the meaning of key words. The semantics problem is particularly severe in the field of management. There is even a difference in the meaning of the word "management." Most people would agree that it means getting things done through and with people, but is it people in formal organizations, or in all group activities? Is it governing, leading, or teaching?

Perhaps the greatest single semantics confusion lies in the word "organization." Most members of the management process school use it to define the activity-authority structure of an enterprise and certainly most practitioners believe that they are "organizing" when they establish a framework of activity groupings and authority relationships. In this case, organization represents the formal framework within an enterprise that furnishes the environment in which people perform. Yet a large number of "organization" theorists conceive of organization as the sum total of human relationships in any group activity; they thus seem to make it equivalent to *social* structure. And some use "organization" to mean "enterprise."

If the meaning of organization cannot be clarified and a standard use of the term adopted by management theorists, understanding and criticism should not be based on this difference. It hardly seems to me to be accurate for March and Simon, for example, to criticize the organization theories of the management process, or "universalist," school for not considering the management planning function as part of organizing, when they have chosen to treat it separately. Nor should those who choose to treat the training, selecting, guiding or leading of people under staffing and direction be criticized for a tendency to "view the employee as an inert instrument" or a "given rather than a variable."[9] Such accusations, proceeding from false premises, are clearly erroneous.

Other semantic entanglements might be mentioned. By some, decision making is regarded as a process of choosing from among alternatives; by others, the total managerial task and environment. Leadership is often made synonymous with managership and is analytically separated by others. Communications may mean everything from a written or oral report to a vast network of formal and informal relationships. Human relations to some implies a psychiatric manipulation of people, but to others the study and art of understanding people and interpersonal relationships.

## Differences in Definition of Management as a Body of Knowledge

As was indicated in the discussion of semantics, "management" has far from a standard meaning, although most agree that it at least involves getting things done through and with people. But, does it mean the dealing with all human relationships? Is a street peddler a manager? Is a parent a manager? Is a leader of a disorganized mob a manager? Does the field of management equal the fields of sociology and social psychology combined? Is it the equivalent of the entire system of social relationships?

While I recognize that sharp lines cannot be drawn in management any more than they are in medicine or engineering, there surely can be a sharper distinction drawn than at present. With the plethora of management writing and experts, calling almost everything under the sun management, can one expect management theory to be regarded as very useful or scientific to the practitioner?

## The A Priori Assumption

Confusion in management theory has also been heightened by the tendency for many newcomers in the field to cast aside significant observations and analyses of the past on the grounds that they are a priori in nature. This is an often-met accusation made by those who wish to cast aside the work of Fayol, Mooney, Brown, Urwick, Gulick, and others who are branded as "universalists." To make the assumption that the distilled experiences of men such as these represent a priori reasoning is to forget that experience in and with managing *is* empirical. While the conclusions that perceptive and experienced practitioners of the art of management draw are not infallible, they represent an experience which is certainly real and not "armchair." No one could deny, I feel sure, that the ultimate test of accuracy of management theory must be practice and management theory and science must be developed from reality.

## The Misunderstanding of Principles

Those who feel that they gain caste or a clean slate for advancing a particular notion or approach often delight in casting away anything which smacks of management principles. Some have referred to them as platitudes, forgetting that a platitude is still a truism and a truth does not become worthless because it is familiar. (As Robert Frost has written, "Most of the changes we think we see in life are merely truths going in or out of favor.") Others cast away principles of Fayol and other practitioners, only to draw apparently different generalizations from their study of management; but many of the generalizations so discovered are often the same fundamental truths in different words that certain criticized "universalists" have discovered.

One of the favorite tricks of the managerial theory trade is to disprove a whole framework of principles by reference to one principle which the observer sees disregarded in practice. Thus, many critics of the universalists point to the well-known cases of dual subordination in organized enterprise, coming to the erroneous conclusion that there is not substance to the principle of unity of command. But this does not prove that there is no cost to the enterprise by designing around, or disregarding, the principle of unity of command; nor does it prove that there were not other advantages which offset the costs, as there often are in cases of establishing functional authorities in organization.

Perhaps the almost hackneyed standby for those who would disprove the validity of all principles by referring to a single one is the misunderstanding around the principle of span of management (or span of control). The usual source of authority quoted by those who criticize is Sir Ian Hamilton, who never intended to state a universal principle, but rather to make a personal observation in a book of reflections on his Army experience, and who did say, offhand, that he found it wise to limit his span to three to six subordinates. No modern universalist relies on this single observation, and, indeed, few can or will state an absolute or universal numerical ceiling. Since Sir Ian was not a management theorist and did not intend to be, let us hope that the ghost of his innocent remark may be laid to deserved rest!

What concerns those who feel that a recognition of fundamental truths, or generalizations, may help in the diagnosis and study of management, and who know from managerial experience that such truths or principles do serve an extremely valuable use, is the tendency for some researchers to prove the wrong things through either misstatement or misapplication of principles. A classic case of such misunderstanding and misapplication is in Chris Argyris's interesting book on *Personality and Organization*.[10] This author, who in this book and his other works has made many noteworthy contributions to management, concludes that "formal organization principles make demands on relatively healthy individuals that are incongruent with their needs," and that "frustration, conflict, failure, and short-time perspective are predicted as results of this basic incongruency."[11] This startling conclusion—the exact opposite of what "good" formal organization based on "sound" organization principles should cause, is explained when one notes that, of four "principles" Argyris quotes, one is not an organization principle at all but the economic principle of specialization and three other "principles" are quoted incorrectly.[12] With such a postulate, and with no attempt to recognize, correctly or incorrectly, any other organization and management principles, Argyris has simply proved that wrong principles badly applied will lead to frustration; and every management practitioner knows this to be true!

### The Inability or Unwillingness of Management Theorists to Understand Each Other

What has been said above leads one to the conclusion that much of the management theory jungle is caused by the unwillingness or inability of the management theorists to understand each other. Doubting that it is inability, because one must assume that a person interested in management theory is able to comprehend, at least in concept and framework, the approaches of the various "schools," I can only come to the conclusion that the roadblock to understanding is unwillingness.

Perhaps this unwillingness comes from the professional "walls" developed by learned disciplines. Perhaps the unwillingness stems from a fear that someone or some new discovery will encroach on professional and academic status. Perhaps it is fear of professional or intellectual obsolescence. But whatever the cause, it seems that these walls will not be torn down until it is realized that they exist, until all cultists are willing to look at the approach and content of other schools, and until, through exchange and understanding of ideas some order may be brought from the present chaos.

## DISENTANGLING THE MANAGEMENT THEORY JUNGLE

It is important that steps be taken to disentangle the management theory jungle. Perhaps, it is too soon and we must expect more years of wandering through a thicket of approaches, semantics, thrusts, and counter thrusts. But in any field as important to society where the many blunders of an unscientifically based managerial art can be so costly, I hope that this will not be long.

There do appear to be some things that can be done. Clearly, meeting what I see to be the major sources of the entanglement should remove much of it. The following considerations are important:

**1. The Need for Definition of a Body of Knowledge.** Certainly, if a field of knowledge is not to get bogged down in a quagmire of misunderstandings, the first need is for definition of the field. Not that it need be defined in sharp, detailed, and inflexible lines, but rather along lines which will give it fairly specific content. Because management is reality, life, practice, my suggestion would be that it be defined in the light of the able and discerning practitioner's frame of reference. A science unrelated to the art for which it is to serve is not likely to be a very productive one.

Although the study of managements in various enterprises, in various countries, and at various levels made by many persons, including myself, may neither be representative nor adequate, I have come to the conclusion that management is the art of getting things done through and with people in *formally organized groups,* the art of creating an environment in such an organized group where people can perform as individuals and yet cooperate toward attainment of group goals, the art of removing blocks to such performance, the art of optimizing efficiency in effectively reaching goals. If this kind of definition of the field is unsatisfactory, I suggest at least an agreement that the area should be defined to reflect the field of the practitioner and that further research and study of practice be done to this end.

In defining the field, too, it seems to me imperative to draw some limits for purposes of analysis and research. If we are to call the entire cultural, biological, and physical universe the field of management, we can no more make progress than could have been done if chemistry or geology had not carved out a fairly specific area and had, instead, studied all knowledge.

In defining the body of knowledge, too, care must be taken to distinguish between tools and content. Thus mathematics, operations research, accounting, economic theory, sociometry, and psychology, to mention a few, are significant *tools* of management but are not, in themselves, a part of the *content* of the field. This is not to mean that they are unimportant or that the practicing manager should not have them available to him, nor does it mean that they may not be the means of pushing back the frontiers of knowledge of management. But they should not be confused with the basic content of the field.

This is not to say that fruitful study should not continue on the underlying disciplines affecting management. Certainly knowledge of sociology, social systems, psychology, economics, political science, mathematics, and other areas, pointed toward contributing to the field of management, should be continued and encouraged. And significant findings in these and other fields of knowledge might well cast important light on, or change concepts in, the field of management. This has certainly happened in other sciences and in every other art based upon significant science.

**2. Integration of Management and Other Disciplines.** If recognition of the proper content of the field were made, I believe that the present crossfire of misunderstanding might tend to disappear. Management would be regarded as a specific discipline and other disciplines would be looked upon as important bases of the field. Under these circumstances, the allied and underlying disciplines would be welcomed by the business and public administration schools, as well as by practitioners, as loyal and helpful associates. Integration of management and other disciplines would then not be difficult.

**3. The Clarification of Management Semantics.** While I would expect the need for clarification and uniformity of management semantics would largely be satisfied by definition of the field as a body of knowledge, semantics problems might require more special attention. There are not too many places where semantics are important enough to cause difficulty. Here again, I would suggest the adoption of the semantics of the intelligent practitioners, unless words are used by them so inexactly as to require special clarification. At least, we should not complicate an already complex field by developing a scientific or academic jargon which would build a language barrier between the theorist and the practitioner.

Perhaps the most expeditious way out of this problem is to establish a commission representing academic societies immediately concerned and associations of practicing managers. This would not seem to be difficult to do. And even if it were, the results would be worth the efforts.

**4. Willingness to Distill and Test Fundamentals.** Certainly, the test of maturity and usefulness of a science is the sharpness and validity of the principles underlying it. No science, now regarded as mature, started out with a complete statement of incontrovertibly valid principles. Even the oldest sciences, such as physics, keep revising their underlying laws and discovering new principles. Yet any science has proceeded, and more than that has been useful, for centuries on the basis of generalizations, some laws, some principles, and some hypotheses.

One of the understandable sources of inferiority of the social sciences is the recognition that they are inexact sciences. On the other hand, even the so-called exact sciences are subject to a great deal of inexactness, have principles which are not completely proved, and use art in the design of practical systems and components. The often-encountered defeatist attitude of the social sciences, of which management is one, overlooks the fact that management may be explained, practice may be improved, and the goals of research may be more meaningful if we encourage attempts at perceptive distillation of experience by stating principles (or generalizations) and placing them in a logical framework. As two scientists recently said on this subject:

> The reason for this defeatist point of view regarding the social sciences may be traceable to a basic misunderstanding of the nature of scientific endeavor. What matters is not whether or to what extent inexactitudes in procedures and predictive capability can eventually be removed . . . : rather it is *objectivity,* i.e., the intersubjectivity of findings independent of any one person's intuitive judgment, which distinguishes science from intuitive guesswork however brilliant. . . . But once a new fact or a new idea has been conjectured, no matter how intuitive a foundation, it must be capable of objective test and confirmation by anyone. And it is this crucial standard of scientific objectivity rather than any purported criterion of exactitude to which the social sciences must conform.[13]

In approaching the clarification of management theory, then, we should not forget a few criteria:

1. The theory should deal with an area of knowledge and inquiry that is "manageable"; no great advances in knowledge were made so long as man contemplated the whole universe.
2. The theory should be *useful* in improving practice and the task and person of the practitioner should not be overlooked.
3. The theory should not be lost in semantics, especially useless jargon not understandable to the practitioner.
4. The theory should give direction and efficiency to research and teaching.
5. The theory must recognize that it is a part of a larger universe of knowledge and theory.

## NOTES AND REFERENCES

1. It is interesting that one of the scholars strongly oriented to human relations and behavioral approaches to management has recently noted that "theory can be viewed as a way of organizing experience" and that "once initial sense is made out of experienced environment, the way is cleared for an even more adequate organization of this experience." See Robert Dubin in "Psyche, Sensitivity, and Social Structure," critical comment in Robert Tannenbaum, I. R. Weschler, and Fred Massarik, *Leadership and Organization: A Behavioral Science Approach* (New York: McGraw-Hill, 1961), p. 401.
2. *The Great Organizers* (New York: McGraw-Hill, 1960), pp. 11–28.

3. Ibid., pp. 11, 26–28, 62–68.
4. R. Tannenbaum, I. R. Weschler, and F. Massarik, *Leadership and Organization* (New York: McGraw-Hill, 1961), p. 9.
5. *Organizations* (New York: John Wiley & Sons, 1958).
6. *The Functions of the Executive* (Cambridge, Mass.: Harvard University Press, 1938).
7. "Comments of the Theory of Organizations," *American Political Science Review* 46, no. 4 (December 1952), p. 1130.
8. *Bonds of Organization* (New York: Harper & Row, 1950). These "bonds" or "devices" of organization are identified by Bakke as (1) the functional specifications system (a system of teamwork arising from job specifications and arrangements for association); (2) the status system (a vertical hierarchy of authority); (3) the communications system; (4) the reward and penalty system; and (5) the organization charter (ideas and means which give character and individuality to the organization, or enterprise).
9. J. G. March and H. A. Simon. *Organizations* (New York: John Wiley & Sons, 1958), pp. 29–33.
10. New York: Harper & Row, 1957.
11. Ibid., p. 74.
12. Ibid., pp. 58–66.
13. O. Helmer and N. Rescher, "On the Epistemology of the Inexact Sciences" (Santa Monica, Cal.: The Rand Corporation, P-1513, 1958), pp. 4–5.

# 4

# What Is Behavioral Science?

*Harold M. F. Rush*

*The question asked in the title of this selection is answered by examining who behavioral scientists are, what they do, and how well they are doing it. The article provides the present or future manager with a basis for understanding the behavioral scientist's function and the use of his or her findings in an organizational setting.—Eds.*

Executives are being exposed increasingly to behavioral science or, as it is also called, behavioral research. Some are in the forefront of this relatively new activity, but many others are familiar with it only to the extent that they hear it mentioned more and more frequently. These executives say they are disturbed about their lack of understanding of behavioral science; they fear that they may fail to improve themselves and their organizations because of their inability to apply relevant findings of the behavioral sciences. In short, they are asking: "What's it all about?"

The purpose of this article is to tell, simply, what behavioral science is. It has not always been possible to avoid the use of technical terms for there has arisen a special language to describe phenomena that are the concern of the behavioral researcher today. Some of these terms amount merely to specialized meanings attached to common words; other terms in vogue may be classified as jargon. Several of the newer coinages have already crept into everyday speech. A subsequent article will discuss a few of the more popular terms and their connotations for the businessman.

"Nothing is permanent except change," contended Heraclitus back in the sixth century, B.C. Succeeding generations have echoed this

---

SOURCE: Reprinted from *The Conference Board Record,* September 1965, vol. 2, no. 9. Reprinted by permission of *The Conference Board Record.*

sentiment, especially in this century of unprecedented change. The business world has taken on so completely new a face in so relatively short a time, that the business manager often finds it difficult to keep abreast with the ever-increasing developments in his field. He may even find that the management concepts he has put into practice for most of his working life are under reexamination.

The conscientious manager who prides himself in being conversant with newer trends probably hears or reads a lot about the widening interest of businessmen in behavioral science. And he may be even a little embarrassed that he isn't quite sure what it's all about. Well, in the most elementary terms, what is it?

A good starting point is to examine the word "behavior." Webster defines it as: "Mode of conducting oneself; the way in which an organism, organ, or substance acts, especially in response to a stimulus."

Behavioral science is interested in studying behavior, specifically, human behavior, in response to various stimuli—internal and mental or external and physical. The term came into popular usage because men working in the field considered it more descriptive than formerly used "social science." The word social, they felt, was associated too much in the layman's mind with sociability, and, possibly more to the point, social science was often confused with socialism.

Behavioral science connotes all the factors that go into man's fundamental personality—his needs, his emotions, his thinking, his ability to relate his thoughts and feelings. His actions are a result and a composite of all these factors.

## WHO IS A BEHAVIORAL SCIENTIST?

The group of academic disciplines which constitute the behavioral sciences is large. In one sense, any person who engages in the study of human behavior is a behavioral scientist; but so broad a definition could be carried to the absurd. (An internal auditor is interested in how people spend money. Is he, then, a behavioral scientist?) A behavioral scientist is simply someone whose *primary* concern is the study of how and why people behave as they do.

The first profession that comes to mind when considering the role of the behavioral scientist is psychology. By definition, psychology is concerned with the study of the mind and its interrelation with an *individual's* behavior. The second profession is sociology. Sociology is concerned with the evolution of society, or the forms, institutions, and functions of human *groups*. In the study of groups, these two areas, for example, overlap so much that it is sometimes difficult to ascertain which of the two disciplines does what. It would be unprofessional to call these situations jurisdictional disputes; but, as an example of overlap, there is an area of specialization within psychology that is interested in groups also. This is called social psychology. The essential difference between a social psychologist and a sociologist is that the former is primarily interested in studying the behavior of an individual as he relates to, or is affected by, the groups in which he lives and functions, while the latter is more concerned with the group as a whole and one group's relationships with another. When directed to "work situations," the efforts of both the psychologist and the sociologist have applicability to the business world.

The behavioral scientist label also has been applied, under certain circumstances, to the economist, the political scientist, the human engineer (who seeks to adapt the work environment to the man), and to a host of other specialists. What the person is called is of less importance than what he does. Social psychologists, industrial sociologists, labor economists, educators, physicians, anthropologists, and many more professionals come under the umbrella of behavioral sciences because all are concerned, to varying degrees, with human behavior.

## WHAT DOES HE DO?

In its raw form "science" refers to knowledge obtained by study and practice or to any department of systematized knowledge. By this definition the behavioral scientist is a scientist, although his counterparts in the natural or physical sciences sometimes may balk at the use of the term as applied to psychologists, sociologists, cultural anthropologists, *et al.* Strictly speaking, the behavioral scientist works within the framework of scientific method, and he applies tests of statistical and clinical validity to the evidence he collects. He approaches a problem in much the same way as the physical scientist: he does basic research by measuring and counting and by observing existing phenomena; he performs experimental work based on a given thesis and postulates a system or approach based on the evidence he gleans. In describing his basic methodology he borrows the language of the physical scientist. He speaks in terms of research, development, and application. But his data, unlike those of the physical scientist, can rarely, if ever, meet the criterion of indisputable universality: he cannot work in the perfectly controlled environment of a laboratory; he cannot extrapolate with rigid authority; he does not deal with properties and conditions that remain constant; he cannot control the quality or quantity of his variables. In short, the properties he is working with are the most complex of all organisms, physically, mentally, and emotionally—people.

Even the most scientifically oriented behavioral scientist recognizes that his field is not at this point an exact science. Still, through adherence to principles of scientific method, through constant observation of his subjects, and thorough validation of his findings, he attempts to predict what is likely to happen to a given person or groups of persons within a given situation.

Most behavioral scientists recognize that they may never reach the point of axiomatic certainty—the variables and complexities of people are great. But their efforts have already produced considerable knowledge about how and why people behave as they do, how their strengths and weaknesses can be evaluated, what their needs and wants are.

There are even persons working within the framework of behavioral research (and particularly as it applies to the business world) who do not follow strict rules of scientific method and inquiry. Many businessmen feel, however, that their theories or philosophies have contributed much to the understanding of people at work and generally of the management process.

Some of the disciplines that are lumped together as behavioral sciences are relatively young; psychology as a modern system was still considered to be an embryo as late as the beginning of this century, for example. But the studies, major ones, have been made possible by an increasing level of sophistication over the past couple of decades. As techniques become refined, many expect that a more finite contribution will be made by the behavioral scientist, particularly to the world of work.

## WHO IS INTERESTED IN HIS WORK?

There has been a recent surge of interest in behavioral science on the part of people in business. But the question may arise: "After all, hasn't industry managed to survive and even thrive without behavioral science in the past?" Business *has* survived and thrived, but not without behavioral science in some form.

Human behavior and its effects upon productivity have been the interest of management for a long time—long before anyone coined a term for the study of this subject. From the early studies on employee learning, in the 1890s, to the first time-and-motion studies, to the development of tests and a more sophisticated approach to employee selection, to on-the-job training, to supervisory training, and on to the advent of management development, companies have become more and more sensitive to how the employee acts and reacts, how he functions in various situations, how his innate abilities can be matched with the job requirements, how to create a work environment conducive to job satisfaction, harmonious relations, and a higher level of production.

Most earlier behavioral scientists were concerned with the physical factors that make for higher levels of production (well designed machines and work areas, healthy working conditions, illumination, temperatures at the workplace, job analysis and selective placement, use of color and music to induce efficiency). They were also interested in keeping the employee loyal and content (rates of pay, paid vacations, insurance benefits and pensions, recreation, coffee breaks, etc.). Broadly speaking, they were interested in manipulating the tangible and/or material environment; and they were, in the main, interested in the rank-and-file worker. Some modern behavioral scientists contend that these earlier studies were concerned with man as an adjunct to a machine, and thus may not be considered behavioral research at all.

It is doubtful whether all of the interest of business in its employees, even in the earlier stages, was initiated out of altruistic concern. Many social pressures, the rise and power of organized labor, the employer's obligation under workmen's compensation laws, and the ever-increasing industrial competition all may have had a part in "forcing" many companies to take a closer look at their relations with their workers. Outside pressures and influences aside, management began to realize that in a competitive free-enterprise economy its only permanent advantage lies in its human resources. With this growing realization, management has intensified its inquiry into the how and why of human behavior.

In this perspective the current activity in behavioral research is, for all practical purposes, a continuation of earlier studies with a new dimension added: the scope of concern.

Whereas early behavioral research concerned itself with workers *en masse,* today's focus is more on the manager and the management process. In the family-owned company the owner did the "hiring and firing," and frequently he kept in close touch with the actual manufacturing operation. In the large modern corporation the head of the company necessarily has a group of technical and administrative specialists who do the jobs the owner-manager used to perform. It has been demonstrated that a good machinist doesn't automatically make a good manager of a machine shop; a crack salesman doesn't necessarily make a good marketing manager. Successful managers need training and special experience in the administration of material and human resources. This need has given rise to the professional manager. The manager of today is rarely the "working group leader." Thus, more than ever, he must depend upon his subordinates to get the work done. Yet, he is accountable to the company for the work output, morale, and performance of those in his unit.

Other factors also have contributed to the change of emphasis. Some of them are: increasing automation; finer distinctions in occupational specialization; refinement of scientific and technical capabilities of the corporation; and the unparalleled affluence of the populace. Society is rapidly becoming one in which the emphasis is shifted from work done by hand to work done by the mind. In this computer age the human mind becomes a more valuable commodity. As machines do the work previously done by men, the professional manager makes his greatest contribution mentally: decision making and management of human resources.

The key to the performance of a manager and to that of his employee is "motivation," a point which is being stressed increasingly by the behavioral scientist in the university and by the businessman. Business has long been concerned about motivation but, for the most part, the interest has been confined to consumer motivation. Researchers have begun to move in their studies from motivation to buy to motivation to work.

What is this thing called motivation? Motivation is defined as a drive within the individual, rather than without, which incites him to action. What the behavioral scientist is interested in is *what* motivates the individual. What are the factors conducive to motivation?

What is involved—or the total concern—can be illustrated by the old saw "You can lead a horse to water but you cannot make him drink." In this folk proverb all the elements are present—you, the horse, the leading, and the water. These are all the external, physical, and material factors. The element missing is the thirst, or the need—or desire—for the water. While modern behavioral scientists recognize that man is infinitely more complex than a horse, the same principle applies. And some behavioral scientists contend that business has for too long tried to do the leading (or actually *has* been leading) without allowing the individual to aspire to or to satisfy his own needs in order to achieve self-realization.

What can the behavioral scientist do about it? For one thing, he can look for the factors that are conducive to motivation. For another, and this, perhaps, is more important, he can determine what the individual's needs *are*. It is an accepted maxim that man is forever a goal-seeking animal, and if it can be determined what those goals *are* and *why* he seeks them, society—or business for that matter—may not only be better equipped to help him reach them, but may also find itself better off.

Some established beliefs about what motivates a person on the job are now being questioned—for example, the long-held assumption that money paid for services is enough to keep a person happy and productive. With high employment and growing affluence, money seems to have lost much of its power as a motivator. Money obviously can be a stimulus to motivation if a man is unemployed and hungry, but it is not a motivator in the real sense. The motivation for the unemployed man is to feed, clothe, and shelter himself, so even then money becomes a means to an end. Some behavioral researchers have shown that above a certain level of responsibility compensation is not a motivating factor at all. If a manager is paid $20,000 annually, for example, it does not necessarily follow that he is more strongly motivated to do a good job if he is raised to $30,000. The salary he receives may make him more *satisfied* with the job, but it won't necessarily make him more highly motivated. A substantial amount of research indicates that compensation, at best, can provide satisfaction only *off* the job.

A prevailing trend in behavioral research as related to human motivation assumes that, in order to reach his inner-directed goals, a man must first know himself and be able to find an outlet for his needs. The atmosphere in which he lives and works must be one that encourages self-expression and self-realization. Furthermore, it is believed that a person's concept of himself determines his attitude toward his contemporaries and the groups in which he functions, because he looks at his world through the only eyes he has—his own. But objectivity about oneself is very difficult to achieve. For this reason much of the behavioral research conducted today is concerned with finding ways to help man know himself, his capabilities, his limitations, and his abilities to relate what is inside him to the external world. Part of his world is composed of the groups in which he moves: his community, his family, and his world of work. His world of work is made up of groups; it is made up of individuals, who make up groups and subgroups. The contemporary manager must communicate with, and work with and around a variety of persons with a wide range of personalities and skills.

## WHAT'S HE WORKING ON NOW?

Many behavioral scientists, sensitive to the personal and social needs of the individual, are engaged in research on the nuances of human relationships and interrelationships. As indicated earlier, they are trying to find the elements that create an environment conducive to personal growth and self-realization. Much of their research is designed to elaborate and elucidate on the individual and the group. A few current concerns with special interest for the business world include:

**Communication.** Upward, downward, and lateral communication within an organization; keeping channels of communication open for flow of accurate and useful information; formal and informal methods of communication; improvement of personal skills in written and oral communication; verbalization of internal needs; "feedback" and effects of communication efforts within the organization.

**Decision Making.** Development of skills in handling "open-ended" or problematic situations; degree of participation at various levels of the organization; rational versus impulsive (or intuitive) approaches; boundaries of "risk-taking."

**Innovation and Change.**  Effecting technological, managerial, and organizational change within an organization; implementing change when indicated and gaining acceptance of novel situations; barriers to innovation; effect of change on productivity and morale; innovation through high motivation.

**Conflict.**  How it arises in an organization; interpersonal and interdepartmental hostility and conflict; optimum resolution of conflict; effect on organizational goals and the group's ability to function under stress.

**Leadership.**  Qualities of effective leaders; development of leadership ability; relative effectiveness of "permissive," "supportive," and "autocratic" approaches to management of an organization; entrepreneurship.

**Authority and Accountability.**  Limits of power; relation of responsibility and authority; span of control, reaction to authority from peer, subordinate, and superior groups; degree of accountability; delegation of responsibility and authority.

**Learning, Perception and Creativity.**  Measurement of learning capacities; individuals and groups within the organization; development of potentialities; refinement of existing skills; creation of climate for personal growth and creative expression; personal creativity within the larger organization's goals and structures.

The above represents only a most cursory overview of the facets of human composition and behavior that occupy the professional behavioral researcher these days. Not only do these capsule listings comprise but a few examples of the topics that might be identified with contemporary behavioral research, but also within the topics there is much overlap.

## HOW'S HE DOING?

With these interests, how is the behavioral scientist doing? At least, how is he doing in terms of the three stages of scientific inquiry, that is, research, development, and application? All three warrant comment on the state of the art.

Research is defined as "diligent and systematic inquiry or investigation into a subject in order to discover facts or principles." The research stage seems to be the most active. There are foundations and other philanthropic organizations whose chief activity is the support of research in human behavior. Their encouragement (and their funds) is being used by an ever-growing number of behavioral scientists to do fundamental research in behavior of individuals and groups, increasingly aimed at the business environment. Some well-known social psychologists, sociologists, (and a few political scientists and economists) have begun adapting older theories about intergroup behavior—previously concerned mainly with community, educational, and ethnic groups—to the world of work.

Aside from the intensive research in the departments of social science at major universities, there can hardly be found a respected business school without a division that is performing behavioral research of some sort, and there are springing up interdisciplinary centers which surmount departmental boundaries for concerted effort in behavioral research.

Research is also being performed by the military services, either directly or through contract with behavioral science institutes, on many of the same problems that confront the business world, e.g., leadership, communications, etc. This reflects the growing realization that group problems are group problems—regardless of where they exist.

Basic research is apparently thriving, judging from the outpouring of books on behavioral research and the numerous research reports in scientific and management journals.

This research most often takes place on the university campus or at some other place where the subjects can be observed closely and where data can be verified with a considerable degree of accuracy. The subjects are often students who contribute time to the experiments and then return to their regular work. Sometimes the subjects are businessmen, but the major extent of their participation is a laboratory session for a specified time away from their places of work. Occasionally behavioral research is conducted in an actual work setting, but most frequently the work force sample is small or restricted to companies whose orientation is in favor of behavioral research to the extent that some researchers question the validity of the findings of these experiments performed with "preconditioned" subjects.

## EARLY APPLICATION

If one accepts the premise that earlier research in physical factors that affect productivity was actually behavioral research, then the application phase is widespread and evident in modern business. Changes in the work environment and production processes that were considered radical innovations a few years ago are now accepted practice.

Another example of popular acceptance and application of behavioral science is the use of employee selection aids, particularly psychological tests, the structured interview, and the weighted application form.

There is some evidence that business is applying the additional findings of the modern group of behavioral researchers. Consumer motivation studies were cited earlier, but perhaps a more significant trend is the acceptance of work-motivation theories by some companies, noticeably in the management development area. Instances of full-scale adoption of current motivational theories are rare, but a few companies have changed complete organization structures in order to put into use some of the more recent theories. And a growing number of companies are enlisting the aid of the behavioral scientist to conduct "laboratory" sessions within the organization, all aimed at achieving a higher degree of communication and motivation among their executives.

While both development and application require removal "from the laboratory to the world," they are sometimes confused. Development implies further research and follow-up, always with the thought in mind that the thing being tried is still research, while application is the putting into practical use a principle or law which is accepted as a concrete phenomenon.

There are those, including some behavioral scientists, who decry application of theories about interpersonal and intergroup relationships until they are more fully developed. One psychologist asserted, "There are a handful of companies that are so concerned about their executives' mental health and performance that they are ready to embrace any new theory put forth. . . . They seem all too willing to try putting into practical application every new fad that comes along. . . . What we need is more developmental research."

Development means "to bring out the capabilities or possibilities; cause to grow or expand into a more advanced or effective state." Development for behavioral scientists, as for physical scientists, involves taking a piece of pure or theoretical research which has been refined in the laboratory and putting it through further tests in a given situation where the variables are not as strictly controlled. In other words, development is an expansion of a piece of basic research to see if it is pragmatic.

For the behavioral researcher concerned with people at work, it means trying out a theory in an actual work setting with constant observance, measurement, validation, and recording of data, with the hope that he will achieve universality.

## THE NEED FOR DEVELOPMENT

The development stage is noticeably missing in the largest segment of business. Development often is indicated for a particular piece of research that already has had some development and application, because conditions for a specific company or type of business may not be the same as for business as a whole. An example of application without appropriate development may be found in the use of psychological tests for screening of employees. Some tests have gained so much in popularity that they have become the *sine qua non* for employment throughout the organization, even though the accepted scores have not been validated for the particular industry, the particular company, and the particular jobs under consideration. To ensure that "cut-off" scores are realistic for the situation in which they are used, development research is indicated in many cases.

Carrying this example further, some companies have begun to stress validation of employment tests. For the most part, however, these validations lack desirable accuracy. The usual procedure in validating a given test is to follow up on the work performance of people after they are employed. It is expected that persons scoring 90, for example, will turn out to be better workers than those scoring 70. In most validation efforts, however, an arbitrary "cut-off" score, say 50, is established, and applicants scoring below that point aren't hired. If the scores established for employment, and taken as an indicator of job success, are to be developed and validated fully, the company would have to hire some people who score in the lower percentiles as well as those who achieve a score in the upper percentiles. Then, the job success of those who scored 10 or 20 could be compared with the higher achievers. Even among those scoring in the upper ranges, the person with a 70 score may show more job success than the person with a 90, if they are in different jobs. If psychological tests are to be given much credence, the need for developmental research is apparent.

For another example of application without thorough development the businessman needs only to look at methods of performance appraisal as they are popularly and widely used. A great deal of basic research has been performed on systems of evaluating an employee's success on the job. The fundamental research showed that such reviews were desirable because they left both the superior and the subordinate with a sense of sympathetic understanding. It was further shown that mutual confidence and trust resulted from the feeling that both parties knew fully what the job required and what was expected of the subordinate in meeting the job's objectives, as well as what he could expect from his superior.

So, a major segment of the business community installed performance appraisals throughout their respective companies at all levels of responsibility.

Did anyone stop to ask: "What effect, if any, does the performance appraisal have on subsequent work performance?" There may have been questions in the minds of some businessmen, but only recently did a large multiplant company, working in collaboration with behav-

ioral scientists from a leading university's school of business, decide
to take a look at the effect of those frank, free-communication appraisals on the performance of the employee afterwards. (Incidentally, at
least in the study cited, the effect of performance appraisals on subsequent work performance had a *negative* correlation.)

Employment tests and performance appraisals are only two examples of the work of behavioral scientists which has been accepted
and put to use without adequate development. Much more fundamental
research is at the stage where development is indicated and needed,
if the knowledge gained through the basic research is ever to be meaningful for the business world. Why, then, is this developmental research
not being conducted?

There are many reasons why the gap exists. Managements' (or
organizations') resistance to change has been offered as one reason.
Also, relatively few companies have been in a position to provide a
climate conducive to behavioral research. Therefore, the developmental research has been restricted, almost exclusively, to a few large
corporations with a management that is more likely to be sensitive to
new concepts and trends, and with the funds to sustain a staff to carry
out the studies. In the main, these efforts have been further restricted
to the corporate offices where product output and manufacturing schedules aren't paramount. Occasionally, development research in human
behavior is conducted by smaller companies—usually very small companies dealing in services, rather than material products, where communication channels are relatively close and controllable.

The reluctance of most companies to participate in behavioral research may be understandable, even to the behavioral scientists, for
many developmental projects can (and do) involve a complete rear-
rangement of interpersonal and intergroup relationships and functions. For this reason, many businessmen have been hesitant to "play
around with profits" by encouraging innovation and change in the
organization's structure. Granted that increased productivity and harmonious relations are still the goals of behavioral research as it relates
to business, these changes may not be observable immediately. For
men accustomed to thinking in terms of manufacturing schedules and
year-end profits truly innovative experiments have often been shunned
in favor of the "tried and true."

The behavioral scientist may feel, on the other hand, that he has
produced theories which have been tested and worked out to their
optimum in the atmosphere of fundamental research. It is, therefore,
the hope of behavioral scientists that more and more companies will
appear upon the scene with both the willingness and the desire to "pick
up the ball" and develop the findings of this basic research. On the
strength of their experience during the past few years, they feel that
their optimism is justified.

# 5

# Toward Organizational Behavior

## L. L. Cummings

*This article presents three bases for conceptualizing organizational behavior as a field of inquiry different from other related fields. OB is characterized by three dimensions and three themes that impact the articulation of these dimensions in teaching, research, and application. Cummings then draws implications for the evolution of OB as a discipline.—Eds.*

Attempting to describe a field as dynamic and as multifaceted, or even as confusing, as Organizational Behavior (OB) is not a task for the timid. It may be a task that only the foolish, yet concerned, would even tackle.

What motivates one toward accepting such an undertaking? Two forces are operating. First, there is a clear need to parcel out knowledge into more understandable and convenient packages. Students, managers, and colleagues in other departments request that we respond to straightforward, honest questions like: What is OB? How is OB different from management? How is it different from human relations? It is difficult for students to understand the philosophy or the systematic nature of a program or curriculum if they cannot define the parts. Our credibility with the managerial world is damaged when OB comes out in executive programs as "a little of everything", as "a combination of behavioral jargon and common sense", or as "touchy-feely" without content. The field's lack of confidence in articulating its structure is occasionally reflected in ambiguous and fuzzy suggestions for improvement in the world that managers face.

---

SOURCE: Reprinted by permission of the publisher from "Toward Organizational Behavior," *Academy of Management Review,* January 1978, pp. 90–98.

Second, identification or assertion of the themes and constructs underlying OB, or any other discipline, represents an important platform for expanding knowledge. Without assumptions about what is included, excluded, and on the boundary, duplication among disciplines results. The efficiency of knowledge generation and transmission is hampered. Until a field is defined in relation to its intellectual cousins, it may develop in redundant directions. This leads to the usual awakening that parallel, and perhaps even superior, developments already have occurred in adjacent fields about which we are ignorant. Repetition of such occurrences in a field lessens its intellectual credibility among scholars. All of this is not to deny the benefits to be gained from cross-fertilization and exchange across subfields once these are delineated and common concerns and interests are discovered.

These are the forces underlying the concern. What is said here represents an unfinished product—a thought in process—not a finished, static, intellectually frozen definition. In fact, the argument is made that stimulating, dynamic fields are defined *in process* and that the processes of emergence and evolution should never end.

## PERSPECTIVES ON ORGANIZATIONAL BEHAVIOR

Several partitions have been used in attempting to distinguish OB from related disciplines. Tracing some of these provides perspective on our task and builds a critical platform for appraising where the field is today.

Probably the most common segmentation of subfields relating behavior and organization is based on *units of analysis* where the units are differentiated by level of aggregation. Typically, using this framework, OB is defined as the study of individuals and groups within organizations. The units of analysis are individual and micro (e.g., dyadic) interactions among individuals. Organizational characteristics (e.g., structure, process, climate) are seen either as "givens" which assume a constant state or as independent variables whose variations are assumed to covary with or cause variations in the relevant dependent variables. These relevant dependent variables are measures of individual or micro unit affective and/or behavioral reactions.

Organizational Theory (OT) is typically defined by its focus upon the *organization as the unit of analysis*. Organizational structure, process, goals, technology, and, more recently, climate are the relevant dependent variables, assumed to vary systematically with variations in environmental characteristics but not with characteristics embedded within systematically clustered individuals. A comparative, cross-organizational framework is essential for development of knowledge in OT. Studies of single organizations add little to understanding of organizations when the unit of analysis and variation is assumed to be the organization itself. This realization is increasingly reflected in the empirical literature of OT.[1]

Some have distinguished the field of inquiry based upon an attribution of *typical* or *modal methodologies* to the respective subfields. OB is defined as studies utilizing laboratory and, occasionally, field experimentation. OT is identified with the predominant use of survey and, occasionally, case designs. While the simplicity of this methodological distinction is attractive, it does not reflect the current diversity of designs underlying current research on people in organizations and on organizations per se.

The adjective pairs "normative-descriptive" and "empirical-theoretical" are attractive labels for describing *epistemological differences*. Certainly, the two predominant versions of classical OT have been characterized, and criticized, as excessively normative and not descriptive of behavioral and organizational realities. Both Taylor and Fayol on the one hand, and Weber on the other, have provided much of the focus for the normative critics. Some OB scholars view their field's mission as adding descriptive, empirically based facts to what they see as the essentially normative and theoretical biases of classical OT. With the advent of data among OT scholars and the infusion of organizational development (OD) into the OB tent, these distinctions are no longer descriptive of our domain. Descriptive, empirical, theoretical, and normative can each be used to characterize some work in both OB and OT. Complexity now overshadows the simple straw man of yesterday.

As OD began to emerge a few years ago, the theme of several corridor conversations was that OB *was becoming the applied cousin of OT*. After all, some claimed, OT deals with the theory of organizations by definition. For a moment the distinctions between OB and OD became blurred, and that opaqueness was attractive for some. Reading between the lines, OT was to become the reservoir of accepted and evolving constructs, and OB would emerge as the behavioral engineering function. For managers and consultants we would have OB; for scholars, OT. The largest obstacle to enacting such a distinction is that scholars and appliers do not generally read or listen to one another. The OB people must have their own constructs and theories. The OT people need their own applications, their own means of establishing credibility within the world of action. From this insulation, two OD camps have emerged with their own strategies for change. One focuses on change via the individual and micro unit within the organization and the other on change through structural and environmental manipulation. Alas, another simple, definitional distinction melts!

My preference among these alternative taxonomic bases is the first. The unit of analysis perspective seems cleanest. The most severe problem with this view is finding intellectual bridges to link the subfields. This linkage is crucial for understanding the way organizations function, the impacts they exert, and the opportunities they provide. Some bridges begin to emerge which are at least suggestive. For example, an organization's structure (i.e., number of levels, average span of supervision, degree of horizontal differentiation) can be viewed as a construct linking OT and OB. In OT, structure is typically positioned in a nomological network as a dependent variable. In OB, structure is typically positioned as an independent variable. This differential positioning of the same construct suggests a possible general role that several constructs might take in linking OT and OB. Structure, climate, task design, reward systems, and leader behavior can each be conceived of as intervening between causal forces in the environment of organizations and the behavior and attitudes of persons within organizations. Each is beginning to be modeled as a dependent variable in one context and an independent variable in another.

This differentiation of subfields by unit of analysis and their integration by intervening constructs is subject to limitations. The boundaries of aggregation between levels of analysis are arbitrary, with no fundamental laws underlying the distinctions. That is a limitation shared with the biological and physical sciences, where subfields have arisen as linking mechanisms (e.g., biophysics, biochemistry, psychopharmacology). The conception also lacks feedback loops with reversible intervening constructs. It is likely that such reciprocal causation reflects reality and that models that omit these loops will not provide a full understanding.

If we were to assume this posture of differentiation, what would be the result? Remembering that the distinctions are based primarily on levels of analysis with a slight nod toward the other distinctions, we can propose the definitions in Figure 1.

## A DIMENSIONAL CHARACTERIZATION OF ORGANIZATIONAL BEHAVIOR

I believe that OB is evolving toward the model presented in Figure 2. The field is being enacted, not defined in some a priori sense, by scholars and teachers in ways that imply the dimensional, thematic conception suggested in that figure.

Three dimensions define the conceptual domain of OB. Most disciplines and emerging fields of inquiry that stand at the interface between science and professional practice are describable in terms of these dimensions. The specific articulation of the dimensions depends

**FIGURE 1**   Distinctions among Organizational Behavior, Organizational
Psychology, Organizational Theory, and Personnel and Human
Resources

| | |
|---|---|
| Organizational Behavior-<br>Organizational Psychology (OP) | Both fields focus upon explaining human behavior within organizations. Their difference centers on the fact that OP restricts its explanatory constructs to those at the psychological level. OB draws constructs from multiple disciplines. As the domain of OP continues to expand, the difference between OB and OP is diminishing, perhaps to the point of identity between the fields. |
| Organizational Behavior-<br>Organizational Theory (OT) | The distinction is based on two differences; unit of analysis and focus of dependent variables. OB is defined as the study of individual and group behavior within organizations and the application of such knowledge. OT is the study of structure, processes, and outcomes of the organization per se. The distinction is neither that OB is atheoretical and concerned only with behavior nor that OT is unique or exclusive in its attention to theory. Alternatively, the distinction can be conceived as between micro and macro perspectives on OB. This removes the awkward differentiation of behavior and theory. |
| Organizational Behavior-<br>Personnel and Human<br>Resources (P&HR) | This distinction usually depicts OB as the more basic of the two and P&HR as more applied in emphasis. OB is seen as more concept oriented while P&HR is |

**FIGURE 1**    (*concluded*)

| Organizational Behavior-Personnel and Human Resources (P&HR) (*continued*) | viewed as emphasizing techniques or technologies. The dependent variables, behavior and affective reactions within organizations, are frequently presented as similar. P&HR can be seen as standing at the interface between the organization and the individual, focusing on developing and implementing the system for attracting, maintaining, and motivating the individual within the organization. |
| --- | --- |

significantly upon the underlying epistemological themes adopted by the discipline.

## A Way of Thinking

OB is a *way of thinking,* a manner of conceiving problems and articulating research and action solutions which can be characterized by five postures. First, problems and questions are typically formulated within an independent variable(s)-dependent variable(s) framework. Recently, OB has begun to incorporate personal and situational moderators into this framework. OB's assertion that behavior within organizations is subject as systematic study is based on conceptualization of the object of study as non-random, systematic, and generally purposive. This way of thinking is significantly influencing our methodologies. The field is engaged in a sometimes painful search for cause and effect within our models.

A second component of OB as a way of thinking is its orientation toward change as a desirable outcome for organizations and persons within organizations. Static phenomena possess diminishing prestige as topics of study. Conditions for stimulating change and models for evaluating change are an increasingly important part of the field.

Third, there is a distinctly humanistic tone within OB, reflected in concern for self-development, personal growth, and self-actualization. Although its influence on research and teaching seems to ebb and flow, and its reflection in scholarship and pedagogy varies by school, it is there, and its presence is causing both strain (given its positioning adjacent to scientism) and excitement, even relevance, within OB. The striving is toward humanism without softness. OB shares this dilemma with most of the person-oriented disciplines that attempt to combine basic, good science with a change orientation. Yet this tone of humanism is only one side of the current, slightly schizophrenic posture of OB. The other side is reflected in a heavy emphasis on operant learning models and behavioral modification techniques, an orientation toward environmental determinism rather than self actualization.

Fourth, OB is becoming increasingly performance oriented, with more studies including a performance-oriented dependent variable. The field is beginning to capture an important distinction between two types of dependent variables. One perspective focuses on description of a behavior, activity, or outcome, that is, the proper focus for scientific analysis and thinking. The other aims at application of a preference function to these behaviors, activities, or outcomes, resulting in a scaling of effectiveness or success. This is the proper focus for an engineering analysis—a managerial mind set.[2] We are beginning to hear the demands for relevance in our research and teaching. Unless OB can increase its performance payoffs, the field may be in danger of losing some of its hard battles for a niche in the curriculum or a moment in the board room.

Finally, OB uses the discipline imposed by the scientific method. The field is substantially influenced by norms of skepticism, caution, replication, and public exposure of knowledge based on facts. In many ways, this posture of "scientism" confuses some students and clients. It can be seen as the antithesis of several other postures that characterize OB thinking. Yet it is generally accepted as a crucial posture. It helps to keep the field straight, and it is the key ingredient in whatever longevity the field may possess. Scientific method, applied to OB, provides the mechanism for feedback and self-renewal.

## A Body of Constructs, Models, and Facts

Even though OB is characterized by some definitional confusion, an implicit agreement is emerging about some of its components. Differences exist concerning the relative weighting of components and the emphasis given to basic science versus application in transmitting the field to others. But most treatments of the field now include coverage of constructs, models, and facts on: motivation, learning or socialization, group structure and process, leader behavior, task design, interpersonal communication, organizational structure, interpersonal change and conflict, and material on relevant dependent variables (e.g. satisfaction, other attitudes, participation measures, performance dimensions, and other behaviors).

This emergence of an identity for the field is evidenced by the second generation of OB textbooks, which are more similar in topical coverage than their ancestors. Some models sell and are thus influential in structuring the introductory level curricula underlying our field. Others stretch the field at its boundaries but do not become a part of the core. That core is gradually developing toward an identifiable body of components.

## A System of Technology

OB is also a system or a collection of technologies. These have evolved out of the primary areas of study identified as the independent variables of OB. Techniques now exist for: training leaders, designing tasks, designing organizations, evaluating performances, rewarding behaviors, and modeling behaviors.

The uncritical eye might be pleased with OB's tool kit. Superficially, it appears that the field is ready to move into the world of action with vigor and confidence. But our posture of scientism keeps the field honest. These technologies are largely exploratory, unvalidated and, in a few cases, under evaluation. The field has even spawned an occasional technology that has been adopted and later found damaging to an organization and its participants. In most cases, even when the technologies work, the field's theoretical models are not sufficiently developed to explain why they were effective. So, a system or collection of technologies? Yes. A behavioral engineering discipline? No.

## THEMES INFLUENCING ORGANIZATIONAL BEHAVIOR

As depicted in Figure 2, three themes span the dimensions defining OB and influence the way each.dimension is articulated. The relative emphasis given to each theme over time, by the various schools of thought within OB, determines our ways of thinking, constructs and facts, and development of technologies.

### Existentialism

The emphasis here is upon the uncertain, contingent environment of people within organizations (and organizations). Existentialism emphasizes that in the face of this type of environment, persons must exercise self-control in pursuit of their own objectives. The ultimate responsibility for designing productive and satisfying organizational environments rests with human beings. It is their responsibility to fashion themselves—to implement self-control. This philosophical pos-

**FIGURE 2**    Dimensions and Themes of Organizational Behavior

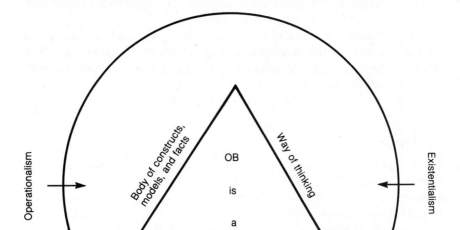

ture leaves a legacy of concepts within OB—goal, purpose, expectation, expectancy, instrumental, path, and contingency.

This theme is forcing OB to become a more complex discipline. It asserts that no meaning exists in absolutes. All meaning derives from comparison; meaning is always relative. Activities and outcomes within organizations are meaningful only within a context including implicit or explicit statements of purpose. This is at the core of one important, current development in conceptualizing the influence of most of the independent variables treated in OB—the concept of contingency.

With the realization that an independent variable's effects depend, the next logical question becomes: Depends upon what? When? etc. *Why* did *who* do *what* with *whom* with what *outcomes?* This seemingly simple question can be applied to most independent-dependent variable linkages currently of concern in OB. The *why* focuses on the causes, the reasons, the antecedents of variance in the dependent variable.

The *who* focuses on the initiating party (individual, group, or organization). The *what* requires description of the behavior in question. The *whom* provides the interaction component, adding dimensionality to the search for meaningfulness. It provides a vertical, horizontal, or diagonal vector to the reality that OB attempts to understand. The *outcomes* provide the ultimate meaning to the field. Existentialism implies that the meaning in any act exists in its consequences, and OB seems to be moving toward this realization.

## Operationalism

Operationalism is reflected in three ways. First, the field is searching for theories of the middle range in most of its subareas. The grand, general, abstract models of motivation, leadership, environment-structure interaction, and change are not yielding satisfying, systematic, cumulative data. Some models posit relations between environmental and organizational characteristics and individual attitudes and behaviors. Models are needed to describe the processes through which environment impacts structure and structure impacts attitudes and behavior.

Second, emphasis is being given to the operations or behaviors through which people within organizations function. Whether describing what managers do or analyzing the impact of leaders, the importance of formulating the issue in operational terms is being realized. The literature is beginning to be characterized by questions like:

1. Through what operations is structure actually designed?
2. Through what operations does a leader impact a subordinate?
3. Through what operations do rewards and punishments effect change?
4. Through what operations do groups actually make decisions?

In each case, the field is beginning to examine the physiology of behavior within organizations. The anatomy of OB is important, but its study has not led to understanding the processes through which persons and organizations interact.

Third, measurement issues are impacting the field. Questions of reliability and validity must be faced, and questions of scaling and measurement confronted. We are increasingly anxious about our inability to explain large amounts of variance in dependent variables. Three rather lengthy streams of research have reached the point where lack of early attention to how we operationalized constructs and validated measures has caused major problems for continued, meaningful work. Cases in point are research on: the two-factor model of motivation (with faulty measurement procedures); expectancy formulations of motivation (with testing of inappropriate models); and the impact of organizational design on attitudes and behaviors (with designs that confound independent variables). While not completely pessimistic, I believe that the field has been extremely inefficient and myopic in the research strategies applied in some areas.

### Neo-behavioralism

Finally, many causal assumptions and models in OB are moving toward a behavioristic orientation with a cognitive overtone. Motivation theory, under the influence of expectancy models, has moved in this direction. Leadership studies reflect the notion of instrumental, goal-oriented behavior with a significant emphasis on leader behavior being partially a function of the consequences which it produces. The concept of contingency plays a major role in several fields within OB, its general intellectual structure deriving directly from the behavioristic notion of structure and process evolving toward forms that are reinforcing to the organism. The behavioristic perspective also has surfaced in literature dealing with organizational design and organizational control and power. Distributions of influence and power are partially explained by environmental consequences of attempts at influence. The exercise of power generates consequences which, in turn, affect structural configurations of the organization.

Radical behaviorism is not the dominant theme, but rather a combination of general behavioral constructs *and* cognitions. It is not clear what functions are provided by the incorporation of cognitions within OB models. Little research has been addressed to the question of the variance explained in most OB models by cognitions beyond that explained by environmental determinants. Perhaps cognitive concepts do explain added variance, or perhaps they constitute a residual reservoir of unexplained variance to which we inappropriately attribute meaning.

## CONCLUSIONS AND IMPLICATIONS

What are the implications of this perspective on the field? First, ultimately the definitions of the domains of OB, OT, OP, and OD are arbitrary. Definitions should be tested by their usefulness in specifying constructs and functional relations. Definitions are needed to guide the field toward middle range and operational theory. Movement toward definition by induction is needed. It may prove fruitful to aim toward definition through describing what is happening in the main streams of research within OB. Definitions established by assertion lead to debate without fruitful results.

Second, realities in organizations change so rapidly that our descriptions (ways of thinking, constructs and technologies) do not keep pace with the rate of change in the objects of our study.[3] I see two implications of this for OB. First, incredibly long periods of time are needed to assess organizations and to identify the fundamental, underlying nature of the field. Second, increasing energy will be devoted to collapsing the time intervals needed to develop relevant constructs and models and to testing these models. This implies that management, as a general field, will accelerate adoption of both simulation and experimental designs. These designs permit the modeling of time lags. Contrary to the usual evaluation of such designs, they will allow us to become more realistic in our modeling and measurement of OB.

Third, what might this line of reasoning mean for the Academy of Management and its members? The Academy is presently the only camp which attempts to house OB, OT, OD, and P&HR. For the moment, these fields have separate tents within the camp, but I believe that the traditional distinctions are beginning to melt. Several examples illustrate this permeability. The 1976 doctoral consortium conducted at the National Academy Convention included topics from both OT and OB. I suspect it is impossible to talk at an advanced level about one domain without the other. The P&HR division's program at the 1976 National Academy Convention consists of about 40 percent OB material. This reflects a healthy trend for both P&HR and OB. It is naive to deal with many of the important issues in P&HR without incorporating OB models and research. The *Academy of Management Journal*, the *Academy of Management Review*, *Organizational Behavior and Human Performance*, and *Administrative Science Quarterly* exhibit trends in submissions that reflect an increasing emphasis on *multiple* levels of analysis in both the independent and dependent variable domains.

I believe we are moving toward an enacted field, perhaps best labeled organizational analysis or organizational science (if we wish to emphasize the scientific lineage of our interests and our aspirations). Basically, we now have five divisions within the Academy, composing organizational analysis or science. These are Organizational Behavior, Organization and Management Theory, Personnel and Human Resources, Organization Development, and Organizational Communication. Such segmentation continues to provide important functions for the Academy and its members, but it remains an open question whether segmentation is the most efficient strategy to advance our common interest in behavior *in* and *of* organizations.

As Thurstone said:

It is the faith of all science that an unlimited number of phenomena can be comprehended in terms of a limited number of concepts or ideal constructs. Without this faith no science could ever have any motivation. To deny this faith is to affirm the primary chaos of nature and the consequent futility of scientific effort. The constructs in terms of which natural phenomena are comprehended are man-made inventions. To discover a scientific law is merely to discover that a man-made scheme serves to unify, and thereby to simplify, comprehension of a certain class of natural phenomena. A scientific law is not to be thought of as having an independent existence which some scientist is fortunate to stumble upon. A scientific law is not a part of nature. It is only a way of comprehending nature.

## NOTES

1. Hannan and Freeman (1) have argued quite convincingly that comparative analyses of organizational effectiveness are inappropriate for scientific purposes.
2. My thinking here has been significantly influenced by Robert Kahn of the University of Michigan. His comments at the 1976 Carnegie-Mellon Workshop on Organizational Effectiveness have been particularly helpful.
3. I am indebted to Professor Lou Pondy for stimulating this notion.

## REFERENCES

1. Hannan, M. T., and J. Freeman. "Obstacles for Comparative Studies." *New Perspectives in Organizational Effectiveness* ed. P. S. Goodman and J. M. Pennings. San Francisco: Jossey-Bass, 1977, pp. 106–31.
2. Thurston, L. S. *Multiple-Factor Analysis.* Chicago: University of Chicago Press, 1947.

# 6

# General Systems Theory: Applications for Organizations and Management

*Fremont E. Kast*

*and*

*James E. Rosenzweig*

*World War II marked the beginning of the Systems Age, although it was not until many years after the war that systems science found its way into the management literature. This article discusses applying systems theory to the real world of organizations and concludes by looking at what steps need to be taken to make general systems theory a more useful model for both organizational analysis and application by practicing managers who must function on a day-to-day basis.—Eds.*

Biological and social scientists generally have embraced systems concepts. Many organization and management theorists seem anxious to identify with this movement and to contribute to the development of an approach which purports to offer the ultimate—the unification of all science into one grand conceptual model. Who possibly could resist? General systems theory seems to provide a relief from the limitations

---

SOURCE: From *Academy of Management Journal,* December 1972, pp. 447–65. Reprinted by permission.

of more mechanistic approaches and a rationale for rejecting "principles" based on relatively "closed-system" thinking. This theory provides the paradigm for organization and management theorists to "crank into their systems model" all of the diverse knowledge from relevant underlying disciplines. It has become almost mandatory to have the word "system" in the title of recent articles and books (many of us have compromised and placed it only in the subtitle).[1]

But where did it all start? This question takes us back into history and brings to mind the long-standing philosophical arguments between mechanistic and organismic models of the nineteenth and early twentieth centuries. As Deutsch says:

> Both mechanistic and organismic models were based substantially on experiences and operations known before 1850. Since then, the experience of almost a century of scientific and technological progress has so far not been utilized for any significant new model for the study of organization and in particular of human thought [12, p. 389].

General systems theory even revives the specter of the "vitalists" and their views on "life force" and most certainly brings forth renewed questions of teleological or purposeful behavior of both living and nonliving systems. Phillips and others have suggested that the philosophical roots of general systems theory go back even further, at least to the German philosopher Hegel (1770–1831) [29, p. 56]. Thus, we should recognize that in the adoption of the systems approach for the study of organizations we are not dealing with newly discovered ideas—they have a rich genealogy.

Even in the field of organization and management theory, systems views are not new. Chester Barnard used a basic systems framework.

> A cooperative system is a complex of physical, biological, personal, and social components which are in a specific systematic relationship by reason of the cooperation of two or more persons for at least one definite end. Such a system is evidently a subordinate unit of larger systems from one point of view; and itself embraces subsidiary systems—physical, biological, etc.—from another point of view. One of the systems comprised within a cooperative system, the one which is implicit in the phrase "cooperation of two or more persons;" is called an "organization" [3, p. 65].

And Barnard was influenced by the "systems views" of Vilfredo Pareto and Talcott Parsons. Certainly this quote (dressed up a bit to give the term "system" more emphasis) could be the introduction to a 1972 book on organizations.

Miller points out that Alexander Bogdanov, the Russian philosopher, developed a theory of tektology or universal organization science in 1912 which foreshadowed general systems theory and used many of the same concepts as modern systems theorists [26, pp. 249–250].

However, in spite of a long history of organismic and holistic thinking, the utilization of the systems approach did not become the accepted model for organization and management writers until relatively recently. It is difficult to specify the turning point exactly. The momentum of systems thinking was identified by Scott in 1961 when he described the relationship between general systems theory and organization theory.

> The distinctive qualities of modern organization theory are its conceptual-analytical base, its reliance on empirical research data, and above all, its integrating nature. These qualities are framed in a philosophy which accepts the premise that the only meaningful way to study organization is to study it as a system. . . . Modern organization theory and general system theory are similar in that they look at organization as an integrated whole [33, pp. 15–21].

Scott said explicitly what many in our field had been thinking and/or implying—he helped us put into perspective the important writings of Herbert Simon, James March, Talcott Parsons, George Homans, E. Wight Bakke, Kenneth Boulding, and many others.

But how far have we really advanced over the past decade in applying general systems theory to organizations and their management? Is it still a "skeleton"; or have we been able to "put some meat on the bones"? The systems approach has been touted because of its potential usefulness in understanding the complexities of "live" organizations. Has this approach really helped us in this endeavor or has it compounded confusion with chaos? Herbert Simon describes the challenge for the systems approach:

> In both science and engineering, the study of "systems" is an increasingly popular activity. Its popularity is more a response to a pressing need for synthesizing and analyzing complexity than it is to any large development of a body of knowledge and technique for dealing with complexity. If this popularity is to be more than a fad, necessity will have to mother invention and provide substance to go with the name [35, p. 114].

In this article we will explore the issue of whether we are providing substance for the term *systems approach* as it relates to the study of organizations and their management. There are many interesting historical and philosophical questions concerning the relationship between the mechanistic and organistic approaches and their applicability to the various fields of science, as well as other interesting digressions into the evolution of systems approaches. However, we will resist those temptations and plunge directly into a discussion of the key concepts of general systems theory, the way in which these ideas have been used by organization theorists, the limitations in their application, and some suggestions for the future.

## KEY CONCEPTS OF GENERAL
## SYSTEMS THEORY

The key concepts of general systems theory have been set forth by many writers [6, 7, 13, 17, 25, 28, 39] and have been used by many organization and management theorists [10, 14, 18, 19, 21, 22, 24, 32]. It is not our purpose here to elaborate on them in great detail because we anticipate that most readers will have been exposed to them in some depth. Figure 1 provides a very brief review of those characteristics of systems which seem to have wide acceptance. The review is far from complete. It is difficult to identify a "complete" list of characteristics derived from general systems theory; moreover, it is merely a first-order classification. There are many derived second- and third-order characteristics which could be considered. For example, James G. Miller sets forth *165* hypotheses, stemming from open systems theory, which might be applicable to two or more levels of systems [25]. He suggests that they are *general* systems theoretical hypotheses and qualifies them by suggesting that they are propositions applicable to general systems *behavior* theory and would thus exclude nonliving systems. He does not limit these propositions to individual organisms, but considers them appropriate for social systems as well. His hypotheses are related to such issues as structure, process, subsystems,

**FIGURE 1**   Key Concepts of General Systems Theory

---

*Subsystems or Components:* A system by definition is composed of interrelated parts or elements. This is true for all systems—mechanical, biological, and social. Every system has at least two elements, and these elements are interconnected.

*Holism, Synergism, Organicism, and Gestalt:* The whole is not just the sum of the parts; the system itself can be explained only as a totality. Holism is the opposite of elementarism, which views the total as the sum of its individual parts.

*Open Systems View:* Systems can be considered in two ways: (1) closed or (2) open. Open systems exchange information, energy, or material with their environments. Biological and social systems are inherently open systems; mechanical systems may be open or closed. The concepts of open and closed systems are difficult to defend in the absolute. We prefer to think of open-closed as a dimension; that is, systems are relatively open or relatively closed.

*Input-Transformation-Output Model:* The open system can be viewed as a transformation model. In a dynamic relationship with its environment, it receives various inputs, transforms these inputs in some way, and exports outputs.

*System Boundaries:* It follows that systems have boundaries which separate them from their environments. The concept of boundaries helps us

**FIGURE 1** (*concluded*)

understand the distinction between open and closed systems. The relatively
closed system has rigid, impenetrable boundaries; whereas the open system
has permeable boundaries between itself and a broader suprasystem.
Boundaries are relatively easily defined in physical and biological systems,
but are very difficult to delineate in social systems, such as organizations.

*Negative Entropy:* Closed, physical systems are subject to the force of
entropy which increases until eventually the entire system fails. The
tendency toward maximum entropy is a movement to disorder, complete
lack of resource transformation, and death. In a closed system, the change
in entropy must always be positive; however, in open biological or social
systems, entropy can be arrested and may even be transformed into
negative entropy—a process of more complete organization and ability to
transform resources—because the system imports resources from its
environment.

*Steady State, Dynamic Equilibrium, and Homeostasis:* The concept of
steady state is closely related to that of negative entropy. A closed system
eventually must attain an equilibrium state with maximum entropy—death
or disorganization. However, an open system may attain a state where the
system remains in dynamic equilibrium through the continuous inflow of
materials, energy, and information.

*Feedback:* The concept of feedback is important in understanding how a
system maintains a steady state. Information concerning the outputs or the
process of the system is fed back as an input into the system, perhaps
leading to changes in the transformation process and/or future outputs.
Feedback can be both positive and negative, although the field of
cybernetics is based on negative feedback. Negative feedback is
informational input which indicates that the system is deviating from a
prescribed course and should readjust to a new steady state.

*Hierarchy:* A basic concept in systems thinking is that of hierarchical
relationships between systems. A system is composed of subsystems of a
lower order and is also part of a suprasystem. Thus, there is a hierarchy of
the components of the system.

*Internal Elaboration:* Closed systems move toward entropy and
disorganization. In contrast, open systems appear to move in the direction of
greater differentiation, elaboration, and a higher level of organization.

*Multiple Goal-Seeking:* Biological and social systems appear to have
multiple goals or purposes. Social organizations seek multiple goals, if for
no other reason than that they are composed of individuals and subunits
with different values and objectives.

*Equifinality of Open Systems:* In mechanistic systems there is a direct
cause and effect relationship between the initial conditions and the final
state. Biological and social systems operate differently. Equifinality suggests
that certain results may be achieved with different initial conditions and in
different ways. This view suggests that social organizations can accomplish
their objectives with diverse inputs and with varying internal activities
(conversion processes).

information, growth, and integration. It is obviously impossible to discuss all of these hypotheses; we want only to indicate the extent to which many interesting propositions are being posed which might have relevance to many different types of systems. It will be a very long time (if ever) before most of these hypotheses are validated; however, we are surprised at how many of them can be agreed with intuitively, and we can see their possible verification in studies of social organizations.

We turn now to a closer look at how successful or unsuccessful we have been in utilizing these concepts in the development of "modern organization theory."

## A BEGINNING: ENTHUSIASTIC BUT INCOMPLETE

We have embraced general systems theory but, really, how completely? We could review a vast literature in modern organization theory which has explicitly or implicitly adopted systems theory as a frame of reference, and we have investigated in detail a few representative examples of the literature in assessing the "state of the art" [18, 19, 21, 22, 31, 38]. It was found that most of these books professed to utilize general systems theory. Indeed, in the first few chapters, many of them did an excellent job of presenting basic systems concepts and showing their relationship to organizations; however, when they moved further into the discussion of more specific subject matter, they departed substantially from systems theory. The studies appear to use a "partial systems approach" and leave for the reader the problem of integrating the various ideas into a systemic whole. It also appears that many of the authors are unable, because of limitations of knowledge about subsystem relationships, to carry out the task of using general systems theory as a conceptual basis for organization theory.

Furthermore, it is evident that each author had many "good ideas" stemming from the existing body of knowledge or current research on organizations which did not fit neatly into a "systems model." For example, they might discuss leadership from a relatively closed-system point of view and not consider it in relation to organizational technology, structure, or other variables. Our review of the literature suggests that much remains to be done in applying general systems theory to organization theory and management practice.

## SOME DILEMMAS IN APPLYING GST TO ORGANIZATIONS

Why have writers embracing general systems theory as a basis for studying organizations had so much difficulty in following through? Part of this difficulty may stem from the newness of the paradigm and our inability to operationalize "all we think we know" about this approach. Or it may be because we know too little about the systems under investigation. Both of these possibilities will be covered later, but first we need to look at some of the more specific conceptual problems.

## Organizations as Organisms

One of the basic contributions of general systems theory was the rejection of the traditional closed-system or mechanistic view of social organizations. But, did general systems theory free us from this constraint only to impose another, less obvious one? General systems theory grew out of the organismic views of von Bertalanffy and other biologists; thus, many of the characteristics are relevant to the living organism. It is conceptually easy to draw the analogy between living organisms and social organizations. "There is, after all, an intuitive similarity between the organization of the human body, and the kinds of organizations men create. And so, undaunted by the failures of the human-social analogy through time, new theorists try afresh in each epoch" [2, p. 660]. General systems theory would have us accept this analogy between organism and social organization. Yet, we have a hard time swallowing it whole. Katz and Kahn warn us of the danger:

> There has been no more pervasive, persistent, and futile fallacy handicapping the social sciences than the use of the physical model for the understanding of social structures. The biological metaphor, with its crude comparisons of the physical parts of the body to the parts of the social system, has been replaced by more subtle but equally misleading analogies between biological and social functioning. This figurative type of thinking ignores the essential difference between the socially contrived nature of social systems and the physical structure of the machine or the human organism. So long as writers are committed to a theoretical framework based upon the physical model, they will miss the essential social-psychological facts of the highly variable, loosely articulated character of social systems [19, p. 31].

In spite of this warning, Katz and Kahn do embrace much of the general systems theory concepts which are based on the biological metaphor. We must be very cautious about trying to make this analogy too literal. We agree with Silverman who says, "It may, therefore, be necessary to drop the analogy between an organization and an organism: organizations may be systems but not necessarily natural systems" [34, p. 31].

## Distinction between Organization and an Organization

General systems theory emphasizes that systems are organized—they are composed of interdependent components in some relationship. The social organization would then follow logically as just another system. But, we are perhaps being caught in circular thinking. It is true that all systems (physical, biological, and social) are by definition organized, but are all systems organizations? Rapoport and Horvath distinguish "organization theory" and "the theory of organizations" as follows:

> We see organization theory as dealing with general and abstract organizational principles; it applies to any system exhibiting organized complexity. As such, organization theory is seen as an extension of mathematical physics or, even more generally, of mathematics designed to deal with organized systems. The theory of organizations, on the other hand, purports to be a social science. It puts real human organizations at the center of interest. It may study the social structure of organizations and so can be viewed as a branch of sociology; it can study the behavior of individuals or groups as members of organizations and can be viewed as a part of social psychology; it can study power relations and principles of control in organizations and so fits into political science [30, pp. 74–75].

Why make an issue of this distinction? It seems to us that there is a vital matter involved. All systems may be considered to be organized, and more advanced systems may display differentiation in the activities of component parts—such as the specialization of human organs. However, all systems *do not* have purposeful entities. Can the heart or lungs be considered as purposeful entities in themselves or are they only components of the larger purposeful system, the human body? By contrast, the social organization is composed of two or more purposeful elements. "An organization consists of elements that have and can exercise their own wills" [1, p. 669]. Organisms, the foundation stone of general systems theory, do not contain purposeful elements which exercise their own will. This distinction between the organism and the social organization is of importance. In much of general systems theory, the concern is primarily with the way in which the organism responds to environmentally generated inputs. Feedback concepts and the maintenance of a steady state are based on internal adaptations to environmental forces. (This is particularly true of cybernetic models.) But, what about those changes and adaptations which occur from *within* social organizations? Purposeful elements within the social organization may initiate activities and adaptations which are difficult to subsume under feedback and steady state concepts.

## Opened and Closed Systems

Another dilemma stemming from general systems theory is the tendency to dichotomize all systems as opened or closed. We have been led to think of physical systems as closed, subject to the laws of entropy, and to think of biological systems as open to their environment and, possibly, becoming negentropic. But applying this strict polarization to social organizations creates many difficulties. In fact, most social organizations and their subsystems are "partially open" and "partially closed." Open and closed are a matter of degree. Unfortunately, there seems to be a widely held view (often more implicit than explicit) that *open-system thinking is good and closed-system thinking is bad*. We have not become sufficiently sophisticated to recognize that both are appropriate under certain conditions. For example, one of the most useful conceptualizations set forth by Thompson is that the social organization *must seek* to use closed-system concepts (particularly at the technical core) to reduce uncertainty and to create more effective performance at this level.

## Still Subsystems Thinking

Even though we preach a general systems approach, we often practice subsystems thinking. Each of the academic disciplines and each of us personally have limited perspective of the system we are studying. While proclaiming a broad systems viewpoint, we often dismiss variables outside our interest or competence as being irrelevant, and we only open our system to those inputs which we can handle with our disciplinary bag of tools. We are hampered because each of the academic disciplines has taken a narrow "partial systems view" and find comfort in the relative certainty which this creates. Of course, this is not a problem unique to modern organization theory. Under the more traditional process approach to the study of management, we were able to do an admirable job of delineating and discussing planning, organizing, and controlling as separate activities. We were much less successful in discussing them as integrated and interrelated activities.

## How Does Our Knowledge Fit?

One of the major problems in utilizing general systems theory is that we know (or think we know) more about certain relationships than we can fit into a general systems model. For example, we are beginning to understand the two-variable relationship between technology and structure. But, when we introduce another variable, say psychosocial relationships, our models become too complex. Consequently, in order to discuss all the things we know about organizations, we depart from a systems approach. Perhaps it is because we know a great deal more about the elements or subsystems of an organization than we do about the interrelationships and interactions between these subsystems. And, general systems theory forces us to consider those relationships about which we know the least—a true dilemma. So we continue to elaborate on those aspects of the organization which we know best—a partial systems view.

## Failure to Delineate a Specific System

When the social sciences embraced general systems theory, the total system became the focus of attention and terminology tended toward vagueness. In the utilization of systems theory, we should be more precise in delineating the specific system under consideration. Failure to do this leads to much confusion. As Murray suggests:

> I am wary of the word "system" because social scientists use it very frequently without specifying which of several possible different denotations they have in mind; but more particularly because, today, "system" is a highly cathected term, loaded with prestige; hence, we are all strongly tempted to employ it even when we have nothing definite in mind and its only service is to indicate that we subscribe to the general premise respecting the interdependence of things—basic to organismic theory, holism, field theory, interactionism, transactionism, etc. ... When definitions of the units of a system are lacking, the term stands for no more than an article of faith, and is misleading to boot, insofar as it suggests a condition of affairs that may not actually exist [27, pp. 50–51].

We need to be much more precise in delineating both the boundaries of the system under consideration and the level of our analysis. There is a tendency for current writers in organization theory to accept general systems theory and then to move indiscriminately across systems boundaries and between levels of systems without being very precise (and letting their readers in on what is occurring). James Miller suggests the need for clear delineation of levels in applying systems theory, "It is important to follow one procedural rule in systems theory in order to avoid confusion. Every discussion should begin with an identification of the level of reference, and the discourse should not change to another level without a specific statement that this is occurring" (25, p. 216]. Our field is replete with these confusions about systems levels. For example, when we use the term "organizational behavior" are we talking about the way the organization behaves as a system or are we talking about the behavior of the individual participants? By goals, do we mean the goals of the organization or the goals of the individuals within the organization? In using systems theory we must become more precise in our delineation of systems boundaries and systems levels if we are to prevent confusing conceptual ambiguity.

### Recognition that Organizations Are "Contrived Systems"

We have a vague uneasiness that general systems theory truly does not recognize the "contrived" nature of social organizations. With its predominate emphasis on natural organisms, it may understate some characteristics which are vital for the social organization. Social organizations do not occur naturally in nature; they are contrived by man. They have structure; but it is the structure of events rather than of physical components, and it cannot be separated from the processes of the system. The fact that social organizations are contrived by human beings suggests that they can be established for an infinite variety of purposes and do not follow the same life-cycle patterns of birth, growth, maturity, and death as biological systems. As Katz and Kahn say:

> Social structures are essentially contrived systems. They are made of men and are imperfect systems. They can come apart at the seams overnight, but they can also outlast by centuries the biological organisms which originally created them. The cement which holds them together is essentially psychological rather than biological. Social systems are anchored in the attitudes, perceptions, beliefs, motivations, habits, and expectations of human beings [19, p. 33].

Recognizing that the social organization is contrived again cautions us against making an exact analogy between it and physical or biological systems.

### Questions of Systems Effectiveness

General systems theory with its biological orientation would appear to have an evolutionary view of system effectiveness. That living system which best adapts to its environment prospers and survives. The primary measure of effectiveness is perpetuation of the organism's species. Teleological behavior is therefore directed toward survival. But, is survival the only criterion of effectiveness of the social system? It is probably an essential but not all-inclusive measure of effectiveness.

General systems theory emphasizes the organism's survival goal and does not fully relate to the question of the effectiveness of the system in its supra-system—the environment. Parsonian functional-structural views provide a contrast. "The *raison d'etre* of complex organizations, according to this analysis, is mainly to benefit the society in which they belong, and that society is, therefore, the appropriate frame of reference for the evaluation of organizational effectiveness" [41, p. 896].

But, this view seems to go to the opposite extreme from the survival view of general systems theory—the organization exists to serve the society. It seems to us that the truth lies somewhere between these two viewpoints. And it is likely that a systems viewpoint (modified from the species survival view of general systems theory) will be most appropriate. Yuchtman and Seashore suggest:

> The organization's success over a period of time in this competition for resources—i.e., its bargaining position in a given environment—is regarded as an expression of its overall effectiveness. Since the resources are of various kinds, and the competitive relationships are multiple, and since there is interchangeability among classes of resources, the assessment of organizational effectiveness must be in terms not of any single criterion but of an open-ended multidimensional set of criteria [41, p. 891].

This viewpoint suggests that questions of organizational effectiveness must be concerned with at least three levels of analysis: the level of the environment, the level of the social organization as a system, and the level of the subsystems (human participants) within the organization. Perhaps much of our confusion and ambiguity concerning organizational effectiveness stems from our failure to clearly delineate the level of our analysis and, even more important, our failure really to understand the relationships among these levels.

Our discussion of some of the problems associated with the application of general systems theory to the study of social organizations might suggest that we completely reject the appropriateness of this model. On the contrary, we see the systems approach as the new paradigm for the study of organizations; but, like all new concepts in the sciences, one which has to be applied, modified, and elaborated to make it as useful as possible.

## SYSTEMS THEORY PROVIDES THE NEW PARADIGM

We hope the discussion of GST and organizations provides a realistic appraisal. We do not want to promote the value of the systems approach as a matter of faith; however, we do see systems theory as vital to the study of social organizations and as providing the major new paradigm for our field of study.

Thomas Kuhn provides an interesting interpretation of the nature of scientific revolution [20]. He suggests that major changes in all fields of science occur with the development of new conceptual schemes or "paradigms." These new paradigms do not just represent a step-by-step advancement in "normal" science (the science generally accepted and practiced) but, rather, a revolutionary change in the way the scientific field is perceived by the practitioners. Kuhn says:

> The historian of science may be tempted to exclaim that when paradigms change, the world itself changes with them. Led by a new paradigm, scientists adopt new instruments and look in new places. Even more important, during revolutions scientists see new and different things when looking with familiar instruments in places they have looked before. It is rather as if the professional community has been suddenly transported to another planet where familiar objects are seen in a different light and are joined by unfamiliar ones as well. . . . Paradigm changes do cause scientists to see the world of their research-engagement differently. Insofar as their only recourse to that world is through what they see and do, we may want to say that after a revolution scientists are responding to a different world [20, p. 110].

New paradigms frequently are rejected by the scientific community. (At first they may seem crude and limited—offering very little more than older paradigms.) They frequently lack the apparent sophistication of the older paradigms which they ultimately replace. They do not display the clarity and certainty of older paradigms which have been refined through years of research and writing. But, a new paradigm does provide for a "new start" and opens up new directions which were not possible under the old. "We must recognize how very limited in both scope and precision a paradigm can be at the time of its first appearance. Paradigms gain their status because they are more successful than their competitors in solving a few problems that the group of practitioners has come to recognize as acute. To be more successful is not, however, to be either completely successful with a single problem or notably successful with any large number" [20, p. 23].

Systems theory does provide a new paradigm for the study of social organizations and their management. At this stage it is obviously crude and lacking in precision. In some ways it may not be much better than older paradigms which have been accepted and used for a long time (such as the management process approach). As in other fields of scientific endeavor, the new paradigm must be applied, clarified, elaborated, and made more precise. But, it does provide a fundamentally different view of the reality of social organizations and can serve as the basis for major advancements in our field.

We see many exciting examples of the utilization of the new systems paradigm in the field of organization and management. Several of these have been referred to earlier [7, 13, 19, 21, 22, 24, 31, 38], and there have been many others. Burns and Stalker made substantial use of systems views in setting forth their concepts of mechanistic and organic managerial systems [8]. Their studies of the characteristics of these two organization types lack precise definition of the variables and relationships, but their colleagues have used the systems approach to look at the relationship of organizations to their environment and also among the technical, structural, and behavioral characteristics within the organization [24]. Chamberlain used a system view in studying enterprises and their environment, which is substantially different from traditional microeconomics [9]. The emerging field of "environmental sciences" and "environmental administration" has found the systems paradigm vital.

Thus, the systems theory paradigm is being used extensively in the investigation of relationships between subsystems within organizations and in studying the environmental interfaces. But, it still has not advanced sufficiently to meet the needs. One of the major problems is that the practical need to deal with comprehensive systems of relationships is overrunning our ability to fully understand and predict these relationships. *We vitally need the systems paradigm but we are not sufficiently sophisticated to use it appropriately.* This is the dilemma. Do our current failures to fully utilize the systems paradigm suggest that we reject it and return to the older, more traditional, and time-tested paradigms? Or do we work with systems theory to make it more precise, to understand the relationships among subsystems, and to gather the informational inputs which are necessary to make the systems approach really work? We think the latter course offers the best opportunity.

Thus, we prefer to accept current limitations of systems theory, while working to reduce them and to develop more complete and sophisticated approaches for its application. We agree with Rapoport who says:

> The system approach to the study of man can be appreciated as an effort to restore meaning (in terms of intuitively grasped understanding of wholes) while adhering to the principles of *disciplined* generalizations and rigorous deduction. It is, in short, an attempt to make the study of man both scientific and meaningful [7, p. xxii].

We are sympathetic with the second part of Rapoport's comment, the need to apply the systems approach but to make disciplined generalizations and rigorous deductions. This is a vital necessity and yet a major current limitation. We do have some indication that progress (although very slow) is being made.

## WHAT DO WE NEED NOW?

Everything is related to everything else—but how? General systems theory provides us with the macro paradigm for the study of social organizations. As Scott and others have pointed out, most sciences go through a macro-micro-macro cycle or sequence of emphasis [33]. Traditional bureaucratic theory provided the first major macro view of organizations. Administrative management theorists concentrated on the development of macro "principles of management" which were applicable to all organizations. When these macro views seemed incomplete (unable to explain important phenomena), attention turned to the micro level—more detailed analysis of components or parts of the organization, thus the interest in human relations, technology, or structural dimensions.

The systems approach returns us to the macro level with a new paradigm. General systems theory emphasizes a very high level of abstraction. Phillips classifies it as a third-order study [29] that attempts to develop macro concepts appropriate for all types of biological, physical, and social systems.

In our view, we are now ready to move down a level of abstraction to consider second-order systems studies or midrange concepts. These will be based on general systems theory but will be more concrete and will emphasize more specific characteristics and relationships in social organizations. They will operate within the broad paradigm of systems theory but at a less abstract level.

What should we call this new midrange level of analysis? Various authors have referred to it as a "contingency view," a study of "patterns of relationships," or a search for "configurations among subsystems." Lorsch and Lawrence reflect this view:

> During the past few years there has been evident a new trend in the study of organizational phenomena. Underlying this new approach is the idea that the internal functioning of organizations must be consistent with the demands of the organization task, technology, or external environment, and the needs of its members if the organization is to be effective. Rather than searching for the panacea of the one best way to organize under all conditions, investigators have more and more tended to examine the functioning of organizations in relation to the needs of their particular members and the external pressures facing them. Basically, this approach seems to be leading to the development of a "contingency" theory of organization with the appropriate internal states and processes of the organization contingent upon external requirements and member needs [21, p. 1].

Numerous others have stressed a similar viewpoint. Thompson suggests that the essence of administration lies in understanding basic configurations which exist between the various subsystems and with the environment. "The basic function of administration appears to be co-alignment, not merely of people (in coalitions) but of institutionalized action—of technology and task environment into a viable domain, and of organizational design and structure appropriate to it [38, p. 157].

Bringing these ideas together we can provide a more precise definition of the contingency view:

> The contingency view of organizations and their management suggests that an organization is a system composed of subsystems and delineated by identifiable boundaries from its environmental suprasystem. The contingency view seeks to understand the interrelationships within and among subsystems as well as between the organization and its environment and to define patterns of relationships or configurations of variables. It emphasizes the multivariate nature of organizations and attempts to understand how organizations operate under varying conditions and in specific circumstances. Contingency views are ultimately directed toward suggesting organizational designs and managerial systems most appropriate for specific situations.

But, it is not enough to suggest that a "contingency view" based on systems concepts of organizations and their management is more appropriate than the simplistic "principles approach." If organization theory is to advance and make contributions to managerial practice, it must define more explicitly certain patterns of relationships between organizational variables. This is the major challenge facing our field.

Just how do we go about using systems theory to develop these midrange or contingency views? We see no alternative but to engage in intensive comparative investigation of many organizations following the advice of Blau:

> A theory of organization, whatever its specific nature, and regardless of how subtle the organizational processes it takes into account, has as its central aim to establish the constellations of characteristics that develop in organizations of various kinds. Comparative studies of many organizations are necessary, not alone to test the hypotheses implied by such a theory, but also to provide a basis for initial exploration and refinement of the theory by indicating the conditions on which relationships, originally assumed to hold universally are contingent. . . . Systematic research on many organizations that provides the data needed to determine the interrelationships between several organizational features is, however, extremely rare [5, p. 332].

Various conceptual designs for the comparative study of organizations and their subsystems are emerging to help in the development of a contingency view. We do not want to impose our model as to what should be considered in looking for these patterns of relationships. However, the tentative matrix shown in Figure 2 suggests this approach. We have used as a starting point the two polar organization types which have been emphasized in the literature—closed/stable/mechanistic and open/adaptive/organic.

We will consider the environment suprasystem and organizational subsystems (goals and values, technical, structural, psychosocial, and managerial) plus various dimensions or characteristics of each of these systems. By way of illustration we have indicated several specific subcategories under the Environmental Suprasystem as well as the Goals and Values subsystem. This process would have to be completed and extended to all of the subsystems. The next step would be the development of appropriate descriptive language (based on research and conceptualization) for each relevant characteristic across the continuum of organization types. For example, on the "stability" dimension for Goals and Values we would have High, Medium, and Low at ap-

**FIGURE 2**    Matrix of Patterns of Relationships between Organization Types and Systems Variables

| Organizational Supra- and Subsystems | Continuum of Organization Types | |
|---|---|---|
| | Closed/Stable/ Mechanistic | Open/Adaptive/ Organic |
| Environmental relationships | | |
| General nature | Placid | Turbulent |
| Predictability | Certain, determinate | Uncertain, indeterminate |
| Boundary relationships | Relatively closed; limited to few participants (sales, purchasing, etc.); fixed and well-defined | Relatively open; many participants have external relationships; varied and not clearly defined |
| Goals and values | | |
| Organizational goals in general | Efficient performance, stability, maintenance | Effective problem-solving innovation, growth |
| Goal set | Single, clear-cut | Multiple, determined by necessity to satisfy a set of constraints |
| Stability | Stable | Unstable |
| Technical | | |
| Structural | | |
| Psychosocial | | |
| Managerial | | |

propriate places on the continuum. If the entire matrix were filled in, it is likely that we would begin to see discernible patterns of relationships among subsystems.

We do not expect this matrix to provide *the* midrange model for everyone. It is highly doubtful that we will be able to follow through with the field work investigations necessary to fill in all the squares. Nevertheless, it does illustrate a possible approach for the translation of more abstract general systems theory into an appropriate midrange model which is relevant for organization theory and management practice. Frankly, we see this as a major long-term effort on the part of many researchers, investigating a wide variety of organizations. In spite of the difficulties involved in such research, the endeavor has practical significance. Sophistication in the study of organizations will come when we have a more complete understanding of organizations as total systems (configurations of subsystems) so that we can prescribe more appropriate organizational designs and managerial systems. Ultimately, organization theory should serve as the foundation for more effective management practice.

## APPLICATION OF SYSTEMS CONCEPTS TO MANAGEMENT PRACTICE

The study of organizations is an applied science because the resulting knowledge is relevant to problem-solving in on-going institutions. Contributions to organization theory come from many sources. Deductive and inductive research in a variety of disciplines provide a theoretical base of propositions which are useful for understanding organizations and for managing them. Experience gained in management practice is also an important input to organization theory. In short, management is based on the body of knowledge generated by practical experience *and* eclectic scientific research concerning organizations. The body of knowledge developed through theory and research should be translatable into more effective organizational design and managerial practices.

Do systems concepts and contingency views provide a panacea for solving problems in organizations? The answer is an emphatic *no;* this approach does not provide "ten easy steps" to success in management. Such cookbook approaches, while seemingly applicable and easy to grasp, are usually shortsighted, narrow in perspective, and superficial—in short, unrealistic. Fundamental ideas, such as systems concepts and contingency views, are more difficult to comprehend. However, they facilitate more thorough understanding of complex situations and increase the likelihood of appropriate action.

It is important to recognize that many managers have used and will continue to use a systems approach and contingency views intuitively and implicitly. Without much knowledge of the underlying body of organization theory, they have an intuitive "sense of the situation," are flexible diagnosticians, and adjust their actions and decisions accordingly. Thus, systems concepts and contingency views are not new. However, if this approach to organization theory and management practice can be made more explicit, we can facilitate better management and more effective organizations.

Practicing managers in business firms, hospitals, and government agencies continue to function on a day-to-day basis. Therefore, they must use whatever theory is available; they cannot wait for the *ultimate* body of knowledge (there is none!). Practitioners should be included in the search for new knowledge because they control access to an essential ingredient—organizational data—and they are the ones who ultimately put the theory to the test. Mutual understanding among managers, teachers, and researchers will facilitate the development of a relevant body of knowledge.

Simultaneously with the refinement of the body of knowledge, a concerted effort should be directed toward applying what we do know. We need ways of making systems and contingency views more usable. Without oversimplification, we need some relevant guidelines for practicing managers.

The general tenor of the contingency view is somewhere between simplistic, specific principles and complex, vague notions. It is a mid-range concept which recognizes the complexity involved in managing modern organizations but uses patterns of relationships and/or configurations of subsystems in order to facilitate improved practice. The art of management depends on a reasonable success rate for actions in a probabilistic environment. Our hope is that systems concepts and contingency views, while continually being refined by scientists/researchers/theorists, will also be made more applicable.

## NOTES

1. An entire article could be devoted to a discussion of ingenious ways in which the term "systems approach" has been used in the literature pertinent to organization theory and management practice.

## REFERENCES

1. Ackoff, Russell L. "Towards a System of Systems Concepts." *Management Science*, July 1971.

2. Back, Kurt W. "Biological Models of Social Change." *American Sociological Review,* August 1971.
3. Barnard, Chester I. *The Functions of the Executive.* Cambridge, Mass.: Harvard University Press, 1938.
4. Berrien, F. Kenneth. *General and Social Systems.* New Brunswick, N.J.: Rutgers University Press, 1968.
5. Blau, Peter M. "The Comparative Study of Organizations." *Industrial and Labor Relations Review,* April 1965.
6. Boulding, Kenneth E. "General Systems Theory: The Skeleton of Science." *Management Science,* April 1956.
7. Buckley, Walter, ed. *Modern Systems Research for the Behavioral Scientist.* Chicago: Aldine, 1968.
8. Burns, Tom, and G. M. Stalker. *The Management of Innovation.* London: Tavistock Publications, 1961.
9. Chamberlain, Neil W. *Enterprise and Environment: The Firm in Time and Place.* New York: McGraw-Hill, 1968.
10. Churchman, C. West. *The Systems Approach.* New York: Dell, 1968.
11. DeGreene, Kenyon, ed. *Systems Psychology.* New York: McGraw-Hill, 1970.
12. Deutsch, Karl W. "Toward A Cybernetic Model of Man and Society." In *Modern Systems Research for the Behavioral Scientist,* ed. Walter Buckley. Chicago: Aldine, 1968.
13. Easton, David. *A Systems Analysis of Political Life.* New York: John Wiley & Sons, 1965.
14. Emery, F. E., and E. L. Trist. "Socio-technical Systems." In *Management Sciences: Models and Techniques,* ed. C. West Churchman and Michele Verhulst. New York: Pergamon, 1960.
15. Emshoff, James R. *Analysis of Behavioral Systems.* New York: Macmillan, 1971.
16. Gross, Bertram M. "The Coming General Systems Models of Social Systems." *Human Relations,* November 1967.
17. Hall, A. D., and R. E. Eagen. "Definition of System." *General Systems, Yearbook for the Society for the Advancement of General Systems Theory.* Vol. 1, 1956.
18. Kast, Fremont E., and James E. Rosenzweig. *Organization and Management Theory: A Systems Approach.* New York: McGraw-Hill, 1970.
19. Katz, Daniel, and Robert L. Kahn. *The Social Psychology of Organizations.* New York: John Wiley & Sons, 1966.
20. Kuhn, Thomas S. *The Structure of Scientific Revolutions.* Chicago: University of Chicago Press, 1962.
21. Litterer, Joseph A. *Organizations: Structure and Behavior.* Vol. 1. New York: John Wiley & Sons, 1969.
22. _____. *Organizations: Systems, Control and Adaptation.* Vol. 2. New York: John Wiley & Sons, 1969.
23. Lorsch, Jay W., and Paul R. Lawrence. *Studies in Organizational Design.* Homewood, Ill.: Irwin-Dorsey, 1970.
24. Miller, E. J., and A. K. Rice. *Systems of Organizations.* London: Tavistock Publications, 1967.

25. Miller, James G. "Living Systems: Basic Concepts." *Behavioral Science,* July 1965.
26. Miller, Robert F. "The New Science of Administration in the USSR." *Administrative Science Quarterly,* September 1971.
27. Murray, Henry A. "Preparation for the Scaffold of a Comprehensive System." In *Psychology: A Study of a Science.* Vol. 3, ed. Sigmund Koch. New York: McGraw-Hill, 1959.
28. Parsons, Talcott. *The Social System.* New York: Free Press of Glencoe, 1951.
29. Phillips, D. C. "Systems Theory—A Discredited Philosophy." In *Management Systems,* ed. Peter P. Schoderbek, New York: John Wiley & Sons, 1971.
30. Rapoport, Anatol, and William J. Horvath. "Thoughts on Organization Theory." In *Modern Systems Research for the Behavioral Scientist,* ed. Walter Buckley. Chicago: Aldine, 1968.
31. Rice, A. K. *The Modern University.* London: Tavistock Publications, 1970.
32. Schein, Edgar. *Organizational Psychology.* Rev. ed. Englewood Cliffs, N.J.: Prentice-Hall, 1970.
33. Scott, William G. "Organization Theory: An Overview and an Appraisal." *Academy of Management Journal,* April 1961.
34. Silverman, David. *The Theory of Organizations.* New York: Basic Books, 1971.
35. Simon, Herbert A. "The Architecture of Complexity." In *Organizations: Systems, Control and Adaptation,* Vol. 2, ed. Joseph A. Litterer. New York: John Wiley & Sons, 1969.
36. Springer, Michael. "Social Indicators, Reports, and Accounts: Toward the Management of Society." *The Annals of the American Academy of Political and Social Science,* March 1970.
37. Terreberry, Shirley. "The Evolution of Organizational Environments." *Administrative Science Quarterly,* March 1968.
38. Thompson, James D. *Organizations in Action.* New York: McGraw-Hill, 1967.
39. von Bertalanffy, Ludwig. *General System Theory.* New York: George Braziller, 1968.
40. _____. "The Theory of Open Systems in Physics and Biology." *Science,* January 13, 1950.
41. Yuchtman, Ephraim, and Stanley E. Seashore. "A System Resource Approach to Organizational Effectiveness." *American Sociological Review,* December 1967.

# PART TWO

# Classical Management Processes

The management processes of planning, organizing, and controlling are among those functions universally recognized as central components of the manager's role. Whether one is a classicist, neoclassicist, or behaviorist, the importance of these managerial functions is not debated. This section of the text presents nine articles that address these three processes.

It has been said that poor managers work on yesterday's problems, good managers work on today's problems, and the truly outstanding managers focus on tomorrow's problems. Focusing on tomorrow's problems clearly requires *planning*. Planning is an essential function of the management process and involves the application of thought, analysis, imagination, and judgment to future activities.

One of the themes of the classical school of management is that there is a distinct difference between planning and executing. Fayol and others argued that managers should plan and nonmanagers should execute. The behaviorists, on the other hand, would counter with the argument that managers and nonmanagers together should be active participants in both planning and executing. Both groups, however, would agree that the planning function includes those activities that result in a definition of goals and the determination of appropriate means to achieve these goals. Simply stated, planning is advance thinking as the basis for doing.

Whenever goals and tasks require the efforts of two or more people, the need for *organizing* arises. For example, when an object is too heavy for one person to lift, the efforts of others must be used. If more than one person is involved in the lifting, the effort must be coordinated. Organizing refers to the process of achieving coordinated effort. The organizing function in management is the means by which managers seek to achieve a coordinated effort through the design of a structure of tasks and authority relationships.

The organizing function is often discussed in terms of dividing tasks, departmentalizing tasks, and delegating authority. The principles of specialization, departmentalization, span of control, and unity of command provide the basic elements for discussing the organizing function. These principles are not ironclad laws or facts but are guidelines that serve to aid the manager faced with organizing decisions. Regardless of what those decisions are, all organizing efforts share a common goal of channelling individual and group behavior into patterns that contribute to effective organizational performance.

For many students of management, the *control* processes are both the least understood and least appreciated managerial functions. Simply stated, control processes are those activities involved in setting standards, measuring performance against these standards, and correcting or adjusting for deviations from the standards. An important implication of this definition is that *plans* have been made and work has been *organized*—very important management activities also addressed in this section. Control, then, is what is necessary to insure that plans and organizations are executed in a manner consistent with achieving the desired results.

## A. Planning

# 7

# Planning

*Henri Fayol*

*Written well over 60 years ago by a true pioneer in discussing planning, this short essay is as current as if it were written yesterday. Fayol identifies the features of a good plan of action and outlines the method of drawing up a plan. Note also the emphasis Fayol places on the human element of planning—Eds.*

The maxim, "managing means looking ahead," gives some idea of the importance attached to planning in the business world and it is true that if foresight is not the whole of management at least it is an essential part of it. To foresee, in this context means both to assess the future and make provision for it; that is, foreseeing is itself action already. Planning is manifested on a variety of occasions and in a variety of ways, its chief manifestation, apparent sign and most effective instrument being the plan of action. The plan of action is, at one and the same time, the result envisaged, the line of action to be followed, the stages to go through, and methods to use. It is a kind of future picture wherein proximate events are outlined with some distinctness, whilst remote events appear progressively less distinct, and it entails the running of the business as foreseen and provided against over a definite period.

The plan of action rests: (1) On the firm's resources (buildings, tools, raw materials, personnel, productive capacity, sales outlets, public relations, etc.). (2) On the nature and importance of work in progress.

---

SOURCE: Reprinted by permission of Pitman Publishing Limited from Chapter V of *General and Industrial Management* by Henri Fayol (London: Sir Isaac Pitman and Sons, Ltd., 1949), pp. 43–52.

(3) On future trends which depend partly on technical, commercial, financial and other conditions, all subject to change, whose importance and occurrence cannot be predetermined. The preparation of the plan of action is one of the most difficult and most important matters of every business and brings into plan all departments and all functions, especially the management function. It is, in effect, in order to carry out his managerial function that the manager takes the initiative for the plan of action, that he indicates its objective and scope, fixes the share of each department in the communal task, coordinates the parts and harmonizes the whole; that he decides, in fine, the line of conduct to be followed. In this line of conduct it is not only imperative that nothing should clash with principles and rules of good management, but also that the arrangement adopted should facilitate application of these principles and rules. Therefore, to the divers technical, commercial, financial and other abilities necessary on the part of a business head and his assistants, there must be added considerable managerial ability.

## GENERAL FEATURES OF A GOOD PLAN OF ACTION

No one disputes the usefulness of a plan of action. Before taking action it is most necessary to know what is possible and what is wanted. It is known that absence of plan entails hesitation, false steps, untimely changes of direction, which are so many causes of weakness, if not of disaster, in business. The question of and necessity for a plan of action, then, does not arise and I think that I am voicing the general opinion in saying that a plan of action is indispensable. But there are plans and plans, there are simple ones, complex ones, concise ones, detailed ones, long- or short-term ones; there are those studied with meticulous attention, those treated lightly; there are good, bad, and indifferent ones. How are the good ones to be singled out from among the others? Experience is the only thing that finally determines the true value of a plan, i.e., on the services it can render to the firm, and even then the manner of its application must be taken into account. There is both instrument and player. Nevertheless, there are certain broad characteristics on which general agreement may be reached beforehand without waiting for the verdict of experience.

Unity of plan is an instance. Only one plan can be put into operation at a time; two different plans would mean duality, confusion, disorder. But a plan may be divided into several parts. In large concerns, there is found alongside the general plan a technical, commercial, and a financial one, or else an overall one with a specific one for each department. But all these plans are linked, welded, so as to make up one only, and every modification brought to bear on any one of them is given expression in the whole plan. The guiding action of the plan must be continuous. Now the limitations of human foresight necessarily set bounds to the duration of plans, so, in order to have no break in the guiding action, a second plan must follow immediately upon the first, a third upon the second, and so on. In large businesses the annual plan is more or less in current use. Other plans of shorter or longer term, always in close accord with the annual plan, operate simultaneously with this latter. The plan should be flexible enough to bend before such adjustments, as it is considered well to introduce, whether from pressure or circumstances or from any other reason. First as last, it is the law to which one bows. Another good point about a plan is to have as much accuracy as is compatible with the unknown factors bearing on the fate of the concern. Usually it is possible to mark out the line of proximate action fairly accurately, while a simple general indication does for remote activities, for before the moment for their execution has arrived sufficient enlightenment will have been forthcoming to settle the line of action more precisely. When the unknown factor occupies a relatively very large place there can be no preciseness in the plan, and then the concern takes on the name of venture.

Unity, continuity, flexibility, precision: such are the broad features of a good plan of action.

As for other specific points which it should have, and which turn on the nature, importance, and condition of the business for which the plan is drawn up, there could be no possibility of settling them beforehand save by comparison with other plans already recognized as effective in similar businesses. In each case, then, comparable elements and models must be sought in business practice, after the fashion of the architect with a building to construct. But the architect, better served than the manager, can call upon books, courses in architecture, whereas there are no books on plans of action, no lessons in foresight, for management theory has yet to be formulated.

There is no lack of good plans, they can be guessed at from the externals of a business but not seen at sufficiently close quarters to be known and judged. Nevertheless, it would be most useful for those whose concern is management to know how experienced managers go about drawing up their plans. By way of information or sample, I am going to set out the method which has long been followed in a great mining and metallurgical concern with which I am well acquainted.

### Method of Drawing Up the Plan of Action in a Large Mining and Metallurgical Firm

This company includes several separate establishments and employs about 10,000 personnel. The entire plan is made up of a series of separate plans called forecasts; and there are yearly forecasts, ten-yearly forecasts, monthly, weekly, daily forecasts, long-term forecasts, special forecasts, and all merge into a single program which operates as a guide for the whole concern.

(1) **Yearly Forecasts.** Each year, two months after the end of the budgetary period, a general report is drawn up of the work and results of this period. The report deals especially with production, sales, technical, commercial, financial position, personnel, economic consequences, etc. The report is accompanied by forecasts dealing with those same matters, the forecasts being a kind of anticipatory summary of the activities and results of the new budgetary period. The two months of the new plan which have elapsed are not left without plan, because of provisional forecasts drawn up fifteen days before the end of the previous period. In a large mining and metallurgical firm not many activities are quite completed during the course of one year. Cooperative projects of a technical, commercial, and financial nature, which provide the business with its activities, need more time for their preparation and execution. From another aspect, account must be taken of the repercussions which proximate activities must have on ultimate ones and of the obligation to prepare far ahead sometimes for a requisite state of affairs.

Finally, thought must be given to constant modifications operating on the technical, commercial, financial, and social condition of the industrial world in general and of the business in particular, to avoid being overtaken by circumstances. These various circumstances come outside the framework of yearly forecasts and lead on to longer-term ones.

(2) **Ten-Yearly Forecasts.** Ten-yearly forecasts deal with the same matters as yearly ones. At the outset these two types of forecasts are identical, the yearly forecast merging into the first year of the ten-yearly one, but from the second year onwards notable divergences make their appearance. To maintain unity of plan each year the ten-yearly forecasts must be reconciled with annual ones so that at the end of some years the ten-yearly forecasts are generally so modified and transformed as to be no longer clear and need redrafting. In effect the custom of redrafting every five years has become established. It is the rule that ten-yearly forecasts always embrace a decade, and that they are revised every five years. Thus there is always a line of action marked out in advance for five years at least.

(3) **Special Forecasts.** There are some activities whose full cycle exceeds one or even several ten-yearly periods; there are others which, occurring suddenly, must sensibly affect the conditions of the business.

**TABLE 1**   Yearly and Ten-Yearly Forecasts

## CONTENTS

*Technical Section*

Mining rights. Premises. Plant.
Extraction. Manufacture. Output.
New workings. Improvements.
Maintenance of plant and buildings.
Production costs.

*Commercial Section*

Sales outlets.
Marketable goods.
Agencies. Contracts.
Customer importance. Credit standing.
Selling price.

*Financial Section*

Capital. Loans. Deposits.

Circulating assets $\begin{cases} \text{Supplies in hand.} \\ \text{Finished goods.} \\ \text{Debtors.} \\ \text{Liquid assets.} \end{cases}$

Available assets.
Reserves and sundry appropriations.

Creditors $\begin{cases} \text{Wages.} \\ \text{Suppliers.} \\ \text{Sundry.} \end{cases}$

Sinking funds. Dividends. Bankers.

*Accounting*

Balance sheet. Profit and Loss account.
Statistics.

*Security*

Accident precautions.
Works police. Claims. Health service.
Insurance.

*Management*

Plan of action.
Organization of personnel. Selection.
Command.
Coordination. Conferences.
Control.

Both the one and the other are the object of special forecasts whose findings necessarily have a place in the yearly and ten-yearly forecasts. But it must never be lost sight of that there is one plan only.

These three sorts of forecasts, yearly, ten-yearly, and special, merged and harmonized, constitute the firm's general plan.

So, having been prepared with meticulous care by each regional management, with the help of departmental management, and then revised, modified, and completed by general management and then submitted for scrutiny and approval to the Board of Directors, these forecasts become the plan which, so long as no other has been put in its place, shall serve as guide, directive, and law for the whole staff.

Fifty years ago I began to use this system of forecasts, when I was engaged in managing a colliery, and it rendered me such good service that I had no hesitation in subsequently applying it to various industries whose running was entrusted to me. I look upon it as a precious managerial instrument and have no hesitation in recommending its use to those who have no better instrument available. It has necessarily some shortcomings, but its shortcomings are very slight compared with the advantages it offers. Let us glance at these advantages and shortcomings.

## Advantages and Shortcomings of Forecasts

1. The study of resources, future possibilities, and means to be used for attaining the objective call for contributions from all departmental heads within the framework of their mandate: each one brings to this study the contribution of his experience together with recognition of the responsibility which will fall upon him in executing the plan.

Those are excellent conditions for ensuring that no resource shall be neglected and that future possibilities shall be prudently and courageously assessed and that means shall be appropriate to ends. Knowing what are its capabilities and its intentions, the concern goes boldly on, confidently tackles current problems and is prepared to align all its forces against accidents and surprises of all kinds which may occur.

2. Compiling the annual plan is always a delicate operation and especially lengthy and laborious when done for the first time, but each repetition brings some simplification and when the plan has become a habit the toil and difficulties are largely reduced. Conversely, the interest it offers increases. The attention demanded for executing the plan, the indispensable comparison between predicted and actual facts, the recognition of mistakes made and successes attained, the search for means of repeating the one and avoiding the other—all go to make the new plan a work of increasing interest and increasing usefulness.

Also, by doing this work the personnel increases in usefulness from year to year, and at the end is considerably superior to what it was in the beginning. In truth, this result is not due solely to the use of planning but everything goes together; a well-thought-out plan is rarely found apart from sound organizational, command, coordination, and control practices. This management element exerts an influence on all the rest.

3. Lack of sequence in activity and unwarranted changes of course are dangers constantly threatening businesses without a plan. The slightest contrary wind can turn from its course a boat which is unfitted to resist. When serious happenings occur, regrettable changes of course may be decided upon under the influence of profound but transitory disturbance. Only a program carefully pondered at an undisturbed time permits of maintaining a clear view of the future and of concentrating maximum possible intellectual ability and material resources upon the danger.

It is in difficult moments above all that a plan is necessary. The best of plans cannot anticipate all unexpected occurrences which may arise, but it does include a place for these events and prepare the weapons which may be needed at the moment of being surprised. The plan protects the business not only against undesirable changes of course which may be produced by grave events, but also against those arising simply from changes on the part of higher authority. Also, it protects against deviations, imperceptible at first, which end by deflecting it from its objective.

## Conditions and Qualities Essential for Drawing Up a Good Plan of Action

To sum up: the plan of action facilitates the utilization of the firm's resources and the choice of best methods to use for attaining the objective. It suppresses or reduces hesitancy, false steps, unwarranted changes of course, and helps to improve personnel. It is a precious managerial instrument.

The question may be asked as to why such an instrument is not in general use and everywhere developed to the farthest extent. The reason is that its compilation demands of managerial personnel a certain number of qualities and conditions rarely to be found in combination. The compilation of a good plan demands for the personnel in charge:

1. The art of handling men.
2. Considerable energy.
3. A measure of moral courage.

4. Some continuity of tenure.

5. A given degree of competence in the specialized requirements of the business.

6. A certain general business experience.

(1) **The Art of Handling Men.**   In a large firm the majority of departmental managers take part in the compiling of the working arrangements. The execution of this task from time to time is in addition to ordinary everyday work and includes a certain responsibility and does not normally carry any special remuneration. So, to have in such conditions loyal and active cooperation from departmental heads an able manager of men is needed who fears neither trouble nor responsibility. The art of handling men is apparent from keenness of subordinates and confidence of superiors.

(2) **Energy.**   Yearly and ten-yearly forecasts and special forecasts demand constant vigilance on the part of management.

(3) **Moral Courage.**   It is well known that the best-thought-out plan is never exactly carried out. Forecasts are not prophecies; their function is to minimize the unknown factor. Nevertheless, the public generally, and even shareholders best informed about the running of a business, are not kindly disposed toward a manager who has raised unfulfilled hopes, or allowed them to be raised. Whence the need for a certain prudence which has to be reconciled with the obligation of making every preparation and seeking out optimum possible results.

The timid are tempted to suppress the plan or else whittle it down to nothing in order not to expose themselves to criticism, but it is a bad policy even from the point of view of self-interest. Lack of plan, which compromises smooth running, also exposes the manager to infinitely graver charges than that of having to explain away imperfectly executed forecasts.

(4) **Continuity of Tenure.**   Some time goes by before a new manager is able to take sufficient cognizance of the course of affairs, its general setup and future possibilities, so as usefully to undertake the compiling of the plan. If, at such a moment, he feels that he will not have enough time to complete the work or only enough to start putting it into execution, or if, on the other hand, he is convinced that such work, condemned to bear no fruit, will only draw criticism upon him, is it to be thought that he will carry it out enthusiastically or even undertake it unless obliged? Human nature must be reckoned with. Without continuity of tenure on the part of management personnel there can be no good plan of action.

**(5 and 6) Professional Competence and General Business Knowledge.**  These are abilities just as necessary for drawing up a plan as for carrying it out.

Such are the conditions essential for compiling a good plan. They presuppose intelligent and experienced management. Lack of plan or a bad plan is a sign of managerial incompetence. To safeguard business against such incompetence:

1. A plan must be compulsory.
2. Good specimen plans must be made generally available. (Successful businesses could be asked to furnish such specimens. Experience and general discussion would single out the best.)
3. Planning (as a subject) must be introduced into education. Thus could general opinion be better informed and react upon management personnel, so that the latter's inefficiency would be less to be feared—a state of affairs which would in no wise detract from the importance of men of proven worth.

# 8

# Long-Range Planning: Challenge to Management Science

*Peter F. Drucker*

*In this article one of the most widely read contributors to the practice of management starts off by identifying what long-range planning is not. From there he defines the proper role of management science in the planning process, stressing that planning is a continuous, ongoing process. Drucker's perspective on planning is a little different from the usual and is well worth examining.—Eds.*

## I

It is easier to define long-range planning by what it is not rather than by what it is. Three things in particular, which it is commonly believed to be, it emphatically is not.

1. *First it is not "forecasting."* It is not masterminding the future, in other words. Any attempt to do so is foolish; human beings can neither predict nor control the future.

If anyone still suffers from the delusion that the ability to forecast beyond the shortest time span is given to us, let him look at the headlines in yesterday's paper, and then ask himself which of them he could possibly have predicted 10 years ago.

SOURCE: Reprinted by permission of the author and publisher from "Long-Range Planning: Challenge to Management Science," *Management Science* 5, no. 3, 1959, pp. 238–49.

- Could he have forecast that by today the Russians would have drawn even with us in the most advanced branches of physical sciences and of engineering?
- Could he have forecast that West Germany in complete ruins and chaos then would have become the most conservative country in the world and one of the most productive ones, let alone that it would become very stable politically?
- Could he have forecast that the Near East would become a central trouble spot, or would he have had to assume that the oil revenues there would take care of all problems?

This is the way the future always behaves. To try to mastermind it is therefore childish; we can only discredit what we are doing by attempting it. We must start out with the conclusion that forecasting is not respectable and not worthwhile beyond the shortest of periods. *Long-range planning is necessary precisely because we cannot forecast.*

But there is another, and even more compelling reason why forecasting is not long-range planning. Forecasting attempts to find the most probable course of events, or at best, a range of probabilities. But the entrepreneurial problem is the unique event that will change the possibilities, for the entrepreneurial universe is not a physical but a value universe. Indeed the central entrepreneurial contribution and the one which alone is rewarded with a profit, is to bring about the unique event, the *innovation* that changes the probabilities.

Let me give an example—a very elementary one which has nothing to do with innovation but which illustrates the importance of the improbable even for purely adaptive business behavior.

A large coffee distributor has for many years struggled with the problem of the location and capacity of its processing plants throughout the country. It had long been known that coffee prices were as important a factor in this, as location of market, volume, or transportation and delivery strategy. Now if we can forecast anything, it is single-commodity prices; and the price forecasts of the company economists have been remarkably accurate. Yet the decisions on plant location and capacity based on these forecasts have again and again proven costly blunders. Extreme pricing events, the probability of which at any one time was exceedingly low, had, even if they lasted only for a week at a time, impact on the economics of the system that were vastly greater than that of the accurately forecast "averages." Forecasting, in other words, obscured economic reality. What was needed (as the Theory of Games could have proven) was to look at the extreme possibilities, and to ask, "which of these can we not afford to disregard?"

The only thing atypical in this example is that it is so simple. Usually things are quite a bit more complex. But despite its (deceptive) simplicity it shows why forecasting is not an adequate basis even for purely adaptive behavior, let alone for the entrepreneurial decisions of long-range planning.

2. The next thing to be said about what long-range planning is not, is that it does not deal with future decisions. It deals with the *futurity of present decisions.*

Decisions exist only in the present. The question that faces the long-range planner is not what we should do tomorrow. It is what do we have to do today to be ready for an uncertain tomorrow. The question is not what will happen in the future. It is: what futurity do we have to factor into our present thinking and doing, what time spans do we have to consider, and how do we converge them to a simultaneous decision in the present?

Decision making is essentially a time machine which synchronizes into one present a great number of divergent time spans. This is, I think, something which we are only learning now. Our approach today still tends toward the making of plans for something we will decide to do in the future. This may be a very entertaining exercise, but it is a futile one.

Again, long-range planning is necessary because we can make decisions only in the present; the rest are pious intentions. And yet we cannot make decisions for the present alone; the most expedient, most opportunist decision—let alone the decision not to decide—may commit us on a long-range basis, if not permanently and irrevocably.

3. Finally, the most common misconception of all, *long-range planning is not an attempt to eliminate risk.* It is not even an attempt to minimize risk. Indeed any such attempt can only lead to irrational and unlimited risk and to certain disaster.

The central fact about economic activity is that, by definition, it commits present resources to future and therefore highly uncertain expectations. To take risk is therefore the essence of economic activity. Indeed one of the most rigorous theorems of economics (Boehm-Bawerk's Law) proves that existing means of production will yield greater economic performance only through greater uncertainty, that is, through greater risk.

But while it is futile to try to eliminate risk, and questionable to try to minimize it, it is essential that the risks taken be the *right risks.* The end result of successful long-range planning must be a capacity to take a greater risk; for this is the only way to improve *entrepreneurial* performance. To do this, however, we must know and understand the risks we take. We must be able to rationally choose among risk-taking courses of action rather than plunge into uncertainty on the basis of hunch, hearsay, or experience (no matter how meticulously quantified).

Now I think we can attempt to define what long-range planning is. It is the continuous process of making *present entrepreneurial (risk taking) decisions* systematically and with the best possible knowledge of their futurity, organizing systematically *the efforts* needed to carry out these decisions, and measuring the results of these decisions against the expectations through *organized, systematic feedback.*

## II

"This is all very well," many experienced businessmen might say (and do say). "But why make a production out of it? Isn't this what the entrepreneur has been doing all along, and doing quite successfully? Why then should it need all this elaborate mumbo jumbo? Why should it be an organized, perhaps even a separate activity? Why in other words, should we even talk about 'long-range planning,' let alone do it?"

It is perfectly true that there is nothing very new to entrepreneurial decisions. They have been made as long as we have had entrepreneurs. There is nothing new in here regarding the essentials of economic activity. It has always been the commitment of present resources to future expectations; and for the last 300 years this has been done in contemplation of change. (This was not true earlier. Earlier economic activity was based on the assumption that there would be no change, which assumption was institutionally guarded and defended. Altogether up to the seventeenth century it was the purpose of all human institutions to prevent change. The business enterprise is a significant and rather amazing novelty in that it is the first human institution having the purpose of bringing about change.)

But there are several things which are new; and they have created the need for the organized, systematic, and above all, specific process that we call "long-range planning."[1]

1. The time span of entrepreneurial and managerial decisions has been lengthening so fast and so much as to make necessary systematic exploration of the uncertainty and risk of decisions.

In 1888 or thereabouts, an old and perhaps apocryphal story goes, the great Thomas Edison, already a world figure, went to one of the big banks in New York for a loan on something he was working on. He had plenty of collateral and he was a great man; so the vice-presidents all bowed and said "Certainly, Mr. Edison, how much do you need?" But one of them, out of idle curiosity asked, "Tell me, Mr. Edison, how long will it be before you have this new product?" Edison looked him in the eye and said, "Son, judging from past experience, it will be about eighteen months before I even know whether I'll have a product or not." Whereupon the vice-presidents collapsed in a body, and, despite the collateral, turned down the loan application. The man was obviously mad; eighteen months of uncertainty was surely not a risk a sane businessman would take!

Today practically every manager takes 10- or 20-year risks without wincing. He takes them in product development, in research, in market development, in the development of a sales organization, and in almost anything. This lengthening of the time span of commitment is one of the most significant features of our age. It underlies our economic advances. But while quantitative in itself, it has changed the qualitative character of entrepreneurial decisions. It has, so to speak, converted time from being a dimension in which business decisions are being made into an essential element of the decisions themselves.

2. Another new feature is the speed and risk of innovation. To define what we mean by this term would go far beyond the scope of this paper.[2]

But we do not need to know more than that industrial research expenditures (that is, business expenditures aimed at innovating primarily peacetime products and processes) have increased in this country from less than $100 million in 1928 to $7 or $8 billion in 1958. Clearly, a technologically slow-moving, if not essentially stable economy has become one of violent technological flux, rapid obsolescence, and great uncertainty.

3. Then there is the growing complexity both of the business enterprise internally, and of the economy and society in which it exists. There is the growing specialization of work which creates increasing need for common vision, common understanding, and common language, without which top management decisions, however right, will never become effective action.

4. Finally—a subtle, but perhaps the most important point—the typical businessman's concept of the basis of entrepreneurial decision is, after all, a misconception.

Most businessmen still believe that these decisions are made by "top management." Indeed practically all text books lay down the dictum that "basic policy decisions" are the "prerogative of top management." At most, top management "delegates" certain decisions.

But this reflects yesterday's rather than today's reality, let alone that of tomorrow. It is perfectly true that top management must have the final say, the final responsibility. But the business enterprise of today is no longer an organization in which there are a handful of "bosses" at the top who make all the decisions while the "workers" carry out orders. It is primarily an organization[3] of professionals of highly specialized knowledge exercising autonomous, responsible judgment. And every one of them—whether manager or individual expert contributor—constantly makes truly entrepreneurial decisions, that is, decisions which affect the economic characteristics and risks of the entire enterprise. He makes them not by "delegation from above" but inevitably in the performance of his own job and work.

For this organization to be functioning, two things are needed: knowledge by the entire organization of what the direction, the goals, the expectations are; and knowledge by top management of what the decisions, commitments, and efforts of the people in the organization are. The needed focus—one might call it a *model of the relevants in internal and external environment*—only a "long-range plan" can provide.

One way to summarize what is new and different in the process of entrepreneurial decision making is in terms of information. The amount, diversity, and ambiguity of the information that is beating in on the decision maker have all been increasing so much that the built-in experience reaction that a good manager has cannot handle it. He breaks down; and his breakdown will take either of the two forms known to any experimental psychologist. One is withdrawal from reality, i.e., "I know what I know and I only go by it; the rest is quite irrelevant and I won't even look at it." Or there is a feeling that the universe has become completely irrational so that one decision is as good as the other, resulting in paralysis. We see both in executives who have to make decisions today. Neither is likely to result in rational or in successful decisions.

There is something else managers and management scientists might learn from the psychologists. Organization of information is often more important to the ability to perceive and act than analysis and understanding of the information. I recall one experience with the organization of research-planning in a pharmaceutical company. The attempt to analyze the research decisions—even to define alternatives of decisions—was a dismal failure. In the attempt, however, the decisions were classified to the point where the research people could know what kind of a decision was possible at what stage. They still did not know what factors should or should not be considered in a given decision, nor what its risks were. They could not explain why they made this decision rather than another one, nor spell out what they expected. But the mere organization of this information enabled them again to apply their experience and to "play hunches"—with measurable and very significant improvement in the performance of the entire research group.

"Long-range planning" is more than organization and analysis of information; it is a decision-making process. But even the information job cannot be done except as part of an organized planning effort—otherwise there is no way of determining which information is relevant.

# III

What then are the requirements of long-range planning? We cannot satisfy all of them as yet with any degree of competence; but we can specify them.

Indeed, we can—and should—give two sets of specifications: One in terms of the characteristics of the process itself; another in terms of its major and specific new-knowledge content.

1. Risk-taking entrepreneurial decisions, no matter whether made rationally or by tea-leaf reading, always embody the same eight elements:

a. *Objectives.* This is, admittedly, an elusive term, perhaps even a metaphysical one. It may be as difficult for Management Science to define "objectives" as it is for biology to define "life." Yet, we will be as unable to do without "objectives" as the biologists are unable to do without "life." Any entrepreneurial decision, let alone the integrated decision system we call a "long-range plan," has objectives, consciously or not.

b. *Assumptions.* These are what is believed by the people who make and carry out decisions to be "real" in the internal and external universe of the business.

c. *Expectations.* The future events or results considered likely or attainable. These three elements can be said to *define the decision.*

d. *Alternative courses of action.* There never is—indeed, in a true uncertainty situation there never can be—"one right decision." There cannot even be "one best decision." There are always "wrong decisions," that is, decisions inadequate to the objectives, incompatible with the assumptions, or grossly improbable in the light of the expectations. But once these have been eliminated, there will still be alternatives left—each a different configuration of objectives, assumptions, and expectations, each with its own risks and its own ratio between risks and rewards, each with its own impact, its specific efforts, and its own results. Every decision is thus a value judgment—it is not the "facts that decide"; people have to choose between imperfect alternatives on the basis of uncertain knowledge and fragmentary understanding.

Two alternatives deserve special mention, if only because they have to be considered in almost every case. One is the alternative of no action (which is, of course, what postponing a decision often amounts to); the other is the very important choice between adaptive and innovating action—each having risks that differ greatly in character though not necessarily in magnitude.

e. The next element in the decision-making process is the *decision itself.*

f. But there is no such thing as one isolated decision; every decision is, of necessity, part of a *decision structure.*

Every financial man knows, for instance, that the original capital appropriation on a new investment implies a commitment to future and usually larger capital appropriations which, however, are almost never as much as mentioned in the proposal submitted. Few of them seem to realize, however, that this implies not only a positive commitment but also, by mortgaging future capital resources, limits future freedom of action. The structuring impact of a decision is even greater in respect to allocations of scarce manpower, such as research people.

g. A decision is only pious intention unless it leads to action. Every decision, therefore, has an *impact stage.*

This impact always follows Newton's Second Law, so to speak; it consists of action and reaction. It requires effort. But it also dislocates. There is, therefore, always the question: what effort is required, by whom, and where? What must people know, what must they do, and what must they achieve? But there is also the question—generally neglected—what does this decision do to other areas? Where does it shift the burden, the weaknesses, and the stress points; and what impact does it have on the outside; in the market, in the supply structure, in the community, and so on?

h. And, finally, there are *results.*

Each of these elements of the process deserves an entire book by itself. But I think I have said enough to show that both, the process itself and each element in it, are *rational*, no matter how irrational and arbitrary they may appear. Both the process and all its elements can therefore be defined, can be studied, and can be analyzed. And both can be improved through systematic and organized work. In particular, as in all rational processes, the entire process is improved and strengthened as we define, clarify, and analyze each of its constituent elements.

2. We can also, as said above, describe long-range planning in terms of its specific new-knowledge content. Among the areas where such new knowledge is particularly cogent, might be mentioned:

a. *The time dimensions of planning.* To say "long-range" or "short-range" planning implies that a given time span defines the planning; and this is actually how businesses look at it when they speak of a "five-year plan" or a "ten-year plan." But the essence of planning is to make present decisions with knowledge of their futurity. It is the futurity that determines the time span, and not vice versa.

Strictly speaking, "short range" and "long range" do not describe time spans but stages in every decision. "Short-range" is the stage before the decision has become fully effective, the stage during which it is only "costs" and not yet "results." The "short-range" of a decision to build a steel mill are the five years or so until the mill is in production. And the "long-range" of any decision is the period of expected performance needed to make the decision a successful one—the 20 or more years above break-even point operations in the case of the steel mill, for instance.

There are limitations on futurity. In business decisions the most precise mathematical statement is often that of my eighth grade teacher that parallels are two lines which do not meet this side of the school yard. Certainly, in the expectations and anticipations of a business the old rule of statistics usually applies that anything beyond 20 years equals infinity; and since expectations more than twenty years hence have normally a present value of zero, they should receive normally only a minimal allocation of present efforts and resources.

Yet it is also true that, if future results require a long gestation period, they will be obtained only if initiated early enough. Hence, long-range planning requires knowledge of futurity: what do we have to do today if we want to be some place in the future? What will not get done at all if we do not commit resources to it today? If we know that it takes 99 years to grow Douglas firs in the Northwest to pulping size, planting seedlings today is the only way we can provide for pulp supply in 99 years. Someone may well develop some speeding-up hormone; but we cannot bank on it if we are in the paper industry. It is quite conceivable, may indeed be highly probable, that we will use trees primarily as a source of chemicals long before these trees grow to maturity. We may even get the bulk of paper supply 30 years hence from less precious, less highly structured sources of cellulose than a tree, which is the most advanced chemical factory in the plant kingdom. This simply means, however, that our forests may put us into the chemical industry some time within the next 30 years; and we had better learn now something about chemistry. If our paper plants depend on Douglas fir, our planning cannot confine itself to 20 years, but must consider 99 years. For we must be able to say whether we have to plant trees today, or whether we can postpone this expensive job.

But on other decisions even five years would be absurdly long. If our business is buying up distress merchandise and selling it at auction, then next week's clearance sale is "long-range future"; and anything beyond is largely irrelevant to us.

It is the nature of the business and the nature of the decision which determine the time spans of planning.

Yet the time spans are not static or "given." The time decision itself is the first and a highly important risk-taking decision in the planning process. It largely determines the allocation of resources and efforts. It largely determines the risks taken (and one cannot repeat too often that to postpone a decision is in itself a risk-taking and often irrevocable decision). Indeed, the time decision largely determines the character and nature of the business.

b. *Decision structure and configuration.* The problem of the time dimension is closely tied in with that of decision structure.

Underlying the whole concept of long-range planning are two simple insights. We need an integrated decision structure for the business as a whole. There are really no isolated decisions on a product, or on markets, or on people. Each major risk-taking decision has impact throughout the whole; and no decision is isolated in time. Every decision is a move in a chess game, except that the rules of enterprise are by no means as clearly defined. There is no finite "board" and the pieces are neither as neatly distinguished nor as few in number. Every move opens some future opportunities for decision, and forecloses others. Every move, therefore, commits positively and negatively.

Let me illustrate these insights with a simple example, that of a major steel company today.

I posit that it is reasonably clear to any student of technology (not of steel technology but of technology in general) that steelmaking is on the threshold of major technological change. *What* they are perhaps the steelmaker knows, but *that* they are I think any study of the pattern, rhythm, and I would say morphology of technological development, might indicate. A logical—rather than metallurgical—analysis of the process would even indicate *where* the changes are likely to occur. At the same time, the steel company faces the need of building new capacity if it wants to keep its share of the market, assuming that steel consumption will continue to increase. A decision to build a plant today, when there is nothing but the old technology available, means in effect that for 15 to 20 years the company cannot go into the new technology except at prohibitive cost. It is very unlikely, looking at the technological pattern, that these changes will be satisfied by minor modifications in existing facilities; they are likely to require new facilities to a large extent. By building today the company closes certain opportunities to itself, or at least it very greatly raises the future entrance price. At the same time, by making the decision to postpone building, it may foreclose other opportunities such as market position, perhaps irrevocably. Management therefore has to understand—without perhaps too much detail—the location of this decision in the continuing process of entrepreneurial decision.

At the same time, entrepreneurial decisions must be fundamentally expedient decisions. It is not only impossible to know all the contingent effects of a decision, even for the shortest time period ahead. The very attempt to know them would lead to complete paralysis.

But the determination of what should be considered and what should be ignored, is in itself a difficult and consequential decision. We need knowledge to make it—I might say that we need a theory of entrepreneurial inference.

c. *The characteristics of risks.* It is not only magnitude of risk that we need to be able to appraise in entrepreneurial decisions. It is above all the character of the risk. Is it, for instance, the kind of risk we can afford to take, or the kind of risk we cannot afford to take? Or is it that rare but singularly important risk, the risk we cannot afford not to take—sometimes regardless of the odds?

The best General Electric scientists, we are told, advised their management in 1945 that it would be at least 40 years before nuclear energy could be used to produce electric power commercially. Yet General Electric—rightly—decided that it had to get into the atomic energy field. It could not afford not to take the risk as long as there was the remotest possibility that atomic energy would, after all, become a feasible source of electric power.

We know from experience that the risk we cannot afford not to take is like a "high-low" poker game. A middle hand will inevitably lose out. But we do not know why this is so. And the other, and much more common kinds of risk we do not really understand at all.

d. *Finally, there is the area of measurements.* I do not have to explain . . . why measurements are needed in management, and especially for the organized entrepreneurial decisions we call "long-range planning."

But it should be said that in human institutions, such as a business enterprise, measurements, strictly speaking, do not and cannot exist. It is the definition of a measurement that it be impersonal and objective, that is, extraneous to the event measured. A child's growth is not dependent on the yardstick or influenced by being recorded. But any measurement in a business enterprise determines action—both on the part of the measurer and the measured—and thereby directs, limits and causes behavior and performance of the enterprise. Measurement in the enterprise is always motivation, that is, moral force, as much as it is *ratio cognoscendi*.

In addition, in long-range planning we do not deal with observable events. We deal with future events, that is, with expectations. And expectations, being incapable of being observed, are never "facts" and cannot be measured.

Measurements, in long-range planning, thus present very real problems, especially conceptual ones. Yet precisely because what we measure and how we measure determines what will be considered relevant, and determines thereby not just what we see, but what we—and others—do, measurements are all-important in the planning process. Above all, unless we build expectations into the planning decision in such a way that we can very early realize whether they are actually fulfilled or not—including a fair understanding of what are significant deviations both in time and in scale—we cannot plan; and we have no feedback, no way of self-control in management.

We obviously also need for long-range planning *managerial* knowledge—the knowledge with respect to the operations of a business. We need such knowledge as that of the resources available, especially the human resources; their capacities and their limitations. We need to know how to "translate" from business needs, business results, and business decisions into functional capacity and specialized effort. There is, after all, no functional decision, there is not even functional data, just as there is no functional profit, no functional loss, no functional investment, no functional risk, no functional customer, no functional product, and no functional image of a company. There is only a unified company product, risk, investment, and so on, hence only company performance and company results. Yet at the same time the work obviously has to be done by people each of whom has to be specialized. Hence for a decision to be possible, we must be able to integrate divergent individual knowledges and capacities into one organization potential; and for a decision to be effective, we must be able to translate it into a diversity of individual and expert, yet focused efforts.

There are also big problems of knowledge in the entrepreneurial task that I have not mentioned—the problems of growth and change, for instance, or those of the moral values of a society and their meaning to business. But these are problems that exist for many areas and disciplines other than management.

And in this paper I have confined myself intentionally to knowledge that is specific to the process of long-range planning. Even so I have barely mentioned the main areas. But I think I have said enough to substantiate three conclusions:

1. Here are areas of genuine knowledge, not just areas in which we need data. What we need above all are basic theory and conceptual thinking.

2. The knowledge we need is new knowledge. It is not to be found in the traditional disciplines of business such as accounting or economics. It is also not available, by and large, in the physical or life sciences. From the existing disciplines we can get a great deal of help, of course, especially in tools and techniques. And we need all we can get. But the knowledge we need is distinct and specific. It pertains not to the physical, the biological, or the psychological universe, though it partakes of them all. It pertains to the specific institution, the enterprise, which is a social institution existing in contemplation of human values. What is "knowledge" in respect to this institution, let alone what is "scientific," must therefore always be determined by reference to the nature, function and purposes of this specific (and very peculiar) institution.

3. It is not within the decision of the entrepreneur whether he wants to make risk-taking decisions with long futurity; he makes them by definition. All that is within his power is to decide whether he wants to make them responsibly or irresponsibly, with a rational chance of effectiveness and success, or as blind gamble against all odds. And both because the process is essentially a rational process, and because the effectiveness of the entrepreneurial decisions depends on the understanding and voluntary efforts of others, the process will be the more responsible and the more likely to be effective, the more it is a rational, organized process based on knowledge.

## IV

Long-range planning is risk-taking decision making. As such it is the responsibility of the policy maker, whether we call him entrepreneur or manager. To do the job rationally and systematically does not change this. Long-range planning does not "substitute facts for judgment," does not "substitute science for the manager." It does not even lessen the importance and role of managerial ability, courage, experience, intuition, or even hunch just as scientific biology and systematic medicine have not lessened the importance of these qualities in the individual physician. On the contrary, the systematic organization of the planning job and the supply of knowledge to it, should make more effective individual managerial qualities of personality and vision.

But at the same time long-range planning offers major opportunity and major challenge to Management Science and to the Management Scientist.[4] We need systematic study of the process itself and of every one of its elements. We need systematic work in a number of big areas of new knowledge—at least we need to know enough to organize our ignorance.

At the same time, long-range planning is the crucial area; it deals with the decisions which, in the last analysis, determine the character and the survival of the enterprise.

So far, it must be said, Management Science has not made much contribution to long-range planning. Sometimes one wonders whether those who call themselves "Management Scientists" are even aware of the risk-taking character of economic activity and of the resultant entrepreneurial job of long-range planning. Yet, in the long run, Management Science and Management Scientists may well, and justly, be judged by their ability to supply the knowledge and thinking needed to make long-range planning possible, simple, and effective.

## NOTES AND REFERENCES

1. *Long-range planning* is not a term I like or would have picked myself. It is a misnomer—as are so many of our terms in economics and management, such as *capitalism, automation, operations research, industrial engineering,* or *depreciation.* But it is too late to do anything about the term; it has become common usage.

2. For a discussion see my book, *The Landmarks of Tomorrow* (New York: Harper & Row, 1958).

3. For a discussion of this "new organization," see again my *The Landmarks of Tomorrow,* mentioned above.

4. I would like to say here that I do not believe that the world is divided into "managers" and "management scientists." One man may well be both. Certainly, management scientists must understand the work and job of the manager, and vice versa. But conceptually and as a kind of work, the two are distinct.

# 9

# Making Long-Range
# Company Planning Pay Off

*George A. Steiner*

*This article makes a strong case for the importance of long-range plan-
ning to American companies. For those interested in prescriptions, the
article outlines a series of "how to" steps designed to lead to effective
plan development. Note particularly his first step—planning to plan.—*
Eds.

This article is devoted to a thumbnail sketch of two major aspects of
long-range planning. First is the methodology or procedure for long-
range planning. The second concerns the payoff to a company that does
long-range planning.

I have chosen to dwell on these two points for several reasons.
First, while long-range planning has grown rapidly in recent years
and has paid off handsomely for many companies, there still are questions raised about its value. Second, while important progress has been
made in the techniques of long-range planning, there are compara-
tively few detailed case studies and principles which are available for
those who wish to initiate the process or improve their planning.

These two factors are related. I suspect, although solid proof is not
available, that the major reason for the fact that more companies do
not engage in long-range planning is that they do not know precisely
how to go about it. Not wishing to admit this even to themselves, other
reasons are given for the lack of long-range planning.[1]

SOURCE: © 1962 by the Regents of the University of California. Reprinted from *California Management Review* IV, 2, pp. 28–41, by permission of the Regents.

## WHAT IS LONG-RANGE PLANNING?

Planning in general is the conscious determination of courses of action to achieve preconceived objectives. It is deciding in advance what is to be done, when it is to be done, by whom it is to be done, and how it is to be done. It can range from the detailed, specific and rigid to the broad, general and flexible design.

Long-range planning does this for extended periods of time. Long-range planning is a process for establishing long-range goals; working out strategies, programs, and policies to achieve these goals; and setting up the necessary machinery to insure that the company gets where it wants to go.

It is a process of choosing from among alternative courses of action and charting the use of time, resources, and effort to achieve the objective sought. The further into the future the plan stretches the less detailed are its specific parts. The subject matter of long-range plans should cover products, services, facilities, manpower, research and development, organization, marketing, financial matters, and various aspects of management itself.[2]

## HOW LONG IS LONG-RANGE?

How long a time should a long-range plan cover? The answer to this question is much like the response of Abraham Lincoln when asked how long a man's legs ought to be. "Long enough to reach the ground," said the President.

Similarly, the length of a planning period will vary considerably from company to company and subject to subject. It is not fixed or rigid. The time span of a plan should cover the period encompassing important financial commitments and their payoff.

For example, depending upon subject matter, coverage should embrace product development time and period of major financial impact following development; resource development time (e.g., sources of supply, management talent, or labor skills); and time required to develop physical facilities plus payoff period for major capital investments. For most businesses such factors will establish a minimum long-range planning period of from 5 to 10 years.

## FORMAL LONG-RANGE PLANNING
## IN INDUSTRY

All managers engage in long-range planning—if only to increase their own salaries. If they do not plan they are not doing their jobs. In the past, when top managers needed help in planning they often hired an assistant or created a vice president for administration.

Large and complex organizations centuries ago had staff positions for planning. Long-range planning, therefore, is not new. What is new is charging someone with full-time responsibility for planning and giving him a staff to do the job. It is the growth of planning departments and staff specialists at the top levels of corporations and major divisions that is new.

Pressures on American companies to establish such formal organizations have been most strong during the past 10 years. Among the major pressures are the following:

1. Business has become increasingly complex because of expanding enterprise size, decentralization of authority, diversification of product lines, mergers, and the growing sensitivity of internal operations to uncontrollable environmental forces.

2. Technological rates of change are increasing and placing a premium on those organizations which can foresee and adapt to them.

3. A variety of forces are squeezing profit margins.

4. End-use markets (domestic) are altering significantly and rapidly with geographic population shifts, changes in population composition, new social trends influencing market behavior of consumers, and growing competition for consumer savings.

5. End-use markets (abroad) are changing rapidly with new commercial alignments, and efforts to industrialize the underdeveloped countries of the world.

6. There has been a rapid development of tools for planning and a growing recognition of the need for skilled technical competence to apply them to long-range planning. This trend promises to accelerate. In mind are not alone the new powerful mathematical tools which have been adapted to business decision making (e.g., linear programming, game theory, probability theory, etc.); but the application of computers, simulation and systems concepts, and new developments in economics, psychology, and other social sciences.

7. Competitors are devoting more attention to long-range planning.[3]

Under such pressures more and more companies in the past 10 years have been developing long-range planning programs and extending the field of inquiry further into the future. I believe, however, that effective long-range planning in industry is not as widespread as it ought to be.

Facts about the growth of formalized long-range planning are not plentiful nor reliable. *Nation's Business* concluded that about 20 percent of businesses had long-range planning in 1953 compared to about 50 percent in 1958.[4] The National Industrial Conference Board concluded in 1956 that of 189 manufacturing companies participating in its survey only one out of four had no formalized forward planning or failed to plan ahead beyond one year. About half of those having long-range plans said they included all the major elements of the enterprise in their planning. Only half said they placed much reliance on the plans.[5]

A survey made by *Management Methods* in 1958 revealed that, among its respondents, only 18 percent had formal advanced plans while another 52 percent had informal advanced plans. No advanced plans were made in 30 percent of the companies covered. When asked whether respondents felt they were doing as much advanced planning as they should, 72 percent replied in the negative. Practically all planning in companies in this survey was for five years or less.

Professors Sord and Welsch found in a study published in the same year that two thirds of the number surveyed had long-range plans, but the subject matter varied greatly. Two thirds had long-range sales plans, but only about one third had long-range research or expense plans. Only about half had long-range profit or cash plans. Practically all plans were for five years or less.[6]

These data, while not conclusive, are helpful. My own empirical observations, together with the data cited, lead me to conclude that, while formal long-range corporate planning has grown by leaps and bounds in the past 10 years, the practice is heavily concentrated in larger enterprises, and it is centered there on a few major problem areas (capital expenditures, product development, and sales) for periods less than 5 years. The coverage, time span, and usage is not great enough in light of potential value.

## HOW TO MAKE A LONG-RANGE PLAN

In developing long-range plans it is helpful to think in terms of a series of steps. But, since the planner must always think in terms of retracing his thinking, allowance must also be made for some overlapping of these steps.

The sequence of steps presented in the next few paragraphs illustrates one concrete framework upon which a company may plan. It is flexible and has been used successfully. This particular sequence has the virtue of focusing attention on product which is usually, although not always, the principal theme of a business long-range plan.

The specific methodology of planning may vary much from one company to another whether or not the steps presented here are followed. This arises because the process must be flexible to accommodate an unusually complex intermeshing of variables which are subject to constant change. In mind are such factors as the technical knowledge and wisdom of the planners, the particular needs of the enterprise, the organization for planning, availability of strategic facts, subject-matter of the plans, and uses to be made of the results.[7]

### First: Plan to Plan

First is *planning to plan*. As the Cleveland Electric Illuminating Company has so well documented, company planning must be planned.[8] This may seem as redundant as Cole Porter's "Begin the Beguine." But planning does not just happen. It must be planned!

A suitable planning climate must be established, and the organization made planning conscious. Policy decisions must be made about who will do what in planning. And, step-by-step procedures must be worked out. In one major planning program of a large corporation in which I participated, the first thing we did was to prepare a detailed letter covering the entire planning procedure for signature by the president. The letter was addressed to all parties involved. In this way everyone knew what was the plan to plan. The newer the plan the more important the thoroughness with which this step should be taken. But even where planning is well established the procedures should be carefully spelled out, as in, for example, the *Westinghouse Planning Guide*.[9]

On the other hand, care should be taken to avoid overdoing this step. It is easily possible to preplan too long, in too much detail, and to spend too much time on clarification of procedures. There is too much feedback in going through the sequences of planning to warrant more than just enough detail in this step to get the process moving.

Basic assumptions must be made at various stages in the planning process. At the outset, however, some of the overall assumptions upon which planning rests should be set forth. In mind, for example, are premises which provide a framework for planning, such as the course of the cold war, population movements, or competitors' activities.

Purely methodological premises may also be established, such as— plans will be based upon constant rather than actual anticipated prices. But, whatever the premises determined, the point is that standards must be developed to guide the planning program. Otherwise, lack of coordination, unnecessary emphasis and study on less important subjects, excessive planning costs, and confusion in drawing conclusions are predictive consequences of poorly devised or neglected premises.

### Second: Define Objectives

Second, *objectives of planning must be clearly specified*. The purpose of the plan, the objectives to be sought in the planning process, and the relation of planning goals to other goals and objectives in the enterprise must be clarified. Setting objectives provides the key to how planning will be done, the strategic factors to be emphasized in plan development, and methods by which planning will become the basis for action.

The objective of every business, of course, is to make a profit. Otherwise the business will not survive. But saying this is far from developing a set of goals which will best serve a company and its long-range planning program.

**Be Specific.**   Goals should be established as concretely as possible. What does this mean? Is the goal to be an aggregate absolute volume of profits? Is the goal to be expressed in terms of a percentage of sales? Is it to be in terms of percentage of investment? If it is return of investment, how is this to be calculated? Is it the E. I. du Pont de Nemours & Company or the Monsanto Chemical Company formula? Will a rising rate of return on investment be accepted even if sales do not increase?

Is sales growth in itself a goal? Is sales stability a goal? How are conflicts among goals to be resolved? Are there other objectives which need to be expressed as a guide to the planning program?

**Defining Corporate Goals.**   There has recently been a growing interest in defining corporate goals, probably in part as an outgrowth of long-range planning needs. Often-stated economic-type objectives, besides those mentioned in preceding paragraphs, are: growth, expressed in terms of sales, assets, employees, profits, or product line; stability, usually expressed in terms of sales, manpower, and profits; flexibility, expressed in numerous ways, such as ability to innovate, speed of response to new environment, especially competition; diversity in preparedness to compete; sensitivity to technological and market changes; and acquisition of a given status of technical skill.

Very frequently, goals express ethical or moral considerations. These are generally described in terms such as leadership of the firm in the industry, integrity and honesty in dealing with others, maintenance of amicable community relations, and assumption of social responsibilities with respect to community problems.[10]

**Must Be Realistic.**   Long-range company goals should be given the greatest thought and formulated as realistically as possible. The validity of goals for planning should be tested upon the basis of past experience of the company and its industry, and future prospects for both. Unrealistic goals are not very helpful.

Sometimes an immediate problem will serve as the focal point for planning. If, for example, rate of return on stockholders' investment for a company has been well below the industry average for the past five years the prime goal for the company planning may be to achieve the industry average or better.

Similarly, actual or anticipated trouble with a product may provide the basis for a concrete goal, e.g., "eliminate the product and substitute others," "undertake new research on the product to improve its salability," or "cut costs of the product by X percent of sales so that it will attract a new level of demand."

Realistic projections of company operations must be placed against any goals established for the future. The difference between the two sets of numbers will reveal the magnitude of the tasks that lie ahead for the corporation. If, for example, a sales objective of 1,000,000 units is established for 5 years in the future, and 1,500,000 for 10 years ahead, and a realistic forecast shows 750,000 units in 1967 and 1,150,000 in 1972, the magnitude of the problem for the company is revealed.

Through this process long-range company goals should be established for sales, profits, capital requirements, new and old product requirements. Then, for each of these, the gap between aspirations and projections on present plans and trends must be measured or defined.

## Third: Explore Possible Strategies

The third step is to *develop strategies to fill the major gaps*. The problem here is to bring to the foreground and examine the principal alternatives open to the company in filling the gaps and then to choose from among them those most acceptable. There obviously are many ways to do this.

In this step companies must come face to face with major questions of policy. If there is a sales gap, for example, to what extent will it be filled with old products, by further penetration of old markets, or entrance into new markets? If this is not enough, to what extent should the old product be importantly modified by research? Where can and should costs be reduced or increased? Should new products be introduced? If so, should they be developed by the present company or acquired through merger? Should all new acquisitions have an affinity with present product lines, or is this not necessary?

While the central focus of planning is naturally on products, the question of strategies is not exclusively concerned with products. Strategies may be developed, for example, for management training, management succession, organization, investments of surplus cash, dividend policy, or public relations.

The precise steps to be followed in developing strategies to answer the kinds of questions given above obviously vary from case to case. One illustrative approach is as follows.

To begin with, tentative alternative courses of action may be set forth for testing in the planning process. These may be suggested by managers at different levels. A planning group itself may, and probably will, think up alternative strategies. The planning process will apply several screenings to the suggestions, the sifting measures which will become more rigorous in successive planning stages.

It is also healthy and often indispensable to undertake an objective and honest appraisal of company strengths and weaknesses in relevant areas. For example, if a company is planning a diversification program, analysis is important in the following areas—management competence to digest proposed mergers; financial capability; marketing abilities for the new product; and, if stock is used to acquire a new company, the ability of the present management to continue control of the enterprise. Other areas of review might include basic research and engineering competence, advertising and promotion skills, labor relations, quality of management, capacity to control costs and production, and product and service acceptability.

Elemental, of course, is the build-up of information important in choosing between alternative courses of action. This is a critical stage in planning because it is frequently difficult to acquire reliable information about the most crucial strategic factors in decision making. It is most important at this stage to concentrate on the strategic data, or those which will have the most significance in choice conclusions.

The range of phenomena about which data should be collected is very wide. For a new product possibility, for example, the analysis may cover technological matters, ranging from projection of prospective scientific advances affecting the product to costs and timing of research, development, tests, and engineering for the product. There are many economic matters of interest, including market changes, possible demand at different pricing levels, estimated fixed and variable costs, break-even volume, prospective return on investment, and probabilities of profit amounts at different price-volume-cost ranges. Where applicable, there are also, of course, social, political, military, and internal administrative matters demanding attention.

The next step is to *select strategies from among alternative possibilities*. More or less simultaneously, four analytical processes merge at this point. The first is the application, where appropriate, of new mathematical techniques to get a quantitative optimization of objectives.

The second is a modification of quantitative conclusions by a broad range of qualitative factors which will have a determining impact on final choices. Included in the latter, for example, would be estimates of what competitors are likely to do under given circumstances.

**Break-Even Calculations.** Third, to the extent practicable, the financial impact of decisions should be measured individually and in their entirety. This should be done by the preparation of break-even calculations, cash flow analyses, and balance sheet and profit and loss statements. The detail of analysis should naturally be tailored to fit the need and importance of the data to the reliability of conclusions. Computer simulation, while not now used very extensively in this step, is a fourth process which promises to grow in importance.

The net results of this stage should be the development of strategies to fill the gaps apparent in step two. These broad plans of action should be either the best possible solutions to the problems or, at the very least, suitable ones. They should be tested for feasibility in terms of management, manpower, finances, competitor actions, technical expectations, and market acceptability. Broad magnitudes and timing should be established.

Resulting strategies can be broad or relatively narrow. One important aerospace company in the United States recently matched a frank appraisal of its strengths and weaknesses in various disciplines of knowledge used in the industry against prospective new product developments. It reasoned that it could not maintain strength in all the areas of knowledge which it now covered. The result was an increase in strength in some areas and an elimination of many other areas.

Some companies have decided to expand through merger even though the resulting product line is heterogeneous. Other companies feel it a better strategy to acquire new products through merger only when there is a close relationship with present product line. Some companies mix these two strategies. Certain companies have decided to lead their industry in research and development. Others are content to follow.

A manufacturer of ceramics ware recently decided to concentrate only on products requiring advanced scientific and engineering skills and to abandon mass production of dinnerware. One electronics producer recently decided, following an agonizing appraisal, to abandon his computer line.

A medium-sized California food processor worked out a completely new detailed strategy for timing of annual sales promotion and new product development. A large oil company recently completed a detailed strategy covering its foreign investment program. These are illustrations of results from this step.

### Fourth: Subplan to Fit Strategy

The fourth step in long-range planning is to *develop derivative operational plans.* A planning process is not complete until subsidiary plans are made to put into effect the strategies developed in step three. This seems elementary but is not always followed in practice. Decisions made without methods to carry them out are ineffective. The following cover the most important functional areas where derivative plans must be made.

Research and development programs should be supported, timed, and controlled to achieve the new product or other requirements needed to reach goals. These other requirements may, for example, include improving old products, reducing production costs, hiring new scientific skills, or increasing basic research.

Production programs should reflect digestion of new equipment, scheduling, new quality controls and inspection methods, and associated activities.

Marketing and promotion plans would, of course, include new selling efforts, advertising programs, reorganization of sales territories, pricing, and perhaps packaging.

Organizational changes may be required as a result of the new program which in turn, of course, needs detailed planning before implementation. Included here might be new management training programs.

Financial plans would include preparations for new equity financing or borrowing, budgeting of capital, and detailed financial forecasts to support the feasibility of the operational plans.

**Parallel Planning.**  An important feature of long-range planning is parallel planning. It would be a waste of time and resources to insist that production await engineering before beginning its derivative plans, or that marketing await production, or that organization await all of them. It is true that what is decided in one functional area will have a determining impact on other areas. But planning in all areas must proceed in parallel to the fullest extent practicable to save time. This can be accomplished by good communications in planning and sharpening of abilities to guess correctly what is going on in other functional areas that will affect planning in another area.

Naturally, the nearer term plans should be sufficiently detailed to permit operations and control. For this purpose detailed budgets or other planning and control techniques should be prepared. The further away in time the less detail should be needed or justified in terms of cost.

## Fifth: Integrate Plans

The fifth and final step is to *assure the integration of long-range and short-range plans and to introduce the necessary controls to be sure operations take place in conformance with plans.*

**Sequential Stages.**  Short-range plans must, of course, be prepared in light of longer-range goals. Meshing the two can be accomplished by developing sequential stages to meet long-range goals, as for example, promotion plans, the near-term aspects of which would be included in specific budgetary items. Where long-range plans are not specified in concrete terms, as for example, outlines to improve the quality of management, the connection is looser.

In such instances, short-range plans should reflect the longer-range goals and policies set to achieve them. In some companies the problem of meshing short-range and long-range plans is accomplished by developing five-year plans in which the first year is the current operating budget.

The control process designed to insure that operations take place in conformance with plans extends too far beyond the planning function discussed in this paper and will not be treated here. It is perhaps unnecessary to say that plans which are not executed are only exercises. They may be important as exercises but they are not plans in the sense the term is used here. Reciprocally, efficient control of operations is rather difficult without the goals and standards of performance which plans establish.

**Organization for Planning.**   Too large a field of inquiry for extended treatment here is the subject of business practices and principles in organizing for long-range planning. But, since it has a direct bearing upon the way planning steps such as the above are performed, a few observations are in order.

First of all, organization for planning is not a simple matter of working out procedural or data flows. It must face the fundamental question of who is going to do what about basic decision making in an organization.

Boards of directors have superior authority but there is great variation in the extent to which they choose to use this power. At E. I. du Pont de Nemours & Company, for example, the board has delegated great power to subcommittees of the board, principally the executive committee. Long-range planning at Du Pont centers in this group. In other companies the board has delegated its planning powers to the president. In some, the president in turn has delegated his powers in varying degrees to committees, departments, or individuals.

**Top Management Support.**   Second, and closely associated with the above issue, long-range planning will be most useful and effective if the top executives of the company have confidence and faith in it. A long-range planning program is not likely to be of much value if the chief executives do not support it actively.

Third, rather widespread participation in the process should be encouraged, but not to the extent that timetables cannot be met, objectivity in analyzing facts is lost, or strategic decisions become known to too many people. Long-range plans are usually rather important to a great many people in an enterprise. Their participation in and execution of the plan will be enhanced if they can point to some contribution of theirs in it, or if they can find in it a goal worth striving for.

Effective planning requires decentralization. It is true that top management itself may define basic long-range planning strategies. But the execution of these programs requires effective coordination of many people. As Peter Drucker has pointed out, planning and doing are separate parts of the same job. They are not separate jobs. Planning proceeds best when both top management and operating people participate fully in it.

## DOES PLANNING PAY OFF?

Determining payoff is a matter of relating the value of planning results to the costs of planning. Every planning program should be examined to determine the margin between value and cost. On the whole, payoff calculations are probably more easily determined for short-range than for long-range plans.

Long-range planning may not pay off for 5, 10, or more years. It is because of the difficulties in making cost-value calculations, together with the length of time needed to draw conclusions, that questions often arise about payoff for long-range planning.

### "Extinct by Instinct"

Two extreme approaches seem to be taken by companies that either ignore or improperly face the question of payoff. One approach is to minimize costs by ignoring basic steps in planning. This method depends upon conclusions derived without encumbrances of carefully developed facts or lines of reasoning. For this approach the practitioner feels little need for a conscious and deliberate assessment of relevant considerations upon which judgments can be developed. In common parlance this is called "flying by the seat of your pants." I prefer to call it the road to becoming extinct by instinct.

### "Paralysis by Analysis"

At the other extreme is overemphasis of value in relation to cost. With this approach there is recognition of the need for planning. An assignment is made to a dedicated hard-working soul with a reputation for thoroughness. Work is begun without much reference to the complexities of the task and before long a large number of people are involved at substantial cost.

Somewhere along the line, usually later than sooner, a voluminous report is prepared and promptly filed away "for future reference." Either the need for decision has long since passed or the report is too complex and bulky for busy people to read and digest. This I call the road to paralysis by analysis.[11]

## Cost-Value Equation

For planning to pay off, a happy balance between the two extremes must be struck. The precise payoff for any particular planning operation is difficult to determine. No one can do this without examining the cost-value equation for that program. But planning has paid off for companies that have considered this equation and achieved the balance required.

The Stanford Research Institute studied the question "Why Companies Grow." One major conclusion of the study was that: "In the cases of both high-growth and low-growth companies, those that now support planning programs have shown a superior growth rate in recent years."[12]

The Stanford study observed that most companies with formalized planning programs were enthusiastic about their value. Well might they be if, partly as a result of planning, their growth rates have been exceptional. For these companies planning has clearly paid off.

## Ford's Experience

Ernest Breech, former Chairman of the Board of the Ford Motor Company, has observed: "We believe it is our business, and that of other large companies, to make trends, not to follow them. A confident aggressive spirit, backed up by intelligent planning and hard-hitting management, can be contagious."[13] For Ford, planning has paid off handsomely as the last 10 years of that company's history will testify.

On the other hand, the path to bankruptcy is strewn with corpses who failed to plan or planned poorly. A study by the Bureau of Business Research at the University of Pittsburgh concluded that among the 10 companies chosen for intensive study every one was guilty of poor planning, and this shortcoming was the major cause of failure in the majority of cases.[14]

It is probably true that the only certainty about long-range planning is that the conclusions will prove to be in error. There is no such thing as 20/20 foresight. But, one great advantage of forward planning is that coming to grips with uncertainty by analysis and study should result in a reduction of the margin of doubt about the future. Despite the fog enshrouding the future many companies have planned ahead and hit goals surprisingly accurately.

## FORWARD PLANNING

Ralph Cordiner, commenting on this point in his book *New Frontiers for Professional Managers*, has observed that one of the three principal new horizons ahead for managers lies in the area of long-range planning. As he put it, "In a time of radical worldwide change, when every day introduces new elements of uncertainty, forward planning may seem to be nearly impossible—an exercise in futility. Yet there never was a more urgent need for long-range planning on the part of every business, and indeed every other important element of our national life."[15]

The argument is often presented that for large companies the choices for investing funds are many and necessitate advance planning. But since a range of choice in investment of funds in a small single-product company does not exist, for it, advance planning is a waste of time.

This idea is most erroneous. Small companies have just as great a need for long-range planning as large ones. They may not have the cash to support technical specialists, but there are other means to acquire the needed expertise. Many small companies, through long-range planning, have opened the door to successful expansion, new products, and new markets by multiplying ranges of desirable choices.

In considering payoff for long-range planning, value is generally considered to lie in the areas of improved profit stability, growth, more efficient sales, capital expenditure, inventory, research and development, or cost reduction programs. Or long-range planning may prove its worth in better management replacement and improvement programs; or some other tangible and concrete activities of the enterprise.

## ANCILLARY BENEFITS

It should also be pointed out that a number of important ancillary and intangible benefits have accrued to companies having formal long-range planning programs. A brief list of them would include the following points. The planning process constitutes an excellent channel of communication throughout the organization. It identifies problems ahead for a firm long before they become acute. It focuses attention on the principal determinants of the business. It provides an organized mechanism for testing value judgments.

It opens new horizons for profitable study. It prevents piecemeal solutions to problems. It is a good training ground for future managers,

**TABLE 1**  Five Steps for Long-Range Planning

---

1—PLANNING TO PLAN

2—SPECIFYING OBJECTIVES OF ENTERPRISE
 · forecasting future prospects
 · measuring the gaps between aspirations and projections

3—DEVELOPING STRATEGIES
 · to fill in the major gaps

4—DEVELOPING DERIVATIVE OR DETAILED PLANS IN MAJOR
FUNCTIONAL AREAS TO FIT THE STRATEGIES
 · research and development
 · production
 · marketing and promotion

5—INTEGRATION OF LONG-RANGE AND SHORT-RANGE PLANS
 · introducing necessary controls

---

and it brings to those responsible for running the business a comprehensive, coordinated, and uniform picture of present and future business.

## CONCLUSIONS

Despite the phenomenal growth of formal long-range planning, and its important payoff to many companies, there are still too many companies that do not employ the process effectively. The reasons are often anchored in their lack of knowledge about how to do it, misunderstanding of its cost-value calculation, or both.

Five operational steps for long-range planning have been set forth and examined. They are recapitulated in graphic form (Table 1).

For long-range planning to pay off, a balance must be struck between minimizing cost by ignoring basic steps and principles of effective planning and incurring overly heavy cost by excessive analysis. While full benefits may not be derived for many years, efforts should be made to measure them and offset them against costs. This article has been devoted to the proposition that available knowledge about how to undertake long-range planning is quite sufficient, and full understanding of the cost-value equation is so pervasive, that all businesses, large and small, should have a more or less formal long-range planning program and reap rich rewards from it.

## NOTES AND REFERENCES

(This article, translated into Italian, appeared abroad under the title "Il rendimento della Programmazione d'impresa a lungo termine" in a recent issue of the *Rivista Internazionale di Scienze Economiche e Commerciali,* a periodical published by the Universita Bocconi in Milan. G.A.S.)

1. For example, other reasons given are: Our business is too cyclical. Our customers do not know their plans, so how can we know ours? Long-range planning is too vague. Not enough time exists for short-range planning, let alone long-range planning. We cannot afford specialists needed to do the job. It costs more than it is worth.

2. For other definitions, see George A. Steiner, "What Do We Know About Using Long-Range Plans?" *California Management Review,* Fall 1959; Peter F. Drucker, "Long-Range Planning, Challenge to Management Science," *Management Science,* April 1959; Bruce Payne and James H. Kennedy, "Making Long-Range Planning Work," *The Management Review,* February 1959; and William H. Newman and Charles E. Summer, Jr., *The Process of Management* (Englewood Cliffs, N.J.: Prentice-Hall, 1961), pp. 430–36.

3. See Charles E. Summer, Jr., "The Future Role of the Corporate Planner," *California Management Review,* Winter 1961.

4. "Planning Tomorrow's Profits," *Nation's Business,* August 1958.

5. "Long-Range Planning Pays Off," *Business Record,* October 1956.

6. Burnard H. Sord and Glenn A. Welsch, *Business Budgeting* (New York: Controllership Foundation, 1958).

7. For other operational planning sequences see David W. Ewing, *Long-Range Planning for Management* (New York: Harper & Row, 1958); William E. Hill, "Planning for Profits: A Four-Stage Method," *California Management Review,* Spring 1959, which is a method much like that presented here; Bruce Payne and James H. Kennedy, "Making Long-Range Planning Work," *The Management Review,* February 1959; *Westinghouse Planning Guide,* Westinghouse Electric Corporation, 1959; *Guide to Profit Improvement Program,* American Brake Shoe Company, 1959; and Arthur W. Lucas and William G. Livingston, "Long-Range Planning and the Capital Appropriations Program," in *Financial Planning for Greater Profits,* American Management Association Report No. 44, 1960. For a detailed analytical planning sequence see Preston P. Le Breton and Dale A. Henning, *Planning Theory* (Englewood Cliffs, N.J.: Prentice-Hall, 1961).

8. Ralph M. Besse, "Company Planning Must Be Planned!" *Dun's Review,* April 1957.

9. See note 7.

10. See, for example, Stewart Thompson, *Management Creeds and Philosophies,* Research Study No. 32, American Management Association, New York, 1958; Richard Fells, *The Meaning of Modern Business,* chapter 6, "Corporate Goals" (New York: Columbia University Press, 1960); Peter Drucker, *The Practice of Management,* chapter 7, "The Objectives of a Business" (New York: Harper & Row, 1954); and George R. Terry, *Principles of Management,* chapter 9, "Management Objectives and Ethics" (Homewood, Ill.: Richard D. Irwin, 1956).

11. From Charles R. Schwartz, "The Return-on-Investment Concept as a Tool for Decision Making" in *Improving the Caliber of Company Management,* General Management Series, no. 183, American Management Association, 1956, p. 46.

12. N. R. Maines, *Why Companies Grow* (Palo Alto, Calif.: Stanford Research Institute, 1957), p. 4.
13. Ernest R. Breech, "Planning the Basic Strategy of a Large Business," in *Planning the Future Strategy of Your Business*, ed. Edward C. Bursk and Dan H. Fenn (New York: McGraw-Hill, 1956), p. 17.
14. A. M. Woodruff and T. G. Alexander, *Success and Failure in Small Manufacturing* (Pittsburgh: University of Pittsburgh Press, 1958), pp. 48 and 100.
15. Ralph Cordiner, *New Frontiers for Professional Managers* (New York: McGraw-Hill, 1956), p. 82.

*B. Organizing*

# 10

# Classifying the Elements
# of Work

*Frank B. Gilbreth*
*and*
*Lillian M. Gilbreth*

*In this article two famous industrial engineers suggest a "one best way"
approach to organizing work. They suggest that their classification system is applicable to all kinds of work and will significantly increase
worker efficiency. This article and the system it describes give an excellent example of the "scientific management" approach, to which the
Gilbreths made major contributions.—Eds.*

This paper presents a complete method of visualizing a classification
of all the subdivisions and the true motion-study elements of The One
Best Way to Do Work.

## NEED FOR SUCH A CLASSIFICATION

Such a classification is vitally necessary, in order that fundamental
super-standards shall be made by the scientific method of selecting and
measuring the best units, for synthesis into methods of least waste.

This classification furnishes the basis of a definite mnemonic classification for filing all motion-study and time-study data for the work
of the industrial engineer, the machine designer, and the behavior
psychologist—that their various pieces of information, usually ob-

SOURCE: Reprinted by permission of the publisher from "Classifying the Elements of
Work," *Management and Administration* 8, no. 2 (August 1924), pp. 151–54.

tained through entirely different channels and methods of attack, may be automatically brought together, to the same filing folders, under the same filing subdivisions.

So far as we are able to learn, there are no other classifications or bases for filing that accomplish this purpose, and we have found that such a classification is absolutely necessary for our work of finding The One Best Way to Do Work, standardizing the trades, and making and enforcing standing orders for best management.

It is hoped that teachers of industrial engineering in our colleges will learn that *one* demonstration of building up The One Best Way to Do Work from the ultimate elements, in any kind of activity, will do more to teach a student the principles of motion study and most efficient methods of management than dozens of lessons dealing with generalities.

The coming generation should be taught a definite filing system for data of scientific management, laid out under a complete classification of all work; should be taught the method of selecting the right units to measure and the methods of measuring these units; and should be furnished with the devices for making the cost of measuring cheap, and with a method for synthesizing the resulting information. This would result in a general progress in world efficiency and an increase in quality of living that would mark an epoch in the history of industry and civilization.

## USE OF FUNDAMENTAL ELEMENTS

The literature of scientific management abounds with examples of units of work improperly called "elements," which are in no sense elements. A classification for finding The One Best Way to Do Work must deal with *true elements,* not merely with subdivisions that are arbitrarily called "elements."

There has recently appeared a well-written biography of a great engineer[1] in which subdivisions of operations, requiring in many instances more than 30 seconds to perform, have been erroneously described as "elements." That error will again mislead many people. These so-called elements should be taken for what they really are, namely, subdivisions and not elements, and not confused with true elements, or fundamental units which cannot be further subdivided.

## SCOPE OF THE CLASSIFICATION

This classification for finding The One Best Way to Do Work is applicable to all kinds of work. It was used by one of the authors while serving as ranking officer in the field under the training committee of the General Staff, standardizing the methods of The One Best Way to

Do Work for teaching the five million men and officers in the World War. It has also been used in analyzing the work of the surgeon, nurse, hospital management, large department stores, selling, a great many kinds of manufacturing, accounting, office work in general, and many other kinds of work.

## TRUE ELEMENTS OF WORK

The classification of all work of any and all organizations for the purpose of finding The One Best Way to Do Work may be visualized as follows:

I. A complete organization, which consists of
II. Processes, such as
    (*a*) Financing
    (*b*) Advertising
    (*c*) Marketing
    (*d*) Distributing
    (*e*) Selling
    (*f*) Accounting
    (*g*) Purchasing
    (*h*) Manufacturing
    (*i*) Planning
    (*j*) Teaching
    (*k*) Charting
    (*l*) Maintaining
    (*m*) Filing

These processes consist of

III. Operations, which consist of
IV. Cycles of motions, which consist of
V. Subdivisions, or events, or therbligs[2] of a cycle of motions, which consist of
    (*a*) Search
    (*b*) Find
    (*c*) Select
    (*d*) Grasp
    (*e*) Transport loaded
    (*f*) Position
    (*g*) Assemble
    (*h*) Use
    (*i*) Disassemble
    (*j*) Inspect
    (*k*) Pre-position for next operation

     (*l*) Release load
    (*m*) Transport empty
    (*n*) Rest for overcoming fatigue
    (*o*) Other periods of unavoidable delay
    (*p*) Avoidable delay
    (*q*) Plan

VI. Variables of motions
    (*a*) Variables of the worker
       1. Anatomy
       2. Brawn
       3. Contentment
       4. Creed
       5. Earning power
       6. Experience
       7. Fatigue
       8. Habits
       9. Health
      10. Mode of living
      11. Nutrition
      12. Size
      13. Skill
      14. Temperament
      15. Training
    (*b*) Variables of the surroundings, equipment, and tools
       1. Appliances
       2. Clothes
       3. Colors
       4. Entertainment, music, reading, etc.
       5. Heating, cooling, ventilating
       6. Lighting
       7. Quality of material
       8. Reward and punishment
       9. Size of unit moved
      10. Special fatigue-eliminating devices
      11. Surroundings
      12. Tools
      13. Union rules
    (*c*) Variables of the motion
       1. Acceleration
       2. Automaticity
       3. Combination with other motions and sequences
       4. Cost
       5. Direction
       6. Effectiveness

7. Foot-pounds of work accomplished
8. Inertia and momentum overcome
9. Length
10. Necessity
11. Path
12. "Play for position"
13. Speed

Under I, a complete organization, are included all kinds of organizations, including financial, industrial, commercial, professional, educational, and social.

Under II, processes, it should be noted that processes are divided in the same way from a motion-study analyst's standpoint, regardless in which department or in which function they are found.

Under III, operations, the operations include mechanical as well as physiological, and mental as well as manual.

The reasons for these inclusions are:

1. From the motion-study standpoint there are not always clear dividing lines between the *operations of devices* and the *mental and manual operations of the human being,* for they are often mutually interchangeable, sometimes in part and sometimes as a whole.[3]

2. Records of many and probably all mental operations can now be obtained by the chronocyclegraph and micromotion photographic methods, and each year such photographic records can more and more be deciphered and used to practical advantage. Enough can already be read and used to serve our present needs. Careful examination of all our old micromotion and chronocyclegraph films taken under conditions of actual practice show that they are literally full of examples of such records of mental processes.

Under IV, cycles of motions are arbitrary subdivisions of operations. They have distinct and natural boundaries of beginning and ending. Usually and preferably there are certain sequences of therbligs that are especially suitable for standardization and transference to other kinds of work, and serve every purpose of finding The One Best Way to Do Work.

Under V, therbligs, we would emphasize that we do not place "motions" as the next subdivision under "cycle of motions" because "motions" have neither distinct and definite boundaries nor beginnings and endings. For example: It is difficult to determine correctly how many "motions" are required to take a fountain pen from the pocket and prepare to write with it. It will be found difficult to agree on just how many "motions" are made and as to where are located the boundaries of the "motions" of so simple a cycle as this, or of any other similarly common cycle of motions.

However, the 17 subdivisions, or events, or therbligs, as they are variously called, seem to be all that are necessary from which to synthesize all of the *cycles of motions* of all the *operations* of all the *processes* of all the *organizations* of every kind whatever. The science of motion study consists, therefore, of finding The One Best Sequence of therbligs for each kind of work and the science of management consists of deriving, installing, and enforcing the conditions that will permit the work to be done repeatedly in The One Best Way. It is conceivable that sometime in the future an eighteenth and possibly more therbligs will be found, and we seem near to their discovery at the present time. The discovery of additional therbligs pertaining to the phenomena of skill and automaticity seems inevitable.[4]

Under VI, variables of motions, provision is made for filing all information regarding any kind of motion made by either hand, device, or machine. It provides for all information regarding the structures in which work is performed. It provides for filing all data regarding human behavior—supernormal, normal, and subnormal. It supplies the basis of filing all data of the educator, psychologist, psychiatrist, and the expert in personnel, placement, and promotion problems.

This classification can be carried on and subdivided indefinitely. It furnishes an efficient and quickly usable plan for synthesizing the components of The One Best Way to Do Work in such shape that they can be cumulatively improved.

However, our present information regarding the 17 therbligs is sufficient to revolutionize all kinds of work, and if the industries of the various nations would eliminate the obviously unnecessary therbligs and standardize the kinds, sequences, and combinations of the remaining efficient therbligs, the resulting savings each year would be sufficient to pay the outstanding debts of most nations.

## HISTORY OF THIS CLASSIFICATION

For many years we have used these therbligs as divisions for dissecting cycles of motions of a great many different kinds of work, but it was not until we began to use photography in motion study in 1892 that we made our greatest progress. It was not until 1912, when we used our first micromotion processes intensively, that we were able to make such great advances as projecting the motions of experts faster and slower, as well as at the speed of experts' demonstration. We were then also able to project and examine therbligs backwards, or in the reversed directions. This enabled us to get a new fund of information that resulted in many suggestions from seeing, measuring, and comparing the therbligs performed in the reversed sequence and opposite directions. This was used to great advantage in finding the methods of least waste and especially in the process of taking machines apart and putting them together again in front of a motion picture camera, and then running the film backwards, showing the films of assembling as disassembling and vice versa.

## EXAMPLES OF PROFITABLE USE

Running films of superexperts backwards, to see what we could get for automatically suggesting inventions, or as "thought detonators" when seeing the operation done thus, presented peculiarities and combinations of therbligs never seen before. This was, of course, supplemented by examining one picture, or frame, at a time which, with motion study experts, will always be the most efficient method for getting facts from the films. Great progress was made, for example, in *pre-positioning for next operation* (therblig *k*) parts and tools so that *grasp* (therblig *d*) was performed with quite the same motions and actions and performed within a time equal to that of *release load* (therblig *l*).

As an example of the importance of recognizing the therblig as the fundamental element, the result of that particular study in 1912 was that our organization enabled a client to have his machine assemblers put together 66 machines per day with less fatigue than they had previously accumulated while assembling 18 machines per day. Because this method was synthesized from fundamentally correct units, the same methods are still in use today in this same factory.[5]

This increase in output should not be considered as an exceptional case. On the contrary, it is quite typical. In fact we have a great many illustrations that we could give where the savings were much greater. For example: One large motion-study laboratory, as a result of this method of attack, synthesized and demonstrated new methods which averaged an output of five times as much product per man. This method used in assembling carburetors enabled messenger boys to do the work in one tenth the time required by skilled mechanics.[6] It has been used on work of assembling pumps with still greater results.[7]

## THERBLIG SEQUENCES

It was early recognized that certain similar operations have similar sequences of therbligs. For example: The operations of feeding pieces into a drill press or into a punch press, time tickets into a time stamp, and paper into a printing press, have practically the same sequence of therbligs. A typical sequence of therbligs for one complete cycle of handling one piece on a drill press is *search, find, select, grasp, transport loaded, position, assemble, use, disassemble, inspect, transport loaded, pre-position for next operation, release load* and *transport empty.* This cycle of motions can and should be done with the following therbligs: *grasp, transport loaded, position, assemble, use, release load* and *transport empty,* which are half the number of therbligs of the usual method.

While the former is the usual sequence of therbligs on a drill press, it is by no means the best one. There is The One Best Sequence of therbligs on each machine and each kind of work, and it should always be found, standardized, taught, and maintained.

## ANOTHER WORK CLASSIFICATION

Now let us look at another method of subdividing and classifying all work. There is another and better known type of division and classification for visualizing all activity which was early recognized. The importance of considering this simple classification can be seen in the unfairness and trouble that have been caused by giving the same piece rate for large lots as for small. This classification divides all work, both large and small, into three parts, as follows:

1. Get ready.
2. Do it, or make it.
3. Clean up.

Now, applying this division to one piece on the drill press, we have:

1. *Get ready,* or pick up the piece and put it under the drill. This consists of all therbligs that come before *use* (therblig *h*).
2. *Drill it* (do it or make it). This consists of only one therblig, namely *use* (therblig *h*).
3. *Clean up,* or take the piece out from under the drill and inspect it and lay it down. This consists of all therbligs that come after *use* (therblig *h*).

## THE IMPORTANCE OF USE

It should be recognized that the therblig *use* is the difficult one to learn in mastering a trade. It is the most productive and, therefore, the most important therblig of all.

All other therbligs of all kinds of work are desirable and necessary only so far as they facilitate, prepare for, or assist in increasing *use.* Any therbligs that do not foster *use* should be under suspicion as being unnecessary. *Use* is the highest paid therblig, because it usually requires the most skill. The more of the therbligs of "get ready" and "clean up" that are performed by less skilled and consequently lower priced workers the better for all workers, for they all will be employed a larger portion of the day at the highest priced work at which they are each individually capable. This is true not only in the consideration of the therbligs but also in the trades in general. For example: The bricklayer, the plumber, the steamfitter, the office executive, and many others, each have their specially assigned helpers, but they still habitually do much pay-reducing work for which in the long run they suffer a loss due to less personal activity. It will help to analyze and classify all work if it is recognized that the hod carrier bears the same relation to the bricklayer, and the secretary to the executive, as do the therbligs that compose "get ready" bear to the therblig *use;* and the laborer's work of "clean up" after the work of the bricklayer, is quite the same as the therbligs that compose "clean up" after therblig *use.*

Further investigations of a typical sequence of therbligs, such as on the drill press or other examples cited, from the standpoint of the classification of the therbligs show that *grasp* (therblig *d*) of "get ready" is used before *use* (therblig *h*) and that *release load* (therblig *l*) done after *use* may be quite the same except that it is performed in motions that are the reverse of those of *grasp.*

## PAIRED THERBLIGS

There are a number of such paired therbligs which are almost always separated by the therblig *use.* For example see Table 1.

It was the absence of a therblig on the other side of *use* to pair with *inspect,* together with the fact that *plan* is actually found in the photographic records regardless of how much planning may be done prior to the beginning of an operation, that caused us to add to the list of therbligs, *plan* (therblig *q*). The therblig *plan* may occur in any place

**TABLE 1**

| *Paired Therblig Usually Performed before Use* | | *Paired Therblig Usually Performed after Use* |
| --- | --- | --- |
| *d.* Grasp | Use | *l.* Release load |
| *e.* Transport loaded | Use | *m.* Transport empty |
| *f.* Position | Use | *k.* Pre-position for next operation |
| *g.* Assemble | Use | *i.* Disassemble |
| *q.* Plan | Use | *j.* Inspect |

**TABLE 2**  Unpaired Therbligs

| Order No. 4 | | Order No. 5 |
| --- | --- | --- |
| a. Search | Use | n. Rest for overcoming fatigue |
| b. Find | Use | o. Other forms of unavoidable delay |
| c. Select | Use | p. Avoidable delay |

in the sequence of therbligs, but we have put it last in the list before cited because it was added last, and also to distinguish it from the "planning" that should be done before any "performing" of the operation is begun.

There are two more kinds of divisions, or orders, making a total of five orders of therbligs, namely, one consisting of *search, find,* and *select* (therbligs *a, b,* and *c*) which usually come before *use,* and *rest for overcoming fatigue, other forms of unavoidable delay* and *avoidable delay* (therbligs *n, o,* and *p*) which usually come after *use.* Thus we have two orders of unpaired therbligs separated by *use,* as . . . shown in Table 2.

In analyzing an operation of any kind a simultaneous motion cycle chart is prepared. The therbligs of motion are applied to this chart in studying it for present methods and determining the altered sequence which should be adopted to establish The One Best Way to Do Work.

## NOTES AND REFERENCES

1. See *Frederick W. Taylor* by F. B. Copley.
2. This word was coined for the purpose of having a short word which will save the motions necessary to write such long descriptions as "The 17 categories into which the motion-study elementary subdivisions of a cycle of motions fall."
3. In 1910 and the years following, we collected and specially devised in our own laboratory many devices for supplying, mechanically, the therbligs of cycles of motions that the crippled soldiers could not perform, due to their injuries. Such collections should be made by all museums and colleges that intend to teach motion study.
4. See *Society of Industrial Engineers Bulletin,* November 1923, pp. 6–7. "A Fourth Dimension for Recording Skill," by Frank B. Gilbreth and L. M. Gilbreth. The lateness in starting or finishing of a therblig performed by any one anatomical member as compared with the time of beginning or finishing of a therblig performed by another anatomical member is a most important unit for measuring skill and automaticity.
5. See *Management Engineering,* February 1923, p. 87. "Ten Years of Scientific Management," by John G. Aldrich, M. E., and also his discussion of paper

1378 on page 1131, Vol. 34, 1912, American Society of Mechanical Engineers Transactions.

6. See *Proceedings of the Institution of Automobile Engineers* (English), "The Fundamentals of Cost Reduction," by H. Kerr Thomas, Member of the Council.

7. See *Society of Industrial Engineers Transactions,* Vol. 2, 1920, "The One Best Way to Do Work," by Frank B. Gilbreth and L. M. Gilbreth.

# 11

# Organization Theory: An Overview and an Appraisal

*William G. Scott*

*Organizing the organization is what organization theory is all about. In this article William Scott identifies three theories of organization which have had considerable impact on management thought and practice: classical, neoclassical, and modern. The article makes a cogent argument for unification of elements of all three theories.—Eds.*

Man is intent on drawing himself into a web of collectivized patterns. "Modern man has learned to accommodate himself to a world increasingly organized. The trend toward ever more explicit and consciously drawn relationships is profound and sweeping; it is marked by depth no less than by extension."[1] This comment by Seidenberg nicely summarizes the pervasive influence of organization in many forms of human activity.

Some of the reasons for intense organizational activity are found in the fundamental transitions which revolutionized our society, changing it from a rural culture, to a culture based on technology, industry, and the city. From these changes, a way of life emerged characterized by the *proximity* and *dependency* of people on each other. Proximity and dependency, as conditions of social life, harbor the threats of human conflict, capricious antisocial behavior, instability of human relationships, and uncertainty about the nature of the social structure with its concomitant roles.

Of course, these threats to social integrity are present to some degree in all societies, ranging from the primitive to the modern. But,

---

SOURCE: Reprinted by permission of the author and publisher from "Organization Theory: An Overview and an Appraisal," *The Academy of Management Journal*, April 1961, pp. 7–26.

these threats become dangerous when the harmonious functioning of a society rests on the maintenance of a highly intricate, delicately balanced form of human collaboration. The civilization we have created depends on the preservation of a precarious balance. Hence, disrupting forces impinging on this shaky form of collaboration must be eliminated or minimized.

Traditionally, organization is viewed as a vehicle for accomplishing goals and objectives. While this approach is useful, it tends to obscure the inner workings and internal purposes of organization itself. Another fruitful way of treating organization is as a mechanism having the ultimate purpose of offsetting those forces which undermine human collaboration. In this sense, organization tends to minimize conflict, and to lessen the significance of individual behavior which deviates from values that the organization has established as worthwhile. Further, organization increases stability in human relationships by reducing uncertainty regarding the nature of the system's structure and the human roles which are inherent to it. Corollary to this point, organization enhances the predictability of human action, because it limits the number of behavioral alternatives available to an individual. As Presthus points out:

> Organization is defined as a system of structural interpersonal relations.
> . . . individuals are differentiated in terms of authority, status, and role
> with the result that personal interaction is prescribed. . . . Anticipated
> reactions tend to occur, while ambiguity and spontaneity are decreased.[2]

In addition to all of this, organization has built-in safeguards. Besides prescribing acceptable forms of behavior for those who elect to submit to it, organization is also able to counterbalance the influence of human action which transcends its established patterns.[3]

Few segments of society have engaged in organizing more intensively than business.[4] The reason is clear. Business depends on what organization offers. Business needs a system of relationships among functions; it needs stability, continuity, and predictability in its internal activities and external contacts. Business also appears to need harmonious relationships among the people and processes which make it up. Put another way, a business organization has to be free, relatively, from destructive tendencies which may be caused by divergent interests.

As a foundation for meeting these needs rests administrative science. A major element of this science is organization theory, which provides the grounds for management activities in a number of significant areas of business endeavor. Organization theory, however, is not a homogeneous science based on generally accepted principles. Various theories of organization have been, and are being evolved. For example, something called "modern organization theory" has recently emerged, raising the wrath of some traditionalists, but also capturing the imagination of a rather elite avant-garde.

The thesis of this paper is that modern organization theory, when stripped of its irrelevancies, redundancies, and "speech defects," is a logical and vital evolution in management thought. In order for this thesis to be supported, the reader must endure a review and appraisal of more traditional forms of organization theory which may seem elementary to him.

In any event, three theories of organization are having considerable influence on management thought and practice. They are arbitrarily labeled in this paper as the classical, the neoclassical, and the modern. Each of these is fairly distinct; but they are not unrelated. Also, these theories are ongoing, being actively supported by several schools of management thought.

## THE CLASSICAL DOCTRINE

For lack of a better method of identification, it will be said that the classical doctrine deals almost exclusively with the *anatomy of formal organization*. This doctrine can be traced back to Frederick W. Taylor's interest in functional foremanship and planning staffs. But most students of management thought would agree that in the United States, the first systematic approach to organization, and the first comprehensive attempt to find organizational universals, is dated 1931 when Mooney and Reiley published *Onward Industry*.[5] Subsequently, numerous books, following the classical vein, have appeared. Two of the more recent are Brech's *Organization*[6] and Allen's *Management and Organization*.[7]

Classical organization theory is built around four key pillars. They are the division of labor, the scalar and functional processes, structure, and span of control. Given these major elements just about all of classical organization theory can be derived.

1. *The division of labor* is without doubt the cornerstone among the four elements.[8] From it the other elements flow as corollaries. For example, *scalar* and *functional* growth requires specialization and departmentalization of functions. Organization *structure* is naturally dependent upon the direction which specialization of activities travels in company development. Finally, *span of control* problems result from the number of specialized functions under the jurisdiction of a manager.

2. *The scalar and functional processes* deal with the vertical and horizontal growth of the organization, respectively.[9] The scalar process

refers to the growth of the chain of command, the delegation of authority and responsibility, unity of command, and the obligation to report.

The division of the organization into specialized parts and the regrouping of the parts into compatible units are matters pertaining to the functional process. This process focuses on the horizontal evolution of the line and staff in a formal organization.

3. *Structure* is the logical relationships of functions in an organization, arranged to accomplish the objectives of the company efficiently. Structure implies system and pattern. Classical organization theory usually works with two basic structures, the line and the staff. However, such activities as committee and liaison functions fall quite readily into the purview of structural considerations. Again, structure is the vehicle for introducing logical and consistent relationships among the diverse functions which comprise the organization.[10]

4. *The span of control* concept relates to the number of subordinates a manager can effectively supervise. Graicunas has been credited with first elaborating the point that there are numerical limitations to the subordinates one man can control.[11] In a recent statement on the subject, Brech points out, "span" refers to ". . . the number of persons, themselves carrying managerial and supervisory responsibilities, for whom the senior manager retains his overembracing responsibility of direction and planning, coordination, motivation, and control."[12] Regardless of interpretation, span of control has significance, in part, for the shape of the organization which evolves through growth. Wide span yields a flat structure; short span results in a tall structure. Further, the span concept directs attention to the complexity of human and functional interrelationships in an organization.

It would not be fair to say that the classical school is unaware of the day-to-day administrative problems of the organization. Paramount among these problems are those stemming from human interactions. But the interplay of individual personality, informal groups, intraorganizational conflict, and the decision-making processes in the formal structure appears largely to be neglected by classical organization theory. Additionally, the classical theory overlooks the contributions of the behavioral sciences by failing to incorporate them in its doctrine in any systematic way. In summary, classical organization theory has relevant insights into the nature of organization, but the value of this theory is limited by its narrow concentration on the formal anatomy of organization.

## NEOCLASSICAL THEORY OF ORGANIZATION

The neoclassical theory of organization embarked on the task of compensating for some of the deficiencies in classical doctrine. The neoclassical school is commonly identified with the human relations movement. Generally, the neoclassical approach takes the postulates of the classical school, regarding the pillars of organization as givens. But these postulates are regarded as modified by people, acting independently or within the context of the informal organization.

One of the main contributions of the neoclassical school is the introduction of behavioral sciences in an integrated fashion into the theory of organization. Through the use of these sciences, the human relationists demonstrate how the pillars of the classical doctrine are affected by the impact of human actions. Further, the neoclassical approach includes a systematic treatment of the informal organization, showing its influence on the formal structure.

Thus, the neoclassical approach to organization theory gives evidence of accepting classical doctrine, but superimposing on it modifications resulting from individual behavior, and the influence of the informal group. The inspiration of the neoclassical school was the Hawthorne studies.[13] Current examples of the neoclassical approach are found in human relations books like Gardner and Moore, *Human Relations in Industry*,[14] and Davis, *Human Relations in Business*.[15] To a more limited extent, work in industrial sociology also reflects a neoclassical point of view.[16]

It would be useful to look briefly at some of the contributions made to organization theory by the neoclassicists. First to be considered are modifications of the pillars of classical doctrine; second is the informal organization.

### Examples of the Neoclassical Approach to the Pillars of Formal Organization Theory

1. The *division of labor* has been a long-standing subject of comment in the field of human relations. Very early in the history of industrial psychology, a study was made of industrial fatigue and monotony caused by the specialization of the work.[17] Later, attention shifted to the isolation of the worker, and his feeling of anonymity resulting from insignificant jobs which contributed negligibly to the final product.[18]

Also, specialization influences the work of management. As an organization expands, the need concomitantly arises for managerial motivation and coordination of the activities of others. Both motivation and coordination in turn relate to executive leadership. Thus, in part, stemming from the growth of industrial specialization, the neoclassical school has developed a large body of theory relating to motivation, coordination, and leadership. Much of this theory is derived from the social sciences.

2. Two aspects of the *scalar and functional* processes which have been treated with some degree of intensity by the neoclassical school are the delegation of authority and responsibility, and gaps in or overlapping of functional jurisdictions. The classical theory assumes something of perfection in the delegation and functionalization processes. The neoclassical school points out that human problems are caused by imperfections in the way these processes are handled.

For example, too much or insufficient delegation may render an executive incapable of action. The failure to delegate authority and responsibility equally may result in frustration for the delegatee. Overlapping of authorities often causes clashes in personality. Gaps in authority cause failures in getting jobs done, with one party blaming the other for shortcomings in performance.[19]

The neoclassical school says that the scalar and functional processes are theoretically valid, but tend to deteriorate in practice. The ways in which they break down are described, and some of the human causes are pointed out. In addition the neoclassicists make recommendations, suggesting various "human tools" which will facilitate the operation of these processes.

3. *Structure* provides endless avenues of analysis for the neoclassical theory of organization. The theme is that human behavior disrupts the best laid organizational plans and thwarts the cleanness of the logical relationships founded in the structure. The neoclassical critique of structure centers on frictions which appear internally among people performing different functions.

Line and staff relations is a problem area, much discussed, in this respect. Many companies seem to have difficulty keeping the line and staff working together harmoniously. Both Dalton[20] and Juran[21] have engaged in research to discover the causes of friction, and to suggest remedies.

Of course, line-staff relations represent only one of the many problems of structural frictions described by the neoclassicists. As often as not, the neoclassicists will offer prescriptions for the elimination of conflict in structure. Among the more important harmony-rendering formulae are participation, junior boards, bottom-up management, joint committees, recognition of human dignity, and "better" communication.

4. An executive's *span of control* is a function of human determinants, and the reduction of span to a precise, universally applicable ratio is silly, according to the neoclassicists. Some of the determinants of span are individual differences in managerial abilities, the type of people and functions supervised, and the extent of communication effectiveness.

Coupled with the span of control question are the human implications of the type of structure which emerges. That is, is a tall structure with a short span or a flat structure with a wide span more conducive to good human relations and high morale? The answer is situational. Short span results in tight supervision; wide span requires a good deal of delegation with looser controls. Because of individual and organizational differences, sometimes one is better than the other. There is a tendency to favor the looser form of organization, however, for the reason that tall structures breed autocratic leadership, which is often pointed out as a cause of low morale.[22]

## The Neoclassical View of the Informal Organization

Nothing more than the barest mention of the informal organization is given even in the most recent classical treatises on organization theory.[23] Systematic discussion of this form of organization has been left to the neoclassicists. The informal organization refers to people in group associations at work, but these associations are not specified in the "blueprint" of the formal organization. The informal organization means natural groupings of people in the work situation.

In a general way, the informal organization appears in response to the social need—the need of people to associate with others. However, for analytical purposes, this explanation is not particularly satisfying. Research has produced the following, more specific determinants underlying the appearance of informal organizations.

1. The *location* determinant simply states that in order to form into groups of any lasting nature, people have to have frequent face-to-face contact. Thus, the geography of physical location in a plant or office is an important factor in predicting who will be in what group.[24]

2. *Occupation* is a key factor determining the rise and composition of informal groups. There is a tendency for people performing similar jobs to group together.[25]

3. *Interests* are another determinant for informal group formation. Even though people might be in the same location,

performing similar jobs, differences of interest among them explain why several small, instead of one large, informal organizations emerge.

4. *Special issues* often result in the formation of informal groups, but this determinant is set apart from the three previously mentioned. In this case, people who do not necessarily have similar interests, occupations, or locations may join together for a common cause. Once the issue is resolved, then the tendency is to revert to the more "natural" group forms.[26] Thus, special issues give rise to a rather impermanent informal association; groups based on the other three determinants tend to be more lasting.

When informal organizations come into being they assume certain characteristics. Since understanding these characteristics is important for management practice, they are noted below:

1. Informal organizations act as agencies of *social control*. They generate a culture based on certain norms of conduct which, in turn, demands conformity from group members. These standards may be at odds with the values set by the formal organization. So an individual may very well find himself in a situation of conflicting demands.

2. The form of human interrelationships in the informal organization requires *techniques of analysis* different from those used to plot the relationships of people in a formal organization. The method used for determining the structure of the informal group is called sociometric analysis. Sociometry reveals the complex structure of interpersonal relations which is based on premises fundamentally unlike the logic of the formal organization.

3. Informal organizations have *status and communication* systems peculiar to themselves, not necessarily derived from the formal systems. For example, the grapevine is the subject of much neoclassical study.

4. Survival of the informal organization requires stable continuing relationships among the people in them. Thus, it has been observed that the informal organization *resists change.*[27] Considerable attention is given by the neoclassicists to overcoming informal resistance to change.

5. The last aspect of analysis which appears to be central to the neoclassical view of the informal organization is the study of the *informal leader*. Discussion revolves around who the informal leader is, how he assumes this role, what characteristics are peculiar to him, and how he can help the manager accomplish his objectives in the formal organization.[28]

This brief sketch of some of the major facets of informal organization theory has neglected, so far, one important topic treated by the neoclassical school. It is the way in which the formal and informal organizations interact.

A conventional way of looking at the interaction of the two is the "live and let live" point of view. Management should recognize that the informal organization exists, nothing can destroy it, and so the executive might just as well work with it. Working with the informal organization involves not threatening its existence unnecessarily, listening to opinions expressed for the group by the leader, allowing group participation in decision-making situations, and controlling the grapevine by prompt release of accurate information.[29]

While this approach is management centered, it is not unreasonable to expect that informal group standards and norms could make themselves felt on formal organizational policy. An honestly conceived effort by managers to establish a working relationship with the informal organization could result in an association where both formal and informal views would be reciprocally modified. The danger which at all costs should be avoided is that "working with the informal organization" does not degenerate into a shallow disguise for human manipulation.

Some neoclassical writing in organization theory, especially that coming from the management-oriented segment of this school, gives the impression that the formal and informal organizations are distinct, and, at times, quite irreconcilable factors in a company. The interaction which takes place between the two is something akin to the interaction between the company and a labor union, or a government agency, or another company.

The concept of the social system is another approach to the interactional climate. While this concept can be properly classified as neoclassical, it borders on the modern theories of organization. The phrase "social system" means that an organization is a complex of mutually interdependent, but variable, factors.

These factors include individuals and their attitudes and motives, jobs, the physical work setting, the formal organization, and the informal organizations. These factors, and many others, are woven into an overall pattern of interdependency. From this point of view, the formal and informal organizations lose their distinctiveness, but find real meaning, in terms of human behavior, in the operation of the system as a whole. Thus, the study of organization turns away from descriptions of its component parts, and is refocused on the system of interrelationships among the parts.

One of the major contributions of the Hawthorne studies was the integration of Pareto's idea of the social system into a meaningful method of analysis for the study of behavior in human organizations.[30]

This concept is still vitally important. But unfortunately some work in the field of human relations undertaken by the neoclassicists has over-looked, or perhaps discounted, the significance of this consideration.[31]

The fundamental insight regarding the social system, developed and applied to the industrial scene by the Hawthorne researchers, did not find much extension in subsequent work in the neoclassical vein. Indeed, the neoclassical school after the Hawthorne studies generally seemed content to engage in descriptive generalizations, or particu-larized empirical research studies which did not have much meaning outside their own context.

The neoclassical school of organization theory has been called bankrupt. Criticisms range from, "human relations is a tool for cynical puppeteering of people," to "human relations is nothing more than a trifling body of empirical and descriptive information." There is a good deal of truth in both criticisms, but another appraisal of the neoclassical school of organization theory is offered here. The neoclassical approach has provided valuable contributions to lore of organization. But, like the classical theory, the neoclassical doctrine suffers from incomplete-ness, a shortsighted perspective, and lack of integration among the many facets of human behavior studied by it. Modern organization theory has made a move to cover the shortcomings of the current body of theoretical knowledge.

## MODERN ORGANIZATION THEORY

The distinctive qualities of modern organization theory are its conceptual-analytical base, its reliance on empirical research data, and, above all, its integrating nature. These qualities are framed in a philosophy which accepts the premise that the only meaningful way to study organization is to study it as a system. As Henderson put it, the study of a system must rely on a method of analysis, ". . . involving the simultaneous variations of mutually dependent variables."[32] Hu-man systems, of course, contain a huge number of dependent variables which defy the most complex simultaneous equations to solve.

Nevertheless, system analysis has its own peculiar point of view which aims to study organization in the way Henderson suggests. It treats organization as a system of mutually dependent variables. As a result, modern organization theory, which accepts system analysis, shifts the conceptual level of organization study above the classical and neoclassical theories. Modern organization theory asks a range of interrelated questions which are not seriously considered by the two other theories.

Key among these questions are: (1) What are the strategic parts of the system? (2) What is the nature of their mutual dependency? (3) What are the main processes in the system which link the parts together, and facilitate their adjustment to each other? (4) What are the goals sought by systems?[33]

Modern organization theory is in no way a unified body of thought. Each writer and researcher has his special emphasis when he considers the system. Perhaps the most evident unifying thread in the study of systems is the effort to look at the organization in its totality. Representative books in this field are March and Simon, *Organizations,*[34] and Haire's anthology, *Modern Organization Theory.*[35]

Instead of attempting a review of different writers' contributions to modern organization theory, it will be more useful to discuss the various ingredients involved in system analysis. They are the parts, the interactions, the processes, and the goals of systems.

## The Parts of the System and Their Interdependency

The first basic part of the system is the *individual,* and the personality structure he brings to the organization. Elementary to an individual's personality are motives and attitudes which condition the range of expectancies he hopes to satisfy by participating in the system.

The second part of the system is the formal arrangement of functions, usually called the *formal organization.* The formal organization is the interrelated pattern of jobs which make up the structure of a system. Certain writers, like Argyris, see a fundamental conflict resulting from the demands made by the system, and the structure of the mature, normal personality. In any event, the individual has expectancies regarding the job he is to perform; and, conversely, the job makes demands on, or has expectancies relating to, the performance of the individual. Considerable attention has been given by writers in modern organization theory to incongruencies resulting from the interaction of organizational and individual demands.[36]

The third part in the organization system is the *informal organization.* Enough has been said already about the nature of this organization. But it must be noted that an interactional pattern exists between the individual and the informal group. This interactional arrangement can be conveniently discussed as the mutual modification of expectancies. The informal organization has demands which it makes on members in terms of anticipated forms of behavior, and the individual has expectancies of satisfaction he hopes to derive from association with people on the job. Both these sets of expectancies interact, resulting in the individual modifying his behavior to accord with the demands of the group, and the group, perhaps, modifying what it expects from an individual because of the impact of his personality on group norms.[37]

Much of what has been said about the various expectancy systems in an organization can also be treated using status and role concepts. Part of modern organization theory rests on research findings in social psychology relative to reciprocal patterns of behavior stemming from role demands generated by both the formal and informal organizations, and role perceptions peculiar to the individual. Bakke's *fusion process* is largely concerned with the modification of role expectancies. The fusion process is a force, according to Bakke, which acts to weld divergent elements together for the preservation of organizational integrity.[38]

The fifth part of system analysis is the *physical setting* in which the job is performed. Although this element of the system may be implicit in what has been said already about the formal organization and its functions, it is well to separate it. In the physical surroundings of work, interactions are present in complex man-machine systems. The human "engineer" cannot approach the problems posed by such interrelationships in a purely technical, engineering fashion. As Haire says, these problems lie in the domain of the social theorist.[39] Attention must be centered on responses demanded from a logically ordered production function, often with the view of minimizing the error in the system. From this standpoint, work cannot be effectively organized unless the psychological, social, and physiological characteristics of people participating in the work environment are considered. Machines and processes should be designed to fit certain generally observed psychological and physiological properties of men, rather than hiring men to fit machines.

In summary, the parts of the system which appear to be of strategic importance are the individual, the formal structure, the informal organization, status and role patterns, and the physical environment of work. Again, these parts are woven into a configuration called the organizational system. The processes which link the parts are taken up next.

### The Linking Processes

One can say, with a good deal of glibness, that all the parts mentioned above are interrelated. Although this observation is quite correct, it does not mean too much in terms of system theory unless some attempt is made to analyze the processes by which the interaction is achieved. Role theory is devoted to certain types of interactional processes. In addition, modern organization theorists point to three other linking activities which appear to be universal to human systems of organized behavior. These processes are communication, balance, and decision making.

1. Communication is mentioned often in neoclassical theory, but the emphasis is on description of forms of communication activity, i.e., formal-informal, vertical-horizontal, line-staff. Communication, as a mechanism which links the segments of the system together, is overlooked by way of much considered analysis.

One aspect of modern organization theory is study of the communication network in the system. Communication is viewed as the method by which action is evoked from the parts of the system. Communication acts not only as stimuli resulting in action but also as a control and coordination mechanism linking the decision centers in the system into a synchronized pattern. Deutsch points out that organizations are composed of parts which communicate with each other, receive messages from the outside world, and store information. Taken together, these communication functions of the parts comprise a configuration representing the total system.[40] More is to be said about communication later in the discussion of the cybernetic model.

2. The concept of *balance* as a linking process involves a series of some rather complex ideas. Balance refers to an equilibrating mechanism whereby the various parts of the system are maintained in a harmoniously structured relationship to each other.

The necessity for the balance concept logically flows from the nature of systems themselves. It is impossible to conceive of an ordered relationship among the parts of a system without also introducing the idea of a stabilizing or an adapting mechanism.

Balance appears in two varieties—quasi-automatic and innovative. Both forms of balance act to insure system integrity in the face of changing conditions, either internal or external to the system. The first form of balance, quasi-automatic, refers to what some think are "homeostatic" properties of systems. That is, systems seem to exhibit built-in propensities to maintain steady states.

If human organizations are open, self-maintaining systems, then control and regulatory processes are necessary. The issue hinges on the degree to which stabilizing processes in systems, when adapting to change, are automatic. March and Simon have an interesting answer to this problem, which in part is based on the type of change and the adjustment necessary to adapt to the change. Systems have programs of action which are put into effect when a change is perceived. If the change is relatively minor, and if the change comes within the purview of established programs of action, then it might be fairly confidently predicted that the adaptation made by the system will be quasi-automatic.[41]

The role of innovative, creative balancing efforts now needs to be examined. The need for innovation arises when adaptation to a change is outside the scope of existing programs designed for the purpose of keeping the system in balance. New programs have to be evolved in order for the system to maintain internal harmony.

New programs are created by trial and error search for feasible action alternatives to cope with a given change. But innovation is subject to the limitations and possibilities inherent in the quantity and variety of information present in a system at a particular time. New combinations of alternatives for innovative purposes depend on:

(a) The possible range of output of the system, or the capacity of the system to supply information.

(b) The range of available information in the memory of the system.

(c) The operating rules (program) governing the analysis and flow of information within the system.

(d) The ability of the system to "forget" previously learned solutions to change problems.[42] A system with too good a memory might narrow its behavioral choices to such an extent as to stifle innovation. In simpler language, old learned programs might be used to adapt to change, when newly innovated programs are necessary.[43]

Much of what has been said about communication and balance brings to mind a cybernetic model in which both these processes have vital roles. Cybernetics has to do with feedback and control in all kinds of systems. Its purpose is to maintain system stability in the face of change. Cybernetics cannot be studied without considering communication networks, information flow, and some kind of balancing process aimed at preserving the integrity of the system.

Cybernetics directs attention to key questions regarding the system. These questions are: How are communication centers connected, and how are they maintained? Corollary to this question: What is the structure of the feedback system? Next, what information is stored in the organization, and at what points? And as a corollary: How accessible is this information to decision-making centers? Third, How conscious is the organization of the operation of its own parts? That is, To what extent do the policy centers receive control information with sufficient frequency and relevancy to create a real awareness of the operation of the segments of the system? Finally, What are the learning (innovating) capabilities of the system?[44]

Answers to the questions posed by cybernetics are crucial to understanding both the balancing and communication processes in systems.[45] Although cybernetics has been applied largely to technical-engineering problems of automation, the model of feedback, control, and regulation in all systems has a good deal of generality. Cybernetics is a fruitful area which can be used to synthesize the processes of communication and balance.

3. A wide spectrum of topics dealing with types of decisions in human systems makes up the core of analysis of another important process in organizations. Decision analysis is one of the major contributions of March and Simon in their book *Organizations*. The two major classes of decisions they discuss are decisions to produce and decisions to participate in the system.[46]

Decisions to produce are largely a result of an interaction between individual attitudes and the demands of organization. Motivation analysis becomes central to studying the nature and results of the interaction. Individual decisions to participate in the organization reflect on such issues as the relationship between organizational rewards versus the demands made by the organization. Participation decisions also focus attention on the reasons why individuals remain in or leave organizations.

March and Simon treat decisions as internal variables in an organization which depend on jobs, individual expectations and motivations, and organizational structure. Marschak[47] looks on the decision process as an independent variable upon which the survival of the organization is based. In this case, the organization is viewed as having, inherent to its structure, the ability to maximize survival requisites through its established decision processes.

## The Goals of Organization

Organization has three goals which may be either intermeshed or independent ends in themselves. They are growth, stability, and interaction. The last goal refers to organizations which exist primarily to provide a medium for association of its members with others. Interestingly enough, these goals seem to apply to different forms of organization at varying levels of complexity, ranging from simple clockwork mechanisms to social systems.

These similarities in organizational purposes have been observed by a number of people, and a field of thought and research called general system theory has developed, dedicated to the task of discovering organizational universals. The dream of general system theory is to create a science of organizational universals, or, if you will, a universal science using common organizational elements found in all systems as a starting point.

Modern organization theory is on the periphery of general system theory. Both general system theory and modern organization theory study:

(1) The parts (individuals) in aggregates, and the movement of individuals into and out of the system.

(2) The interaction of individuals with the environment found in the system.

(3) The interactions among individuals in the system.

(4) General growth and stability problems of systems.[48]

Modern organization theory and general system theory are similar in that they look at organization as an integrated whole. They differ, however, in terms of their generality. General system theory is concerned with every level of system, whereas modern organizational theory focuses primarily on human organization.

The question might be asked, What can the science of administration gain by the study of system levels other than human? Before attempting an answer, note should be made of what these other levels are. Boulding presents a convenient method of classification:

(1) The static structure—a level of framework, the anatomy of a system; for example, the structure of the universe.

(2) The simple dynamic system—the level of clockworks, predetermined necessary motions.

(3) The cybernetic system—the level of the thermostat, the system moves to maintain a given equilibrium through a process of self-regulation.

(4) The open system—level of self-maintaining systems, moves toward and includes living organisms.

(5) The genetic-societal system—level of cell society, characterized by a division of labor among cells.

(6) Animal systems—level of mobility, evidence of goal-directed behavior.

(7) Human systems—level of symbol interpretation and idea communication.

(8) Social system—level of human organization.

(9) Transcendental systems—level of ultimates and absolutes which exhibit systematic structure but are unknowable in essence.[49]

This approach to the study of systems by finding universals common at all levels of organization offers intriguing possibilities for administrative organization theory. A good deal of light could be thrown on social systems if structurally analogous elements could be found in the simpler types of systems. For example, cybernetic systems have characteristics which seem to be similar to feedback, regulation, and control phenomena in human organizations. Thus, certain facets of cybernetic models could be generalized to human organization. Considerable danger, however, lies in poorly founded analogies. Superficial similarities between simpler system forms and social systems are apparent everywhere. Instinctually based ant societies, for example, do not yield particularly instructive lessons for understanding rationally conceived human organizations. Thus, care should be taken that analogies used to bridge system levels are not mere devices for literary enrichment. For analogies to have usefulness and validity, they must exhibit inherent structural similarities or implicitly identical operational principles.[50]

Modern organization theory leads, as it has been shown, almost inevitably into a discussion of general system theory. A science of organizational universals has some strong advocates, particularly among biologists.[51] Organization theorists in administrative science cannot afford to overlook the contributions of general system theory. Indeed, modern organization concepts could offer a great deal to those working with general system theory. But the ideas dealt with in the general theory are exceedingly elusive.

Speaking of the concept of equilibrium as a unifying element in all systems, Easton says, "It (equilibrium) leaves the impression that we have a useful general theory when in fact, lacking measurability, it is a mere pretense for knowledge."[52] The inability to quantify and measure universal organization elements undermines the success of pragmatic tests to which general system theory might be put.

## Organization Theory: Quo Vadis?

Most sciences have a vision of the universe to which they are applied, and administrative science is not an exception. This universe is composed of parts. One purpose of science is to synthesize the parts into an organized conception of its field of study. As a science matures, its theorems about the configuration of its universe change. The direction of change in three sciences, physics, economics, and sociology, are noted briefly for comparison with the development of an administrative view of human organization.

The first comprehensive and empirically verifiable outlook of the physical universe was presented by Newton in his *Principia*. Classical physics, founded on Newton's work, constitutes a grand scheme in which a wide range of physical phenomena could be organized and predicted. Newtonian physics may rightfully be regarded as "macro" in nature, because its system of organization was concerned largely with gross events of which the movement of celestial bodies, waves, energy forms, and strain are examples. For years classical physics was supreme, being applied continuously to smaller and smaller classes of phenomena in the physical universe. Physicists at one time adopted the view that everything in their realm could be discovered by simply subdividing problems. Physics thus moved into the "micro" order.

But in the nineteenth century a revolution took place motivated largely because events were being noted which could not be explained adequately by the conceptual framework supplied by the classical school. The consequences of this revolution are brilliantly described by Eddington:

> From the point of view of philosophy of science the conception associated with entropy must I think be ranked as the great contribution of the nineteenth century to scientific thought. It marked a reaction from the view that everything to which science need pay attention is discovered by microscopic dissection of objects. It provided an alternative standpoint in which the centre of interest is shifted from the entities reached by the customary analysis (atoms, electric potentials, etc.) to qualities possessed by the system as a whole, which cannot be split up and located—a little bit here, and a little bit there. . . .
>
> We often think that when we have completed our study of *one* we know all about *two,* because "two" is "one and one." We forget that we have still to make a study of "and." Secondary physics is the study of "and"—that is to say, of organization.[53]

Although modern physics often deals in minute quantities and oscillations, the conception of the physicist is on the "macro" scale. He is concerned with the "and," or the organization of the world in which the events occur. These developments did not invalidate classical physics as to its usefulness for explaining a certain range of phenomena. But classical physics is no longer the undisputed law of the universe. It is a special case.

Early economic theory, and Adam Smith's *Wealth of Nations* comes to mind, examined economic problems in the macro order. The *Wealth of Nations* is mainly concerned with matters of national income and welfare. Later, the economics of the firm, micro-economics, dominated the theoretical scene in this science. And, finally, with Keynes's *The General Theory of Employment, Interest and Money,* a systematic approach to the economic universe was re-introduced on the macro level.

The first era of the developing science of sociology was occupied by the great social "system builders." Comte, the so-called father of sociology, had a macro view of society in that his chief works are devoted to social reorganization. Comte was concerned with the interrelationships among social, political, religious, and educational institutions.

As sociology progressed, the science of society compressed. Emphasis shifted from the macro approach of the pioneers to detailed, empirical study of small social units. The compression of sociological analysis was accompanied by study of social pathology or disorganization.

In general, physics, economics, and sociology appear to have two things in common. First, they offered a macro point of view as their initial systematic comprehension of their area of study. Second, as the science developed, attention fragmented into analysis of the parts of the organization, rather than attending to the system as a whole. This is the micro phase.

In physics and economics, discontent was evidenced by some scientists at the continual atomization of the universe. The reaction to the micro approach was a new theory or theories dealing with the total system, on the macro level again. This third phase of scientific development seems to be more evident in physics and economics than in sociology.

The reason for the "macro-micro-macro" order of scientific progress lies, perhaps, in the hypothesis that usually the things which strike man first are of great magnitude. The scientist attempts to discover order in the vastness. But after macro laws or models of systems are postulated, variations appear which demand analysis, not so much in terms of the entire system, but more in terms of the specific parts which make it up. Then, intense study of microcosm may result in new general laws, replacing the old models of organization. Or, the old and the new models may stand together, each explaining a different class of phenomenon. Or, the old and the new concepts of organization may be welded to produce a single creative synthesis.

Now, what does all this have to do with the problem of organization in administrative science? Organization concepts seem to have gone through the same order of development in this field as in the three just mentioned. It is evident that the classical theory of organization, particularly as in the work of Mooney and Reiley, is concerned with principles common to all organizations. It is a macro-organizational view. The classical approach to organization, however, dealt with the gross anatomical parts and processes of the formal organization. Like classical physics, the classical theory of organization is a special case. Neither is especially well equipped to account for variation from its established framework.

Many variations in the classical administrative model result from human behavior. The only way these variations could be understood was by a microscopic examination of particularized, situational aspects of human behavior. The mission of the neoclassical school thus is "microanalysis."

It was observed earlier, that somewhere along the line the concept of the social system, which is the key to understanding the Hawthorne studies, faded into the background. Maybe the idea is so obvious that it was lost to the view of researchers and writers in human relations. In any event, the press of research in the microcosmic universes of the informal organization, morale and productivity, leadership, participation, and the like forced the notion of the social system into limbo. Now, with the advent of modern organization theory, the social system has been resurrected.

Modern organization theory appears to be concerned with Eddington's "and." This school claims that its operational hypothesis is based on a macro point of view; that is, the study of organization as a whole. This nobility of purpose should not obscure, however, certain difficulties faced by this field as it is presently constituted. Modern organization theory raises two questions which should be explored further. First, Would it not be more accurate to speak of modern organization theories? Second, Just how much of modern organization theory is modern?

The first question can be answered with a quick affirmative. Aside from the notion of the system, there are few, if any, other ideas of a unifying nature. Except for several important exceptions,[54] modern organization theorists tend to pursue their pet points of view,[55] suggesting they are part of system theory, but not troubling to show by what mystical means they arrive at this conclusion.

The irony of it all is that a field dealing with systems has, indeed, little system. Modern organization theory needs a framework, and it needs an integration of issues into a common conception of organization. Admittedly, this is a large order. But it is curious not to find serious analytical treatment of subjects like cybernetics or general system theory in Haire's *Modern Organization Theory,* which claims to be a representative example of work in this field. Beer has ample evidence in his book *Cybernetics and Management* that cybernetics, if imaginatively approached, provides a valuable conceptual base for the study of systems.

The second question suggests an ambiguous answer. Modern organization theory is in part a product of the past; system analysis is not a new idea. Further, modern organization theory relies for supporting data on microcosmic research studies, generally drawn from the journals of the last 10 years. The newness of modern organization theory, perhaps, is its effort to synthesize recent research contributions of many fields into a system theory characterized by a reoriented conception of organization.

One might ask, but what is the modern theorist reorienting? A clue is found in the almost snobbish disdain assumed by some authors of the neoclassical human relations school, and particularly, the classical school. Reevaluation of the classical school of organization is overdue. However, this does not mean that its contributions to organization theory are irrelevant and should be overlooked in the rush to get on the "behavioral science bandwagon."

Haire announces that the papers appearing in *Modern Organization Theory* constitute "the ragged leading edge of a wave of theoretical development."[56] Ragged, yes; but leading, no! The papers appearing in this book do not represent a theoretical breakthrough in the concept of organization. Haire's collection is an interesting potpourri with several contributions of considerable significance. But readers should beware that they will not find vastly new insights into organizational behavior in this book, if they have kept up with the literature of the social sciences, and have dabbled to some extent in the esoterica of biological theories of growth, information theory, and mathematical model building. For those who have not maintained the pace, *Modern Organization Theory* serves the admirable purpose of bringing them up to date on a rather diversified number of subjects.

Some work in modern organization theory is pioneering, making its appraisal difficult and future uncertain. While the direction of this endeavor is unclear, one thing is patently true. Human behavior in organizations, and indeed, organization itself, cannot be adequately understood within the ground rules of classical and neoclassical doctrines. Appreciation of human organization requires a *creative* synthesis of massive amounts of empirical data, a high order of deductive reasoning, imaginative research studies, and a taste for individual and social values. Accomplishment of all these objectives, and the inclusion of them into a framework of the concept of the system, appears to be the goal of modern organization theory. The vitality of administrative science rests on the advances modern theorists make along this line.

Modern organization theory, 1960 style, is an amorphous aggregation of synthesizers and restaters, with a few extending leadership on the frontier. For the sake of these few, it is well to admonish that pouring old wine into new bottles may make the spirits cloudy. Unfortunately, modern organization theory has almost succeeded in achieving the status of a fad. Popularization and exploitation contributed to the disrepute into which human relations has fallen. It would be a great waste if modern organization theory yields to the same fate, particularly since both modern organization theory and human relations draw from the same promising source of inspiration—system analysis.

Modern organization theory needs tools of analysis and a conceptual framework uniquely its own, but it must also allow for the incorporation of relevant contributions of many fields. It may be that the framework will come from general system theory. New areas of research such as decision theory, information theory, and cybernetics also offer reasonable expectations of analytical and conceptual tools. Modern organization theory represents a frontier of research which has great significance for management. The potential is great, because it offers the opportunity for uniting what is valuable in classical theory with the social and natural sciences into a systematic and integrated conception of human organization.

## NOTES AND REFERENCES

1. Roderick Seidenberg, *Post Historic Man* (Boston: Beacon Press, 1951), p. 1.
2. Robert V. Presthus, "Toward a Theory of Organizational Behavior," *Administrative Science Quarterly,* June 1958, p. 50.
3. Regulation and predictability of human behavior are matters of degree varying with different organizations on something of a continuum. At one extreme are bureaucratic type organizations with tight bonds of regulation. At the other extreme are voluntary associations, and informal organizations with relatively loose bonds of regulation.

   This point has an interesting sidelight. A bureaucracy with tight controls and a high degree of predictability of human action appears to be unable to distinguish between destructive and creative deviations from established values. Thus, the only thing which is safeguarded is the status quo.
4. The monolithic institutions of the military and government are other cases of organizational preoccupation.
5. James D. Mooney and Alan C. Reiley, *Onward Industry* (New York: Harper & Row, 1931). Later published by James D. Mooney under the title *Principles of Organization.*
6. E. F. L. Brech, *Organization* (London: Longmans, Green, 1957).
7. Louis A. Allen, *Management and Organization* (New York: McGraw-Hill, 1958).
8. Usually the division of labor is treated under a topical heading of departmentation; see, for example: Harold Koontz and Cyril O'Donnell, *Principles of Management.* (New York: McGraw-Hill, 1959), chap. 7.
9. These processes are discussed at length in Ralph Currier Davis, *The Fundamentals of Top Management* (New York: Harper & Row, 1951), chap. 7.
10. For a discussion of structure see William H. Newman, *Administrative Action* (Englewood Cliffs, N.J.: Prentice-Hall, 1951), chap. 16.
11. V. A. Graicunas, "Relationships in Organization," *Papers on the Science of Administration* (New York: Columbia University, 1937).
12. Brech, p. 78 (see note 6).
13. See: F. J. Roethlisberger and William J. Dickson, *Management and the Worker* (Cambridge, Mass.: Harvard University Press, 1939).
14. Burleigh B. Gardner and David G. Moore, *Human Relations in Industry* (Homewood, Ill.: Richard D. Irwin, 1955).
15. Keith Davis, *Human Relations in Business* (New York: McGraw-Hill, 1957).
16. For example, see Delbert C. Miller and William H. Form, *Industrial Sociology* (New York: Harper & Row, 1951).

17. See Hugo Munsterberg, *Psychology and Industrial Efficiency* (Boston: Houghton Mifflin, 1913).

18. Probably the classic work is Elton Mayo, *The Human Problems of an Industrial Civilization* (Cambridge, Mass.: Harvard University Press, 1946, first printed 1933).

19. For further discussion of the human relations implications of the scalar and functional processes see Keith Davis, pp. 60–66 (see note 15).

20. Melville Dalton, "Conflicts between Staff and Line Managerial Officers," *American Sociological Review,* June 1950, pp. 342–51.

21. J. M. Juran, "Improving the Relationship between Staff and Line," *Personnel,* May 1956, pp. 515–24.

22. Gardner and Moore, pp. 237–43 (see note 14).

23. For example: Brech, pp. 27–29 (see note 6); and Allen, pp. 61–62 (see note 7).

24. See Leon Festinger, Stanley Schachter, and Kurt Back, *Social Pressures in Informal Groups* (New York: Harper & Row, 1950), pp. 153–63.

25. For example see W. Fred Cottrell, *The Railroader* (Palo Alto, Calif.: Stanford University Press, 1940), chap. 3.

26. Except in cases where the existence of an organization is necessary for the continued maintenance of employee interest. Under these conditions the previously informal association may emerge as a formal group, such as a union.

27. Probably the classic study of resistance to change is Lester Coch and John R. P. French, Jr., "Overcoming Resistance to Change," in *Human Factors in Management,* ed. Schuyler Dean Hoslett (New York: Harper & Row, 1951), pp. 242–268.

28. For example see Robert Saltonstall, *Human Relations in Administration* (New York: McGraw-Hill, 1959), pp. 330–31; and Keith Davis, pp. 99–101 (see note 15).

29. For an example of this approach see John T. Doutt, "Management Must Manage the Informal Group, Too," *Advanced Management,* May 1959, pp. 26–28.

30. See Roethlisberger and Dickson, chap. 24 (see note 13).

31. A check of management human relations texts, the organization and human relations chapters of principles of management texts, and texts on conventional organization theory for management courses reveals little or no treatment of the concept of the social system.

32. Lawrence J. Henderson, *Pareto's General Sociology* (Cambridge, Mass.: Harvard University Press, 1935), p. 13.

33. There is another question which cannot be treated in the scope of this paper. It asks, What research tools should be used for the study of the system?

34. James G. March and Herbert A. Simon, *Organizations* (New York: John Wiley & Sons, 1958).

35. Mason Haire, ed., *Modern Organization Theory* (New York: John Wiley & Sons, 1959).

36. See Chris Argyris, *Personality and Organization* (New York: Harper & Row, 1957), especially chaps. 2, 3, 7.

37. For a larger treatment of this subject, see George C. Homans, *The Human Group* (New York: Harcourt Brace Jovanovich, 1950), chap. 5.
38. E. Wight Bakke, "Concept of the Social Organization," *Modern Organization Theory,* ed. Mason Haire (New York: John Wiley & Sons, 1959), pp. 60–61.
39. Mason Haire, "Psychology and the Study of Business: Joint Behavioral Sciences," *Social Science Research on Business: Product and Potential* (New York: Columbia University Press, 1959), pp. 53–59.
40. Karl W. Deutsch, "On Communication Models in the Social Sciences," *Public Opinion Quarterly,* 16 (1952), pp. 356–80.
41. March and Simon, pp. 139–40 (see note 34).
42. Mervyn L. Cadwallader, "The Cybernetic Analysis of Change in Complex Social Organization," *The American Journal of Sociology,* September 1959, p. 156.
43. It is conceivable for innovative behavior to be programmed into the system.
44. These are questions adapted from Deutsch, pp. 368–70 (see note 40).
45. Answers to these questions would require a comprehensive volume. One of the best approaches currently available is Stafford Beer, *Cybernetics and Management* (New York: John Wiley & Sons, 1959).
46. March and Simon, chaps. 3 and 4 (see note 34).
47. Jacob Marschak, "Efficient and Viable Organizational Forms," *Modern Organization Theory,* ed. Mason Haire (New York: John Wiley & Sons, 1959), pp. 307–20.
48. Kenneth E. Boulding, "General System Theory—The Skeleton of a Science," *Management Science,* April 1956, pp. 200–202.
49. Ibid., pp. 202–205.
50. Seidenberg, p. 136 (see note 1). The fruitful use of the type of analogies spoken of by Seidenberg is evident in the application of thermodynamic principles, particularly the entropy concept, to communication theory. See Claude E. Shannon and Warren Weaver, *The Mathematical Theory of Communication* (Urbana: University of Illinois Press, 1949). Further, the existence of a complete analogy between the operational behavior of thermodynamic systems, electrical communications systems, and biological systems has been noted by Y. S. Touloukian, *The Concept of Entropy in Communication, Living Organisms, and Thermodynamics,* Research Bulletin 130, Purdue Engineering Experiment Station.
51. For example, see Ludwig von Bertalanffy, *Problem of Life* (London: Watts, 1952).
52. David Easton, "Limits of the Equilibrium Model in Social Research," *Profits and Problems of Homeostatic Models in the Behavioral Sciences,* Publication 1, Chicago Behavioral Sciences, 1953, p. 39.
53. Sir Arthur Eddington, *The Nature of the Physical World* (Ann Arbor: University of Michigan Press, 1958), pp. 103–4.
54. For example, E. Wight Bakke, pp. 18–75 (see note 38).
55. There is a large selection including decision theory, individual-organization interaction, motivation, vitality, stability, growth, and graph theory, to mention a few.
56. Mason Haire, "General Issues," in *Modern Organization Theory,* ed. Mason Haire (New York: John Wiley & Sons, 1959), p. 2.

# 12
# Parkinson's Law

### C. Northcote Parkinson

*One of the most famous articles on management, "Parkinson's Law," focuses on a specific aspect of organizing, namely staff size, and demonstrates how work expands to fill the time available for its completion. Many would argue that the Law of Multiplication of Subordinates and the Law of Multiplication of Work are validated constantly in organizations throughout the world.—Eds.*

It is a commonplace observation that work expands so as to fill the time available for its completion. Thus, an elderly lady of leisure can spend an entire day in writing and despatching a postcard to her niece at Bognor Regis. An hour will be spent in finding the postcard, another in hunting for spectacles, half-an-hour in a search for the address, an hour and a quarter in composition, and twenty minutes in deciding whether or not to take an umbrella when going to the pillar-box in the next street. The total effort which would occupy a busy man for three minutes all told may in this fashion leave another person prostrate after a day of doubt, anxiety and toil.

Granted that work (and especially paper work) is thus elastic in its demands of time, it is manifest that there need be little or no relationship between the work to be done and the size of the staff to which it may be assigned. Before the discovery of a new scientific law— herewith presented to the public for the first time, and to be called Parkinson's Law—there has, however, been insufficient recognition of the implication of this fact in the field of public administration. Politicians and taxpayers have assumed (with occasional phases of doubt) that a rising total in the number of civil servants must reflect a growing volume of work to be done. Cynics, in questioning this belief, have

SOURCE: From *Parkinson's Law* by C. Northcote Parkinson, published by Houghton Mifflin Company. Copyright © 1957 by C. Northcote Parkinson. Reprinted by permission.

imagined that the multiplication of officials must have left some of them idle or all of them able to work for shorter hours. But this is a matter in which faith and doubt seem equally misplaced. The fact is that the number of the officials and the quantity of the work to be done are not related to each other at all. The rise in the total of those employed is governed by Parkinson's Law, and would be much the same whether the volume of the work were to increase, diminish or even disappear. The importance of Parkinson's Law lies in the fact that it is a law of growth based upon an analysis of the factors by which the growth is controlled.

The validity of this recently discovered law must rely mainly on statistical proofs, which will follow. Of more interest to the general reader is the explanation of the factors that underlie the general tendency to which this law gives definition. Omitting technicalities (which are numerous) we may distinguish, at the outset, two motive forces. They can be represented for the present purpose by two almost axiomatic statements, thus:

Factor I. An official wants to multiply subordinates, not rivals; and

Factor II. Officials make work for each other. We must now examine these motive forces in turn.

## THE LAW OF MULTIPLICATION OF SUBORDINATES

To comprehend Factor I, we must picture a civil servant called A who finds himself overworked. Whether this overwork is real or imaginary is immaterial; but we should observe, in passing, that A's sensation (or illusion) might easily result from his own decreasing energy—a normal symptom of middle-age. For this real or imagined overwork there are, broadly speaking, three possible remedies:

1. He may resign.
2. He may ask to halve the work with a colleague called B.
3. He may demand the assistance of two subordinates to be called C and D.

There is probably no instance in civil service history of A choosing any but the third alternative. By resignation he would lose his pension rights. By having B appointed, on his own level in the hierarchy, he would merely bring in a rival for promotion to W's vacancy when W (at long last) retires. So A would rather have C and D, junior men, below him. They will add to his consequence; and, by dividing the work into two categories, as between C and D, he will have the merit of being the only man who comprehends them both.

It is essential to realize, at this point, that C and D are, as it were, inseparable. To appoint C alone would have been impossible. Why? Because C, if by himself, would divide the work with A and so assume almost the equal status which has been refused in the first instance to B: a status the more emphasized if C is A's only possible successor. Subordinates must thus number two or more, each being kept in order by fear of the other's promotion. When C complains in turn of being overworked (as he certainly will), A will, with the concurrence of C, advise the appointment of two assistants to help C. But he can then avert internal friction only by advising the appointment of two more assistants to help D, whose position is much the same. With this recruitment of E, F, G and H, the promotion of A is now practically certain.

## THE LAW OF MULTIPLICATION OF WORK

Seven officials are now doing what one did before. This is where Factor II comes into operation. For these seven make so much work for each other that all are fully occupied and A is actually working harder than ever. An incoming document may well come before each of them in turn. Official E decides that it falls within the province of F, who places a draft reply before C, who amends it drastically before consulting D, who asks G to deal with it. But G goes on leave at this point, handing the file over to H, who drafts a minute, which is signed by D and returned to C, who revises his draft accordingly and lays the new version before A.

What does A do? He would have every excuse for signing the thing unread, for he has many other matters on his mind. Knowing now that he is to succeed W next year, he has to decide whether C or D should succeed to his own office. He had to agree to G going on leave, although not yet strictly entitled to it. He is worried whether H should not have gone instead, for reasons of health. He has looked pale recently—partly but not solely because of his domestic troubles. Then there is the business of F's special increment of salary for the period of the conference, and E's application for transfer to the Ministry of Pensions. A has heard that D is in love with a married typist and that G and F are no longer on speaking terms—no one seems to know why. So A might be tempted to sign C's draft and have done with it.

But A is a conscientious man. Beset as he is with problems created by his colleagues for themselves and for him—created by the mere fact of these officials' existence—he is not the man to shirk his duty. He reads through the draft with care, deletes the fussy paragraphs added by C and H and restores the thing back to the form preferred in the first instance by the able (if quarrelsome) F. He corrects the English—none of these young men can write grammatically—and finally produces the same reply he would have written if officials C to H have never been born. Far more people have taken far longer to produce the same result. No one has been idle. All have done their best. And it is late in the evening before A finally quits his office and begins the return journey to Ealing. The last of the office lights are being turned off in the gathering dusk which marks the end of another day's administrative toil. Among the last to leave, A reflects, with bowed shoulders and a wry smile, that late hours, like grey hairs, are among the penalties of success.

## THE SCIENTIFIC PROOFS

From this description of the factors at work the student of political science will recognize that administrators are more or less bound to multiply. Nothing has yet been said, however, about the period of time likely to elapse between the date of A's appointment and the date from which we can calculate the pensionable service of H. Vast masses of statistical evidence have been collected and it is from a study of this data that Parkinson's Law has been deduced. Space will not allow of detailed analysis, but research began in the British Navy Estimates. These were chosen because the Admiralty's responsibilities are more easily measurable than those of (say) the Board of Trade.

The accompanying table is derived from Admiralty statistics for 1914 and 1928. The criticism voiced at the time centered on the comparison between the sharp fall in numbers of those available for fighting and the sharp rise in those available only for administration, the creation, it was said, of "a magnificent Navy on land." But that comparison is not to the present purpose. What we have to note is that the 2,000 Admiralty officials of 1914 had become the 3,569 of 1928; and that this growth was unrelated to any possible increase in their work. The Navy during that period had diminished, in point of fact, by a third in men and two thirds in ships. Nor, from 1922 onwards, was its strength even expected to increase, for its total of ships (unlike its total of officials) was limited by the Washington Naval Agreement of that year. Yet in these circumstances we had a 78.45 percent increase in Admiralty officials over a period of 14 years, an average increase of 5.6 percent a year on the earlier total. In fact, as we shall see, the rate of increase was not as regular as that. All we have to consider, at this stage, is the percentage rise over a given period.

|  | 1914 | 1928 | Percentage Increase or Decrease |
|---|---|---|---|
| Capital ships in commission | 62 | 20 | − 67.74 |
| Officers and men in Royal Navy | 146,000 | 100,000 | − 31.50 |
| Dockyard workers | 57,000 | 62,439 | + 9.54 |
| Dockyard officials and clerks | 3,249 | 4,558 | + 40.28 |
| Admiralty officials | 2,000 | 3,569 | + 78.45 |

Can this rise in the total number of civil servants be accounted for except on the assumption that such a total must always rise by a law governing its growth? It might be urged, at this point, that the period under discussion was one of rapid development in naval technique. The use of the flying machine was no longer confined to the eccentric. Submarines were tolerated if not approved. Engineer officers were beginning to be regarded as almost human. In so revolutionary an age we might expect the storekeepers would have more elaborate inventories to compile. We might not wonder to see more draughtsmen on the payroll, more designers, more technicians and scientists. But these, the dockyard officials, increased only by 40 percent in number, while the men of Whitehall increased by nearly 80 percent. For every new foreman or electrical engineer at Portsmouth there had to be two or more clerks at Charing Cross. From this we might be tempted to conclude, provisionally, that the rate of increase in administrative staff is likely to be double that of the technical staff at a time when the actually useful strength (in this case, of seamen) is being reduced by 31.5 percent. It has been proved, however, statistically, that this last percentage is irrelevant. *The Officials would have multiplied at the same rate had there been no actual seamen at all.*

It would be interesting to follow the further progress by which the 8,118 Admiralty staff of 1935 came to number 33,788 by 1954. But the staff of the Colonial Office affords a better field of study during a period of Imperial decline. The relevant statistics are set down below. Before showing what the rate of increase is, we must observe that the extent of this department's responsibilities was far from constant during these 20 years. The colonial territories were not much altered in area or population between 1935 and 1939. They were considerably diminished by 1943, certain areas being in enemy hands. They were increased again in 1947, but have since then shrunk steadily from year to year as successive colonies achieve self-government.

Colonial Office Officials

| 1935 | 1939 | 1943 | 1947 | 1954 |
|------|------|------|------|------|
| 372 | 450 | 817 | 1,135 | 1,661 |

It would be rational, prior to the discovery of Parkinson's Law, to suppose that these changes in the scope of Empire would be reflected in the size of its central administration. But a glance at the figures shows that the staff totals represent automatic stages in an inevitable increase. And this increase, while related to that observed in other departments, has nothing to do with the size—or even the existence—of the Empire. What are the percentages of increase? We must ignore, for this purpose, the rapid increase in staff which accompanied the diminution of responsibility during World War II. We should note rather the peacetime rates of increase over 5.24 percent between 1935 and 1939, and 6.55 percent between 1947 and 1954. This gives an average increase of 5.89 percent each year, a percentage markedly similar to that already found in the Admiralty staff increase between 1914 and 1928.

Further and detailed statistical analysis of departmental staffs would be inappropriate in such an article as this. It is hoped, however, to reach a tentative conclusion regarding the time likely to elapse between a given official's first appointment and the later appointment of his two or more assistants. Dealing with the problem of pure staff accumulation, all the researches so far completed point to average increase of about 5.75 percent per year. This fact established, it now becomes possible to state Parkinson's Law in mathematical form, thus:

In any public administrative department not actually at war the staff increase may be expected to follow this formula:

$$x = \frac{2k^m + p}{n}$$

where $k$ is the number of staff seeking promotion through the appointment of subordinates; $p$ represents the difference between the ages of appointment and retirement; $m$ is the number of man-hours devoted to answering minutes within the department; and $n$ is the number of effective units being administered. Then $x$ will be the number of new staff required each year.

Mathematicians will, of course, realize that to find the percentage increase they must multiply $x$ by 100 and divide by the total of the previous year, thus:

$$\frac{100(2k^m + p)}{yn}\%$$

where $y$ represents the total original staff. And this figure will invariably prove to be between 5.17 percent and 6.56 percent, irrespective of any variation in the amount of work (if any) to be done.

The discovery of this formula and of the general principles upon which it is based has, of course, no emotive value. No attempt has been made to inquire whether departments ought to grow in size. Those who hold that this growth is essential to gain full employment are fully entitled to their opinion. Those who doubt the stability of an economy based upon reading each other's minutes are equally entitled to theirs. Parkinson's Law is a purely scientific discovery, inapplicable except in theory to the politics of the day. It is not the business of the botanist to eradicate the weeds. Enough for him if he can tell us just how fast they grow.

# 13

# The Ideal Bureaucracy

*Max Weber*

*To Max Weber control is an essential element in the efficient functioning of any enterprise and the best control is that which is attained in a bureaucratic form of organizational arrangement. If you are one of those people who associate bureaucracy with inefficiency and red tape this article should convince you that that is not Weber's definition of an ideal bureaucracy at all. Rather, he sees it as the best known means of carrying out imperative control of human beings.—Eds.*

The purest type of exercise of legal authority is that which employs a bureaucratic administrative staff. Only the supreme chief of the organization occupies his position of authority by virtue of appropriation, of election, or of having been designated for the succession. But even his authority consists in a sphere of legal "competence." The whole administrative staff under the supreme authority then consists, in the purest type, of individual officials who are appointed and function according to the following criteria:

1. They are personally free and subject to authority only with respect to their impersonal official obligations.

2. They are organized in a clearly defined hierarchy of offices.

3. Each office has a clearly defined sphere of competence in the legal sense.

---

SOURCE: Reprinted with permission of Macmillan Publishing Company, Inc., from *The Theory of Social and Economic Organizations* by Max Weber, translated by Talcott Parsons and A. M. Henderson. Copyright © 1947, 1975 by Talcott Parsons.

4. The office is filled by a free contractual relationship. Thus, in principle, there is free selection.

5. Candidates are selected on the basis of technical qualifications. In the most rational case, this is tested by examination or guaranteed by diplomas certifying technical training, or both. They are appointed, not elected.

6. They are remunerated by fixed salaries in money, for the most part with a right to pensions. Only under certain circumstances does the employing authority, especially in private organizations, have a right to terminate the appointment, but the official is always free to resign. The salary scale is primarily graded according to rank in the hierarchy; but in addition to this criterion, the responsibility of the position and the requirements of the incumbent's social status may be taken into account.

7. The office is treated as the sole, or at least the primary, occupation of the incumbent.

8. It constitutes a career. There is a system of "promotion" according to seniority or to achievement, or both. Promotion is dependent on the judgment of superiors.

9. The official works entirely separated from ownership of the means of administration and without appropriation of his position.

10. He is subject to strict and systematic discipline and control in the conduct of the office.

This type of organization is in principle applicable with equal facility to a wide variety of different fields. It may be applied in profit-making business or in charitable organizations, or in any number of other types of private enterprises serving ideal or material ends. It is equally applicable to political and to religious organizations. With varying degrees of approximation to a pure type, its historical existence can be demonstrated in all these fields.

1. For example, this type of bureaucracy is found in private clinics as well as in endowed hospitals or the hospitals maintained by religious orders. Bureaucratic organization has played a major role in the Catholic Church. It is well illustrated by the administrative role of the priesthood in the modern church, which has expropriated almost all the old church benefices which were in former days to a large extent subject to private appropriation. It is also illustrated by the conception of the universal Episcopate, which is thought of as formally constituting a universal legal competence in religious matters. Similarly, the doctrine of papal infallibility is thought of as in fact involving a universal competence,

but only one which functions ex cathedra in the sphere of the office, thus implying the typical distinction between the sphere of office and that of the private affairs of the incumbent. The same phenomena are found in the large-scale capitalistic enterprise; and the larger it is, the greater their role. And this is not less true of political parties, which will be discussed separately. Finally, the modern army is essentially a bureaucratic organization administered by that peculiar type of military functionary, the "officer."

2. Bureaucratic authority is carried out in its purest form where it is most clearly dominated by the principle of appointment. There is no such thing as a hierarchy of elected officials in the same sense as there is a hierarchical organization of appointed officials. In the first place, election makes it impossible to attain a stringency of discipline even approaching that in the appointed type; for it is open to a subordinate official to compete for elective honors on the same terms as his superiors, and his prospects are not dependent on the superior's judgment.

3. Appointment by free contract, which makes free selection possible, is essential to modern bureaucracy. Where there is a hierarchical organization with impersonal spheres of competence but occupied by unfree officials—like slaves or dependents, who, however, function in a formally bureaucratic manner—the term "patrimonial bureaucracy" will be used.

4. The role of technical qualifications in bureaucratic organizations is continually increasing. Even an official in a party or a trade union organization is in need of specialized knowledge, though it is usually of an empirical character, developed by experience rather than by formal training. In the modern state, the only "offices" for which no technical qualifications are required are those of ministers and presidents. This only goes to prove that they are "officials" only in a formal sense and not substantively, as is true of the managing director or president of a large business corporation. Thus at the top of a bureaucratic organization, there is necessarily an element which is at least not purely bureaucratic. The category of bureaucracy is one applying only to the exercise of control by means of a particular kind of administrative staff.

5. The bureaucratic official normally receives a fixed salary. By contrast, sources of income which are privately appropriated will be called "benefices." Bureaucratic salaries are also normally paid in money. Though this is not essential to the concept of bureaucracy, it is the arrangement which best fits the pure type. Payments in kind are apt to have the character of benefices, and the receipt of a benefice normally implies the appropriation of

opportunities for earnings and of positions. There are, however, gradual transitions in this field with many intermediate types. Appropriation by virtue of leasing or sale of offices or the pledge of income from office are phenomena foreign to the pure type of bureaucracy.

6. "Offices" which do not constitute the incumbent's principal occupation, in particular "honorary" offices, belong in other categories. The typical "bureaucratic" official occupies the office as his principal occupation.

7. With respect to the separation of the official from ownership of the means of administration, the situation is essentially the same in the field of public administration and in private bureaucratic organizations, such as the large-scale capitalistic enterprise.

8. Collegial bodies are rapidly decreasing in importance in favor of types of organization which are in fact, and for the most part formally as well, subject to the authority of a single head. For example, the collegial "governments" in Prussia have long since given way to the monocratic "district president." The decisive factor in this development has been the need for rapid, clear decisions, free of the necessity of compromise between different opinions and also free of shifting majorities.

9. The modern army officer is a type of appointed official who is clearly marked off by certain class distinctions. In this respect such officers differ radically from elected military leaders, from charismatic condottieri, from the type of officers who recruit and lead mercenary armies as a capitalistic enterprise, and, finally, from the incumbents of commissions which have been purchased. There may be gradual transitions between these types. The patrimonial "retainer," who is separated from the means of carrying out his function and the proprietor of a mercenary army for capitalistic purposes have, along with the private capitalistic entrepreneur, been pioneers in the organization of the modern type of bureaucracy.

## THE MONOCRATIC TYPE OF BUREAUCRATIC ADMINISTRATION

Experience tends universally to show that the purely bureaucratic type of administrative organization—that is, the monocratic variety of bureaucracy—is, from a purely technical point of view, capable of attaining the highest degree of efficiency and is in this sense formally the most rational known means of carrying out imperative control over human beings. It is superior to any other form in precision, in stability, in the stringency of its discipline, and in its reliability. It thus makes possible a particularly high degree of calculability of results for the heads of the organization and for those acting in relation to it. It is finally superior both in intensive efficiency and in the scope of its operations and is formally capable of application to all kinds of administrative tasks.

The development of the modern form of the organization of corporate groups in all fields is nothing less than identical with the development and continual spread of bureaucratic administration. This is true of church and state, of armies, political parties, economic enterprises, organizations to promote all kinds of causes, private associations, clubs, and many others. Its development is, to take the most striking case, the most crucial phenomenon of the modern Western state. However many forms there may be which do not appear to fit this pattern—such as collegial representative bodies, parliamentary committees, soviets, honorary officers, lay judges, and what not—and however much people may complain about the "evils of bureaucracy," it would be sheer illusion to think for a moment that continuous administrative work could be carried out in any field except by means of officials working in offices. The whole pattern of everyday life is cut to fit this framework. For bureaucratic administration is, other things being equal, always, from a formal, technical point of view, the most rational type. For the needs of mass administration today, it is completely indispensable. The choice is only that between bureaucracy and dilettantism in the field of administration.

The primary source of the superiority of bureaucratic administration lies in the role of technical knowledge which, through the development of modern technology and business methods in the production of goods, has become completely indispensable. In this respect, it makes no difference whether the economic system is organized on a capitalistic or a socialistic basis. Indeed, if in the latter case a comparable level of technical efficiency were to be achieved, it would mean a tremendous increase in the importance of specialized bureaucracy.

When those subject to bureaucratic control seek to escape the influence of the existing bureaucratic apparatus, this is normally possible only by creating an organization of their own which is equally subject to the process of bureaucratization. Similarly the existing bureaucratic apparatus is driven to continue functioning by the most powerful interests which are material and objective, but also ideal in character. Without it, a society like our own—with a separation of officials, employees, and workers from ownership of the means of administration, dependent on discipline and on technical training—could no longer function. The only exception would be those groups, such as the peasantry, who are still in possession of their own means of subsistence. Even in case of revolution by force or of occupation by an enemy, the bureaucratic machinery will normally continue to function just as it had for the previous legal government.

The question is always who controls the existing bureaucratic machinery. And such control is possible only to a very limited degree for persons who are not technical specialists. Generally speaking, in the long run the trained permanent official is more likely to get his way than his nominal superior, the Cabinet minister, who is not a specialist.

Though by no means alone, the capitalistic system has undeniably played a major role in the development of bureaucracy. Indeed, without it capitalistic production could not continue, and any rational type of socialism would have simply to take it over and increase its importance. Its development, largely under capitalistic auspices, has created an urgent need for stable, strict, intensive, and calculable administration. It is this need which gives bureaucracy a crucial role in our society as the central element in any kind of large-scale administration. Only by reversion in every field—political, religious, economic, and so forth— to small-scale organization would it be possible to any considerable extent to escape its influence. On the one hand, capitalism in its modern stages of development strongly tends to foster the development of bureaucracy, although both capitalism and bureaucracy have arisen from many different historical sources. Conversely, capitalism is the most rational economic basis for bureaucratic administration and enables it to develop in the most rational form, especially because, from a fiscal point of view, it supplies the necessary money resources.

Along with these fiscal conditions of efficient bureaucratic administration, there are certain extremely important conditions in the field of communication and transportation. The precision of its functioning requires the services of the railway, the telegraph, and the telephone and becomes increasingly dependent on them. A socialistic form of organization would not alter this fact. It would be a question whether in a socialistic system it would be possible to provide conditions for carrying out as stringent bureaucratic organization as has been possible in a capitalistic order. For socialism would, in fact, require a still higher degree of formal bureaucratization than capitalism. If this should prove not to be possible, it would demonstrate the existence of another of those fundamental elements of irrationality in social systems—a conflict between formal and substantive rationality of the sort which sociology so often encounters.

Bureaucratic administration means fundamentally the exercise of control on the basis of knowledge. This is the feature of it which makes it specifically rational. This consists on the one hand in technical knowledge which, by itself, is sufficient to ensure it a position of extraordinary power. But in addition to this, bureaucratic organizations, or the holders of power who make use of them, have the tendency to increase their power still further by the knowledge growing out of experience in the service; for they acquire through the conduct of office a special knowledge of facts and have available a store of documentary material peculiar to themselves. While not peculiar to bureaucratic organizations, the concept of "official secrets" is certainly typical of them. It stands in relation to technical knowledge in somewhat the same position as commercial secrets do to technological training. It is a product of the striving for power.

Bureaucracy is superior in knowledge, including both technical knowledge and knowledge of the concrete fact within its own sphere of interest, which is usually confined to the interests of a private business—a capitalistic enterprise. The capitalistic entrepreneur is, in our society, the only type who has been able to maintain at least relative immunity from subjection to the control of rational bureaucratic knowledge. All the rest of the population have tended to be organized in large-scale corporate groups which are inevitably subject to bureaucratic control. This is as inevitable as the dominance of precision machinery in the mass production of goods.

The following are the principal more general social consequences of bureaucratic control:

1. The tendency to "leveling" in the interest of the broadest possible basis of recruitment in terms of technical competence.
2. The tendency to plutocracy growing out of the interest in the greatest possible length of technical training. Today this often lasts up to the age of 30.
3. The dominance of a spirit of formalistic impersonality, without hatred or passion, and hence without affection or enthusiasm. The dominant norms are concepts of straightforward duty without regard for personal considerations. Everyone is subject to formal equality of treatment—that is, everyone in the same empirical situation. This is the spirit in which the ideal official conducts his office.

The development of bureaucracy greatly favors the leveling of social classes, and this can be shown historically to be the normal tendency. Conversely, every process of social leveling creates a favorable situation for the development of bureaucracy; for it tends to eliminate class privileges, which include the appropriation of means of administration and the appropriation of authority as well as the occupation of offices on an honorary basis or as an avocation by virtue of wealth. This combination everywhere inevitably foreshadows the development of mass democracy.

The "spirit" of rational bureaucracy normally has the following general characteristics:

1. Formalism, which is promoted by all the interests which are concerned with the security of their own personal situation, whatever this may consist in. Otherwise the door would be open to arbitrariness, and hence formalism in the line of least resistance.

2. There is another tendency, which is apparently in contradiction to the above—a contradiction which is in part genuine. It is the tendency of officials to treat their official function from what is substantively a utilitarian point of view in the interest of the welfare of those under their authority. But this utilitarian tendency is generally expressed in the enactment of corresponding regulatory measures which themselves have a formal character and tend to be treated in a formalistic spirit. This tendency to substantive rationality is supported by all those subject to authority who are not included in the class mentioned above as interested in the security of advantages already controlled. The problems which open up at this point belong in the theory of "democracy."

# 14

# Leaders' Control and
# Members' Compliance

*Amitai Etzioni*

*Etzioni suggests that organizations can be categorized in terms of how their leaders exercise control through the use of coercive, remunerative, or normative power. This classification may be developed further by examining how organizational members respond to these control attempts. He suggests three categories of response: involvement, commitment, and alienation. It is the discussion of the relationship between types of control and responses to them that makes this article such a significant one.—Eds.*

## A CLASSIFICATION OF POWER

*Power* is an actor's ability to induce or influence another actor to carry out his directives or any other norms he supports.[1] Goldhamer and Shils state that "a person may be said to have power to the extent that he influences the behavior of others in accordance with his own intentions."[2] Of course, "his own intentions" might be to influence a person to follow others' "intentions" or those of a collectivity. In organizations, enforcing the collectivity norms is likely to be a condition determining the powerholder's access to the means of power.

*Power positions* are positions whose incumbents regularly have access to means of power. Statements about power positions imply a particular group (or groups) who are subject to this power. For instance, to state that prison guards have a power position implies the subordination of inmates. In the following analysis we focus on power re-

SOURCE: Reprinted with permission of Macmillan Publishing Company, Inc., from *A Comparative Analysis of Complex Organizations* by Amitai Etzioni. Copyright © 1961 by Free Press of Glencoe, Inc.

lations in organizations between those higher and those lower in rank. We refer to those in power positions, who are higher in rank, as *elites* or as organizational *representatives*. We refer to those in subject positions, who are lower in rank, as *lower participants*.

Power differs according to the means employed to make the subjects comply. These means may be physical, material, or symbolic.[3]

*Coercive* power rests on the application, or the threat of application, of physical sanctions such as infliction of pain, deformity, or death; generation of frustration through restriction of movement; or controlling through force the satisfaction of needs such as those for food, sex, comfort, and the like.

*Remunerative* power is based on control over material resources and rewards through allocation of salaries and wages, commissions and contributions, "fringe benefits," services, and commodities.

*Normative* power rests on the allocation and manipulation of symbolic rewards and deprivations through employment of leaders, manipulation of mass media, allocation of esteem and prestige symbols, administration of ritual, and influence over the distribution of "acceptance" and "positive response." (A more eloquent name for this power would be persuasive, or manipulative, or suggestive power. But all these terms have negative value connotations which we wish to avoid.)

There are two kinds of normative power. One is based on the manipulation of esteem, prestige, and ritualistic symbols (such as a flag or a benediction); the other, on allocation and manipulation of acceptance and positive response.[4] Although both powers are found both in vertical and in horizontal relationships, the first is more frequent in vertical relations, between actors who have different ranks, whereas the second is more common in horizontal relations, among actors equal in rank—in particular, in the power of an "informal" or primary group over its members. Lacking better terms, we refer to the first kind as *pure normative power* and to the second as *social power.*[5] Social power could be treated as a distinct kind of power. But since powers are here classed according to the means of control employed, and since both social and pure normative power rest on the same set of means—manipulation of symbolic rewards—we treat these two powers as belonging to the same category.

From the viewpoint of the organization, pure normative power is more useful, since it can be exercised directly down the hierarchy. Social power becomes organizational power only when the organization can influence the group's powers, as when a teacher uses the class climate to control a deviant child or a union steward agitates the members to use their informal power to bring a deviant into line.

Organizations can be ordered according to their power structure, taking into account which power is predominant, how strongly it is stressed compared with other organizations in which the same power is predominant, and which power constitutes the secondary source of control. . . .

## NEUTRALIZATION OF POWER

Most organizations employ all three kinds of power, but the degree to which they rely on each differs from organization to organization. Most organizations tend to emphasize only one means of power, relying less on the other two.[6] Evidence to this effect is presented below in the analysis of the compliance structures of various organizations. The major reason for power specialization seems to be that when two kinds of power are emphasized at the same time, over the same subject group, they tend to neutralize each other.

Applying force, for instance, usually creates such a high degree of alienation that it becomes impossible to apply normative power successfully. This is one of the reasons that rehabilitation is rarely achieved in traditional prisons, that custodial measures are considered as blocking therapy in mental hospitals, and that teachers in progressive schools tend to oppose corporal punishment.

Similarly, the application of remunerative powers makes appeal to "idealistic" (pure normative) motives less fruitful. In a study of the motives which lead to purchase of war bonds, Merton pointed out that in one particularly effective drive (the campaign of Kate Smith), all "secular" topics were omitted and the appeal was centered on patriotic, "sacred" themes. Merton asked a sample of 978 people: "Do you think that it is a good idea to give things to people who buy bonds?"

> Fifty percent were definitely opposed in principle to premiums, bonuses, and other such inducements, and many of the remainder thought it a good idea only for "other people" who might not buy otherwise.[7]
>
> By omitting this [secular] argument, the authors of her scripts were able to avoid the strain and incompatibility between the two main lines of motivation: unselfish, sacrificing love of country and economic motives of sound investment.[8]

It is possible to make an argument for the opposite position. It might be claimed that the larger the number of personal needs whose satisfaction the organization controls, the more power it has over the participants. For example, labor unions that cater to and have control over the social as well as the economic needs of their members have more power over those members than do unions that focus only on economic needs. There may be some tension between the two modes of control, some ambivalence and uneasy feeling among members about the combinations, but undoubtedly the total control is larger. Similarly, it is obvious that the church has more power over the priest than over the average parishioner. The parishioner is exposed to normative power, whereas the priest is controlled by both normative and remunerative powers.

The issue is complicated by the fact that the *amount* of each kind of power applied must be taken into account. If a labor union with social powers has economic power which is much greater than that of another union, this fact may explain why the first union has greater power in sum, despite some "waste" due to neutralization. A further complication follows from the fact that neutralization may also occur through application of the "wrong" power in terms of the cultural definition of what is appropriate to the particular organization and activity. For example, application of economic power in religious organizations may be less effective than in industries, not because two kinds of power are mixed, but because it is considered illegitimate to use economic pressures to attain religious goals. Finally, some organizations manage to apply two kinds of power abundantly and without much waste through neutralization, because they segregate the application of one power from that of the other. The examination below of combat armies and labor unions supplies an illustration of this point.

We have discussed some of the factors related to the tendency of organizations to specialize their power application. In conclusion, it seems that although there can be little doubt that such a tendency exists, its scope and a satisfactory explanation for it have yet to be established.

## THREE KINDS OF INVOLVEMENT: A COMPARATIVE DIMENSION

### Involvement, Commitment, and Alienation

Organizations must continually recruit means if they are to realize their goals. One of the most important of these means is the positive orientation of the participants to the organizational power. *Involvement*[9] refers to the cathectic-evaluative orientation of an actor to an object, characterized in terms of intensity and direction.

The intensity of involvement ranges from high to low. The direction is either positive or negative. We refer to positive involvement as *commitment*[10] and to negative involvement as *alienation*.[11] (The advantage of having a third term, *involvement,* is that it enables us to refer to the continuum in a neutral way.[12]) Actors can accordingly be placed on an involvement continuum which ranges from a highly intense negative zone through mild negative and mild positive zones to a highly positive zone.[13]

## Three Kinds of Involvement

We have found it helpful to name three zones of the involvement continuum, as follows: *alienative,* for the high alienation zone; *moral,* for the high commitment zone; and *calculative,* for the two mild zones. This classification of involvement can be applied to the orientations of actors in all social units and to all kinds of objects. Hence the definitions and illustrations presented below are not limited to organizations but are applicable to orientations in general.

**Alienative Involvement.**   Alienative involvement designates an intense negative orientation; it is predominant in relations among hostile foreigners. Similar orientations exist among merchants in "adventure" capitalism, where trade is built on isolated acts of exchange, each side trying to maximize immediate profit.[14] Such an orientation seems to dominate the approach of prostitutes to transient clients.[15] Some slaves seem to have held similar attitudes to their masters and to their work. Inmates in prisons, prisoners of war, people in concentration camps, enlisted men in basic training, all tend to be alienated from their respective organizations.[16]

**Calculative Involvement.**   Calculative involvement designates either a negative or a positive orientation of low intensity. Calculative orientations are predominant in relationships of merchants who have continuous business contacts. Attitudes of (and toward) permanent customers are often predominantly calculative, as are relationships among entrepreneurs in modern (rational) capitalism. Inmates in prisons who have established contact with prison authorities, such as "rats" and "peddlers," often have predominantly calculative attitudes toward those in power.[17]

**Moral Involvement.**[18]   Moral involvement designates a positive orientation of high intensity. The involvement of the parishioner in his church, the devoted member in his party, and the loyal follower in his leader are all "moral."

There are two kinds of moral involvement, pure and social. They differ in the same way pure normative power differs from social power. Both are intensive modes of commitment, but they differ in their foci of orientation and in the structural conditions under which they develop. Pure moral commitments are based on internalization of norms and identification with authority (like Riesman's inner-directed "mode of conformity"); social commitment rests on sensitivity to pressures of primary groups and their members (Riesman's "other-directed"). Pure moral involvement tends to develop in vertical relationships, such as those between teachers and students, priests and parishioners, leaders and followers. Social involvement tends to develop in horizontal relationships like those in various types of primary groups. Both pure moral and social orientations might be found in the same relationships, but, as a rule, one orientation predominates.

Actors are means to each other in alienative and in calculative relations; but they are ends to each other in "social" relationships. In pure moral relationships the means-orientation tends to predominate; hence, for example, the willingness of devoted members of totalitarian parties or religious orders to use each other. But unlike the means-orientation of calculative relationships, the means-orientation here is expected to be geared to needs of the collectivity in serving its goals, and not to those of an individual.

## NOTES AND REFERENCES

1. T. Parsons, *The Social System* (New York: Free Press of Glencoe, 1951), p. 121.
2. H. Goldhamer and E. A. Shils, "Types of Power and Status," *American Journal of Sociology* 45 (1939), p. 171.
3. We suggest that this typology is exhaustive, although the only way we can demonstrate this is by pointing out that every type of power we have encountered so far can be classified as belonging to one of the categories or to a combination of them.
4. T. Parsons, *The Social System* (New York: Free Press of Glencoe, 1951), p. 108.
5. This distinction draws on the difference between social and normative integration, referred to by T. Parsons, R. F. Bales, and E. A. Shils, *Working Papers in the Theory of Action* (New York: Free Press of Glencoe, 1953), p. 182, as the distinction between the "integrative" and the "latent pattern maintenance" phases. . . . Shils distinguishes between social and ideological primary groups (private communication). J. S. Coleman, "Multidimensional Scale Analysis," *American Journal of Sociology* 63 (1957), p. 255, has pointed to the difference between group-oriented and idea-oriented attachments.
6. In more technical language, one can say that the three continua of power constitute a three-dimensional property space. If we collapse each dimension into high, medium, and low segments, there are 27 possible combinations or cells. Our hypothesis reads that most organizations fall into cells which are high on one dimension and low or medium on the others; this excludes 18 cells (not counting three types of dual structures discussed below).
7. R. K. Merton, *Mass Persuasion: The Social Psychology of a War Bond Drive* (New York: Harper & Row, 1946), p. 47.
8. Ibid., p. 45.
9. *Involvement* has been used in a similar manner by Nancy C. Morse, *Satisfactions in the White-Collar Job* (Survey Research Center, University

of Michigan, 1953), pp. 76–96. The term is used in a somewhat different way by students of voting, who refer by it to the psychological investment in the outcome of an election rather than in the party, which would be parallel to Morse's usage and ours. See, for example, A. Campbell, G. Gurin, and W. E. Miller, *The Voter Decides* (New York: Harper & Row, 1954), pp. 33–40.

10. Mishler defined *commitment* in a similar though more psychological way: "An individual is committed to an organization to the extent that central tensions are integrated through organizationally relevant instrumental acts." Cited by C. Argyris, *Personality and Organization* (New York: Harper & Row, 1957), p. 202.

11. We draw deliberately on the associations this term has acquired from its usage by Marx and others. For a good analysis of the idea of alienation in Marxism, and of its more recent development, see D. Bell, "The 'Rediscovery' of Alienation," *Journal of Philosophy* 56 (1959), pp. 933–952; and D. Bell, *The End of Ideology* (New York: Free Press of Glencoe, 1960), pp. 335–68. See also D. G. Dean, "Alienation and Political Apathy," *Social Forces* 38 (1960), pp. 185–89.

12. An example of empirical indicators which can be used to translate the involvement continuum into directly observable terms is offered by E. A. Shils and M. Janowits, "Cohesion and Disintegration in the Wehrmacht in World War II," *Public Opinion Quarterly* 12, no. 2 (1948), pp. 282–83. They classify "modes of social disintegration" in the armed forces as follows: desertion, active surrender, passive surrender, routine resistance, "last-ditch" resistance. In the terms used here, these measures indicate varying degrees of involvement, from highest alienation (desertion) to highest commitment (last-ditch resistance).

   Nettler (1958) has developed a 17-item unidimensional scale which measures alienation from society. It seems that a similar scale could be constructed for measuring alienation from or commitment to organizational power without undue difficulties. A. Kornhauser, H. L. Sheppard, and A. J. Mayer, *When Labor Votes* (New York: University Books, 1956), pp. 147–48, have developed a six-item scale, measuring the orientation of union members to their organization, which supplies another illustration of the wide use and measurability of these concepts, which are central to our analysis.

13. Several sociologists have pointed out that the relationship between intensity and direction of involvement is a curvilinear one: the more positive or negative the orientation, the more intensely it is held. L. Guttman, "The Cornell Technique for Scale and Intensity Analysis," *Education and Psychology Measurement* 7 (4197), pp. 247–79.

14. H. H. Gerth and C. W. Mills, *From Max Weber: Essays in Sociology* (New York: Oxford University Press, 1946), p. 67.

15. K. Davis, "The Sociology of Prostitution," *American Sociological Review* 2 (1937), pp. 748–49.

16. For a description of this orientation in prisons, see D. Clemmer, *The Prison Community* (New York: Holt, Rinehart & Winston, 1958), p. 152ff. Attitudes

toward the police, particularly on the part of members of the lower class, are often strictly alienative. See, for example, E. Banfield, *The Moral Basis of a Backward Society* (New York: Free Press of Glencoe, 1958).

17. G. M. Sykes, *The Society of Captives* (Princeton: Princeton University Press, 1958), pp. 87–95.

18. The term *moral* is used here . . . to refer to an orientation of the actor; it does not involve a value-position of the observer. See T. Parsons et al., *Toward a General Theory of Action* (Cambridge, Mass.: Harvard University Press, 1952), pp. 170ff.

# 15

# Human Organizational Measurements: Key to Financial Success

*Rensis Likert*

*A significant objective of the control process is to identify deviations from planned objectives. Clearly the sooner a deviation is identified the more rapidly a correction can be made. In this article, Rensis Likert suggests that we need no longer rely on "after-the-fact" measurements to tell us of problems. By measuring certain aspects of the human part of the organization, it may be possible to identify future problems in advance and greatly improve upon our control processes.—Eds.*

Managers and administrators need no longer wait until "after-the-fact" measurements tell them that they are in trouble before taking corrective steps. All performance, accounting, and financial data are after-the-fact measurements. They reveal the state of a department or organization as it was *yesterday*. As a consequence, often before a problem becomes sufficiently clear to be recognized, it has reached serious proportions.

Recent research developments in the social sciences, however, now can enable any administrator to have data one or more years in advance of trouble. These data can reveal the operating and performance problems which his organization is likely to encounter, the probable causes of these problems, and the steps which if taken now will correct the situation and prevent the problem from developing.

These *lead time data* are measurements of the state of the human organization of an agency or department. They include such measure-

SOURCE: Reprinted by permission from the May 1971 issue of the *Michigan Business Review*, published by the Graduate School of Business Administration, The University of Michigan.

ments as the leadership behavior of administrators and reveal the extent to which the agency is capable of performing in a highly efficient, productive manner. These measurements of the human organization are objective, impartial, and replicable. They can be used to:

1. Reveal the extent to which the organization as a whole and each of its administrators and supervisors are using managerial principles and practices which yield the highest productivity and the best performance. They will show how well each manager or administrator is building his subordinates into a highly motivated, highly effective unit.

2. Provide evidence concerning the condition for each firm, department, or subordinate unit of such variables as communication, decision making, attitudes and loyalty, motivation, performance goals, and commitment to the organization's success.

3. Increase the lead time by one to three years concerning awareness of operational and performance problems caused by deterioration of the human organization and its productive capability. Lead time measurements will reveal problems at their early stages, point to the major causes of each incipient problem, provide clues to the course of action most likely to correct the situation, show at an early stage how effective each attempt to solve a problem is proving to be, and indicate the further steps likely to bring additional improvement.

4. Reveal the extent to which greater productivity and better performance represent true improvement, in contrast to that achieved by costly liquidation of the human organization.

5. Establish the basis for improving the compensation of managers and supervisors by providing more objective and more accurate data concerning the effectiveness of each administrator's managerial practices.

6. Improve labor relations by facilitating early awareness of problem situations, more accurate diagnosis of these causes, and early action of a remedial character.

7. Detect at an early stage new innovative improvements in organizational structure or in managerial or supervisory behavior. This early detection of better principles and methods of administration will enable the more rapid dissemination of these principles and methods to other parts of the organization. In this manner, all managers and supervisors in the organization can be aided in rapidly adopting better practices.

## MANAGEMENT AND ACHIEVEMENT

These and similar uses of lead time measurements are based on the capacity of these measurements to describe correctly the condition of the human organization of a firm and to predict the trends in the performance capability of that firm. A large number of studies of business firms and governmental agencies by the Institute for Social Research, involving thousands of managers and tens of thousands of employees, reveal a relatively consistent relationship between the leadership style and management system of a business firm and the extent to which the organization is able to achieve its objectives fully and efficiently. In widely different kinds of organizations, the managers who are achieving the greatest productivity, lowest cost, best quality of operation, and best labor relations are using the same basic principles of management. These principles differ significantly from those used by managers who achieve average or below average information.

The kind of organization created by the most successful managers can be described briefly: This human system is made up of interlocking work groups with a high degree of group loyalty among members and favorable attitudes and trust between supervisors and subordinates. Sensitivity to others and relatively high levels of skill in personal interaction and the functioning of groups also are present. These skills permit effective participation in decisions on common problems. Participation is used, for example, to establish organizational objectives which are a satisfactory integration of the needs and desires of all members of the organization and of persons functionally related to it. High levels of reciprocal influence occur, and high levels of total coordinated influence are achieved in the organization. Responsibility for the organization's success is felt individually by the members and each initiates action, when necessary to assure that the organization accomplishes its objectives. Communication is efficient and effective. There is a flow from one part of the organization to another of all relevant information important for each decision and action. The leadership in the organization has developed what might well be called a highly effective social system for interaction and mutual influence.

The system of management based on this theory has been labelled "System 4" for convenient reference. Prevailing systems of management and administration which are more authoritarian in character will be referred to as "System 2." System 4 is an appreciably more effective management system than is System 2.

## SIGNIFICANCE OF TRENDS

These relationships between the management systems of an organization and the excellence of its performance are, however, *much more marked if trends and relationships over time* are examined instead of using measurements made only at one point in time.

In a recent study of a continuous process plant, for example, the relationship was examined between managerial behavior and cost performance of 40 departments. When both measurements were obtained at the same point in time, the relationships were so slight as to be not statistically significant. But when these measurements of managerial behavior obtained in 1966 were related to cost performance by departments in 1967, i.e., one year later, one fourth of the variation in costs among departments was accounted for by the behavior of the managers one year earlier. When the time interval was two years, one half of the variation in costs among departments could be attributed to managerial behavior two years earlier.

These findings and other recent studies reveal that measurements of such causal variables as the behavior of administrators and supervisors can be used to predict subsequent trends in organizational performance. As a consequence, these measurements are highly valuable for the uses suggested for lead time purposes.

Any business firm, governmental agency, or educational institution that wishes to do so can use both lead time human organizational measurements and System 4 to achieve excellent performance at low cost. A number of studies show that when an organization does this, productivity is higher and costs lower by 15 to 30 percent or more. The use of System 4 and human organizational measurements can pay off handsomely.

## PLANNING-PROGRAMMING-BUDGETING

There are, moreover, other valuable uses of these human organizational measurements which reveal the productive capability of an agency and the probable trends in this capability. For example, these data can be used in conjunction with P.P.B. (Planning-Programming-Budgeting).

P.P.B. is a powerful administrative management tool but it can be effective only in situations where objectives and progress toward their achievement can be expressed in quantitative dimensions. For many governmental operations, it is very difficult, if not impossible, to state organizational objectives so that the extent to which they are being achieved can be measured quantitatively and at a reasonable cost.

When this condition exists, it is still possible to make effective use of the powerful resources of P.P.B. This involves shifting the P.P.B activity from focusing on end-result variables to dealing with human organizational variables. For this purpose, all of the major human organizational variables should be used, including both *causal*—such as managerial behavior—and *intervening*—such as communication, motivation, and control.

This application of the human organizational variables as the fundamental dimension for P.P.B. is based on the substantial body of research findings which show that when an organization is functioning well, as revealed by measurements of its human organizational variables, it is, or soon will be, achieving its performance, service, and other end-result objectives well. This application of P.P.B. requires that objectives be stated and progress toward their achievement measured in terms of human organizational variables. To date, this combined use of P.P.B. and human organizational variables has not been tried. It is, however, perfectly feasible and is likely to yield highly profitable results.

P.P.B. is used commonly in situations where some, but not all, of the objectives of an organization can be dealt with quantitatively. In some of these situations, P.P.B. may work well. In many, however, it may give the appearance of working well when its use is actually producing costly adverse consequences. This occurs when P.P.B. causes an agency to focus its efforts on activities which, when carried out, may achieve the quantitatively stated subobjective, but with considerable adverse consequences so far as the total objectives of the organization are concerned.

## IMPACTS OF COST REDUCTION PROGRAM

The typical cost reduction program can be used to illustrate this point. These cost reduction programs, like P.P.B., focused on a quantitatively defined subobjective, usually accomplish their immediate cost reduction goals, but with serious financial losses to the agency or firm. A study was made recently of a typical cost reduction program in a plant of about 700 persons. This cost reduction program employed the usual methods of "tightening up." The work was analyzed with the aid of outside consultants to see whether the work could be reorganized so as to require less labor. This analysis revealed that in some departments savings in labor could be achieved. For each of these departments, teams consisting of persons from other departments, staff, and outside consultants were established to study the department and recommend how the estimated labor savings could be achieved. The manager of each affected department was ordered to introduce the specific changes and achieve the designated labor savings. The total annual savings amounted to approximately $250,000.

This saving, viewed by itself, was a nice reduction in costs. But measurements of the human organizational variables for this plant and especially for the departments most affected by the cost reduction effort, showed an appreciable drop. Leadership behavior, motivation, communication, control, coordination, and similar variables all showed an adverse shift. When scores on these variables worsen, research findings show that productivity and earnings drop subsequently. The unfavorable shift in these variables for this plant indicate that an annual drop in earnings of approximately one million dollars is likely to occur in each of the next several years.

Recent data from this plant concerning production, costs, quality, and labor relations indicate that the poorer results forecast by the adverse shift in the human organizational variables are occurring. Moreover, the estimated loss mentioned above understates the total drop since it ignores all losses due to downtime and any losses caused by customer dissatisfaction due to poor quality.

Long-range survival and financial success are more important in this company's total objectives than are short-range cash flows erroneously labelled "savings." This cash flow was accompanied in this plant by a liquidation of the firm's human assets far greater in amount than the increased cash flow reported as savings. This cost reduction program illustrates the unfavorable consequences to an organization of concentrating on those subobjectives which can be measured with traditional methods, ignoring the extent to which the total objectives are, or are not, being realized.

## PROMISE AND PROBLEMS IN P.P.B.

Education is a good example of a situation where it is possible to deal with subobjectives quantitatively, but where it is virtually impossible at any reasonable cost to measure the extent to which each teacher, class, school, and school system is performing efficiently as an educational institution. It is extremely difficult to eliminate or partial out from measurements of educational achievement such influences as each student's native ability and the environment of his home. It is extremely difficult, consequently, and would be prohibitively costly to attempt to measure the overall effectiveness of a school system in achieving its total educational objectives efficiently. For these reasons, P.P.B. cannot be applied to the overall operation of a school system.

P.P.B. is used at present, however, for such specific educational subobjectives as teaching students to read or having a designated proportion of students achieve a specified score on a standardized achievement test. The danger of this use of P.P.B., when only a fractional part of an agency's total objectives is dealt with in quantitative dimensions, is that the subobjective may be accomplished but often serious adverse consequences for the organization's total objectives may ensue. The cost of teaching youngsters to read might be reduced, for example, by focusing intensive effort on it and by putting pressure on each teacher to achieve specified results and on each pupil to learn. Such a program could achieve the P.P.B. objective in reducing the costs of teaching students to read, but it could simultaneously create resentful attitudes in teachers and develop hostile attitudes among students toward reading, school, and education. Hostile attitudes toward schools and education lead to dropouts. If the least costly way of teaching reading led to dropouts years later, it would be a high cost to pay for a 5 percent reduction in the cost of learning to read. This would be as inefficient and undesirable as the typical cost reduction programs which yield immediate cash flows accompanied by financial losses over many subsequent years.

It is perfectly feasible for an organization to use P.P.B. to gain the benefit of achieving some of its subobjectives efficiently, without suffering overall adverse consequences. This requires measurements of both the causal and intervening human organizational variables and their use in conjunction with the P.P.B. effort focused on achieving the subobjective. If these human organizational variables are measured and examined regularly, trends in these variables can be used to prevent costly overall consequences while achieving the subobjective. Thus, when P.P.B. is used to reduce the costs of teaching students to read, measurements of the human organizational variables of the school system should be obtained. If the latter measurements reveal an adverse shift in the motivation, values, attitudes, and behavior of teachers and students, the effort to achieve the specified subobjective should be modified appropriately.

These are a few examples of the use of human organizational variables to improve the capacity of any agency or organization to achieve its objectives efficiently.

# PART THREE

# Managing Individual Behavior

The individual employee is the basic building block of the organization. To a very large degree, overall organizational performance is a function of the individual performance of all organizational members. Although the link between individual level effectiveness and total organizational effectiveness is not simply an additive one, it is clear that successful performance at the individual level is necessary (although perhaps not sufficient) for organizational success.

It has been said that the two basic questions which the field of organizational behavior attempts to answer are, Why do people in organizational settings behave the way they do, and How can we get them to behave differently? It is not oversimplifying too much to say that it was not until the famous Hawthorne studies conducted at Western Electric over 60 years ago that we realized the importance of even asking the first question.

To successfully manage individual behavior in organizations requires that various aspects of what shapes and energizes behavior be recognized, and, when feasible, taken into consideration while carrying out the job of managing organizational behavior. These variables that are so critical in determining individual behavior include individual abilities and skills, personality makeup, psychological variables of perception, attitudes, and needs, socialization experiences, and even such demographic variables as age, gender, and race.

Effective management of individual behavior also requires recognition of the need to obtain the best possible fit between the individual and the larger organization. Aspects of such fit include matching individual needs with organizational rewards, and matching individual skills, abilities, and expertise with job requirements and expectations. The potential dysfunctional consequences of a lack of fit have been both speculated upon and studied by numerous writers and researchers. Such consequences include increases in absenteeism, turnover, waste, sabotage, goldbricking, rate setting, and errors. Similarly, decreases in quantity and quality of output, morale, willingness to take initiatives and accept responsibilities, and commitment to organizational goals and objectives may also occur.

The readings in this section touch upon a variety of individual behavior considerations relevant to managers, including a discussion of the Hawthorne research, an overview of the problems and the promises of dealing with individualized organizations, a look at the cause and effects of role conflict and ambiguity in work settings, and a model for maximizing individual levels of commitment and performance.

# 16

## The Western Electric Researches

*George C. Homans*

*Perhaps no single research study has had a greater impact on management theory and practice than that conducted at the Hawthorne Works of Western Electric. This article describes part of this multiyear project and the conclusions which flowed from it. No study of management is complete without a look at the "Hawthorne Research," credited by many as giving birth to the behavioral management thrust.—Eds.*

Perhaps the most important program of research studied by the Committee on Work in Industry of the National Research Council is that which has been carried on at the Hawthorne (Chicago) Works of the Western Electric Company. This program was described by H. A. Wright and M. L. Putnam of the Western Electric Company and by F. J. Roethlisberger, now Professor of Human Relations, Graduate School of Business Administration, Harvard University, particularly at a meeting of the Committee held on March 9, 1938. These men, together with Elton Mayo and G. A. Pennock, both members of the committee, had been intimately associated with the research.

A word about the Western Electric Company is a necessary introduction to what follows. This company is engaged in manufacturing equipment for the telephone industry. Besides doing this part of its work, it has always shown concern for the welfare of its employees. In the matter of wages and hours, it has maintained a high standard. It has provided good physical conditions for its employees; and it has tried to make use of every established method of vocational guidance in the effort to suit the worker to his work. The efforts of the company

SOURCE: Reprinted from *Fatigue of Workers* by George C. Homans (Reinhold, 1941), pp. 56–65, by permission from the author.

have been rewarded in good industrial relations: there has been no strike or other severe symptom of discontent for over 20 years. In short, there is no reason to doubt that while these researches were being carried out, the morale of the company was high and that the employees, as a body, had confidence in the abilities and motives of the company management. These facts had an important bearing on the results achieved.

The program of research which will be described grew out of a study conducted at Hawthorne by the Western Electric Company in collaboration with the National Research Council, the aim of which was to determine the relation between intensity of illumination and efficiency of workers, measured in output. One of the experiments made was the following: Two groups of employees doing similar work under similar conditions were chosen, and records of output were kept for each group. The intensity of the light under which one group worked was varied, while that under which the other group worked was held constant. By this method the investigators hoped to isolate from the effect of other variables the effect of changes in the intensity of illumination on the rate of output.

In this hope they were disappointed. The experiment failed to show any simple relation between experimental changes in the intensity of illumination and observed changes in the rate of output. The investigators concluded that this result was obtained, not because such a relation did not exist, but because it was in fact impossible to isolate it from the other variables entering into any determination of productive efficiency. This kind of difficulty, of course, has been encountered in experimental work in many fields. Furthermore, the investigators were in agreement as to the character of some of these other variables. They were convinced that one of the major factors which prevented their securing a satisfactory result was psychological. The employees being tested were reacting to changes in light intensity in the way in which they assumed that they were expected to react. That is, when light intensity was increased they were expected to produce more; when it was decreased they were expected to produce less. A further experiment was devised to demonstrate this point. The light bulbs were changed, as they had been changed before, and the workers were allowed to assume that as a result there would be more light. They commented favorably on the increased illumination. As a matter of fact, the bulbs had been replaced with others of just the same power. Other experiments of the sort were made, and in each case the results could be explained as a "psychological" reaction rather than as a "physiological" one.

This discovery seemed to be important. It suggested that the relations between other physical conditions and the efficiency of workers might be obscured by similar psychological reactions. Nevertheless, the investigators were determined to continue in their course. They recognized the existence of the psychological factors, but they thought of them only as disturbing influences. They were not yet ready to turn their attention to the psychological factors themselves. Instead, they were concerned with devising a better way of eliminating them from the experiments, and the experiments they wanted to try by no means ended with illumination. For instance, there was the question of what was called "fatigue." Little information existed about the effect on efficiency of changes in the hours of work and the introduction of rest pauses. The investigators finally came to the conclusion that, if a small group of workers were isolated in a separate room and asked to co-operate, the psychological reaction would in time disappear, and they would work exactly as they felt. That is, changes in their rate of output would be the direct result of changes in their physical conditions of work and nothing else.

The decision to organize such a group was in fact taken. A small number of workers was to be selected and placed in a separate room, where experiments were to be made with different kinds of working conditions in order to see if more exact information could be secured. Six questions were asked by those setting up the experiment. They were the following:

1. Do employees actually get tired out?
2. Are rest pauses desirable?
3. Is a shorter working day desirable?
4. What is the attitude of employees toward their work and toward the company?
5. What is the effect of changing the type of working equipment?
6. Why does production fall off in the afternoon?

It is obvious that several of these questions could be answered only indirectly by the proposed experiment, and several of them touched upon the "psychological" rather than the "physiological" factors involved. Nevertheless, all of them arose out of the bewilderment of men of experience faced with the problem of dealing with fellow human beings in a large industrial organization. In fact, one of the executives of the company saw the purpose of the experiment in even simpler and more general terms. He said that the experiment grew out of a desire on the part of the management to "know more about our workers." In this way began the experiment which is referred to as the Relay Assembly Test Room. With this experiment and the others that followed, members of the Department of Industrial Research of the Graduate School of Business Administration, Harvard University, came to be closely associated.

In April 1927, six girls were selected from a large shop department of the Hawthorne Works. They were chosen as average workers, neither inexperienced nor expert, and their work consisted of the assembling of telephone relays. A coil, armature, contact springs, and insulators were put together on a fixture and secured in position by means of four machine screws. The operation at that time was being completed at the rate of about five relays in six minutes. This particular operation was chosen for the experiment because the relays were being assembled often enough so that even slight changes in output rate would show themselves at once on the output record. Five of the girls were to do the actual assembly work; the duty of the sixth was to keep the others supplied with parts.

The test room itself was an area divided from the main department by a wooden partition eight feet high. The girls sat in a row on one side of a long workbench. Their bench and assembly equipment was identical with that used in the regular department, except in one respect. At the right of each girl's place was a hole in the bench, and into this hole she dropped completed relays. It was the entrance to a chute, in which there was a flapper gate opened by the relay in its passage downward. The opening of the gate closed an electrical circuit which controlled a perforating device, and this in turn recorded the completion of the relay by punching a hole in a tape. The tape moved at the rate of one quarter of an inch a minute and had space for a separate row of holes for each operator. When punched, it thus constituted a complete output record for each girl for each instant of the day. Such records were kept for five years.

In this experiment then, as in the earlier illumination experiments, great emphasis was laid on the rate of output. A word of caution is needed here. The Western Electric Company was not immediately interested in increasing output. The experiments were not designed for that purpose. On the other hand, output is easily measured; i.e., it yields precise quantitative data, and experience suggested that it was sensitive to at least some of the conditions under which the employees worked. Output was treated as an index. In short, the nature of the experimental conditions made the emphasis on output inevitable.

From their experience in the illumination experiments, the investigators were well aware that factors other than those experimentally varied might affect the output rate. Therefore, arrangements were made that a number of other records should be kept. Unsuitable parts supplied by the firm were noted down, as were assemblies rejected for any reason upon inspection. In this way the type of defect could be known and related to the time of day at which it occurred. Records were kept of weather conditions in general and of temperature and humidity in the test room. Every six weeks each operator was given a medical examination by the company doctor. Every day she was asked to tell how many hours she had spent in bed the night before and, during a part of the experiment, what food she had eaten. Besides all these records, which concerned the physical condition of the operators, a log was kept in which were recorded the principal events in the test room hour by hour, including among the entries snatches of conversation between the workers. At first these entries related largely to the physical condition of the operators: how they felt as they worked. Later the ground they covered somewhat widened, and the log ultimately became one of the most important of the test room records. Finally, when the so-called Interviewing Program was instituted at Hawthorne, each of the operators was interviewed several times by an experienced interviewer.

The girls had no supervisor in the ordinary sense, such as they would have had in a regular shop department, but a "test room observer" was placed in the room, whose duty it was to maintain the records, arrange the work, and secure a cooperative spirit on the part of the girls. Later, when the complexity of his work increased, several assistants were assigned to help him.

When the arrangements had been made for the test room, the operators who had been chosen to take part were called in for an interview in the office of the superintendent of the Inspection Branch, who was in general charge of the experiment and of the researches which grew out of it. The superintendent described this interview as follows:

> The nature of the test was carefully explained to these girls and they readily consented to take part in it, although they were very shy at the first conference. An invitation to six shop girls to come up to a superintendent's office was naturally rather startling. They were assured that the object of the test was to determine the effect of certain changes in working conditions, such as rest periods, midmorning lunches, and shorter working hours. They were expressly cautioned to work at a comfortable pace, and under no circumstances to try to make a race out of the test.

This conference was only the first of many. Whenever any experimental change was planned, the girls were called in, the purpose of the change was explained to them, and their comments were requested. Certain suggested changes which did not meet with their approval were abandoned. They were repeatedly asked, as they were asked in the first interview, not to strain but to work "as they felt."

The experiment was now ready to begin. Put in its simplest terms, the idea of those directing the experiment was that if an output curve was studied for a long enough time under various changes in working conditions, it would be possible to determine which conditions were the most satisfactory. Accordingly, a number of so-called experimental periods were arranged. For two weeks before the operators were placed in the test room, a record was kept of the production of each one without her knowledge. In this way the investigators secured a measure of her productive ability while working in the regular department under the usual conditions. This constituted the first experimental period. And for five weeks after the girls entered the test room no change was made in working conditions. Hours remained what they had been before. The investigators felt that this period would be long enough to reveal any changes in output incidental merely to the transfer. This constituted the second experimental period.

The third period involved a change in the method of payment. In the regular department, the girls had been paid according to a scheme of group piecework, the group consisting of a hundred or more employees. Under these circumstances, variations in an individual's total output would not be immediately reflected in her pay, since such variations tended to cancel one another in a large group. In the test room, the six operators were made a group by themselves. In this way each girl received an amount more nearly in proportion to her individual effort, and her interests became more closely centered on the experiment. Eight weeks later, the directly experimental changes began. An outline will reveal their general character: Period IV: two rest pauses, each five minutes in length, were established, one occurring in midmorning and the other in the early afternoon. Period V: these rest pauses were lengthened to ten minutes each. Period VI: six five-minute rests were established. Period VII: the company provided each member of the group with a light lunch in the midmorning and another in the midafternoon accompanied by rest pauses. This arrangement became standard for subsequent Periods VIII through XI. Period VIII: work stopped a half hour earlier every day—at 4:30 P.M. Period IX: work stopped at 4 P.M. Period X: conditions returned to what they were in Period VII. Period XI: a five-day work week was established. Each of these experimental periods lasted several weeks.

Period XI ran through the summer of 1928, a year after the beginning of the experiment. Already the results were not what had been expected. The output curve, which had risen on the whole slowly and steadily throughout the year, was obviously reflecting something other than the responses of the group to the imposed experimental conditions. Even when the total weekly output had fallen off, as it could hardly fail to do in such a period as Period XI, when the group was working only five days a week, daily output continued to rise. Therefore, in accordance with a sound experimental procedure, as a control on what had been done, it was agreed with the consent of the operators that in experimental Period XII a return should be made to the original conditions of work, with no rest pauses, no special lunches, and a full-length working week. This period lasted for 12 weeks. Both daily and weekly output rose to a higher point than ever before: the working day and the working week were both longer. The hourly output rate declined somewhat but it did not approach the level of Period III, when similar conditions were in effect.

The conclusions reached after Period XII may be expressed in terms of another observation. Identical conditions of work were repeated in three different experimental periods: Periods VII, X, and XII. If the assumptions on which the study was based had been correct, that is to say, if the output rate were directly related to the physical conditions of work, the expectation would be that in these three experimental periods there would be some similarity in output. Such was not the case. The only apparent uniformity was that in each experimental period output was higher than in the preceding one. In the Relay Assembly Test Room, as in the previous illumination experiments, something was happening which could not be explained by the experimentally controlled conditions of work.

There is no need here to go into the later history of the test room experiment, which came to an end in 1933. It is enough to say that the output of the group continued to rise until it established itself on a high plateau from which there was no descent until the time of discouragement and deepening economic depression which preceded the end of the test. The rough conclusions reached at the end of experimental Period XII were confirmed and sharpened by later research. T. N. Whitehead, Associate Professor of Business in the Graduate School of Business Administration, Harvard University, has made a careful statistical analysis of the output records. He shows that the changes which took place in the output of the group have no simple correlation with the experimental changes in working conditions. Nor can they be correlated with changes in other physical conditions of which records were kept, such as temperature, humidity, hours of rest, and changes of relay type. Even when the girls themselves complained of mugginess or heat, these conditions were not apparently affecting their output. This statement, of course, does not mean that there is never any relation between output rate and these physical conditions. There is such a thing as heat prostration. It means only that, within the limits in which these conditions were varying in the test room, they apparently did not affect the rate of work.

The question remains: with what facts, if any, can the changes in the output rate of the operators in the test room be correlated? Here the statements of the girls themselves are of first importance. Each girl knew that she was producing more in the test room than she ever

had in the regular department, and each said that the increase had
come about without any conscious effort on her part. It seemed easier
to produce at the faster rate in the test room than at the slower rate
in the regular department. When questioned further, each girl stated
her reasons in slightly different words, but there was uniformity in
the answers in two respects. First, the girls liked to work in the test
room: "it was fun." Secondly, the new supervisory relation or, as they
put it, the absence of the old supervisory control, made it possible for
them to work freely without anxiety.

For instance, there was the matter of conversation. In the regular
department, conversation was in principle not allowed. In practice it
was tolerated if it was carried on in a low tone and did not interfere
with work. In the test room an effort was made in the beginning to
discourage conversation, though it was soon abandoned. The observer
in charge of the experiment was afraid of losing the cooperation of the
girls if he insisted too strongly on this point. Talk became common and
was often loud and general. Indeed the conversation of the operators
came to occupy an important place in the log. T. N. Whitehead has
pointed out that the girls in the test room were far more thoroughly
supervised than they ever had been in the regular department. They
were watched by an observer of their own, an interested management,
and outside experts. The point is that the character and purpose of the
supervision were different and were felt to be so.

The operators knew that they were taking part in what was considered an important and interesting experiment. They knew that their
work was expected to produce results—they were not sure what results—which would lead to the improvement of the working conditions
of their fellow employees. They knew that the eyes of the company
were upon them. Whitehead has further pointed out that, although the
experimental changes might turn out to have no physical significance,
their social significance was always favorable. They showed that the
management of the company was still interested, that the girls were
still part of a valuable piece of research. In the regular department,
the girls, like the other employees, were in the position of responding
to changes the source and purpose of which were beyond their knowledge. In the test room, they had frequent interviews with the superintendent, a high officer of the company. The reasons for the
contemplated experimental changes were explained to them. Their
views were consulted and in some instances they were allowed to veto
what had been proposed. Professor Mayo has argued that it is idle to
speak of an experimental period like Period XII as being in any sense
what it purported to be—a return to the original conditions of work.
In the meantime, the entire industrial situation of the girls had been
reconstructed.

Another factor in what occurred can only be spoken of as the social development of the group itself. When the girls went for the first time to be given a physical examination by the company doctor, someone suggested as a joke that ice cream and cake ought to be served. The company provided them at the next examination, and the custom was kept up for the duration of the experiment. When one of the girls had a birthday, each of the others would bring her a present, and she would respond by offering the group a box of chocolates. Often one of the girls would have some good reason for feeling tired. Then the others would "carry" her. That is, they would agree to work especially fast to make up for the low output expected from her. It is doubtful whether this "carrying" did have any effect, but the important point is the existence of the practice, not its effectiveness. The girls made friends in the test room and went together socially after hours. One of the interesting facts which has appeared from Whitehead's analysis of the output records is that there were times when variations in the output rates of two friends were correlated to a high degree. Their rates varied simultaneously and in the same direction—something, of course, which the girls were not aware of and could not have planned. Also, these correlations were destroyed by such apparently trivial events as a change in the order in which the girls sat at the workbench.

Finally, the group developed leadership and a common purpose. The leader, self-appointed, was an ambitious young Italian girl who entered the test room as a replacement after two of the original members had left. She saw in the experiment a chance for personal distinction and advancement. The common purpose was an increase in the output rate. The girls had been told in the beginning and repeatedly thereafter that they were to work without straining, without trying to make a race of the test, and all the evidence shows that they kept this rule. In fact, they felt that they were working under less pressure than in the regular department. Nevertheless, they knew that the output record was considered the most important of the records of the experiment and was always closely scrutinized. Before long they had committed themselves to a continuous increase in production. In the long run, of course, this ideal was an impossible one, and when the girls found out that it was, the realization was an important element of the change of tone which was noticeable in the second half of the experiment. But for a time they felt that they could achieve the impossible. In brief, the increase in the output rate of the girls in the Relay Assembly Test Room could not be related to any changes in their physical conditions of work, whether experimentally induced or not. It could, however, be related to what can only be spoken of as the development of an organized social group in a peculiar and effective relation with its supervisors.

Many of these conclusions were not worked out in detail until long after the investigators at Hawthorne had lost interest in the Relay Assembly Test Room, but the general meaning of the experiment was clear at least as early as Period XII. A continuous increase in productivity had taken place irrespective of changing physical conditions of work. In the words of a company report made in January 1931, on all the research which had been done up to that date:

> Upon analysis, only one thing seemed to show a continuous relationship with this improved output. This was the mental attitude of the operators. From their conversations with each other and their comments to the test observers, it was not only clear that their attitudes were improving but it was evident that this area of employee reactions and feelings was a fruitful field for industrial research.

# 17

## The Individualized Organization: Problems and Promise

*Edward E. Lawler III*

*Concluding that research on reward systems, job design, leadership, selection, and training demonstrates that individuals respond differently to policies and practices, Lawler argues that organizations should be "individualized" through the use of cafeteria-style pay plans and selective job enrichment programs.—Eds.*

Two easily identified and distinctly different approaches to the study of behavior in organizations have dominated the organizational behavior literature for the past half century. One emphasizes the differences among people, the other the similarities.

The first and least dominant approach has its foundation in differential psychology and is concerned with the study of individual differences. The basic assumptions underlying this approach are that people differ in their needs, skills, and abilities; that these differences can be measured; that valid data about people's competence and motivation can be obtained by organizations; and that these data can be used to make organizations more effective.

When behavioral scientists who take this approach look at organizations, they tend to see selection and placement. Their concern is

SOURCE: Edward E. Lawler, "The Individualized Organization: Problems and Promise," *California Management Review* 17 (Winter 1974) pp. 31–39. © 1974 by the Regents of the University of California. Reprinted from *California Management Review* 17, no. 2, pp. 31–39, by permission of the Regents.

with selecting those people who are right for a given job by measuring
the characteristics of both the people and jobs and then trying to achieve
the best fit. Their paradigm of the ideal organization would seem to
be one where everyone has the ability and motivation to do the job to
which he is assigned. Rarely do behavioral scientists with this orientation try to change the design of jobs or of organizations. Jobs are
taken as a given, and the focus is on finding the right people for them.
Where efforts at job redesign have been made, they typically are instituted in the tradition of human engineering. That is, jobs have been
made simpler so that more people can do them.

What is needed if this approach is to work?

1. People must differ in meaningful ways.
2. Valid data about the characteristics of people must exist.
3. People who are suited for the jobs must apply.
4. A favorable selection ratio must exist (a large number of qualified
   applicants must apply for the job).

The second approach has generally assumed that all employees in
an organization are similar in many ways and that certain general
rules or principles can and should be developed for the design of organizations. It is universalistic, propounding that there is a right way
to deal with all people in organizations. This type of thinking is present
in the work of such traditional organization theorists as Urwick and
Taylor. It is also present in the writings of the human relations theorists
such as Mayo and in the work of the human resource theorists such
as McGregor and Likert. As John Morse notes, all these approaches
contain either implicitly or explicitly the assumption that there is a
right way to manage people.[1]

Douglas McGregor's discussion of Theory X and Theory Y points
out that, although scientific management and the more modern theories make different assumptions about the nature of man, both emphasize the similarities among people rather than differences.[2] Based
upon the Theory Y view of the nature of people, McGregor develops a
normative organization theory that, like Theory X, stresses universal
principles of management. For any of the universality theories to be
generally valid, a certain type of person must populate society: one
that fits its assumptions about the nature of people. In the case of the
human resource theorists, this universal person will respond favorably
to such things as enriched jobs, participative leadership, and interpersonal relationships characterized by openness, trust, and leveling.
For the scientific management theorists, the universal type responds
well to the use of financial rewards and the simplification of work.
Thus, the validity of all these theories rests upon the correctness of
the assumptions about the nature of people.

The work of those behavioral scientists who are concerned with individual differences suggests that the assumptions of all the universal theorists are dangerous over-simplifications for one very important reason: they fail to acknowledge the significant differences (in needs, personalities, and abilities) that cause individuals to react differently to organization practices concerned with job design, pay systems, leadership, training, and selection. Although many studies of individual behavior in organizations have not looked for individual differences, there are some that have found significant diversities. They are worth reviewing briefly since they clearly illustrate what is wrong with all organization theories which make universal assumptions about the nature of people.

## JOB DESIGN

Job enrichment is one of the key ideas in most of the recent human resource theories of organization. According to the argument presented by Frederick Herzberg and others, job enrichment can lead to appreciable increases in employee motivation, performance, and satisfaction.[3] In fact, there is a fairly large body of evidence to support this view.[4]

There is, however, also a considerable amount of evidence that all individuals do not respond to job enrichment with higher satisfaction, productivity, and quality. In many studies, the researchers have not been concerned with explaining these individual differences and have treated them as error variance. In others, however, attempts have been made to find out what distinguishes those people who respond positively to job enrichment. It has been pointed out that the type of background a person comes from may be related to how he or she responds to an enriched job.[5] According to some analyses, employees from rural backgrounds are more likely to respond positively to enrichment than are workers from urban environments.

More recent findings have shown that individual differences in need strength determine how people respond to jobs; the reason previous researchers have found urban-rural differences to be important lies in the kind of needs that people from these backgrounds have.[6] Rural background people have stronger higher-order needs (self-actualization, competence, self-esteem), and people with these needs respond positively to job enrichment, while those who don't fail to respond. It is argued that job enrichment creates conditions under which people can experience growth and self-esteem, motivating them to perform well. Clearly, for those employees who do not want to experience competence and growth, the opportunity to experience them will not be motivating, and not everyone should be expected to respond well to enriched jobs.[7]

## PAY SYSTEMS

The scientific management philosophy strongly emphasizes the potential usefulness of pay as a motivator as in many piece-rate, bonus, profit-sharing, and other pay incentive plans. There is abundant evidence to support the point that, when pay is tied to performance, motivation and performance are increased.[8] However, there is also evidence to indicate that not everyone responds to pay incentive plans by performing better. In one study, certain types of employees responded to a piece-rate incentive system while others did not.[9] Who responded? Workers from rural backgrounds who owned their homes, were Protestants, and social isolates—workers who, in short, saw money as a way of getting what they wanted and for whom social relations were not highly important.

There are many different kinds of pay incentive systems; and the kind of pay system that will motivate one person often does not motivate others. For example, group plans apparently work best with people who have strong social needs.[10] This suggests that not only do the members of an organization have to be treated differently according to whether they will or will not respond to a pay incentive, but that those who will respond to pay systems may have to be subdivided according to the type of system to which they will respond.

There is abundant evidence that individuals differ in their responses to the fringe benefits they receive. Large differences, determined by such things as age, marital status, education, and so on, exist among individuals in the kind of benefits they want and need.[11] Most organizations ignore this and give everyone the same benefits, thereby often giving high-cost benefits to people who do not want them. Maximizing individual satisfaction with fringe benefits would require a unique plan for each employee.

## LEADERSHIP

Research on leadership style during the past two decades has stressed the advantages that can be gained from the use of the various forms of power equalization. Participation, flat organizations, decentralization, and group decision making are all power-equalization approaches to motivating and satisfying employees. There is a considerable body of evidence to suggest that power equalization can lead to higher subordinate satisfaction, greater subordinate motivation, and better decision making.[12] Unfortunately, much of this literature has only given brief mention to the fact that not all subordinates respond in the same way to power equalization and the fact that not all superiors can practice power equalization.

Victor Vroom was one of the first to point out that at least one type of subordinate does not respond positively to participative management.[13] His data show that subordinates who are high on the F-scale (a measure of authoritarianism) do not respond well when they are subordinates to a boss who is oriented toward participative management. Later studies have shown that at times the majority of the membership of a work group may not respond positively to power-equalization efforts on the part of superiors.[14]

Many superiors cannot manage in a democratic manner.[15] This, combined with the poor responses of many employees to democratic management styles, raises the question of whether it is advisable even to think of encouraging most managers to lead in a democratic manner. Many superiors probably *cannot* adopt a democratic leadership style, and because of the likely responses of some of their subordinates they *shouldn't*—regardless of task and situational considerations.

## TRAINING

To most modern organization theorists, training is an important element of organization design. It is particularly helpful in resolving individual differences. T-groups, managerial grid seminars, and leadership courses are some examples of the kinds of human relations training that organizations use. These training approaches help assure that most people in the organization have certain basic skills and abilities and that some valid assumptions about the capacity of the people in the organization can be made.

Once again, the problem is that the very individual employee differences greatly affect the ability to learn from things such as T-groups and managerial grid seminars; this type of training is simply wasted on many people.[16] In fact, the training may end up increasing the range of individual differences in an organization rather than reducing it. It is also likely that while one type of human relations training may not affect a person, another type could have a significant impact. The same point can be made with respect to training people in the area of occupational skills. One person may learn best from a teaching machine while another learns the same material best from a lecture format.

## SELECTION

In the work on selection, the assumption has typically been made that people are sufficiently similar so that the same selection instruments can be used for everyone. Thus, all applicants for a job are often given the same battery of selection criteria—overlooking the fact that different instruments might work better as predictors for some groups than for others. This would not be a serious problem if individual difference factors were not related to the ability of the selection instruments to predict performance; but recent evidence suggests that they are. Certain kinds of tests work better for some segments of the population than for others.[17] However, this uniformity in selection testing is not the only reason for poor job performance prediction.

Differential psychologists have developed numerous valid tests of people's ability to perform jobs, but they have failed to develop tests that measure how employees will fit into particular organizational climates and how motivated they will be in particular organizations. All too often, they have tried to predict individual behavior in organizations without measuring the characteristics of the organization. Trying to predict behavior by looking only at personal characteristics must inevitably lead to predictions whose validity is questionable.

All this is beginning to change, but it is doubtful if highly accurate predictions will ever be obtained. The measurement problems are too great and both organizations and people change too much. The research evidence also shows that people sometimes don't give valid data in selection situations and that some important determinants of individual behavior in organizations are difficult to measure.[18]

## INDIVIDUAL DIFFERENCES

One clear implication of the research on individual differences is that, for any of the universalistic theories to operate efficiently in a given organization or situation, one of two things must occur: either the organization must deal with the individuals it hires so that they will change to meet the assumptions of the theory, or it must hire only those individuals who fit the kind of system that the organization employs. Unfortunately, there is no solid evidence that individuals can be trained or dealt with in ways that will increase the degree to which they respond to such things as enriched jobs and democratic supervision. Proponents of job enrichment often stress that people will come to like it once they have tried it, but this point remains to be proven.

The validity of most selection instruments is so low that organizations should not count on finding instruments that will allow them to select only those who fit whatever system they use. There is always the prospect that the differential psychologist can develop appropriate measures and that this will lead to organizations being able to select more homogenous work forces. This, in turn, would allow approaches such as the human resources approach to be effectively utilized in some situations. However, it seems unlikely that they could ever be used in large complex organizations. Even if measures are developed, it may not be possible for large homogenous populations of workers to be selected by organizations. Effective selection depends on favorable selection ratios, which are rare, and on the legal ability of organizations to run selection programs. It is also obvious that there has been and will continue to be a large influx into the labor market and into organizations of people from different socioeconomic backgrounds. This has and will continue to create more diversity rather than homogeneity in the work forces of most organizations, decreasing the likelihood that large organizations can ever be completely staffed by people who fit the assumptions of scientific management, Theory X, Theory Y, or any other organization theory that is based upon the view that people are similar in important ways.

Further, it soon may not be legally possible for organizations to conduct the kind of selection programs that will by themselves produce good individual-organization fits. The federal government restrictions on testing for selection purposes soon could create conditions under which testing will no longer be practical. Organizations may find themselves in a situation where they must randomly select from among the "qualified applicants" for a job. Thus, even if valid tests were developed, work forces probably could not be selected that would contain only people that fit either the human resources or the scientific management assumptions about people.

There is evidence in the literature that some organization theorists are moving away from the view that one style of management or one organization design is right for most organizations.[19] However, the focus so far has been on environmental variables such as degree of uncertainty and stability, and production variables such as whether the task is predictable and whether the product can be mass, process, or unit produced. The researchers point out that different structures and different management styles are appropriate under different conditions. Some of the evidence they present is persuasive: products and environmental factors need to be considered when organizations are being designed. However, they often fail to point out that the nature of the work force also needs to be considered and they fail to suggest organization structures that allow for the fact that the people in any organization will vary in their response to such things as tight controls, job enrichment, and so on.

What seems to be needed is an organization theory based upon assumptions like the following, which recognize the existence of differences among individuals:

1. Most individuals are goal-oriented in their behavior but there are large differences in the goals people pursue.
2. Individuals differ both in what they enjoy doing and in what they can do.

3. Some individuals need to be closely supervised while others can exercise high levels of self-control.

In order to design an organization based on these assumptions, it is necessary to utilize various normative theories as guides to how different members of the same organization should be treated. In addition, measures of individual needs and abilities, like those developed by differential psychologists, are needed. As will become apparent, it probably also is necessary to depend on the ability of individuals to help make decisions about where and how they will work. In short, it requires a synthesis of the individual differences approach and the work of the organization theorists into a new paradigm of how organizations should be designed—a new paradigm that emphasizes structuring organizations so that they can better adapt themselves to the needs, desires, and abilities of their members.

## STRUCTURING THE INDIVIDUALIZED ORGANIZATION

The research on job design, training, reward systems, and leadership provides a number of suggestions about what an organization designed on the basis of individual differences assumptions would look like. A brief review will help to illustrate how an individualized organization might operate and identify some of the practical problems of the approach.

The research on job design shows that jobs can be fit to people if organizations can tolerate having a wide range of jobs and tasks. One plant in Florida has done this by having an assembly line operating next to a bench assembly of the same product. Employees are given a choice of which kind of job they want. The fact that some want to work to each kind is impressive evidence of the existence of individual differences. Robert Kahn has suggested that the fit process can be facilitated by allowing individuals to choose among different groups of tasks or modules that would be several hours long.[20] In his system, workers would bid for those tasks which they would like to do. For this system to work, all individuals would, of course, have to know a considerable amount about the nature of the different modules, and the approach would probably have to take place in conjunction with some job enrichment activities. Otherwise, the employee might be faced with choosing among modules made up of simple, repetitive tasks, thus giving them no real choice. As Kahn notes, the work module concept is also intriguing because it should make it easier for individuals to choose not to work a standard 40-hour workweek. This is important because of the difference in people's preferences with respect to hours of work. The whole module approach rests on the ability of individuals to make valid choices about when and where they should work.

The leadership research shows that people respond to different types of leadership. This could be handled by fitting the superior's style to the personality of subordinates—the superior who can only behave in an authoritarian manner will be given subordinates who perform well under that type of supervision; the superior who can only behave participatively could be given only people who respond to that style; and the superior who is capable of varying his style could be given either people who respond to different styles in different conditions or a mix of people with which he or she would be encouraged to behave differently.

The research shows that training needs to be individualized so that it will fit the needs and abilities of the employee. Implementation requires careful assessment of the individual's abilities and motivation, and good career counseling. Once it has been accepted that not everyone in the organization can profit from a given kind of training, then training becomes a matter of trying to develop people as much as possible with the kind of training to which they will respond. It requires accepting the fact that people may develop quite different leadership styles or ways of behaving in general and trying to capitalize on these by fitting the job the person holds and the groups he supervises to his style.

The research shows that pay systems need to be fit to the person. Fringe benefit packages are a good example of this; several companies have already developed cafeteria-style fringe benefit packages that allow employees to select the benefits they want. The research also suggests that those individuals whose desire for money is strong should be placed on jobs that lend themselves to pay incentive plans.

In summary, an organization based on individual differences assumptions would have a job environment for each person which fits his or her unique skills and abilities. It would accomplish this by a combination of good selection and self-placement choices in the areas of fringe benefits, job design, hours of work, style of supervision, and training programs. But creating truly individualized job situations presents many practical problems in organization design—it is difficult to create gratifying jobs for both the person who responds to an enriched job and the person who responds to a routinized job. One way of accomplishing this could be by creating relatively autonomous subunits that vary widely in climate, job design, leadership style, and so on. For example, within the same organization the same product might be produced by mass production in one unit and by unit production using enriched jobs in another. One subunit might have a warm, supportive climate while another might have a cold, demanding one. The size of the subunit would also vary depending upon the type of climate that is desired and the type of production it uses. This variation is desirable as long as the placement process is able to help people find the modules that fit them.

An organization would have to have an immense number of subunits if it were to try to have one to represent each of the possible combinations of climate, leadership style, incentive systems, and job design. Since such a large number is not practical, a selection should be made based on a study of the labor market, attention to the principles of motivation and satisfaction, and the nature of the product and market. A study of the labor market to see what type of people the organization is likely to attract should help determine what combinations will be needed to fit the characteristics of most of the workers. In most homogeneous labor markets, this may be only a few of the many possible combinations. Traditional selection instruments can help the organization decide who will fit into the subunits; and, if individuals are given information about the nature of the subunits, they can often make valid decisions themselves.

Motivation theory argues that when important rewards are tied to performance, it is possible to have both high satisfaction and high performance.[21] This suggests that all new work modules must meet one crucial condition: some rewards that are valued by members of that part of the organization must be tied to performance. This rules out many situations. For example, a situation in which no extrinsic rewards such as pay and promotion are tied to performance and which has authoritarian management and repetitive jobs should not exist. Finally, the research on job design and organization structure shows that the type of product and type of market limit the kind of subunit which can be successful. For example, authoritarian management, routine jobs, and tall organization structures are not effective when the product is technically sophisticated and must be marketed in a rapidly changing environment.

Creating subunits with distinctly different climates and practices is one way, but not the only way, to create an individualized organization. In small organizations, this probably is not possible; thus, it is important to encourage differences within the same unit. This may mean training supervisors to deal differently with subordinates who have distinctly different personal characteristics. It may also mean designing jobs that can be done in various ways. For example, in one group a product might be built by a team and passed from one member to another while in another group everyone might build the entire product without help. Obviously, this approach generally will not allow for as much variation as does the approach of building distinctive subunits, but it permits some degree of individualization.

It is not yet entirely clear how such divergent organization practices as work modules, cafeteria-style pay plans, and job enrichment that is guided by individual difference measures can be integrated in practice. Research on how organizations can be individualized and on how individual differences affect behavior in organizations is sorely needed.

## RESEARCH ON INDIVIDUAL DIFFERENCES

The work on measuring individual differences that has been done so far has focused largely on measuring the "can do" aspects of behavior for the purpose of selection. The effective individualization of organizations depends on the development of measures which tap the "will do" aspects of behavior, such as measures of motivation and reactions to different organizational climates, and measures that can be used for placing people in positions that best fit their needs.

This is not to say that selection should be ignored; the kinds of individual differences that exist in an organization should be kept at a manageable number and those who clearly cannot do the job should be excluded. But it is important that, in selection, measures of such things as motivation, reactions to different leadership styles, and preferred organization climate be collected and evaluated in relationship to the climate of the organization, the psychological characteristics of the jobs in the organizations, and the leadership style of various managers. The same measures are obviously relevant when consideration is given to placing new employees in different parts of the organization or in different jobs. The difficulty in doing this kind of selection and placement is that there are few measures of the relevant individual differences, of the organization climate, and of the psychological characteristics of jobs. In many cases, it is not even known what the relevant individual difference variables are when consideration is being given to predicting how people will react to different administrative practices, policies, and to different organization climates. This is where the differential psychologist can make a major contribution.

Also needed is research on selection that is responsive to the new demands that society is placing on organizations and which recognizes that individuals can contribute to better selection decisions. Since organizations are rapidly losing the ability to select who their members will be, research is needed on how the selection situation can be turned into more of a counseling situation so that enlightened self-selection will operate. There is evidence that when job applicants are given valid information about the job, they will make better choices. Joseph Weitz showed this long ago with insurance agents, and more recently it has been illustrated with West Point cadets and telephone operators.[22] In the future, the most effective selection programs will have to emphasize providing individuals with valid data about themselves and about the nature of the organization. After this information is presented to the applicants, they will make the decision of whether to join the organization. Before this kind of "selection" system can be put into effect, however, much research is needed to determine how this process can be handled. We need to know, for example, what kind of information should be presented to individuals and how it should be presented. However, the problems involved in the approach are solvable and, given the current trends in society, this approach represents the most viable selection approach in many situations.

## CONCLUSIONS

The research on reward systems, job design, leadership, selection, and training shows that significant individual differences exist in how individuals respond to organizational policies and practices. Because of this, an effective normative organization theory has to suggest an organization design that will treat individuals differently. Existing normative theories usually fail to emphasize this point. There are, however, a number of things that organizations can do now to deal with individual differences. These include cafeteria-style pay plans and selective job enrichment. Unfortunately, a fully developed practical organization theory based upon an individual difference approach cannot be yet stated. Still, it is important to note that approaches to shaping organizations to individuals are developing. It seems logical, therefore, to identify these and other similar efforts as attempts to individualize organizations. It is hoped that the identification of these efforts and the establishment of the concept of individualization will lead to two very important developments: the generation of more practices that will individualize organizations and work on how these different practices can simultaneously be made operational in organizations. Only if these developments take place will individualized organizations ever be created.

## NOTES

1. John J. Morse, "A Contingency Look at Job Design," *California Management Review,* Fall 1973, pp. 67–75.
2. Douglas McGregor, *The Human Side of Enterprise* (New York: McGraw-Hill, 1960).
3. Frederick Herzberg, *Work and the Nature of Man* (Cleveland: World, 1966).
4. Robert Blauner, *Alienation and Freedom* (Chicago: University of Chicago Press, 1964); and Edward E. Lawler, "Job Design and Employee Motivation," *Personnel Psychology* 22 (1969), pp. 426–35.

5. Arthur Turner and Paul R. Lawrence, *Industrial Jobs and the Worker* (Boston: Harvard University School of Business Administration, 1965); and Charles L. Hulin and Milton R. Blood, "Job Enlargement, Individual Differences, and Worker Responses," *Psychological Bulletin* 69 (1968), pp. 41–55.
6. J. Richard Hackman and Edward E. Lawler, "Employee Reactions to Job Characteristics," *Journal of Applied Psychology* 55 (1971), pp. 259–86.
7. John J. Morse, "A Contingency Look at Job Design."
8. Edward E. Lawler, *Pay and Organizational Effectiveness: A Psychological View* (New York: McGraw-Hill, 1971).
9. William F. Whyte, *Money and Motivation* (New York: Harper & Row, 1955).
10. Edward E. Lawler, *Pay and Organizational Effectiveness: A Psychological View.*
11. Stanley Nealy, "Pay and Benefit Preferences," *Industrial Relations* 3 (1963), pp. 17–28.
12. Chris Argyris, "Personality and Organization Revisited," *Administrative Science Quarterly* 18 (1973), pp. 141–67.
13. Victor H. Vroom, *Some Personality Determinants of the Effects of Participation* (Englewood Cliffs, N.J.: Prentice-Hall, 1960).
14. John R. P. French, J. Israel, and Dagfin As, "An Experiment on Participation in a Norwegian Factory," *Human Relations* 13 (1960), pp. 3–19; and George Strauss, "Some Notes on Power-Equalization," in *The Social Science of Organizations,* ed. H. J. Leavitt. (Englewood Cliffs, N.J.: Prentice-Hall, 1963).
15. Frederick E. Fiedler, "Predicting the Effects of Leadership Training and Experience from the Contingency Model," *Journal of Applied Psychology* 56 (1972), pp. 114–19.
16. John P. Campbell and Marvin D. Dunnette, "Effectiveness of T-Group Experiences in Managerial Training and Development," *Psychological Bulletin* 70 (1968), pp. 73–104.
17. Edwin E. Ghiselli, "Moderating Effects and Differential Reliability and Validity," *Journal of Applied Psychology* 47 (1963), pp. 81–86.
18. Robert M. Guion, *Personnel Testing* (New York: McGraw-Hill, 1965).
19. Joan Woodward, *Industrial Organization: Theory and Practice* (London: Oxford University Press, 1965); Paul R. Lawrence and Jay W. Lorsch, *Organization and Environment* (Boston: Division of Research, Graduate School of Business Administration, Harvard University, 1967); Chris Argyris, *Integrating the Individual and the Organization* (New York: John Wiley & Sons, 1964); and Tom Burns and G. M. Stalker, *The Management of Innovation* (London: Tavistock Publications Limited, 1961).
20. Robert Kuhn, "The Work Module—A Tonic for Lunchpail Lassitude," *Psychology Today* 6 (1973), pp. 94–95.
21. Victor Vroom, *Work and Motivation* (New York: John Wiley & Sons, 1964).
22. Joseph Weitz, "Job Expectancy and Survival," *Journal of Applied Psychology* 40 (1956), pp. 245–47; and John P. Wanous, "Effect of a Realistic Job Preview on Job Acceptance, Job Survival and Job Attitudes," *Journal of Applied Psychology,* in press.

# 18

# Role Conflict and Ambiguity in Organizations

## Robert L. Kahn

*Each individual organizational member has numerous roles to play. These roles, the relationships between and among them, and, particularly, the conflict that can result from them, is the focus of this article. The dynamics of several different types of role conflict are discussed in the context of what the authors call role episodes.—Eds.*

Our studies of role conflict and ambiguity in industry are among a number of researches which share a common and distant goal: to make understandable the effects of the contemporary environment on the person including his physical and mental health. We begin by thinking of the environment of any individual as consisting very largely of formal organizations and groups. From this point of view the life of the person can be seen as an array of roles which he plays in the particular set of organizations and groups to which he belongs. These groups and organizations, or rather the subparts of each which affect the person directly, together make up his objective environment. Characteristics of these organizations and groups (company, union, church, family, and others) affect the physical and emotional state of the person and are major determinants of his behavior.

The first requirement for linking the individual and the organization is to locate the individual in the total set of ongoing relationships and behaviors comprised by the organization. The key concept for doing this is office, by which we mean a unique point in organizational space, where space is defined in terms of a structure of interrelated offices and the pattern of activities associated with them. Associated with

SOURCE: Reprinted with permission from *The Personnel Administrator* 9 (March–April 1964), pp. 8–13.

each office is a set of activities or potential behaviors. These activities constitute the role to be performed by any person who occupies that office. Each office in an organization is directly related to certain others, less directly to still others, and, perhaps only remotely to the remaining offices included in the organization. Consider the office of press foreman in a factory manufacturing external trim parts for automobiles. The offices most directly related to that of press foreman might include general foreman and superintendent, from which press foreman's work assignments emanate and to which he turns for approval of work done. Also directly related to the office of press foreman will be the foreman of the sheet metal shop, which provides stock for the presses, the inspector who must pass or reject the completed stampings, the shipping foreman who receives and packages the stampings, and, of course, the 14 press operators for whose work press foreman is responsible. We can imagine the organizational chart spread before us like a vast fish net, in which each knot represents an office and each string a functional relationship between offices. If we pick up the net by seizing any office, we see immediately the other offices to which it is directly attached. Thus, when we pick the office of press foreman, we find it attached directly to 19 others—general foreman, superintendent, sheet metal foreman, inspector, shipping room foreman, and 14 press operators. These 19 offices make up the role set for the office of press foreman.

In similar fashion each member of an organization is directly associated with a relatively small number of others, usually the occupants of offices adjacent to his in the work flow structure. They constitute his role set and usually include his immediate supervisor (and perhaps his supervisor's direct superior), his immediate subordinates, and certain members of his own and other departments with whom he must work closely. These offices are defined into his role set by virtue of his work flow, technology, and authority structure of the organization. Also included in a person's role set may be people who are related to him in other ways—close friends, respected "identification models," and others within or outside the organization who for one reason or another are concerned with his behavior in his organization role. (Figure 1.)

All members of a person's role set depend upon his performance in some fashion; they are rewarded by it, or they require it in order to perform their own tasks. Because they have a stake in his performance, they develop beliefs and attitudes about what he should and should not do as his role. These preferences, which we will refer to as role expectations, are by no means restricted to the job description as it might be given by the head of the organization or prepared by some specialist in personnel.

For each person in an organization, then, there is a pattern of role expectations which exists in the minds of members of his role

**FIGURE 1**    Focal Person and Role Set

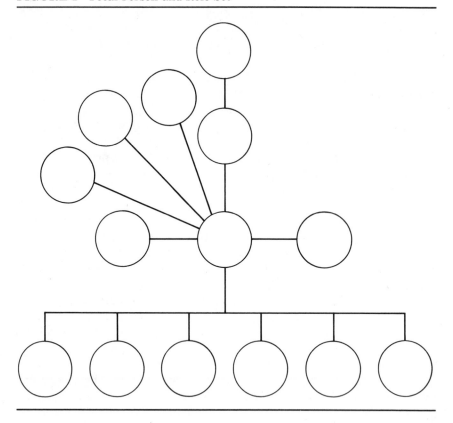

set, and represent standards in terms of which they evaluate his performance. The expectations do not remain in the minds of members of the role set, however. They are communicated in many ways— sometimes directly, as when a supervisor instructs a subordinate in the requirements of his job; sometimes indirectly, as when a colleague expresses admiration or disappointment in some behavior. The crucial point is that the activities which define a role consist of the expectations of members of the role set, and that these expectations are communicated or sent to the focal person (the person occupying the role being studied).

It is apparent from the approach to social role described above that various members of the role set for a given office may hold quite different role expectations toward the focal person. At any given time, they may impose pressures on him toward different kinds of behavior. To the extent that these role pressures are felt by him, he experiences psychological conflict. In the objective sense, then, role conflict may be defined as the simultaneous occurrence of two or more sets of pressures such that compliance with one would make more difficult or render impossible compliance with the other. For example, a person's superior may make it clear to him that he is expected to hold his subordinates strictly to company rules and to high production schedules. At the same time, his subordinates may indicate in various ways that they would like loose, relaxed supervision, and that they will make things difficult if they are pushed too hard. The pressures from above and below in this case are incompatible, since the style of supervision which satisfies one set of pressures violates the other set. Cases of this kind are so common that a whole literature has been created on the problem of the first line supervisor as the man in the middle, or the master and victim of double-talk.

Several types of role conflict can be identified. One might be termed intra-sender conflict: different prescriptions and proscriptions from a given member of the role set may be incompatible, as for example when a supervisor requests a man to acquire material which is unavailable through normal channels and at the same time prohibits violations of normal channels.

A second type might be termed inter-sender conflict: pressures from one role sender oppose pressures from another sender. The pressures for close versus loose supervisory styles cited above constitute an example of this type of conflict.

A third type of conflict we refer to as inter-role conflict. In this case the role pressure is associated with membership in one organization and in conflict with pressures which stem from membership in other groups. For example, demands on the job for overtime or take-home work may conflict with pressures from one's wife to give undivided attention to family affairs during evening hours. The conflict arises between the role of the person as worker and his role as husband and father.

All three of these types of role conflict begin in the objective environment although they will regularly result in psychological conflicts for the focal person. Other types of conflict, however, are generated directly by a combination of environmental pressures and internal forces. A major example is the conflict which may exist between the needs and values of a person and the demands of others in his role set. This fourth type of conflict we will call person-role conflict. It can occur when role requirements violate moral values—for example, when pressures on an executive to enter price fixing conspiracies are opposed by his personal code of ethics. In other cases a person's needs and aspirations may lead to behaviors which are unacceptable to members of his role set; for example, an ambitious young man may be called up short by his associates for stepping on their toes while trying to advance in the organization.

All the types of role conflict discussed above have in common one major characteristic—members of a role set exerting pressure to change the behavior of a focal person. When such pressures are generated and sent, they do not enter an otherwise empty field; the focal person is already in role, already behaving, already maintaining some kind of equilibrium among the disparate forces and motives which he experiences. Pressures to change, therefore, represent new and additional forces with which he must cope; by definition they threaten an existing equilibrium. Moreover, the stronger the pressures from role senders toward change in the behavior of the focal person, the greater the conflict created for him.

This approach to the understanding of behavior in organizations in general and the understanding of role conflict in particular is summarized in Figure 2 which illustrates a role episode: that is, a complete cycle of role sending, response by the focal person, and the effects of that response on the role senders.

The four boxes in Figure 2 represent events that constitute a role episode. The arrows connecting them imply a causal sequence. Role pressures are assumed to originate in the expectations held by members of the role set. Role senders have expectations regarding the way in which the focal role should be performed. They also have perceptions regarding the way in which the focal person is actually performing. They correlate the two, and exert pressures to make his performance congruent with their expectations. These pressures induce in the focal person an experience which has both perceptual and cognitive properties, and which leads in turn to certain adjustive (or maladjustive) responses. The responses of the focal person are typically perceived by those exerting the pressures, and their expectations are correspondingly adjusted. Thus, for both the role senders and the focal person the

**FIGURE 2**    A Model of the Role Episode

| Role Senders | | Focal Person | |
|---|---|---|---|
| Experience | Response | Experience | Response |
| Role expectations; perception of focal person's behavior; evaluations. | Role pressures; objective role conflict; objective ambiguity. | Psychological conflict; experienced ambiguity; perception of role and role senders. | Coping efforts; compliance; symptom formation. |
| I | II | III | IV |

episode involves experience and the response to experience. Let us look in more detail at the contents of the four boxes in Figure 2 and at the relations among them.

A role episode starts with the existence of a set of role expectations held by other persons about a focal person and his behavior on the job. Speaking of the members of a person's role set as a group is a matter of convenience. In fact, each member of the role set behaves toward the focal person in ways determined by his own expectations and his own anticipations of the focal person's responses. Under certain circumstances a member of the role set, responding to his own immediate experience, expresses his expectations overtly; he attempts to influence the focal person in the direction of greater conformity with his expectations. Arrow 1 indicates that the total set of such influence attempts affects the immediate experience of the focal person in a given situation (Box III in Figure 2). This experience includes for example the focal person's perception of the demands and requirements placed on him by members of his role set, and his awareness or experience of psychological conflict. The specific reactions of each focal person to a situation are immediately determined by the nature of his experience in that situation. Any person who is confronted with a situation of role conflict, however, must respond to it in some fashion. One or more members of his role set are exerting pressure on him to change his behavior, and he must cope somehow with the pressure they are exerting. Whatever pattern of response he adopts may be regarded as an attempt to attain or regain an adequately gratifying experience in the work situation. He may attempt a direct solution of the objective problem by compliance or by persuading others to modify their incompatible demands. He may attempt to avoid the sources of stress, perhaps by using defense mechanisms which distort the reality of a conflictful or ambiguous situation. There is also the possibility that coping with the pressures of the work will involve the formation of affective or physiological symptoms. Regardless of which of these, singly or in combination, the focal person uses, his behavior can be assessed in relation to the expectations of each of his role senders.

The degree to which the focal person's behavior conforms to the expectations held for him will affect the state of those expectations at the next moment. If his response is essentially a hostile counter-attack, members of his role set are apt to think of him and behave toward him in ways quite different than if he were submissively compliant. If he complies partially under pressure they may increase the pressure; if he is obviously overcome with tension and anxiety, they may "lay off." In some, the role episode is abstracted from a process which is cyclic and ongoing; the response of the focal person to role pressure feeds back on the senders of those pressures in ways that alter or reinforce them. The next role sendings of each member of the set depend on his evaluations of the response to his last sendings, and thus a new episode begins.

In order to understand more fully the causal dynamics of such episodes and their consequences for the person's adjustment, the model must be extended to include three additional classes of variables— organizational factors, personality factors, and the character of interpersonal relations between the focal person and other members of his role set. Taken in combination, these factors represent the context within which the episode occurs. In Figure 3 the role episode is shown in the context of these three additional classes of variables. Figure 2 forms the core of Figure 3. However, the circles in Figure 3 represent not momentary events, but enduring states of the organization, the person, and the interpersonal relations between focal person and other members of his role set. An analysis of these factors makes more understandable the sequence of events in a role episode. Figure 3 provides a convenient framework within which to summarize the major research findings obtained from an intensive study of fifty-four role sets in a

**FIGURE 3**    A Theoretical Model of Factors Involved in Adjustment to Role
Conflict and Ambiguity

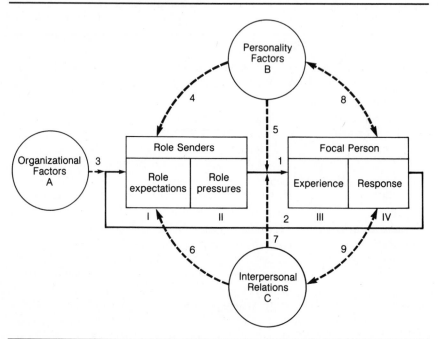

number of different industries, and from a national survey of approximately 1,500 households.

## EFFECTS OF CONFLICT AND AMBIGUITY

### Role Conflict

The experience of role conflict is common indeed in the work situation. Almost half of our respondents reported being caught "in the middle" between two conflicting persons or factions. These conflicts are usually hierarchical; 88 percent of the people involved in them report at least one party to the conflict as being above them in the organization. Somewhat less than half report that one of the conflicting parties is outside the organization. One of the dominant forms of role conflict is overload, which can be thought of as a conflict among legitimate tasks, or a problem in the setting of priorities; almost half of all respondents reported this problem.

The intensive study, in which role senders and focal persons were interviewed independently, deals more directly with the causal sequences initiated by conditions of conflict. Measures of objective conflict, as derived from the expectations of individual role senders, are strongly associated with the subjective experience of conflict, as reported by the focal person, who is target of incompatible expectations. These, in turn, are linked to affective and behavioral responses of that person.

For the focal person, the emotional costs of role conflict include low job satisfaction, low confidence in the organization, and high scores on the multi-item index of tension. The most frequent behavioral response to role conflict is withdrawal or avoidance of those who are seen as creating the conflict. Symptomatic of this is the attempt of the conflicted person to reduce communication with his co-workers and to assert (sometimes unrealistically) that they lack power over him. Case material indicates that such withdrawal, while a mechanism of defense is not a mechanism of solution. It appears to reduce the possibility of subsequent collaborative solutions to role conflict.

### Role Ambiguity

The prevalence of role ambiguity appears to be approximately comparable to that of role conflict. Four specific subjects of ambiguity are cited as disturbing and troublesome in approximately equal numbers of respondents. These include uncertainty about the way in which one's supervisor evaluates one's work, about opportunities for advancement, about scope of responsibility and about the expectations of others regarding one's performance. Each of these areas of ambiguity was mentioned by approximately one third of the respondents. In all, about two persons out of five considered that they were given insufficient information to perform their jobs adequately.

Among the major sources of role ambiguity about which we speculated were complexity of task and technology, rapidity of organizational change, interconnectedness of organizational positions, and that managerial philosophy which advocates restriction of information on the assumption that the division of labor makes broad information unnecessary for most positions.

The individual consequences of ambiguity conditions are in general comparable to the individual effects of role conflict. These include, for ambiguity: low job satisfaction, low self-confidence, a high sense of futility, and a high score on the tension index. There is evidence, however, that the response of the person to ambiguity is highly selective. For example, ambiguity regarding the evaluations of others does not decrease the intrinsic satisfaction of the employee with the job, although it does decrease his self-confidence and weaken his positive effect for co-workers.

**Determinants of Conflict and Ambiguity.**   The major organizational determinants of conflict and ambiguity include three kinds of role requirements—the requirement for crossing organizational boundaries, the requirement for producing innovative solutions to nonroutine problems, and the requirement for being responsible for the work of others (Arrow 3).

Let us consider first the requirement for crossing a company boundary. Both the frequency and the importance of making contacts outside one's company are associated with the experience of role conflict. Crossing the company boundary is associated also with experienced tension, but the relationship is curvilinear; greatest tension is experienced by those who have discontinuous contacts outside the organization. We propose the hypothesis that in positions which require extra-company contacts on a continuous basis, there are special facilities or some other organizational acknowledgment of boundary difficulties which renders them less painful.

Hypothetical explanations for the stressfulness of boundary crossing are available primarily from case materials. It appears that the person who must frequently deal with people outside the company usually has limited control over these outsiders. He cannot strongly influence their demands and the resources which they supply to him. Moreover, a person in a boundary position is likely to be blamed by people in his own company for what his outside contacts do or fail to do. They in turn may blame him for shortcomings in his own company.

The difficulties of living at the boundary of an organization are intensified when the boundary-dweller must coordinate his extra-organizational activities with people in other departments within the company.

In general, living "near" a departmental or other intra-organizational boundary has effects very like those just remarked for boundaries of the organization itself. Nearness to a departmental boundary and frequency of dealing across such boundaries are associated with felt conflict and with experienced tension.

Roles which demand creative problem solving are associated with high role conflict and with tension. The occupants of such roles appear to become engaged in conflict primarily with older and often more powerful individuals in the organization, who want to maintain the *status quo*. Among the major role conflicts which persons in innovative jobs complain of is the conflict of priority between the nonroutine activities which are at the core of the creative job and the routine activities of administration or paper work. These latter, according to the people who fill innovative positions, are unduly time consuming, disrupt the continuity of their creative work, and are generally unpalatable.

There is considerable evidence that organizations exercise selective effort in choosing people for innovative positions. People in such positions tend to be characterized by high self-confidence, high mobility aspirations, high job involvement, low apathy, and a tendency to rate the importance of a job extremely high compared to the importance of other areas of their lives.

Supervisory responsibility emerges as a major organizational determinant of role conflict. Either the supervision of rank and file employees or the supervision of people who are themselves supervisors appears to have substantial effects on the degree of objective conflict and the amount of experienced conflict. In combination, direct and indirect supervisory responsibility produce very substantial role conflict and tension. There is a systematic relationship also between rank and role conflict, as there is between rank and tension. The often heard assertion that the lowest levels of supervision are subjected to the greatest conflict is not borne out by these data. Rather, there is a curvilinear relationship in which the maximum of conflict and conflict experience occurs at what might be called the "upper middle" levels of management. We interpret this in part as a consequence of the still unfulfilled mobility aspirations of middle management, in contrast to the better actualized aspirations of top management people.

**Interpersonal Relations and Role Conflict.** The sources of pressure and conflict for a person can be expressed rather fully in terms of his interpersonal relations with these pressure sources. The greatest pressure is directed to a person from other people who are in the same department as he is, who are his superiors in the hierarchy, and who are sufficiently dependent on his performance to care about his adequacy without being so completely dependent as to be inhibited in making their demands known (Arrow 6). The people who are least likely to apply such pressures are a person's peers and role senders outside his own department.

The kinds of pressure which people are prepared to apply, as well as the degree of that pressure, vary considerably with their formal interpersonal relationship to the potential target of their pressures. Thus, supervisors seem to refrain from exerting coercive power where it might impede the performance of the focal person and perhaps reflect upon the supervisor himself. On the other hand, the techniques used by subordinates to apply coercive power are precisely those which threaten the efficiency of the organization. They include the withholding of aid and information.

When a person is surrounded by others who are highly dependent on him and who have high power over him and exert high pressure on him, his response is typically one of apathy and withdrawal (Arrow 7). Moreover, under such circumstances, his experience of role conflict is very high and his job satisfaction correspondingly reduced. Emotionally he experiences a sense of futility and attempts a hopeless withdrawal from his co-workers.

There is significant evidence that close and positive interpersonal relations between a focal person and members of his role set can mediate substantially the effects of role conflict (Arrow 7). A given degree of objective role conflict is experienced as less stressful in the context of positive affective relations with others. Nevertheless, experienced conflict and ambiguity appear to cause deterioration in interpersonal relations (Arrow 9). Thus, a consequence of role conflict is decreased trust, respect, and liking for co-workers, and in the presence of experienced ambiguity there is a similar attempt on the part of the focal person to weaken interpersonal relations. As with conflict, this weakening of interpersonal relations is self-defeating, since he finds himself withdrawing in the face of ambiguity from the very persons from whom he requires information.

**Personality Variables in Conflict and Ambiguity.** Several personality dimensions mediate significantly (Arrow 8) the degree to which a given intensity of objective conflict is experienced as strain by the focal person. These personality dimensions include emotional sensitivity, sociability, and flexibility-rigidity. With respect to sociability, we find that the effects of objective role conflict on interpersonal bonds and on tension are more pronounced for people who are unsociable (independent). The independent person, in other words, develops social relations which, while often congenial and trusting, are easily under-mined by conditions of stress. The preference of such people for auton-omy becomes manifest primarily when social contacts are stressful; that is, when others are exerting strong pressures and thereby creating conflict for the persons. In similar fashion, emotional sensitivity con-ditions very sharply the relationship between objective conflict and tension, with emotionally sensitive persons showing substantially higher tension scores for any given degree of objective conflict. There is also a tendency for people of different personality characteristics to be exposed by their senders to differing degrees of objective conflict (Arrow 4). Thus, people who are relatively flexible are subjected to stronger pressures than those who have already demonstrated by their rigidity the futility of applying such pressures.

## CONCLUSION

Much of the role conflict in industry takes the form of overload, especially in managerial positions. The focal person has more demands flooding in on him than he can possibly satisfy. He may try to deal with such pressures by exporting his work-induced tensions to outside groups, such as his family, but this a form of industrial drainage which the community can ill afford. Some persons shut off communication from others in the work situation and thus reduce their own pressures—at the same time reducing the effectiveness of the orga-nization and increasing the pressures of those people who try in vain to communicate with them.

It is not exaggeration to say that most of the responses which we have observed for coping with conflict, ambiguity, and overload are less than satisfactory for individual and for organization. It seems that more constructive resolution of pressure situations ought to be possible. For example, why should the person who experiences role conflict or ambiguity not convene the members of his role set, who have in effect created the situation which he finds stressful, so that they can make a joint attack on the problem? None of the people in the set knows the totality of the focal person's job requirements (any more than he knows theirs), but this is something he can explain to them. Each person in an organization is the ultimate expert in this single respect: He knows better than anyone else the combination of demands which are being made upon him and what their immediate sources are.

A ceremony of confrontation and joint problem solving would seem to be a useful mode of conflict resolution. Why does it not happen? Two factors may work to prevent it. The first is subjective, a feeling that such an approach is unorthodox, unlikely to work, or even downright dangerous. The second may be inherent in the structure of hierarchical organizations.

Regarding the subjective factor, it is indeed difficult to find people who are willing and able to undertake such a confrontation of superiors, subordinates, and peers. A person may have deliberately created overload, conflict, or ambiguity in order to further his own organizational ambitions or to increase his power. More often, his feelings of insecurity and embarrassment prevent him from attempting such a group solution to his problems. Regarding the organizational factor, the risks and rewards of industrial life often cause individuals to keep their information sources private and hold as much power as possible in their own hands. Confrontation under such circumstances could be viewed as a giving away of precious power and information, or even as an admission of incompetence. More frequently, perhaps, the person in conflict feels that he lacks the power to convene the members of his role set in the first place. How many people in industry can recall taking the initiative in bringing together their subordinates, supervisors, and peers to consider the incompatibilities in their various expectations?

Nevertheless, there is in many managements a growing interest in solving the human problems of large scale organizations, a growing realization that the solutions will involve structural changes as well as gains in interpersonal skills, and a growing willingness to innovate and evaluate in the effort to put organizations more fully into the service of human needs. These attitudes of management, in combination with research, offer new possibilities for understanding organized human behavior. We know of no goal more deserving of our effort.

# 19

# New Approaches in
# Management Organization
# and Job Design

*Frederick Herzberg*

*The relationship between the nature of individuals and the satisfaction
of individual's needs and the implications of this relationship on how
jobs are structured is the thrust of this selection. Herzberg suggests that
organizations will be most effective in situations where work is structured to maximize the opportunity for need satisfaction.—Eds.*

To clarify my remarks this morning, I should like to qualify, at the
beginning, many of the points that I am about to make. I must necessarily oversimplify certain positions in order to stay within allotted
time limits, and also because I wish to emphasize a particular view of
the problems of psychiatry in industry. Much that may appear icono-
clastic is meant only for the negative aspects of the position I will be
criticizing. I should like to begin by stating certain propositions regarding the goals of the American industrial enterprise.

The first two goals are traditional and provide for little or no
disagreement. The third proposition will allow, I believe, for some disagreement in either its philosophy, or its practicality or both. Let me
state them:

First, the function of any industrial or business enterprise is to
produce goods and services required or desired by the society of which
it is a part. No argument here. Second, the business should make a
profit if for no other reason than to insure its survival. Again, there

SOURCE: Reprinted by permission of the author from the *Journal of Industrial Medicine*,
November 1962.

is no conflict. Third, the business organization, or any organization for that matter, should provide a meaningful existence for its employees during the process of producing the goods and services and maintaining its integrity. If industry is an institution to serve society, then surely its provision of the material needs of the people should not be at the cost of denying its members the psychological income that should come from work. That it has been so is abundantly clear. That this is a tragedy is not so clear to many.

Two recent studies are relevant to this last point. In the large epidemiological survey sponsored by the Joint Commission on Mental Health and reported in *Americans View Their Mental Health,* it was discovered that tensions related to jobs are credited by the persons surveyed as the second major source for bringing them to the verge of a "nervous" breakdown. This is hardly a favorable commentary on the world of work.

In another recent study by Arthur Kornhauser of Wayne University, mental health scores of workers in the Detroit area show a strong and ominous relationship with the skill level of the jobs performed. It is the skill required by the jobs, and not other factors associated with the type of persons in the various echelons of job hierarchy, that Kornhauser claims to be the crucial factor from the analysis of his data. Only 16 percent of middle aged workers doing repetitive semiskilled jobs showed "high" mental scores. This percentage dropped to a minuscule 7 percent for those classified in the "young" age bracket.

The student of social history and the perceptive observer of the industrial scene require little in the way of experimental proof to affirm what is so apparent—the jobs most people do are not a rich source for psychological health and, in fact, they may often best be classified as mental health hazards.

## CONCEPTS OF THE WORKER

Every society develops myths to sustain its institutional forms. Paramount among these myths are those dealing with human nature. Just as each of us has beliefs about what makes people tick that satisfy our own wishes, so do institutions define the needs and nature of men to suit their own desires. Let us look at what the industrial institution has variously served up as the psychology of man.

### The Economic Man

The economic man arose out of the dominant myths of the Industrial Revolution and the larger myths of the Protestant ethic. Business is religion and religion is business became the dominant theme of the rise of the modern business system. Making money was a prominent sign of religious virtue and the motivation to succeed in making money was the true reflection of natural and supernatural man. This religious justification for the social and human evils of the revolution was buttressed by the pseudoscientism of the social Darwin doctrine which suggested that the economically successful were the survival of the fittest in an inexorable law of competition. The worker was inferior from both a scientific evolutionary point of view as well as from an ethical religious point of view—a happy and expedient view of man to justify conditions wrought by the factory system. Humanitarian efforts, largely dictated by the fear of radicalism, were sufficient as a philosophy of employee relations, particularly when various economic incentives were added to complete the carrot and the stick by stimulating the supposed rawest motivational nerve of all—the desire for money.

### The Social Man

The social man got his clearest definition and boost from the work of Elton Mayo, F. Roethlisberger, et al. The interpretation of the Hawthorne studies that the overriding need of the worker was to be accepted by his fellow employee fitted in perfectly with the growth of scientific management, industrial engineering, and the consequent rationalization of jobs. Since the myth of the Horatio Alger story of the Protestant ethic no longer had pragmatic validity and since the work required by industry became more suited for the feebleminded, what more useful concept of man than as a seeker of acceptance by people? His work contribution was relegated to an unreliable and interchangeable part of the work process, but he didn't mind as long as you paid him and offered him an opportunity to belong to informal work groups. Welfare capitalism combined with the newer science of group dynamics for a more complete view of employee relations.

### The Emotional Man

While Sigmund Freud did not discover emotional man, he certainly defined him. Man is determined and is a victim of biological urges and childhood frustrations of these urges. Man is not really responsible for his irrational behavior, and in fact his behavior is not really irrational. Understanding and dealing with man as a victim of emotions precipitated the modern emphasis on human relations programs at all job levels and at all levels of sophistication. This concept fitted in nicely with the burgeoning bureaucracies that developed to manage the huge production plants that emerged. How to manage a rank and file of managers became a problem, particularly when the industrial engineering principles of job rationalization and restriction of individual variability and responsibility were adopted for the utilization of managerial manpower. These principles found their expression by the bureaucratic techniques of policies, rules, regulations, committees, and organizational theory. Just as the assembly line reduces the effect of the industrial worker at the production line, so do the bureaucratic techniques reduce the effect of the manager at the office. Denigrating the potentiality of the worker calls for scientific handling of the resulting partial man. Human relations becomes a means of avoiding the unpleasantness arising from the use of the adult as a child on the job. What is cause and effect here? Is the employee acting as a child because the circumstances force this kind of behavior or, as assumed by the "emotional" school, are the circumstances forced by the emotional nature of man? My thesis is the former explanation.

The economic man, the social man, and the emotional man today have been combined, with each representing one aspect of the total. This definition parallels the weird assortment of premises and practices of contemporary industrial relations. We have developed from experience and research a plethora of facts, principles, and, in many instances, workable techniques with which to deal more effectively with people on the job.

## SATISFYING WORKERS' NEEDS

How to handle the economic motive has given rise to an unimaginable array of wage, salary, bonus, and benefit programs of such intricacy that an interdisciplinary team of lawyers, economists, financiers, physicians, sociologists, psychologists, and welfarists are involved in their creation, planning, and administration. Research on this aspect of man is mainly at the level of new models of economic prizes, reminiscent of the frantic efforts of the give-away shows to tantalize the audience with exotic variations of payoffs. Recently the personnel director of a local restaurant chain advertised his intention to stay awake nights to think up new variations of benefits to motivate his automaton employees.

The social needs of man have given rise to some of our most ingenious and in some cases fruitful research in industry. The problems of leadership, supervision, organizational structure, group functioning, and other social psychological issues have multiplied both our scientific and applied literature beyond anything that could be imagined a few years ago. Unfortunately, the value of this work has been tarnished by some of the evangelical zeal of its proponents, but it is of significance, because of the premise that man is essentially a social animal primarily in search of social gratification. It has already defined the form of social criticism for this era in the writings of David Reisman and his attack on the Lonely Crowd and William H. Whyte's attack on the Organization Man. Nevertheless, there is a gold mine to be worked in this research for improving personnel relations, organizational efficiency, and human happiness.

Closely allied with the work being done on the social psychology of industry has been the emphasis on understanding the role played by personal adjustment on the effectiveness of our industrial concerns. The clinical insights of psychiatry and psychology have become germane to the problems of people at work. The implementation of clinical psychiatry and psychology to industry has found expression ranging from the crude and often obnoxious misuse of personality assessment for hiring and promoting, through some of the naive psychology programs in supervisory training, to the more sophisticated managerial programs such as the one at the Menninger Foundation and the current wave of group therapy in sensitivity programs. Personal counseling initiated as a product of the original Hawthorne studies has never crystallized as a promised land of psychological amelioration in our companies. It is perhaps too early to forecast the impact that these newer uses of clinical psychiatry and psychology will have, but I believe its effectiveness will be limited by the view of emotionally sick man carried over from the pathological settings where the clinician is trained. This has often led to the embarrassing necessity of labelling effective behaviors by negative terms: the well-adjusted man who earns a million dollars is overcompensating; the star football guard is a masochist relieving an Oedipus complex.

Perhaps the greatest contribution that the behavioral sciences have made during the last half century of research on the industrial scene has been to broaden the concept of the needs and nature of man from a solely determined economic organism to one that encompasses some of the more human aspects—the emotional and social needs.

However, I do not believe that we have yet developed a complete picture. It has been only recently that the truly human needs of man have emerged in the research and writings of the behavioral scientists. I refer to such men as Maslow with his emphasis on the higher actualizing needs, McGregor in the *Human Side of Enterprise*, Argyris in the conflict of *Human Personality and Organizations*, and, hopefully, myself in the *Motivation to Work*.

I should like now to concentrate on a view of man that I believe is emerging and challenging our concepts of managing men. To begin, I will briefly review certain concepts derived from research on job motivation and reported in the book just mentioned, *The Motivation to Work*, and in other journal publications.

## FACTORS INFLUENCING JOB SATISFACTION

The implication of this research for job design and organizational structure I believe are important although difficult to conceive and implement. But a lack of proved hardware should not lead to an alternative understanding of the problems, which may have techniques but violates reality.

Essentially the initial study consisted of interviewing engineers and accountants representing a fair cross-section of Pittsburgh industry, on events that they had experienced on jobs that resulted in either a marked improvement in their job satisfaction or a marked reduction in their job satisfaction.

Figure 1 shows the major findings of this study. The factors listed in this figure are a kind of shorthand for summarizing the "objective" events that each respondent described. The length of each box represents the frequency with which each factor appeared in the events presented, and the width of the box indicates the duration of time the good or bad job attitude lasted, in terms of a classification of short duration and long duration. A short duration was usually not longer than two weeks while a long duration attitude change may have lasted for years.

Five factors stand out as high determiners of job satisfaction: achievement, recognition, work itself, responsibility, and advancement; with the last three of greater importance for lasting change of attitudes. These five factors appeared very infrequently when the respondents described events that paralleled job dissatisfaction feelings. A further word on recognition. When it appeared in a "high" sequence of events, it referred to recognition for a task rather than recognition as a human relations tool divorced from any accomplishment. The latter type of recognition does not serve as a "satisfier."

When we coded the factors involved in the job dissatisfaction events, an entirely different set of factors evolved. These factors were similar to the "satisfiers" in their unidimensional effect. This time, however, they served only to bring about job dissatisfaction and were rarely involved in events which led to positive job attitudes. Also contrary to the "satisfiers," the "dissatisfiers" consistently produced short-term job attitude changes.

There is a fundamental distinction between the "satisfiers" and the "dissatisfiers." The "satisfiers" all refer to the job content or job task: achievement of a task, recognition for task achievement, nature of the task, responsibility for the task, and professional growth or advancement in task capability. In contrast, the "dissatisfiers" refer to the job context or job environment: the nature of the company's policies and administrative practices under which the job is performed, the

**FIGURE 1**   Comparison of Satisfiers and Dissatisfiers

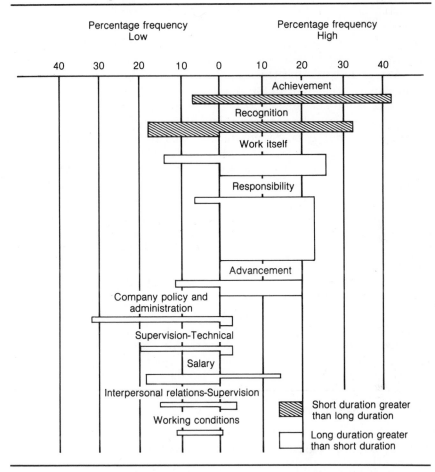

type of supervision received when doing the job, the quality of the working conditions in which the job is done, and the salary received for doing the job. Another factor that belongs on the "dissatisfiers" list and not shown in the figure, is status. Again this popular factor defines the job context.

Since the "dissatisfier" factors describe essentially the environment and serve primarily to prevent job satisfaction while having little effect on positive job attitudes, they have been named the hygiene factors, in analogy with the medical use of this term as preventative and environmental. The "satisfier" factors were named the "motivators," since other findings of the study suggest that they are effective in motivating the individual to superior performance and effort.

So far, I have reported on that part of the interview that was restricted to determining the actual objective events as reported by our respondents. We also asked them to interpret the events for us; that is to tell us why the particular event led to a change in their feelings about their jobs. The principal result of the analysis of this data was to suggest that the hygiene events led to job dissatisfaction because of a "need" to avoid unpleasantness; the motivator events led to job satisfaction because of a "need" for growth or self-actualization. At the psychological level the two dimensions of job attitudes reflected a two dimensional "need" structure: one need system for avoidance and a parallel need system for personal growth.

In summary, there are two essential findings from this study. First, the factors which make people happy on the job are not the *same* factors that make people unhappy on the job. The distinguishing characteristic of these two sets of factors is whether they describe the job content or the job context. Second, the effects of hygiene factors on job attitudes are of a relatively short duration in contrast with the motivator factors which, three of them at least, have long lasting attitude effects.

A number of studies have subsequently been completed on a variety of different populations and with significant alterations in methods which suggest that the motivation-hygiene concept has a considerable degree of general validity.

The two sets of factors emerge with Air Force personnel, nonsupervisory employees in the auto industry, general managers, schizophrenic patients, and physical rehabilitation patients. Age, job tenure, place of work, and other demographic variables show no substantial effect on these relationships.

## EMPHASIS ON SELF-ACTUALIZATION

The importance of two distinct sets of factors to research in job satisfaction can hardly be overestimated. Traditional research in job attitudes has consistently emphasized the betterment of surrounding conditions, largely neglecting the self-actualizing factors. The self-actualizing need of man is certainly not new; Jung wrote eloquently of this need. Freud observing the Moses of Michelangelo was moved to write ". . . so that the giant frame with its tremendous physical power becomes only a concrete expression of the highest mental achievement that is possible in man, that of struggling against an inward passion for the sake of a cause to which he had devoted himself." The achievement and growth motives appear throughout our literature and experience. Why, then, has it not become a guiding principle in our employee relations philosophy? Briefly I offer these reasons.

First, it has, but mostly in a cultural noise manner. It is something to be talked about but not really implemented.

Second, it has been warped by what is now called in our national science the new wave of conservatism. Self-actualization and individual freedom come out as a fight against Social Security deductions to provide medical care for our aged. Hygiene is the battleground for apostles of individual integrity. They use the language of the motivators but they do not comprehend its significance.

Third, the investment in the hardware or hygiene is too great and the number of people involved in the perpetuation too many, to relegate hygiene programs to their proper place as only maintenance needs of employees.

Fourth, and most important, we have decided that we cannot economically afford to make jobs meaningful in the sense that I have asked.

What should we do?

First, we need a new kind of therapy program. The traditional therapies are directed to the avoidance needs of man, the anxiety, the psychological pain of emotional conflict. We need, in addition, a therapy program to orient people to the satisfaction of individual accomplishment. Psychological growth does not simply unleash when we remove some discomfort.

Second, we need to reverse the philosophy of employee relations, as primarily oriented to hygiene with such motivator programs as management development merely tacked on, and put the development of man as the basic philosophy with the hygiene programs subsumed under them.

Third, we must recognize that our greatest mental health challenge is to provide jobs that have meaning. Specifically, this calls for research on job enlargement, and not the meaningless stringing of snippets of tasks that have often been defined as job enlargement. We have to go back to the traditional concepts of matching talent to the job, good, old fashioned classification of people. At the organizational level, we need to increase its variability. Line staff relations, span of control, all organizational theory has to be re-looked at, not so much to increase the hygiene effectiveness of the organization, but to increase individual responsibility and individual psychological income from jobs. We need a fluid structure to match achievement needs of people.

I would like to suggest the concept of the collateral organization; that is, every organization should be able to provide jobs beyond the usual organizational structure for creativity when individuals on jobs no longer are being challenged. If we sent out 100 collaterals and only one man is creative, it will pay for the other 99.

I have attempted here briefly to provide ingredients, not the recipe. Perhaps as part of this conference the recipe might be forthcoming.

# PART FOUR

# Managing Group Behavior

Groups form because of managerial action, but also because of individual efforts. An organization has technical requirements that arise from its stated goals. The accomplishment of these goals requires that certain tasks be performed and that employees be assigned to perform these tasks. As a result, most employees will be members of a group based on their position in the organization. Groups such as these, created by managerial decisions, are termed *formal* groups.

However, groups also form as a consequence of employees' actions. Such groups, termed *informal* groups, develop around common interests and friendships. Informal groups are natural groupings of people in the work situation in response to social needs. In other words, informal groups do not arise as a result of deliberate design but rather evolve naturally. Though not sanctioned by management, groups of this kind can most definitely affect organizational and individual performance.

Group behavior is more than simply the sum of the behavior of the individuals who comprise the group. The nature of groups is such that they exhibit behaviors which are a function of certain characteristics common to all groups. These characteristics include norms (generally agreed-upon standards of behavior for group members), cohesiveness (the field of forces operating to maintain group membership), roles (the position played by group members), and social control (the mechanisms employed by the group to insure member conformance with group norms.

For a manager to disregard or to underestimate the influence potential of groups in organizational settings is to seriously limit his or her effectiveness as a manager. Increasingly, the concern shown in recent years by United States corporations in the areas of quantity and quality of production are focusing on *group* factors. Quality circles, to use just one example, not only use groups (rather than individuals) as their basic building block for performance improvement but also deliberately attempt to strengthen group cohesion and identity precisely because of the recognition that groups are potent determinants of managerial and organizational success.

# 20

# The Development and Enforcement of Group Norms

*Daniel C. Feldman*

*Why group norms are enforced and how such norms develop are the focus of this article. The author suggests that groups will bring under normative control those behaviors that ensure group survival, increase the predictability of member behavior, or give expression to the central values of the group. The development of norms is the result of explicit statements by group members, past events, or primacy.—Eds.*

Group norms are the informal rules that groups adopt to regulate and regularize group members' behavior. Although these norms are infrequently written down or openly discussed, they often have a powerful, and consistent, influence on group members' behavior (Hackman, 1976).

Most of the theoretical work on group norms has focused on identifying the types of group norms (March, 1954) or on describing their structural characteristics (Jackson, 1966). Empirically, most of the focus has been on examining the impact that norms have on other social phenomena. For example, Seashore (1954) and Schachter, Ellertson, McBride, and Gregory (1951) use the concept of group norms to discuss group cohesiveness; Trist and Bamforth (1951) and Whyte (1955a) use norms to examine production restriction; Janis (1972) and Longley and Pruitt (1980) use norms to illuminate group decision making; and Asch (1951) and Sherif (1936) use norms to examine conformity.

This paper focuses on two frequently overlooked aspects of the group norms literature. First, it examines *why* group norms are enforced. Why do groups desire conformity to these informal rules? Sec-

SOURCE: Reprinted with permission from the publisher from "The Development and Enforcement of Group Norms," *Academy of Management Review,* January 1984, pp. 47–53.

ond, it examines *how* group norms develop. Why do some norms develop in one group but not in another? Much of what is known about group norms comes from post hoc examination of their impact on outcome variables; much less has been written about how these norms actually develop and why they regulate behavior so strongly.

Understanding how group norms develop and why they are enforced is important for two reasons. First, group norms can play a large role in determining whether the group will be productive or not. If the work group feels that management is supportive, groups norms will develop that facilitate—in fact, enhance—group productivity. In contrast, if the work group feels that management is antagonistic, group norms that inhibit and impair group performance are much more likely to develop. Second, managers can play a major role in setting and changing group norms. They can use their influence to set task-facilitative norms; they can monitor whether the group's norms are functional; they can explicitly address counterproductive norms with subordinates. By understanding how norms develop and why norms are enforced, managers can better diagnose the underlying tensions and problems their groups are facing, and they can help the group develop more effective behavior patterns.

## WHY NORMS ARE ENFORCED

As Shaw (1981) suggests, a group does not establish or enforce norms about every conceivable situation. Norms are formed and enforced only with respect to behaviors that have some significance for the group. The frequent distinction between task maintenance duties and social maintenance duties helps explain why groups bring selected behaviors under normative control.

Groups, like individuals, try to operate in such a way that they maximize their chances for task success and minimize their chances of task failure. First of all, a group will enforce norms that facilitate its very survival. It will try to protect itself from interference from groups external to the organization or harassment from groups internal to the organization. Second, the group will want to increase the predictability of group members' behaviors. Norms provide a basis for predicting the behavior of others, thus enabling group members to anticipate each other's actions and to prepare quick and appropriate responses (Shaw, 1981; Kiesler and Kiesler, 1970).

In addition, groups want to ensure the satisfaction of their members and prevent as much interpersonal discomfort as possible. Thus, groups also will enforce norms that help the group avoid embarrassing interpersonal problems. Certain topics of conversation might be sanctioned, and certain types of social interaction might be openly discouraged. Moreover, norms serve an expressive function for groups

(Katz and Kahn, 1978). Enforcing group norms gives group members a chance to express what their central values are, and to clarify what is distinctive about the group and central to its identity (Hackman, 1976).

Each of these four conditions under which group norms are most likely to be enforced is discussed in more detail below.

(1) *Norms are likely to be enforced if they facilitate group survival.* A group will enforce norms that protect it from interference or harassment by members of other groups. For instance, a group might develop a norm not to discuss its salaries with members of other groups in the organization, so that attention will not be brought to pay inequities in its favor. Groups might also have norms about not discussing internal problems with members of other units. Such discussions might boomerang at a later date if other groups use the information to develop a better competitive strategy against the group.

Enforcing group norms also makes clear what the "boundaries" of the group are. As a result of observation of deviant behavior and the consequences that ensue, other group members are reminded of the *range* of behavior that is acceptable to the group (Dentler and Erikson, 1959). The norms about productivity that frequently develop among piecerate workers are illustrative here. By observing a series of incidents (a person produces 50 widgets and is praised; a person produces 60 widgets and receives sharp teasing; a person produces 70 widgets and is ostracized), group members learn the limits of the group's patience: "This far, and no further." The group is less likely to be "successful" (i.e., continue to sustain the low productivity expectations of management) if it allows its jobs to be reevaluated.

The literature on conformity and deviance is consistent with this observation. The group is more likely to reject the person who violates group norms when the deviant has not been a "good" group member previously (Hollander, 1958, 1964). Individuals can generate "idiosyncrasy credits" with other group members by contributing effectively to the attainment of group goals. Individuals expend these credits when they perform poorly or dysfunctionally at work. When a group member no longer has a positive "balance" of credits to draw on when he or she deviates, the group is much more likely to reject that deviant (Hollander, 1961).

Moreover, the group is more likely to reject the deviant when the group is failing in meeting its goals successfully. When the group is successful it can afford to be charitable or tolerant towards deviant behavior. The group may disapprove, but it has some margin for error. When the group is faced with failure, the deviance is much more sharply punished. Any behavior that negatively influences the success of the group becomes much more salient and threatening to group members (Alvarez, 1968; Wiggins, Dill, and Schwartz, 1965).

(2) *Norms are likely to be enforced if they simplify, or make predictable, what behavior is expected of group members.* If each member of the group had to decide individually how to behave in each interaction, much time would be lost performing routine activities. Moreover, individuals would have more trouble predicting the behaviors of others and responding correctly. Norms enable group members to anticipate each other's actions and to prepare the most appropriate response in the most timely manner (Hackman, 1976; Shaw, 1981).

For instance, when attending group meetings in which proposals are presented and suggestions are requested, do the presenters really want feedback or are they simply going through the motions? Groups may develop norms that reduce this uncertainty and provide a clearer course of action, for example, make suggestions in small, informal meetings but not in large, formal meetings.

Another example comes from norms that regulate social behavior. For instance, when colleagues go out for lunch together, there can be some awkwardness about how to split the bill at the end of the meal. A group may develop a norm that gives some highly predictable or simple way of behaving, for example, split evenly, take turns picking up the tab, or pay for what each ordered.

Norms also may reinforce specific individual members' roles. A number of different roles might emerge in groups. These roles are simply expectations that are shared by group members regarding who is to carry out what types of activities under what circumstances (Bales and Slater, 1955). Although groups obviously create pressure toward uniformity among members, there also is a tendency for groups to create and maintain *diversity* among members (Hackman, 1976). For instance, a group might have one person whom others expect to break the tension when tempers become too hot. Another group member might be expected to keep track of what is going on in other parts of the organization. A third member might be expected to take care of the "creature" needs of the group—making the coffee, making dinner reservations, and so on. A fourth member might be expected by others to take notes, keep minutes, or maintain files.

None of these roles are *formal* duties, but they are activities that the group needs accomplished and has somehow parcelled out among members. If the role expectations are not met, some important jobs might not get done, or other group members might have to take on additional responsibilities. Moreover, such role assignments reduce individual members' ambiguities about what is expected specifically of them. It is important to note, though, that who takes what role in a group also is highly influenced by individuals' personal needs. The person with a high need for structure often wants to be in the note-taking role to control the structuring activity in the group; the person who breaks the tension might dislike conflict and uses the role to circumvent it.

(3) *Norms are likely to be enforced if they help the group avoid embarrassing interpersonal problems.* Goffman's work on "facework" gives some insight on this point. Goffman (1955) argues that each person in a group has a "face" he or she presents to other members of a group. This "face" is analogous to what one would call "self-image," the person's perceptions of himself or herself and how he or she would like to be seen by others. Groups want to insure that no one's self-image is damaged, called into question, or embarrassed. Consequently, the group will establish norms that discourage topics of conversation or situations in which face is too likely to be inadvertently broken. For instance, groups might develop norms about not discussing romantic involvements (so that differences in moral values do not become salient) or about not getting together socially in people's homes (so that differences in taste or income do not become salient).

A good illustration of Goffman's facework occurs in the classroom. There is always palpable tension in a room when either a class is totally unprepared to discuss a case or a professor is totally unprepared to lecture or lead the discussion. One part of the awkwardness stems from the inability of the other partner in the interaction to behave as he or she is prepared to or would like to behave. The professor cannot teach if the students are not prepared, and the students cannot learn if the professors are not teaching. Another part of the awkwardness, though, stems from self-images being called into question. Although faculty are aware that not all students are serious scholars, the situation is difficult to handle if the class as a group does not even show a pretense of wanting to learn. Although students are aware that many faculty are mainly interested in research and consulting, there is a problem if the professor does not even show a pretense of caring to teach. Norms almost always develop between professor and students about what level of preparation and interest is expected by the other because both parties want to avoid awkward confrontations.

(4) *Norms are likely to be enforced if they express the central values of the group and clarify what is distinctive about the group's identity.* Norms can provide the social justification for group activities to its members (Katz and Kahn, 1978). When the production group labels rate-busting deviant, it says: "We care more about maximizing group security than about individual profits." Group norms also convey what is distinctive about the groups to outsiders. When an advertising agency labels unstylish clothes deviant, it says: "We think of ourselves, personally and professionally, as trend-setters, and being fashionably dressed conveys that to our clients and our public."

One of the key expressive functions of group norms is to define and legitimate the power of the group itself over individual members (Katz and Kahn, 1978). When groups punish norm infraction, they reinforce in the minds of group members the authority of the group. Here, too, the literature on group deviance sheds some light on the issue at hand.

It has been noted frequently that the amount of deviance in a group is rather small (Erikson, 1966; Schur, 1965). The group uses norm enforcement to show the *strength* of the group. However, if a behavior becomes so widespread that it becomes impossible to control, then the labeling of the widespread behavior as deviance becomes problematic. It simply reminds members of the *weakness* of the group. At this point, the group will redefine what is deviant more narrowly, or it will define its job as that of keeping deviants *within bounds* rather than that of obliterating it altogether. For example, though drug use is and always has been illegal, the widespread use of drugs has led to changes in law enforcement over time. A greater distinction now is made between "hard" drugs and other controlled substances; less penalty is given to those apprehended with small amounts than large amounts; greater attention is focused on capturing large scale smugglers and traffickers than the occasional user. A group, unconsciously if not consciously, learns how much behavior it is capable of labeling deviant *and* punishing effectively.

Finally, this expressive function of group norms can be seen nicely in circumstances in which there is an inconsistency between what group members *say* is the group norm and how people actually *behave*. For instance, sometimes groups will engage in a lot of rhetoric about how much independence its managers are allowed and how much it values entrepreneurial effort; yet the harder data suggest that the more conservative, deferring, or dependent managers get rewarded. Such an inconsistency can reflect conflicts among the group's expressed values. First, the group can be ambivalent about independence; the group knows it needs to encourage more entrepreneurial efforts to flourish, but such efforts create competition and threaten the status quo. Second, the inconsistency can reveal major subgroup differences. Some people may value and encourage entrepreneurial behavior, but others do not— and the latter may control the group's rewards. Third, the inconsistency can reveal a source of the group's self-consciousness, a dichotomy between what the group is really like and how it would like to be perceived. The group may realize that it is too conservative, yet be unable or too frightened to address its problem. The expressed group norm allows the group members a chance to present a "face" to each other and to outsiders that is more socially desirable than reality.

## HOW GROUP NORMS DEVELOP

Norms usually develop gradually and informally as group members learn what behaviors are necessary for the group to function more effectively. However, it also is possible for the norm development process to be short-cut by a critical event in the group or by conscious group decision (Hackman, 1976).

Most norms develop in one or more of the following four ways: explicit statements by supervisors or co-workers; critical events in the group's history; primacy; and carry-over behaviors from past situations.

(1) *Explicit statements by supervisors or co-workers.* Norms that facilitate group survival or task success often are set by the leader of the group or powerful members (Whyte, 1955b). For instance, a group leader might explicitly set norms about not drinking at lunch because subordinates who have been drinking are more likely to have problems dealing competently with clients and top management or they are more likely to have accidents at work. The group leader might also set norms about lateness, personal phone calls, and long coffee breaks if too much productivity is lost as a result of time away from the work place.

Explicit statements by supervisors also can increase the predictability of group members' behavior. For instance, supervisors might have particular preferences for a way of analyzing problems or presenting reports. Strong norms will be set to ensure compliance with these preferences. Consequently, supervisors will have increased certainty about receiving work in the format requested, so they can plan accordingly; workers will have increased certainty about what is expected, so they will not have to outguess their boss or redo their projects.

Managers or important group members also can define the specific role expectations of individual group members. For instance, a supervisor or a co-worker might go up to a new recruit after a meeting to give the proverbial advice: "New recruits should be seen and not heard." The senior group member might be trying to prevent the new recruit from appearing brash or incompetent or from embarrassing other group members. Such interventions set specific role expectations for the new group member.

Norms that cater to supervisor preferences also are frequently established even if they are not objectively necessary to task accomplishment. For example, although organizational norms may be very democratic in terms of everybody calling each other by their first names, some managers have strong preferences about being called Mr., Ms., or Mrs. Although the form of address used in the work group does not influence group effectiveness, complying with the norm bears little cost to the group member, whereas noncompliance could cause daily friction with the supervisor. Such norms help group members avoid embarrassing interpersonal interactions with their managers.

Fourth, norms set explicitly by the supervisor frequently express the central values of the group. For instance, a dean can set very strong norms about faculty keeping office hours and being on campus daily. Such norms reaffirm to members of the academic community their teaching and service obligations, and they send signals to individuals outside the college about what is valued in faculty behavior or distinctive about the school. A dean also could set norms that allow faculty to consult or do executive development two or three days a week. Such norms, too, legitimate other types of faculty behavior and send signals to both insiders and outsiders about some central values of the college.

(2) *Critical events in the group's history.* At times there is a critical event in the group's history that established an important precedent. For instance, a group member might have discussed hiring plans with members of other units in the organization, and as a result new positions were lost or there was increased competition for good applicants. Such indiscretion can substantially hinder the survival and task success of the group; very likely the offender will be either formally censured or informally rebuked. As a result of such an incident, norms about secrecy might develop that will protect the group in similar situations in the future.

An example from Janis's *Victims of Groupthink* (1972) also illustrates this point nicely. One of President Kennedy's closest advisors, Arthur Schlesinger, Jr., had serious reservations about the Bay of Pigs invasion and presented his strong objections to the Bay of Pigs plan in a memorandum to Kennedy and Secretary of State Dean Rusk. However, Schlesinger was pressured by the President's brother, Attorney General Robert Kennedy, to keep his objections to himself. Remarked Robert Kennedy to Schlesinger: "You may be right or you may be wrong, but the President has made his mind up. Don't push it any further. Now is the time for everyone to help him all they can." Such critical events led group members to silence their views and set up group norms about the bounds of disagreeing with the president.

Sometimes group norms can be set by a conscious decision of a group after a particularly good or bad experience the group has had. To illustrate, a group might have had a particularly constructive meeting and be very pleased with how much it accomplished. Several people might say, "I think the reason we got so much accomplished today is that we met really early in the morning before the rest of the staff showed up and the phone started ringing. Let's try to continue to meet at 7:30 A.M." Others might agree, and the norm is set. On the other hand, if a group notices it accomplished way too little in a meeting, it might openly discuss setting norms to cut down on ineffective behavior (e.g., having an agenda, not interrupting others while they were talking). Such norms develop to facilitate task success and to reduce uncertainty about what is expected from each individual in the group.

Critical events also can identify awkward interpersonal situations that need to be avoided in the future. For instance, a divorce between two people working in the same group might have caused a lot of acrimony and hard feeling in a unit, not only between the husband and wife but also among various other group members who got involved in the marital problems. After the unpleasant divorce, a group might develop a norm about not hiring spouses to avoid having to deal with such interpersonal problems in the future.

Finally, critical events also can give rise to norms that express the central, or distinctive, values of the group. When a peer review panel finds a physician or lawyer guilty of malpractice or malfeasance, first it establishes (or reaffirms) the rights of professionals to evaluate and criticize the professional behavior of their colleagues. Moreover, it clarifies what behaviors are inconsistent with the group's self-image or its values. When a faculty committee votes on a candidate's tenure, it, too, asserts the legitimacy of influence of senior faculty over junior faculty. In addition, it sends (hopefully) clear messages to junior faculty about its values in terms of quality of research, teaching, and service. There are important "announcement effects" of peer reviews; internal group members carefully reexamine the group's values, and outsiders draw inferences about the character of the group from such critical decisions.

(3) *Primacy.* The first behavior pattern that emerges in a group often sets group expectations. If the first group meeting is marked by very formal interaction between supervisors and subordinates, then the group often expects future meetings to be conducted in the same way. Where people sit in meetings or rooms frequently is developed through primacy. People generally continue to sit in the same seats they sat in at their first meeting, even though those original seats are not assigned and people could change where they sit at every meeting. Most friendship groups of students develop their own "turf" in a lecture hall and are surprised/dismayed when an interloper takes "their" seats.

Norms that develop through primacy often do so to simplify, or make predictable, what behavior is expected of group members. There may be very little task impact from where people sit in meetings or how formal interactions are. However, norms develop about such behaviors to make life much more routine and predictable. Every time a group member enters a room, he or she does not have to "decide" where to sit or how formally to behave. Moreover, he or she also is much more certain about how other group members will behave.

(4) *Carry-over behaviors from past situations.* Many group norms in organizations emerge because individual group members bring set expectations with them from other work groups in other organizations. Lawyers expect to behave towards clients in Organization I (e.g., confidentiality, setting fees) as they behaved towards those in Organization II. Doctors expect to behave toward patients in Hospital I (e.g., "bedside manner," professional distance) as they behaved in Hospital II. Accountants expect to behave towards colleagues at Firm I (e.g., dress code, adherence to statutes) as they behaved towards those at Firm II. In fact, much of what goes on in professional schools is giving new members of the profession the same standards and norms of behavior that practitioners in the field hold.

Such carry-over of individual behaviors from past situations can increase the predictability of group members' behaviors in new settings and facilitate task accomplishment. For instance, students and professors bring with them fairly constant sets of expectations from class to class. As a result, students do not have to relearn continually their roles from class to class; they know, for instance, if they come in late to take a seat quietly at the back of the room without being told. Professors also do not have to relearn continually their roles; they know, for instance, no to mumble, scribble in small print on the blackboard, or be vague when making course assignments. In addition, presumably the most task-successful norms will be the ones carried over from organization to organization.

Moreover, such carry-over norms help avoid embarrassing interpersonal situations. Individuals are more likely to know which conversations and actions provoke annoyance, irritation, or embarrassment to their colleagues. Finally, when groups carry over norms from one organization to another, they also clarify what is distinctive about the occupational or professional role. When lawyers maintain strict rules of confidentiality, when doctors maintain a consistent professional distance with patients, when accountants present a very formal physical appearance, they all assert: "These are the standards we sustain *independent* of what we could 'get away with' in this organization. This is *our* self-concept."

## SUMMARY

Norms generally are enforced only for behaviors that are viewed as important by most group members. Groups do not have the time or energy to regulate each and every action of individual members. Only those behaviors that ensure group survival, facilitate task accomplishment, contribute to group morale, or express the group's central values are likely to be brought under normative control. Norms that reflect these group needs will develop through explicit statements of supervisors, critical events in the group's history, primacy, or carry-over behaviors from past situations.

Empirical research on norm development and enforcement has substantially lagged descriptive and theoretical work. In large part, this may be due to the methodological problems of measuring norms and getting enough data points either across time or across groups. Until such time as empirical work progresses, however, the usefulness of group norms as a predictive concept, rather than as a post hoc explanatory device, will be severely limited. Moreover, until it is known more concretely why norms develop and why they are strongly enforced, attempts to *change* group norms will remain haphazard and difficult to accomplish.

# REFERENCES

Alvarez, R. Informal reactions to deviance in simulated work organizations: A laboratory experiment. *American Sociological Review.* 1968, 33, 895–912.

Asch, S. Effects of group pressure upon the modification and distortion of judgment. In M. H. Guetzkow (Ed.) *Groups, leadership, and men.* Pittsburgh: Carnegie, 1951, 117–190.

Bales, R. F., & Slater, P. E. Role differentiation in small groups. In T. Parsons, R. F. Bales, J. Olds, M. Zelditch, & P. E. Slater (Eds.), *Family, socialization, and interaction process.* Glencoe, Ill.: Free Press, 1955, 35–131.

Dentler, R. A., & Erikson, K. T. The functions of deviance in groups. *Social Problems,* 1959, 7, 98–107.

Erikson, K. T. *Wayward Puritans.* New York: Wiley, 1966.

Goffman, E. On face-work: An analysis of ritual elements in social interaction. *Psychiatry,* 1955, 18, 213–231.

Hackman, J. R. Group influences on individuals. In M. Dunnette (Ed.). *Handbook of industrial and organizational psychology* Chicago: Rand McNally, 1976, 1455–1525.

Hollander, E. P. Conformity, status, and idiosyncrasy credit. *Psychological Review,* 1958, 65, 117–127.

Hollander, E. P. Some effects of perceived status on responses to innovative behavior. *Journal of Abnormal and Social Psychology,* 1961, 63, 247–250.

Hollander, E. P. *Leaders, groups, and influence.* New York: Oxford University Press, 1964.

Jackson, J. A conceptual and measurement model for norms and roles. *Pacific Sociological Review,* 1966, 9, 35–47.

Janis, I. *Victims of groupthink: A psychological study of foreign-policy decisions and fiascos.* New York: Houghton-Mifflin, 1972.

Katz, D., & Kahn, R. L. *The social psychology of organizations.* 2nd ed. New York: Wiley, 1978.

Kiesler, C. A., & Kiesler, S. B. *Conformity.* Reading, Mass.: Addison-Wesley, 1970.

Longley, J., & Pruitt, D. C. Groupthink: A critique of Janis' theory. In Ladd Wheeler. (Ed.). *Review of personality and social psychology.* Beverly Hills: Sage, 1980, 74–93.

March, J. Group norms and the active minority. *American Sociological Review,* 1954, 19, 733–741.

Schachter, S., Ellertson, N., McBride, D., & Gregory, D. An experimental study of cohesiveness and productivity. *Human Relations,* 1951, 4, 229–238.

Schur, E. M. *Crimes without victims.* Englewood Cliffs, N.J.: Prentice-Hall, 1965.

Seashore, S. *Group cohesiveness in the industrial work group.* Ann Arbor: Institute for Social Research, University of Michigan, 1954.

Shaw, M. *Group dynamics.* 3rd ed. New York: Harper, 1936.

Trist, E. L., & Bamforth, K. W. Some social and psychological consequences of the longwall method of coal-getting. *Human Relations,* 1951, 4, 1–38.

Whyte, W. F. *Money and motivation.* New York: Harper, 1955a.

Whyte, W. F. *Street corner society.* Chicago: University of Chicago Press, 1955b.

Wiggins, J. A., Dill, F., & Schwartz, R. D. On status-liability. *Sociometry,* 1965, 28, 197–209.

# 21

# Assets and Liabilities in Group Problem Solving: The Need for an Integrative Function

## Norman R. F. Maier

*One of the long-standing debates in management has centered on the pros and cons of individual versus group decision making. Norman Maier examines this question in this article and in so doing considers three forces which operate in group decision situations: forces that are assets, forces that are liabilities, and forces that can be either, depending upon the skills of the members of the group.—Eds.*

A number of investigations have raised the question of whether group problem solving is superior, inferior, or equal to individual problem solving. Evidence can be cited in support of each position so that the answer to this question remains ambiguous. Rather than pursue this generalized approach to the question, it seems more fruitful to explore the forces that influence problem solving under the two conditions (see reviews by Hoffman, 1965; Kelly and Thibaut, 1954). It is hoped that a better recognition of these forces will permit clarification of the varied dimensions of the problem-solving process, especially in groups.

The forces operating in such groups include some that are assets, some that are liabilities, and some that can be either assets or liabilities, depending upon the skills of the members, especially those of the discussion leader. Let us examine these three sets of forces.

SOURCE: Reprinted from *Psychological Review* (1967) 74, pp. 239–49. Copyright 1967 by the American Psychological Association. Reprinted by permission.

# GROUP ASSETS

## Greater Sum Total of Knowledge and Information

There is more information in a group than in any of its members. Thus problems that require the utilization of knowledge should give groups an advantage over individuals. Even if one member of the group (e.g., the leader) knows much more than anyone else, the limited unique knowledge of lesser-informed individuals could serve to fill in some gaps in knowledge. For example, a skilled machinist might contribute to an engineer's problem solving and an ordinary workman might supply information on how a new machine might be received by workers.

## Greater Number of Approaches to a Problem

It has been shown that individuals get into ruts in their thinking (Duneker, 1945; Maier, 1930; Wertheimer, 1959). Many obstacles stand in the way of achieving a goal, and a solution must circumvent these. The individual is handicapped in that he tends to persist in his approach and thus fails to find another approach that might solve the problem in a simpler manner. Individuals in a group have the same failing, but the approaches in which they are persisting may be different. For example, one researcher may try to prevent the spread of a disease by making man immune to the germ, another by finding and destroying the carrier of the germ, and still another by altering the environment so as to kill the germ before it reaches man. There is no way of determining which approach will best achieve the desired goal, but undue persistence in any one will stifle new discoveries. Since group members do not have identical approaches, each can contribute by knocking others out of ruts of thinking.

## Participation in Problem Solving Increases Acceptance

Many problems require solutions that depend upon the support of others to be effective. Insofar as group problem solving permits participation and influence, it follows that more individuals accept solutions when a group solves the problem than when one person solves it. When one individual solves a problem he still has the task of persuading others. It follows, therefore, that when groups solve such problems, a greater number of persons accept and feel responsible for making the solution work. A low-quality solution that has good acceptance can be more effective than a higher-quality solution that lacks acceptance.

## Better Comprehension of the Decision

Decisions made by an individual, which are to be carried out by others, must be communicated from the decision maker to the decision executors. Thus individual problem solving often requires an additional stage—that of relaying the decision reached. Failure in this communication process detracts from the merits of the decision and can even cause its failure or create a problem of greater magnitude than the initial problem that was solved. Many organizational problems can be traced to inadequate communication of decisions made by superiors and transmitted to subordinates, who have the task of implementing the decision.

The chances for communication failures are greatly reduced when the individuals who must work together in executing the decision have participated in making it. They not only understand the solution because they saw it develop, but they are also aware of the several other alternatives that were considered and the reasons why they were discarded. The common assumption that decisions supplied by superiors are arbitrarily reached therefore disappears. A full knowledge of goals, obstacles, alternatives, and factual information is essential to communication, and this communication is maximized when the total problem-solving process is shared.

## GROUP LIABILITIES

### Social Pressure

Social pressure is a major force making for conformity. The desire to be a good group member and to be accepted tends to silence disagreement and favors consensus. Majority opinions tend to be accepted regardless of whether or not their objective quality is logically and scientifically sound. Problems requiring solutions based upon facts, regardless of feelings and wishes, can suffer in group problem-solving situations.

It has been shown (Maier and Solem, 1952) that minority opinions in leaderless groups have little influence in the solution reached, even when these opinions are the correct ones. Reaching agreement in a group often is confused with finding the right answer, and it is for this reason that the dimensions of a decision's acceptance and its objective quality must be distinguished (Maier, 1963).

### Valence of Solutions

When leaderless groups (made up of three or four persons) engage in problem solving, they propose a variety of solutions. Each solution may receive both critical and supportive comments, as well as descriptive and explorative comments from other participants. If the number of negative and positive comments for each solution are algebraically summed, each may be given a *valence index* (Hoffman and Maier, 1964). The first solution that receives a positive valence value of .15 tends to be adopted to the satisfaction of all participants about 85 percent of the time, regardless of its quality. Higher quality solutions introduced after the critical value for one of the solutions has been reached have little chance of achieving real consideration. Once some degree of consensus is reached, the jelling process seems to proceed rather rapidly.

The critical valence value of .15 appears not to be greatly altered by the nature of the problem or the exact size of the group. Rather, it seems to designate a turning point between the idea-getting process and the decision-making process (idea evaluation). A solution's valence index is not a measure of the number of persons supporting the solution, since a vocal minority can build up a solution's valence by actively pushing it. In this sense, valence becomes an influence in addition to social pressure in determining an outcome.

Since a solution's valence is independent of its objective quality, this group factor becomes an important liability in group problem solving, even when the value of a decision depends upon objective criteria (facts and logic). It becomes a means whereby skilled manipulators can have more influence over the group process than their proportion of membership deserves.

## Individual Domination

In most leaderless groups a dominant individual emerges and captures more than his share of influence on the outcome. He can achieve this end through a greater degree of participation (valence), persuasive ability, or stubborn persistence (fatiguing the opposition). None of these factors is related to problem-solving ability, so that the best problem solver in the group may not have the influence to upgrade the quality of the group's solution (which he would have had if left to solve the problem by himself).

Hoffman and Maier (1967) found that the mere fact of appointing a leader causes this person to dominate a discussion. Thus, regardless of his problem-solving ability a leader tends to exert a major influence on the outcome of a discussion.

## Conflicting Secondary Goal: Winning the Argument

When groups are confronted with a problem, the initial goal is to obtain a solution. However, the appearance of several alternatives causes individuals to have preferences and once these emerge the desire to support a position is created. Converting those with neutral viewpoints and refuting those with opposed viewpoints now enter into the problem-solving process. More and more the goal becomes that of winning the decision rather than finding the best solution. This new goal is unrelated to the quality of the problem's solution and therefore can result in lowering the quality of the decision (Hoffman and Maier, 1967).

## FACTORS THAT SERVE AS ASSETS OR LIABILITIES, DEPENDING LARGELY UPON THE SKILL OF THE DISCUSSION LEADER

### Disagreement

The fact that discussion may lead to disagreement can serve either to create hard feelings among members or lead to a resolution of conflict and hence to an innovative solution (Hoffman, 1961; Hoffman, Harburg, & Maier, 1962; Hoffman and Maier, 1961; Maier, 1958, 1963; Maier and Hoffman, 1965). The first of these outcomes of disagreement is a liability, especially with regard to the acceptance of solutions; while the second is an asset, particularly where innovation is desired. A leader can treat disagreement as undesirable and thereby reduce the probability of both hard feelings and innovation, or he can maximize disagreement and risk hard feelings in his attempts to achieve innovation. The skill of a leader requires his ability to create a climate for disagreement which will permit innovation without risking hard feelings. The leader's perception of disagreement is one of the critical factors in this skill area (Maier and Hoffman, 1965). Others involve permissiveness (Maier, 1953), delaying the reaching of a solution (Maier and Hoffman, 1960b; Maier and Solem, 1962), techniques for processing information and opinions (Maier, 1963; Maier and Hoffman, 1960b; Maier and Maier, 1957), and techniques for separating idea-getting from idea-evaluation (Maier, 1960, 1963; Osborn, 1953).

### Conflicting Interests versus Mutual Interests

Disagreement in discussion may take many forms. Often participants disagree with one another with regard to solutions, but when issues are explored one finds that these conflicting solutions are designed to solve different problems. Before one can rightly expect agreement on a solution, there should be agreement on the nature of the problem. Even before this, there should be agreement on the goal, as well as on the various obstacles that prevent the goal from being reached. Once distinctions are made between goals, obstacles, and solutions (which represent ways of overcoming obstacles), one finds increased opportunities for cooperative problem solving and less conflict (Hoffman and Maier, 1959; Maier, 1960, 1963; Maier and Solem, 1962; Solem, 1965).

Often there is also disagreement regarding whether the objective of a solution is to achieve quality or acceptance (Maier and Hoffman, 1964b), and frequently a stated problem reveals a complex of separate problems, each having separate solutions so that a search for a single solution is impossible (Maier, 1963). Communications often are inadequate because the discussion is not synchronized and each person is engaged in discussing a different aspect. Organizing discussion to synchronize the exploration of different aspects of the problem and to follow a systematic procedure increases solution quality (Maier & Hoffman, 1960a; Maier and Maier, 1957). The leadership function of influencing discussion procedure is quite distinct from the function of evaluating or contributing ideas (Maier, 1950, 1953).

When the discussion leader aids in the separation of the several aspects of the problem-solving process and delays the solution-mindedness of the group (Maier, 1958, 1963; Maier and Solem, 1962), both solution quality and acceptance improve; when he hinders or fails to facilitate the isolation of these varied processes, he risks a deterioration in the group process (Solem, 1965). His skill thus determines whether a discussion drifts toward conflicting interests or whether mutual interests are located. Cooperative problem solving can only occur after the mutual interests have been established and it is surprising how often they can be found when the discussion leader makes this his task (Maier, 1952, 1963; Maier and Hayes, 1962).

## Risk Taking

Groups are more willing than individuals to reach decisions involving risks (Wallach and Kogan, 1965; Wallach, Kogan, and Bem, 1962). Taking risks is a factor in acceptance of change, but change may represent either a gain or a loss. The best guard against the latter outcome seems to be primarily a matter of a decision's quality. In a group situation this depends upon the leader's skill in utilizing the factors that represent group assets and avoiding those that make for liabilities.

## Time Requirements

In general, more time is required for a group to reach a decision than for a single individual to reach one. Insofar as some problems require quick decisions, individual decisions are favored. In other situations acceptance and quality are requirements, but excessive time without sufficient returns also represents a loss. On the other hand, discussion can resolve conflicts, whereas reaching consensus has limited value (Wallach and Kogan, 1965). The practice of hastening a meeting can prevent full discussion, but failure to move a discussion forward can lead to boredom and fatigue-type solutions, in which members agree merely to get out of the meeting. The effective utilization of discussion time (a delicate balance between permissiveness and control on the part of the leader), therefore, is needed to make the time factor an asset rather than a liability. Unskilled leaders tend to be too concerned with reaching a solution and therefore terminate a discussion before the group potential is achieved (Maier and Hoffman, 1960b).

## Who Changes

In reaching consensus or agreement, some members of a group must change. Persuasive forces do not operate in individual problem solving in the same way they operate in a group situation; hence, the changing of someone's mind is not an issue. In group situations, however, who changes can be an asset or a liability. If persons with the most constructive views are induced to change, the end-product suffers; whereas if persons with the least constructive point of view change, the end-product is upgraded. The leader can upgrade the quality of a decision because his position permits him to protect the person with a minority view and increase his opportunity to influence the majority position. This protection is a constructive factor because a minority viewpoint influences only when facts favor it (Maier, 1950, 1952; Maier and Solem, 1952).

The leader also plays a constructive role insofar as he can facilitate communications and thereby reduce misunderstandings (Maier, 1952; Solem, 1965). The leader has an adverse effect on the end-product when he suppresses minority views by holding a contrary position and when he uses his office to promote his own views (Maier and Hoffman, 1960b, 1962; Maier and Solem, 1952). In many problem-solving discussions the untrained leader plays a dominant role in influencing the outcome, and when he is more resistant to changing his views than are the other participants, the quality of the outcome tends to be lowered. This negative leader-influence was demonstrated by experiments in which untrained leaders were asked to obtain a second solution to a problem after they had obtained their first one (Maier and Hoffman, 1960a). It was found that the second solution tended to be superior to the first. Since the dominant individual had influenced the first solution, he had won his point and therefore ceased to dominate the subsequent discussion which led to the second solution. Acceptance of a solution also increases as the leader sees disagreement as idea-producing rather than as a source of difficulty or trouble (Maier and Hoffman, 1965). Leaders who see some of their participants as troublemakers obtain fewer innovative solutions and gain less acceptance of decisions made than leaders who see disagreeing members as persons with ideas.

# THE LEADER'S ROLE FOR INTEGRATED GROUPS

## Two Differing Types of Group Process

In observing group problem solving under various conditions it is rather easy to distinguish between cooperative problem-solving activity and persuasion or selling approaches. Problem-solving activity includes searching, trying out ideas on one another, listening to understand rather than to refute, making relatively short speeches, and reacting to differences in opinion as stimulating. The general pattern is one of rather complete participation, involvement. Persuasion activity includes the selling of opinions already formed, defending a position held, either not listening at all or listening in order to be able to refute, talking dominated by a few members, unfavorable reactions to disagreement, and a lack of involvement of some members. During problem solving the behavior observed seems to be that of members interacting as segments of a group. The interaction pattern is not between certain individual members, but with the group as a whole. Sometimes it is difficult to determine who should be credited with an idea. "It just developed," is a response often used to describe the solution reached. In contrast, discussions involving selling or persuasive behavior seem to consist of a series of interpersonal interactions with each individual retaining his identity. Such groups do not function as integrated units but as separate individuals, each with an agenda. In one situation the solution is unknown and is sought; in the other, several solutions exist and conflict occurs because commitments have been made.

## The Starfish Analogy

The analysis of these two group processes suggests an analogy with the behavior of the rays of a starfish under two conditions; one with the nerve ring intact, the other with the nerve ring sectioned (Hamilton, 1922; Moore, 1924; Moore and Doudoroff, 1939; Schneirla and Maier, 1940). In the intact condition, locomotion and righting behavior reveal that the behavior of each ray is not merely a function of local stimulation. Locomotion and righting behavior reveal a degree of coordination and interdependence that is centrally controlled. However, when the nerve ring is sectioned, the behavior of one ray still can influence others, but internal coordination is lacking. For example, if one ray is stimulated, it may step forward, thereby exerting pressure on the sides of the other four rays. In response to these external pressures (tactile stimulation), these rays show stepping responses on the stimulated side so that locomotion successfully occurs without the aid of neural coordination. Thus integrated behavior can occur on the basis of external control. If, however, stimulation is applied to opposite rays, the specimen may be "locked" for a time, and in some species the conflicting locomotions may divide the animal, thus destroying it (Crozier, 1920; Moore and Doudoroff, 1939).

Each of the rays of the starfish can show stepping responses even when sectioned and removed from the animal. Thus each may be regarded as an individual. In a starfish with a sectioned nerve ring the five rays become members of a group. They can successfully work together for locomotion purposes by being controlled by the dominant ray. Thus if uniformity of action is desired, the group of five rays can sometimes be more effective than the individual ray in moving the group toward a source of stimulation. However, if "locking" or the division of the organism occurs, the group action becomes less effective than individual action. External control, through the influence of a dominant ray, therefore can lead to adaptive behavior for the starfish as a whole, but it can also result in a conflict that destroys the organism. Something more than external influence is needed.

In the animal with an intact nerve ring, the function of the rays is coordinated by the nerve ring. With this type of internal organization the group is always superior to that of the individual actions. When the rays function as a part of an organized unit, rather than as a group that is physically together, they become a higher type of organization—a single intact organism. This is accomplished by the nerve ring, which in itself does not do the behaving. Rather, it receives and processes the data which the rays relay to it. Through this central organization, the responses of the rays become part of a larger pattern so that together they constitute a single coordinated total response rather than a group of individual responses.

### The Leader as the Group's Central Nervous System

If we now examine what goes on in a discussion group we find that members can problem-solve as individuals, they can influence others by external pushes and pulls, or they can function as a group with varying degrees of unity. In order for the latter function to be maximized, however, something must be introduced to serve the function of nerve ring. In our conceptualization of group problem solving and group decision (Maier, 1963), we see this as the function of the leader. Thus the leader does not serve as a dominant ray and produce the solution. Rather, his function is to receive information, facilitate communications between the individuals, relay messages, and integrate the incoming responses so that a single unified response occurs.

Solutions that are the product of good group discussions often come as surprises to discussion leaders. One of these is unexpected generosity. If there is a weak member, this member is given less to do, in much the same way as an organism adapts to an injured limb and alters the function of other limbs to keep the locomotion on course. Experimental evidence supports the point that group decisions award special consideration to needy members of groups (Hoffman and Maier, 1959). Group decisions in industrial groups often give smaller assignments to the less gifted (Maier, 1952). A leader could not effectually impose such differential treatment on group members without being charged with discriminatory practices.

Another unique aspect of group discussion is the way fairness is resolved. In a simulated problem situation involving the problem of how to introduce a new truck into a group of drivers, the typical group solution involves a trading of trucks so that several or all members stand to profit. If the leader makes the decision the number of persons who profit is often confined to one (Maier and Hoffman, 1962; Maier and Zerfoss, 1952). In industrial practice, supervisors assign a new truck to an individual member of a crew after careful evaluation of needs. This practice results in dissatisfaction, with the charge of *unfair* being leveled at him. Despite those repeated attempts to do justice, supervisors in the telephone industry never hit upon the notion of a general reallocation of trucks, a solution that crews invariably reach when the decision is theirs to make.

In experiments involving the introduction of change, the use of group discussion tends to lead to decisions that resolve differences (Maier, 1952, 1953; Maier and Hoffman, 1961, 1964a, 1964b). Such decisions tend to be different from decisions reached by individuals because of the very fact that disagreement is common in group problem solving. The process of resolving differences in a constructive setting causes the exploration of additional areas and leads to solutions that are integrative rather than compromises.

Finally, group solutions tend to be tailored to fit the interests and personalities of the participants; thus group solutions to problems involving fairness, fears, face-saving, etc., tend to vary from one group to another. An outsider cannot process these variables because they are not subject to logical treatment.

If we think of the leader as serving a function in the group different from that of its membership, we might be able to create a group that can function as an intact organism. For a leader, such functions as rejecting or promoting ideas according to his personal needs are out of bounds. He must be receptive to information contributed, accept contributions without evaluating them (posting contributions on a chalk board to keep them alive), summarize information to facilitate integration, stimulate exploratory behavior, create awareness of problems of one member by others, and detect when the group is ready to resolve differences and agree to a unified solution.

Since higher organisms have more than a nerve ring and can store information, a leader might appropriately supply information, but according to our model of a leader's role, he must clearly distinguish between supplying information and promoting a solution. If his knowledge indicates the desirability of a particular solution, sharing this knowledge might lead the group to find this solution, but the solution should be the group's discovery. A leader's contributions do not receive the same treatment as those of a member of the group. Whether he likes it or not, his position is different. According to our conception of the leader's contribution to discussion, his role not only differs in influence, but gives him an entirely different function. He is to serve much as the nerve ring in the starfish and to further refine this function so as to make it a higher type of nerve ring.

This model of a leader's role in group process has served as a guide for many of our studies in group problem solving. It is not our claim that this will lead to the best possible group function under all conditions. In sharing it we hope to indicate the nature of our guidelines in exploring group leadership as a function quite different and apart from group membership. Thus the model serves as a stimulant for research problems and as a guide for our analyses of leadership skills and principles.


## CONCLUSIONS

On the basis of our analysis, it follows that the comparison of the merits of group versus individual problem solving depends on the nature of the problem, the goal to be achieved (high quality solution, highly accepted solution, effective communication and understanding of the solution, innovation, a quickly reached solution, or satisfaction), and the skill of the discussion leader. If liabilities inherent in groups are avoided, assets capitalized upon, and conditions that can serve either favorable or unfavorable outcomes are effectively used, it follows that groups have a potential which in many instances can exceed that of a superior individual functioning alone, even with respect to creativity.

This goal was nicely stated by Thibaut and Kelley (1961) when they

> wonder whether it may not be possible for a rather small, intimate group to establish a problem solving process that capitalizes upon the total pool of information and provides for great interstimulation of ideas without any loss of innovative creativity due to social restraints [p. 268].

In order to accomplish this high level of achievement, however, a leader is needed who plays a role quite different from that of the members. His role is analogous to that of the nerve ring in the starfish which permits the rays to execute a unified response. If the leader can contribute the integrative requirement, group problem solving may emerge as a unique type of group function. This type of approach to group processes places the leader in a particular role in which he must cease to contribute, avoid evaluation, and refrain from thinking about solutions or group *products*. Instead, he must concentrate on the group *process,* listen in order to understand rather than to appraise or refute, assume responsibility for accurate communication between members, be sensitive to unexpressed feelings, protect minority points of view, keep the discussion moving, and develop skills in summarizing.

## NOTES AND REFERENCES

1. Crozier, W. J. Notes on some problems of adaptation. *Biological Bulletin,* 1920, 39, 116–129.
2. Dunkeker, K. On problem solving. *Psychological Monographs,* 1945, 58 (5, Whole No. 270).
3. Hamilton, W. F. Coordination in the starfish. III. The righting reaction as a phase of locomotion (righting and locomotion). *Journal of Comparative Psychology,* 1922, 2, 81–94.
4. Hoffman, L. R. Conditions for creative problem solving. *Journal of Psychology,* 1961, 52, 429–444.
5. Hoffman, L. R. Group problem solving in L. Berkowitz (ed.)., *Advances in Experimental Social Psychology,* Vol. 2. New York: Academic Press, 1965, pp. 99–132.
6. Hoffman, L. R., Harburg, E., & Maier, N. R. F. Differences and disagreement as factors in creative group problem solving. *Journal of Abnormal and Social Psychology,* 1962, 64, 206–214.
7. Hoffman, L. R. & Maier, N. R. F. The use of group decision to resolve a problem of fairness. *Personnel Psychology,* 1959, 12, 545–559.
8. Hoffman, L. R., & Maier, N. R. F. Quality and acceptance of problem solutions by members of homogeneous and heterogeneous groups. *Journal of Abnormal and Social Psychology,* 1961, 62, 401–407.

9. Hoffman, L. R., & Maier, N. R. F. Valence in the adoption of solutions by problem-solving groups: I. Concept, method, and results. *Journal of Abnormal and Social Psychology,* 1964, 69, 264–271.
10. Hoffman, L. R., & Maier, N. R. F. Valence in the adoption of solutions by problem-solving groups: II. Quality and acceptance as goals of leaders and members. Unpublished manuscript, 1967 (Mimeo).
11. Kelley, H. H., & Thibaut, J. W. Experimental studies of group problem solving and process. In G. Lindzey (ed.), *Handbook of Social Psychology,* Cambridge, Mass.: Addison Wesley, 1954, pp. 735–785.
12. Maier, N. R. F. Reasoning in humans. I. On direction. *Journal of Comparative Psychology,* 1930, 10, 115–143.
13. Maier, N. R. F. The quality of group decisions as influenced by the discussion leader. *Human Relations,* 1950, 3, 155–174.
14. Maier, N. R. F. *Principles of Human Relations.* New York: Wiley, 1952.
15. Maier, N. R. F. An experimental test of the effect of training on discussion leadership. *Human Relations,* 1953, 6, 161–173.
16. Maier, N. R. F. *The Appraisal Interview.* New York: Wiley, 1958.
17. Maier, N. R. F. Screening solutions to upgrade quality: A new approach to problem solving under conditions of uncertainty. *Journal of Psychology,* 1960, 49, 217–231.
18. Maier, N. R. F. *Problem solving discussions and conferences: Leadership methods and skills.* New York: McGraw-Hill, 1963.
19. Maier, N. R. F., & Hayes, J. A. *Creative Management,* New York: Wiley, 1962.
20. Maier, N. R. F., & Hoffman, L. R. Using trained "developmental" discussion leaders to improve further the quality of group decisions. *Journal of Applied Psychology,* 1960, 44, 274–251. (a)
21. Maier, N. R. F., & Hoffmann, L. R. Quality of first and second solutions in group decisions. *Journal of Applied Psychology,* 1960, 44, 278–283. (b)
22. Maier, N. R. F., & Hoffman, L. R. Organization and creative problem solving. *Journal of Applied Psychology,* 1961, 45, 277–280.
23. Maier, N. R. F., & Hoffman, L. R. Group decision in England and the United States. *Personnel Psychology,* 1962, 15, 78–87.
24. Maier, N. R. F., & Hoffman, L. R. Financial incentives and group decision in motivation change. *Journal of Social Psychology,* 1964, 64, 369–378. (a)
25. Maier, N. R. F., & Hoffman, L. R. Types of problems confronting managers. *Personnel Psychology,* 1964, 17, 261–266. (b)
26. Maier, N. R. F., & Hoffman, L. R. Acceptance and quality of solutions as related to leaders' attitudes toward disagreement in group problem solving. *Journal of Applied Behavioral Science,* 1965, 1, 273–386.
27. Maier, N. R. F., & Maier, R. A. An experimental test of the effects of "developmental" vs. "free" discussions on the quality of group decisions. *Journal of Applied Psychology,* 1957, 41, 320–323.
28. Maier, N. R. F., & Solem, A. R. The contribution of a discussion leader to the quality of group thinking: The effective use of minority opinions. *Human Relations,* 1952, 5, 277–288.

29. Maier, N. R. F., & Solem, A. R. Improving solutions by turning choice situations into problems. *Personnel Psychology,* 1962, 15, 151–157.
30. Maier, N. R. F., & Zerfoss, I. F. MRP: A technique for training large groups of supervisors and its potential use in social research. *Human Relations,* 1952, 5, 177–186.
31. Moore, A. R. The nervous mechanism of coordination in the crinoid Antedon rosaceus. *Journal of Genetic Psychology,* 1924, 6, 281–288.
32. Moore, A. R., & Doudoroff, M. Injury, recovery and function in an aganglionic central nervous system. *Journal of Comparative Psychology,* 1939, 28, 313–328.
33. Osborn, A. F. *Applied imagination.* New York: Scribner's, 1953.
34. Schneirla, T. C., & Maier, N. R. F. Concerning the status of the starfish. *Journal of Comparative Psychology,* 1940, 30, 103–110.
35. Solem, A. R. Almost anything I can do, we can do better. *Personnel Administration,* 1965, 28, 6–16.
36. Thibaut, J. W., & Kelley, H. H. *The social psychology of groups.* New York: Wiley, 1961.
37. Wallach, M. A., and Kogan, N. The roles of information, discussion and consensus in group risk taking. *Journal of Experimental and Social Psychology,* 1965, 1, 1–19.
38. Wallach, M. A., Kogan, N., & Bem, D. J. Group influence on individual risk taking. *Journal of Abnormal and Social Psychology,* 1962, 65, 75–86.
39. Wertheimer, M. *Productive thinking.* New York: Harper, 1959.

# 22

# Groupthink

## Irving L. Janis

*Using the infamous Bay of Pigs invasion as an example, Janis identifies a dysfunctional consequence of group activity. Groupthink is seen as replacing rational and independent critical thinking in some group settings. The article identifies the symptoms of groupthink, as well as outlining preventive actions which can be taken to lessen the chance of its occurrence.—Eds.*

"How could we have been so stupid?" President John F. Kennedy asked after he and a close group of advisers had blundered into the Bay of Pigs invasion. For the last two years I have been studying that question, as it applies not only to the Bay of Pigs decision makers but also to those who led the United States into such other major fiascos as the failure to be prepared for the attack on Pearl Harbor, the Korean War stalemate, and the escalation of the Vietnam War.

Stupidity certainly is not the explanation. The men who participated in making the Bay of Pigs decision, for instance, comprised one of the greatest arrays of intellectual talent in the history of American government—Dean Rusk, Robert McNamara, Douglas Dillon, Robert Kennedy, McGeorge Bundy, Arthur Schlesinger, Jr., Allen Dulles and others.

It also seemed to me that explanations were incomplete if they concentrated only on disturbances in the behavior of each individual within a decision-making body: temporary emotional states of elation, fear, or anger that reduce a man's mental efficiency, for example, or chronic blind spots arising from a man's social prejudices or idiosyncratic biases.

---

SOURCE: *Psychology Today,* November 1971. Copyright © 1971 Ziff-Davis Publishing Company. Reprinted by permission of *Psychology Today* magazine.

I preferred to broaden the picture by looking at the fiascos from the standpoint of group dynamics as it has been explored over the past three decades, first by the great social psychologist Kurt Lewin and later in many experimental situations by myself and other behavioral scientists. My conclusion after poring over hundreds of relevant documents—historical reports about formal group meetings and informal conversations among the members—is that the groups that committed the fiascos were victims of what I call "groupthink."

## "GROUPY"

In each case study, I was surprised to discover the extent to which each group displayed the typical phenomena of social conformity that are regularly encountered in studies of group dynamics among ordinary citizens. For example, some of the phenomena appear to be completely in line with findings from social-psychological experiments showing that powerful social pressures are brought to bear by the members of a cohesive group whenever a dissident begins to voice his objections to a group consensus. Other phenomena are reminiscent of the shared illusions observed in encounter groups and friendship cliques when the members simultaneously reach a peak of "groupy" feelings.

Above all, there are numerous indications pointing to the development of group norms that bolster morale at the expense of critical thinking. One of the most common norms appears to be that of remaining loyal to the group by sticking with the policies to which the group has already committed itself, even when those policies are obviously working out badly and have unintended consequences that disturb the conscience of each member. This is one of the key characteristics of groupthink.

## 1984

I use the term groupthink as a quick and easy way to refer to the mode of thinking that persons engage in when *concurrence-seeking* becomes so dominant in a cohesive ingroup that it tends to override realistic appraisal of alternative courses of action. Groupthink is a term of the same order as the words in the newspeak vocabulary George Orwell used in his dismaying world of *1984*. In that context, groupthink takes on an invidious connotation. Exactly such a connotation is intended, since the term refers to a deterioration in mental efficiency, reality testing, and moral judgments as a result of group pressures.

The symptoms of groupthink arise when the members of decision-making groups become motivated to avoid being too harsh in their judgments of their leaders' or their colleagues' ideas. They adopt a soft line of criticism, even in their own thinking. At their meetings, all the members are amiable and seek complete concurrence on every important issue, with no bickering or conflict to spoil the cozy, "we-feeling" atmosphere.

## KILL

Paradoxically, soft-headed groups are often hard-hearted when it comes to dealing with outgroups or enemies. They find it relatively easy to resort to dehumanizing solutions—they will readily authorize bombing attacks that kill large numbers of civilians in the name of the noble cause of persuading an unfriendly government to negotiate at the peace table. They are unlikely to pursue the more difficult and controversial issues that arise when alternatives to a harsh military solution come up for discussion. Nor are they inclined to raise ethical issues that carry the implication that *this fine group of ours, with its humanitarianism and its high-minded principles, might be capable of adopting a course of action that is inhumane and immoral.*

## NORMS

There is evidence from a number of social-psychological studies that as the members of a group feel more accepted by the others, which is a central feature of increased group cohesiveness, they display less overt conformity to group norms. Thus we would expect that the more cohesive a group becomes, the less the members will feel constrained to censor what they say out of fear of being socially punished for antagonizing the leader or any of their fellow members.

In contrast, the groupthink type of conformity tends to increase as group cohesiveness increases. Groupthink involves nondeliberate suppression of critical thoughts as a result of internalization of the group's norms, which is quite different from deliberate suppression on the basis of external threats of social punishment. The more cohesive the group, the greater the inner compulsion on the part of each member to avoid creating disunity, which inclines him to believe in the soundness of whatever proposals are promoted by the leader or by a majority of the group's members.

In a cohesive group, the danger is not so much that each individual will fail to reveal his objections to what the others propose but that he will think the proposal is a good one, without attempting to carry out a careful, critical scrutiny of the pros and cons of the alternatives. When groupthink becomes dominant, there also is considerable suppression of deviant thoughts, but it takes the form of each person's deciding that his misgivings are not relevant and should be set aside, that the benefit of the doubt regarding any lingering uncertainties should be given to the group consensus.

## STRESS

I do not mean to imply that all cohesive groups necessarily suffer from groupthink. All ingroups may have a mild tendency toward groupthink, displaying one or another of the symptoms from time to time, but it need not be so dominant as to influence the quality of the group's final decision. Neither do I mean to imply that there is anything necessarily inefficient or harmful about group decisions in general. On the contrary, a group whose members have properly defined roles, with traditions concerning the procedures to follow in pursuing a critical inquiry, probably is capable of making better decisions than any individual group member working alone.

The problem is that the advantages of having decisions made by groups are often lost because of powerful psychological pressures that arise when the members work closely together, share the same set of values and, above all, face a crisis situation that puts everyone under intense stress.

The main principle of groupthink, which I offer in the spirit of Parkinson's Law, is:

> The more amiability and esprit de corps there is among the members of a policy-making ingroup, the greater the danger that independent critical thinking will be replaced by groupthink, which is likely to result in irrational and dehumanizing actions directed against outgroups.

## SYMPTOMS

In my studies of high-level governmental decision makers, both civilian and military, I have found eight main symptoms of groupthink.

### 1.  Invulnerability

Most or all of the members of the ingroup share an *illusion* of invulnerability that provides for them some degree of reassurance about obvious dangers and leads them to become overoptimistic and willing to take extraordinary risks. It also causes them to fail to respond to clear warnings of danger.

The Kennedy ingroup, which uncritically accepted the Central Intelligence Agency's disastrous Bay of Pigs plan, operated on the false assumption that they could keep secret the fact that the United States was responsible for the invasion of Cuba. Even after news of the plan began to leak out, their belief remained unshaken. They failed even to consider the danger that awaited them: a worldwide revulsion against the U.S.

A similar attitude appeared among the members of President Lyndon B. Johnson's ingroup, the "Tuesday Cabinet," which kept escalating the Vietnam War despite repeated setbacks and failures. "There was a belief," Bill Moyers commented after he resigned, "that if we indicated a willingness to use our power, they [the North Vietnamese] would get the message and back away from an all-out confrontation. . . . There was a confidence—it was never bragged about, it was just there—that when the chips were really down, the other people would fold."

A most poignant example of an illusion of invulnerability involves the ingroup around Admiral H. E. Kimmel, which failed to prepare for the possibility of a Japanese attack on Pearl Harbor despite repeated warnings. Informed by his intelligence chief that radio contact with Japanese aircraft carriers had been lost, Kimmel joked about it: "What, you don't know where the carriers are? Do you mean to say that they could be rounding Diamond Head (at Honolulu) and you wouldn't know it?" The carriers were in fact moving full-steam toward Kimmel's command post at the time. Laughing together about a danger signal, which labels it as a purely laughing matter, is a characteristic manifestation of groupthink.

## 2. Rationale

As we see, victims of groupthink ignore warnings; they also collectively construct rationalizations in order to discount warnings and other forms of negative feedback that, taken seriously, might lead the group members to reconsider their assumptions each time they recommit themselves to past decisions. Why did the Johnson ingroup avoid reconsidering its escalation policy when time and again the expectations on which they based their decisions turned out to be wrong? James C. Thompson, Jr., a Harvard historian who spent five years as an observing participant in both the State Department and the White House, tells us that the policymakers avoided critical discussion of their prior decisions and continually invented new rationalizations so that they could sincerely recommit themselves to defeating the North Vietnamese.

In the fall of 1964, before the bombing of North Vietnam began, some of the policymakers predicted that six weeks of air strikes would induce the North Vietnamese to seek peace talks. When someone asked, "What if they don't?" the answer was that another four weeks certainly would do the trick.

Later, after each setback, the ingroup agreed that by investing just a bit more effort (by stepping up the bomb tonnage a bit, for instance), their course of action would prove to be right. *The Pentagon Papers* bear out these observations.

In *The Limits of Intervention,* Townsend Hoopes, who was acting Secretary of the Air Force under Johnson, says that Walt A. Rostow in particular showed a remarkable capacity for what has been called "instant rationalization." According to Hoopes, Rostow buttressed the group's optimism about being on the road to victory by culling selected scraps of evidence from news reports or, if necessary, by inventing "plausible" forecasts that had no basis in evidence at all.

Admiral Kimmel's group rationalized away their warnings, too. Right up to December 7, 1941, they convinced themselves that the Japanese would never dare attempt a full-scale surprise assault against Hawaii because Japan's leaders would realize that it would precipitate an all-out war which the United States would surely win. They made no attempt to look at the situation through the eyes of the Japanese leaders—another manifestation of groupthink.

### 3.  Morality

Victims of groupthink believe unquestioningly in the inherent morality of their ingroup; this belief inclines the members to ignore the ethical or moral consequences of their decisions.

Evidence that this symptom is at work usually is of a negative kind—the things that are left unsaid in group meetings. At least two influential persons had doubts about the morality of the Bay of Pigs adventure. One of them, Arthur Schlesinger, Jr., presented his strong objections in a memorandum to President Kennedy and Secretary of State Rusk but suppressed them when he attended meetings of the Kennedy team. The other, Senator J. William Fullbright, was not a member of the group, but the President invited him to express his misgivings in a speech to the policymakers. However, when Fullbright finished speaking the President moved on to other agenda items without asking for reactions of the group.

David Kraslow and Stuart H. Loory, in *The Secret Search for Peace in Vietnam,* report that during 1966 President Johnson's ingroup was concerned primarily with selecting bomb targets in North Vietnam. They based their selection on four factors—the military advantage, the risk to American aircraft and pilots, the danger of forcing other countries into the fighting, and the danger of heavy civilian casualties. At their regular Tuesday luncheons, they weighed these factors the way school teachers grade examination papers, averaging them out. Though evidence on this point is scant, I suspect that the group's ritualistic adherence to a standardized procedure induced the members to feel morally justified in their destructive way of dealing with the Vietnamese people—after all, the danger of heavy civilian casualties from U.S. air strikes was taken into account on their checklists.

### 4.  Stereotypes

Victims of groupthink hold stereotyped views of the leaders of enemy groups: they are so evil that genuine attempts at negotiating differences with them are unwarranted, or they are too weak or too stupid to deal effectively with whatever attempts the ingroup makes to defeat their purposes, no matter how risky the attempts are.

Kennedy's groupthinkers believed that Premier Fidel Castro's air force was so ineffectual that obsolete B-26s could knock it out completely in a surprise attack before the invasion began. They also believed that Castro's army was so weak that a small Cuban-exile brigade could establish a well-protected beachhead at the Bay of Pigs. In addition, they believed that Castro was not smart enough to put down any possible internal uprisings in support of the exiles. They were wrong on all three assumptions. Though much of the blame was attributable to faulty intelligence, the point is that none of Kennedy's advisers even questioned the CIA planners about these assumptions.

The Johnson advisers' sloganistic thinking about "the Communist apparatus" that was "working all around the world" (as Dean Rusk put it) led them to overlook the powerful nationalistic strivings of the North Vietnamese government and its efforts to ward off Chinese domination. The crudest of all stereotypes used by Johnson's inner circle to justify their policies was the domino theory ("If we don't stop the Reds in South Vietnam, tomorrow they will be in Hawaii and next week they will be in San Francisco," Johnson once said). The group so firmly accepted this stereotype that it became almost impossible for any adviser to introduce a more sophisticated viewpoint.

In the documents on Pearl Harbor, it is clear to see that the Navy commanders stationed in Hawaii had a naive image of Japan as a midget that would not dare to strike a blow against a powerful giant.

### 5.  Pressure

Victims of groupthink apply direct pressure to any individual who momentarily expresses doubts about any of the group's shared illusions or who questions the validity of the arguments supporting a policy alternative favored by the majority. This gambit reinforces the concurrence-seeking norm that loyal members are expected to maintain.

President Kennedy probably was more active than anyone else in raising skeptical questions during the Bay of Pigs meetings, and yet he seems to have encouraged the group's docile, uncritical acceptance of defective arguments in favor of the CIA's plan. At every meeting, he allowed the CIA representatives to dominate the discussion. He permitted them to give their immediate refutations in response to each tentative doubt that one of the others expressed, instead of asking whether anyone shared the doubt or wanted to pursue the implications of the new worrisome issue that had just been raised. And at the most crucial meeting, when he was calling on each member to give his vote for or against the plan, he did not call on Arthur Schlesinger, the one man there who was known by the President to have serious misgivings.

Historian Thomson informs us that whenever a member of Johnson's ingroup began to express doubts, the group used subtle social pressures to "domesticate" him. To start with, the dissenter was made to feel at home, provided that he lived up to two restrictions: (1) that he did not voice his doubts to outsiders, which would play into the hands of the opposition; and (2) that he kept his criticisms within the bounds of acceptable deviation, which meant not challenging any of the fundamental assumptions that went into the group's prior commitments. One such "domesticated dissenter" was Bill Moyers. When Moyers arrived at a meeting, Thomson tells us, the President greeted him with, "Well, here comes Mr. Stop-the-Bombing."

## 6.  Self-Censorship

Victims of groupthink avoid deviating from what appears to be group consensus; they keep silent about their misgivings and even minimize to themselves the importance of their doubts.

As we have seen, Schlesinger was not at all hesitant about presenting his strong objections to the Bay of Pigs plan in a memorandum to the President and the Secretary of State. But he became keenly aware of his tendency to suppress objections at the White House meetings. "In the months after the Bay of Pigs I bitterly reproached myself for having kept so silent during those crucial discussions in the cabinet room," Schlesinger writes in *A Thousand Days*. "I can only explain my failure to do more than raise a few timid questions by reporting that one's impulse to blow the whistle on this nonsense was simply undone by the circumstances of the discussion."

## 7.  Unanimity

Victims of groupthink share an *illusion* of unanimity within the group concerning almost all judgments expressed by members who speak in favor of the majority view. This symptom results partly from the preceding one, whose effects are augmented by the false assumption that any individual who remains silent during any part of the discussion is in full accord with what the others are saying.

When a group of persons who respect each other's opinions arrives at a unanimous view, each member is likely to feel that the belief must be true. This reliance on consensual validation within the group tends to replace individual critical thinking and reality testing, unless there are clear-cut disagreements among the members. In contemplating a course of action such as the invasion of Cuba, it is painful for the members to confront disagreements within their group, particularly if it becomes apparent that there are widely divergent views about whether the preferred course of action is too risky to undertake at all. Such disagreements are likely to arouse anxieties about making a serious error. Once the sense of unanimity is shattered, the members no longer can feel complacently confident about the decision they are inclined to make. Each man must then face the annoying realization that there are troublesome uncertainties and he must diligently seek out the best information he can get in order to decide for himself exactly how serious the risks might be. This is one of the unpleasant consequences of being in a group of hardheaded, critical thinkers.

To avoid such an unpleasant state, the members often become inclined, without quite realizing it, to prevent latent disagreements from surfacing when they are about to initiate a risky course of action. The group leader and the members support each other in playing up the areas of convergence in their thinking, at the expense of fully exploring divergencies that might reveal unsettled issues.

"Our meetings took place in a curious atmosphere of assumed consensus," Schlesinger writes. His additional comments clearly show that, curiously, the consensus was an illusion—an illusion that could be maintained only because the major participants did not reveal their own reasoning or discuss their idiosyncratic assumptions and vague reservations. Evidence from several sources makes it clear that even the three principals—President Kennedy, Rusk, and McNamara—had widely differing assumptions about the invasion plan.

### 8.  Mindguards

Victims of groupthink sometimes appoint themselves as mindguards to protect the leader and fellow members from adverse information that might break the complacency they shared about the effectiveness and morality of past decisions. At a large birthday party for his wife, Attorney General Robert F. Kennedy, who had been constantly informed about the Cuban invasion plan, took Schlesinger aside and asked him why he was opposed. Kennedy listened coldly and said, "You may be right or you may be wrong, but the President has made his mind up. Don't push it any further. Now is the time for everyone to help him all they can."

Rusk also functioned as a highly effective mindguard by failing to transmit to the group the strong objections of three "outsiders" who had learned of the invasion plan—Undersecretary of State Chester Bowles, USIA Director Edward R. Murrow, and Rusk's intelligence chief, Roger Hilsman. Had Rusk done so, their warnings might have reinforced Schlesinger's memorandum and jolted some of Kennedy's ingroup, if not the President himself, into reconsidering the decision.

## PRODUCTS

When a group of executives frequently displays most or all of these interrelated symptoms, a detailed study of their deliberations is likely to reveal a number of immediate consequences. These consequences are, in effect, products of poor decision-making practices because they lead to inadequate solutions to the problems being dealt with.

First, the group limits its discussions to a few alternative courses of action (often only two) without an initial survey of all the alternatives that might be worthy of consideration.

Second, the group fails to reexamine the course of action initially preferred by the majority after they learn of risks and drawbacks they had not considered originally.

Third, the members spend little or no time discussing whether there are nonobvious gains they may have overlooked or ways of reducing the seemingly prohibitive costs that made rejected alternatives appear undesirable to them.

Fourth, members make little or no attempt to obtain information from experts within their own organizations who might be able to supply more precise estimates of potential losses and gains.

Fifth, members show positive interest in facts and opinions that support their preferred policy; they tend to ignore facts and opinions that do not.

Sixth, members spend little time deliberating about how the chosen policy might be hindered by bureaucratic inertia, sabotaged by political opponents, or temporarily derailed by common accidents. Consequently, they fail to work out contingency plans to cope with foreseeable setbacks that could endanger the overall success of their chosen course.

## SUPPORT

The search for an explanation of why groupthink occurs has led me through a quagmire of complicated theoretical issues in the murky area of human motivation. My belief, based on recent social psychological research, is that we can best understand the various symptoms of groupthink as a mutual effort among the group members to maintain self-esteem and emotional equanimity by providing social support to each other, especially at times when they share responsibility for making vital decisions.

Even when no important decision is pending, the typical administrator will begin to doubt the wisdom and morality of his past decisions each time he receives information about setbacks, particularly if the information is accompanied by negative feedback from prominent men who originally had been his supporters. It should not be surprising, therefore, to find that individual members strive to develop unanimity and esprit de corps that will help bolster each other's morale, to create an optimistic outlook about the success of pending decisions, and to reaffirm the positive value of past policies to which all of them are committed.

## PRIDE

Shared illusions of invulnerability, for example, can reduce anxiety about taking risks. Rationalizations help members believe that the risks are really not so bad after all. The assumption of inherent morality helps the members to avoid feelings of shame or guilt. Negative stereotypes function as stress-reducing devices to enhance a sense of moral righteousness as well as pride in a lofty mission.

The mutual enhancement of self-esteem and morale may have functional value in enabling the members to maintain their capacity to take action, but it has maladaptive consequences insofar as concurrence-seeking tendencies interfere with critical, rational capacities and lead to serious errors of judgment.

While I have limited my study to decision-making bodies in Government, groupthink symptoms appear in business, industry, and any other field where small, cohesive groups make the decisions. It is vital, then, for all sorts of people—and especially group leaders—to know what steps they can take to prevent groupthink.

## REMEDIES

To counterpoint my case studies of the major fiascos, I have also investigated two highly successful group enterprises, the formulation of the Marshall Plan in the Truman Administration and the handling of the Cuban missile crisis by President Kennedy and his advisers. I have found it instructive to examine the steps Kennedy took to change his group's decision-making processes. These changes ensured that the mistakes made by his Bay of Pigs ingroup were not repeated by the missile-crisis ingroup, even though the membership of both groups was essentially the same.

The following recommendations for preventing groupthink incorporate many of the good practices I discovered to be characteristic of the Marshall Plan and missile-crisis groups:

1. The leader of a policy-forming group should assign the role of critical evaluator to each member, encouraging the group to give high priority to open airing of objections and doubts. This practice needs to be reinforced by the leader's acceptance of criticism of his own judgments in order to discourage members from soft-pedaling their disagreements and from allowing their striving for concurrence to inhibit criticism.

2. When the key members of a hierarchy assign a policy-planning mission to any group within their organization, they should adopt an impartial stance instead of stating preferences and expectations at the beginning. This will encourage open inquiry and impartial probing of a wide range of policy alternatives.

3. The organization routinely should set up several outside policy-planning and evaluation groups to work on the same policy question, each deliberating under a different leader. This can prevent the insulation of an ingroup.

4. At intervals before the group reaches a final consensus, the leader should require each member to discuss the group's deliberations with associates in his own unit of the organization—assuming that those associates can be trusted to adhere to the same security regulations that govern the policy makers—and then to report back their reactions to the group.

5. The group should invite one or more outside experts to each meeting on a staggered basis and encourage the experts to challenge the views of the core members.

6. At every general meeting of the group, whenever the agenda calls for an evaluation of policy alternatives, at least one member should play devil's advocate, functioning as a good lawyer in challenging the testimony of those who advocate the majority position.

7. Whenever the policy issue involves relations with a rival nation or organization, the group should devote a sizable block of time, perhaps an entire session, to a survey of all warning signals from the rivals and should write alternative scenarios on the rivals' intentions.

8. When the group is surveying policy alternatives for feasibility and effectiveness, it should from time to time divide

into two or more subgroups to meet separately, under different chairmen, and then come back together to hammer out differences.

9. After reaching a preliminary consensus about what seems to be the best policy, the group should hold a "second-chance" meeting at which every member expresses as vividly as he can all his residual doubts, and rethinks the entire issue before making a definitive choice.

## HOW

These recommendations have their disadvantages. To encourage the open airing of objections, for instance, might lead to prolonged and costly debates when a rapidly growing crisis requires immediate solution. It also could cause rejection, depression, and anger. A leader's failure to set a norm might create cleavage between leader and members that could develop into a disruptive power struggle if the leader looks on the emerging consensus as anathema. Setting up outside evaluation groups might increase the risk of security leakage. Still, inventive executives who know their way around the organizational maze probably can figure out how to apply one or another of the prescriptions successfully, without harmful side effects.

They also could benefit from the advice of outside experts in the administrative and behavioral sciences. Though these experts have much to offer, they have had few chances to work on policy-making machinery within large organizations. As matters now stand, executives innovate only when they need new procedures to avoid repeating serious errors that have deflated their self-images.

In this era of atomic warheads, urban disorganization and ecocatastrophes, it seems to me that policy makers should collaborate with behavioral scientists and give top priority to preventing groupthink and its attendant fiascos.

# 23

# Participative Management: Time for a Second Look

*Robert C. Albrook*

*Participative management might not be for everyone, cautions this article. Albrook calls for a reexamination of some of the notions we have about the democratic approach to management, noting that some assumptions about the utility of participation in decision making and the showing of authority are not always valid. Note particularly the discussion of the special difficulties involved in moving a traditionally authoritarian organization toward a participative style.—Eds.*

The management of change has become a central preoccupation of U.S. business. When the directors have approved the record capital budget and congratulated themselves on "progress," when the banquet speaker has used his last superlative to describe the "world of tomorrow," the talk turns, inevitably, to the question: "Who will make it all work?" Some people resist change. Some hold the keys to it. Some admit the need for new ways but don't know how to begin. The question becomes what kind of management can ease the inevitable pains, unlock the talent, energy, and knowledge where they're needed, help valuable men to contribute to and shape change rather than be flattened by it.

The recipe is elusive, and increasingly business has turned to the academic world for help, particularly to the behavioral scientists—the psychologists, sociologists, and anthropologists whose studies have now become the showpieces of the better business schools. A number of major corporations, such as General Electric, Texas Instruments, and Standard Oil (N.J.), have brought social scientists onto their staffs. Some companies collaborate closely with university based scholars and

SOURCE: Reprinted by permission of the publisher from "Participative Management: Time for a Second Look," *Fortune*, May 1967, pp. 166–70, 197–200.

are contributing importantly to advanced theoretical work, just as industry's physicists, chemists, and engineers have become significant contributors of new knowledge in their respective realms. Hundreds of companies, large and small, have tried one or another formulation of basic behavioral theory, such as the many schemes for sharing their savings with employees and actively soliciting their ideas for improved efficiency.

For 40 years the quantity and quality of academic expertise in this field have been steadily improving, and there has lately been a new burst of ideas which suggest that the researchers in the business schools and other centers of learning are really getting down to cases. The newest concepts already represent a considerable spin off from the appealingly simple notions on which the behavioral pioneers first concentrated. The essential message these outriders had for business was this: recognize the social needs of employees in their work, as well as their need for money; they will respond with a deeper commitment and better performance, help to shape the organization's changing goals and make them their own. To blue-collar workers this meant such steps as organizing work around tasks large enough to have meaning and inviting workers' ideas; for middle and upper management it meant more participation in decision making, more sharing of authority and responsibility, more open and more candid communication, up, down, and sideways.

The new work suggests that neither the basic philosophy nor all of the early prescriptions of this management style were scientifically sound or universally workable. The word from the behavioral scientists is becoming more specific and "scientific," less simple and moralistic. At Harvard, M.I.T., the University of Michigan, Chicago, U.C.L.A., Stanford, and elsewhere, they are mounting bigger, longer, and more rigorous studies of the human factors in management than ever before undertaken.

One conclusion is that the "participative" or "group" approach doesn't seem to work with all people and in all situations. Research has shown that satisfied, happy workers are sometimes more productive—and sometimes merely happy. Some managers and workers are able to take only limited responsibility, however much the company tries to give them. Some people will recognize the need to delegate but "can't let go." In a profit squeeze the only way to get costs under control fast enough often seems to be with centralized, "get tough" management.

Few, if any, behaviorists espouse a general return to authoritarian management. Instead, they are seeking a more thorough, systematic way to apply participative principles on a sustained schedule that will give the theory a better chance to work. Others are insisting that management must be tailor-made, suited to the work or the people, rather than packaged in a standard mixture. Some people aren't and never will be suited for "democracy" on the job, according to one viewpoint, while others insist that new kinds of psychological training can fit most executives for the rugged give-and-take of successful group management.

As more variables are brought into their concepts, and as they look increasingly at the specifics of a management situation, the behaviorists are also being drawn toward collaboration with the systems designers and the theorists of data processing. Born in reaction to the cold scientism of the earlier "scientific management" experts with their stopwatches and measuring tapes, the "human relations" or behavioral school of today may be getting ready at last to bury that hatchet in a joint search for a broadly used "general theory" of management.

## WHY EXECUTIVES DON'T PRACTICE WHAT THEY PREACH

Before any general theory can be evolved, a great deal more has to be known about the difficulty of putting theory into practice—i.e., of transforming a simple managerial attitude into an effective managerial style. "There are plenty of executives," observes Stanley Seashore, a social psychologist at the University of Michigan's Institute for Social Research, "who'll decide one morning they're going to be more participative and by the afternoon have concluded it doesn't work."

What's often lacking is an understanding of how deeply and specifically management style affects corporate operations. The executive who seeks a more effective approach needs a map of the whole terrain of management activity. Rensis Likert, director of the Michigan institute, has developed a chart to assist managers in gaining a deeper understanding of the way they operate. A simplified version appears (in Table 1). By answering the questions in the left-hand column of the chart (e.g., "Are subordinates' ideas sought and used?"), an executive sketches a profile of the way his company is run and whether it leans to the "authoritative" or the "participative." Hundreds of businessmen have used the chart, under Likert's direction, and many have discovered a good deal they didn't realize about the way they were handling people.

Likert leads his subjects in deliberate steps to a conclusion that most of them do not practice what they say they believe. First, the executive is asked to think of the most successful company (or division of a company) he knows intimately. He then checks off on the chart his answers as they apply to that company. When the executive has finished this exercise, he has nearly always traced the profile of a strongly "participative" management system, well to the right on Likert's chart. He is next asked to repeat the procedure for the least successful company (or division) he knows well. Again, the profiles are nearly always the same, but this time they portray a strongly "authoritative" system, far to the left on the chart.

Then comes the point of the exercise. The executive is asked to describe his own company or division. Almost always, the resulting profile is that of a company somewhere in the middle, a blend of the "benevolent authoritative" and the "consultative"—well to the left of what the executive had previously identified as the most successful style. To check out the reliability of this self-analysis, Likert sometimes asks employees in the same company or division to draw its profile, too. They tend to rate it as slightly more "authoritative" than the boss does.

Likert believes that the predominant management style in U.S. industry today falls about in the middle of his chart, even though most managers seem to know from personal observation of other organizations that a more participative approach works better. What accounts for their consistent failure to emulate what they consider successful? Reaching for a general explanation, Likert asks his subjects one final question: "In your experience, what happens when the senior officer becomes concerned about earnings and takes steps to cut costs, increase productivity, and improve profits?" Most reply that the company's management profile shifts left, toward the authoritarian style. General orders to economize—and promptly—often result in quick, across-the-board budget cuts. Some programs with high potential are sacrificed along with obvious losers. Carefully laid, logical plans go down the drain. Some people are laid off—usually the least essential ones. But the best people in the organization sooner or later rebel at arbitrary decisions, and many of them leave.

At the outset, the arbitrary cost cutting produces a fairly prompt improvement in earnings, of course. But there is an unrecognized trade-off in the subsequent loss of human capital, which shows up still later in loss of business. In due course, management has to "swing right" again, rebuilding its human assets at great expense in order to restore good performance. Yet the manager who puts his firm through this dreary cycle, Likert observes, is often rewarded with a bonus at the outset, when things still look good. Indeed, he may be sent off to work his magic in another division!

Likert acknowledges that there are emergencies when sharp and sudden belt-tightening is inescapable. The trouble, he says, is that it is frequently at the expense of human assets and relationships that have taken years to build. Often it would make more sense to sell off inventory or dispose of a plant. But such possibilities are overlooked because human assets do not show up in the traditional balance sheet

**TABLE 1**

| | System 1 Exploitative Authoritative | System 2 Benevolent Authoritative | System 3 Consultative | System 4 Participative Group |
|---|---|---|---|---|
| **Leadership** | | | | |
| How much confidence is shown in subordinates? | None | Condescending | Substantial | Complete |
| How free do they feel to talk to superiors about job? | Not at all | Not very | Rather free | Fully free |
| Are subordinates' ideas sought and used, if worthy? | Seldom | Sometimes | Usually | Always |
| **Motivation** | | | | |
| Is predominant use made of (1) fear, (2) threats, (3) punishment, (4) rewards, (5) involvement? | 1, 2, 3, occasionally 4 | 4, some 3 | 4, some 3 and 5 | 5, 4 based on group set goals |
| Where is responsibility felt for achieving organization's goals? | Mostly at top | Top and middle | Fairly general | At all levels |
| **Communication** | | | | |
| How much communication is aimed at achieving organization's objectives? | Very little | Little | Quite a bit | A great deal |
| What is the direction of information flow? | Downward | Mostly downward | Down and up | Down, up, and sideways |
| How is downward communication accepted? | With suspicion | Possibly with suspicion | With caution | With an open mind |
| How accurate is upward communication? | Often wrong | Censored for the boss | Limited accuracy | Accurate |

| | Know little | Some knowledge | Quite well | Very well |
|---|---|---|---|---|
| How well do superiors know problems faced by subordinates? | Know little | Some knowledge | Quite well | Very well |
| **Decisions** | | | | |
| At what level are decisions formally made? | Mostly at top | Policy at top, some delegation | Broad policy at top, more delegation | Throughout but well integrated |
| What is the origin of technical and professional knowledge used in decision making | Top management | Upper and middle | To a certain extent, throughout | To a great extent, throughout |
| Are subordinates involved in decisions related to their work? | Not at all | Occasionally consulted | Generally consulted | Fully involved |
| What does decision-making process contribute to motivation? | Nothing, often weakens it | Relatively little | Some contribution | Substantial contribution |
| **Goals** | | | | |
| How are organizational goals established? | Orders issued | Orders, some comment invited | After discussion, by orders | By group action (except in crisis) |
| How much covert resistance to goals is present? | Strong resistance | Moderate resistance | Some resistance at times | Little or none |
| **Control** | | | | |
| How concentrated are review and control functions? | Highly at top | Relatively highly at top | Moderate delegation to lower levels | Quite widely shared |
| Is there an informal organization resisting the formal one? | Yes | Usually | Sometimes | No—same goals as formal |
| What are cost, productivity, and other control data used for? | Policing, punishment | Reward and punishment | Reward, some self-guidance | Self-guidance, problem solving |

SOURCE: Adapted, with permission, from *The Human Organization: Its Management and Value*, by Rensis Likert. Published in April 1967, by McGraw-Hill.

the way physical assets do. A company can, of course, lose $100,000 worth of talent and look better on its statement than if it sells off $10,000 worth of inventory at half price.

A dollars-and-cents way of listing the value of a good engineering staff, an experienced shop crew, or an executive group with effective, established working relations might indeed steady the hand of a hard-pressed president whose banker is on the phone. Likert believes he is now on the trail of a way to assign such values—values that should be at least as realistic as the often arbitrary and outdated figures given for real estate and plant. It will take some doing to get the notion accepted by bankers and accountants, however sophisticated his method turns out to be. But today's executives are hardly unaware that their long payrolls of expensive scientific and managerial talent represent an asset as well as an expense. Indeed, it is an asset that is often bankable. A merely more regular, explicit recognition of human assets in cost-cutting decisions would help to ensure that human assets get at least an even break with plant and inventory in time of trouble.

Likert and his institute colleagues are negotiating with several corporations to enlist them in a systematic five-year study, in effect a controlled experiment, that should put a firmer footing under tentative conclusions and hypotheses. This study will test Likert's belief that across-the-board participative management, carefully developed, sustained through thick and thin, and supported by a balance sheet that somehow reckons the human factor, will show better long-run results than the cyclical swing between authoritarian and participative styles reflected in the typical middle-ground profile on his chart.

## CONVERSION IN A PAJAMA FACTORY

Already there's enough evidence in industry experience to suggest that participative management gets in trouble when it is adopted too fast. In some cases, an authoritarian management has abruptly ordered junior executives or employees to start taking on more responsibility, not recognizing that the directive itself reasserted the fact of continuing centralized control. Sometimes, of course, a hard shove may be necessary, as in the recent experience of Harwood Manufacturing Corp. of Marion, Virginia, which has employed participative practices widely for many years. When it acquired a rival pajama maker, Weldon Manufacturing Co., the latter's long-held authoritarian traditions were hard to crack. With patient but firm prodding by outside consultants, who acknowledge an initial element of "coercion," the switch in style was finally accomplished.

Ideally, in the view of Likert and others, a move of this kind should begin with the patient education of top executives, followed by the development of the needed skills in internal communication, group leadership, and the other requisites of the new system. Given time, this will produce better employee attitudes and begin to harness personal motivation to corporate goals. Still later, there will be improved productivity, less waste, lower turnover and absence rates, fewer grievances and slow-downs, improved product quality, and, finally, better customer relations.

The transformation may take several years. A checkup too early in the game might prove that participative management, even when thoroughly understood and embraced at the top, doesn't produce better results. By the same token, a management that is retreating from the new style in a typical cost squeeze may still be nominally participative, yet may already have thrown away the fruits of the system. Some research findings do indicate that participation isn't producing the hoped-for results. In Likert's view, these were spot checks, made without regard to which way the company was tending and where it was in the cycle of change.

A growing number of behaviorists, however, have begun to question whether the participative style is an ideal toward which all management should strive. If they once believed it was, more as a matter of faith in their long struggle against the "scientific" manager's machine-like view of man than as a finding from any new science of their own, they are now ready to take a second look at the proposition.

It seems plain enough that a research scientist generally benefits from a good deal of freedom and autonomy, and that top executives, confronted every day by new problems that no routine can anticipate, operate better with maximum consultation and uninhibited contributions from every member of the team. If the vice-president for finance can't talk candidly with the vice-president for production about financing the new plant, a lot of time can be wasted. In sales, group effort—instead of the usual competition—can be highly productive. But in the accounting department, things must go by the book. "Creative accounting" sounds more like a formula for jail than for the old behaviorists' dream of personal self-fulfillment on the job. And so with quality control in the chemical plant. An inspired adjustment here and there isn't welcome, thank you; just follow the specifications.

In the production department, automation has washed out a lot of the old problem of man as a prisoner of the assembly line, the kind of problem that first brought the "human relations" experts into the factories in the 1920s and 1930s. If a shop is full of computer-controlled machine tools busily reproducing themselves, the boy with the broom who sweeps away the shavings may be the only one who can put a personal flourish into his work. The creativity is all upstairs in the engineering and programming departments. But then, so are most of the people.

"Look what's happened in the last twenty years," says Harold J. Leavitt, a social psychologist who recently moved to Stanford after some years at Carnegie Tech. "Originally the concern of the human relations people was with the blue-collar worker. Then the focus began to shift to foremen and to middle management. Now it's concentrated in special areas like research and development and in top management. Why? Because the 'group' style works best where nobody knows exactly and all the time what they're supposed to be doing, where there's a continuous need to change and adapt."

## DEMOCRACY WORKS BETTER IN PLASTICS

One conclusion that has been drawn from this is that management style has to be custom designed to fit the particular characteristics of each industry. The participative approach will work best in those industries that are in the vanguard of change. A Harvard Business School study has compared high performance companies in three related, but subtly different, fields: plastics, packaged food, and standard containers. The plastics company faced the greatest uncertainties and change in research, new products, and market developments. The food company's business was somewhat more stable, while the container company encountered little or no requirement for innovation. The three achieved good results using markedly different management styles. The plastics firm provided for wide dispersal of responsibility for major decisions, the food company for moderate decentralization of authority, and the container company operated with highly centralized control.

Less successful enterprises in each of the three industries were also examined, and their managements were compared with those of the high performance companies. From this part of the study, Harvard researchers Paul Lawrence and Jay Lorsch drew another conclusion; not only may each industry have its own appropriate management style, but so may the individual operations within the same company. The companies that do best are those which allow for variations among their departments and know how to take these variations into account in coordinating the whole corporate effort.

Both the sales and the research departments in a fast-moving plastics company, for example, may adopt a style that encourages employees to participate actively in departmental decision making. But in special ways the two operations still need to differ. The research worker, for example, thinks in long-range terms, focusing on results expected in two or three years. The sales executive has his sights set on results next week or next month. This different sense of time may make it hard for the two departments to understand each other. But if top management recognizes the reasons and the need for such differences, each department will do its own job better, and they can be better coordinated. On the other hand, if top management ignores the differences and insists for example, on rigidly uniform budgeting and planning timetables, there will be a loss of effectiveness.

It seems an obvious point that sales must be allowed to operate like sales, accounting like accounting, and production like production. But as Lawrence comments, "The mark of a good idea in this field is that as soon as it is articulated, it does seem obvious. People forget that, five minutes before, it wasn't. One curse of the behavioral scientist is that anything he comes up with is going to seem that way, because anything that's good *is* obvious."

## PEOPLE, TOO, HAVE THEIR STYLES

Other behavioral scientists take the view that management style should be determined not so much by the nature of the particular business operation involved, but by the personality traits of the people themselves. There may be some tendency for certain kinds of jobs to attract certain kinds of people. But in nearly any shop or office a wide range of personality types may be observed. There is, for example, the outgoing, socially oriented scientist as well as the supposedly more typical introverted recluse. There are mature, confident managers, and there are those who somehow fill the job despite nagging self-doubt and a consuming need for reassurance.

For a long time, personality tests seemed to offer a way to steer people into the psychologically right kind of work. Whether such testing for placement is worthwhile is now a matter of some dispute. In any case, the whole question of individual differences is often reduced to little more than an office guessing game. Will Sue cooperate with Jane? Can Dorothy stand working for Jim? Will Harry take suggestions?

The participative approach to management may be based upon a greatly oversimplified notion about people, in the view of psychologist Clare Graves of Union College in Schenectady, New York. On the basis of limited samplings, he tentatively concludes that as many as half the people in the northeastern U.S., and a larger proportion nation-wide, are not and many never will be the eager beaver workers on whom the late Douglas McGregor of M.I.T. based his "Theory Y." Only some variation of old-style authoritarian management will meet their psychological needs, Graves contends.

Graves believes he has identified seven fairly distinct personality types, although he acknowledges that many people are not "purebreds" who would fit his abstractions perfectly and that new and higher personality forms may still be evolving. At the bottom of his well-ordered hierarchy he places the childlike "autistic" personality, which requires "close care and nurturing." Next up the scale are the "animistic" type, which must be dealt with by sheer force or enticement; the "ordered" personality that responds best to a moralistic management; and the "materialistic" individual who calls for pragmatic, hard bargaining. None of these are suited for the participative kind of management.

At the top of Graves's personality ladder are the "sociocentric," the "cognitive," and the "apprehending" types of people. They are motivated, respectively, by a need for "belonging," for "information," and for an "understanding" of the total situation in which they are involved. For each of these levels some form of participative management will work. However, those at the very top, the unemotional "apprehending" individuals, must be allowed pretty much to set their own terms for work. Management can trust such people to contribute usefully only according to their own cool perception of what is needed. They will seldom take the trouble to fight authority when they disagree with it, but merely withdraw, do a passable but not excellent job, and wait for management to see things their way. In that sense, these highest-level people are probably not ideal participators.

Graves believes most adults are stuck at one level throughout their lifetimes or move up a single notch, at best. He finds, incidentally, that there can be bright or dull, mature or immature behavior at nearly all levels. The stages simply represent psychological growth toward a larger and larger awareness of the individual's relationship to society.

If a company has a mixture of personality types, as most do, it must somehow sort them out. One way would be to place participative-type managers in charge of some groups, and authoritarian managers in charge of others. Employees would then be encouraged to transfer into sections where the management style best suits them. This would hardly simplify corporate life. But companies pushing the group approach might at least avoid substituting harmful new rigidities—"participate, or else!"—for the old ones.

## THE ANTHROPOLOGICAL VIEW

Behaviorists who have been studying management problems from an anthropological viewpoint naturally stress cultural rather than individual differences. Manning Nash, of the University of Chicago's business school, for example, observes that the American emphasis on egalitarianism and performance has always tempered management style in the U.S. "No matter what your role is, if you don't perform, no one in this country will defer to you," he says. "Americans won't act unless they respect you. You couldn't have an American Charge of the Light Brigade." But try to export that attitude to a country with a more autocratic social tradition, and, in the words of Stanley Davis of Harvard, "it won't be bought and may not be workable."

Within the U.S. there are many cultural differences that might provide guides to managerial style if they could be successfully analyzed. Recent research by Lawrence and Arthur N. Turner at the Harvard Business School hints at important differences between blue-collar workers in cities and those in smaller towns, although religious and other factors fog the results. Town workers seem to seek "a relatively large amount of variety, autonomy, interaction, skill and responsibility" in their work, whereas city workers "find more simple tasks less stress-producing and more satisfying."

In managerial areas where democratic techniques *are* likely to work, the problem is how to give managers skill and practice in participation. The National Education Association's National Training Laboratories 20 years ago pioneered a way of doing this called "sensitivity training" (see "Two Weeks in a T-Group," *Fortune,* August 1961). Small groups of men, commonly drawn from the executive ranks, sit down with a professional trainer but without agenda or rule book and "see what happens." The "vacuum" draws out first one and then another participant, in a way that tends to expose in fairly short order how he comes across to others.

The technique has had many critics, few more vocal than William Gomberg of the University of Pennsylvania's Wharton School. Renewing his assault recently, he called the "training" groups "titillating therapy, management development's most fashionable fad." When people from the same company are in the group, he argues, the whole exercise is an invasion of privacy, an abuse of the therapeutic technique to help the company, not the individual. For top executives in such groups, Gomberg and others contend, the technique offers mainly a catharsis for their loneliness or insecurity.

## "PSYCHING OUT THE BOSS"

Undoubtedly the T-groups can be abused, intentionally or otherwise. But today's sensitivity trainers are trying to make sure the experience leads to useful results for both the individual and his firm. They realize that early groups, made up of total strangers gathered at some remote "cultural island," often gave the executive little notion of how to apply his new knowledge back on the job. To bring more realism to the exercise, the National Training Laboratories began 10 years ago to make up groups of executives and managers from the same company, but not men who had working relationships with one another. These "cousin labs" have led, in turn, to some training of actual management "families," a boss and his subordinates. At the West Coast headquarters of the T-group movement, the business school at U.C.L.A., some now call such training "task-group therapy."

Many businessmen insist T-groups have helped them. Forty-three presidents and chairmen and hundreds of lesser executives are National Training Laboratories alumni. U.C.L.A. is besieged by applicants, and many are turned away.

Sensitivity training is supposed to help most in business situations where there is a great deal of uncertainty, as there is in the training sessions themselves. In such situations in the corporate setting there is sometimes a tendency for executives to withdraw, to defer action, to play a kind of game with other people in the organization to see who will climb out on a limb first. A chief ploy is "psyching out the boss," which means trying to anticipate the way the winds of ultimate decision will blow and to set course accordingly.

The aim of sensitivity training is to stop all this, to get the executive's nerve up so that he faces facts, or, in the words of U.C.L.A.'s James V. Clark, to "lay bare the stress and strain faster and get a resolution of the problem." In that limited sense, such therapy could well serve any style of management. In Clark's view, this kind of training, early in the game, might save many a company a costly detour on the road to company-wide "democracy." He cites the experience of Non-Linear Systems, Inc., of Del Mar, California, a manufacturer of such electronic gear as digital voltmeters and data-logging equipment and an important supplier to aerospace contractors. The company is headed by Andrew Kay, a leading champion of the participative style. At the lower levels, Kay's application of participative concepts worked well. He gave workers responsibility for "the whole black box" instead of for pieces of his complex finished products. Because it was still a box, with some definite boundaries, the workers seized the new opportunity without fear or hesitation. The psychological magic of meaningful work, as opposed to the hopelessly specialized chore, took hold. Productivity rose.

## VICE PRESIDENTS IN MIDAIR

But at the executive level, Kay moved too quickly, failing to prepare his executives for broad and undefined responsibilities—or failing to choose men better suited for the challenge. One vice president was put in charge of "innovation." Suspended in midair, without the support of departments or functional groups and lacking even so much as a job description, most of the VPs became passive and incapable of making decisions. "They lost touch with reality—including the reality of the market," recalls Clark. When the industry suffered a general slump and new competition entered the field, Non-Linear wasn't ready. Sales dropped 16 percent, according to Kay. In time he realized he was surrounded with dependent men, untrained to participate in the fashion he had peremptorily commanded. He trimmed his executive group and expects to set a new sales record this year.

Sheldon Davis of TRW Systems in Redondo Beach, California, blames the behavioral scientists themselves for breakdowns like Non-Linear's. Too often, he argues, "their messages come out sounding soft and easy, as if what we are trying to do is build happy teams of employees who feel 'good' about things, rather than saying we're trying to build effective organizations with groups that function well and that can zero in quickly on their problems and deal with them rationally."

To Davis, participation should mean "tough, open exchange," focused on the problem, not the organizational chart. Old-style managers who simply dictate a solution are wrong, he argues, and so are those new-style managers who think the idea is simply to go along with a subordinate's proposals if they're earnestly offered. Neither approach taps the full potential of the executive group. When problems are faced squarely, Davis believes, the boss—who should remain boss—gets the best solution because all relevant factors are thoroughly considered. And because everyone has contributed to the solution and feels responsible for it, it is also the solution most likely to be carried out.

One of the most useful new developments in the behavioral study of management is a fresh emphasis on collaboration with technology. In the early days of the human-relations movement in industry, technology was often regarded as "the enemy," the source of the personal and social problems that the psychologists were trying to treat. But from the beginning, some social scientists wanted to move right in and help fashion machines and industrial processes so as to reduce or eliminate their supposedly antihuman effects. Today this concept is more than mere talk. The idea is to develop so-called "sociotechnical" systems that permit man and technology *together* to produce the best performance.

Some early experimentation in the British coal mines, by London's Tavistock Institute, as well as scattered work in this country and in Scandinavia, have already demonstrated practical results from such a collaboration. Tavistock found that an attempt to apply specialized factory-style technology to coal mining had isolated the miners from one another. They missed the sense of group support and self-direction that had helped them cope with uncertainty and danger deep in the coal faces. Productivity suffered. In this case, Tavistock's solution was to redesign the new system so that men could still work in groups.

In the U.S. a manufacturer of small household appliances installed some highly sophisticated new technical processes that put the company well in the front of its field. But the engineers had broken down the jobs to such an extent that workers were getting no satisfaction out of their performance and productivity declined. Costs went up and, in the end, some of the new machinery had to be scrapped.

Some technologists seem more than ready to welcome a partnership with the human-relations expert. Louis Davis, a professor of engineering, has joined the U.C.L.A. business-school faculty to lead a six-man sociotechnical research group that includes several behaviorists. Among them is Eric Trist, a highly respected psychologist from the Tavistock Institute. Davis hopes today's collaboration will lead in time to a new breed of experts knowledgeable in both the engineering and the social disciplines.

## "IT'S TIME WE STOPPED BUILDING RIVAL DICTIONARIES"

The importance of time, the nature of the task, the differences within a large organization, the nature of the people, the cultural setting, the psychological preparation of management, the relationship to technology—all these and other variables are making the search for effective managerial style more and more complex. But the growing recognition of these complexities has drained the human-relations movement of much of its antagonism toward the "superrationalism" of management science. Humanists must be more systematic and rational if they are to make some useful sense of the scattered and half-tested concepts they have thus far developed, and put their new theories to a real test.

A number of behaviorists believe it is well past time to bury the hatchet and collaborate in earnest with the mathematicians and economists. Some business schools and commercial consulting groups are already realigning their staffs to encourage such work. It won't be easy. Most "systems" thinkers are preoccupied with bringing all the relevant knowledge to bear on a management problem in a systematic way, seeking the theoretically "best" solution. Most behaviorists have tended to assume that the solution which is *most likely to be carried out* is the best one, hence their focus on involving lots of people in the decision making so that they will follow through. Where the "experts" who shape decisions are also in charge of getting the job done, the two approaches sometimes blend, in practice. But in many organizations, it is a long, long road from a creative and imaginative decision to actual performance. A general theory of management must show how to build systematic expertise into a style that is also well suited to people.

The rapprochement among management theorists has a distinguished herald, Fritz J. Roethlisberger of Harvard Business School, one of the human-relations pioneers who first disclosed the potential of the "small group" in industrial experiments 40 years ago. He laughs quickly at any suggestion that a unified approach will come easily. "But after all, we are all looking at the same thing," he says. "It's time we stopped building rival dictionaries and learned to make some sentences that really say something."

PART FIVE

# Managing Organizational Behavior

In this last section our focus is on management processes that extend beyond an individual or group focus and encompass actions and behaviors at all levels of the organization. Managing behavior at the organizational level includes the topics of leadership, motivation, decision making, and organizational development. Each of these comprises a portion of this section.

Probably no other area of managerial endeavor has received as much interest and emphasis for so long a time as leadership. The earliest writings bearing on leadership date back to around 1100 B.C. and the constitution of Chow, indicating the Chinese were cognizant of the importance of this process. Specific principles of leadership were addressed by Sun Tzu around 500 B.C. Since this time numerous writers have studied leadership, resulting in a myriad of many times confusing and sometimes contradictory approaches, schools, theories, and styles. Nonetheless, significant strides have been made in understanding the dynamics of leadership.

Leadership is influence, and influence is what we are trying to exert when we talk about motivation. Motivation may be thought of as external (something we do to someone) and typified by the carrot-and-stick approach, or it may be conceived as internal (something someone does to him or herself) and typified by the behavioral science approaches. A variety of perspectives are represented by the articles in this portion of Part Five.

Of all the management processes, decision making is in many respects the most complex. It has been said that management *is* decision making, and thus the very essence of the entire managerial process is to be found in its study. The earliest managers made decisions on the basis of hunch, guesswork, intuition, and, in some cases, palmists and the phases of the moon. Today's managers have at their disposal a variety of decision-making tools and techniques their predecessors lacked, including the computer and a host of such quantitative techniques as decision theory, linear programming, and simulation.

Organizations, and the environments in which they operate, are constantly changing. Organizational development is a term used to refer to the process of preparing for and managing change. Organizational development efforts are typically intended to affect people's beliefs, values, attitudes, and behaviors. Regardless of the focus, the payoff is to be found in increased organizational effectiveness and efficiency, and in an enhanced capability to deal successfully with change.

*A. Leadership*

# 24

---

# The Manager's Job:
# Folklore and Fact

## Henry Mintzberg

*Mintzberg's article explores the popular notion that a manager's time is spent planning, organizing, controlling, and directing. He argues that, instead, managerial time is spent in a variety of roles—most of which are a far cry from the usual perception of the job. Note that he argues for better training of managers by our business schools.—Eds.*

If you ask a manager what he does, he will most likely tell you that he plans, organizes, coordinates, and controls. Then watch what he does. Don't be surprised if you can't relate what you see to these four words.

When he is called and told that one of his factories has just burned down, and he advises the caller to see whether temporary arrangements can be made to supply customers through a foreign subsidiary, is he planning, organizing, coordinating, or controlling? How about when he presents a gold watch to a retiring employee? Or when he attends a conference to meet people in the trade? Or on returning from that conference, when he tells one of his employees about an interesting product idea he picked up there?

The fact is that these four words, which have dominated management vocabulary since the French industrialist Henri Fayol first introduced them in 1916, tell us little about what managers actually do.

---

At best, they indicate some vague objectives managers have when they work.

The field of management, so devoted to progress and change, has for more than half a century not seriously addressed *the* basic question: What do managers do? Without a proper answer, how can we teach management? How can we design planning or information systems for managers? How can we improve the practice of management at all?

Our ignorance of the nature of managerial work shows up in various ways in the modern organization—in the boast by the successful manager that he never spent a single day in a management training program; in the turnover of corporate planners who never quite understood what it was the manager wanted; in the computer consoles gathering dust in the back room because the managers never used the fancy on-line MIS some analyst thought they needed. Perhaps most important, our ignorance shows up in the inability of our large public organizations to come to grips with some of their most serious policy problems.

Somehow, in the rush to automate production, to use management science in the functional areas of marketing and finance, and to apply the skills of the behavioral scientist to the problem of worker motivation, the manager—that person in charge of the organization or one of its subunits—has been forgotten.

My intention in this article is simple: to break the reader away from Fayol's words and introduce him to a more supportable, and what I believe to be a more useful, description of managerial work. This description derives from my review and synthesis of the available research on how various managers have spent their time.

In some studies, managers were observed intensively ("shadowed" is the term some of them used); in a number of others, they kept detailed diaries of their activities; in a few studies, their records were analyzed. All kinds of managers were studied—foremen, factory supervisors, staff managers, field sales managers, hospital administrators, presidents of companies and nations, and even street gang leaders. These "managers" worked in the United States, Canada, Sweden, and Great Britain. The insert (on the next page) is a brief review of the major studies that I found most useful in developing this description, including my own study of five American chief executive officers.

A synthesis of these findings paints an interesting picture, one as different from Fayol's classical view as a cubist abstract is from a Renaissance painting. In a sense, this picture will be obvious to anyone who has ever spent a day in a manager's office, either in front of the desk or behind it. Yet, at the same time, this picture may turn out to be revolutionary, in that it throws into doubt so much of the folklore that we have accepted about the manager's work.

I first discuss some of the folklore and contrast it with some of the discoveries of systematic research—the hard facts about how managers spend their time. Then I synthesize these research findings in a description of ten roles that seem to describe the essential content of all managers' jobs. In a concluding section, I discuss a number of implications of this synthesis for those trying to achieve more effective management, both in classrooms and in the business world.

## SOME FOLKLORE AND FACTS ABOUT MANAGERIAL WORK

There are four myths about the manager's job that do not bear up under careful scrutiny of the facts.

### 1

*Folklore: The manager is a reflective, systematic planner.* The evidence on this issue is overwhelming, but not a shred of it supports this statement.

*Fact: Study after study has shown that managers work at an unrelenting pace, that their activities are characterized by brevity, variety, and discontinuity, and that they are strongly oriented to action and dislike reflective activities.* Consider this evidence:

Half the activities engaged in by the five chief executives of my study lasted less than nine minutes, and only 10 percent exceeded one hour.[1] A study of 56 U.S. foremen found that they averaged 583 activities per eight-hour shift, an average of 1 every 48 seconds.[2] The work pace for both chief executives and foremen was unrelenting. The chief executives met a steady stream of callers and mail from the moment they arrived in the morning until they left in the evening. Coffee breaks and lunches were inevitably work related, and ever-present subordinates seemed to usurp any free moment.

A diary study of 160 British middle and top managers found that they worked for a half hour or more without interruption only about once every two days.[3]

Of the verbal contacts of the chief executives in my study, 93 percent were arranged on an ad hoc basis. Only 1 percent of the executives' time was spent in open-ended observational tours. Only 1 out of 368 verbal contacts was unrelated to a specific issue and could be called general planning. Another researcher finds that "in *not one single case* did a manager report the obtaining of important external

Considering its central importance to every aspect of management, there has been surprisingly little research on the manager's work, and virtually no systematic building of knowledge from one group of studies to another. In seeking to describe managerial work, I conducted my own research and also scanned the literature widely to integrate the findings of studies from many diverse sources with my own. These studies focused on two very different aspects of managerial work. Some

company's stand on some proposed legislation in order to change a regulation. A few of the studies of managerial work are widely known, but most have remained buried as single journal articles or isolated books. Among the more important ones I cite (with full references in the footnotes) are the following:

☐

Sune Carlson developed the diary method to study the work characteristics of nine Swedish managing directors. Each kept a

"anthropological," Sayles studied the work content of middle- and lower-level managers in a large U.S. corporation. Sayles moved freely in the company, collecting whatever information struck him as important.

☐

Perhaps the best-known source is *Presidential Power*, in which Richard Neustadt analyzes the power and managerial behavior of Presidents Roosevelt, Truman, and Eisenhower. Neustadt used secondary sources—documents and interviews

emotional roles were divided among the three managers.

☐

William F. Whyte, from his study of a street gang during the Depression, wrote *Street Corner Society*. His findings about the gang's leadership, which George C. Homans analyzed in *The Human Group*, suggest some interesting similarities of job content between street gang leaders and corporate managers.

My own study involved five American CEOs of middle-to large-size organizations—a consulting firm, a technology company, a hospital, a consumer goods company, and a school system. Using a method called "structural observation," during one intensive week of observation for each executive I recorded various aspects of every piece of mail and every verbal contact. My method was designed to capture data on both work characteristics and job content. In all, I analyzed 890 pieces of incoming and outgoing mail and 368 verbal contacts.

were concerned with the characteristics of the work—how long managers work, where, at what pace and with what interruptions, with whom they work, and through what media they communicate. Other studies were more concerned with the essential content of the work—what activities the managers actually carry out, and why. Thus, after a meeting, one researcher might note that the manager spent 45 minutes with three government officials in their Washington office, while another might record that he presented his

detailed log of his activities. Carlson's results are reported in his book *Executive Behavior*. A number of British researchers, notably Rosemary Stewart, have subsequently used Carlson's method. In *Managers and Their Jobs*, she describes the study of 160 top and middle managers of British companies during four weeks, with particular attention to the differences in their work.

□ Leonard Sayles's book *Managerial Behavior* is another important reference. Using a method he refers to as

with other parties—to generate his data.

□ Robert H. Guest, in *Personnel*, reports on a study of the foreman's working day. Fifty-six U.S. foremen were observed and each of their activities recorded during one eight-hour shift.

□ Richard C. Hodgson, Daniel J. Levinson, and Abraham Zaleznik studied a team of three top executives of a U.S. hospital. From that study they wrote *The Executive Role Constellation*. These researchers addressed in particular the way in which work and socio-

information from a general conversation or other undirected personal communication."[4]

No study has found important patterns in the way managers schedule their time. They seem to jump from issue to issue, continually responding to the needs of the moment.

Is this the planner that the classical view describes? Hardly. How, then, can we explain this behavior? The manager is simply responding to the pressures of his job. I found that my chief executives terminated many of their own activities, often leaving meetings before the end, and interrupted their desk work to call in subordinates. One president not only placed his desk so that he could look down a long hallway but also left his door open when he was alone—an invitation for subordinates to come in and interrupt him.

Clearly, these managers wanted to encourage the flow of current information. But more significantly, they seemed to be conditioned by their own work loads. They appreciated the opportunity cost of their own time, and they were continually aware of their ever-present obligations—mail to be answered, callers to attend to, and so on. It seems that no matter what he is doing, the manager is plagued by the possibilities of what he might do and what he must do.

When the manager must plan, he seems to do so implicitly in the context of daily actions, not in some abstract process reserved for two weeks in the organization's mountain retreat. The plans of the chief executives I studied seemed to exist only in their heads—as flexible, but often specific, intentions. The traditional literature notwithstanding, the job of managing does not breed reflective planners; the manager is a real-time responder to stimuli, an individual who is conditioned by his job to prefer live to delayed action.

## 2

*Folklore: The effective manager has no regular duties to perform.* Managers are constantly being told to spend more time planning and delegating, and less time seeing customers and engaging in negotiations. These are not, after all, the true tasks of the manager. To use the popular analogy, the good manager, like the good conductor, carefully orchestrates everything in advance, then sits back to enjoy the fruits of his labor, responding occasionally to an unforeseeable exception.

But here again the pleasant abstraction just does not seem to hold up. We had better take a closer look at those activities managers feel compelled to engage in before we arbitrarily define them away.

*Fact: In addition to handling exceptions, managerial work involves performing a number of regular duties, including ritual and ceremony, negotiations, and processing of soft information that links the organi-*

*zation with its environment.* Consider some evidence from the research studies:

A study of the work of the presidents of small companies found that they engaged in routine activities because their companies could not afford staff specialists and were so thin on operating personnel that a single absence often required the president to substitute.[5]

One study of field sales managers and another of chief executives suggest that it is a natural part of both jobs to see important customers, assuming the managers wish to keep those customers.[6]

Someone, only half in jest, once described the manager as that person who sees visitors so that everyone else can get his work done. In my study, I found that certain ceremonial duties—meeting visiting dignitaries, giving out gold watches, presiding at Christmas dinners— were an intrinsic part of the chief executive's job.

Studies of managers' information flow suggest that managers play a key role in securing "soft" external information (much of it available only to them because of their status) and in passing it along to their subordinates.

### 3

*Folklore: The senior manager needs aggregated information, which a formal management information system best provides.* Not too long ago, the words *total information system* were everywhere in the management literature. In keeping with the classical view of the manager as that individual perched on the apex of a regulated, hierarchical system, the literature's manager was to receive all his important information from a giant, comprehensive MIS.

But lately, as it has become increasingly evident that these giant MIS systems are not working—that managers are simply not using them—the enthusiasm has waned. A look at how managers actually process information makes the reason quite clear. Managers have five media at their command—documents, telephone calls, scheduled and unscheduled meetings, and observational tours.

*Fact: Managers strongly favor the verbal media—namely, telephone calls and meetings.* The evidence comes from every single study of managerial work. Consider the following:

In two British studies, managers spent an average of 66 percent and 80 percent of their time in verbal (oral) communication.[7] In my study of five American chief executives, the figure was 78 percent.

These five chief executives treated mail processing as a burden to be dispensed with. One came in Saturday morning to process 142 pieces of mail in just over three hours, to "get rid of all the stuff." This same manager looked at the first piece of "hard" mail he had received all week, a standard cost report, and put it aside with the comment, "I never look at this."

These same five chief executives responded immediately to 2 of the 40 routine reports they received during the five weeks of my study and to 4 items in the 104 periodicals. They skimmed most of these periodicals in seconds, almost ritualistically. In all, these chief executives of good-sized organizations initiated on their own—that is, not in response to something else—a grand total of 25 pieces of mail during the 25 days I observed them.

An analysis of the mail the executives received reveals an interesting picture—only 13 percent was of specific and immediate use. So now we have another piece in the puzzle: not much of the mail provides live, current information—the action of a competitor, the mood of a government legislator, or the rating of last night's television show. Yet this is the information that drove the managers, interrupting their meetings and rescheduling their workdays.

Consider another interesting finding. Managers seem to cherish "soft" information, especially gossip, hearsay, and speculation. Why? The reason is its timeliness; today's gossip may be tomorrow's fact. The manager who is not accessible for the telephone call informing him that his biggest customer was seen golfing with his main competitor may read about a dramatic drop in sales in the next quarterly report. But then it's too late.

To assess the value of historical, aggregated, "hard" MIS information, consider two of the manager's prime uses for his information— to identify problems and opportunities[8] and to build his own mental models of the things around him (e.g., how his organization's budget system works, how his customers buy his product, how changes in the economy affect his organization, and so on). Every bit of evidence suggests that the manager identifies decision situations and builds models not with the aggregated abstractions an MIS provides, but with specific tidbits of data.

Consider the words of Richard Neustadt, who studied the information-collecting habits of Presidents Roosevelt, Truman, and Eisenhower:

> It is not information of a general sort that helps a President see personal stakes; not summaries, not surveys, not the *bland amalgams*. Rather . . . it is the odds and ends of *tangible detail* that pieced together in his mind illuminate the underside of issues put before him. To help himself he must reach out as widely as he can for every scrap of fact, opinion, gossip, bearing on his interests and relationships as President. He must become his own director of his own central intelligence.[9]

The manager's emphasis on the verbal media raises two important points:

First, verbal information is stored in the brains of people. Only when people write this information down can it be stored in the files of the organization—whether in metal cabinets or on magnetic tape—and managers apparently do not write down much of what they hear. Thus the strategic data bank of the organization is not in the memory of its computers but in the minds of its managers.

Second, the manager's extensive use of verbal media helps to explain why he is reluctant to delegate tasks. When we note that most of the manager's important information comes in verbal form and is stored in his head, we can well appreciate his reluctance. It is not as if he can hand a dossier over to someone; he must take the time to "dump memory"—to tell that someone all he knows about the subject. But this could take so long that the manager may find it easier to do the task himself. Thus the manager is damned by his own information system to a "dilemma of delegation"—to do too much himself or to delegate to his subordinates with inadequate briefing.

### 4

*Folklore: Management is, or at least is quickly becoming, a science and a profession.* By almost any definitions of science and profession, this statement is false. Brief observation of any manager will quickly lay to rest the notion that managers practice a science. A science involves the enaction of systematic, analytically determined procedures or programs. If we do not even know what procedures managers use, how can we prescribe them by scientific analysis? And how can we call management a profession if we cannot specify what managers are to learn? For after all, a profession involves "knowledge of some department of learning or science" (*Random House Dictionary*).[10]

*Fact: The Managers' programs—to schedule time, process information, make decisions, and so on—remain locked deep inside their brains.* Thus, to describe these programs, we rely on words like *judgment* and *intuition,* seldom stopping to realize that they are merely labels for our ignorance.

I was struck during my study by the fact that the executives I was observing—all very competent by any standard—are fundamentally indistinguishable from their counterparts of a hundred years ago (or a thousand years ago, for that matter). The information they need differs, but they seek it in the same way—by word of mouth. Their decisions concern modern technology, but the procedures they use to make them are the same as the procedures of the nineteenth-century manager. Even the computer, so important for the specialized work of the organization, has apparently had no influence on the work procedures of general managers. In fact, the manager is in a kind of loop, with increasingly heavy work pressures but no aid forthcoming from management science.

Considering the facts about managerial work, we can see that the manager's job is enormously complicated and difficult. The manager is overburdened with obligations; yet he cannot easily delegate his tasks. As a result, he is driven to overwork and is forced to do many tasks superficially. Brevity, fragmentation, and verbal communication characterize his work. Yet these are the very characteristics of managerial work that have impeded scientific attempts to improve it. As a result, the management scientist has concentrated his efforts on the specialized functions of the organization, where he could more easily analyze the procedures and quantify the relevant information.[11]

But the pressures of the manager's job are becoming worse. Where before he needed only to respond to owners and directors, now he finds that subordinates with democratic norms continually reduce his freedom to issue unexplained orders, and a growing number of outside influences (consumer groups, government agencies, and so on) expect his attention. And the manager has had nowhere to turn for help. The first step in providing the manager with some help is to find out what his job really is.

## BACK TO A BASIC DESCRIPTION OF MANAGERIAL WORK

Now let us try to put some of the pieces of this puzzle together. Earlier, I defined the manager as that person in charge of an organization or one of its subunits. Besides chief executive officers, this definition would include vice presidents, bishops, foremen, hockey coaches, and prime ministers. Can all of these people have anything in common? Indeed they can. For an important starting point, all are vested with formal authority over an organizational unit. From formal authority comes status, which leads to various interpersonal relations, and from these comes access to information. Information, in turn, enables the manager to make decisions and strategies for his unit.

The manager's job can be described in terms of various "roles," or organized sets of behaviors identified with a position. My description, shown in Exhibit 1, comprises 10 roles. As we shall see, formal authority gives rise to the three interpersonal roles, which in turn give rise to the three informational roles; these two sets of roles enable the manager to play the four decisional roles.

**EXHIBIT 1**    The Manager's Roles

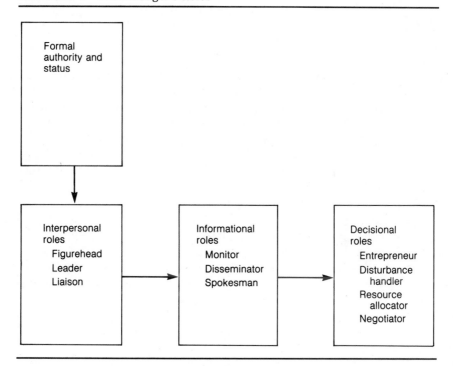

## Interpersonal Roles

Three of the manager's roles arise directly from his formal authority and involve basic interpersonal relationships.

**1**

First is the *figurehead* role. By virtue of his position as head of an organizational unit, every manager must perform some duties of a ceremonial nature. The president greets the touring dignitaries, the foreman attends the wedding of a lathe operator, and the sales manager takes an important customer to lunch.

The chief executives of my study spent 12 percent of their contact time on ceremonial duties; 17 percent of their incoming mail dealt with acknowledgments and requests related to their status. For example, a letter to a company president requested free merchandise for a crippled schoolchild; diplomas were put on the desk of the school superintendent for his signature.

Duties that involve interpersonal roles may sometimes be routine, involving little serious communication and no important decision making. Nevertheless, they are important to the smooth functioning of an organization and cannot be ignored by the manager.

## 2

Because he is in charge of an organizational unit, the manager is responsible for the work of the people of that unit. His actions in this regard constitute the *leader* role. Some of these actions involve leadership directly—for example, in most organizations the manager is normally responsible for hiring and training his own staff.

In addition, there is the indirect exercise of the leader role. Every manager must motivate and encourage his employees, somehow reconciling their individual needs with the goals of the organization. In virtually every contact the manager has with his employees, subordinates seeking leadership clues probe his actions: "Does he approve?" "How would he like the report to turn out?" "Is he more interested in market share than high profits?"

The influence of the manager is most clearly seen in the leader role. Formal authority vests him with great potential power; leadership determines in large part how much of it he will realize.

## 3

The literature of management has always recognized the leader role, particularly those aspects of it related to motivation. In comparison, until recently it has hardly mentioned the *liaison* role, in which the manager makes contacts outside his vertical chain of command. This is remarkable in light of the finding of virtually every study of managerial work that managers spend as much time with peers and other people outside their units as they do with their own subordinates—and, surprisingly, very little time with their own superiors.

In Rosemary Stewart's diary study, the 160 British middle and top managers spent 47 percent of their time with peers, 41 percent of their time with people outside their unit, and only 12 percent of their time with their superiors. For Robert H. Guest's study of U.S. foremen, the figures were 44 percent, 46 percent, and 10 percent. The chief executives of my study averaged 44 percent of their contact time with people outside their organizations, 48 percent with subordinates, and 7 percent with directors and trustees.

The contacts the five CEOs made were with an incredibly wide range of people: subordinates; clients, business associates, and suppliers; and peers—managers of similar organizations, government and trade organization officials, fellow directors on outside boards, and independents with no relevant organizational affiliations. The chief

**EXHIBIT 2**    The Chief Executives' Contacts

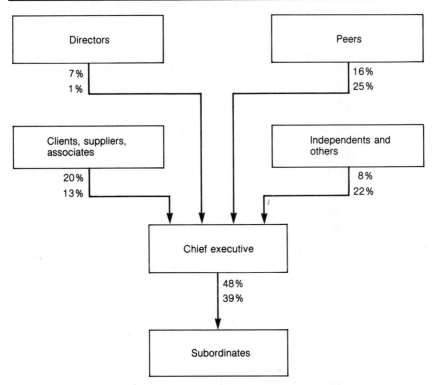

Note: The top figure indicates the proportion of total contact time spent with each group, and the bottom figure the proportion of mail from each group.

executives' time with and mail from these groups is shown in Exhibit 2. Guest's study of foremen shows, likewise, that their contacts were numerous and wide ranging, seldom involving fewer than 25 individuals, and often more than 50.

As we shall see shortly, the manager cultivates such contacts largely to find information. In effect, the liaison role is devoted to building up the manager's own external information system—informal, private, verbal, but, nevertheless, effective.

## Informational Roles

By virtue of his interpersonal contacts, both with his subordinates and with his network of contacts, the manager emerges as the nerve center of his organizational unit. He may not know everything, but he typically knows more than any member of his staff.

Studies have shown this relationship to hold for all managers, from street gang leaders to U.S. presidents. In *The Human Group,* George C. Homans explains how, because they were at the center of the information flow in their own gangs and were also in close touch with other gang leaders, street gang leaders were better informed than any of their followers.[12] And Richard Neustadt describes the following account from his study of Franklin D. Roosevelt:

> The essence of Roosevelt's technique for information-gathering was competition. "He would call you in," one of his aides told me, "and he'd ask you to get the story on some complicated business, and you'd come back after a couple of days of hard labor and present the juicy morsel you'd uncovered under a stone somewhere, and *then* you'd find out he knew all about it, along with something else you *didn't* know. Where he got this information from he wouldn't mention, usually, but after he had done this to you once or twice you got damn careful about *your* information."[13]

We can see where Roosevelt "got this information" when we consider the relationship between the interpersonal and informational roles. As leader, the manager has formal and easy access to every member of his staff. Hence, as noted earlier, he tends to know more about his own unit than anyone else does. In addition, his liaison contacts expose the manager to external information to which his subordinates often lack access. Many of these contacts are with other managers of equal status, who are themselves nerve centers in their own organization. In this way, the manager develops a powerful data base of information.

The processing of information is a key part of the manager's job. In my study, the chief executives spent 40 percent of their contact time on activities devoted exclusively to the transmission of information; 70 percent of their incoming mail was purely informational (as opposed to requests for action). The manager does not leave meetings or hang up the telephone in order to get back to work. In large part, communication *is* his work. Three roles describe these informational aspects of managerial work.

## 1

As *monitor,* the manager perpetually scans his environment for information, interrogates his liaison contacts and his subordinates, and receives unsolicited information, much of it as a result of the network of personal contacts he has developed. Remember that a good part of the information the manager collects in his monitor role arrives in verbal form, often as gossip, hearsay, and speculation. By virtue of his contacts, the manager has a natural advantage in collecting this soft information for his organization.

## 2

He must share and distribute much of this information. Information he gleans from outside personal contacts may be needed within his organization. In his *disseminator* role, the manager passes some of his privileged information directly to his subordinates, who would otherwise have no access to it. When his subordinates lack easy contact with one another, the manager will sometimes pass information from one to another.

## 3

In his *spokesman role*, the manager sends some of his information to people outside his unit—a president makes a speech to lobby for an organization cause, or a foreman suggests a product modification to a supplier. In addition, as part of his role as spokesman, every manager must inform and satisfy the influential people who control his organizational unit. For the foreman, this may simply involve keeping the plant manager informed about the flow of work through the shop.

The president of a large corporation, however, may spend a great amount of his time dealing with a host of influences. Directors and shareholders must be advised about financial performance; consumer groups must be assured that the organization is fulfilling its social responsibilities; and government officials must be satisfied that the organization is abiding by the law.

### Decisional Roles

Information is not, of course, an end in itself; it is the basic input to decision making. One thing is clear in the study of managerial work: the manager plays the major role in his unit's decision-making system. As its formal authority, only he can commit the unit to important new courses of action; and as its nerve center, only he has full and current information to make the set of decisions that determines the unit's strategy. Four roles describe the manager as decision maker.

## 1

As *entrepreneur,* the manager seeks to improve his unit, to adapt it to changing conditions in the environment. In his monitor role, the president is constantly on the lookout for new ideas. When a good one appears, he initiates a development project that he may supervise himself or delegate to an employee (perhaps with the stipulation that he must approve the final proposal).

There are two interesting features about these development projects at the chief executive level. First, these projects do not involve single decisions or even unified clusters of decisions. Rather, they emerge as a series of small decisions and actions sequenced over time. Apparently, the chief executive prolongs each project so that he can fit it bit by bit into his busy, disjointed schedule and so that he can gradually come to comprehend the issue, if it is a complex one.

Second, the chief executives I studied supervised as many as 50 of these projects at the same time. Some projects entailed new products or processes; others involved public relations campaigns, improvement of the cash position, reorganization of a weak department, resolution of a morale problem in a foreign division, integration of computer operations, various acquisitions at different stages of development, and so on.

The chief executive appears to maintain a kind of inventory of the development projects that he himself supervises—projects that are at various stages of development, some active and some in limbo. Like a juggler, he keeps a number of projects in the air; periodically, one comes down, is given a new burst of energy, and is sent back into orbit. At various intervals, he puts new projects on-stream and discards old ones.

## 2

While the entrepreneur role describes the manager as the voluntary initiator of change, the *disturbance handler* role depicts the manager involuntarily responding to pressures. Here change is beyond the manager's control. He must act because the pressures of the situation are too severe to be ignored: strike looms, a major customer has gone bankrupt, or a supplier reneges on his contract.

It has been fashionable, I noted earlier, to compare the manager to an orchestra conductor, just as Peter F. Drucker wrote in *The Practice of Management:*

> The manager has the task of creating a true whole that is larger than the sum of its parts, a productive entity that turns out more than the sum of the resources put into it. One analogy is the conductor of a symphony orchestra, through whose effort, vision and leadership individual instrumental parts that are so much noise by themselves become the living whole of music. But the conductor has the composer's score; he is only interpreter. The manager is both composer and conductor.[14]

Now consider the works of Leonard R. Sayles, who has carried out systematic research on the manager's job:

> [The manager] is like a symphony orchestra conductor, endeavoring to maintain a melodious performance in which the contributions of the various

instruments are coordinated and sequenced, patterned and paced, while the orchestra members are having various personal difficulties, stage hands are moving music stands, alternating excessive heat and cold are creating audience and instrument problems, and the sponsor of the concert is insisting on irrational changes in the program.[15]

In effect, every manager must spend a good part of his time responding to high-pressure disturbances. No organization can be so well run, so standardized, that it has considered every contingency in the uncertain environment in advance. Disturbances arise not only because poor managers ignore situations until they reach crisis proportions, but also because good managers cannot possibly anticipate all the consequences of the actions they take.

## 3

The third decisional role is that of *resource allocator*. To the manager falls the responsibility of deciding who will get what in his organizational unit. Perhaps the most important resource the manager allocates is his own time. Access to the manager constitutes exposure to the unit's nerve center and decision maker. The manager is also charged with designing his unit's structure, that pattern of formal relationships that determines how work is to be divided and coordinated.

Also, in his role as resource allocator, the manager authorizes the important decisions of his unit before they are implemented. By retaining this power, the manager can ensure that decisions are interrelated; all must pass through a single brain. To fragment this power is to encourage discontinuous decision making and a disjointed strategy.

There are a number of interesting features about the manager's authorizing others' decisions. First, despite the widespread use of capital budgeting procedures—a means of authorizing various capital expenditures at one time—executives in my study made a great many authorization decisions on an ad hoc basis. Apparently, many projects cannot wait or simply do not have the quantifiable costs and benefits that capital budgeting requires.

Second, I found that the chief executives faced incredibly complex choices. They had to consider the impact of each decision on other decisions and on the organization's strategy. They had to ensure that the decision would be acceptable to those who influence the organization, as well as ensure that resources would not be overextended. They had to understand the various costs and benefits as well as the feasibility of the proposal. They also had to consider questions of timing. All this was necessary for the simple approval of someone else's proposal. At the same time, however, delay could lose time, while quick approval could be ill considered and quick rejection might discourage the subordinate who had spent months developing a pet project.

One common solution to approving projects is to pick the man instead of the proposal. That is, the manager authorizes those projects presented to him by people whose judgment he trusts. But he cannot always use this simple dodge.

## 4

The final decisional role is that of *negotiator*. Studies of managerial work at all levels indicate that managers spend considerable time in negotiations: the president of the football team is called in to work out a contract with the holdout superstar; the corporation president leads his company's contingent to negotiate a new strike issue; the foreman argues a grievance problem to its conclusion with the shop steward. As Leonard Sayles puts it, negotiations are a "way of life" for the sophisticated manager.

These negotiations are duties of the manager's job; perhaps routine, they are not to be shirked. They are an integral part of his job, for only he has the authority to commit organizational resources in "real time," and only he has the nerve center information that important negotiations require.

### The Integrated Job

It should be clear by now that the 10 roles I have been describing are not easily separable. In the terminology of the psychologist, they form a gestalt, an integrated whole. No role can be pulled out of the framework and the job be left intact. For example, a manager without liaison contacts lacks external information. As a result, he can neither disseminate the information his employees need nor make decisions that adequately reflect external conditions. (In fact, this is a problem for the new person in a managerial position, since he cannot make effective decisions until he has built up his network of contacts.)

Here lies a clue to the problems of team management.[16] Two or three people cannot share a single managerial position unless they can act as one entity. This means that they cannot divide up the ten roles unless they can very carefully reintegrate them. The real difficulty lies with the informational roles. Unless there can be full sharing of managerial information—and, as I pointed out earlier, it is primarily verbal—team management breaks down. A single managerial job cannot be arbitrarily split, for example, into internal and external roles, for information from both sources must be brought to bear on the same decisions.

To say that the 10 roles form a gestalt is not to say that all managers give equal attention to each role. In fact, I found in my review of the various research studies that

... sales managers seem to spend relatively more of their time in the interpersonal roles, presumably a reflection of the extrovert nature of the marketing activity;

... production managers give relatively more attention to the decisional roles, presumably a reflection of their concern with efficient work flow;

... staff managers spend the most time in the informational roles, since they are experts who manage departments that advise other parts of the organization.

Nevertheless, in all cases the interpersonal, informational, and decisional roles remain inseparable.

## TOWARD MORE EFFECTIVE MANAGEMENT

What are the messages for management in this description? I believe, first and foremost, that this description of managerial work should prove more important to managers than any prescription they might derive from it. That is to say, *the manager's effectiveness is significantly influenced by his insight into his own work*. His performance depends on how well he understands and responds to the pressures and dilemmas of the job. Thus managers who can be introspective about their work are likely to be effective at their jobs. The insert (on the next two pages) offers 14 groups of self-study questions for managers. Some may sound rhetorical; none is meant to be. Even though the questions cannot be answered simply, the manager should address them.

Let us take a look at three specific areas of concern. For the most part, the managerial logjams—the dilemma of delegation, the data base centralized in one brain, the problems of working with the management scientist—revolve around the verbal nature of the manager's information. There are great dangers in centralizing the organization's data bank in the minds of its managers. When they leave, they take their memory with them. And when subordinates are out of convenient verbal reach of the manager, they are at an information disadvantage.

### 1

*The manager is challenged to find systematic ways to share his privileged information.* A regular debriefing session with key subordinates, a weekly memory dump on the dictating machine, the main-

**Self-Study Questions for Managers**

1

Where do I get my information, and how? Can I make greater use of my contacts to get information? Can other people do some of my scanning for me? In what areas is my knowledge weakest, and how can I get others to provide me with the information I need? Do I have powerful enough mental models of those things I must understand within the organization and in its environment?

2

What information do I disseminate in my organization? How important is it that my subordinates get my information? Do I keep too much information to myself because dissemination of it is time-consuming or inconvenient? How can I get more information to others so they can make better decisions?

3

Do I balance information collecting with action taking? Do I tend to act before information is in? Or do I wait so long for all the information that opportunities pass me by and I become a bottleneck in my organization?

4

What pace of change am I asking my organization to tolerate? Is this change balanced so that our operations are neither excessively static nor overly disrupted? Have we sufficiently analyzed the impact of this change on the future of our organization?

5

Am I sufficiently well informed to pass judgment on the proposals that my subordinates make? Is it possible to leave final authorization for more of the proposals with subordinates? Do we have problems of coordination because subordinates in fact now make too many of these decisions independently?

6

What is my vision of direction for this organization? Are these plans primarily in my own mind in loose form? Should I make them explicit in order to guide the decisions of others in the organizations better? Or do I need flexibility to change them at will?

7

How do my subordinates react to my managerial style? Am I sufficiently sensitive to the powerful influence my actions have on them? Do I fully understand their reactions to my actions? Do I find an appropriate balance between encouragement and pressure? Do I stifle their initiative?

8

What kind of external relationships do I maintain, and how? Do I spend too much of my time maintaining these relationships? Are there certain types of people whom I should get to know better?

9

Is there any system to my time scheduling, or am I just reacting to the pressures of the mo-

10

Do I overwork? What effect does my work load have on my efficiency? Should I force myself

11

Am I too superficial in what I do? Can I really shift moods as quickly and frequently as my

12

Do I orient myself too much toward current, tangible activities? Am I a slave to the action

318

ment? Do I find the appropriate mix of activities, or do I tend to concentrate on one particular function or one type of problem just because I find it more interesting? Am I more efficient with particular kinds of work at special times of the day or week? Does my schedule reflect this? Can someone else (in addition to my secretary take responsibility for much of my scheduling and do it more systematically?

13
Do I use the different media appropriately? Do I know how to make the most of written communication? Do I rely excessively on face-to-face communication, thereby putting all but a few of my subordinates at an informational disadvantage? Do I schedule enough of my meetings on a regular basis? Do I spend time touring my organization to observe activity at first hand? Am I too detached from the heart of my organization's activities, seeing things only in an abstract way?

to take breaks or to reduce the pace of my activity?

14
How do I blend my personal rights and duties? Do my obligations consume all my time? How can I free myself sufficiently from obligations to ensure that I am taking this organization where I want it to go? How can I turn my obligations to my advantage?

work patterns require? Should I attempt to decrease the amount of fragmentation and interruption in my work?

and excitement of my work, so that I am no longer able to concentrate on issues? Do key problems receive the attention they deserve? Should I spend more time reading and probing deeply into certain issues? Could I be more reflective? Should I be?

taining of a diary of important information for limited circulation, or other similar methods may ease the logjam of work considerably. Time spent disseminating this information will be more than regained when decisions must be made. Of course, some will raise the question of confidentiality. But managers would do well to weigh the risks of exposing privileged information against having subordinates who can make effective decisions.

If there is a single theme that runs through this article, it is that the pressures of his job drive the manager to be superficial in his actions—to overload himself with work, encourage interruption, respond quickly to every stimulus, seek the tangible and avoid the abstract, make decisions in small increments, and do everything abruptly.

## 2

*Here again, the manager is challenged to deal consciously with the pressures of superficiality by giving serious attention to the issues that require it, by stepping back from his tangible bits of information in order to see a broad picture, and by making use of analytical inputs.* Although effective managers have to be adept at responding quickly to numerous and varying problems, the danger in managerial work is that they will respond to every issue equally (and that means abruptly) and that they will never work the tangible bits and pieces of informational input into a comprehensive picture of their world.

As I noted earlier, the manager uses these bits of information to build models of his world. But the manager can also avail himself of the models of the specialists. Economists describe the functioning of markets, operations researchers simulate financial flow processes, and behavioral scientists explain the needs and goals of people. The best of these models can be searched out and learned.

In dealing with complex issues, the senior manager has much to gain from a close relationship with the management scientists of his own organization. They have something important that he lacks—time to probe complex issues. An effective working relationship hinges on the resolution of what a colleague and I have called "the planning dilemma."[17] Managers have the information and the authority; analysts have the time and the technology. A successful working relationship between the two will be effected when the manager learns to share his information and the analyst learns to adapt to the manager's needs. For the analyst, adaptation means worrying less about the elegance of the method and more about its speed and flexibility.

It seems to me that analysts can help the top manager especially to schedule his time, feed in analytical information, monitor projects under his supervision, develop models to aid in making choices, design contingency plans for disturbances that can be anticipated, and conduct "quick-and-dirty" analysis for those that cannot. But there can be no cooperation if the analysts are out of the mainstream of the manager's information flow.

### 3

*The manager is challenged to gain control of his own time by turning obligations to his advantage and by turning those things he wishes to do into obligations.* The chief executives of my study initiated only 32 percent of their own contacts (and another 5 percent by mutual agreement). And yet to a considerable extent they seemed to control their time. There were two key factors that enabled them to do so.

First, the manager has to spend so much time discharging obligations that, if he were to view them as just that, he would leave no mark on his organization. The unsuccessful manager blames failure on the obligations; the effective manager turns his obligations to his own advantage. A speech is a chance to lobby for a cause; a meeting is a chance to reorganize a weak department; a visit to an important customer is a chance to extract trade information.

Second, the manager frees some of his time to do those things that he—perhaps no one else—thinks important by turning them into obligations. Free time is made, not found, in the manager's job; it is forced into the schedule. Hoping to leave some time open for contemplation or general planning is tantamount to hoping that the pressures of the job will go away. The manager who wants to innovate initiates a project and obligates others to report back to him; the manager who needs certain environmental information establishes channels that will automatically keep him informed; the manager who has to tour facilities commits himself publicly.

### The Educator's Job

Finally, a word about the training of managers. Our management schools have done an admirable job of training the organization's specialists—management scientists, marketing researchers, accountants, and organizational development specialists. But for the most part they have not trained managers.[18]

Management schools will begin the serious training of managers when skill training takes a serious place next to cognitive learning. Cognitive learning is detached and informational, like reading a book or listening to a lecture. No doubt much important cognitive material must be assimilated by the manager-to-be. But cognitive learning no more makes a manager than it does a swimmer. The latter will drown the first time he jumps into the water if his coach never takes him out of the lecture hall, gets him wet, and gives him feedback on his performance.

In other words, we are taught a skill through practice plus feedback, whether in a real or a simulated situation. Our management schools need to identify the skills manager use, select students who show potential in these skills, put the students into situations where these skills can be practiced, and then give them systematic feedback on their performance.

My description of managerial work suggests a number of important managerial skills—developing peer relationships, carrying out negotiations, motivating subordinates, resolving conflicts, establishing information networks and subsequently disseminating information, making decisions in conditions of extreme ambiguity, and allocating resources. Above all, the manager needs to be introspective about his work so that he may continue to learn on the job.

Many of the manager's skills can, in fact, be practiced, using techniques that range from role playing to videotaping real meetings. And our management schools can enhance the entrepreneurial skills by designing programs that encourage sensible risk taking and innovation.

No job is more vital to our society than that of the manager. It is the manager who determines whether our social institutions serve us well or whether they squander our talents and resources. It is time to strip away the folklore about managerial work, and time to study it realistically so that we can begin the difficult task of making significant improvements in its performance.

## NOTES AND REFERENCES

1. All the data from my study can be found in Henry Mintzberg, *The Nature of Managerial Work* (New York: Harper & Row, 1973).
2. Robert H. Guest, "Of Time and the Foreman," *Personnel*, May 1956, p. 478.
3. Rosemary Stewart, *Managers and Their Jobs* (London: Macmillan, 1967); see also Sune Carlson, *Executive Behaviour* (Stockholm: Strömbergs, 1951), the first of the diary studies.
4. Francis J. Aguilar, *Scanning the Business Environment* (New York: Macmillan, 1967), p. 102.
5. Unpublished study by Irving Choran, reported in Mintzberg, *The Nature of Managerial Work.*
6. Robert T. Davis, *Performance and Development of Field Sales Managers* (Boston: Division of Research, Harvard Business School, 1957); George H. Copeman, *The Role of the Managing Director* (London: Business Publications, 1963).
7. Stewart, *Managers and Their Jobs;* Tom Burns, "The Directions of Activity and Communication in a Departmental Executive Group," *Human Relations* 7, no. 1 (1954); p. 73.

8. H. Edward Wrapp, "Good Managers Don't Make Policy Decisions," *HBR*, September–October 1967, p. 91. Wrapp refers to this as spotting opportunities and relationships in the stream of operating problems and decisions; in his article Wrapp raises a number of excellent points related to this analysis.

9. Richard E. Neustadt, *Presidential Power* (New York: John Wiley & Sons, 1960), pp. 153–54; italics added.

10. For a more thorough, though rather different, discussion of this issue, see Kenneth R. Andrews, "Toward Professionalism in Business Management," *HBR*, March–April 1969, p. 49.

11. C. Jackson Grayson, Jr., in "Management Science and Business Practice," *HBR*, July–August 1973, p. 41, explains in similar terms why, as chairman of the Price Commission, he did not use those very techniques that he himself promoted in his earlier career as a management scientist.

12. George C. Homans, *The Human Group* (New York: Harcourt, Brace & World, 1950), based on the study by William F. Whyte entitled *Street Corner Society*, Rev. ed. (Chicago: University of Chicago Press, 1955).

13. Neustadt, *Presidential Power*, p. 157.

14. Peter S. Drucker, *The Practice of Management* (New York: Harper & Row, 1954), pp. 341–42.

15. Leonard R. Sayles, *Managerial Behavior* (New York: McGraw-Hill, 1964), p. 162.

16. See Richard C. Hodgson, Daniel J. Levinson, and Abraham Zaleznik, *The Executive Role Constellation* (Boston: Division of Research, Harvard Business School, 1965), for a discussion of the sharing of roles.

17. James S. Hekimian and Henry Mintzberg, "The Planning Dilemma," *The Management Review*, May 1968, p. 4.

18. See J. Sterling Livingston, "Myth of the Well-Educated Manager," *HBR*, January–February 1971, p. 79.

# 25

# How to Choose a
# Leadership Pattern

*Robert Tannenbaum*
*and*
*Warren H. Schmidt*

*Tannenbaum and Schmidt see the leadership problem as being one of how managers can be democratic and still retain necessary control. By looking at forces in the manager, forces in the subordinates, and forces in the situation, they present a guide for making appropriate leadership decisions. It is interesting to note that this article written over 30 years ago anticipates modern-day contingency theory.—Eds.*

- "I put most problems into my group's hands and leave it to them to carry the ball from there. I serve merely as a catalyst, mirroring back the people's thoughts and feelings so that they can better understand them."
- "It's foolish to make decisions oneself on matters that affect people. I always talk things over with my subordinates, but I make it clear to them that I'm the one who has to have the final say."
- "Once I have decided on a course of action, I do my best to sell my ideas to my employees."
- "I'm being paid to lead. If I let a lot of other people make the decisions I should be making, then I'm not worth my salt."

SOURCE: Robert Tannenbaum and Warren H. Schmidt, "How to Choose a Leadership Pattern," *Harvard Business Review*, May–June 1973, pp. 162–64, 168, 170, 173, 175, 178–80. © 1973 by the President and Fellows of Harvard College; all rights reserved. This article, an "HBR Classic," was originally published in 1958.

- "I believe in getting things done. I can't waste time calling meetings. Someone has to call the shots around here, and I think it should be me."

Each of these statements represents a point of view about "good leadership." Considerable experience, factual data, and theoretical principles could be cited to support each statement, even though they seem to be inconsistent when placed together. Such contradictions point up the dilemma in which the modern manager frequently finds himself.

## NEW PROBLEMS

The problem of how the modern manager can be "democratic" in his relations with subordinates and at the same time maintain the necessary authority and control in the organization for which he is responsible has come into focus increasingly in recent years.

Earlier in the century this problem was not so acutely felt. The successful executive was generally pictured as possessing intelligence, imagination, initiative, the capacity to make rapid (and generally wise) decisions, and the ability to inspire subordinates. People tended to think of the world as being divided into "leaders" and "followers."

### New Focus

Gradually, however, from the social sciences emerged the concept of "group dynamics" with its focus on *members* of the group rather than solely on the leader. Research efforts of social scientists underscored the importance of employee involvement and participation in decision making. Evidence began to challenge the efficiency of highly directive leadership, and increasing attention was paid to problems of motivation and human relations.

Through training laboratories in group development that sprang up across the country, many of the newer notions of leadership began to exert an impact. These training laboratories were carefully designed to give people a first-hand experience in full participation and decision making. The designated "leaders" deliberately attempted to reduce their own power and to make group members as responsible as possible for setting their own goals and methods within the laboratory experience.

It was perhaps inevitable that some of the people who attended the training laboratories regarded this kind of leadership as being truly "democratic" and went home with the determination to build fully participative decision making into their own organizations. Whenever their bosses made a decision without convening a staff meeting, they tended to perceive this as authoritarian behavior. The true symbol of democratic leadership to some was the meeting—and the less directed from the top, the more democratic it was.

Some of the more enthusiastic alumni of these training laboratories began to get the habit of categorizing leader behavior as "democratic" or "authoritarian." The boss who made too many decisions himself was thought of as an authoritarian, and his directive behavior was often attributed solely to his personality.

### New Need

The net result of the research findings and of the human relations training based upon them has been to call into question the stereotype of an effective leader. Consequently, the modern manager often finds himself in an uncomfortable state of mind.

Often he is not quite sure how to behave; there are times when he is torn between exerting "strong" leadership and "permissive" leadership. Sometimes new knowledge pushes him in one direction ("I should really get the group to help make this decision"), but at the same time his experience pushes him in another direction ("I really understand the problem better than the group and therefore I should make the decision"). He is not sure when a group decision is really appropriate or when holding a staff meeting serves merely as a device for avoiding his own decision-making responsibility.

The purpose of our article is to suggest a framework which managers may find useful in grappling with this dilemma. First, we shall look at the different patterns of leadership behavior that the manager can choose from in relating himself to his subordinates. Then, we shall turn to some of the questions suggested by this range of patterns. For instance, how important is it for a manager's subordinates to know what type of leadership he is using in a situation? What factors should he consider in deciding on a leadership pattern? What difference do his long-run objectives make as compared to his immediate objectives?

### RANGE OF BEHAVIOR

Figure 1 presents the continuum or range of possible leadership behavior available to a manager. Each type of action is related to the degree of authority used by the boss and to the amount of freedom available to his subordinates in reaching decisions. The actions seen on the extreme left characterize the manager who maintains a high degree of control while those seen on the extreme right characterize the manager who releases a high degree of control. Neither extreme is absolute; authority and freedom are never without their limitations.

**FIGURE 1** Continuum of Leadership Behavior

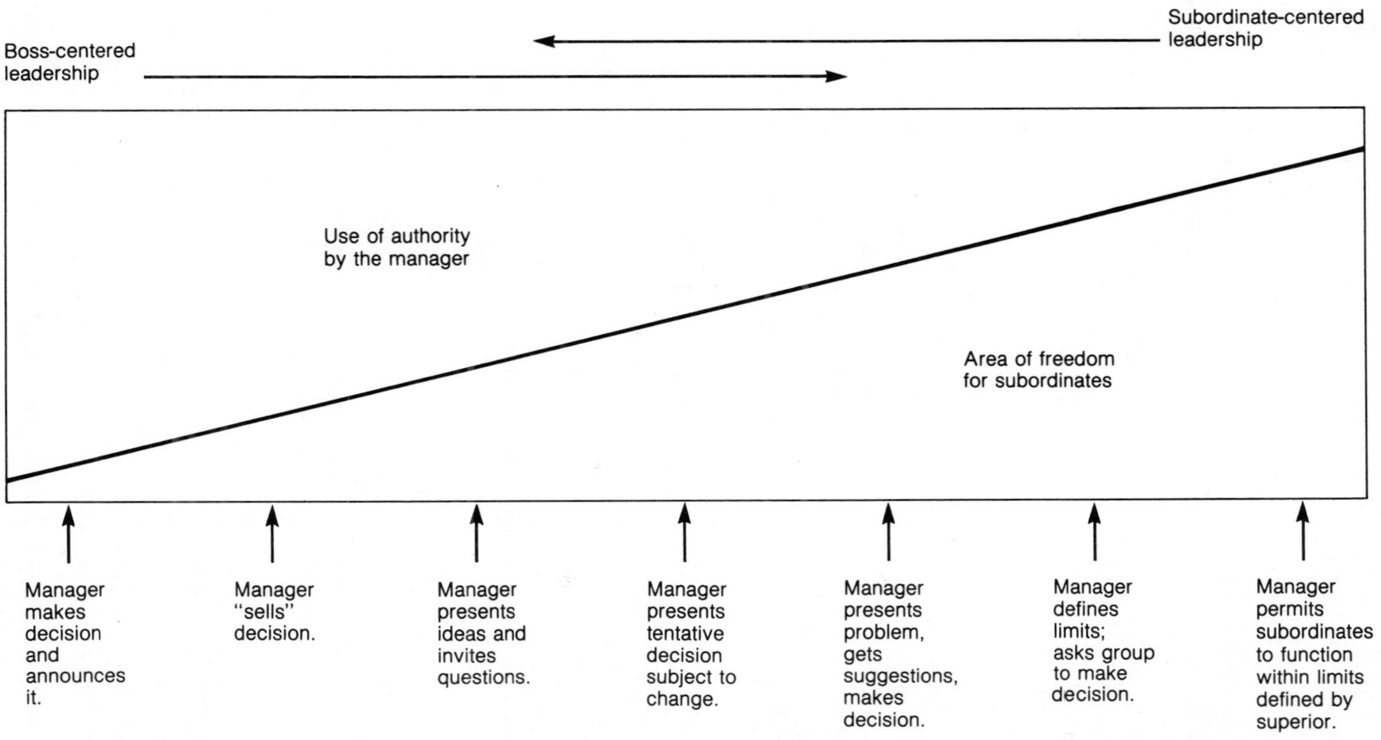

Boss-centered
leadership

Subordinate-centered
leadership

Use of authority
by the manager

Area of freedom
for subordinates

Manager
makes
decision
and
announces
it.

Manager
"sells"
decision.

Manager
presents
ideas and
invites
questions.

Manager
presents
tentative
decision
subject to
change.

Manager
presents
problem,
gets
suggestions,
makes
decision.

Manager
defines
limits;
asks group
to make
decision.

Manager
permits
subordinates
to function
within limits
defined by
superior.

Now let us look more closely at each of the behavior points occurring along this continuum.

- The manager makes the decision and announces it.

In this case the boss identifies a problem, considers alternative solutions, chooses one of them, and then reports this decision to his subordinates for implementation. He may or may not give consideration to what he believes his subordinates will think or feel about his decision; in any case, he provides no opportunity for them to participate directly in the decision-making process. Coercion may or may not be used or implied.

- The manager "sells" his decision.

Here the manager, as before, takes responsibility for identifying the problem and arriving at a decision. However, rather than simply announcing it, he takes the additional step of persuading his subordinates to accept it. In doing so, he recognizes the possibility of some resistance among those who will be faced with the decision, and seeks to reduce this resistance by indicating, for example, what the employees have to gain from his decision.

- The manager presents his ideas, invites questions.

Here the boss who has arrived at a decision and who seeks acceptance of his ideas provides an opportunity for his subordinates to get a fuller explanation of his thinking and his intentions. After presenting the ideas, he invites questions so that his associates can better understand what he is trying to accomplish. This "give and take" also enables the manager and the subordinates to explore more fully the implications of the decision.

- The manager presents a tentative decision subject to change.

This kind of behavior permits the subordinates to exert some influence on the decision. The initiative for identifying and diagnosing the problem remains with the boss. Before meeting with his staff, he has thought the problem through and arrived at a decision—but only a tentative one. Before finalizing it, he presents his proposed solution for the reaction of those who will be affected by it. He says, in effect, "I'd like to hear what you have to say about this plan that I have developed. I'll appreciate your frank reactions, but will reserve for myself the final decision."

- The manager presents the problem, gets suggestions, and then makes his decision.

Up to this point the boss has come before the group with a solution of his own. Not so in this case. The subordinates now get the first chance to suggest solutions. The manager's initial role involves identifying the problem. He might, for example, say something of this sort: "We are faced with a number of complaints from newspapers and the general public on our service policy. What is wrong here? What ideas do you have for coming to grips with this problem?"

The function of the group becomes one of increasing the manager's repertory of possible solutions to the problem. The purpose is to capitalize on the knowledge and experience of those who are on the "firing line." From the expanded list of alternatives developed by the manager and his subordinates, the manager then selects the solution that he regards as most promising.[1]

- The manager defines the limits and requests the group to make a decision.

At this point the manager passes to the group (possibly including himself as a member) the right to make decisions. Before doing so, however, he defines the problem to be solved and the boundaries within which the decision must be made.

An example might be the handling of a parking problem at a plant. The boss decides that this is something that should be worked on by the people involved, so he calls them together and points up the existence of the problem. Then he tells them:

"There is the open field just north of the main plant which has been designated for additional employee parking. We can build underground or surface multilevel facilities as long as the cost does not exceed $100,000. Within these limits we are free to work out whatever solution makes sense to us. After we decide on a specific plan, the company will spend the available money in whatever way we indicate."

- The manager permits the group to make decisions within prescribed limits.

This represents an extreme degree of group freedom only occasionally encountered in formal organizations, as, for instance, in many research groups. Here the team of managers or engineers undertakes the identification and diagnosis of the problem, develops alternative procedures for solving it, and decides on one or more of these alternative solutions. The only limits directly imposed on the group by the organization are those specified by the superior of the team's boss. If the boss participates in the decision-making process, he attempts to do so with no more authority than any other member of the group. He commits himself in advance to assist in implementing whatever decision the group makes.

## Key Questions

As the continuum in Figure 1 demonstrates, there are a number of alternative ways in which a manager can relate himself to the group or individuals he is supervising. At the extreme left of the range, the emphasis is on the manager—on what *he* is interested in, how *he* sees things, how *he* feels about them. As we move toward the subordinate-centered end of the continuum, however, the focus is increasingly on the subordinates—on what *they* are interested in, how *they* look at things, how *they* feel about them.

When business leadership is regarded in this way, a number of questions arise. Let us take four of especial importance:

1. Can a boss ever relinquish his responsibility by delegating it to someone else?

Our view is that the manager must expect to be held responsible by his superior for the quality of the decisions made, even though operationally these decisions may have been made on a group basis. He should, therefore, be ready to accept whatever risk is involved whenever he delegates decision-making power to his subordinates. Delegation is not a way of "passing the buck." Also, it should be emphasized that the amount of freedom the boss gives to his subordinates cannot be greater than the freedom which he himself has been given by his own superior.

2. Should the manager participate with his subordinates once he has delegated responsibility to them?

The manager should carefully think over this question and decide on his role prior to involving the subordinate group. He should ask if his presence will inhibit or facilitate the problem-solving process. There may be some instances when he should leave the group to let it solve the problem for itself. Typically, however, the boss has useful ideas to contribute, and should function as an additional member of the group. In the latter instance, it is important that he indicate clearly to the group that he sees himself in a *member* role rather than in an authority role.

3. How important is it for the group to recognize what kind of leadership behavior the boss is using?

It makes a great deal of difference. Many relationship problems between boss and subordinate occur because the boss fails to make clear how he plans to use his authority. If, for example, he actually intends to make a certain decision himself, but the subordinate group gets the impression that he has delegated this authority, considerable confusion and resentment are likely to follow. Problems may also occur when the boss uses a "democratic" facade to conceal the fact that he has already made a decision which he hopes the group will accept as its own. The attempt to "make them think it was their idea in the first place" is a risky one. We believe that it is highly important for the manager to be honest and clear in describing what authority he is keeping and what role he is asking his subordinates to assume in solving a particular problem.

4. Can you tell how "democratic" a manager is by the number of decisions his subordinates make?

The sheer *number* of decisions is not an accurate index of the amount of freedom that a subordinate group enjoys. More important is the *significance* of the decisions which the boss entrusts to his subordinates. Obviously a decision on how to arrange desks is of an entirely different order from a decision involving the introduction of new electronic data-processing equipment. Even though the widest possible limits are given in dealing with the first issue, the group will sense no particular degree of responsibility. For a boss to permit the group to decide equipment policy, even within rather narrow limits, would reflect a greater degree of confidence in them on his part.

## Deciding How to Lead

Now let us turn from the types of leadership which are possible in a company situation to the question of what types are *practical* and *desirable*. What factors or forces should a manager consider in deciding how to manage? Three are of particular importance:

- Forces in the manager.
- Forces in the subordinates.
- Forces in the situation.

We should like briefly to describe these elements and indicate how they might influence a manager's action in a decision-making situation.[2] The strength of each of them will, of course, vary from instance to instance, but the manager who is sensitive to them can better assess the problems which face him and determine which mode of leadership behavior is most appropriate for him.

**Forces in the Manager.**  The manager's behavior in any given instance will be influenced greatly by the many forces operating within his own personality. He will, of course, perceive his leadership problems in a unique way on the basis of his background, knowledge, and experience. Among the important internal forces affecting him will be the following:

1. His value system.

How strongly does he feel that individuals should have a share in making the decisions which affect them? Or, how convinced is he that the official who is paid to assume responsibility should personally carry the burden of decision making? The strength of his convictions on questions like these will tend to move the manager to one end or the other of the continuum shown in Figure 1. His behavior will also be influenced by the relative importance that he attaches to organizational efficiency, personal growth of subordinates, and company profits.[3]

2. His confidence in his subordinates.

Managers differ greatly in the amount of trust they have in other people generally, and this carries over to the particular employees they supervise at a given time. In viewing his particular group of subordinates, the manager is likely to consider their knowledge and competence with respect to the problem. A central question he might ask himself is: "Who is best qualified to deal with this problem?" Often he may, justifiably or not, have more confidence in his own capabilities than in those of his subordinates.

3. His own leadership inclinations.

There are some managers who seem to function more comfortably and naturally as highly directive leaders. Resolving problems and issuing orders come easily to them. Other managers seem to operate more comfortably in a team role, where they are continually sharing many of their functions with their subordinates.

4. His feelings of security in an uncertain situation.

The manager who releases control over the decision-making process thereby reduces the predictability of the outcome. Some managers have a greater need than others for predictability and stability in their environment. This "tolerance for ambiguity" is being viewed increasingly by psychologists as a key variable in a person's manner of dealing with problems.

The manager brings these and other highly personal variables to each situation he faces. If he can see them as forces which, consciously or unconsciously, influence his behavior, he can better understand what makes him prefer to act in a given way. And understanding this, he can often make himself more effective.

**Forces in the Subordinate.**    Before deciding how to lead a certain group, the manager will also want to consider a number of forces affecting his subordinates' behavior. He will want to remember that each employee, like himself, is influenced by many personality variables. In addition, each subordinate has a set of expectations about how the boss should act in relation to him (the phrase "expected behavior" is one we hear more and more often these days at discussions of leadership and teaching). The better the manager understands these factors, the more accurately he can determine what kind of behavior on his part will enable his subordinates to act most effectively.

Generally speaking, the manager can permit his subordinates greater freedom if the following essential conditions exist:

- If the subordinates have relatively high needs for independence. (As we all know, people differ greatly in the amount of direction that they desire.)
- If the subordinates have a readiness to assume responsibility for decision making. (Some see additional responsibility as a tribute to their ability; others see it as "passing the buck.")
- If they have a relatively high tolerance for ambiguity. (Some employees prefer to have clear-cut directives given to them; others prefer a wider area of freedom.)
- If they are interested in the problem and feel that it is important.
- If they understand and identify with the goals of the organization.
- If they have the necessary knowledge and experience to deal with the problem.
- If they have learned to expect to share in decision making. (Persons who have come to expect strong leadership and are then suddenly confronted with the request to share more fully in decision making are often upset by this new experience. On the other hand, persons who have enjoyed a considerable amount of freedom resent the boss who begins to make all the decisions himself.)

The manager will probably tend to make fuller use of his own authority if the above conditions do *not* exist; at times there may be no realistic alternative to running a "one-man show."

The restrictive effect of many of the forces will, of course, be greatly modified by the general feeling of confidence which subordinates have in the boss. Where they have learned to respect and trust him, he is free to vary his behavior. He will feel certain that he will not be perceived as an authoritarian boss on those occasions when he makes decisions by himself. Similarly, he will not be seen as using staff meetings to avoid his decision-making responsibility. In a climate of mutual confidence and respect, people tend to feel less threatened by deviations from normal practice, which in turn makes possible a higher degree of flexibility in the whole relationship.

**Forces in the Situation.** In addition to the forces which exist in the manager himself and in his subordinates, certain characteristics of the general situation will also affect the manager's behavior. Among the more critical environmental pressures that surround him are those which stem from the organization, the work group, the nature of the problem, and the pressures of time. Let us look briefly at each of these:

1. Type of organization.

Like individuals, organizations have values and traditions which inevitably influence the behavior of the people who work in them. The manager who is a newcomer to a company quickly discovers that certain kinds of behavior are approved while others are not. He also discovers that to deviate radically from what is generally accepted is likely to create problems for him.

These values and traditions are communicated in numerous ways—through job descriptions, policy pronouncements, and public statements by top executives. Some organizations, for example, hold to the notion that the desirable executive is one who is dynamic, imaginative, decisive, and persuasive. Other organizations put more emphasis upon the importance of the executive's ability to work effectively with people—his human relations skills. The fact that his superiors have a defined concept of what the good executive should be will very likely push the manager toward one end or the other of the behavioral range.

In addition to the above, the amount of employee participation is influenced by such variables as the size of the working units, their geographical distribution, and the degree of inter- and intra-organizational security required to attain company goals. For example, the wide geographical dispersion of an organization may preclude a practical system of participative decision making, even though this would otherwise be desirable. Similarly, the size of the working units or the need for keeping plans confidential may make it necessary for the boss to exercise more control than would otherwise be the case. Factors like these may limit considerably the manager's ability to function flexibly on the continuum.

2. Group effectiveness.

Before turning decision-making responsibility over to a subordinate group, the boss should consider how effectively its members work together as a unit.

One of the relevant factors here is the experience the group has had in working together. It can generally be expected that a group which has functioned for some time will have developed habits of cooperation and thus be able to tackle a problem more effectively than a new group. It can also be expected that a group of people with similar backgrounds and interests will work more quickly and easily than people with dissimilar backgrounds, because the communication problems are likely to be less complex.

The degree of confidence that the members have in their ability to solve problems as a group is also a key consideration. Finally, such group variables as cohesiveness, permissiveness, mutual acceptance, and commonality of purpose will exert subtle but powerful influence on the group's functioning.

3. The problem itself.

The nature of the problem may determine what degree of authority should be delegated by the manager to his subordinates. Obviously he will ask himself whether they have the kind of knowledge which is needed. It is possible to do them a real disservice by assigning a problem that their experience does not equip them to handle.

Since the problems faced in larger or growing industries increasingly require knowledge of specialists from many different fields, it might be inferred that the more complex a problem, the more anxious a manager will be to get some assistance in solving it. However, this is not always the case. There will be times when the very complexity of the problem calls for one person to work it out. For example, if the manager has most of the background and factual data relevant to a given issue, it may be easier for him to think it through himself than to take the time to fill in his staff on all the pertinent background information.

The key question to ask, of course, is: "Have I heard the ideas of everyone who has the necessary knowledge to make a significant contribution to the solution of this problem?"

4. The pressure of time.

This is perhaps the most clearly felt pressure on the manager (in spite of the fact that it may sometimes be imagined). The more that he feels the need for an immediate decision, the more difficult it is to involve other people. In organizations which are in a constant state of "crisis" and "crash programming" one is likely to find managers personally using a high degree of authority with relatively little delegation to subordinates. When the time pressure is less intense, however, it becomes much more possible to bring subordinates in on the decision-making process.

These, then, are the principal forces that impinge on the manager in any given instance and that tend to determine his tactical behavior in relation to his subordinates. In each case his behavior ideally will be that which makes possible the most effective attainment of his immediate goal within the limits facing him.

## Long-Run Strategy

As the manager works with his organization on the problems that come up day by day, his choice of a leadership pattern is usually limited. He must take account of the forces just described and within the restrictions they impose on him, do the best that he can. But as he looks ahead months or even years, he can shift his thinking from tactics to large-scale strategy. No longer need he be fettered by all of the forces mentioned, for he can view many of them as variables over which he has some control. He can, for example, gain new insights or skills for himself, supply training for individual subordinates, and provide participative experiences for his employee group.

In trying to bring about a change in these variables, however, he is faced with a challenging question: At which point along the continuum *should* he act?

**Attaining Objectives.**    The answer depends largely on what he wants to accomplish. Let us suppose that he is interested in the same objectives that most modern managers seek to attain when they can shift their attention from the pressure of immediate assignments:

1. To raise the level of employee motivation.

2. To increase the readiness of subordinates to accept change.

3. To improve the quality of all managerial decisions.

4. To develop teamwork and morale.

5. To further the individual development of employees.

In recent years the manager has been deluged with a flow of advice on how best to achieve these longer-run objectives. It is little wonder that he is often both bewildered and annoyed. However, there are some guidelines which he can usefully follow in making a decision.

Most research and much of the experience of recent years give a strong factual basis to the theory that a fairly high degree of subordinate-centered behavior is associated with the accomplishment of the five purposes mentioned.[4] This does not mean that a manager should always leave all decisions to his assistants. To provide the individual or the group with greater freedom than they are ready for at any given time may very well tend to generate anxieties and therefore inhibit rather than facilitate the attainment of desired objectives. But this should not keep the manager from making a continuing effort to confront his subordinates with the challenge of freedom.

## CONCLUSION

In summary, there are two implications in the basic thesis that we have been developing. The first is that the successful leader is one who is keenly aware of those forces which are most relevant to his behavior at any given time. He accurately understands himself, the individuals and group he is dealing with, and the company and broader social environment in which he operates. And certainly he is able to assess the present readiness for growth of his subordinates.

But this sensitivity or understanding is not enough, which brings us to the second implication. The successful leader is one who is able to behave appropriately in the light of these perceptions. If direction is in order, he is able to direct; if considerable participative freedom is called for, he is able to provide such freedom.

Thus, the successful manager of men can be primarily characterized neither as a strong leader nor as a permissive one. Rather, he is one who maintains a high batting average in accurately assessing the forces that determine what his most appropriate behavior at any given time should be and in actually being able to behave accordingly. Being both insightful and flexible, he is less likely to see the problems of leadership as a dilemma.

## RETROSPECTIVE COMMENTARY

Since this HBR Classic was first published in 1958, there have been many changes in organizations and in the world that have affected leadership patterns. While the article's continued popularity attests to its essential validity, we believe it can be reconsidered and updated to reflect subsequent societal changes and new management concepts.

The reasons for the article's continued relevance can be summarized briefly:

- The article contains insights and perspectives which mesh well with, and help clarify, the experiences of managers, other leaders, and students of leadership. Thus it is useful to individuals in a wide variety of organizations—industrial, governmental, educational, religious, and community.

- The concept of leadership the article defines is reflected in a continuum of leadership behavior (see Figure 1 in original article). Rather than offering a choice between two styles of leadership, democratic or authoritarian, it sanctions a range of behavior.

- The concept does not dictate to managers but helps them to analyze their own behavior. The continuum permits them to review their behavior within a context of other alternatives, without any style being labeled right or wrong.

(We have sometimes wondered if we have, perhaps, made it too easy for anyone to justify his or her style of leadership. It may be a small step between being nonjudgmental and giving the impression that all behavior is equally valid and useful. The latter was not our intention. Indeed, the thrust of our endorsement was for the manager who is insightful in assessing relevant forces within himself, others, and the situation, and who can be flexible in responding to these forces.)

In recognizing that our article can be updated, we are acknowledging that organizations do not exist in a vacuum but are affected by changes that occur in society. Consider, for example, the implications for organizations of these recent social developments:

- The youth revolution that expresses distrust and even contempt for organizations identified with the establishment.
- The civil rights movement that demands all minority groups be given a greater opportunity for participation and influence in the organizational processes.
- The ecology and consumer movements that challenge the right of managers to make decisions without considering the interest of people outside the organization.
- The increasing national concern with the quality of working life and its relationship to worker productivity, participation, and satisfaction.

These and other societal changes make effective leadership in this decade a more challenging task, requiring even greater sensitivity and flexibility than was needed in the 1950s. Today's manager is more likely to deal with employees who resent being treated as subordinates, who may be highly critical of any organizational system, who expect to be consulted and to exert influence, and who often stand on the edge of alienation from the institution that needs their loyalty and commitment. In addition, he is frequently confronted by a highly turbulent, unpredictable environment.

In response to these social pressures, new concepts of management have emerged in organizations. Open-system theory, with its emphasis on subsystems' interdependency *and* on the interaction of an organization with its environment, has made a powerful impact on managers' approach to problems. Organization development has emerged as a new behavioral science approach to the improvement of individual, group, organizational, and interorganizational performance. New research has added to our understanding of motivation in the work situation. More and more executives have become concerned with social responsibility and have explored the feasibility of social audits. And a growing number of organizations, in Europe and in the United States, have conducted experiments in industrial democracy.

In light of these developments, we submit the following thoughts on how we would rewrite certain points in our original article.

The article described forces in the manager, subordinates, and the situation as givens, with the leadership pattern a resultant of these forces. We would now give more attention to the *interdependency* of these forces. For example, such interdependency occurs in: (a) the interplay between the manager's confidence in his subordinates, their readiness to assume responsibility, and the level of group effectiveness; and (b) the impact of the behavior of the manager on that of his subordinates, and vice versa.

In discussing the forces in the situation, we primarily identified organizational phenomena. We would now include forces lying outside the organization, and would explore the relevant interdependencies between the organization and its environment.

In the original article, we presented the size of the rectangle in Figure 1 as a given, with its boundaries already determined by external forces—in effect, a closed system. We would now recognize the possibility of the manager and/or his subordinates taking the initiative to change those boundaries through interaction with relevant external forces—both within their own organization and in the larger society.

The article portrayed the manager as the principal and almost unilateral actor. He initiated and determined group functions, assumed responsibility, and exercised control. Subordinates made inputs and assumed power only at the will of the manager. Although the manager might have taken into account forces outside himself, it was *he* who decided where to operate on the continuum—that is, whether to announce a decision instead of trying to sell his idea to his subordinates, whether to invite questions, to let subordinates decide an issue, and so on. While the manager has retained this clear prerogative in many organizations, it has been challenged in others. Even in situations where he has retained it, however, the balance in the relationship between manager and subordinates at any given time is arrived at by interaction—direct or indirect—between the two parties.

Although power and its use by the manager played a role in our article, we now realize that our concern with cooperation and collaboration, common goals, commitment, trust, and mutual caring limited our vision with respect to the realities of power. We did not attempt to deal with unions, other forms of joint worker action, or with individual workers' expressions of resistance. Today, we would recognize much more clearly the power available to *all* parties, and the factors that underlie the interrelated decisions on whether to use it.

In the original article, we used the terms "manager" and "subordinate." We are now uncomfortable with "subordinate" because of its demeaning, dependency-laden connotations and prefer "nonmanager." The titles "manager" and "nonmanager" make the terminological difference functional rather than hierarchical.

**FIGURE 2**  Continuum of Manager-Nonmanager Behavior

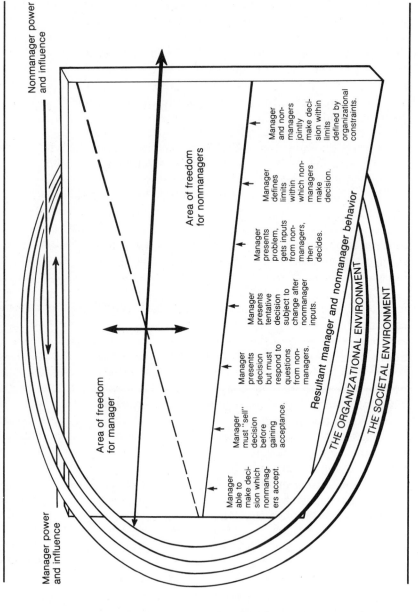

Manager power and influence

Nonmanager power and influence

Area of freedom for manager

Area of freedom for nonmanagers

Manager able to make decision which nonmanagers accept.

Manager must "sell" decision before gaining acceptance.

Manager presents decision but must respond to questions from nonmanagers.

Manager presents tentative decision subject to change after nonmanager inputs.

Manager presents problem, gets inputs from nonmanagers, then decides.

Manager defines limits within which nonmanagers make decision.

Manager and nonmanagers jointly make decision within limits defined by organizational constraints.

Resultant manager and nonmanager behavior

THE ORGANIZATIONAL ENVIRONMENT

THE SOCIETAL ENVIRONMENT

We assumed fairly traditional organizational structures in our original article. Now we would alter our formulation to reflect newer organizational modes which are slowly emerging, such as industrial democracy, intentional communities, and "phenomenarchy."[5] These new modes are based on observations such as the following:

- Both managers and nonmanagers may be governing forces in their group's environment, contributing to the definition of the total area of freedom.
- A group can function without a manager, with managerial functions being shared by group members.
- A group, as a unit, can be delegated authority and can assume responsibility within a larger organizational context.

Our thoughts on the question of leadership have prompted us to design a new behavior continuum (see Figure 2) in which the total area of freedom shared by manager and nonmanagers is constantly redefined by interactions between them and the forces in the environment.

The arrows in the figure indicate the continual flow of interdependent influence among systems and people. The points on the continuum designate the types of manager and nonmanager behavior that become possible with any given amount of freedom available to each. The new continuum is both more complex and more dynamic than the 1958 version, reflecting the organizational and societal realities of 1973.

## NOTES AND REFERENCES

1. For a fuller explanation of this approach, see Leo Moore, "Too Much Management, Too Little Change," *Harvard Business Review,* January–February 1956, p. 41.
2. See also Robert Tannenbaum and Fred Massarik, "Participation by Subordinates in the Managerial Decision-Making Process," *Canadian Journal of Economics and Political Science,* August 1950, p. 413.
3. See Chris Argyris, "Top Management Dilemma: Company Needs vs. Individual Development," *Personnel,* September 1955, pp. 123–34.
4. For example, see Warren H. Schmidt and Paul C. Buchanan, *Techniques that Produce Teamwork* (New London: Arthur C. Croft Publications, 1954); and Morris S. Viteles, *Motivation and Morale in Industry* (New York: W. W. Norton, 1953).
5. For a description of phenomenarchy, see Will McWhinney, "Phenomenarchy: A Suggestion for Social Redesign," *Journal of Applied Behavioral Science,* May 1973.

# 26

# The Ambiguity of Leadership

*Jeffrey Pfeffer*

*This article addresses several problems with the concept of leadership including the ambiguity of its definition and measurement, the issue of whether leadership affects organizational performance, and the process of selecting leaders, which frequently emphasizes irrelevant criteria.—* Eds.

Leadership has for some time been a major topic in social and organizational psychology. Underlying much of this research has been the assumption that leadership is causally related to organizational performance. Through an analysis of leadership styles, behaviors, or characteristics (depending on the theoretical perspective chosen), the argument has been made that more effective leaders can be selected or trained or, alternatively, the situation can be configured to provide for enhanced leader and organizational effectiveness.

Three problems with emphasis on leadership as a concept can be posed: (a) ambiguity in definition and measurement of the concept itself; (b) the question of whether leadership has discernible effects on organizational outcomes; and (c) the selection process in succession to leadership positions, which frequently uses organizationally irrelevant criteria and which has implications for normative theories of leadership. The argument here is that leadership is of interest primarily as a phenomenological construct. Leaders serve as symbols for repre-

---

SOURCE: Reprinted with permission from the publisher from "The Ambiguity of Leadership," *Academy of Management Review*, January 1977, pp. 104–12.

senting personal causation of social events. How and why are such attributions of personal effects made? Instead of focusing on leadership and its effects, how do people make inferences about and react to phenomena labelled as leadership (5)?

## THE AMBIGUITY OF THE CONCEPT

While there have been many studies of leadership, the dimensions and definition of the concept remain unclear. To treat leadership as a separate concept, it must be distinguished from other social influence phenomena. Hollander and Julian (24) and Bavelas (2) did not draw distinctions between leadership and other processes of social influence. A major point of the Hollander and Julian review was that leadership research might develop more rapidly if more general theories of social influence were incorporated. Calder (5) also argued that there is no unique content to the construct of leadership that is not subsumed under other, more general models of behavior.

Kochan, Schmidt, and DeCotiis (33) attempted to distinguish leadership from related concepts of authority and social power. In leadership, influence rights are voluntarily conferred. Power does not require goal compatibility—merely dependence—but leadership implies some congruence between the objectives of the leader and the led. These distinctions depend on the ability to distinguish voluntary from involuntary compliance and to assess goal compatibility. Goal statements may be retrospective inferences from action (46, 53) and problems of distinguishing voluntary from involuntary compliance also exist (32). Apparently there are few meaningful distinctions between leadership and other concepts of social influence. Thus, an understanding of the phenomena subsumed under the rubric of leadership may not require the construct of leadership (5).

While there is some agreement that leadership is related to social influence, more disagreement concerns the basic dimensions of leader behavior. Some have argued that there are two tasks to be accomplished in groups—maintenance of the group and performance of some task or activity—and thus leader behavior might be described along these two dimensions (1, 6, 8, 25). The dimensions emerging from the Ohio State leadership studies—consideration and initiating structure—may be seen as similar to the two components of group maintenance and task accomplishment (18).

Other dimensions of leadership behavior have also been proposed (4). Day and Hamblin (10) analyzed leadership in terms of the closeness and punitiveness of the supervision. Several authors have conceptualized leadership behavior in terms of the authority and discretion subordinates are permitted (23, 36, 51). Fiedler (14) analyzed leadership in terms of the least-preferred-co-worker scale (LPC), but the meaning and behavioral attributes of this dimension of leadership behavior remain controversial.

The proliferation of dimensions is partly a function of research strategies frequently employed. Factor analysis on a large number of items describing behavior has frequently been used. This procedure tends to produce as many factors as the analyst decides to find, and permits the development of a large number of possible factor structures. The resultant factors must be named and further imprecision is introduced. Deciding on a summative concept to represent a factor is inevitably a partly subjective process.

Literature assessing the effects of leadership tends to be equivocal. Sales (45) summarized leadership literature employing the authoritarian-democratic typology and concluded that effects on performance were small and inconsistent. Reviewing the literature on consideration and initiating structure dimensions, Korman (34) reported relatively small and inconsistent results, and Kerr and Schriesheim (30) reported more consistent effects of the two dimensions. Better results apparently emerge when moderating factors are taken into account, including subordinate personalities (50), and situational characteristics (23, 51). Kerr, et al. (31) list many moderating effects grouped under the headings of subordinate considerations, supervisor considerations, and task considerations. Even if each set of considerations consisted of only one factor (which it does not), an attempt to account for the effects of leader behavior would necessitate considering four-way interactions. While social reality is complex and contingent, it seems desirable to attempt to find more parsimonious explanations for the phenomena under study.

## THE EFFECTS OF LEADERS

Hall asked a basic question about leadership: is there any evidence on the magnitude of the effects of leadership (17, p. 248)? Surprisingly, he could find little evidence. Given the resources that have been spent studying, selecting, and training leaders, one might expect that the question of whether or not leaders matter would have been addressed earlier (12).

There are at least three reasons why it might be argued that the observed effects of leaders on organizational outcomes would be small. First, those obtaining leadership positions are selected, and perhaps only certain, limited styles of behavior may be chosen. Second, once in the leadership position, the discretion and behavior of the leader are constrained. And third, leaders can typically affect only a few of the variables that may impact organizational performance.

## Homogeneity of Leaders

Persons are selected to leadership positions. As a consequence of this selection process, the range of behaviors or characteristics exhibited by leaders is reduced, making it more problematic to empirically discover an effect of leadership. There are many types of constraints on the selection process. The attraction literature suggests that there is a tendency for persons to like those they perceive as similar (3). In critical decisions such as the selections of persons for leadership positions, compatible styles of behavior probably will be chosen.

Selection of persons is also constrained by the internal system of influence in the organization. As Zald (56) noted, succession is a critical decision, affected by political influence and by environmental contingencies faced by the organization. As Thompson (49) noted, leaders may be selected for their capacity to deal with various organizational contingencies. In a study of characteristics of hospital administrators, Pfeffer and Salancik (42) found a relationship between the hospital's context and the characteristics and tenure of the administrators. To the extent that the contingencies and power distribution within the organization remain stable, the abilities and behaviors of those selected into leadership positions will also remain stable.

Finally, the selection of persons to leadership positions is affected by a self-selection process. Organizations and roles have images, providing information about their character. Persons are likely to select themselves into organizations and roles based upon their preferences for the dimensions of the organizational and role characteristics as perceived through these images. The self-selection of persons would tend to work along with organizational selection to limit the range of abilities and behaviors in a given organizational role.

Such selection processes would tend to increase homogeneity more within a single organization than across organizations. Yet many studies of leadership effect at the work group level have compared groups within a single organization. If there comes to be a widely shared, socially constructed definition of leadership behaviors or characteristics which guides the selection process, then leadership activity may come to be defined similarly in various organizations, leading to the selection of only those who match the constructed image of a leader.

## Constraints on Leader Behavior

Analyses of leadership have frequently presumed that leadership style or leader behavior was an independent variable that could be selected or trained at will to conform to what research would find to be optimal. Even theorists who took a more contingent view of appropriate leadership behavior generally assumed that with proper training, appropriate behavior could be produced (51). Fiedler (13), noting how hard it was to change behavior, suggested changing the situational characteristics rather than the person, but this was an unusual suggestion in the context of prevailing literature which suggested that leadership style was something to be strategically selected according to the variables of the particular leadership theory.

But the leader is embedded in a social system, which constrains behavior. The leader has a role set (27), in which members have expectations for appropriate behavior and persons make efforts to modify the leader's behavior. Pressures to conform to the expectations of peers, subordinates, and superiors are all relevant in determining actual behavior.

Leaders, even in high-level positions, have unilateral control over fewer resources and fewer policies than might be expected. Investment decisions may require approval of others, while hiring and promotion decisions may be accomplished by committees. Leader behavior is constrained by both the demands of others in the role set and by organizationally prescribed limitations on the sphere of activity and influence.

### External Factors

Many factors that may affect organizational performance are outside a leader's control, even if he or she were to have complete discretion over major areas of organizational decisions. For example, consider the executive in a construction firm. Costs are largely determined by operation of commodities and labor markets; and demand is largely affected by interest rates, availability of mortgage money, and economic conditions which are affected by governmental policies over which the executive has little control. School superintendents have little control over birth rates and community economic development, both of which profoundly affect school system budgets. While the leader may react to contingencies as they arise, or may be a better or worse forecaster, in accounting for variation in organizational outcomes, he or she may account for relatively little compared to external factors.

Second, the leader's success or failure may be partly due to circumstances unique to the organization but still outside his or her control. Leader positions in organizations vary in terms of the strength and position of the organization. The choice of a new executive does not fundamentally alter a market and financial position that has developed over years and affects the leader's ability to make strategic changes and the likelihood that the organization will do well or poorly. Organizations have relatively enduring strengths and weaknesses. The choice of a particular leader for a particular position has limited impact on these capabilities.

## Empirical Evidence

Two studies have assessed the effects of leadership changes in major positions in organizations. Lieberson and O'Connor (35) examined 167 business firms in 13 industries over a 20-year period, allocating variance in sales, profits, and profit margins to one of four sources: year (general economic conditions), industry, company effects, and effects of changes in the top executive position. They concluded that compared to other factors, administration had a limited effect on organizational outcomes.

Using a similar analytical procedure, Salancik and Pfeffer (44) examined the effects of mayors on city budgets for 30 U.S. cities. Data on expenditures by budget category were collected for 1951–1968. Variance in amount and proportion of expenditures was apportioned to the year, the city, or the mayor. The mayoral effect was relatively small, with the city accounting for most of the variance, although the mayor effect was larger for expenditure categories that were not as directly connected to important interest groups. Salancik and Pfeffer argued that the effects of the mayor were limited both by absence of power to control many of the expenditures and tax sources, and by construction of policies in response to demands from interests in the environment.

If leadership is defined as a strictly interpersonal phenomenon, the relevance of these two studies for the issue of leadership effects becomes problematic. But such a conceptualization seems unduly restrictive, and is certainly inconsistent with Selznick's (47) conceptualization of leadership as strategic management and decision making. If one cannot observe differences when leaders change, then what does it matter who occupies the positions or how they behave?

Pfeffer and Salancik (41) investigated the extent to which behaviors selected by first-line supervisors were constrained by expectations of others in their role set. Variance in task and social behaviors could be accounted for by role-set expectations, with adherence to various demands made by role-set participants a function of similarity and relative power. Lowin and Craig (37) experimentally demonstrated that leader behavior was determined by the subordinate's own behavior. Both studies illustrate that leader behaviors are responses to the demands of the social context.

The effect of leadership may vary depending upon level in the organizational hierarchy, while the appropriate activities and behaviors may also vary with organizational level (26, 40). For the most part, empirical studies of leadership have dealt with first line supervisors or leaders with relatively low organizational status (17). If leadership has any impact, it should be more evident at higher organizational levels or where there is more discretion in decisions and activities.

## THE PROCESS OF SELECTING LEADERS

Along with the suggestion that leadership may not account for much variance in organizational outcomes, it can be argued that merit or ability may not account for much variation in hiring and advancement of organizational personnel. These two ideas are related. If competence is hard to judge, or if leadership competence does not greatly affect organizational outcomes, then other, person-dependent criteria may be sufficient. Effective leadership styles may not predict career success when other variables such as social background are controlled.

Belief in the importance of leadership is frequently accompanied by belief that persons occupying leadership positions are selected and trained according to how well they can enhance the organization's performance. Belief in a leadership effect leads to development of a set of activities oriented toward enhancing leadership effectiveness. Simultaneously, persons managing their own careers are likely to place emphasis on activities and developing behaviors that will enhance their own leadership skills, assuming that such a strategy will facilitate advancement.

Research on the bases for hiring and promotion has been concentrated in examination of academic positions (e.g., 7, 19, 20). This is possibly the result of availability of relatively precise and unambiguous measures of performance, such as number of publications or citations. Evidence on criteria used in selecting and advancing personnel in industry is more indirect.

Studies have attempted to predict either the compensation or the attainment of general management positions of MBA students, using personality and other background information (21, 22, 54). There is some evidence that managerial success can be predicted by indicators of ability and motivation such as test scores and grades, but the amount of variance explained is typically quite small.

A second line of research has investigated characteristics and backgrounds of persons attaining leadership positions in major organizations in society. Domhoff (11), Mills (38), and Warner and Abbeglin (52) found a strong preponderance of persons with upper-class backgrounds occupying leadership positions. The implication of these findings is that studies of graduate success, including the success of MBAs, would explain more variance if the family background of the person were included.

A third line of inquiry uses a tracking model. The dynamic model developed is one in which access to elite universities is affected by social status (28) and, in turn, social status and attendance at elite universities affect later career outcomes (9, 43, 48, 55).

Unless one is willing to make the argument that attendance at elite universities or coming from an upper class background is perfectly correlated with merit, the evidence suggests that succession to leadership positions is not strictly based on meritocratic criteria. Such a conclusion is consistent with the inability of studies attempting to predict the success of MBA graduates to account for much variance, even when a variety of personality and ability factors are used.

Beliefs about the bases for social mobility are important for social stability. As long as persons believe that positions are allocated on meritocratic grounds, they are more likely to be satisfied with the social order and with their position in it. This satisfaction derives from the belief that occupational position results from application of fair and reasonable criteria, and that the opportunity exists for mobility if the person improves skills and performance.

If succession to leadership positions is determined by person-based criteria such as social origins or social connections (16), then efforts to enhance managerial effectiveness with the expectation that this will lead to career success divert attention from the process of stratification actually operating within organizations. Leadership literature has been implicitly aimed at two audiences. Organizations were told how to become more effective, and persons were told what behaviors to acquire in order to become effective, and hence, advance in their careers. The possibility that neither organizational outcomes nor career success are related to leadership behaviors leaves leadership research facing issues of relevance and importance.

## THE ATTRIBUTION OF LEADERSHIP

Kelley conceptualized the layman as:

> an applied scientist, that is, as a person concerned about applying his knowledge of causal relationships in order to *exercise control* of his world [29, p. 2].

Reviewing a series of studies dealing with the attributional process, he concluded that persons were not only interested in understanding their world correctly, but also in controlling it.

> The view here proposed is that attribution processes are to be understood not only as a means of providing the individual with a veridical view of his world, but as a means of encouraging and maintaining his effective exercise of control in that world [29, p. 22].

Controllable factors will have high salience as candidates for causal explanation, while a bias toward the more important causes may shift the attributional emphasis toward causes that are not controllable (29, p. 23). The study of attribution is a study of naive psychology—an examination of how persons make sense out of the events taking place around them.

If Kelley is correct that individuals will tend to develop attributions that give them a feeling of control, then emphasis on leadership may derive partially from a desire to believe in the effectiveness and importance of individual action, since individual action is more controllable than contextual variables. Lieberson and O'Connor (35) made essentially the same point in introducing their paper on the effects of top management changes on organizational performance. Given the desire for control and a feeling of personal effectiveness, organizational outcomes are more likely to be attributed to individual actions, regardless of their actual causes.

Leadership is attributed by observers. Social action has meaning only through a phenomenological process (46). The identification of certain organizational roles as leadership positions guides the construction of meaning in the direction of attributing effects to the actions of those positions. While Bavelas (2) argued that the functions of leadership, such as task accomplishment and group maintenance, are shared throughout the group, this fact provides no simple and potentially controllable focus for attributing causality. Rather, the identification of leadership positions provides a simpler and more readily changeable model of reality. When causality is lodged in one or a few persons rather than being a function of a complex set of interactions among all group members, changes can be made by replacing or influencing the occupant of the leadership position. Causes of organizational actions are readily identified in this simple causal structure.

Even if, empirically, leadership has little effect, and even if succession to leadership positions is not predicated on ability or performance, the belief in leadership effects and meritocratic succession provides a simple causal framework and a justification for the structure of the social collectivity. More importantly, the beliefs interpret social actions in terms that indicate potential for effective individual intervention or control. The personification of social causality serves too many uses to be easily overcome. Whether or not leader behavior actually influences performance or effectiveness, it is important because people believe it does.

One consequence of the attribution of causality to leaders and leadership is that leaders come to be symbols. Mintzberg (39), in his discussion of the roles of managers, wrote of the symbolic role, but more in terms of attendance at formal events and formally representing the organization. The symbolic role of leadership is more important than implied in such a description. The leader as a symbol provides a target for action when difficulties occur, serving as a scapegoat when things go wrong. Gamson and Scotch (15) noted that, in baseball, the firing of the manager served a scapegoating purpose. One cannot fire the whole team, yet when performance is poor, something must be done. The firing of the manager conveys to the world and to the actors involved that success is the result of personal actions, and that steps can and will be taken to enhance organizational performance.

The attribution of causality to leadership may be reinforced by organizational actions, such as the inauguration process, the choice process, and providing the leader with symbols and ceremony. If leaders are chosen by using a random number table, persons are less likely to believe in their effects than if there is an elaborate search or selection process followed by an elaborate ceremony signifying the changing of control, and if the leader then has a variety of perquisites and symbols that distinguish him or her from the rest of the organization. Construction of the importance of leadership in a given social context is the outcome of various social processes, which can be empirically examined.

Since belief in the leadership effect provides a feeling of personal control, one might argue that efforts to increase the attribution of causality to leaders would occur more when it is more necessary and more problematic to attribute causality to controllable factors. Such an argument would lead to the hypothesis that the more the *context* actually effects organizational outcomes, the more efforts will be made to ensure attribution to *leadership*. When leaders really do have effects, it is less necessary to engage in rituals indicating their effects. Such rituals are more likely when there is uncertainty and unpredictability associated with the organization's operations. This results both from the desire to feel control in uncertain situations and from the fact that in ambiguous contexts, it is easier to attribute consequences to leadership without facing possible disconfirmation.

The leader is, in part, an actor. Through statements and actions, the leader attempts to reinforce the operation of an attribution process which tends to vest causality in that position in the social structure. Successful leaders, as perceived by members of the social system, are those who can separate themselves from organizational failures and associate themselves with organizational success. Since the meaning of action is socially constructed, this involves manipulation of symbols to reinforce the desired process of attribution. For instance, if a manager knows that business in his or her division is about to improve because of the economic cycle, the leader may, nevertheless, write recommendations and undertake actions and changes that are highly visible and that will tend to identify his or her behavior closely with the division. A manager who perceives impending failure will attempt to associate the division and its policies and decisions with others, particularly persons in higher organizational positions, and to disassociate himself or herself from the division's performance, occasionally even transferring or moving to another organization.

## CONCLUSION

The theme of this article has been that analysis of leadership and leadership processes must be contingent on the intent of the researcher. If the interest is in understanding the causality of social phenomena as reliably and accurately as possible, then the concept of leadership may be a poor place to begin. The issue of the effects of leadership is open to question. But examination of situational variables that accompany more or less leadership effect is a worthwhile task.

The more phenomenological analysis of leadership directs attention to the process by which social causality is attributed, and focuses on the distinction between causality as perceived by group members and causality as assessed by an outside observer. Leadership is associated with a set of myths reinforcing a social construction of meaning which legitimates leadership role occupants, provides belief in potential mobility for those not in leadership roles, and attributes social causality to leadership roles, thereby providing a belief in the effectiveness of individual control. In analyzing leadership, this mythology and the process by which such mythology is created and supported should be separated from analysis of leadership as a social influence process, operating within constraints.

## REFERENCES

1. Bales, R. F. *Interaction Process Analysis: A Method for the Study of Small Groups.* Reading, Mass.: Addison-Wesley, 1950.
2. Bavelas, Alex. "Leadership: Man and Function." *Administrative Science Quarterly* 4 (1960), pp. 491–98.
3. Berscheid, Ellen, and Elaine Walster. *Interpersonal Attraction.* Reading, Mass.: Addison-Wesley, 1969.
4. Bowers, David G., and Stanley E. Seashore. "Predicting Organizational Effectiveness with a Four-Factor Theory of Leadership." *Administrative Science Quarterly* 11 (1966), pp. 238–63.
5. Calder, Bobby J. "An Attribution Theory of Leadership." In *New Directions in Organizational Behavior,* ed. B. Staw and G. Salancik. Chicago: St. Clair Press, 1976; in press.
6. Cartwright, Dorwin C., and Alvin Zander. *Group Dynamics: Research and Theory.* 3rd ed. Evanston, Ill.: Row, Peterson, 1960.
7. Cole, Jonathan R., and Stephen Cole. *Social Stratification in Science.* Chicago: University of Chicago Press, 1973.

8. Collins, Barry E., and Harold Guetzkow. *A Social Psychology of Group Processes for Decision-Making.* New York: John Wiley & Sons, 1964.
9. Collins, Randall. "Functional and Conflict Theories of Stratification," *American Sociological Review* 36 (1971), pp. 1002–19.
10. Day, R. C., and R. L. Hamblin. "Some Effects of Close and Punitive Styles of Supervision." *American Journal of Sociology* 69 (1964), pp. 499–510.
11. Domhoff, G. William. *Who Rules America?* Englewood Cliffs, N.J.: Prentice-Hall, 1967.
12. Dubin, Robert. "Supervision and Productivity: Empirical Findings and Theoretical Considerations." In *Leadership and Productivity* ed. R. Dubin, G. C. Homans, F. C. Mann, and D. C. Miller. San Francisco: Chandler, 1965, pp. 1–50.
13. Fiedler, Fred E. "Engineering the Job to Fit the Manager." *Harvard Business Review* 43 (1965), pp. 115–22.
14. Fiedler, Fred E. *A Theory of Leadership Effectiveness.* New York: McGraw-Hill, 1967.
15. Gamson, William A., and Norman A. Scotch. "Scapegoating in Baseball." *American Journal of Sociology* 70 (1964), pp. 69–72.
16. Granovetter, Mark. *Getting a Job.* Cambridge, Mass.: Harvard University Press, 1974.
17. Hall, Richard H. *Organizations: Structure and Process.* Englewood Cliffs, N.J.: Prentice-Hall, 1972.
18. Halpin, A. W., and J. Winer. "A Factorial Study of the Leader Behavior Description Questionnaire." In *Leader Behavior: Its Description and Measurement,* ed. R. M. Stogdill and A. E. Coons. Columbus, Ohio: Bureau of Business Research, Ohio State University, 1957, pp. 39–51.
19. Hargens, L. L. "Patterns of Mobility of New Ph.D.'s Among American Academic Institutions." *Sociology of Education* 42 (1969), pp. 18–37.
20. Hargens, L. L., and W. O. Hagstrom. "Sponsored and Contest Mobility of American Academic Scientists." *Sociology of Education* 40 (1967), pp. 24–38.
21. Harrell, Thomas W. "High Earning MBA's." *Personnel Psychology* 25 (1972), pp. 523–30.
22. Harrell, Thomas W., and Margaret S. Harrell. "Predictors of Management Success." *Stanford University Graduate School of Business, Technical Report no. 3 to the Office of Naval Research.*
23. Heller, Frank, and Gary Yukl. "Participation, Managerial Decision-Making, and Situational Variables." *Organizational Behavior and Human Performance* 4 (1969), pp. 227–41.
24. Hollander, Edwin P., and James W. Julian. "Contemporary Trends in the Analysis of Leadership Processes." *Psychological Bulletin* 71 (1969), pp. 387–97.
25. House, Robert J. "A Path Goal Theory of Leader Effectiveness." *Administrative Science Quarterly* 16 (1971), pp. 321–38.
26. Hunt, J. G. "Leadership-Style Effects at Two Managerial Levels in a Simulated Organization." *Administrative Science Quarterly* 16 (1971), pp. 476–85.

27. Kahn, R. L., D. M. Wolfe, R. P. Quinn, and J. D. Snoek. *Organizational Stress: Studies in Role Conflict and Ambiguity.* New York: John Wiley & Sons, 1964.
28. Karabel, J., and A. W. Astin. "Social Class, Academic Ability, and College 'Quality'." *Social Forces* 53 (1975), pp. 381–98.
29. Kelley, Harold H. *Attribution in Social Interaction.* Morristown, N.J.: General Learning Press, 1971.
30. Kerr, Steven, and Chester Schriesheim. "Consideration, Initiating Structure and Organizational Criteria—An Update of Korman's 1966 Review." *Personnel Psychology* 27 (1974), pp. 555–68.
31. Kerr, S., C. Schriesheim, C. J. Murphy, and R. M. Stogdill. "Toward A Contingency Theory of Leadership Based upon the Consideration and Initiating Structure Literature." *Organizational Behavior and Human Performance* 12 (1974), pp. 62–82.
32. Kiesler, C., and S. Kiesler. *Conformity.* Reading, Mass.: Addison-Wesley, 1969.
33. Kochan, T. A., S. M. Schmidt, and T. A. DeCotiis. "Superior-Subordinate Relations: Leadership and Headship." *Human Relations* 28 (1975), pp. 279–94.
34. Korman, A. K. "Consideration, Initiating Structure, and Organizational Criteria—A Review," *Personnel Psychology* 19 (1966), pp. 349–62.
35. Lieberson, Stanley, and James F. O'Connor. "Leadership and Organizational Performance: A Study of Large Corporations." *American Sociological Review* 37 (1972), pp. 117–30.
36. Lippitt, Ronald. "An Experimental Study of the Effect of Democratic and Authoritarian Group Atmospheres." *University of Iowa Studies in Child Welfare* 16 (1940), pp. 43–195.
37. Lowin, A., and J. R. Craig. "The Influence of Level of Performance on Managerial Style: An Experimental Object-Lesson in the Ambiguity of Correlational Data." *Organizational Behavior and Human Performance* 3 (1968), pp. 440–58.
38. Mills, C. Wright. "The American Business Elite: A Collective Portrait." In C. W. Mills, *Power, Politics, and People.* New York: Oxford University Press, 1963, pp. 110–39.
39. Mintzberg, Henry. *The Nature of Managerial Work.* New York: Harper & Row, 1973.
40. Nealey, Stanley M., and Milton R. Blood. "Leadership Performance of Nursing Supervisors at Two Organizational Levels." *Journal of Applied Psychology* 52 (1968), pp. 414–42.
41. Pfeffer, Jeffrey, and Gerald R. Salancik. "Determinants of Supervisory Behavior: A Role Set Analysis." *Human Relations* 28 (1975), pp. 139–54.
42. Pfeffer, Jeffrey, and Gerald R. Salancik. "Organizational Context and the Characteristics and Tenure of Hospital Administrators." *Academy of Management Journal* 20 (1977), in press.
43. Reed, R. H., and H. P. Miller. "Some Determinants of the Variation in Earnings for College Men." *Journal of Human Resources* 5 (1970), pp. 117–90.

44. Salancik, Gerald R., and Jeffrey Pfeffer. "Constraints on Administrator Discretion: The Limited Influence of Mayors on City Budgets." *Urban Affairs Quarterly*, in press.
45. Sales, Stephen M. "Supervisory Style and Productivity: Review and Theory," *Personnel Psychology* 19 (1966), pp. 275–86.
46. Schutz Alfred. *The Phenomenology of the Social World.* Evanston, Ill.: Northwestern University Press, 1967.
47. Selznick, P. *Leadership in Administration.* Evanston, Ill.: Row, Peterson, 1957.
48. Spaeth, J. L., and A. M. Greeley. *Recent Alumni and Higher Education.* New York: McGraw-Hill, 1970.
49. Thompson, James D. *Organizations in Action.* New York: McGraw-Hill, 1967.
50. Vroom, Victor H. "Some Personality Determinants of the Effects of Participation." *Journal of Abnormal and Social Psychology* 59 (1959), pp. 322–27.
51. Vroom, Victor H., and Phillip W. Yetton. *Leadership and Decision-Making.* Pittsburgh: University of Pittsburgh Press, 1973.
52. Warner, W. L., and J. C. Abbeglin. *Big Business Leaders in America.* New York: Harper & Row, 1955.
53. Weick, Karl E. *The Social Psychology of Organizing.* Reading, Mass.: Addison-Wesley, 1969.
54. Weinstein, Alan G., and V. Srinivasan. "Predicting Managerial Success of Master of Business Administration (MBA) Graduates." *Journal of Applied Psychology* 59 (1974), pp. 207–12.
55. Wolfle, Dael. *The Uses of Talent.* Princeton: Princeton University Press, 1971.
56. Zald, Mayer N. "Who Shall Rule? A Political Analysis of Succession in a Large Welfare Organization." *Pacific Sociological Review* 8 (1965), pp. 52–60.

# 27

# The Contingency Model— New Directions for Leadership Utilization

## Fred E. Fiedler

*An early proponent of the contingency approach, Fiedler suggests that what constitutes effective leadership is dependent upon the situation in which the leadership attempt is made. Fiedler goes on to clearly spell out what aspects of the situation are important, namely the state of leader-member relations, task structure and the leader's formal power. These three factors combine to determine situational favorableness, a key variable in the model. While the theory has its problems, it is a classical example of the contingency approach.—Eds.*

Leadership research has come a long way from the simple concepts of earlier years which centered on the search for the magic leadership trait. We have had to replace the old cherished notion that "leaders are born and not made." These increasingly complex formulations postulate that some types of leaders will behave and perform differently in a given situation than other types. The Contingency Model is one of the earliest and most articulated of these theories;[1] taking into account the personality of the leader as well as aspects of the situation which affect the leader's behavior and performance. This model has given rise to well over 100 empirical studies. This article briefly reviews the current status of the Contingency Model and then discusses several new developments which promise to have considerable impact on our

SOURCE: From the *Journal of Contemporary Business* 3, no. 4, (Autumn 1974), pp. 65–80. Reprinted by permission of the publisher.

thinking about leadership as well as on the management of executive manpower.

## THE CONTINGENCY MODEL

The theory holds that the effectiveness of a task group or of an organization depends on two main factors: the personality of the leader and the degree to which the situation gives the leader power, control, and influence over the situation or, conversely, the degree to which the situation confronts the leader with uncertainty.[2]

**Leader Personality.**    The first of these factors distinguishes leader personality in terms of two different motivational systems, i.e., the basic or primary goals as well as the secondary goals which people pursue once their more pressing needs are satisfied. One type of person, whom we shall call "relationship-motivated," primarily seeks to maintain good interpersonal relationships with coworkers. These basic goals become very apparent in uncertain and anxiety provoking situations in which we try to make sure that the important needs are secured. Under these conditions the relationship-motivated individual will seek out others and solicit their support; however, under conditions in which he or she feels quite secure and relaxed—because this individual has achieved the major goals of having close relations with subordinates—he or she will seek the esteem and admiration of others. In a leadership situation where task performance results in esteem and admiration from superiors, this leader will tend to concentrate on behaving in a task-relevant manner, sometimes to the detriment of relations with immediate subordinates.

The relationship-motivated leader's counterpart has as a major goal the accomplishment of some tangible evidence of his or her worth. This person gets satisfaction from the task itself and from knowing that he or she has done well. In a leadership situation which is uncertain and anxiety provoking, this person will, therefore, put primary emphasis on completing the task. However, when this individual has considerable control and influence and knows, therefore, the task will get done, he or she will relax and be concerned with subordinates' feelings and satisfactions. In other words, business before pleasure, but business *with* pleasure whenever possible.

Of course, these two thumbnail sketches are oversimplified, but they do give a picture which tells us, first, that we are dealing with different types of people and, second, that they differ in their primary and secondary goals and, consequently, in the way they behave under various conditions. Both the relationship-motivated and the task-motivated persons may be pleasant and considerate toward their members. How-

ever, the task-motivated leader will be considerate in situations in which
he or she is secure, i.e., in which the individual's power and influence
are high; the relationship-motivated leader will be considerate when his
or her control and influence are less assured, when some uncertainty is
present.

These motivational systems are measured by the Least Preferred
Coworker score (LPC) which is obtained by first asking an individual
to think of all people with whom he or she has ever worked, and then
to describe the one person with whom this individual has been able to
work least well. The description of the least preferred coworker is made
on a short, bipolar eight-point scale, from 16 to 22 item-scale of the
semantic differential format. The LPC score is the sum of the item
scores; e.g.:

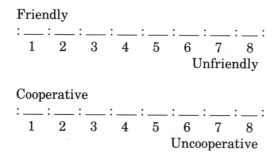

High-LPC persons, i.e., individuals who describe their LPC in relatively positive terms, seem primarily relationship-motivated. Low-
LPC persons, those who describe their least preferred coworker in very
unfavorable terms, are basically task-motivated. Therefore, as can be
seen, the LPC score is not a description of leader behavior because the
behavior of high- and low-LPC people changes with different situations.

Relationship-motivated people seem more open, more approach-
able and more like McGregor's "Theory Y" managers, while the task-
motivated leaders tend to be more controlled and more controlling
persons, even though they may be as likeable and pleasant as their
relationship-motivated colleagues.[3]

Current evidence suggests that the LPC scores and the personality
attributes they reflect are almost as stable as most other personality
measures. (For example, test-retest reliabilities for military leaders
have been .72 over an eight-month period[4] and .67 over a two-year
period for faculty members.[5]) Changes do occur, but in the absence of
major upsets in the individual's life, they tend to be gradual and relatively small.

**The Leadership Situation.** The second variable, "situational favorableness,"[6] indicates the degree to which the situation gives the leader control and influence and the ability to predict the consequences of his or her behavior.[7] A situation in which the leader cannot predict the consequences of the decision tends to be stressful and anxiety arousing.

One rough but useful method for defining situational favorableness is based on three subscales. These are the degree to which (a) the leader is, or feels, accepted and supported by his or her members (leader-member relations); (b) the task is clear-cut, programmed and structured as to goals, procedures and measurable progress and success (task structure); and (c) the leader's position provides power to reward and punish and, thus, to obtain compliance from subordinates (position power).

Groups then can be categorized as being high or low on each of these three dimensions by dividing them at the median or, on the basis of normative scores, into those with good and poor leader-member relations, task structure, and position power. This leads to an eight-celled classification shown on the horizontal axis of Figure 1. The eight cells or "octants" are scaled from "most favorable" (octant I) to the left of the graph to "least favorable" (octant VIII) to the right. A leader obviously will have the most control and influence in groups that fall into octant I; i.e., in which this leader is accepted, has high position power and a structured task. The leader will have somewhat less control and influence in octant II, where he or she is accepted and has a structured task, but little position power, and so on to groups in octant VIII where control and influence will be relatively small because the leader is not accepted by his or her group, has a vague, unstructured task and little position power. Situational favorableness and LPC are, of course, neither empirically nor logically related to each other.

## The Personality-Situation Interaction

The basic findings of the Contingency Model are that task-motivated leaders perform generally best in very "favorable" situations, i.e., either under conditions in which their power, control and influence are very high (or, conversely, where uncertainty is very low) or where the situation is unfavorable, where they have low power, control, and influence. Relationship-motivated leaders tend to perform best in situations in which they have moderate power, control, and influence. The findings are summarized in Figure 1. The horizontal axis indicates the eight cells of the situational favorableness dimension, with the most favor-

**FIGURE 1**

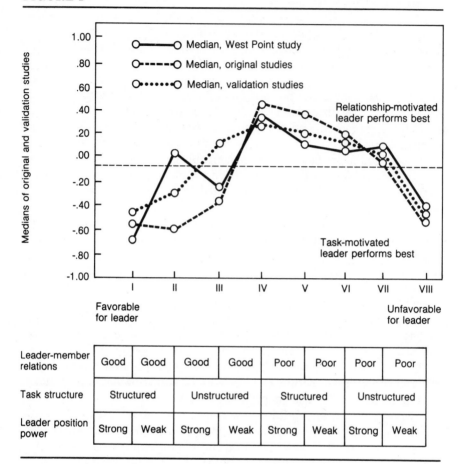

able end on the left side of the graph's axis. The vertical axis indicates the *correlation coefficients* between the leader's LPC score and the group's performance. A high correlation in the positive direction, indicated by a point above the midline of the graph, shows that the relationship-motivated leaders performed better than the task-motivated leaders. A negative correlation, shown by a point which falls below the midline of the graph, indicates that the task-motivated leaders performed better than relationship-motivated leaders, i.e., the higher the LPC score, the lower the group's performance.

The solid curve connects the median correlations within each of the octants obtained in the original studies (before 1963) on which the model was based. The broken line connects the median correlations obtained in various validation studies from 1964–1971.[8] As can be seen, the two curves are very similar, and the points on the curves correlate .76 (p < .01). Only in octant 2 is there a major discrepancy. However, it should be pointed out that there are very few groups in real life which have a highly structured task while the leader has low position power, e.g., in high school basketball teams and student surveying parties. Most of the validation evidence for octant II comes from laboratory studies in which this type of situation may be difficult to reproduce. However, the field study results for this octant are in the negative direction, just as the model predicts.

The most convincing validation evidence comes from a well-controlled experiment conducted by Chemers and Skrzypek at the U.S. Military Academy at West Point.[9] LPC scores as well as sociometric performance ratings to predict leader-member relations were obtained several weeks *prior* to the study, and groups then were assembled in advance, based on having the leader's LPC score and the expressed positive or negative feelings of group members about one another. The results of the Chemers and Skrzypek study are shown in the figure as a dotted line and give nearly a point-for-point replication of the original model with a correlation of .86 (p < .01). A subsequent reanalysis of the Chemers and Skrzypek data by Shiflett showed that the Contingency Model accounted for no less than 28 percent of the variance in group performance.[10] This is a very high degree of prediction, especially in a study in which variables such as the group members' intelligence, the leader's ability, the motivational factors of participants and similar effects were uncontrolled. Of course, it is inconceivable that data of this nature could be obtained by pure chance.

A different and somewhat clearer description of the Contingency Model is presented schematically in Figure 2. As before, the situational favorableness dimension is indicated on the horizontal axis, extending from the most favorable situation on the left to the relatively least favorable situation on the right. However, here the vertical axis indicates the group or organizational performance; the solid line on the graph is the schematic performance curve of relationship-motivated (high-LPC) leaders, while the dashed line indicates the performance of task-motivated (low-LPC) leaders.

These curves show, first of all, that both the relationship- and the task-motivated leaders perform well under some situations but not under others. Therefore, it is not accurate to speak of a "good" or a "poor" leader; rather, a leader may perform well in one type of situation but not in another. Outstanding directors of research teams do not necessarily make good production foremen or military leaders, and outstanding battle field commanders, like General Patton, do not necessarily make good chiefs of staff or good chairmen of volunteer school picnic committees.

**FIGURE 2**    The Performance of Relationship- and Task-Motivated Leaders in Different Situational-Favorableness Conditions

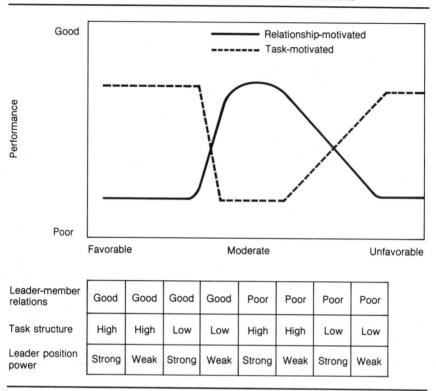

| Leader-member relations | Good | Good | Good | Good | Poor | Poor | Poor | Poor |
|---|---|---|---|---|---|---|---|---|
| Task structure | High | High | Low | Low | High | High | Low | Low |
| Leader position power | Strong | Weak | Strong | Weak | Strong | Weak | Strong | Weak |

The second major implication of Figure 2 is that leader performance depends as much on the situation to which the organization assigns him (her) as on his or her own personality. Hence, organizational improvement can be achieved either by changing the leader's personality and motivational system—which is at best a very difficult and uncertain process—or by modifying the degree to which the situation provides the leader with power and influence. It should be obvious from the graph that certain leaders perform better with less rather than more power, i.e., some leaders let the power "go to their heads," they become cocky and arrogant, while others need security to function well.

## Extensions of the Contingency Model

Two important tests of any theory are the degree to which it allows us to understand phenomena which do not follow common-sense expectations and, second, the extent to which it predicts nonobvious findings. In both of these respects, the Contingency Model has demonstrated its usefulness. We present here several important findings from recent studies, and then discuss some implications for management.

**Effects of Experience and Training.**    One of the major research efforts in the area of leadership and management has been the attempt to develop training methods which will improve organizational performance. However, until now the various training programs have failed to live up to their expectations. Stogdill concluded that:

> The research on leadership training is generally inadequate in both design and execution. It has failed to address itself to the most crucial problem of leadership—. . . [the] effects of leadership on group performance and member satisfaction.[11]

The Contingency Model would predict that training should increase the performance of some leaders and also decrease the performance of others. However, it raises the question of whether any current method of training logically can result in an across-the-board increase in organizational leadership performance.[12]

As pointed out before, a group's performance depends on the leader's personality as well as the degree to which the situation provides him or her with control, power and influence. If the leader's power and influence are increased by experience and training, the "match" between leader personality and situational favorableness would change. However, increasing the leader's power and influence is exactly the goal of most leadership training. For example, technical training increases the leader's expert power; coaching and orthodox training programs which use the case study and lecture method are designed to increase the structure of the task by providing the leader with methods for dealing with problems which, otherwise, would require him or her to think of new solutions. Human relations training is designed to develop better relations with group members, thus enabling the leader to exert more personal influence or "referent power."

For example, let us take a newly promoted supervisor of a production department in which he has not worked before. As he begins his new job, some of the tasks may seem unfamiliar and he will be unsure of his exact duties and responsibilities. He also may be uncertain of the power his position provides—how, for example, will the group react if he tries to dock an old, experienced worker who had come in late? Is this type of disciplinary measure acceptable to the group even though it may be allowed by the union contract? He may wonder how he should handle a problem with a fellow supervisor in the plant on whom he has to depend for parts and supplies. Should he file a formal complaint or should he talk to him personally?

After several years on the job, our supervisor will have learned the ropes; he will know how far he can go in disciplining his workers, how to troubleshoot various machines and how to deal with other managers in the organization. Thus, for the experienced supervisor the job is structured, his position power is high and his relations with his group are probably good. In other words, his situation is very favorable.

When he first started on the job, his leadership situation probably was only moderately favorable. If you will recall, relationship-motivated leaders tend to perform best in moderately favorable situations, while task-motivated leaders perform better in very favorable situations. Therefore, a relationship-motivated leader will perform well at first before gaining experience (e.g., by using the resources of group members and inviting their participation); a task-motivated leader will perform well after becoming experienced. In other words, the relationship-motivated leader actually should perform less well after gaining experience, while the task-motivated leader's performance should increase with greater experience.

A substantial number of studies now support this prediction.[13] A good example comes from a longitudinal study of infantry squad leaders who were assigned to newly organized units.[14] Their performance was evaluated by the same judges shortly after they joined their squads and, again, approximately five months later after their squads had passed the combat readiness test. As Figure 3 shows, the data are exactly as predicted by the Contingency Model. Similar results have been obtained in studies on the effects of training and experience of post office managers, managers of consumer cooperatives, police patrol supervisors, and leaders of various military units.

The effect of leadership training on performance also was demonstrated by a very ingenious experiment conducted at the University of Utah.[15] ROTC cadets and students were assembled *a priori* into four-man teams with high- and low-LPC leaders. One-half of the team leaders were given training in decoding cryptographic messages, i.e., they were shown how to decode simple messages easily by first counting all the letters in the message and considering the most frequent letter an "e." A three-letter word, ending with the supposed "e" is then likely to be a "the," etc. The other half of the leaders were given no training of this type. All teams operated under a fairly high degree of tension, as indicated by subsequent ratings of the group atmosphere. Because the task is by definition unstructured, the situation was moderately favorable for the trained leaders but unfavorable for the untrained leaders. Therefore, we would expect that the relationship-motivated leaders would perform better with training, while the task-motivated leaders would perform more effectively in the unfavorable situation, i.e., without the benefit of training. As can be seen in Figure 4, the findings support the predictions of the model.

**FIGURE 3**    Performance of High- and Low-LPC Leaders as a Function of Increased Experience and More Structured Task Assignment over Five Months

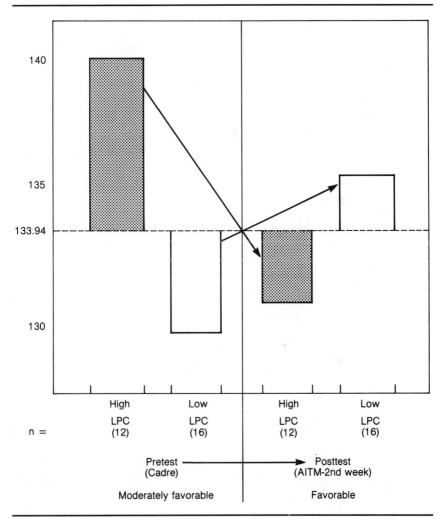

## FURTHER IMPLICATIONS

**Selection.**    It seems highly likely from these and similar findings that we need to reconsider our management selection strategies. Obviously, the old adage calling for "the right man for the right job" is not as simple as it once appeared. The right person for a particular job today may be the wrong person in six months or in one or two years.

**FIGURE 4**   Interaction of Training and LPC on Group Productivity

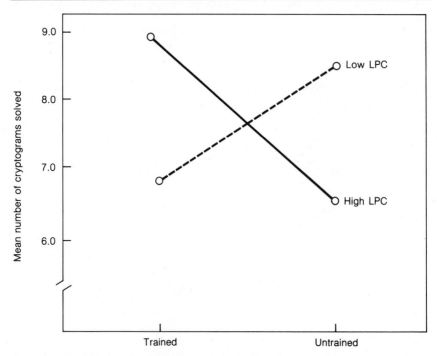

In a Harvard study, a group of underachieving 14-year-olds was given a six-week course designed to help them do better in school. Some of the boys were also given training in achievement motivation, or *n* Ach (solid lines). As graph reveals, the only boys who continued to improve after a two-year period were the middle-class boys with the special *n* Ach training. Psychologists suspect the lower-class boys dropped back, even with *n* Ach training, because they returned to an environment in which neither parents nor friends encouraged achievement.

As we have seen, the job which presents a very favorable leadership situation for the experienced leader presents a moderately favorable situation for the leader who is new and inexperienced or untrained. Hence, under these conditions a relationship-motivated leader should be chosen for the long run. The job which is moderately favorable for the experienced and trained leader is likely to represent an unfavorable leadership situation for the inexperienced leader. Hence, a task-motivated leader should be selected for the short run, and a relationship-motivated leader should be selected for the long run.

**Rotation.**   Figure 4 suggests that certain types of leaders will reach a "burn-out point" after they have stayed on the job for a given length of time. They will become bored, stale, disinterested and no longer challenged. A rational rotation policy obviously must be designed to rotate these leaders at the appropriate time to new and more challenging jobs. The other types of leaders, e.g., the task-motivated leaders represented in Figure 4, should be permitted to remain on the job so that they can become maximally efficient.

Most organizations and, in particular, the military services, have a rotation system which (at least in theory) moves all officers to new jobs after a specified period of time. Such a rigid system is likely to be dysfunctional because it does not properly allow for individual differences which determine the time required by different types of people to reach their best performance. Recent research by Bons also has shown that the behavior and performance of leaders is influenced by such other organizational changes as the transfer of a leader from one unit to a similar unit and by a reorganization which involves the reassignment of the leader's superiors.[16]

The Contingency Model clearly is a very complex formulation of the leadership problem. Whether it is more complex than is necessary, as some of its critics have claimed, or whether it is still not sufficiently complex, as others have averred, remains an open question. It is clear at this point that the theory not only predicts leadership performance in field studies and laboratory experiments, but also that it serves as a very important and fruitful source of new hypotheses in the area of leadership.

## NOTES AND REFERENCES

1. F. E. Fiedler, "A Contingency Model of Leadership Effectiveness," in *Advances in Experimental Social Psychology,* ed. L. Berkowitz. Academic Press, 1964. Also, *A Theory of Leadership Effectiveness* (New York: McGraw-Hill, 1967) and F. E. Fiedler and M. M. Chemers, *Leadership and Effective Management* (Glenview, Ill.: Scott, Foresman, 1974).
2. D. Nebeker, "Situational Favorability and Environmental Uncertainty: An Integrative Study," *Administrative Science Quarterly,* 1974.
3. L. K. Michaelsen, "Leader Orientation, Leader Behavior, Group Effectiveness and Situational Favorability: An Empirical Extension of the Contingency Model," *Organizational Behavior and Human Performance* 9 (1973), pp. 226–45.
4. P. M. Bons, "The Effect of Changes in Leadership Environment on the Behavior of Relationship- and Task-Motivated Leaders" (Ph.D. dissertation, University of Washington, 1974).
5. Joyce Prothero, "Personality and Situational Effects on the Job-Related Behavior of Faculty Members" (Honors thesis, University of Washington, 1974).
6. F. E. Fiedler, *Leadership Effectiveness.*
7. D. Nebeker, "Situational Favorability."

8. F. E. Fiedler, "Validation and Extension of the Contingency Model of Leadership Effectiveness: A Review of Empirical Findings," *Psychological Bulletin* 76 (1971), pp. 128–48.
9. M. M. Chemers and G. J. Skrzypek, "Experimental Test of the Contingency Model of Leadership Effectiveness, *Journal of Personality and Social Psychology* 24 (1972), pp. 172–77.
10. S. C. Shiflett, "The Contingency Model of Leadership Effectiveness: Some Implications of Its Statistical and Methodological Properties," *Behavioral Science* 18 (1973), pp. 429–41.
11. R. M. Stogdill, *Handbook of Leadership: A Survey of Theory and Research* (New York: Free Press, 1974).
12. F. E. Fiedler, "The Effects of Leadership Training and Experience: A Contingency Model Interpretation," *Administrative Science Quarterly* 17 (1972), pp. 453–70.
13. Ibid.
14. F. E. Fiedler; P. M. Bons; and L. L. Hastings, "New Strategies for Leadership Utilization," in W. T. Singleton and P. Spurgeon, eds., *Defense Psychology,* NATO, Division of Scientific Affairs, 1974.
15. M. M. Chemers et al., "Leader LPC, Training and Effectiveness: An Experimental Examination," *Journal of Personality and Social Psychology,* 1974.
16. P. M. Bons, "Changes in Leadership."

*B. Motivation*

# 28

## A Theory of Human Motivation

*Abraham H. Maslow*

*A classic among classics, Maslow's article sets forth the well-known idea that all human needs may be grouped into five major categories which, in turn, are arranged into a hierarchy of importance so that the needs at one level must be minimally satisfied before higher level needs become active. This is important because, according to Maslow, only unsatisfied needs are motivators of behavior. The article includes an important discussion of the implications of the theory.—Eds.*

In a previous paper (13) various propositions were presented which would have to be included in any theory of human motivation that could lay claim to being definitive. These conclusions may be briefly summarized as follows:

1. The integrated wholeness of the organism must be one of the foundation stones of motivation theory.

2. The hunger drive (or any other physiological drive) was rejected as a centering point or model for a definitive theory of motivation. Any drive that is somatically based and localizable was shown to be atypical rather than typical in human motivation.

SOURCE: Abraham H. Maslow, "A Theory of Human Motivation," *Psychological Review* 50 (1943), pp. 370–96. Copyright 1943 by the American Psychological Association. Reprinted by permission.

3. Such a theory should stress and center itself upon ultimate or basic goals rather than partial or superficial ones, upon ends rather than means to these ends. Such a stress would imply a more central place for unconscious than for conscious motivations.

4. There are usually available various cultural paths to the same goal. Therefore conscious, specific, local-cultural desires are not as fundamental in motivation theory as the more basic, unconscious goals.

5. Any motivated behavior, either preparatory or consummatory, must be understood to be a channel through which many basic needs may be simultaneously expressed or satisfied. Typically an act has *more* than one motivation.

6. Practically all organismic states are to be understood as motivated and as motivating.

7. Human needs arrange themselves in hierarchies of prepotency. That is to say, the appearance of one need usually rests on the prior satisfaction of another, more prepotent need. Man is a perpetually wanting animal. Also no need or drive can be treated as if it were isolated or discrete; every drive is related to the state of satisfaction or dissatisfaction of other drives.

8. *Lists* of drives will get us nowhere for various theoretical and practical reasons. Furthermore any classification of motivations must deal with the problem of levels of specificity or generalization of the motives to be classified.

9. Classifications of motivations must be based upon goals rather than upon instigating drives or motivated behavior.

10. Motivation theory should be human-centered rather than animal-centered.

11. The situation or the field in which the organism reacts must be taken into account but the field alone can rarely serve as an exclusive explanation for behavior. Furthermore the field itself must be interpreted in terms of the organism. Field theory cannot be a substitute for motivation theory.

12. Not only the integration of the organism must be taken into account, but also the possibility of isolated, specific, partial or segmental reactions.

It has since become necessary to add to these another affirmation.

13. Motivation theory is not synonymous with behavior theory. The motivations are only one class of determinants of behavior. While behavior is almost always motivated, it is also almost always biologically, culturally and situationally determined as well.

The present paper is an attempt to formulate a positive theory of motivation which will satisfy these theoretical demands and at the same time conform to the known facts, clinical and observational as well as experimental. It derives most directly, however, from clinical experience. This theory is, I think, in the functionalist tradition of James and Dewey, and is fused with the holism of Wertheimer (19), Goldstein (6), and Gestalt Psychology, and with the dynamicism of Freud (4) and Adler (1). This fusion or synthesis may arbitrarily be called a "general-dynamic" theory.

It is far easier to perceive and to criticize the aspects in motivation theory than to remedy them. Mostly this is because of the very serious lack of sound data in this area. I conceive this lack of sound facts to be due primarily to the absence of a valid theory of motivation. The present theory then must be considered to be a suggested program or framework for future research and must stand or fall, not so much on facts available or evidence presented, as upon researches yet to be done, researches suggested perhaps by the questions raised in this paper.

## THE BASIC NEEDS

### The "Physiological" Needs

The needs that are usually taken as the starting point for motivation theory are the so-called physiological drives. Two recent lines of research make it necessary to revise our customary notions about these needs, first, the development of the concept of homeostasis, and second, the finding that appetites (preferential choices among foods) are a fairly efficient indication of actual needs or lacks in the body.

Homeostasis refers to the body's automatic efforts to maintain a constant, normal state of the blood stream. Cannon (2) has described this process for (1) the water content of the blood, (2) salt content, (3) sugar content, (4) protein content, (5) fat content, (6) calcium content, (7) oxygen content, (8) constant hydrogen-ion level (acid-base balance) and (9) constant temperature of the blood. Obviously this list can be extended to include other minerals, the hormones, vitamins, etc.

Young in a recent article (21) has summarized the work on appetite in its relation to body needs. If the body lacks some chemical, the individual will tend to develop a specific appetite or partial hunger for that food element.

Thus it seems impossible as well as useless to make any list of fundamental physiological needs for they can come to almost any number one might wish, depending on the degree of specificity of description. We cannot identify all physiological needs as homeostatic. That sexual desire, sleepiness, sheer activity and maternal behavior in animals, are homeostatic, has not yet been demonstrated. Furthermore, this list would not include the various sensory pleasures (tastes, smells, tickling, stroking) which are probably physiological and which may become the goals of motivated behavior.

In a previous paper (13) it has been pointed out that these physiological drives or needs are to be considered unusual rather than typical because they are isolable, and because they are localizable somatically. That is to say, they are relatively independent of each other, of other motivations and of the organism as a whole, and secondly, in many cases, it is possible to demonstrate a localized, underlying somatic base for the drive. This is true less generally than has been thought (exceptions are fatigue, sleepiness, maternal responses) but it is still true in the classic instances of hunger, sex, and thirst.

It should be pointed out again that any of the physiological needs and the consummatory behavior involved with them serve as channels for all sorts of other needs as well. That is to say, the person who thinks he is hungry may actually be seeking more for comfort, or dependence, than for vitamins or proteins. Conversely, it is possible to satisfy the hunger need in part by other activities such as drinking water or smoking cigarettes. In other words, relatively isolable as these physiological needs are, they are not completely so.

Undoubtedly these physiological needs are the most prepotent of all needs. What this means specifically is that in the human being who is missing everything in life in an extreme fashion, it is most likely that the major motivation would be the physiological needs rather than any others. A person who is lacking food, safety, love, and esteem would most probably hunger for food more strongly than for anything else.

If all the needs are unsatisfied, and the organism is then dominated by the physiological needs, all other needs may become simply nonexistent or be pushed into the background. It is then fair to characterize the whole organism by saying simply that it is hungry, for consciousness is almost completely preempted by hunger. All capacities are put into the service of hunger-satisfaction, and the organization of these capacities is almost entirely determined by the one purpose of satisfying hunger. The receptors and effectors, the intelligence, memory, habits, all may now be defined simply as hunger-gratifying tools. Capacities that are not useful for this purpose lie dormant, or are pushed into the background. The urge to write poetry, the desire to acquire an automobile, the interest in American history, the desire for a new pair of shoes are, in the extreme case, forgotten or become of secondary importance. For the man who is extremely and dangerously hungry, no other interests exist but food. He dreams food, he remembers food, he thinks about food, he emotes only about food, he perceives only food and he wants only food. The more subtle determinants that ordinarily fuse with the physiological drives in organizing even feeding, drinking or sexual behavior, may now be so completely overwhelmed as to allow us to speak at this time (but *only* at this time) of pure hunger drive and behavior, with the one unqualified aim of relief.

Another peculiar characteristic of the human organism when it is dominated by a certain need is that the whole philosophy of the future tends also to change. For our chronically and extremely hungry man, Utopia can be defined very simply as a place where there is plenty of food. He tends to think that if only he is guaranteed food for the rest of his life, he will be perfectly happy and will never want anything more. Life itself tends to be defined in terms of eating. Anything else will be defined as unimportant. Freedom, love, community feeling, respect, philosophy, may all be waved aside as fripperies which are useless since they fail to fill the stomach. Such a man may fairly be said to live by bread alone.

It cannot possibly be denied that such things are true but their *generality* can be denied. Emergency conditions are, almost by definition, rare in the normally functioning peaceful society. That this truism can be forgotten is due mainly to two reasons. First, rats have few motivations other than physiological ones, and since so much of the research upon motivation has been made with these animals, it is easy to carry the rat picture over to the human being. Secondly, it is too often not realized that culture itself is an adaptive tool, one of whose main functions is to make the physiological emergencies come less and less often. In most of the known societies, chronic extreme hunger of the emergency type is rare, rather than common. In any case, this is still true in the United States. The average American citizen is experiencing appetite rather than hunger when he says "I am hungry." He is apt to experience sheer life-and-death hunger only by accident and then only a few times through his entire life.

Obviously a good way to obscure the "higher" motivations, and to get a lopsided view of human capacities and human nature, is to make the organism extremely and chronically hungry or thirsty. Anyone who attempts to make an emergency picture into a typical one, and who will measure all of man's goals and desires by his behavior during extreme physiological deprivation is certainly being blind to many things. It is quite true that man lives by bread alone—when there is no bread. But what happens to man's desires when there *is* plenty of bread and when his belly is chronically filled?

*At once other (and "higher") needs emerge* and these, rather than physiological hungers, dominate the organism. And when these in turn are satisfied, again new (and still "higher") needs emerge and so on. This is what we mean by saying that the basic human needs are organized into a hierarchy of relative prepotency.

One main implication of this phrasing is that gratification becomes as important a concept as deprivation in motivation theory, for it releases the organism from the domination of a relatively more physiological need, permitting thereby the emergence of other more social goals. The physiological needs, along with their partial goals, when chronically gratified cease to exist as active determinants or organizers of behavior. They now exist only in a potential fashion in the sense that they may emerge again to dominate the organism if they are thwarted. But a want that is satisfied is no longer a want. The organism is dominated and its behavior organized only by unsatisfied needs. If hunger is satisfied, it becomes unimportant in the current dynamics of the individual.

This statement is somewhat qualified by a hypothesis to be discussed more fully later, namely that it is precisely those individuals in whom a certain need has always been satisfied who are best equipped to tolerate deprivation of that need in the future, and that furthermore, those who have been deprived in the past will react differently to current satisfactions than the one who has never been deprived.

## The Safety Needs

If the physiological needs are relatively well gratified, there then emerges a new set of needs, which we may categorize roughly as the safety needs. All that has been said of the physiological needs is equally true, although in lesser degree, of these desires. The organism may equally well be wholly dominated by them. They may serve as the almost exclusive organizers of behavior, recruiting all the capacities of the organism in their service, and we may then fairly describe the whole organism as a safety-seeking mechanism. Again we may say of the receptors, the effectors, of the intellect and the other capacities that they are primarily safety-seeking tools. Again, as in the hungry man, we find that the dominating goal is a strong determinant not only of his current world outlook and philosophy but also of his philosophy of the future. Practically everything looks less important than safety (even sometimes the physiological needs which, being satisfied, are now underestimated). A man, in this state, if it is extreme enough and chronic enough, may be characterized as living almost for safety alone.

Although in this paper we are interested primarily in the needs of the adult, we can approach an understanding of his safety needs perhaps more efficiently by observation of infants and children, in whom these needs are much more simple and obvious. One reason for the clearer appearance of the threat or danger reaction in infants is that they do not inhibit this reaction at all, whereas adults in our society have been taught to inhibit it at all costs. Thus even when adults do feel their safety to be threatened we may not be able to see this on the surface. Infants will react in a total fashion and as if they were endangered, if they are disturbed or dropped suddenly, startled by loud noises, flashing light, or other unusual sensory stimulation, by rough handling, by general loss of support in the mother's arms, or by inadequate support.[1]

In infants we can also see a much more direct reaction to bodily illnesses of various kinds. Sometimes these illnesses seem to be immediately and per se threatening and seem to make the child feel unsafe. For instance, vomiting, colic or other sharp pains seem to make the child look at the whole world in a different way. At such a moment of pain, it may be postulated that, for the child, the appearance of the whole world suddenly changes from sunniness to darkness, so to speak, and becomes a place in which anything at all might happen, in which previously stable things have suddenly become unstable. Thus a child who because of some bad food is taken ill may, for a day or two, develop fear, nightmares, and a need for protection and reassurance never seen in him before his illness.

Another indication of the child's need for safety is his preference for some kind of undisrupted routine or rhythm. He seems to want a predictable, orderly world. For instance, injustice, unfairness, or inconsistency in the parents seems to make a child feel anxious and unsafe. This attitude may be not so much because of the injustice per se or any particular pains involved, but rather because this treatment threatens to make the world look unreliable, or unsafe, or unpredictable. Young children seem to thrive better under a system which has at least a skeletal outline of rigidity, in which there is a schedule of a kind, some sort of routine, something that can be counted upon, not only for the present but also far into the future. Perhaps one could express this more accurately by saying that the child needs an organized world rather than an unorganized or unstructured one.

The central role of the parents and the normal family setup are indisputable. Quarreling, physical assault, separation, divorce or death within the family may be particularly terrifying. Also parental outbursts of rage or threats of punishment directed to the child, calling him names, speaking to him harshly, shaking him, handling him roughly, or actual physical punishment sometimes elicit such total panic and terror in the child that we must assume more is involved than the physical pain alone. While it is true that in some children this terror may represent also a fear of loss of parental love, it can also occur in completely rejected children, who seem to cling to the hating parents more for sheer safety and protection than because of hope of love.

Confronting the average child with new, unfamiliar, strange, unmanageable stimuli or situations will too frequently elicit the danger
or terror reaction, as for example, getting lost or even being separated
from the parents for a short time, being confronted with new faces,
new situations or new tasks, the sight of strange, unfamiliar or uncontrollable objects, illness or death. Particularly at such times, the
child's frantic clinging to his parents is eloquent testimony to their
role as protectors (quite apart from their roles as food-givers and love-
givers).

From these and similar observations, we may generalize and say
that the average child in our society generally prefers a safe, orderly,
predictable, organized world, which he can count on, and in which
unexpected, unmanageable or other dangerous things do not happen,
and in which, in any case, he has all-powerful parents who protect and
shield him from harm.

That these reactions may so easily be observed in children is in a
way a proof of the fact that children in our society feel too unsafe (or,
in a word, are badly brought up). Children who are reared in an un-
threatening, loving family do *not* ordinarily react as we have described
above (17). In such children the danger reactions are apt to come mostly
to objects or situations that adults too would consider dangerous.[2]

The healthy, normal, fortunate adult in our culture is largely satisfied in his safety needs. The peaceful, smoothly running, "good" society ordinarily makes its members feel safe enough from wild animals,
extremes of temperature, criminals, assault and murder, tyranny, etc.
Therefore, in a very real sense, he no longer has any safety needs as
active motivators. Just as a sated man no longer feels hungry, a safe
man no longer feels endangered. If we wish to see these needs directly
and clearly we must turn to neurotic or near-neurotic individuals, and
to the economic and social underdogs. In between these extremes, we
can perceive the expressions of safety needs only in such phenomena
as, for instance, the common preference for a job with tenure and
protection, the desire for a savings account, and for insurance of various
kinds (medical, dental, unemployment, disability, old age).

Other broader aspects of the attempt to seek safety and stability
in the world are seen in the very common preference for familiar rather
than unfamiliar things, or for the known rather than the unknown.
The tendency to have some religion or world-philosophy that organizes
the universe and the men in it into some sort of satisfactorily coherent,
meaningful whole is also in part motivated by safety-seeking. Here
too we may list science and philosophy in general as partially motivated
by the safety needs (we shall see later that there are also other motivations to scientific, philosophical or religious endeavor).

Otherwise the need for safety is seen as an active and dominant
mobilizer of the organism's resources only in emergencies, e.g., war,

disease, natural catastrophies, crime waves, societal disorganization, neurosis, brain injury, chronically bad situation.

Some neurotic adults in our society are, in many ways, like the unsafe child in their desire for safety, although in the former it takes on a somewhat special appearance. Their reaction is often to unknown, psychological dangers in a world that is perceived to be hostile, over-whelming and threatening. Such a person behaves as if a great catastrophe were almost always impending, i.e., he is usually responding as if to an emergency. His safety needs often find specific expression in a search for a protector, or a stronger person on whom he may depend, or perhaps, a Fuehrer.

The neurotic individual may be described in a slightly different way with some usefulness as a grownup person who retains his childish attitudes toward the world. That is to say, a neurotic adult may be said to behave "as if" he were actually afraid of a spanking, or of his mother's disapproval, or of being abandoned by his parents, or having his food taken away from him. It is as if his childish attitudes of fear and threat reaction to a dangerous world had gone underground, and untouched by the growing up and learning processes, were now ready to be called out by any stimulus that would make a child feel endan-gered and threatened.[3]

The neurosis in which the search for safety takes its clearest form is in the compulsive-obsessive neurosis. Compulsive-obsessives try frantically to order and stabilize the world so that no unmanageable, unexpected or unfamiliar dangers will ever appear (14). They hedge themselves about with all sorts of ceremonials, rules and formulas so that every possible contingency may be provided for and so that no new contingencies may appear. They are much like the brain injured cases, described by Goldstein (6), who manage to maintain their equi-librium by avoiding everything unfamiliar and strange and by ordering their restricted world in such a neat, disciplined, orderly fashion that everything in the world can be counted upon. They try to arrange the world so that anything unexpected (dangers) cannot possibly occur. If, through no fault of their own, something unexpected does occur, they go into a panic reaction as if this unexpected occurrence constituted a grave danger. What we can see only as a none too strong preference in the healthy person, e.g., preference for the familiar, becomes a life-and-death necessity in abnormal cases.

### The Love Needs

If both the physiological and the safety needs are fairly well grat-ified, then there will emerge the love and affection and belongingness needs, and the whole cycle already described will repeat itself with this new center. Now the person will feel keenly, as never before, the absence of friends, or a sweetheart, or a wife, or children. He will hunger for affectionate relations with people in general, namely, for a place in his group, and he will strive with great intensity to achieve this goal. He will want to attain such a place more than anything else in the world and may even forget that once, when he was hungry, he sneered at love.

In our society the thwarting of these needs is the most commonly found core in cases of maladjustment and more severe psychopathology. Love and affection, as well as their possible expression in sexuality, are generally looked upon with ambivalence and are customarily hedged about with many restrictions and inhibitions. Practically all theorists of psychopathology have stressed thwarting of the love needs as basic in the picture of maladjustment. Many clinical studies have therefore been made of this need and we know more about it perhaps than any of the other needs except the physiological ones (14).

One thing that must be stressed at this point is that love is not synonymous with sex. Sex may be studied as a purely physiological need. Ordinarily sexual behavior is multidetermined, that is to say, determined not only by sexual but also by other needs, chief among which are the love and affection needs. Also not to be overlooked is the fact that the love needs involve both giving *and* receiving love.[4]

## The Esteem Needs

All people in our society (with a few pathological exceptions) have a need or desire for a stable, firmly based, (usually) high evaluation of themselves, for self-respect, or self-esteem, and for the esteem of others. By firmly based self-esteem, we mean that which is soundly based upon real capacity, achievement and respect from others. These needs may be classified into two subsidiary sets. These are, first, the desire for strength, for achievement, for adequacy, for confidence in the face of the world, and for independence and freedom.[5] Secondly, we have what we may call the desire for reputation or prestige (defining it as respect or esteem from other people), recognition, attention, importance or appreciation.[6] These needs have been relatively stressed by Alfred Adler and his followers, and have been relatively neglected by Freud and the psychoanalysts. More and more today however there is appearing widespread appreciation of their central importance.

Satisfaction of the self-esteem need leads to feelings of self-confidence, worth, strength, capability and adequacy of being useful and necessary in the world. But thwarting of these needs produces feelings of inferiority, of weakness and of helplessness. These feelings in turn give rise to either basic discouragement or else compensatory or neurotic trends. An appreciation of the necessity of basic self-confidence and an understanding of how helpless people are without it, can be easily gained from a study of severe traumatic neurosis (8).[7]

## The Need for Self-Actualization

Even if all these needs are satisfied, we may still often (if not always) expect that a new discontent and restlessness will soon develop, unless the individual is doing what he is fitted for. A musician must make music, an artist must paint, a poet must write, if he is to be ultimately happy. What a man *can* be, he *must* be. This need we may call self-actualization.

This term, first coined by Kurt Goldstein, is being used in this paper in a much more specific and limited fashion. It refers to the desire for self-fulfillment, namely, to the tendency for him (a person) to become actualized in what he is potentially. This tendency might be phrased as the desire to become more and more what one is, to become everything that one is capable of becoming.

The specific form that these needs will take will of course vary greatly from person to person. In one individual it may take the form of the desire to be an ideal mother, in another it may be expressed athletically, and in still another it may be expressed in painting pictures or in inventions. It is not necessarily a creative urge although in people who have any capacities for creation it will take this form.

The clear emergence of these needs rests upon prior satisfaction of the physiological, safety, love and esteem needs. We shall call people who are satisfied in these needs, basically satisfied people, and it is from these that we may expect the fullest (and healthiest) creativeness.[8] Since, in our society, basically satisfied people are the exception, we do not know much about self-actualization, either experimentally or clinically. It remains a challenging problem for research.

## The Preconditions for the Basic Need Satisfactions

There are certain conditions which are immediate prerequisites for the basic need satisfactions. Danger to these is reacted to almost as if it were a direct danger to the basic needs themselves. Such conditions as freedom to speak, freedom to do what one wishes so long as no harm is done to others, freedom to express one's self, freedom to investigate and seek for information, freedom to defend one's self, justice, fairness, honesty, orderliness in the group are examples of such preconditions for basic need satisfactions. Thwarting in these freedoms will be reacted to with a threat or emergency response. These conditions are not ends in themselves but they are *almost* so since they are so closely related to the basic needs, which are apparently the only ends in themselves. These conditions are defended because without them the basic satisfactions are quite impossible, or at least, very severely endangered.

If we remember that the cognitive capacities (perceptual, intellectual, learning) are a set of adjustive tools, which have among other functions, that of satisfaction of our basic needs, then it is clear that any danger to them, any deprivation or blocking of their free use, must also be indirectly threatening to the basic needs themselves. Such a statement is a partial solution of the general problems of curiosity, the search for knowledge, truth and wisdom, and the ever-persistent urge to solve the cosmic mysteries.

We must therefore introduce another hypothesis and speak of degrees of closeness to the basic needs, for we have already pointed out that *any* conscious desires (partial goals) are more or less important as they are more or less close to the basic needs. The same statement may be made for various behavior acts. An act is psychologically important if it contributes directly to satisfaction of basic needs. The less directly it so contributes, or the weaker this contribution is, the less important this act must be conceived to be from the point of view of dynamic psychology. A similar statement may be made for the various defense or coping mechanisms. Some are very directly related to the protection or attainment of the basic needs, others are only weakly and distantly related. Indeed if we wished, we could speak of more basic and less basic defense mechanisms, and then affirm that danger to the more basic defenses is more threatening than danger to less basic defenses (always remembering that this is so only because of their relationship to the basic needs).

## The Desires to Know and to Understand

So far, we have mentioned the cognitive needs only in passing. Acquiring knowledge and systematizing the universe have been considered as, in part, techniques for the achievement of basic safety in the world, or, for the intelligent man, expressions of self-actualization. Also freedom of inquiry and expression have been discussed as preconditions of satisfactions of the basic needs. True though these formulations may be, they do not constitute definitive answers to the question as to the motivation role of curiosity, learning, philosophizing, experimenting, etc. They are, at best, no more than partial answers.

This question is especially difficult because we know so little about the facts. Curiosity, exploration, desire for the facts, desire to know may certainly be observed easily enough. The fact that they often are pursued even at great cost to the individual's safety is an earnest of the partial character of our previous discussion. In addition, the writer must admit that, though he has sufficient clinical evidence to postulate the desire to know as a very strong drive in intelligent people, no data are available for unintelligent people. It may then be largely a function of relatively high intelligence. Rather tentatively, then, and largely in the hope of stimulating discussion and research, we shall postulate a basic desire to know, to be aware of reality, to get the facts, to satisfy curiosity, or, as Wertheimer phrases it, to see rather than to be blind.

This postulation, however, is not enough. Even after we know, we are impelled to know more and more minutely and microscopically on the one hand, and on the other, more and more extensively in the direction of a world philosophy, religion, etc. The facts that we acquire, if they are isolated or atomistic, inevitably get theorized about, and either analyzed or organized or both. This process has been phrased by some as the search for "meaning." We shall then postulate a desire to understand, to systematize, to organize, to analyze, to look for relations and meanings.

Once these desires are accepted for discussion, we see that they, too, form themselves into a small hierarchy in which the desire to know is prepotent over the desire to understand. All the characteristics of a hierarchy of prepotency that we have described above, seem to hold for this one as well.

We must guard ourselves against the too easy tendency to separate these desires from the basic needs we have discussed above, i.e., to make a sharp dichotomy between "cognitive" and "conative" needs. The desires to know and to understand are themselves conative, i.e., have a striving character, and are as much personality needs as the "basic needs" we have already discussed (19).

## FURTHER CHARACTERISTICS OF THE BASIC NEEDS

### The Degree of Fixity of the Hierarchy of Basic Needs

We have spoken so far as if this hierarchy were a fixed order but actually it is not nearly as rigid as we may have implied. It is true that most of the people with whom we have worked have seemed to have these basic needs in about the order that has been indicated. However, there have been a number of exceptions.

(1) There are some people in whom, for instance, self-esteem seems to be more important than love. This most common reversal in the hierarchy is usually due to the development of the notion

that the person who is most likely to be loved is a strong or powerful person, one who inspires respect or fear, and who is self-confident or aggressive. Therefore, such people who lack love and seek it, may try hard to put on a front of aggressive, confident behavior. But essentially they seek high self-esteem and its behavior expressions more as a means to an end than for its own sake; they seek self-assertion for the sake of love rather than for self-esteem itself.

(2) There are other, apparently innately creative people in whom the drive to creativeness seems to be more important than any other counter-determinant. Their creativeness might appear not as self-actualization released by basic satisfaction, but in spite of lack of basic satisfaction.

(3) In certain people the level of aspiration may be permanently deadened or lowered. That is to say, the less prepotent goals may simply be lost, and may disappear forever, so that the person who has experienced life at a very low level, i.e., chronic unemployment, may continue to be satisfied for the rest of his life if only he can get enough food.

(4) The so-called psychopathic personality is another example of permanent loss of the love needs. These are people who, according to the best data available (9), have been starved for love in the earliest months of their lives and have simply lost forever the desire and the ability to give and to receive affection (as animals lose sucking or pecking reflexes that are not exercised soon enough after birth).

(5) Another cause of reversal of the hierarchy is that when a need has been satisfied for a long time, this need may be underevaluated. People who have never experienced chronic hunger are apt to underestimate its effects and to look upon food as a rather unimportant thing. If they are dominated by a higher need, this higher need will seem to be the most important of all. It then becomes possible, and indeed does actually happen, that they may, for the sake of this higher need, put themselves into the position of being deprived in a more basic need. We may expect that after a long-time deprivation of the more basic need there will be a tendency to reevaluate both needs so that the more prepotent need will actually become consciously prepotent for the individual who may have given it up very lightly. Thus, a man who has given up his job rather than lose his self-respect, and who then starves for six months or so, may be willing to take his job back even at the price of losing his self-respect.

(6) Another partial explanation of *apparent* reversals is seen in the fact that we have been talking about the hierarchy of prepotency in terms of consciously felt wants or desires rather than of behavior. Looking at behavior itself may give us the wrong impression. What we have claimed is that the person will *want* the more basic of two needs when deprived in both. There is no necessary implication here that he will act upon his desires. Let us say again that there are many determinants of behavior other than the needs and desires.

(7) Perhaps more important than all these exceptions are the ones that involve ideals, high social standards, high values and the like. With such values people become martyrs; they will give up everything for the sake of a particular ideal, or value. These people may be understood, at least in part, by reference to one basic concept (or hypothesis) which may be called "increased frustration-tolerance through early gratification." People who have been satisfied in their basic needs throughout their lives, particularly in their earlier years, seem to develop exceptional power to withstand present or future thwarting of these needs simply because they have strong, healthy character structure as a result of basic satisfaction. They are the "strong" people who can easily weather disagreement or opposition who can swim against the stream of public opinion and who can stand up for the truth at great personal cost. It is just the ones who have loved and been well loved, and who have had many deep friendships, who can hold out against hatred, rejection or persecution.

I say all this in spite of the fact that there is a certain amount of sheer habituation which is also involved in any full discussion of frustration tolerance. For instance, it is likely that those persons who have been accustomed to relative starvation for a long time, are partially enabled thereby to withstand food deprivation. What sort of balance must be made between these two tendencies, of habituation on the one hand, and of past satisfaction breeding present frustration tolerance on the other hand, remains to be worked out by further research. Meanwhile we may assume that they are both operative, side by side, since they do not contradict each other. In respect to this phenomenon of increased frustration tolerance, it seems probable that the most important gratifications come in the first two years of life. That is to say, people who have been made secure and strong in the earliest years, tend to remain secure and strong thereafter in the face of whatever threatens.

## Degrees of Relative Satisfaction

So far, our theoretical discussion may have given the impression that these five sets of needs are somehow in a stepwise, all-or-none relationship to each other. We have spoken in such terms as the following: "If one need is satisfied, then another emerges." This statement might give the false impression that a need must be satisfied 100 percent before the next need emerges. In actual fact, most members of our society who are normal, are partially satisfied in all their basic needs and partially unsatisfied in all their basic needs at the same time. A more realistic description of the hierarchy would be in terms of decreasing percentages of satisfaction as we go up the hierarchy of prepotency. For instance, if I may assign arbitrary figures for the sake of illustration, it is as if the average citizen is satisfied perhaps 85 percent in his physiological needs, 70 percent in his safety needs, 50 percent in his love needs, 40 percent in his self-esteem needs, and 10 percent in his self-actualization needs.

As for the concept of emergence of a new need after satisfaction of the prepotent need, this emergence is not a sudden, saltatory phenomenon but rather a gradual emergence by slow degrees from nothingness. For instance, if prepotent need A is satisfied only 10 percent, then need B may not be visible at all. However, as this need A becomes satisfied 25 percent, need B may emerge 5 percent; as need A becomes satisfied 75 percent, need B may emerge 90 percent, and so on.

## Unconscious Character of Needs

These needs are neither necessarily conscious nor unconscious. On the whole, however, in the average person, they are more often unconscious rather than conscious. It is not necessary at this point to overhaul the tremendous mass of evidence which indicates the crucial importance of unconscious motivation. It would by now be expected, on a priori grounds alone, that unconscious motivations would on the whole be rather more important than the conscious motivations. What we have called the basic needs are very often largely unconscious although they may, with suitable techniques, and with sophisticated people become conscious.

## Cultural Specificity and Generality of Needs

This classification of basic needs makes some attempt to take account of the relative unity behind the superficial differences in specific desires from one culture to another. Certainly in any particular culture an individual's conscious motivational content will usually be extremely different from the conscious motivational content of an individual in another society. However, it is the common experience of anthropologists that people, even in different societies, are much more alike than we would think from our first contact with them, and that as we know them better we seem to find more and more of this commonness. We then recognize the most startling differences to be superficial rather than basic, e.g., differences in style of hairdress, clothes, tastes in food, etc. Our classification of basic needs is in part an attempt to account for this unity behind the apparent diversity from culture to culture. No claim is made that it is ultimate or universal for all cultures. The claim is made only that it is relatively *more* ultimate, more universal, more basic, than the superficial conscious desires from culture to culture, and makes a somewhat closer approach to common human characteristics. Basic needs are *more* common-human than superficial desires or behaviors.

## Multiple Motivations of Behavior

These needs must be understood *not* to be *exclusive* or single determiners of certain kinds of behavior. An example may be found in any behavior that seems to be physiologically motivated, such as eating, or sexual play or the like. The clinical psychologists have long since found that any behavior may be a channel through which flow various determinants. Or to say it in another way, most behavior is multimotivated. Within the sphere of motivational determinants any behavior tends to be determined by several or *all* of the basic needs simultaneously rather than by only one of them. The latter would be more an exception than the former. Eating may be partially for the sake of filling the stomach, and partially for the sake of comfort and amelioration of other needs. One may make love not only for pure sexual release, but also to convince one's self of one's masculinity, or to make a conquest, to feel powerful, or to win more basic affection. As an illustration, I may point out that it would be possible (theoretically if not practically) to analyze a single act of an individual and see in it the expression of his physiological needs, his safety needs, his love needs, his esteem needs and self-actualization. This contrasts sharply with the more naive brand of trait psychology in which one trait or one motive accounts for a certain kind of act, i.e., an aggressive act is traced solely to a trait of aggressiveness.

## Multiple Determinants of Behavior

Not all behavior is determined by the basic needs. We might even say that not all behavior is motivated. There are many determinants of behavior other than motives.[9] For instance, one other important class of determinants is the so-called field determinants. Theoretically, at least, behavior may be determined completely by the field, or even by specific isolated external stimuli, as in association of ideas, or certain conditioned reflexes. If in response to the stimulus word "table," I immediately perceive a memory image of a table, this response certainly has nothing to do with my basic needs.

Secondly, we may call attention again to the concept of "degree of closeness to the basic needs" or "degree of motivation." Some behavior is highly motivated, other behavior is only weakly motivated. Some is not motivated at all (but all behavior is determined).

Another important point[10] is that there is a basic difference between expressive behavior and coping behavior (functional striving, purposive goal seeking). An expressive behavior does not try to do anything; it is simply a reflection of the personality. A stupid man behaves stupidly, not because he wants to, or tries to, or is motivated to, but simply because he *is* what he is. The same is true when I speak in a bass voice rather than tenor or soprano. The random movements of a healthy child, the smile on the face of a happy man even when he is alone, the springiness of the healthy man's walk, and the erectness of his carriage are other examples of expressive, nonfunctional behavior. Also the *style* in which a man carries out almost all his behavior, motivated as well as unmotivated, is often expressive.

We may then ask, is *all* behavior expressive or reflective of the character structure? The answer is no. Rote, habitual, automatized, or conventional behavior may or may not be expressive. The same is true for most "stimulus-bound" behaviors.

It is finally necessary to stress that expressiveness of behavior, and goal-directedness of behavior are not mutually exclusive categories. Average behavior is usually both.

## Goals as Centering Principle in Motivation Theory

It will be observed that the basic principle in our classification has been neither the instigation nor the motivated behavior but rather the functions, effects, purposes, or goals of the behavior. It has been proven sufficiently by various people that this is the most suitable point for centering in any motivation theory.[11]

## Animal- and Human-Centering

This theory starts with the human being rather than any lower and presumably "simpler" animal. Too many of the findings that have been made in animals have been proven to be true for animals but not for the human being. There is no reason whatsoever why we should start with animals in order to study human motivation. The logic or rather illogic behind this general fallacy of "pseudosimplicity" has been exposed often enough by philosophers and logicians as well as by scientists in each of the various fields. It is no more necessary to study animals before one can study man than it is to study mathematics before one can study geology or psychology or biology.

We may also reject the old, naive behaviorism which assumed that it was somehow necessary, or at least more "scientific" to judge human beings by animal standards. One consequence of this belief was that the whole notion of purpose and goal was excluded from motivational psychology simply because one could not ask a white rat about his purposes. Tolman (18) has long since proven in animal studies themselves that this exclusion was not necessary.

## Motivation and the Theory of Psychopathogenesis

The conscious motivational content of everyday life has, according to the foregoing, been conceived to be relatively important or unimportant accordingly as it is more or less closely related to the basic goals. A desire for an ice cream cone might actually be an indirect expression of a desire for love. If it is, then this desire for the ice cream cone becomes extremely important motivation. If however the ice cream is simply something to cool the mouth with, or a casual appetitive reaction, then the desire is relatively unimportant. Everyday conscious desires are to be regarded as symptoms, as surface indicators of more basic needs. If we were to take these superficial desires at their face value we would find ourselves in a state of complete confusion which could never be resolved, since we would be dealing seriously with symptoms rather than with what lay behind the symptoms.

Thwarting of unimportant desires produces no psychopathological results; thwarting of a basically important need does produce such results. Any theory of psychopathogenesis must then be based on a sound theory of motivation. A conflict or a frustration is not necessarily pathogenic. It becomes so only when it threatens or thwarts the basic needs, or partial needs that are closely related to the basic needs (10).

## The Role of Gratified Needs

It has been pointed out above several times that our needs usually emerge only when more prepotent needs have been gratified. Thus gratification has an important role in motivation theory. Apart from this, however, needs cease to play an active determining or organizing role as soon as they are gratified.

What this means is that, e.g., a basically satisfied person no longer has the needs for esteem, love, safety, etc. The only sense in which he might be said to have them is in the almost metaphysical sense that a sated man has hunger, or a filled bottle has emptiness. If we are interested in what *actually* motivates us, and not in what has, will, or might motivate us, then a satisfied need is not a motivator. It must be considered for all practical purposes simply not to exist, to have disappeared. This point should be emphasized because it has been either overlooked or contradicted in every theory of motivation I know.[12] The perfectly healthy, normal, fortunate man has no sex needs or hunger needs, or needs for safety, or for love, or for prestige, or self-esteem, except in stray moments of quickly passing threat. If we were to say otherwise, we should also have to aver that every man had all the pathological reflexes, e.g., Babinski, etc., because if his nervous system were damaged, these would appear.

It is such considerations as these that suggest the bold postulation that a man who is thwarted in any of his basic needs may fairly be envisaged simply as a sick man. This is a fair parallel to our designation as "sick" of the man who lacks vitamins or minerals. Who is to say that a lack of love is less important than a lack of vitamins? Since we know the pathogenic effects of love starvation, who is to say that we are invoking value-questions in an unscientific or illegitimate way, any more than the physician does who diagnoses and treats pellagra or scurvy? If I were permitted this usage, I should then say simply that a healthy man is primarily motivated by his needs to develop and actualize his fullest potentialities and capacities. If a man has any other basic needs in any active, chronic sense, then he is simply an unhealthy man. He is as surely sick as if he had suddenly developed a strong salt hunger or calcium hunger.[13]

If this statement seems unusual or paradoxical the reader may be assured that this is only one among many such paradoxes that will appear as we revise our ways of looking at man's deeper motivations. When we ask what man wants of life, we deal with his very essence.

## SUMMARY

1. There are at least five sets of goals, which we may call basic needs. These are briefly physiological, safety, love, esteem, and self-actualization. In addition, we are motivated by the desire to achieve or maintain the various conditions upon which these basic satisfactions rest and by certain more intellectual desires.

2. These basic goals are related to each other, being arranged in a hierarchy of prepotency. This means that the most prepotent

goal will monopolize consciousness and will tend of itself to organize the recruitment of the various capacities of the organism. The less prepotent needs are minimized, even forgotten or denied. But when a need is fairly well satisfied, the next prepotent ("higher") need emerges, in turn to dominate the conscious life and to serve as the center of organization of behavior, since gratified needs are not active motivators.

Thus man is a perpetually wanting animal. Ordinarily the satisfaction of these wants is not altogether mutually exclusive, but only tends to be. The average member of our society is most often partially satisfied and partially unsatisfied in all of his wants. The hierarchy principle is usually empirically observed in terms of increasing percentages of nonsatisfaction as we go up the hierarchy. Reversals of the average order of the hierarchy are sometimes observed. Also it has been observed that an individual may permanently lose the higher wants in the hierarchy under special conditions. There are not only ordinarily multiple motivations for usual behavior, but in addition many determinants other than motives.

3. Any thwarting or possibility of thwarting of these basic human goals, or danger to the defenses which protect them, or to the conditions upon which they rest, is considered to be a psychological threat. With a few exceptions, all psychopathology may be partially traced to such threats. A basically thwarted man may actually be defined as a "sick" man, if we wish.

4. It is such basic threats which bring about the general emergency reactions.

5. Certain other basic problems have not been dealt with because of limitations of space. Among these are (a) the problem of values in any definitive motivation theory, (b) the relation between appetites, desires, needs and what is "good" for the organism, (c) the etiology of the basic needs and their possible derivation in early childhood, (d) redefinition of motivational concepts, i.e., drive, desire, wish, need, goal, (e) implication of our theory for hedonistic theory, (f) the nature of the uncompleted act, of success and failure, and of aspiration level, (g) the role of association, habit and conditioning, (h) relation to the theory of interpersonal relations, (i) implications for psychotherapy, (j) implication for theory of society, (k) the theory of selfishness, (l) the relation between needs and cultural patterns, (m) the relation between this theory and Allport's theory of functional autonomy. These as well as certain other less important questions must be considered as motivation theory attempts to become definitive.

# NOTES

1. As the child grows up, sheer knowledge and familiarity as well as better motor development make these "dangers" less and less dangerous and more and more manageable. Throughout life it may be said that one of the main conative functions of education is this neutralizing of apparent dangers through knowledge, e.g., I am not afraid of thunder because I know something about it.

2. A "test battery" for safety might be confronting the child with a small exploding firecracker, or with a bewhiskered face, having the mother leave the room, putting him upon a high ladder, a hypodermic injection, having a mouse crawl up to him, etc. Of course I cannot seriously recommend the deliberate use of such "tests" for they might very well harm the child being tested. But these and similar situations come up by the score in the child's ordinary day-to-day living and may be observed. There is no reason why these stimuli should not be used with, for example, young chimpanzees.

3. Not all neurotic individuals feel unsafe. Neurosis may have at its core a thwarting of the affection and esteem needs in a person who is generally safe.

4. For further details see (12) and (16, Ch. 5).

5. Whether or not this particular desire is universal we do not know. The crucial question, especially important today, is "Will men who are enslaved and dominated inevitably feel dissatisfied and rebellious?" We may assume on the basis of commonly known clinical data that a man who has known true freedom (not paid for by giving up safety and security but rather built on the basis of adequate safety and security) will not willingly or easily allow his freedom to be taken away from him. But we do not know that this is true for the person born into slavery. The events of the next decade should give us our answer. See discussion of this problem in (5).

6. Perhaps the desire for prestige and respect from others is subsidiary to the desire for self-esteem or confidence in oneself. Observation of children seems to indicate that this is so, but clinical data give no clear support for such a conclusion.

7. For more extensive discussion of normal self-esteem, as well as for reports of various researches, see (11).

8. Clearly creative behavior, like painting, is like any other behavior in having multiple determinants. It may be seen in "innately creative" people whether they are satisfied or not, happy or unhappy, hungry or sated. Also it is clear that creative activity may be compensatory, ameliorative or purely economic. It is my impression (as yet unconfirmed) that it is possible to distinguish the artistic and intellectual products of basically satisfied people from those of basically unsatisfied people by inspection alone. In any case, here too we must distinguish, in a dynamic fashion, the overt behavior itself from its various motivations or purposes.

9. I am aware that many psychologists and psychoanalysts use the term "motivated" and "determined" synonymously, e.g., Freud. But I consider this an obfuscating usage. Sharp distinctions are necessary for clarity of thought, and precision in experimentation.

10. Discussed fully in a subsequent publication.

11. The interested reader is referred to the very excellent discussion of this point in Murray's *Explorations in Personality* (15).
12. Note that acceptance of this theory necessitates basic revision of the Freudian theory.
13. If we were to use the word "sick" in this way, we should then also have to face squarely the relations of man to his society. One clear implication of our definition would be that (1) since a man is to be called sick who is basically thwarted, and (2) since such basic thwarting is made possible ultimately only by forces outside the individual, then (3) sickness in the individual must come ultimately from a sickness in the society. The "good" or healthy society would then be defined as one that permitted man's highest purposes to emerge by satisfying all his prepotent basic needs.

# REFERENCES

1. Adler, A. *Social Interest*. London: Faber & Faber, 1938.
2. Cannon, W. B. *Wisdom of the Body*. New York: W. W. Norton, 1932.
3. Freud, A. *The Ego and the Mechanisms of Defense*. London: Hogarth, 1937.
4. Freud, S. *New Introductory Lectures on Psychoanalysis* (New York: W. W. Norton, 1933).
5. Fromm, E. *Escape from Freedom*. New York: Farrar and Rinehart, 1941.
6. Goldstein, K. *The Organism*. New York: American Book, 1939.
7. Horney, K. *The Neurotic Personality of Our Time*. New York: W. W. Norton, 1937.
8. Kardiner, A. *The Traumatic Neuroses of War*. New York: Hoeber, 1941.
9. Levy, D. M. "Primary Affect Hunger." *American Journal of Psychiatry* 94 (1937), pp. 643–52.
10. Maslow, A. H. "Conflict, Frustration, and the Theory of Threat." *Journal of Abnormal (Social) Psychology* 38 (1943), pp. 81–86.
11. _____. "Dominance, Personality and Social Behavior in Women." *Journal of Social Psychology* 10 (1939), pp. 3–39.
12. _____. "The Dynamics of Psychological Security-Insecurity." *Character and Personality* 10 (1942), pp. 331–44.
13. _____. "A Preface to Motivation Theory." *Psychosomatic Medicine* 5 (1943), pp. 85–92.
14. Maslow, A. H. and B. Mittelmann. *Principles of Abnormal Psychology*. New York: Harper & Row, 1941.
15. Murray, H. A. et al. *Explorations in Personality*. New York: Oxford University Press, 1938.
16. Plant, J. *Personality and the Cultural Pattern*. New York: Commonwealth Fund, 1937.
17. Shirley, M. "Children's Adjustments to a Strange Situation." *Journal of Abnormal (Social) Psychology* 37 (1942), pp. 201–17.
18. Tolman, E. C. *Purposive Behavior in Animals and Men*. New York: Century, 1932.
19. Wertheimer, M. Unpublished lectures at the New School for Social Research.
20. Young, P. T. *Motivation of Behavior*. New York: John Wiley & Sons, 1936.
21. _____. "The Experimental Analysis of Appetite." *Psychology Bulletin* 38 (1941), pp. 129–64.

# 29

## That Urge to Achieve

### David C. McClelland

*Foremost among the factors which serve to spur individuals to greater and greater efforts is thought by many to be the need to achieve. In this article, McClelland, who has devoted his professional life to understanding this need, describes what achievement motivation is, how it is measured, and, most importantly, how it can be taught. McClelland argues that the urge to achieve is an essential ingredient in business success for individuals as well as for nations.—Eds.*

Most people in this world, psychologically, can be divided into two broad groups. There is that minority which is challenged by opportunity and willing to work hard to achieve something, and the majority which really does not care all that much.

For nearly 20 years now, psychologists have tried to penetrate the mystery of this curious dichotomy. Is the need to achieve (or the absence of it) an accident, is it hereditary, or is it the result of environment? Is it a single, isolatable human motive, or a combination of motives—the desire to accumulate wealth, power, fame? Most important of all, is there some technique that could give this will to achieve to people, even whole societies, who do not now have it?

While we do not yet have complete answers for any of these questions, years of work have given us partial answers to most of them and insights into all of them. There is a distinct human motive, distinguishable from others. It can be found, in fact tested for, in any group.

Let me give you one example. Several years ago, a careful study was made of 450 workers who had been thrown out of work by a plant

SOURCE: From *THINK Magazine* 32, no. 6 (November–December 1966), pp. 19–23. Reprinted by permission from *THINK Magazine,* published by IBM, copyright 1966 by International Business Machines Corporation.

shutdown in Erie, Pennsylvania. Most of the unemployed workers stayed home for a while and then checked back with the United States Employment Service to see if their old jobs or similar ones were available. But a small minority among them behaved differently; the day they were laid off, they started job-hunting.

They checked both the United States and the Pennsylvania Employment Offices; they studied the "Help Wanted" sections of the papers; they checked through their union, their church, and various fraternal organizations; they looked into training courses to learn a new skill; they even left town to look for work, while the majority when questioned said they would not under any circumstances move away from Erie to obtain a job. Obviously the members of that active minority were differently motivated. All the men were more or less in the same situation objectively: they needed work, money, food, shelter, job security. Yet only a minority showed initiative and enterprise in finding what they needed. Why? Psychologists, after years of research, now believe they can answer that question. They have demonstrated that these men possessed in greater degree a specific type of human motivation. For the moment let us refer to this personality characteristic as "Motive A" and review some of the other characteristics of the men who have more of the motive than other men.

Suppose they are confronted by a work situation in which they can set their own goals as to how difficult a task they will undertake. In the psychological laboratory, such a situation is very simply created by asking them to throw rings over a peg from any distance they may choose. Most men throw more or less randomly, standing now close, now far away, but those with Motive A seem to calculate carefully where they are most likely to get a sense of mastery. They stand nearly always at moderate distances, not so close as to make the task ridiculously easy, nor so far away as to make it impossible. They set moderately difficult, but potentially achievable goals for themselves, where they objectively have only about a 1-in-3 chance of succeeding. In other words, they are always setting challenges for themselves, tasks to make them stretch themselves a little.

But they behave like this only if *they* can influence the outcome by performing the work themselves. They prefer not to gamble at all. Say they are given a choice between rolling dice with one in three chances of winning and working on a problem with a one-in-three chance of solving in the time allotted, they choose to work on the problem even though rolling the dice is obviously less work and the odds of winning are the same. They prefer to work at a problem rather than leave the outcome to chance or to others.

Obviously they are concerned with personal achievement rather than with the rewards of success *per se,* since they stand just as much chance of getting those rewards by throwing the dice. This leads to another characteristic the Motive A men show—namely, a strong preference for work situations in which they get concrete feedback on how well they are doing, as one does, say in playing golf, or in being a salesman, but as one does not in teaching, or in personnel counseling. A golfer always knows his score and can compare how well he is doing with par or with his own performance yesterday or last week. A teacher has no such concrete feedback on how well he is doing in "getting across" to his students.

## THE *n* Ach MEN

But why do certain men behave like this? At one level the reply is simple: because they habitually spend their time thinking about doing things better. In fact, psychologists typically measure the strength of Motive A by taking samples of a man's spontaneous thoughts (such as making up a story about a picture they have been shown) and counting the frequency with which he mentions doing things better. The count is objective and can even be made these days with the help of a computer program for content analysis. It yields what is referred to technically as an individual's *n* Ach score (for "need for Achievement"). It is not difficult to understand why people who think constantly about "doing better" are more apt to do better at job-hunting, to set moderate, achievable goals for themselves, to dislike gambling (because they get no achievement satisfaction from success) and to prefer work situations where they can tell easily whether they are improving or not. But why some people and not others come to think this way is another question. The evidence suggests it is not because they are born that way, but because of special training they get in the home from parents who set moderately high achievement goals but who are warm, encouraging and nonauthoritarian in helping their children reach these goals.

Such detailed knowledge about one motive helps correct a lot of common sense ideas about human motivation. For example, much public policy (and much business policy) is based on the simpleminded notion that people will work harder "if they have to." As a first approximation, the idea isn't totally wrong, but it is only a half-truth. The majority of unemployed workers in Erie "had to" find work as much as those with higher *n* Ach, but they certainly didn't work as hard at it. Or again, it is frequently assumed that *any* strong motive will lead to doing things better. Wouldn't it be fair to say that most of the Erie workers were just "unmotivated"? But our detailed knowledge of various human motives shows that each one leads a person to behave in *different* ways. The contrast is not between being "motivated" or "unmotivated" but between being motivated toward A or B or C, etc.

A simple experiment makes the point nicely: subjects were told that they could choose as a working partner either a close friend or a stranger who was known to be an expert on the problem to be solved. Those with higher $n$ Ach (more "need to achieve") chose the experts over their friends, whereas those with more $n$ Aff (the "need to affiliate with others") chose friends over experts. The latter were not "unmotivated"; their desire to be with someone they liked was simply a stronger motive than their desire to excel at the task. Other such needs have been studied by psychologists. For instance, the need for Power is often confused with the need for Achievement because both may lead to "outstanding" activities. There is a distinct difference. People with a strong need for Power want to command attention, get recognition, and control others. They are more active in political life and tend to busy themselves primarily with controlling the channels of communication both up to the top and down to the people so that they are more "in charge." Those with high $n$ Power are not as concerned with improving their work performance daily as those with high $n$ Ach.

It follows, from what we have been able to learn, that not all "great achievers" score high $n$ Ach. Many generals, outstanding politicians, great research scientists do not, for instance, because their work requires other personality characteristics, other motives. A general or a politician must be more concerned with power relationships, a research scientist must be able to go for long periods without the immediate feedback the person with high $n$ Ach requires, etc. On the other hand, business executives, particularly if they are in positions of real responsibility or if they are salesmen, tend to score high in $n$ Ach. This is true even in a Communist country like Poland: apparently there, as well as in a private enterprise economy, a manager succeeds if he is concerned about improving all the time, setting moderate goals, keeping track of his or the company's performance, etc.

## MOTIVATION AND HALF-TRUTHS

Since careful study has shown that common sense notions about motivation are at best half-truths, it also follows that you cannot trust what people tell you about their motives. After all, they often get their own motives from common sense. Thus a general may say he is interested in achievement (because he has obviously achieved), or a businessman that he is interested only in making money (because he has made money), or one of the majority of unemployed in Erie that he desperately wants a job (because he knows he needs one); but a careful check of what each one thinks about and how he spends his time may show that each is concerned about quite different things. It requires special measurement techniques to identify the presence of $n$ Ach and other such motives. Thus what people say and believe is not very closely related to these "hidden" motives which seem to affect a person's "style of life" more than his political, religious or social attitudes. Thus n Ach produces enterprising men among labor leaders or managers, Republicans or Democrats, Catholics or Protestants, capitalists or communists.

Wherever people begin to think often in n Ach terms things begin to move. Men with higher n Ach get more raises and are promoted more rapidly, because they keep actively seeking ways to do a better job. Companies with many such men grow faster. In one comparison of two firms in Mexico, it was discovered that all but one of the top executives of a fast-growing firm had higher n Ach scores than the highest-scoring executive in an equally large but slow-growing firm. Countries with many such rapidly growing firms tend to show above-average rates of economic growth. This appears to be the reason why correlations have regularly been found between the n Ach content in popular literature (such as popular songs or stories in children's textbooks) and subsequent rates of national economic growth. A nation which is thinking about doing better all the time (as shown in its popular literature) actually does do better economically speaking. Careful quantitative studies have shown this to be true in Ancient Greece, in Spain in the Middle Ages, in England from 1400–1800, as well as among contemporary nations, whether capitalist or communist, developed or underdeveloped.

Contrast these two stories for example. Which one contains more n Ach? Which one reflects a state of mind which ought to lead to harder striving to improve the way things are?

*Excerpt from story A* (4th grade reader): "Don't Ever Owe a Man— The world is an illusion. Wife, children, horses, and cows are all just ties of fate. They are ephemeral. Each after fulfilling his part in life disappears. So we should not clamour after riches which are not permanent. As long as we live it is wise not to have any attachments and just think of God. We have to spend our lives without trouble, for is it not time that there is an end to grievances? So it is better to live knowing the real state of affairs. Don't get entangled in the meshes of family life."

*Excerpt from story B* (4th grade reader): "How I Do Like to Learn— I was sent to an accelerated technical high school. I was so happy I cried. Learning is not very easy. In the beginning I couldn't understand what the teacher taught us. I always got a red cross mark on my papers. The boy sitting next to me was very enthusiastic and also an outstanding student. When he found I couldn't do the problems he offered to show me how he had done them. I could not copy his work. I must learn through my own reasoning. I gave his paper back and explained I had to do it myself. Sometimes I worked on a problem until midnight. If I couldn't finish, I started early in the morning. The red cross marks on my work were getting less common. I conquered my difficulties. My marks rose. I graduated and went on to college."

Most readers would agree without any special knowledge of the $n$ Ach coding system, that the second story shows more concern with improvement than the first, which comes from a contemporary reader used in Indian public schools. In fact the latter has a certain Horatio Alger quality that is reminiscent of our own McGuffey readers of several generations ago. It appears today in the textbooks of Communist China. It should not, therefore, come as a surprise if a nation like Communist China, obsessed as it is with improvement, tended in the long run to outproduce a nation like India, which appears to be more fatalistic.

The $n$ Ach level is obviously important for statesmen to watch and in many instances to try to do something about, particularly if a nation's economy is lagging. Take Britain, for example. A generation ago (around 1925) it ranked fifth among 25 countries where children's readers were scored for $n$ Ach—and its economy was doing well. By 1950 the $n$ Ach level had dropped to 27th out of 39 countries—well below the world average—and today, its leaders are feeling the severe economic effects of this loss in the spirit of enterprise.

## ECONOMICS AND $n$ Ach

If psychologists can detect $n$ Ach levels in individuals or nations, particularly before their effects are widespread, can't the knowledge somehow be put to use to foster economic development? Obviously detection or diagnosis is not enough. What good is it to tell Britain (or India for that matter) that it needs more $n$ Ach, a greater spirit of enterprise? In most such cases, informed observers of the local scene know very well that such a need exists, though they may be slower to discover it than the psychologist hovering over $n$ Ach in individuals or nations.

Since about 1960, psychologists in my research group at Harvard have been experimenting with techniques designed to accomplish this goal, chiefly among business executives whose work requires the action characteristics of people with high $n$ Ach. Initially, we had real doubts as to whether we could succeed, partly because like most American psychologists we had been strongly influenced by the psychoanalytic view that basic motives are laid down in childhood and cannot really be changed later, and partly because many studies of intensive psychotherapy and counseling have shown minor if any long-term personality effects. On the other hand we were encouraged by the nonprofessionals: those enthusiasts like Dale Carnegie, the communist ideologue or the church missionary, who felt they could change adults and in fact seemed to be doing so. At any rate we ran some brief (7 to 10 days) "total push" training courses for businessmen, designed to increase their $n$ Ach.

## FOUR MAIN GOALS

In broad outline the courses had four main goals: (1) They were designed to teach the participants how to think, talk and act like a person with high $n$ Ach, based on our knowledge of such people gained through 17 years of research. For instance, men learned how to make up stories that would code high in $n$ Ach (i.e., how to think in $n$ Ach terms), how to set moderate goals for themselves in the ring toss game (and in life). (2) The courses stimulated the participants to set higher but carefully planned and realistic work goals for themselves over the next two years. Then we checked back with them every six months to see how well they were doing in terms of their own objectives. (3) The courses also utilized techniques for giving the participants knowledge about themselves. For instance, in playing the ring toss game, they could observe that they behaved differently from others—perhaps in refusing to adjust a goal downward after failure. This would then become a matter for group discussion and the man would have to explain what he had in mind in setting such unrealistic goals. Discussion could then lead on to what a man's ultimate goals in life were, how much he cared about actually improving performance versus making a good impression or having many friends. In this way the participants would be freer to realize their achievement goals without being blocked by old habits and attitudes. (4) The courses also usually created a group *esprit de corps* from learning about each other's hopes and fears, successes and failures, and from going through an emotional experience together, away from everyday life, in a retreat setting. This membership in a new group helps a man achieve his goals, partly because he knows he has their sympathy and support and partly because he knows they will be watching to see how well he does. The same effect has been noted in other therapy groups like Alcoholics Anonymous. We are not sure which of these course "inputs" is really absolutely essential—that remains a research question—but we were taking no chances at the outset in view of the general pessimism about such efforts, and we wanted to include any and all techniques that were thought to change people.

The courses have been given: to executives in a large American firm, and in several Mexican firms; to underachieving high school boys; and to businessmen in India from Bombay and from a small city—Kakinada in the state of Andhra Pradesh. In every instance save one (the Mexican case), it was possible to demonstrate statistically, some two years later, that the men who took the course had done better (made more money, got promoted faster, expanded their businesses faster) than comparable men who did not take the course or who took some other management course.

Consider the Kakinada results, for example. In the two years preceding the course 9 men, 18 percent of the 52 participants, had shown "unusual" enterprise in their businesses. In the 18 months following the course 25 of the men, in other words nearly 50 percent, were unusually active. And this was not due to a general upturn of business in India. Data from a control city some 45 miles away, show the same base rate of "unusually active" men as in Kakinada before the course—namely, about 20 percent. Something clearly happened in Kakinada: the owner of a small radio shop started a chemical plant; a banker was so successful in making commercial loans in an enterprising way that he was promoted to a much larger branch of his bank in Calcutta; the local political leader accomplished his goal (it was set in the course) to get the federal government to deepen the harbor and make it into an all-weather port; plans are far along for establishing a steel rolling mill, etc. All this took place without any substantial capital input from outside. In fact, the only costs were for four 10-day courses plus some brief follow-up visits every six months. The men are raising their own capital and using their own resources for getting business and industry moving in a city that had been considered stagnant and unenterprising.

The promise of such a method of developing achievement motivation seems very great. It has obvious applications in helping underdeveloped countries, or "pockets of poverty" in the United States, to move faster economically. It has great potential for businesses that need to "turn around" and take a more enterprising approach toward their growth and development. It may even be helpful in developing more *n* Ach among low-income groups. For instance, data show that lower-class Negro Americans have a very low level of *n* Ach. This is not surprising. Society has systematically discouraged and blocked their achievement striving. But as the barriers to upward mobility are broken down, it will be necessary to help stimulate the motivation that will lead them to take advantage of new opportunities opening up.

## EXTREME REACTIONS

But a word of caution: Whenever I speak of this research and its great potential, audience reaction tends to go to opposite extremes. Either people remain skeptical and argue that motives can't really be changed, that all we are doing is dressing Dale Carnegie up in fancy "psychologese," or they become converts and want instant course descriptions by return mail to solve their local motivational problems. Either response is unjustified. What I have described here in a few pages has taken 20 years of patient research effort, and hundreds of thousands of dollars in basic research costs. What remains to be done will involve even larger sums or more time for development to turn a promising idea into something of wide practical utility.

## ENCOURAGEMENT NEEDED

To take only one example, we have not learned to develop $n$ Ach really well among low-income groups. In our first effort—a summer course for bright underachieving 14-year-olds—we found that boys from the middle class improved steadily in grades in school over a two-year period, but boys from the lower class showed an improvement after the first year followed by a drop back in their beginning low grade average. (See the accompanying chart.) Why? We speculate that it was

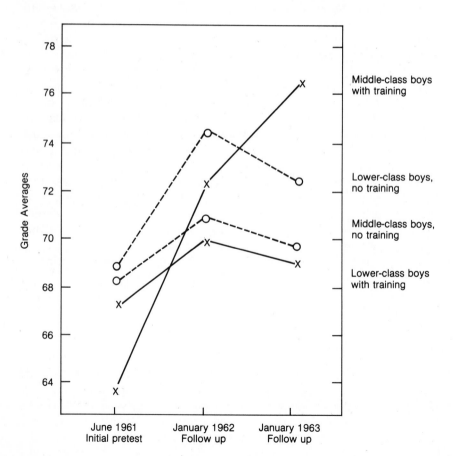

because they moved back into an environment in which neither parents nor friends encouraged achievement or upward mobility. In other words, it isn't enough to change a man's motivation if the environment in which he lives doesn't support at least to some degree his new efforts. Negroes striving to rise out of the ghetto frequently confront this problem: they are faced by skepticism at home and suspicion on the job, so that even if their $n$ Ach is raised, it can be lowered again by the heavy odds against their success. We must learn not only to raise $n$ Ach but also to find methods of instructing people in how to manage it, to create a favorable environment in which it can flourish.

Many of these training techniques are now only in the pilot testing stage. It will take time and money to perfect them, but society should be willing to invest heavily in them in view of their tremendous potential for contributing to human betterment.

# 30

# On the Folly of Rewarding A, while Hoping for B

*Steven Kerr*

*Supposedly, we reward people for doing what we want them to and don't reward them when they do something else. While it sounds very simple and straightforward, this article by Steven Kerr suggests that it isn't that way at all. He notes that all too often organizations create motivational forces which lead to unwanted and unintended consequences by rewarding behaviors that are not desired and by discouraging behaviors that are desired.—Eds.*

Whether dealing with monkeys, rats, or human beings, it is hardly controversial to state that most organisms seek information concerning what activities are rewarded, and then seek to do (or at least pretend to do) those things, often to the virtual exclusion of activities not rewarded. The extent to which this occurs of course will depend on the perceived attractiveness of the rewards offered, but neither operant nor expectancy theorists would quarrel with the essence of this notion.

Nevertheless, numerous examples exist of reward systems that are fouled up in that behaviors which are rewarded are those which the rewarder is trying to *discourage,* while the behavior he desires is not being rewarded at all.

In an effort to understand and explain this phenomenon, this paper presents examples from society, from organizations in general, and from profit-making firms in particular. Data from a manufacturing company and information from an insurance firm are examined to demonstrate the consequences of such reward systems for the organizations involved, and possible reasons why such reward systems continue to exist are considered.

---

SOURCE: Reprinted from *Academy of Management Journal* 18 (1975), pp. 769–83.

## SOCIETAL EXAMPLES

### Politics

Official goals are "purposely vague and general and do not indicate
. . . the host of decisions that must be made among alternative ways
of achieving official goals and the priority of multiple goals . . ." (8,
p. 66). They usually may be relied on to offend absolutely no one, and
in this sense can be considered high-acceptance, low-quality goals. An
example might be "build better schools." Operative goals are higher in
quality but lower in acceptance, since they specify where the money
will come from, what alternative goals will be ignored, etc.

The American citizenry supposedly wants its candidates for public
office to set forth operative goals, making their proposed programs
"perfectly clear," specifying sources and uses of funds, etc. However,
since operative goals are lower in acceptance, and since aspirants to
public office need acceptance (from at least 50.1 percent of the people),
most politicians prefer to speak only of official goals, at least until after
the election. They of course would agree to speak at the operative level
if "punished" for not doing so. The electorate could do this by refusing
to support candidates who do not speak at the operative level.

Instead, however, the American voter typically punishes (with-
holds support from) candidates who frankly discuss where the money
will come from, rewards politicians who speak only of official goals,
but hopes that candidates (despite the reward system) will discuss the
issues operatively. It is academic whether it was moral for Nixon, for
example, to refuse to discuss his 1968 "secret plan" to end the Vietnam
war, his 1972 operative goals concerning the lifting of price controls,
the reshuffling of his cabinet, etc. The point is that the reward system
made such refusal rational.

It seems worth mentioning that no manuscript can adequately
define what is "moral" and what is not. However, examination of costs
and benefits, combined with knowledge of what motivates a particular
individual, often will suffice to determine what for him is "rational."[1]
If the reward system is so designed that it is irrational to be moral,
this does not necessarily mean that immorality will result. But is this
not asking for trouble?

### War

If some oversimplification may be permitted, let it be assumed that
the primary goal of the organization (Pentagon, Luftwaffe, or whatever)
is to win. Let it be assumed further that the primary goal of most
individuals on the front lines is to get home alive. Then there appears

to be an important conflict in goals—personally rational behavior by those at the bottom will endanger goal attainment by those at the top.

But not necessarily! It depends on how the reward system is set up. The Vietnam war was indeed a study of disobedience and rebellion, with terms such as "fragging" (killing one's own commanding officer) and "search and evade" becoming part of the military vocabulary. The difference in subordinates' acceptance of authority between World War II and Vietnam is reported to be considerable, and veterans of the Second World War often have been quoted as being outraged at the mutinous actions of many American soldiers in Vietnam.

Consider, however, some critical differences in the reward system in use during the two conflicts. What did the GI in World War II want? To go home. And when did he get to go home? When the war was won! If he disobeyed the orders to clean out the trenches and take the hills, the war would not be won and he would not go home. Furthermore, what were his chances of attaining his goal (getting home alive) if he obeyed the orders compared to his chances if he did not? What is being suggested is that the rational soldier in World War II, *whether patriotic or not,* probably found it expedient to obey.

Consider the reward system in use in Vietnam. What did the man at the bottom want? To go home. And when did he get to go home? When his tour of duty was over! This was the case *whether or not* the war was won. Furthermore, concerning the relative chance of getting home alive by obeying orders compared to the chance if they were disobeyed, it is worth noting that a mutineer in Vietnam was far more likely to be assigned rest and rehabilitation (on the assumption that fatigue was the cause) than he was to suffer any negative consequence.

In his description of the "zone of difference," Barnard stated that "a person can and will accept a communication as authoritative only when . . . at the time of his decision, he believes it to be compatible with his personal interests as a whole" (1, p. 165). In light of the reward system used in Vietnam, would it not have been personally irrational for some orders to have been obeyed? Was not the military implementing a system which *rewarded* disobedience, while *hoping* that soldiers (despite the reward system) would obey orders?

## Medicine

Theoretically, a physician can make either of two types of error, and intuitively one seems as bad as the other. A doctor can pronounce a patient sick when he is actually well, thus causing him needless anxiety and expense, curtailment of enjoyable foods and activities, and even physical danger by subjecting him to needless medication and surgery. Alternately, a doctor can label a sick person well, and thus avoid treating what may be a serious, even fatal ailment. It might be natural to conclude that physicians seek to minimize both types of error.

Such a conclusion would be wrong.[2] It is estimated that numerous Americans are presently afflicted with iatrogenic (physician *caused*) illnesses (9). This occurs when the doctor is approached by someone complaining of a few stray symptoms. The doctor classifies and organizes these symptoms, gives them a name, and obligingly tells the patient what further symptoms may be expected. This information often acts as a self-fulfilling prophecy, with the result that from that day on the patient for all practical purposes is sick.

Why does this happen? Why are physicians so reluctant to sustain a type 2 error (pronouncing a sick person well) that they will tolerate many type 1 errors? Again, a look at the reward system is needed. The punishments for a type 2 error are real: guilt, embarrassment, and the threat of lawsuit and scandal. On the other hand, a type 1 error (labeling a well person sick) "is sometimes seen as sound clinical practice, indicating a healthy conservative approach to medicine" (9, p. 69). Type 1 errors also are likely to generate increased income and a stream of steady customers who, being well in a limited physiological sense, will not embarrass the doctor by dying abruptly.

Fellow physicians and the general public therefore are really *rewarding* type 1 errors and at the same time *hoping* fervently that doctors will try not to make them.

## GENERAL ORGANIZATIONAL EXAMPLES

### Rehabilitation Centers and Orphanages

In terms of the prime beneficiary classification (2, p. 42) organizations such as these are supposed to exist for the "public-in-contact," that is, clients. The orphanage therefore theoretically is interested in placing as many children as possible in good homes. However, often orphanages surround themselves with so many rules concerning adoption that it is nearly impossible to pry a child out of the place. Orphanages may deny adoption unless the applicants are a married couple, both of the same religion as the child, without history of emotional or vocational instability, with a specified minimum income and a private room for the child, etc.

If the primary goal is to place children in good homes, then the rules ought to constitute means toward that goal. Goal displacement results when these "means become ends-in-themselves that displace the original goals" (2, p. 229).

To some extent these rules are required by law. But the influence of the reward system on the orphanage's management should not be ignored. Consider, for example, that the:

1. Number of children enrolled often is the most important determinant of the size of the allocated budget.
2. Number of children under the director's care also will affect the size of his staff.
3. Total organizational size will determine largely the director's prestige at the annual conventions, in the community, etc.

Therefore, to the extent that staff size, total budget, and personal prestige are valued by the orphanage's executive personnel, it becomes rational for them to make it difficult for children to be adopted. After all, who wants to be the director of the smallest orphanage in the state?

If the reward system errs in the opposite direction, paying off only for placements, extensive goal displacement again is likely to result. A common example of vocational rehabilitation in many states, for example, consists of placing someone in a job for which he has little interest and few qualifications, for two months or so, and then "rehabilitating" him again in another position. Such behavior is quite consistent with the prevailing reward system, which pays off for the number of individuals placed in any position for 60 days or more. Rehabilitation counselors also confess to competing with one another to place relatively skilled clients, sometimes ignoring persons with few skills who would be harder to place. Extensively disabled clients find that counselors often prefer to work with those whose disabilities are less severe.[3]

## Universities

Society *hopes* that teachers will not neglect their teaching responsibilities but *rewards* them almost entirely for research and publications. This is most true at the large and prestigious universities. Clichés such as "good research and good teaching go together" notwithstanding, professors often find that they must choose between teaching and research-oriented activities when allocating their time. Rewards for good teaching usually are limited to outstanding teacher awards, which are given to only a small percentage of good teachers and which usually bestow little money and fleeting prestige. Punishments for poor teaching also are rare.

Rewards for research and publications, on the other hand, and punishments for failure to accomplish these, are commonly administered by universities at which teachers are employed. Furthermore, publication-oriented resumés usually will be well received at other universities, whereas teaching credentials, harder to document and quantify, are much less transferable. Consequently it is rational for university teachers to concentrate on research, even if to the detriment of teaching and at the expense of their students.

By the same token, it is rational for students to act based upon the goal displacement which has occurred within universities concerning what they are rewarded for. If it is assumed that a primary goal of a university is to transfer knowledge from teacher to student, then grades become identifiable as a means toward that goal, serving as motivational, control, and feedback devices to expedite the knowledge transfer. Instead, however, the grades themselves have become much more important for entrance to graduate school, successful employment, tuition refunds, parental respect, etc., than the knowledge or lack of knowledge they are supposed to signify.

It therefore should come as no surprise that information has surfaced in recent years concerning fraternity files for examinations, term-paper writing services, organized cheating at the service academies, and the like. Such activities constitute a personally rational response to a reward system which pays off for grades rather than knowledge.

## BUSINESS-RELATED EXAMPLES

### Ecology

Assume that the president of XYZ Corporation is confronted with the following alternatives:

1. Spend $11 million for antipollution equipment to keep from poisoning fish in the river adjacent to the plant; or

2. Do nothing, in violation of the law, and assume a 1-in-10 chance of being caught, with a resultant $1 million fine plus the necessity of buying the equipment.

Under this not unrealistic set of choices it requires no linear program to determine that XYZ Corporation can maximize its probabilities by flouting the law. Add the fact that XYZ's president is probably being rewarded (by creditors, stockholders, and other salient parts of his task environment) according to criteria totally unrelated to the number of fish poisoned, and his probable course of action becomes clear.

### Evaluation of Training

It is axiomatic that those who care about a firm's well-being should insist that the organization get fair value for its expenditures. Yet it is commonly known that firms seldom bother to evaluate a new GRID, MBO, job enrichment program, or whatever, to see if the company is getting its money's worth. Why? Certainly it is not because people have not pointed out that this situation exists; numerous practitioner-oriented articles are written each year to just this point.

The individuals (whether in personnel, manpower planning, or wherever) who normally would be responsible for conducting such evaluations are the same ones often charged with introducing the change effort in the first place. Having convinced top management to spend the money, they usually are quite animated afterwards in collecting rigorous vignettes and anecdotes about how successful the program was. The last thing many desire is a formal, systematic, and revealing evaluation. Although members of top management may actually *hope* for such systematic evaluation, their reward systems continue to *reward* ignorance in this area. And if the personnel department abdicates its responsibility, who is to step into the breach? The change agent himself? Hardly! He is likely to be too busy collecting anecdotal "evidence" of his own, for use with his next client.

## Miscellaneous

Many additional examples could be cited of systems which in fact are rewarding behaviors other than those supposedly desired by the rewarder. A few of these are described briefly below.

Most coaches disdain to discuss individual accomplishments, preferring to speak of teamwork, proper attitude, and a one-for-all spirit. Usually, however, rewards are distributed according to individual performance. The college basketball player who feeds his teammates instead of shooting will not compile impressive scoring statistics and is less likely to be drafted by the pros. The ballplayer who hits to right field to advance the runners will win neither the batting nor home run titles, and will be offered smaller raises. It therefore is rational for players to think of themselves first, and the team second.

In business organizations where rewards are dispensed for unit performance or for individual goals achieved, without regard for overall effectiveness, similar attitudes often are observed. Under most Management by Objectives (MBO) systems, goals in areas where quantification is difficult often go unspecified. The organization therefore often is in a position where it *hopes* for employee effort in the areas of team building, interpersonal relations, creativity, etc., but it formally *rewards* none of these. In cases where promotions and raises are formally tied to MBO, the system itself contains a paradox in that it "asks employees to set challenging, risky goals, only to face smaller paychecks and possibly damaged careers if these goals are not accomplished" (5, p. 40).

It is *hoped* that administrators will pay attention to long-run costs and opportunities and will institute programs which will bear fruit later on. However, many organizational reward systems pay off for short-run sales and earnings only. Under such circumstances it is personally rational for officials to sacrifice long-term growth and profit (by selling off equipment and property, or by stifling research and development) for short-term advantages. This probably is most pertinent in the public sector, with the result that many public officials are unwilling to implement programs which will not show benefits by election time.

As a final, clear-cut example of a fouled-up reward system, consider the cost-plus contract or its next of kin, the allocation of next year's budget as a direct function of this year's expenditures. It probably is conceivable that those who award such budgets and contracts really hope for economy and prudence in spending. It is obvious, however, that adopting the proverb "to him who spends shall more be given," rewards not economy, but spending itself.

## TWO COMPANIES' EXPERIENCES

### A Manufacturing Organization

A Midwest manufacturer of industrial goods had been troubled for some time by aspects of its organizational climate it believed dysfunctional. For research purposes, interviews were conducted with many employees and a questionnaire was administered on a company-wide basis, including plants and offices in several American and Canadian locations. The company strongly encouraged employee participation in the survey, and made available time and space during the workday for completion of the instrument. All employees in attendance during the day of the survey completed the questionnaire. All instruments were collected directly by the researcher, who personally administered each session. Since no one employed by the firm handled the questionnaires, and since respondent names were not asked for, it seems likely that the pledge of anonymity given was believed.

A modified version of the Expect Approval scale (7) was included as part of the questionnaire. The instrument asked respondents to indicate the degree of approval or disapproval they could expect if they performed each of the described actions. A seven-point Likert scale was used, with 1 indicating that the action would probably bring strong disapproval and 7 signifying likely strong approval.

Although normative data for this scale from studies of other organizations are unavailable, it is possible to examine fruitfully the data obtained from this survey in several ways. First, it may be worth noting that the questionnaire data corresponded closely to information gathered through interviews. Furthermore, as can be seen from the results summarized in Table 1, sizable differences between various work units, and between employees at different job levels within the

**TABLE 1**  Summary of Two Divisions' Data Relevant to Conforming and Risk-Avoidance Behaviors (extent to which subjects expect approval)

| Dimension | Item | Division and Sample | Total Responses | Percentage of Workers Responding | | |
|---|---|---|---|---|---|---|
| | | | | 1, 2, or 3 (Disapproval) | 4 | 5, 6, or 7 (Approval) |
| Risk avoidance | Making a risky decision based on the best information available at the time, but which turns out wrong. | A, levels 1–4 (lowest) | 127 | 61 | 25 | 14 |
| | | A, levels 5–8 | 172 | 46 | 31 | 23 |
| | | A, levels 9 and above | 17 | 41 | 30 | 30 |
| | | B, levels 1–4 (lowest) | 31 | 58 | 26 | 16 |
| | | B, levels 5–8 | 19 | 42 | 42 | 16 |
| | | B, levels 9 and above | 10 | 50 | 20 | 30 |
| Risk | Setting extremely high and challenging standards and goals, and then narrowly failing to make them. | A, levels 1–4 | 122 | 47 | 28 | 25 |
| | | A, levels 5–8 | 168 | 33 | 26 | 41 |
| | | A, levels 9 + | 17 | 24 | 6 | 70 |

| | | | | |
|---|---|---|---|---|
| B, levels 1–4 | 31 | 48 | 23 | 29 |
| B, levels 5–8 | 18 | 17 | 33 | 50 |
| B, levels 9+ | 10 | 30 | 0 | 70 |
| Setting goals which are extremely easy to make and then making them. | | | | |
| A, levels 1–4 | 124 | 35 | 30 | 35 |
| A, levels 5–8 | 171 | 47 | 27 | 26 |
| A, levels 9+ | 17 | 70 | 24 | 6 |
| B, levels 1–4 | 32 | 58 | 26 | 16 |
| B, levels 5–8 | 19 | 63 | 16 | 21 |
| B, levels 9+ | 10 | 80 | 0 | 20 |
| Being a "yes man" and always agreeing with the boss. | | | | |
| A, levels 1–4 | 126 | 46 | 17 | 37 |
| A, levels 5–8 | 180 | 54 | 14 | 31 |
| A, levels 9+ | 17 | 88 | 12 | 0 |
| B, levels 1–4 | 32 | 53 | 28 | 19 |
| B, levels 5–8 | 19 | 68 | 21 | 11 |
| B, levels 9+ | 10 | 80 | 10 | 10 |

**TABLE 1** (*concluded*)

| Dimension | Item | Division and Sample | Total Responses | Percentage of Workers Responding | | |
|---|---|---|---|---|---|---|
| | | | | 1, 2, or 3 (Disapproval) | 4 | 5, 6, or 7 (Approval) |
| | Always going along with the majority. | A, levels 1–4 | 125 | 40 | 25 | 35 |
| | | A, levels 5–8 | 173 | 47 | 21 | 32 |
| | | A, levels 9+ | 17 | 70 | 12 | 18 |
| | | B, levels 1–4 | 31 | 61 | 23 | 16 |
| | | B, levels 5–8 | 19 | 68 | 11 | 21 |
| | | B, levels 9+ | 10 | 80 | 10 | 10 |
| | Being careful to stay on the good side of everyone, so that everyone agrees that you are a great guy. | A, levels 1–4 | 124 | 45 | 18 | 37 |
| | | A, levels 5–8 | 173 | 45 | 22 | 33 |
| | | A, levels 9+ | 17 | 64 | 6 | 30 |
| | | B, levels 1–4 | 31 | 54 | 23 | 23 |
| | | B, levels 5–8 | 19 | 73 | 11 | 16 |
| | | B, levels 9+ | 10 | 80 | 10 | 10 |

same work unit, were obtained. This suggests that response bias effects (social desirability in particular loomed as a potential concern) are not likely to be severe.

Most importantly, comparisons between scores obtained on the Expect Approval scale and a statement of problems which were the reason for the survey revealed that the same behaviors which managers in each division thought dysfunctional were those which lower level employees claimed were rewarded. As compared to job levels 1 to 8 in Division B (see Table 1), those in Division A claimed a much higher acceptance by management of "conforming" activities. Between 31 and 37 percent of Division A employees at levels 1–8 stated that going along with the majority, agreeing with the boss, and staying on everyone's good side brought approval; only once (level 5–8 responses to one of the three items) did a majority suggest that such actions would generate disapproval.

Furthermore, responses from Division A workers at levels 1–4 indicate that behaviors geared toward risk avoidance were as likely to be rewarded as to be punished. Only at job levels 9 and above was it apparent that the reward system was positively reinforcing behaviors desired by top management. Overall, the same "tendencies toward conservatism and apple-polishing at the lower levels" which divisional management had complained about during the interviews were those claimed by subordinates to be the most rational course of action in light of the existing reward system. Management apparently was not getting the behaviors it was *hoping* for, but it certainly was getting the behaviors it was perceived by subordinates to be *rewarding*.

## An Insurance Firm

The Group Health Claims Division of a large eastern insurance company provides another rich illustration of a reward system which reinforces behaviors not desired by top management.

Attempting to measure and reward accuracy in paying surgical claims, the firm systematically keeps track of the number of returned checks and letters of complaint received from policyholders. However, underpayments are likely to provoke cries of outrage from the insured, while overpayments often are accepted in courteous silence. Since it often is impossible to tell from the physician's statement which of two surgical procedures, with different allowable benefits, was performed, and since writing for clarifications will interfere with other standards used by the firm concerning "percentage of claims paid within two days of receipt," the new hire in more than one claims section is soon acquainted with the informal norm: "When in doubt, pay it out!"

The situation would be even worse were it not for the fact that other features of the firm's reward system tend to neutralize those described. For example, annual "merit" increases are given to all employees, in one of the following three amounts:

1. If the worker is "outstanding" (a select category, into which no more than two employees per section may be placed): 5 percent

2. If the worker is "above average" (normally all workers not "outstanding" are so rated): 4 percent

3. If the worker commits gross acts of negligence and irresponsibility for which he might be discharged in many other companies: 3 percent.

Now, since (a) the difference between the 5 percent theoretically attainable through hard work and the 4 percent attainable merely by living until the review date is small and (b) since insurance firms seldom dispense much of a salary increase in cash (rather, the worker's insurance benefits increase, causing him to be further overinsured), many employees are rather indifferent to the possibility of obtaining the extra one percent reward and therefore tend to ignore the norm concerning indiscriminant payments.

However, most employees are not indifferent to the rule which states that, should absences or latenesses total three or more in any six-month period, the entire 4 or 5 percent due at the next "merit" review must be forfeited. In this sense the firm may be described as *hoping* for performance, while *rewarding* attendance. What it gets, of course, is attendance. (If the absence-lateness rule appears to the reader to be stringent, it really is not. The company counts "times" rather than "days" absent, and a 10-day absence therefore counts the same as one lasting 2 days. A worker in danger of accumulating a third absence within six months merely has to remain ill [away from work] during his second absence until his first absence is more than six months old. The limiting factor is that at some point his salary ceases, and his sickness benefits take over. This usually is sufficient to get the younger workers to return, but for those with 20 or more years' service, the company provides sickness benefits of 90 percent of normal salary, tax-free! Therefore . . .)

## CAUSES

Extremely diverse instances of systems which reward behavior A although the rewarder apparently hopes for behavior B have been given. These are useful to illustrate the breadth and magnitude of the phenomenon, but the diversity increases the difficulty of determining commonalities and establishing causes. However, four general factors may be pertinent to an explanation of why fouled-up reward systems seem to be so prevalant.

### Fascination with an "Objective" Criterion

It has been mentioned elsewhere that:

Most "objective" measures of productivity are objective only in that their subjective elements are (a) determined in advance, rather than coming into play at the time of the formal evaluation, and (b) well concealed on the rating instrument itself. Thus industrial firms seeking to devise objective rating systems first decide, in an arbitrary manner, what dimensions are to be rated, ... usually including some items having little to do with organizational effectiveness while excluding others that do. Only then does Personnel Division churn out official-looking documents on which all dimensions chosen to be rated are assigned point values, categories, or whatever [6, p. 92:].

Nonetheless, many individuals seek to establish simple, quantifiable standards against which to measure and reward performance. Such efforts may be successful in highly predictable areas within an organization, but are likely to cause goal displacement when applied anywhere else. Overconcern with attendance and lateness in the insurance firm and with number of people placed in the vocational rehabilitation division may have been largely responsible for the problems described in those organizations.

### Overemphasis on Highly Visible Behaviors

Difficulties often stem from the fact that some parts of the task are highly visible while other parts are not. For example, publications are easier to demonstrate than teaching, and scoring baskets and hitting home runs are more readily observable than feeding teammates and advancing base runners. Similarly, the adverse consequences of pronouncing a sick person well are more visible than those sustained by labeling a well person sick. Team-building and creativity are other examples of behaviors which may not be rewarded simply because they are hard to observe.

### Hypocrisy

In some of the instances described the rewarder may have been getting the desired behavior, notwithstanding claims that the behavior was not desired. This may be true, for example, of management's attitude toward apple-polishing in the manufacturing firm (a behavior which subordinates felt was rewarded, despite management's avowed dislike of the practice). This also may explain politicians' unwillingness to revise the penalties for disobedience of ecology laws, and the failure of top management to devise reward systems which would cause systematic evaluation of training and development programs.

### Emphasis on Morality or Equity Rather than Efficiency

Some consideration of other factors prevents the establishment of a system which rewards behaviors desired by the rewarder. The felt obligation of many Americans to vote for one candidate or another, for example, may impair their ability to withhold support from politicians who refuse to discuss the issues. Similarly, the concern for spreading the risks and costs of wartime military service may outweigh the advantage to be obtained by committing personnel to combat until the war is over.

It should be noted that only with respect to the first two causes are reward systems really paying off for other than desired behaviors. In the case of the third and fourth causes the system *is* rewarding behaviors desired by the rewarder, and the systems are fouled up only from the standpoints of those who believe the rewarder's public statements (cause 3), or those who seek to maximize efficiency rather than other outcomes (cause 4).

## CONCLUSIONS

Modern organization theory requires a recognition that the members of organizations and society possess divergent goals and motives. It therefore is unlikely that managers and their subordinates will seek the same outcomes. Three possible remedies for this potential problem are suggested.

### Selection

It is theoretically possible for organizations to employ only those individuals whose goals and motives are wholly consonant with those of management. In such cases the same behaviors judged by subordinates to be rational would be perceived by management as desirable. State-of-the-art reviews of selection techniques, however, provide scant grounds for hope that such an approach would be successful (for example, see 12).

## Training

Another theoretical alternative is for the organization to admit those employees whose goals are not consonant with those of management and then, through training, socialization, or whatever, alter employee goals to make them consonant. However, research on the effectiveness of such training programs, though limited, provides further grounds for pessimism (for example, see 3).

### Altering the Reward System

What would have been the result if:

1. Nixon had been assured by his advisors that he could not win reelection except by discussing the issues in detail?
2. Physicians' conduct was subjected to regular examination by review boards for type 1 errors (calling healthy people ill) and to penalties (fines, censure, etc.) for errors of either type?
3. The president of XYZ Corporation had to choose between (a) spending $11 million for antipollution equipment, and (b) incurring a 50-50 chance of going to jail for five years?

Managers who complain that their workers are not motivated might do well to consider the possibility that they have installed reward systems which are paying off for behaviors other then those they are seeking. This, in part, is what happened in Vietnam, and this is what regularly frustrates societal efforts to bring about honest politicians, civic-minded managers, etc. This certainly is what happened in both the manufacturing and the insurance companies.

A first step for such managers might be to find out what behaviors currently are being rewarded. Perhaps an instrument similar to that used in the manufacturing firm could be useful for this purpose. Chances are excellent that these managers will be surprised by what they find—that their firms are not rewarding what they assume they are. In fact, such undesirable behavior by organizational members as they have observed may be explained largely by the reward systems in use.

This is not to say that all organizational behavior is determined by formal rewards and punishments. Certainly it is true that in the absence of formal reinforcement some soldiers will be patriotic, some presidents will be ecology-minded, and some orphanage directors will care about children. The point, however, is that in such cases the rewarder is not *causing* the behaviors desired but is only a fortunate bystander. For an organization to *act* upon its members, the formal reward system should positively reinforce desired behaviors, not constitute an obstacle to be overcome.

It might be wise to underscore the obvious fact that there is nothing really new in what has been said. In both theory and practice these matters have been mentioned before. Thus in many states Good Samaritan laws have been installed to protect doctors who stop to assist a stricken motorist. In states without such laws it is commonplace for doctors to refuse to stop, for fear of involvement in a subsequent lawsuit. In college basketball additional penalties have been instituted against players who foul their opponents deliberately. It has long been argued by Milton Friedman and others that penalties should be altered so as to make it irrational to disobey the ecology laws, and so on.

By altering the reward system the organization escapes the necessity of selecting only desirable people or of trying to alter undesirable ones. In Skinnerian terms (as described in 11, p. 704), "As for responsibility and goodness—as commonly defined—no one . . . would want or need them. They refer to a man's behaving well despite the absence of positive reinforcement that is obviously sufficient to explain it. Where such reinforcement exists, 'no one needs goodness.' "

## NOTES

1. In Simon's (10, pp. 76–77) terms, a decision is "subjectively rational" if it maximizes an individual's valued outcomes so far as his knowledge permits. A decision is "personally rational" if it is oriented toward the individual's goals.
2. In one study (4) of 14,867 films for signs of tuberculosis, 1,216 positive readings turned out to be clinically negative; only 24 negative readings proved clinically active, a ratio of 50 to 1.
3. Personal interviews conducted during 1972–73.

## REFERENCES

1. Barnard, Chester I. *The Functions of the Executive.* Cambridge, Mass.: Harvard University Press, 1968. (First published in 1936.)
2. Blau, Peter M., and W. Richard Scott. *Formal Organizations.* San Francisco: Chandler, 1962.
3. Fiedler, Fred E. "Predicting the effects of leadership training and experience from the contingency model." *Journal of Applied Psychology* 56 (1972), pp. 114–19.
4. Garland, L. H. "Studies of the accuracy of diagnostic procedures." *American Journal Roentgenological, Radium Therapy Nuclear Medicine* 82 (1959), pp. 25–28.
5. Kerr, Steven. "Some modifications in MBO as an OD strategy." *Academy of Management Proceedings,* 1973, pp. 39–42.

6. Kerr, Steven. "What price objectivity?" *American Sociologist* 8 (1973), pp. 92–93.
7. Litwin, G. H., and R. A. Stringer, Jr. *Motivation and Organizational Climate.* Cambridge, Mass.: Harvard University Press, 1968.
8. Perrow, Charles. "The analysis of goals in complex organizations." In *Readings on Modern Organizations,* ed. A. Etzioni. Englewood Cliffs, N.J.: Prentice-Hall, 1969.
9. Scheff, Thomas J. "Decision rules, types of error, and their consequences in medical diagnosis." In *Mathematical Explorations in Behavioral Science,* ed. F. Massarik and P. Ratoosh. Homewood, Ill.: Richard D. Irwin, 1965.
10. Simon, Herbert A. *Administrative Behavior.* New York: Free Press, 1957.
11. Swanson, G. E. "Review symposium: Beyond freedom and dignity." *American Journal of Sociology* 78 (1972), pp. 702–5.
12. Webster, E. *Decision Making in the Employment Interview.* Montreal: Industrial Relations Center, McGill University, 1964.

# 31

# A New Strategy for Job Enrichment

*J. Richard Hackman,*
*Greg Oldham,*
*Robert Janson,*
*and*
*Kenneth Purdy*

*The authors of this selection present a strategy for the redesign of work,*
*in general, and for job enrichment, in particular. They argue that there*
*are three critical psychological states which determine a person's mo-*
*tivation on the job: meaningfulness, responsibility, and knowledge of*
*results.—Eds.*

Practitioners of job enrichment have been living through a time of excitement, even euphoria. Their craft has moved from the psychology and management journals to the front page and the Sunday supplement. Job enrichment, which began with the pioneering work of Herzberg and his associates, originally was intended as a means to increase the motivation and satisfaction of people at work—and to improve productivity in the bargain. (Herzberg 1966, 1968; Herzberg, Mausner, and Snyderman 1959; Paul, Robertson, and Herzberg 1969; Ford 1969). Now it is being acclaimed in the popular press as a cure for problems ranging from inflation to drug abuse.

Much current writing about job enrichment is enthusiastic, sometimes even messianic, about what it can accomplish. But the hard questions of exactly what should be done to improve jobs, and how,

SOURCE: Reprinted from *California Management Review* 17, pp. 57–71, by permission of the Regents; © 1975, by the Regents of the University of California.

tend to be glossed over. Lately, because the harder questions have not been dealt with adequately, critical winds have begun to blow. Job enrichment has been described as yet another "management fad," as "nothing new," even as a fraud. And reports of job enrichment failures are beginning to appear in management and psychology journals.

This article attempts to redress the excesses that have characterized some of the recent writings about job enrichment. As the technique increases in popularity as a management tool, top managers inevitably will find themselves making decisions about its use. The intent of this paper is to help both managers and behavioral scientists become better able to make those decisions on a solid basis of fact and data.

Succinctly stated, we present here a new strategy for going about the redesign of work. The strategy is based on three years of collaborative work and cross-fertilization among the authors—two of whom are active practitioners in job enrichment. Our approach is new, but it has been tested in many organizations. It draws on the contributions of both management practice and psychological theory, but it is firmly in the middle ground between them. It builds on and complements previous work by Herzberg and others, but provides for the first time a set of tools for *diagnosing* existing jobs—and a map for translating the diagnostic results into specific action steps for change.

What we have, then, is the following:

1. A theory that specifies when people will get personally "turned on" to their work. The theory shows what kinds of jobs are most likely to generate excitement and commitment about work, and what kinds of employees it works best for.

2. A set of action steps for job enrichment based on the theory, which prescribe in concrete terms what to do to make jobs more motivating for the people who do them.

3. Evidence that the theory holds water and that it can be used to bring about measurable—and sometimes dramatic—improvements in employee work behavior, in job satisfaction, and in the financial performance of the organizational unit involved.

## THE THEORY BEHIND THE STRATEGY

*What makes people get turned on to their work?* For workers who are really prospering in their jobs, work is likely to be a lot like play. Consider, for example, a golfer at a driving range, practicing to get rid of a hook. His activity is *meaningful* to him; he has chosen to do it because he gets a "kick" from testing his skills by playing the game. He knows that he alone is *responsible* what happens when he hits the ball. And he has *knowledge of the results* within a few seconds.

Behavioral scientists have found that the three "psychological states" experienced by the golfer in the above example also are critical in determining a person's motivation and satisfaction on the job.

- *Experienced meaningfulness:* The individual must perceive his work as worthwhile or important by some system of values he accepts.

- *Experienced responsibility:* He must believe that he personally is accountable for the outcomes of his efforts.

- *Knowledge of results:* He must be able to determine, on some fairly regular basis, whether or not the outcomes of his work are satisfactory.

When these three conditions are present, a person tends to feel very good about himself when he performs well. And those good feelings will prompt him to try to continue to do well—so he can continue to earn the positive feelings in the future. That is what is meant by "internal motivation"—being turned on to one's work because of the positive internal feelings that are generated by doing well, rather than being dependent on external factors (such as incentive pay or compliments from the boss) for the motivation to work effectively.

What if one of the three psychological states is missing? Motivation drops markedly. Suppose, for example, that our golfer has settled in at the driving range to practice for a couple of hours. Suddenly a fog drifts in over the range. He can no longer see if the ball starts to tail off to the left a hundred yards out. The satisfaction he got from hitting straight down the middle—and the motivation to try to correct something whenever he didn't—are both gone. If the fog stays, it's likely that he soon will be packing up his clubs.

The relationship between the three psychological states and on-the-job outcomes is illustrated in Figure 1. When all three are high, then internal work motivation, job satisfaction, and work quality are high, and absenteeism and turnover are low.

*What job characteristics make it happen?* Recent research has identified five "core" characteristics of jobs that elicit the psychological states described above (Turner and Lawrence 1965; Hackman and Lawler 1971; Hackman and Oldham 1974). These five core job dimensions provide the key to objectively measuring jobs and to changing them so that they have high potential for motivating people who do them.

- Toward meaningful work. Three of the five core dimensions contribute to a job's meaningfulness for the worker;

1. Skill variety—the degree to which a job requires the worker to perform activities that challenge his skills and abilities. When even

**FIGURE 1**    Relationships among Core Job Dimensions, Critical
Psychological States, and On-the-Job Outcomes

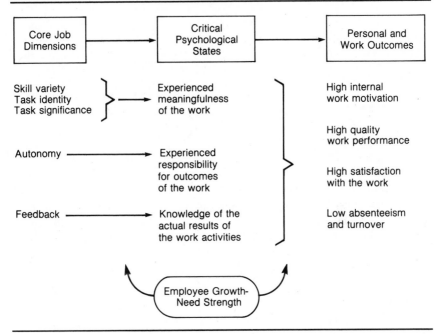

a single skill is involved, there is at least a seed of potential meaningfulness. When several are involved, the job has the potential of
appealing to more of the whole person, and also of avoiding the
monotony of performing the same task repeatedly, no matter how
much skill it may require.

2. Task identity—the degree to which the job requires completion of
   a "whole" and identifiable piece of work—doing a job from beginning
   to end with visible outcome. For example, it is clearly more meaningful to an employee to build complete toasters than to attach
   electrical cord after electrical cord, especially if he never sees a
   completed toaster. (Note that the whole job, in this example, probably would involve greater skill variety as well as task identity.)

3. Task significance—the degree to which the job has a substantial
   and perceivable impact on the lives of other people, whether in the
   immediate organization or the world at large. The worker who tight-
   ens nuts on aircraft brake assemblies is more likely to perceive his
   work as significant than the worker who fills small boxes with paper
   clips—even though the skill levels involved may be comparable.

Each of these three job dimensions represents an important route to experienced meaningfulness. If the job is high in all three, the worker is quite likely to experience his job as very meaningful. It is not necessary, however, for a job to be very high in all three dimensions. If the job is low in any one of them, there will be a drop in overall experienced meaningfulness. But even when two dimensions are low the worker may find the job meaningful if the third is high enough.

- Toward personal responsibility. A fourth core dimension leads a worker to experience increased responsibility in his job. This is *autonomy*, the degree to which the job gives the worker freedom, independence, and discretion in scheduling work and determining how he will carry it out. People in highly autonomous jobs know that they are personally responsible for successes and failures. To the extent that their autonomy is high, then, how the work goes will be felt to depend more on the individual's own efforts and initiatives rather than on detailed instructions from the boss or from a manual of job procedures.

- Toward knowledge of results. The fifth and last core dimension is *feedback*. This is the degree to which a worker, in carrying out the work activities required by the job, gets information about the effectiveness of his efforts. Feedback is most powerful when it comes directly from the work itself—for example, when a worker has the responsibility for gauging and otherwise checking a component he has just finished and learns in the process that he has lowered his reject rate by meeting specifications more consistently.

- The overall "motivating potential" of a job. Figure 1 shows how the five core dimensions combine to affect the psychological states that are critical in determining whether or not an employee will be internally motivated to work effectively. Indeed, when using an instrument to be described later, it is possible to compute a "motivating potential score" (MPS) for any job. The MPS provides a single summary index of the degree to which the objective characteristics of the job will prompt high internal work motivation. Following the theory outlined above, a job high in motivating potential must be high in at least one (and hopefully more) of the three dimensions that lead to experienced meaningfulness and high in both autonomy and feedback as well. The MPS provides a quantitative index of the degree to which this is in fact the case. As will be seen later, the MPS can be very useful in diagnosing jobs and in assessing the effectiveness of job enrichment activities.

*Does the theory work for everybody?* Unfortunately not. Not everyone is able to become internally motivated in his work, even when the motivating potential of a job is very high indeed.

Research has shown that the *psychological needs* of people are very important in determining who can (and who cannot) become internally motivated at work. Some people have strong needs for personal accomplishment, for learning and developing themselves beyond where they are now, for being stimulated and challenged, and so on. These people are high in "growth-need strength."

Figure 2 shows diagrammatically the proposition that individual growth needs have the power to moderate the relationship between the characteristics of jobs and work outcomes. Many workers with high growth needs will turn on eagerly when they have jobs that are high in the core dimensions. Workers whose growth needs are not so strong may respond less eagerly—or, at first, even balk at being "pushed" or "stretched" too far.

Psychologists who emphasize human potential argue that everyone has within him at least a spark of the need to grow and develop personally. Steadily accumulating evidence shows, however, that unless that spark is pretty strong, chances are it will get snuffed out by one's experiences in typical organizations. So, a person who has worked for 20 years in stultifying jobs may find it difficult or impossible to become internally motivated overnight when given the opportunity.

We should be cautious, however, about creating rigid categories of people based on their measured growth-need strength at any particular time. It is true that we can predict from these measures who is likely to become internally motivated on a job and who will be less willing or able to do so. But what we do not know yet is whether or not the growth-need "spark" can be rekindled for those individuals who have

FIGURE 2    The Moderating Effect of Employee Growth-Need Strength

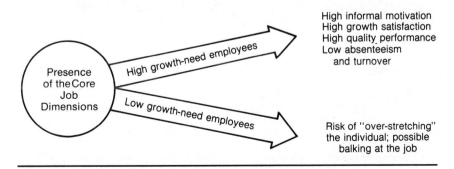

had their growth needs dampened by years of growth-depressing experience in their organizations.

Since it is often the organization that is responsible for currently low levels of growth desires, we believe that the organization also should provide the individual with the chance to reverse that trend whenever possible, even if that means putting a person in a job where he may be "stretched" more than he wants to be. He can always move back to the old job—and in the meantime the embers of his growth needs just might burst back into flame, to his surprise and pleasure, and for the good of the organization.

## FROM THEORY TO PRACTICE: A TECHNOLOGY FOR JOB ENRICHMENT

When job enrichment fails, it often fails because of inadequate *diagnosis* of the target job and employees' reactions to it. Often, for example, job enrichment is assumed by management to be a solution to "people problems" on the job and is implemented even though there has been no diagnostic activity to indicate that the root of the problem is in fact how the work is designed. At other times, some diagnosis is made—but it provides no concrete guidance about what specific aspects of the job require change. In either case, the success of job enrichment may wind up depending more on the quality of the intuition of the change agent—or his luck—than on a solid base of data about the people and the work.

In the paragraphs to follow, we outline a new technology for use in job enrichment which explicitly addresses the diagnostic as well as the action components of the change process. The technology has two parts: (1) a set of diagnostic tools that are useful in evaluating jobs and people's reactions to them prior to change—and in pinpointing exactly what aspects of specific jobs are most critical to a successful change attempt; and (2) a set of "implementing concepts" that provide concrete guidance for action steps in job enrichment. The implementing concepts are tied directly to the diagnostic tools; the output of the diagnostic activity specifies which action steps are likely to have the most impact in a particular situation.

*The diagnostic tools.* Central to the diagnostic procedure we propose is a package of instruments to be used by employees, supervisors, and outside observers in assessing the target job and employees' reactions to it (Hackman and Oldham 1975). These instruments gauge the following:

1. The objective characteristics of the jobs themselves, including both an overall indication of the "motivating potential" of the job as it

exists (that is, the MPS score) and the score of the job on each of the five core dimensions described previously. Because knowing the strengths and weaknesses of the job is critical to any work redesign effort, assessments of the job are made by supervisors and outside observers as well as the employees themselves—and the final assessment of a job uses data from all three sources.

2. The current levels of motivation, satisfaction, and work performance of employees on the job. In addition to satisfaction with the work itself, measures are taken of how people feel about other aspects of the work setting, such as pay, supervision, and relationships with co-workers.

3. The level of growth-need strength of the employees. As indicated earlier, employees who have strong growth needs are more likely to be more responsive to job enrichment than employees with weak growth needs. Therefore, it is important to know at the outset just what kinds of satisfactions the people who do the job are (and are not) motivated to obtain from their work. This will make it possible to identify which persons are best to start changes with, and which may need help in adapting to the newly enriched job.

What, then, might be the actual steps one would take in carrying out a job diagnosis using these tools? Although the approach to any particular diagnosis depends upon the specifics of the particular work situation involved, the sequence of questions listed below is fairly typical.

- *Step 1. Are motivation and satisfaction central to the problem?* Sometimes organizations undertake job enrichment to improve the work motivation and satisfaction of employees when in fact the real problem with work performance lies elsewhere—for example, in a poorly designed production system, in an error-prone computer, and so on. The first step is to examine the scores of employees on the motivation and satisfaction portions of the diagnostic instrument. (The questionnaire taken by employees is called the Job Diagnostic Survey and will be referred to hereafter as the JDS.) If motivation and satisfaction are problematic, the change agent would continue to Step 2; if not, he would look to other aspects of the work situation to identify the real problem.

- *Step 2. Is the job low in motivating potential?* To answer this question, one would examine the motivating potential score of the target job and compare it to the MPS's of other jobs to determine whether or not *the job itself* is a probable cause of the motivational problems documented in Step 1. If the job turns out to be low on the MPS, one would continue to Step 3; if it scores high, attention should be given to other possible reasons for the motivational difficulties (such as the pay system, the nature of supervision, and so on).

• *Step 3. What specific aspects of the job are causing the difficulty?* This step involves examining the job on each of the five core dimensions to pinpoint the specific strengths and weaknesses of the job as it is currently structured. It is useful at this stage to construct a "profile" of the target job, to make visually apparent where improvements need to be made. An illustrative profile for two jobs (one "good" job and one job needing improvement) is shown in Figure 3.

Job A is an engineering maintenance job and is high on all of the core dimensions; the MPS of this job is a very high 260. (MPS scores can range from 1 to about 350; an "average" score would be about 125.) Job enrichment would not be recommended for this job; if employees working on the job were unproductive

**FIGURE 3**    The JDS Diagnostic Profile for a "Good" and a "Bad" Job

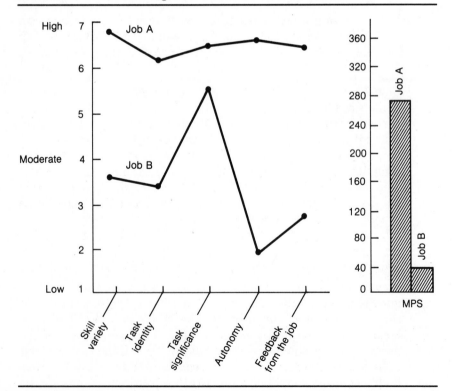

and unhappy, the reasons are likely to have little to do with the nature or design of the work itself.

Job B, on the other hand, has many problems.

This job involves the routine and repetitive processing of checks in the "back room" of a bank. The MPS is 30, which is quite low—and indeed, would be even lower if it were not for the moderately high task significance of the job. (Task significance is moderately high because the people are handling large amounts of other people's money, and therefore the quality of their efforts potentially has important consequences for their unseen clients.) The job provides the individuals with very little direct feedback about how effectively they are doing it; the employees have little autonomy in how they go about doing the job; and the job is moderately low in both skill variety and task identity.

For Job B, then, there is plenty of room for improvement—and many avenues to examine in planning job changes. For still other jobs, the avenues for change often turn out to be considerably more specific: for example, feedback and autonomy may be reasonably high, but one or more of the core dimensions that contribute to the experienced meaningfulness of the job (skill variety, task identity, and task significance) may be low. In such a case, attention would turn to ways to increase the standing of the job on these latter three dimensions.

- *Step 4. How "ready" are the employees for change?* Once it has been documented that there is need for improvement in the job—and the particularly troublesome aspects of the job have been identified—then it is time to begin to think about the specific action steps which will be taken to enrich the job. An important factor in such planning is the level of growth needs of the employees, since employees high on growth needs usually respond more readily to job enrichment than do employees with little need for growth. The JDS provides a direct measure of the growth-need strength of the employees. This measure can be very helpful in planning how to introduce the changes to the people (for instance, cautiously versus dramatically), and in deciding who should be among the first group of employees to have their jobs changed.

*The implementing concepts.* Five "implementing concepts" for job enrichment are identified and discussed below (Walters and Associates, 1975). Each one is a specific action step aimed at improving both the quality of the working experience for the individual and his work productivity. They are: (1) forming natural work units, (2) combining tasks, (3) establishing client relationships, (4) vertical loading, (5) opening feedback channels.

The links between the implementing concepts and the core dimensions are shown in Figure 4—which illustrates our theory of job enrichment, ranging from the concrete action steps through the core dimensions and the psychological states to the actual personal and work outcomes.

After completing the diagnosis of a job, a change agent would know which of the core dimensions were most in need of remedial attention. He could then turn to Figure 4 and select those implementing concepts that specifically deal with the most troublesome parts of the existing job. How this would take place in practice will be seen below.

- Forming natural work units. The notion of distributing work in some logical way may seem to be an obvious part of the design of any job. In many cases, however, the logic is one imposed by just about any consideration except job-holder satisfaction and motivation. Such considerations include technological dictates, level of worker training or experience, "efficiency" as defined by industrial engineering, and current workload. In many cases the

**FIGURE 4**    The Full Model: How Use of the Implementing Concepts Can Lead to Positive Outcomes

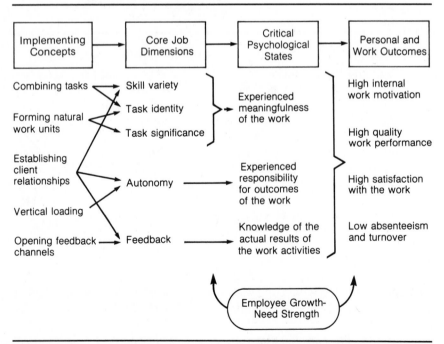

cluster of tasks a worker faces during a typical day or week is natural to anyone *but* the worker.

For example, suppose that a typing pool (consisting of one supervisor and 10 typists) handles all work for one division of a company. Jobs are delivered in rough draft or dictated form to the supervisor, who distributes them as evenly as possible among the typists. In such circumstances the individual letters, reports, and other tasks performed by a given typist in one day or week are randomly assigned. There is no basis for identifying with the work or the person or department for whom it is performed, or for placing any personal value upon it.

The principle underlying natural units of work, by contrast, is "ownership"—a worker's sense of continuing responsibility for an identifiable body of work. Two steps are involved in creating natural work units. The first is to identify the basic work items. In the typing pool, for example, the items might be "pages to be typed." The second step is to group the items in natural categories. For example, each typist might be assigned continuing responsibility for all jobs requested by one or several specific departments. The assignments should be made, of course, in such a way that workloads are about equal in the long run. (For example, one typist might end up with all the work from one busy department, while another handles jobs from several smaller units.)

At this point we can begin to see specifically how the job-design principles relate to the core dimensions (cf. Figure 4). The ownership fostered by natural units of work can make the difference between a feeling that work is meaningful and rewarding and the feeling that it is irrelevant and boring. As the diagram shows, natural units of work are directly related to two of the core dimensions: task identity and task significance.

A typist whose work is assigned naturally rather than randomly—say, by departments—has a much greater chance of performing a whole job to completion. Instead of typing one section of a large report, the individual is likely to type the whole thing, with knowledge of exactly what the product of the work is (task identity). Furthermore, over time the typist will develop a growing sense of how the work affects co-workers in the department serviced (task significance).

- Combining tasks. The very existence of a pool made up entirely of persons whose sole function is typing reflects a fractionalization of jobs that has been a basic precept of "scientific management." Most obvious in assembly-line work, fractionalization has been applied to nonmanufacturing jobs as well. It is typically justified by efficiency, which is usually defined in terms of either low costs or some time-and-motion type of criteria.

It is hard to find fault with measuring efficiency ultimately in terms of cost-effectiveness. In doing so, however, a manager should be sure to consider *all* the costs involved. It is possible, for example, for highly fractionalized jobs to meet all the time-and-motion criteria of efficiency, but if the resulting job is so unrewarding that performing it day after day leads to high turnover, absenteeism, drugs and alcohol, and strikes, then productivity is really lower (and costs higher) than data on efficiency might indicate.

The principle of combining tasks, then, suggests that whenever possible existing and fractionalized tasks should be put together to form new and larger modules of work. At the Medfield, Massachusetts, plant of Corning Glass Works the assembly of a laboratory hot plate has been redesigned along the lines suggested here. Each hot plate now is assembled from start to finish by one operator, instead of going through several separate operations that are performed by different people.

Some tasks, if combined into a meaningfully large module of work, would be more than an individual could do by himself. In such cases, it is often useful to consider assigning the new, larger task to a small *team* of workers—who are given great autonomy for its completion. At the Racine, Wisconsin, plant of Emerson Electric, the assembly process for trash disposal appliances was restructured this way. Instead of a sequence of moving the appliance from station to station, the assembly now is done from start to finish by one team. Such teams include both men and women to permit switching off the heavier and more delicate aspects of the work. The team responsible is identified on the appliance. In case of customer complaints, the team often drafts the reply.

As a job-design principle, task combination, like natural units of work, expands the task identity of the job. For example, the hot plate assembler can see and identify with finished product ready for shipment, rather than a nearly invisible junction of solder. Moreover, the more tasks that are combined into a single worker's job, the greater the variety of skills he must call on in performing the job. So task combination also leads to greater skill variety—the third core dimension that contributes to the overall experienced meaningfulness of the work.

- Establishing client relationships. One consequence of fractionalization is that the typical worker has little or no contact with (or even awareness of) the ultimate use of his product or service. By encouraging and enabling employees to establish direct relationships with the clients of their work, improvements often can be realized simultaneously often on three of the core dimensions. Feedback increases, because of additional opportunities for the individual to receive praise or criticism of his work outputs directly. Skill variety often increases, because of the necessity to develop and exercise one's interpersonal skills in maintaining the client relationship. And autonomy can increase because the individual often is given personal responsibility for deciding how to manage his relationships with the clients of his work.

Creating client relationships is a three-step process. First, the client must be identified. Second, the most direct contact possible between the worker and the client must be established. Third, criteria must be set up by which the client can judge the quality of the product or service he receives. And whenever possible, the client should have a means of relaying his judgements directly back to the worker.

The contact between worker and client should be as great as possible and as frequent as necessary. Face-to-face contact is highly desirable, at least occasionally. Where that is impossible or impractical, telephone and mail can suffice. In any case, it is important that the performance criteria by which the worker will be rated by the client must be mutually understood and agreed upon.

- Vertical loading. Typically the split between the "doing" of a job and the "planning" and "controlling" of the work has evolved along with horizontal fractionalization. Its rationale, once again, has been "efficiency through specialization." And once again, the excess of specialization that has emerged has resulted in unexpected but significant costs in motivation, morale, and work quality. In vertical loading, the intent is to partially close the gap between the doing and the controlling parts of the job—and thereby reap some important motivational advantages.

Of all the job-design principles, vertical loading may be the single most crucial one. In some cases, where it has been impossible to implement any other changes, vertical loading alone has had significant motivational effects.

When a job is vertically loaded, responsibilities and controls that formerly were reserved for higher levels of management are added to the job. There are many ways to accomplish this:

- Return to the jobholder greater discretion in setting schedules, deciding on work methods, checking on quality, and advising or helping to train less-experienced workers.

- Grant additional authority. The objective should be to advance workers from a position of no authority or highly restricted authority to positions of reviewed, and eventually, near-total authority for their own work.

- Time management. The jobholder should have the greatest possible freedom to decide when to start and stop work, when to break, and how to assign priorities.

- Troubleshooting and crisis decisions. Workers should be encouraged to seek problem solutions on their own, rather than calling immediately for the supervisor.

- Financial controls. Some degree of knowledge and control over budgets and other financial aspects of a job can often be highly motivating. However, access to this information frequently tends to be restricted. Workers can benefit from knowing something about the costs of their jobs, the potential effect upon profit, and various financial and budgetary alternatives.

    When a job is vertically loaded it will inevitably increase in *autonomy*. And as shown in Figure 4, this increase in objective personal control over the work will also lead to an increased feeling of personal responsibility for the work, and ultimately to higher internal work motivation.

- Opening feedback channels. In virtually all jobs there are ways to open channels of feedback to individuals or teams to help them learn whether their performance is improving, deteriorating, or remaining at a constant level. While there are numerous channels through which information about performance can be provided, it generally is better for a worker to learn about his performances *directly as he does his job*—rather than from management on an occasional basis.

    Job-provided feedback usually is more immediate and private than supervisor-supplied feedback, and it increases the worker's feelings of personal control over his work in the bargain. Moreover, it avoids many of the potentially disruptive interpersonal problems that can develop when the only way a worker has to find out how he is doing is through direct messages or subtle cues from his boss.

    Exactly what should be done to open channels for job-provided feedback will vary from job to job and organization to organization. Yet in many cases the changes involve simply removing existing blocks that isolate the worker from naturally occuring data about performance—rather than generating entirely new feedback mechanisms. For example:

- Establishing direct client relationships often removes blocks between the worker and natural external sources of data about his work.

- Quality control efforts in many organizations often eliminate a natural source of feedback. The quality check on a product or service is done by a person other than those responsible for the work. Feedback to the workers—if there is any—is belated and diluted. It often fosters a tendency to think of quality as "someone else's concern." By placing control close to the worker (perhaps even in his own hands), the quantity and quality of data about performance available to him can dramatically increase.

- Tradition and established procedure in many organizations dictate that records about performance be kept by a supervisor and transmitted up (not down) in the organizational hierarchy. Sometimes supervisors even check the work and correct any errors themselves. The worker who made the error never knows it occured—and is denied the very information that could enhance both his internal work motivation and the technical adequacy of his performance. In many cases it is possible to provide standard summaries of performance records directly to the worker (as well as to his superior), thereby giving him personally and regularly the data he needs to improve his performance.

- Computers and other automated operations sometimes can be used to provide the individual with data now blocked from him. Many clerical operations, for example, are now performed on computer consoles. These consoles often can be programmed to provide the clerk with immediate feedback in the form of a CRT display or a printout indicating that an error has been made. Some systems even have been programmed to provide the operator with a positive feedback message when a period of error-free performance has been sustained.

   Many organizations simply have not recognized the importance of feedback as a motivator. Data on quality and other aspects of performance are viewed as being of interest only to management. Worse still, the *standards* for acceptable performance often are kept from workers as well. As a result, workers who would be interested in following the daily or weekly ups and downs of their performance, and in trying accordingly to improve, are deprived of the very guidelines they need to do so. They are like the golfer we mentioned earlier, whose efforts to correct his hook are stopped dead by fog over the driving range.

## CONCLUSIONS

In this article we have presented a new strategy for the redesign of work in general and for job enrichment in particular. The approach has four main characteristics:

1. It is grounded in a basic psychological theory of what motivates people in their work.
2. It emphasizes the planning for job changes should be done on the basis of *data* about the jobs and the people who do them—and a set of diagnostic instruments is provided to collect such data.
3. It provides a set of specific implementing concepts to guide actual job changes, as well as a set of theory-based rules for selecting *which* action steps are likely to be most beneficial in a given situation.
4. The strategy is buttressed by a set of findings showing that the theory holds water, that the diagnostic procedures are practical and informative, and that the implementing concepts can lead to changes that are beneficial both to organizations and to the people who work in them.

We believe that job enrichment is moving beyond the stage where it can be considered "yet another management fad." Instead, it represents a potentially powerful strategy for change that can help organizations achieve their goals for higher quality work—and at the same time further the equally legitimate needs of contemporary employees for a more meaningful work experience. Yet there are pressing questions about job enrichment and its use that remain to be answered.

Prominent among these is the question of employee participation in planning and implementing work redesign. The diagnostic tools and implementing concepts we have presented are neither designed nor intended for use only by management. Rather, our belief is that the effectiveness of job enrichment is likely to be enhanced when the tasks of diagnosing and changing jobs are undertaken *collaboratively* by management and by the employees whose work will be affected.

Moreover, the effects of work redesign on the broader organization remain generally uncharted. Evidence now is accumulating that when jobs are changed, turbulence can appear in the surrounding organization—for example, in supervisory-subordinate relationships, in pay and benefit plans, and so on. Such turbulence can be viewed by management either as a problem with job enrichment, or as an opportunity for further and broader organizational development by teams of managers and employees. To the degree that management takes the latter view, we believe, the oftespoused goal of achieving basic organizational change through the redesign of work may come increasingly within reach.

The diagnostic tools and implementing concepts we have presented are useful in deciding on and designing basic changes in the jobs themselves. They do not address the broader issues of who plans the changes, how they are carried out, and how they are followed up. The way these broader questions are dealt with, we believe, may determine whether job enrichment will grow up—or whether it will die an early and unfortunate death, like so many other fledgling behavioral science approaches to organizational change.

*C. Decision Making*

# 32

# The Myth of Management

## C. West Churchman

*The myth, according to the author, is that of believing that the really great manager has a special ability to solve the puzzling problems found in large, complex organizations. Effective managerial decision making is seen not as a result of hidden special abilities but as a reasoned logical approach to problem analysis.—Eds.*

Making decisions is, on the one hand, one of the most fascinating manifestations of biological activity and, on the other hand, a matter of terrifying implications for the whole of the human race. Although this activity is both fascinating and awesome, it is difficult to find a satisfactory name for it in any of the common languages. In English we use such terms as *manager, administrator, executive,* or simply *decision maker.* Yet each of these terms fails somehow to capture the true significance of this important activity of the human being. Because we need a label to conduct our discussion, I shall risk choosing the term *manager* and begin to say some things that will generalize on this term beyond its ordinary usage in English.

The manager is the man who decides among alternative choices. He must decide which choice he believes will lead to a certain desired objective or set of objectives. But his decision is not an abstract one, because it creates a type of reality. The manager is the man with the magic that enables him to create in the world a state of affairs that would not have occurred except for him. We say that the manager is one who has the authority to make such choices. He is also a person

SOURCE: From *Challenge to Reason*, by C. West Churchman. Copyright © 1968 by McGraw-Hill, Inc. Used with permission of McGraw-Hill Book Company.

who has the responsibility for the choices he has made in the sense that the rest of his fellow men may judge whether he should be rewarded or punished for his choices; he is the person who justifiably is the object of praise or blame.

So broad a description of the manager makes managers of us all. It is a common failing of the labels that language applies to things that they may be generalized to encompass everything, as philosophers have long recognized in the case of such labels as *matter* and *mind*. It takes no great sophomoric talent to see that the world is basically matter and that everything could be reduced thereto. Nor does it take any great astuteness to see that everything a human being recognizes as natural reality is the product of some mind or collection of minds. So, too, the label *manager* may become appropriately applied to practically everything or at least to every human, once we describe the manager as someone having the authority and responsibility for making choices. I am interested in the broad aspects of decision making, but for present purposes I want to add one more stipulation that makes the label *manager* less general. This is the stipulation that managerial activity take place within a "system": The manager must concern himself with interrelated parts of a complex organization of activities, and he is responsible for the effectiveness of the whole system. . . .

But even this further stipulation concerning the use of the label *manager* permits us to describe many activities as management. It is true that in the history of England and the United States, the term *management* has often been narrowed to mean the managing of industrial activities, especially for the purpose of generating profit for an enterprise. In this connection management is contrasted with labor. In government activities our use of the term *manager* is often labelled *administrator,* and the term *executive* is often used to describe people who are given the legal authority to put into practice the laws of the land. All these activities, whether they be at the level of government or industry or education or health, or whatever, have a common ground which we wish to explore. The common ground is the burden of making choices about system improvement and the responsibility of responding to the choices made in a human environment in which there is bound to be opposition to what the manager has decided. Thus the head of a labor union, the state legislator, the head of a government agency, the foreman of a shop are all managers in our sense. So is a man in his own family a manager; so is the captain of a football team. Probably all of us at some time or other in our lives become managers when, because of appointment to a committee or because of our political activities, we take on the authority and responsibility of making decisions in complex systems. Managing is an activity of which we are all aware, and its consequences concern each one of us.

I said that managers must bear the burden of the decisions they make. I could have added, in a more optimistic tone, that they enjoy the pleasures accompanying the power to make decisions. And certainly many managers in today's society do find a great deal of psychic satisfaction in the roles they play which society so clearly recognizes as important and which it credits with a great deal of prestige.

Now managing is a type of behavior, and since it's a very important type of behavior, you might expect that we know a great deal about it. But we don't at all. We could also explore the many ways in which managers often think they know how they manage, but observers of their behavior often differ from them quite radically. The manager is frequently astonished to hear a sociologist's description of his activities, which he believes he himself knows so well, and he resents the inclination on the part of the "detached" scientist to try to describe the activity that he performs.

Imagine an observer carefully trained to study such activities as bees in a hive, or fish in a school, or birds in a flock, and suppose such a student of nature becomes curious about the behavior of judges during a trial. How might such a scientist describe what the judge actually does? He might learn a little bit from some of the reflective judges, and perhaps a little bit more from the sociologists and other scientists who have attempted to describe legal behavior, but he would find that most of the activity remains a huge mystery to the whole of humanity— a mystery that no one has ever felt inclined to investigate in detail.

The whole activity of managing, important as it is for the human race, is still largely an unknown aspect of the natural world. When man detaches himself and tries to observe what kind of living animal he is, he finds that he knows very little about the things most important to him and precious little about his role as a decision maker. Few managers are capable of describing how they reach their decisions in a way that someone else can understand; few can tell us how they feel about the decisions once they have been made. Of course, despite our ignorance about managerial phenomena, a great deal is written on the subject in popular magazines and managerial journals. It appears that the less we know about a subject, the more we are inclined to write extensively about it with great conviction. Some writings describe the various rituals followed in organizations prior and posterior to the actual managerial decision. But most of these descriptions pay little attention to the very puzzling question of *when* a decision actually occurred and *who* made it. A great deal is said about committee deliberations and other aspects of organizational rationality that go into the making of a decision, and the many checks and controls that are exerted to determine whether the decisions have been made properly. Much attention is paid to these aspects of organizational decision making, because they show up on the surface, so to speak. But the facts that a committee deliberated for three hours and then a decision emerged do not tell us *who* made the decision, *how* it was made, or *when* it was made. It might be added that the verbal assertions of the committee often do not tell us *what* decision is made.

So there is a great mystery of the natural world: the *who, when, how,* and *what* of man's decision making.

But even if we were to succeed in discovering a great deal more than we have about management, the result would be at best descriptive. It would be merely the background of the basic problem before us, namely, the question of how the manager *should* decide.

Am I right in claiming that we know so little about management? After all, most of us are quite willing, even eager, to express an opinion about managers, because we love to praise and complain. We don't hesitate to say that some men are better managers than others. We are constantly criticizing our political leaders. Biographers are accustomed to choose the most "outstanding" leaders of the age as the subject of their texts. These leaders may be great political leaders, leaders of industry, leaders of social movements, of religion, and so on. What is the quality these men of success have that their less successful colleagues lack? Since we believe we can identify "successful" leaders, surely we also believe we know a great deal about what a manager *should* decide. For example, in the case of the Presidents of the United States, we are told in our school-boy texts that we can readily recognize that some of these Presidents were "great" and some of them far from great. What is the quality of greatness that we are led to ascribe to some of these Presidents?

A ready answer is at hand—the successful and great Presidents were those who made decisions that today we clearly recognize to be correct, and those who made these decisions in the face of severe opposition. We are led to believe that the activity of great Presidents is a marvelous example of successful decision making in large complex systems.

But the skeptics among us will find this answer quite unsatisfactory as an explanation of what constitutes greatness in a President. In the first place, history has no record of what would have happened had the opposition's point of view succeeded or if serious modifications had been made in the choices of the so-called great Presidents. What if the Union had *not* been saved, or our independence declared? History seems only to have recorded the episodes that followed upon the particular decision that was made and does not provide us with an analysis of events that might have occurred if an alternative had been adopted.

More curious still is the implicit assumption that a successful President made his great decisions on the basis of his own particular abilities. Since evidence is so often lacking that great Presidents of the past had these abilities, there is a natural inclination on the part of many of us to ascribe either determinism or randomness to the activities of so-called successful managers. In the case of determinism, we might argue that the events of the world occur by the accidental conglomeration of many forces unknown to man, and that these forces produce "decisions" that man in his innocence believes that he himself makes. The decision of independence in 1776 was, according to this view, simply the outgrowth of many complex human and physical inter-relationships. Those who adopt the idea of randomness simply add to the physical determinism of events a random fluctuation of the sort occurring in a roulette wheel or in the shuffling of cards. They would then be willing to admit that other decisions might have been made in 1776 or later, but that these decisions would be very much like the outcome of another spin of the roulette wheel. In either event, whether we choose to describe the world of decision making as determinism or as randomness, we conclude that ascribing greatness to the decision makers in Independence Hall would be a mistake unless one meant by greatness some recognizable features of the determined or random events occurring in the world. By analogy one might say that the man who spins the roulette wheel is its "manager" who decides nothing about the outcome of his spins; a multitude of hidden physical forces determine where the wheel will stop. Calling a President great is like calling the spinner of a roulette wheel that happens to have a satis-factory result a great spinner.

This is certainly a crass and impolite way to describe the great managerial minds of the past. Surely we can do more for their memories than to describe them as irrelevant aspects of the history of society. We might try to look into the story of their lives to find evidence that they really had superior methods of deliberation. We might try to show that they had the sort of brilliance and courage that creates an ability to handle confusing pieces of information and to reach appropriate decisions. Perhaps the great manager is an extremely adept informa-tion processor who can act so rapidly that he himself is not even aware of the comparisons and computations he has made.

Indeed, this last is more or less the popular image of the great manager. For example, many scientists who advise politicians, corpo-rate managers, and other decision makers often state that they cannot possibly attempt to tell such men what decisions *should* be made. At best they believe they can merely tell the decision maker about certain outcomes if the decisions are adopted. Thus the more modest among the advisers believe that they have no intent of "replacing" the man-agers they advise. And yet if these scientific advisers are capable of discerning at least some aspects of the managerial decision, what is it they lack? What are they incapable of doing that the politician and corporate manager are so successful in accomplishing? What is this secret ingredient of the great presidents of corporations, universities, and countries that no scientist or ordinary man could ever hope to acquire?

The answer usually given is that the President has information about many different aspects of the world and has an ability to put these aspects together in a way that no analysis could possibly do. In other words, he has a vision of the whole system and can relate the effectiveness of the parts to the effectiveness of the whole. The hidden secret of the great manager, so goes the myth, is his ability to solve the puzzling problems of whole systems that we have been discussing so far.

This answer is a myth, because it is totally unsatisfactory to the reasoning of an intellectually curious person. Are "great" managers fantastically high-speed data processors? Do great managerial minds outstrip any machinery now on the market or contemplated for decades to come? From what we know of the brain and its capabilities, the answer seems to be no. Indeed, it is doubtful whether the great manager in reaching decisions uses very much of the information he has received from various sources. It is also doubtful whether the manager scans many of the alternatives open to him. . . . We described how the scientist, when he comes to grips with the problems of decision making, discovers that they can only be represented by fairly complicated mathematical models. Even in fairly simple decision-making situations we have come to learn how complicated is the problem of developing a sensible way of using available information. It seems incredible that the so-called successful managers really have inbuilt models that are rich and complicated enough to include the subtleties of large-scale systems.

Suppose for the moment we descend from the lofty heights of the decision makers in Independence Hall and the White House and begin to describe a very mundane and easily recognized managerial problem concerning the number of tellers that should be available to customers in a bank. All of us have experienced the annoyance of going into a bank in a hurry and spending a leisurely but frustrating half hour behind the wrong line. How should the bank manager decide on the allocation of tellers at various times of the day?

This is a fairly simple managerial problem and its like is encountered by thousands of middle managers every day. Furthermore, this problem has been studied quite extensively in operations research and its "solution" is often found in the elementary texts. The texts say that the scientist should try to answer the managerial question by considering both the inconvenience of the customers who wait in the lines and the possible idle time of the tellers who wait at their stations when no customers are there. Thus the "successful" manager can be identified in an objective way, and we need not take a poll of greatness or lack thereof to ascertain whether the manager has performed well. The successful manager will be someone who has properly balanced the two costs of the operation of servicing customers in a bank: the cost of waiting customers and the cost of idle tellers. He will insist that the cost of a minute's waiting of a customer in a line must be compared to a minute's idle time of the teller. On the basis of this comparison, together with suitable evidence concerning the arrival rate of customers and the time required to service each customer, the successful manager will determine the policy concerning allocation of tellers to various stations during the day. Perhaps no one will feel inclined to write the biography of so ordinary a man as the manager of a branch of a local bank, but in any case if this manager decides according to the rational methods just outlined, his biographer may at least be honest about his "greatness."

Nevertheless, the analysis just outlined leaves much unanswered. For example, an idle teller need not be idle while waiting at a station where there are no customers. Instead he may be occupied with other routine matters requiring attention in the administration of the bank. Consequently, if the manager can design the entire operation of his bank's many functions properly, he may be able to decrease the cost of idle time of personnel who are servicing customers. If we look on the other side of the picture, that is, the inconvenience to a customer, we may find that in fact waiting in line is not an inconvenience at all if the customer happens to meet an acquaintance there. Perhaps the manager should serve coffee and doughnuts to waiting customers. Furthermore, if the manager could somehow or other hope to control the behavior of his customers, he might be able to recognize their arrivals in such a way that inconvenience costs are vastly reduced. Add to these considerations other innovations that might be introduced: For example, in many cases banks set up Express Windows to handle customers who would normally have very low service times. Hence, an overall average waiting time may not make sense if there are different types of service tailored to the various needs of the customers.

But then another, broader consideration occurs to us: Handling the public's financial matters by branch banking methods may be completely wrong. Modern technology may provide ways of developing financial servicing methods far cheaper for both bank and customer. After all, handling cash and checks is an extremely awkward way for a person to acquire goods at a price. With adequately designed information centers, the retail markets need only input information about a customer purchase, and the customer's employers need only input information about his income. Thus every purchase would become simply a matter of centralized information processing, as would a man's weekly or monthly paycheck. There would therefore be no real need for any of us to carry money about and no need to go to a bank and stand patiently in line. But this idea of automated purchasing and income recording is followed by another thought. We realize that any such automated financial system would probably end in eliminating a number of clerical and managerial jobs. Consequently we must examine the social problems of displaced personnel and the need for retraining, otherwise total social costs of automated banking might be far greater than the convenience gained by introducing new technology.

Before we can decide whether the manager of the branch bank is performing "satisfactorily," we must decide a much broader issue—whether the particular system that the manager operates is an appropriate one. This question leads to deeper considerations concerning the potentials of modern technology and their implications with respect to automation, job training, and the future economics of many lives.

The simple illustration with which we started has now driven us to an almost absurd concept of the "great" manager of even so little a system as a branch bank. The really successful manager must be able to understand the optimal design of the whole bank, as well as the optimal behavior patterns of his customers, and the optimal development of the technology of automation. The great manager of a little enterprise needs to be the great manager of the great enterprise.

This is a curious concept of human behavior that we have been developing. The manager cannot manage well unless he in some sense manages all. Specifically, he must have some idea of what the whole relevant world is like to be able to justify that what he manages is managed correctly.

At the present time we understand very little about managerial behavior, because in all studies of behavior we concentrate our attention on what the observer sees the manager doing; even if we broaden our perspective of his behavior to include the manager's objectives, we usually narrow the scope of these objectives so we are capable of understanding them, that is, of representing them in some kind of analytical form. We have no apparatus in our scientific kit that enables us to observe an activity which must encompass so broad a scope as managerial activity actually implies.

In other words, when we undertake studies to assist managers, or when we try to understand how managers themselves behave, we are incapable of deciding what the behavior of the manager really means because we are incapable of understanding or observing the manager's whole system. When a system scientist tries to solve a production problem or a government agency problem, he feels there are symptoms of trouble and he wishes to remove them. But he has no means by which he can decide whether the entire activity ought to be redesigned, thereby eliminating both the trouble and the far more serious loss entailed in a useless set of activities. This is true whether or not he claims he has used the "systems approach."

We have certainly failed to live up to the lessons that Greek philosophy tried to teach mankind, namely, that knowledge of oneself is the most important knowledge man can gain. We have undoubtedly done much in biology and psychology to study certain properties of living organisms and their minds. Our efforts in sociology have been mainly of a descriptive nature, since the sociologist typically does not try to judge that which he observes, nor even to understand what the characteristics of an excellent or healthy decision maker might be. Hence there is a serious question whether what is observed by the "behavioral sciences" is really relevant at all with respect to the healthy life of the organization. The study of the health of organizations is thus largely neglected, even though it is the most important health problem that exists.

The heritage of Western science with its emphasis on observation and logic seems to have provided us with no tools to study managerial activity, even though this is undoubtedly the most important problem ever faced by man. We simply do not understand the part of the natural world that is of most concern to us. At best we are able to say that the good manager is one who has a faith of a proper sort in what will happen in the world, a faith that he does not attempt to examine or control. Abraham Lincoln, for example, had the faith that, by trying to preserve the Union through war, an excellent democracy would result. No matter that he failed to understand or have any evidence concerning the implications of the Civil War in the late decades of the nineteenth and early twentieth centuries. No matter either that Lincoln's whole concept of political activity might have been wrong. No matter that today we have no adequate information about what other courses of action were available in the 1860s and what their implications might have been. We too have a simple faith that Lincoln was a "great" President, or else—south of the Mason-Dixon line—an equally simple faith that he was not.

If we are to be honest about our ignorance, we will have to admit that some managers become great simply because there is common agreement that they are great. The scientist, the public, and the manager all agree that the decisions made by these great managers were correct, and they agree that there were no other alternatives that would have led to far better results. They also agree that the enterprise in which the manager was engaged was a meaningful one. The scientist might contribute to this agreement by using whatever resources he has available to study the alternatives that were open to the great manager; the public can recognize the benefits they have received from the great manager's activities because they "worked out" well, and the managers themselves through their experience can appreciate what the great manager has accomplished. The public, science, and management come to agree that certain managerial activities are beneficial to the whole system. What results is a judgment of excellence of management based upon such common agreement—not too bad a basis after all in view of the powerful role that common agreement often plays.

We must admit, though, that agreement is a dangerous basis for rational conclusions. Agreement always has its opposite side and often becomes disagreement in the next generation, especially in healthy societies where social change is bound to occur. A rational mind will want to find a far better basis for the judgment of excellence. He will want to find the rational basis in whose terms he can really prove the excellence of managerial decisions, based on an accurate account of the whole system.

Actually, we humans are quite incapable of understanding the agreements we reach. We often take common agreement as expressed in majority opinion to be the end of the matter, even though we frankly recognize that our own judgments are so often inadequate, no matter how strong the agreement behind them.

It may be that as men become politically more astute, they will begin to develop that part of their mentality which enables them to so look at themselves that they can examine the common agreements they hold and adopt a critical attitude toward them. Instead of gaining moral support from the agreements of his fellow man, a person may instead begin to regard agreement as a kind of evidence of danger ahead. He will then be on his way toward what we may call a theory of management, that is, a knowledge about what management really is and not what it is merely perceived to be.

We have been discussing the manager as though he were an object of study of the scientist, and we have been using as an analogy the way in which the scientist observes any kind of living activity. We have seen, however, that science is incapable as yet of generating an adequate science of management simply because it has no basis or technique by which it can adequately judge the difference between good and bad, or healthy and unhealthy, types of managerial behavior. We recognize that there must be such things as a good and a bad manager, but we have no basis on which to decide whether a specific activity falls in one category or the other.

We have also been speaking as though the scientist's interest in management is based mainly on the kind of intellectual curiosity that motivates him to discover the meaning of various mysteries of nature, that is, to transform myth into objectivity.

There is, however, another way in which we should look at the matter: We should realize that science itself is an organized activity, that is, a complex system, and we should examine what the management characteristics of this system are. The typical scientist regards the manager as someone who provides resources and creates the kind of environment in which "high-level" intellectual activity can occur. The scientist has failed to see that the whole problem of management is fundamental to every aspect of his own activities. Rather, he did see this three centuries ago, but saw it in a way that for later science turned out to be unsatisfactory. Thus the idea that management is fundamental to science disappeared in favor of other types of foundations of science. But the scientist is clearly a manager in the broad sense of the term. . . . If the concept of a great manager is a myth or a mystery, cannot the same be said of the great scientist?

# 33
## Administrative Decision Making

*Herbert A. Simon*

*This article surveys the broad area of managerial decisions in organizations and summarizes the current state of the art with respect to decision-making concepts and language. Of particular importance is the discussion of the role played in advancing our knowledge by (1) developments in management science, (2) the application of the experimental method to the investigation of decision making, and (3) the computer.—Eds.*

There is no need, at this late date, to justify the study of organization and administration in terms of the decision-making process, for decision-making concepts and language have become highly popular in writing about administration.[1] This paper will describe some of the progress that has been made over the past quarter century, employing this approach, toward deepening our scientific knowledge—what new facts have been learned about human behavior in organizations, what new scientific procedures for ascertaining facts, what new concepts for describing them, and what new generalizations for explaining them. This progress extends both to descriptive and normative matters: to the pure science of administration, and its application to the practical business of managing.

To satisfy limits on . . . space, your patience, and my time, the account will be highly selective. Only a few notable and significant advances have been selected; others for which equally plausible claims might be made are ignored. A frequent practice in the social sciences is to bemoan our present ignorance while making optimistic predictions

SOURCE: Reprinted by permission of the author and the American Society for Public Administration from *Public Administration Review*, March 1965, pp. 31–37.

about future knowledge. It is a pleasure to survey an area of social science where, by contrast, we can speak without blushing about our present knowledge—indeed, where only a small sample of the gains in knowledge that have been achieved in the past quarter century can be presented.

## OPERATIONS RESEARCH AND MANAGEMENT SCIENCE

One obvious answer to the question "What's new?" is the spectacular development in the normative theory of decision making that goes under the labels of "operations research" and "management science." Through these activities, many classes of administrative decisions have been formalized, mathematics has been applied to determine the characteristics of the "best" or "good" decisions, and myriads of arithmetic calculations are carried out routinely in many business and governmental organizations to reach the actual decisions from day to day. A number of sophisticated and mathematical tools—linear programming, queuing theory, dynamic programming, combinatorial mathematics, and others—have been invented or developed to this end.

Like all scientific developments, this one has a long intellectual history, and did not spring, full-grown, from the brow of Zeus. Nevertheless, the state of the art today is so remarkably advanced beyond its position before World War II that the difference of degree becomes one of kind.[2]

The quantitative decision-making tools of operations research have perhaps had more extensive application in business than in governmental organizations. It is worth recalling, however, that many of these tools underwent their early development in the American and British military services during and just after the Second World War (where the terms "operations research" and "operations analysis" were coined). Among the inventors of linear programming, for example, were Tjalling Koopmans, seeking, as statistician with the Combined Shipping Adjustment Board, a means for scheduling tanker operations efficiently; and George B. Dantzig and Marshall K. Wood, in the Office of the Air Force Controller, who used as one of their first (hypothetical) programming problems the scheduling of the Berlin Airlift.

Operations research, particularly in its governmental applications, has retained close intellectual ties with classical economic theory, and has sought to find effective ways of applying that theory to public budgeting and expenditure decisions. This has been a central preoccupation of the RAND Corporation effort, as exemplified by such works as Charles J. Hitch and Roland N. McKean, *The Economics of Defense in the Nuclear Age*.[3] In the past several years, Hitch, as Controller of the Department of Defense, and a number of his former RAND associates have played major roles in bringing the new tools to bear on Defense Department budget decisions. Thus, while the quarter century begins with V. O. Key's plaint about "The Lack of a Budgetary Theory,"[4] it ends with a distinct revitalization of the whole field of public expenditure theory, and with a burgeoning of new analytic tools to assist in allocating public resources.

## OPTIMALITY AND ALL THAT

In many ways the contributions of operations research and management science to decision-making theory have been very pragmatic in flavor. The goal, after all, is to devise tools that will help management make better decisions. One example of a pragmatic technique that has proved itself very useful and has been rapidly and widely adopted over the past five years, is the scheduling procedure variously called PERT, or critical path scheduling. This technique does not use any very deep or sophisticated mathematics (which may account partly for the speed of its adoption), but is mainly an improvement of the common sense underlying the traditional Gantt Chart.

Contrasting with this pragmatic flavor, advances in operations research have been paralleled by developments in the pure theory of rational choice—a theory that has reached a very high level of mathematical and logical elegance and rigor. Among these developments perhaps the most important are: (1) rigorous, formal axiom systems for defining the concept of utility in operational terms, (2) extension of the theory of rational choice to encompass the maximization of expected utility under conditions of uncertainty, (3) extension of the theory to repeated choices over time—dynamic optimization, and (4) extension of the theory to competitive "gaming" situations. These formal advances have had an important influence, in turn, on directions of work in theoretical statistics (statistical decision theory, Bayesian statistics), and on the kinds of models that are preferred by operations researchers—or at least by the theorists among their number.[5]

An evaluation of these contributions on the pure theory of rational choice would return a mixed verdict. On the positive side, they have provided enormous conceptual clarification for discussions of "rationality." For example, it has always been unclear what rationality meant in a pure outwitting or bargaining situation, where each party is trying to outguess, and perhaps bluff, the other. If the theory of games, due to von Neumann and Morgenstern, did not solve this problem for all situations, it at least made painfully clear exactly what the problem is.

On the negative side, fascination with the pure theory of rational choice has sometimes distracted attention from the problems of decision makers who possess modest calculating powers in the face of a world of enormous complexity. (In the real world, the calculating powers of electronic computers as well as men must be described as "modest.") A normative theory, to be useful, must call only for information that can be obtained and only for calculations that can be performed. The classical theory of rational choice has generally ignored these information processing limitations. It has assumed that rationality was concerned with choice among alternatives that were already specified, and whose consequences were known or were readily calculable. It has assumed, also, comparability of consequences—that is, a practically measurable utility index.

Since these conditions, on which the classical theory rests, are so seldom satisfied in the real world, great interest attaches to procedures that make less heroic assumptions about the "givens" and the knowns; and, there is considerable progress in devising less than optimal decision procedures for situations where the optimum is unknown and practically undiscoverable. These procedures, often called *heuristic methods,* are distinguishable from optimizing techniques in three respects: they grapple, as most optimizing techniques do not, with the problems of designing and discovering alternatives, as well as with choosing among given alternatives; they frequently "satisfice," or settle for good-enough answers in despair at finding best answers; they commonly do not guarantee the qualities of the solutions they provide, and often do not even guarantee they will find a solution. The second and third of these characteristics are, of course, not virtues, but are the price that must be paid for extending our theory and tools for decision making to the wide range of real-world situations not encompassed by the classical models.

By way of illustration, a common problem of business and governmental management involves locating a system of warehouses over a country so that products can be distributed from production points to ultimate users as economically as possible. Attempts to formulate the warehousing problem so that the optimizing methods known as linear programming can be used have failed because the computations become too lengthy. However, heuristic techniques have been applied successfully to find "good" solutions to the problem where "best" solutions are unattainable.[6]

It is traditional to observe, in any discussion of the modern decision-making tools, that knowledge of these tools runs far in advance of application, and that the domain of application has been limited largely to decisions that are well-structured or "programmed," and quantitative in character. The warehousing problem described above has both of these characteristics. Whether this limitation on applications is inherent or temporary is a more controversial question. One of the important tasks before us now is to see how far we can go in extending the applicability of the new decision-making tools to areas that are ill structured, and qualitative, calling for "judgment," "experience," and even "creativity." To do this, we shall presumably have to understand what "judgment," "experience," and "creativity" are, a topic discussed later.

## EXPERIMENTS ON DECISION MAKING

A second area of significant advance has been in applying the experimental method to the investigation of decision making. This has been done both by arranging for experiments on live real-world organizations—on the model of the Hawthorne experiments—and/or by bringing organizations, or organizationoid systems into the laboratory. For obvious reasons, the latter has been done more often than the former.

The first volume of the *Public Administration Review* contained a report of a large-scale field experiment on the decision-making processes of social workers,[7] but similar experiments have been exceedingly rare in the succeeding 25 years. One of the few other examples to which I can refer is the study done in the Prudential Life Insurance Company by the Survey Research Center of the University of Michigan.[8] Either researchers on organizations decided that the information attainable from field experiments was not worth the trouble and cost of carrying out such experiments, or they found it difficult to secure the cooperation of business and governmental organizations in arranging such experiments—or both. Whatever the reason, field experiments have not been an important procedure for learning about organizational decision making.

In a few cases researchers have tried to import relatively sizeable organizations into the laboratory—hence, their studies lie on the boundary line between field and laboratory experiments. The Systems Research Laboratory of the RAND Corporation, for example, studied decision making by simulating, under controlled conditions, an entire air defense control center and associated early warning stations, manned on a full-time basis over a period of several months by a staff of some 30 subjects. While the studies conducted by the Systems Research Laboratory had as their direct outgrowth a major Air Force training program, the laboratory proved less tractable as a setting for obtaining data for testing theories of the decision-making process, and there has been no subsequent rash of studies of this kind.[9]

In contrast to the dearth of field experiments and large-scale laboratory experiments, laboratory experimentation with relatively small groups has been a thriving enterprise. Several examples of methodological advances in the art of small-group experimentation can be mentioned. Fred Bales, with his interaction process analysis, developed a scheme of data processing useful for studying the interaction of task-oriented and social-system oriented behavior in small problem-solving groups. Alex Bavelas devised a small-group task that permitted the experimenter to alter the decision-making process by opening or closing particular channels of communication between members of the group. In succeeding years, the Bales coding scheme and the Bavelas small-group task have both been used in a substantial number of studies, manipulating a great many different independent variables. Both have proved exceedingly valuable in permitting the cumulation of comparable knowledge from a whole series of experiments carried out by different investigators in different laboratories.

It is impossible to summarize here, or even to reference, the numerous contributions to the substantive knowledge of decision making that have been contributed by the small-group experiments. A single example will convey the flavor of such work. Cyert and March were able to produce bias in the estimates of members of a simulated organization by creating partial conflict of interest among them, but showed that under certain circumstances this bias did not affect organizational performance.[10]

New knowledge about organizational decision making can be obtained from appropriately planned experiments on individuals as well as from small-group experiments. Andrew Stedry, for example, has tested in this way theories about how budget controls affect behavior in organizations.[11] The series of studies of influence processes carried out at Yale by the late Carl Hovland and his associates belong in the same category.[12]

## PERSUASION AND EVOCATION

Mention of the Yale research on influence processes marks a good point in our discussion to turn to several substantive developments in the theory of decision making. The notion that a decision is like a conclusion derived from a set of premises has been a useful metaphor for analyzing the decision-making process. Following the metaphor a step further, we can view each member of an organization as "inputting" certain premises, and "outputting" certain conclusions, or decisions. But each member's conclusions become, in turn, the inputs, that is to say, the premises, for other members. For one person to influence another involves inducing him to use appropriate premises in his decision making.

What happens in an organization, or in any kind of social system, when there are conflicting premises pushing a particular decision in different directions? Much of the research on influence processes has been aimed at answering this question. In much of this research, influence has been conceived as a kind of "force," so that when several influences are brought to bear simultaneously, the outcome is interpreted as a "resultant" of the impinging forces. Persuasion is then a process of exerting such a force.

An important advance in understanding decision making has been to complement the notion of persuasion with the notion of evocation. When we want someone to carry out a particular action, we may think of our task as one of inducing him to *accept* latent decision premises favorable to the action that he already possesses. Thus, writing about food will often make a reader hungry, but we would hardly say that we had "persuaded" him that he was hungry; it would be better to say that we had "reminded" him.

Processes of persuasion play their largest role in decision making in conflict situations—where the issue is already posed, and the alternatives present. This is the framework within which most of the Yale studies on attitude change were carried out. It is also the framework for the important and well-known study of *Voting* by Berelson, Lazarsfeld, and McPhee.[13]

On the other hand, in studies of decision making where the focus of attention of the participants is one of the main independent variables, the evoking processes take on larger importance. The recent study of the Trade Agreements Act renewal, by Raymond Bauer, Ithiel Pool, and Lewis Dexter indicates that these processes played a major role in deciding the issue.[14] The authors describe the setting of their study thus (p. 5): "We are interested in the sources of information for each of these populations, the bases of its attitudes on the trade issue, *and the circumstances which lead some individuals to take active roles in the making of policy.*" (Emphasis supplied.) They demonstrate convincingly that the behavior of particular Congressmen on the trade issue depended as much on the alternative claims on their time and attention as on the distribution of interests of their constituents.

To the extent that the mechanism of evocation is important for decision making, many new ways arise in which organizational arrangements may affect behavior. As example, one of the findings of the study just mentioned (p. 229) can be cited:

> In summary, we would suggest that most significant of all to an understanding of what communication went out from business on foreign trade was neither self-interest nor ideology, but the institutional structure which facilitated or blocked the production of messages. Whether a letter to a congressman would get written depended on whether organization facilitated it, whether the writer's round of daily conversations would lead up to it, whether a staff was set up to produce it, and whether the writer conceived writing this letter to be part of his job.

Evoking mechanisms take on special prominence wherever dynamic change is occurring. Studies of the diffusion of innovations show that the timing of adoption of an innovation depends critically on the means for getting people to attend to it.[15] From every point of view, the new knowledge gained about evoking and attention-directing processes is a major substantive advance in our understanding of organizational decision making.

## THE STRUCTURE OF DECISIONS

A decision is not a simple, unitary event, but the product of a complex social process generally extending over a considerable period of time. As noted, decision making includes attention-directing or intelligence processes that determine the occasions of decision, processes for discovering and designing possible courses of action, and processes for evaluating alternatives and choosing among them. The complexity of decision making has posed grave difficulties in its study and description, difficulties only now being overcome by recent methodological innovations.

Traditionally, a decision-making process was captured and recorded by the common sense tools of the historian using everyday language. The notion that a decision might be viewed as a conclusion drawn from premises—a notion mentioned earlier—introduced a modicum of system into the description of decision making. According to this view, in order to record a decision-making process it was necessary to discover the sources of the decision premises, and the channels of communication they followed through the organization to the point where they became the raw materials of decision.

Studies that adopted this general approach to the description of decisions, while remaining within the traditional case study framework, became increasingly frequent during the period under discussion. One example is Herbert Kaufman's excellent study of *The Forest Ranger,* aimed at analyzing "the way their decisions and behavior are influenced within and by the Service."[16] Another is the study by the Carnegie Tech group of the influence of accounting information on operating decisions in large companies.[17]

The method of these studies is best described as "systematized common sense." The decision premise concept provides an ordering and organizing principle; it reduces somewhat the subjectivity of the description and the dangers of observer bias; but it falls far short of allowing complete formalization of the description. And it cannot, of course, solve the problem of how to validate generalizations with data from single cases.

The invention of the modern digital computer radically changed the situation. As gradually became apparent to those who came into contact with computers, the computer is a device that is capable of making decisions. (One demonstration of this is its use to implement the analytic decision-making schemes introduced by operations research.) Hence, a language suitable for describing the processes going on in computers might well be appropriate for describing decision making in organizations. At least the notion appeared to be worth a trial: to equate "decision premise" with the concepts of data input and program of instructions in a computer, and to equate the concept of a conclusion with the concept of the output of a computer program.

An early, and rather primitive, attempt to describe an organization decision-making process in computer programming terms appeared in 1956.[18] In this study the authors recounted the steps taken by a business firm to reach a decision about the installation of an electronic computer. They then showed how this sequence of events could be explained by a program composed of an organized system of relatively simple and general information gathering, searching, problem solving, and evaluating processes. Of particular interest was the fact that the decision examined in this study was not a highly structured, quantitative one, but one that called for large amounts of professional and administrative judgment.

Encouraging results from early studies of this kind raised hopes that it might be possible to use computer programming languages formally as well as informally to construct theories of organizational decision making, and to test those theories by simulating the decision process on the computer. Computer programs seeking to explain several kinds of organizational decision-making situations have, in fact, been constructed, and have shown themselves adequate to simulate important aspects of the human behavior in these situations. The decisions that have been simulated in this way to date are still relatively simple ones, but they encompass behavior that would generally be regarded as professional, and as involving judgment. Two of the best-developed examples are a simulation of a department store buyer and a simulation of a bank trust investment officer.[19]

I am not aware that any single comparable simulation of a decision-making process in the area of public administration has yet been carried out, but it appears that several are under way in current research. Perhaps the most likely target for initial attempts is public budgeting. If we examine the strategies described in recent empirical studies, like those of Wildavsky,[20] we will see that they can be rather directly translated into components of computer programs.

Parallel with these simulations of administrative decision making there has been a considerable exploration of individual thinking and problem solving processes, also using computer simulation as the tool of theory formulation and theory testing.[21] Today, we have a considerable specific knowledge on how human beings accomplish complex cognitive tasks. We have reasons for optimism, too, that this body of knowledge will increase rapidly, for in the digital computer language we have an analytic tool and a means for accurate expression whose powers are commensurate with the complexity of the phenomena we wish to describe and understand.

## LANDMARKS AND NEW ROADS

These, then, are some of the more prominent landmarks along the road of decision-making research over the past 25 years. On the normative side, the analytic tools of modern operations research have secured an important place in the practical work of management. Their role in everyday decision making promises to be much enlarged as present techniques are supplemented by new heuristic approaches.

On the side of the pure science of administration, there have been equally fruitful developments. The experimental method, in the small-group laboratory, can now be used to study a wide range of decision-making behaviors that are relevant to organizations. We have introduced the concept of evocation into our theories of influence, and have used it to gain new understanding of the decision-making process in changing environments. Finally, the modern digital computer, a powerful new tool, has provided both a language for expressing our theories of decision making and an engine for calculating their empirical implications. Theories can now be compared with data of the real world of organizations.

The attention-directing mechanisms so important in decision making also have played their part in determining the particular developments sampled in this paper. Another scientist, with a different set of research concerns, would choose a different sample. The fact that even one such sample exists shows how far we have come during the past 25 years toward understanding human behavior in organizations.

## NOTES AND REFERENCES

1. The term "decision making" occurred 3 times in the titles of articles in the first 15 volumes of the *Public Administration Review*—that is, through 1955; it occurred 10 times in the next 8 volumes, or about 6 times as often per annum as in the earlier period.
2. Some notion of the state of proto-operations-research just before World War II, as it applied to municipal administration, can be obtained from Ridley and Simon, *Measuring Municipal Activities* (Chicago: International City Managers' Association, first edition, 1938).
3. Cambridge, Mass.: Harvard University Press, 1960.
4. *American Political Science Review*, December 1940, p. 1142. Labels have an unfortunate tendency to compartmentalize knowledge. Thus, the

literature of "budgeting" has been only partly informed by the literature on "decision making," and vice versa, and both of these have sometimes been isolated from the economics literature on resources allocation and public expenditure theory. Variants on the same basic sets of ideas are rediscovered each generation: "measurement of public services," "program budgeting," "performance budgeting," "engineering economy," "cost-benefit analysis," "operations analysis." What is genuinely new in this area in the past decade is the power and sophistication of the analytic and computational tools. Some impression of these tools may be gained from the Hitch and McKean book previously mentioned; from Roland N. McKean, *Efficiency in Government through Systems Analysis* (New York: John Wiley & Sons, 1958); Arthur Maass et al., *Design of Water Resource Systems* (Cambridge, Mass.: Harvard University Press, 1962); or Allen V. Kneese, *The Economics of Regional Water Quality Management* (Baltimore: John Hopkins University Press, 1964), and the references cited therein.

5. Since I have discoursed at length on these matters elsewhere, I shall be brief here. See "Theories of Decision Making in Economics and Behavioral Science," *American Economic Review* 49 (June 1959), pp. 253–83, and Part 4 of *Models of Man* (New York: John Wiley & Sons, 1957).

6. Alfred A. Kuehn and Michael J. Hamberger, "A Heuristic Program for Locating Warehouses," *Management Science*, July 1963.

7. Herbert A. Simon and William R. Divine, "Human Factors in an Administrative Experiment," *Public Administration Review* 1 (Autumn 1941), pp. 485–92.

8. N. C. Morse and E. Reimer, "Experimental Change of a Major Organizational Variable," *Journal of Abnormal and Social Psychology* 52 (1955), pp. 120–29.

9. Robert L. Chapman et al., "The System Research Laboratory's Air Defense Experiments," *Management Science* 5 (April 1959), pp. 250–69.

10. Richard M. Cyert and James G. March, *The Behavioral Theory of the Firm* (Englewood Cliffs, N.J.: Prentice-Hall, 1963), pp. 67–77.

11. *Budget Control and Cost Behavior* (Englewood Cliffs, N.J.: Prentice-Hall, 1960), chap. 4.

12. See the "Yale Studies in Attitude and Communication," edited by Hovland and Rosenberg, and published by the Yale University Press.

13. Chicago: University of Chicago Press, 1954.

14. *American Business and Public Policy: The Politics of Foreign Trade* (Atherton Press, 1963).

15. See J. Coleman, E. Katz, and H. Menzel, "Diffusion of an Innovation Among Physicians," *Sociometry* 20 (1957), pp. 253–70; also, H. A. Simon and J. G. March, *Organizations* (New York: John Wiley & Sons, 1957), chap. 7.

16. Johns Hopkins University Press, 1960, p. 4.

17. *Centralization versus Decentralization in Organizing the Controller's Department* (New York: The Controllership Foundation, 1954). The study is summarized in John M. Pfiffner and Frank P. Sherwood, *Administrative Organization* (Englewood Cliffs, N.J.: Prentice-Hall, 1960), chap. 21.

18. R. M. Cyert, H. A. Simon, and D. B. Trow, "Observation of a Business Decision," *Journal of Business* 29 (1956), pp. 237–48.

19. Descriptions of these two simulations may be found in chapters 7 and 10, respectively, of Cyert and March, *Behavioral Theory of the Firm* (see note 10).

20. Aaron Wildavsky, *The Politics of the Budgetary Process* (Boston: Little, Brown, 1964).

21. For a survey, and numerous examples, see Edward Feigenbaum and Julian Feldman, *Computers and Thought* (New York: McGraw-Hill, 1963).

# 34

# Interpersonal Barriers to Decision Making

*Chris Argyris*

*Human decision making is very much an interpersonal process. This article discusses this sometimes neglected aspect of the decision process and identifies such factors as lack of awareness, subordinate gamesmanship, restricted commitment, blindspots, and distrust and antagonism as contributors to ineffectiveness in decision making. The damage these do to the decision process and what can be done to overcome them are discussed.—Eds.*

- The actual behavior of top executives during decision-making meetings often does not jibe with their attitudes and prescriptions about effective executive action.

- The gap that often exists between what executives say and how they behave helps create barriers to openness and trust, to the effective search for alternatives, to innovation, and to flexibility in the organization.

- These barriers are more destructive in important decision-making meetings than in routine meetings, and they upset effective managers more than ineffective ones.

- The barriers cannot be broken down simply by intellectual exercises. Rather, executives need feedback concerning their behavior and opportunities to develop self-awareness in action. To this end, certain kinds of questioning are valuable; playing back and analyzing tape recordings of meetings has proved to be a helpful step; and laboratory education programs are valuable.

These are a few of the major findings of a study of executive decision making in six representative companies. The findings have vital im-

SOURCE: Chris Argyris, "Interpersonal Barriers to Decision Making," *Harvard Business Review*, March–April 1966, pp. 84–97. © 1966 by the President and Fellows of Harvard College; all rights reserved.

plications for management groups everywhere; for while some organizations are less subject to the weaknesses described than are others,
*all* groups have them in some degree. In this article I shall discuss the
findings in detail and examine the implications for executives up and
down the line. For information on the company sample and research
methods used in the study, see Table 1.

## WORDS VS. ACTIONS

According to top management, the effectiveness of decision-making
activities depends on the degree of innovation, risk taking, flexibility,
and trust in the executive system. (Risk taking is defined here as any
act where the executive risks his self-esteem. This could be a moment,
for example, when he goes against the group view; when he tells someone, especially the person with the highest power, something negative
about his impact on the organization; or when he seeks to put millions
of dollars in a new investment.)

Nearly 95 percent of the executives in our study emphasize that
an organization is only as good as its top people. They constantly repeat
the importance of their responsibility to help themselves and others
to develop their abilities. Almost as often they report that the qualities
just mentioned—motivation, risk taking, and so on—are key characteristics of any successful executive system. "People problems" head
the list as the most difficult, perplexing, and crucial.

In short, the executives vote overwhelmingly for executive systems
where the contributions of each executive can be maximized and where
innovation, risk taking, flexibility, and trust reign supreme. Nevertheless, the *behavior* of these same executives tends to create decision-
making processes that are *not* very effective. Their behavior can be
fitted into two basic patterns:

*Pattern A—thoughtful, rational, and mildly competitive.* This is the
behavior most frequently observed during the decision-making meetings. Executives following this pattern own up to their ideas in a style
that emphasizes a serious concern for ideas. As they constantly battle
for scarce resources and "sell" their views, their openness to others'
ideas is relatively high, not because of a sincere interest in learning
about the point of view of others, but so they can engage in a form of
"one-upmanship"—that is, gain information about the others' points
of view in order to politely discredit them.

*Pattern B—competitive first, thoughtful and rational second.* In this
pattern, conformity to ideas replaces concern for ideas as the strongest
norm. Also, antagonism to ideas is higher—in many cases higher than
openness to ideas. The relatively high antagonism scores usually indicate, in addition to high competitiveness, a high degree of conflict
and pent-up feelings.

**TABLE 1**    Nature of the Study

- The six companies studied include: (1) an electronics firm with 40,000 employees, (2) a manufacturer and marketer of a new innovative product with 4,000 employees, (3) a large research and development company with 3,000 employees, (4) a small research and development organization with 150 employees, (5) a consulting-research firm with 400 employees, (6) a producer of heavy equipment with 4,000 employees.
- The main focus of the investigation reported here was on the behavior of 165 top executives in these companies. The executives were board members, executive committee members, upper-level managers, and (in a few cases) middle-level managers.
- Approximately 265 decision-making meetings were studied and nearly 10,000 units of behavior analyzed. The topics of the meetings ranged widely, covering investment decisions, new products, manfacturing problems, marketing strategies, new pricing policies, administrative changes, and personnel issues. An observer took notes during all but 10 of the meetings; for research purposes, these 10 were analyzed "blind" from tapes (i.e., without ever meeting the executives). All other meetings were taped also, but analyzed at a later time.
- The major device for analyzing the tapes was a new system of categories for scoring decision-making meetings.* Briefly, the executives' behavior was scored according to how often they
  - owned up to and accepted responsibility for their ideas or feelings;
  - opened up to receive others' ideas or feelings;
  - experimented and took risks with ideas or feelings;
  - helped others to own up, be open, and take risks;
  - did not own up; were not open; did not take risks; and did not help others in any of these activities.
- A second scoring system was developed to produce a quantitative index of the *norms* of the executive culture. There were both positive and negative norms. The positive norms were:
  1. *Individuality,* especially rewarding behavior that focused on and valued the uniqueness of each individual's ideas and feelings.
  2. *Concern* for others' ideas and feelings.
  3. *Trust* in others' ideas and feelings.
  The negative norms were:
  1. *Conformity* to others' ideas and feelings.
  2. *Antagonism* toward these ideas and feelings.
  3. *Mistrust* of these ideas and feelings.
- In addition to our observations of the men at work, at least one semistructured interview was conducted with each executive. All of these interviews were likewise taped, and the typewritten protocols served as the basis for further analysis.

*For a detailed discussion of the system of categories and other aspects of methodology, see my book, *Organization and Innovation* (Homewood, Illinois: Richard D. Irwin, 1965).

Table 2 summarizes data for four illustrative groups of managers—
two groups with Pattern A characteristics and two with Pattern B
characteristics.

## Practical Consequences

In both patterns executives are rarely observed:

- taking risks or experimenting with new ideas or feelings;
- helping others to own up, be open, and take risks;
- using a style of behavior that supports the norm of individuality
  and trust as well as mistrust;
- expressing feelings, positive or negative.

These results should not be interpreted as implying that the executives do not have feelings. We know from interviews that many of
the executives have strong feelings indeed. However, the overwhelming
majority (84 percent) feel that it is a sign of immaturity to express
feelings openly *during decison-making meetings*. Nor should the results be interpreted to mean that the executives do not enjoy risk
taking. The data permit us to conclude only that few risk-taking actions
were *observed* during the meetings. (Also, we have to keep in mind
that the executives were always observed in groups; it may be that
their behavior in groups varies significantly from their behavior as
individuals.)

Before I attempt to give my views about the reasons for the discrepancy between executives' words and actions, I should like to point
out that these results are not unique to business organizations. I have
obtained similar behavior patterns from leaders in education, research,
the ministry, trade unions, and government. Indeed, one of the fascinating questions for me is why so many different people in so many
different kinds of organizations tend to manifest similar problems.

## WHY THE DISCREPANCY?

The more I observe such problems in different organizations possessing different technologies and varying greatly in size, the more I
become impressed with the importance of the role played by the values
or assumptions top people hold on the nature of effective human relationships and the best ways to run an organization.

### Basic Values

In the studies so far I have isolated three basic values that seem
to be very important:

**TABLE 2**  Management Groups with Pattern A and Pattern B Characteristics*

*Total Number of Units Analyzed*

| Units Characterized by: | Pattern A | | | | Pattern B | | | |
| --- | --- | --- | --- | --- | --- | --- | --- | --- |
| | Group 1 (198) | | Group 2 (143) | | Group 3 (201) | | Group 4 (131) | |
| | Number | Percent | Number | Percent | Number | Percent | Number | Percent |
| Owning up to own ideas and feelings | 146 | 74% | 105 | 74% | 156 | 78% | 102 | 78% |
| Concern for others' ideas and feelings | 122 | 62 | 89 | 62 | 52 | 26 | 56 | 43 |
| Conformity to others' ideas and feelings | 54 | 27 | 38 | 26 | 87 | 43 | 62 | 47 |
| Openness to others' ideas and feelings | 46 | 23 | 34 | 24 | 31 | 15 | 25 | 19 |
| Individuality | 4 | 2 | 12 | 8 | 30 | 15 | 8 | 6 |
| Antagonism to others' ideas and feelings | 18 | 9 | 4 | 3 | 32 | 16 | 5 | 4 |
| Unwillingness to help others own up to their ideas | 5 | 2 | 3 | 2 | 14 | 7 | 4 | 3 |

*A unit is an instance of a manager speaking on a topic. If during the course of speaking he changes to a new topic, another unit is created.

1. *The significant human relationships are the ones which have to do with achieving the organization's objective.* My studies of over 265 different types and sizes of meetings indicate that executives almost always tend to focus their behavior on "getting the job done." In literally thousands of units of behavior, almost none are observed where the men spend some time in analyzing and maintaining their group's effectiveness. This is true even though in many meetings the group's effectiveness "bogged down" and the objectives were not being reached because of interpersonal factors. When the executives are interviewed and asked why they did not spend some time in examining the group operations or processes, they reply that they were there to get a job done. They add: "If the group isn't effective, it is up to the leader to get it back on the track by directing it."

2. *Cognitive rationality is to be emphasized; feelings and emotions are to be played down.* This value influences executives to see cognitive, intellectual discussions as "relevant," "good," "work," and so on. Emotional and interpersonal discussions tend to be viewed as "irrelevant," "immature," "not work," and so on.

As a result, when emotions and interpersonal variables become blocks to group effectiveness, all the executives report feeling that they should *not* deal with them. For example, in the event of an emotional disagreement, they would tell the members to "get back to facts" or "keep personalities out of this."

3. *Human relationships are most effectively influenced through unilateral direction, coercion, and control, as well as by rewards and penalties that sanction all three values.* This third value of direction and control is implicit in the chain of command and also in the elaborate managerial controls that have been developed within organizations.

## Influence on Operations

The impact of these values can be considerable. For example, to the extent that individuals dedicate themselves to the value of intellectual rationality and "getting the job done," they will tend to be aware of and emphasize the intellectual aspects of issues in an organization and (consciously or unconsciously) to suppress the interpersonal and emotional aspects, especially those which do not seem relevant to achieving the task.

As the interpersonal and emotional aspects of behavior become suppressed, organizational norms that coerce individuals to hide their feelings or to disguise them and bring them up as technical, intellectual problems will tend to arise.

Under these conditions the individual may tend to find it very difficult to develop competence in dealing with feelings and interpersonal relationships. Also, in a world where the expression of feelings is not valued, individuals may build personal and organizational defenses to help them suppress their own feelings or inhibit others in such expression. Or they may refuse to consider ideas which, if explored, could expose suppressed feelings.

Such a defensive reaction in an organization could eventually inhibit creativity and innovation during decision making. The participants might learn to limit themselves to those ideas and values that were not threatening. They might also decrease their openness to new ideas and values. And as the degree of openness decreased, the capacity to experiment would also decrease, and fear of taking risk would increase. This would reduce the *probability* of experimentation, thus decreasing openness to new ideas still further and constricting risk taking even more than formerly. We would thereby have a closed circuit which could become an important cause of loss of vitality in an organization.

## SOME CONSEQUENCES

Aside from the impact of values on vitality, what are some other consequences of the executive behavior patterns earlier described on top management decision making and on the effective functioning of the organization? For the sake of brevity, I shall include only examples of those consequences that were found to exist in one form or another in all organizations studied.

### Restricted Commitment

One of the most frequent findings is that, in major decisions that are introduced by the president, there tends to be less than open discussion of the issues, and the commitment of the officers tends to be less than complete (although they may assure the president to the contrary). For instance, consider what happened in one organization where a major administrative decision made during the period of the research was the establishment of several top management committees to explore basic long-range problems:

> As is customary with major decisions, the president discussed it in advance at a meeting of the executive committee. He began the meeting by circulating, as a basis for discussion, a draft of the announcement of the committees. Most of the members' discussion was concerned with raising questions about the wording of the proposal:

- "Is the word 'action' too strong?"
- I recommend that we change 'steps can be taken' to 'recommendations can be made.' "
- "We'd better change the word 'lead' to 'maintain.' "

As the discussion seemed to come to an end, one executive said he was worried that the announcement of the committees might be interpreted by the people below as an implication "that the executive committee believes the organization is in trouble. Let's get the idea in that all is well."

There was spontaneous agreement by all executives: "Hear, hear!"

A brief silence was broken by another executive who apparently was not satisfied with the concept of the committees. He raised a series of questions. The manner in which it was done was interesting. As he raised each issue, he kept assuring the president and the group that he was not against the concept. He just wanted to be certain that the executive committee was clear on what it was doing. For example, he assured them:

- "I'm not clear. Just asking."
- "I'm trying to get a better picture."
- "I'm trying to get clarification."
- "Just so that we understand what the words mean."

The president nodded in agreement, but he seemed to become slightly impatient. He remarked that many of these problems would not arise if the members of these new committees took an overall company point of view. An executive commented (laughingly), "Oh, I'm for motherhood too!"

The proposal was tabled in order for the written statement to be revised and discussed further during the next meeting. It appeared that the proposal was the president's personal "baby," and the executive committee members would naturally go along with it. The most responsibility some felt was that they should raise questions so the president would be clear about *his* (not *their*) decision.

At the next meeting the decision-making process was the same as at the first. The president circulated copies of the revised proposal. During this session a smaller number of executives asked questions. Two pushed (with appropriate care) the notion that the duties of one of the committees were defined too broadly.

The president began to defend his proposal by citing an extremely long list of examples, indicating that in his mind "reasonable" people should find the duties clear. This comment and the long list of examples may have communicated to others a feeling that the president was becoming impatient. When he finished, there was a lengthy silence. The president then turned to one of the executives and asked directly, "Why are you worried about this?" The executive explained, then quickly added that as far as he could see the differences were not major ones and his point of view could be integrated with the president's by "changing some words."

The president agreed to the changes, looked up, and asked, "I take it now there is common agreement?" All executives replied "yes" or nodded their heads affirmatively.

As I listened, I had begun to wonder about the commitment of the executive committee members to the idea. In subsequent interviews I asked each about his view of the proposal. Half felt that it was a good proposal. The other half had reservations ranging from moderate to serious. However, being loyal members, they would certainly do their best to make it work, they said.

### Subordinate Gamesmanship

I can best illustrate the second consequence by citing from a study of the effectiveness of product planning and program review activities in another of the organizations studied:

It was company policy that peers at any given level should make the decisions. Whenever they could not agree or whenever a decision went beyond their authority, the problem was supposed to be sent to the next higher level. The buck passing stopped at the highest level. A meeting with the president became a great event. Beforehand, a group would "dry run" its presentation until all were satisfied that they could present their view effectively.

Few difficulties were observed when the meeting was held to present a recommendation agreed to by all at the lower levels. The difficulties arose when "negative" information had to be fed upward. For example, a major error in the program, a major delay, or a major disagreement among the members was likely to cause such trouble.

The dynamics of these meetings was very interesting. In one case the problem to present was a major delay in a development project. In the dry run the subordinates planned to begin the session with information that "updated" the president. The information was usually presented in such a way that slowly and carefully the president was alerted to the fact that a major problem was about to be announced. One could hear such key phrases as:

- "We are a bit later than expected."
- "We're not on plan."
- "We have had greater difficulties than expected."
- "It is now clear that no one should have promised what we did."

These phrases were usually followed by some reassuring statement, such as:

- "However, we're on top of this."
- "Things are really looking better now."
- "Although we are late, we have advanced the state of the art."

- "If you give us another three months, we are certain that we can solve this problem."

To the observer's eyes, it is difficult to see how the president could deny the request. Apparently he felt the same way because he granted it. However, he took nearly 20 minutes to say that this shocked him; he was wondering if everyone was *really* doing everything they could; this was a serious program; this was not the way he wanted to see things run; he was sure they would agree with him; and he wanted their assurances that this would be the final delay.

A careful listening to the tape after the meeting brought out the fact that no subordinate gave such assurances. They simply kept saying that they were doing their best; they had poured a lot into this; or they had the best technical know-how working on it.

Another interesting observation is that most subordinates in this company, especially in presentations to the president, tended to go along with certain unwritten rules:

1. Before you give any bad news, give good news. Especially emphasize the capacity of the department to work hard and to rebound from a failure.

2. Play down the impact of a failure by emphasizing how close you came to achieving the target or how soon the target can be reached. If neither seems reasonable, emphasize how difficult it is to define such targets, and point out that because the state of the art is so primitive, the original commitment was not a wise one.

3. In a meeting with the president it is unfair to take advantage of another department that is in trouble, even if it is a "natural enemy." The sporting thing to do is say something nice about the other department and offer to help it in any way possible. (The offer is usually not made in concrete form, nor does the department in difficulty respond with the famous phrase, "What do you have in mind?")

The subordinates also were in agreement that too much time was spent in long presentations in order to make the president happy. The president, however, confided to the researcher that he did not enjoy listening to long and, at times, dry presentations (especially when he had seen most of the key data anyway). However, he felt that it was important to go through this because it might give the subordinates a greater sense of commitment to the problem!

## Lack of Awareness

One of our most common observations in company studies is that executives lack awareness of their own behavioral patterns as well as of the negative impact of their behavior on others. This is not to imply that they are completely unaware; each individual usually senses some aspects of a problem. However, we rarely find an individual or group of individuals who is aware of enough of the scope and depth of a problem so that the need for effective action can be fully understood.

For example, during the study of the decision-making processes of the president and the nine vice presidents of a firm with nearly 3,000 employees, I concluded that the members unknowingly behaved in such a way as *not* to encourage risk taking, openness, expression of feelings, and cohesive, trusting relationships. But subsequent interviews with the 10 top executives showed that they held a completely different point of view from mine. They admitted that negative feelings were not expressed, but said the reason was that "we trust each other and respect each other." According to six of the men, individuality was high and conformity low; where conformity was agreed to be high, the reason given was the necessity of agreeing with the man who is boss. According to eight of the men, "We help each other all the time." Issues loaded with conflict were not handled during meetings, it was reported, for these reasons:

- "We should not discuss emotional disagreements before the executive committee because when people are emotional, they are not rational."
- "We should not air our dirty linen in front of the people who may come in to make a presentation."
- "Why take up people's time with subjective debates?"
- "Most members are not acquainted with all the details. Under our system the person who presents the issues has really thought them through."
- "Pre-discussion of issues helps to prevent anyone from sandbagging the executive committee."
- "Rarely emotional; when it does happen, you can pardon it."

The executive committee climate or emotional tone was characterized by such words as:

- "Friendly."
- "Not critical of each other."
- "Not tense."
- "Frank and no tensions because we've known each other for years."

How was I to fit the executives' views with mine? I went back and listened to all the interviews again. As I analyzed the tapes, I began to realize that an interesting set of contradictions arose during many of the interviews. In the early stages of the interviews the executives tended to say things that they contradicted later; Table 3 contains examples of contradictions repeated by 6 or more of the 10 top executives.

What accounts for these contradictions? My explanation is that

**TABLE 3**

| DURING ONE PART OF THE INTERVIEW AN EXECUTIVE SAID: | YET LATER IN THE SAME INTERVIEW HE SAID: |
|---|---|
| The relationship among the executive committee members is "close," "friendly," and based on years of working together. | I do not know how (my peers) feel about me. That's a tough question to answer. |
| The strength of this company lies in its top people. They are a dedicated, friendly group. We never have the kinds of disagreements and fights that I hear others do. | Yes, the more I think of it, the more I feel this is a major weakness of the company. Management is afraid to hold someone accountable to say, "You said you would do it. What happened?" |
| I have an open relationship with my superior. | I have no direct idea how my superior evaluates my work and feels about me. |
| The group discussions are warm, friendly, not critical. | We trust each other not to upset one another. |
| We say pretty much what we think. | We are careful not to say anything that will antagonize anyone. |
| We respect and have faith in each other. | People do not knowingly upset each other, so they are careful in what they say. |
| The executive committee tackles all issues. | The executive committee tends to spend too much time talking about relatively unimportant issues. |
| The executive committee makes decisions quickly and effectively. | A big problem of the executive committee is that it takes forever and a day to make important decisions. |
| The members trust each other. | The members are careful not to say something that may make another member look bad. It may be misinterpreted. |
| The executive committee makes the major policy decisions. | On many major issues, decisions are really made outside the executive committee meetings. The executive committee convenes to approve a decision and have "holy water" placed on it. |

over time the executives had come to mirror, in their behavior, the values of their culture (e.g., be rational, nonemotional, diplomatically open, and so on). They had created a culture that reinforced their own leadership styles. If an executive wanted to behave differently, he probably ran the risk of being considered a deviant. In most of the cases the executives decided to forgo this risk, and they behaved like the majority. These men, in order to live with themselves, probably had to develop various defenses and blinders about their acquiescence to an executive culture that may not have been the one they personally preferred and valued.

Incidentally, in this group there were two men who had decided to take the other route. Both men were viewed by the others as "a bit rough at the edges" or "a little too aggressive."

To check the validity of some of the findings reported, we interviewed the top 25 executives below the executive committee. If our analysis was correct, we knew, then they should tend to report that the members of the executive committee were low in openness to uncomfortable information, risk taking, trust, and capacity to deal with conflicts openly, and high in conformity. The results were as predicted (see Table 4).

## Blind Spots

Another result found in all organizations studied is the tendency for executives to be unaware of the negative feelings that their subordinates have about them. This finding is not startling in view of the fact that the executive problem-solving processes do not tend to reward

**TABLE 4**  How the Executive Committee Was Rated by 25 Executives below It

|  | Number of Managers Rating the Committee as: | | |
| Characteristic Rated | Low | Moderate | High |
|---|---|---|---|
| Openness to uncomfortable information* | 12 | 6 | 4 |
| Risk taking | 20 | 4 | 1 |
| Trust | 14 | 9 | 2 |
| Conformity | 0 | 2 | 23 |
| Ability to deal with details | 19 | 6 | 0 |

*Three executives gave a "don't know" response.

the upward communication of information about interpersonal issues that is emotionally laden and risky to communicate. To illustrate:

In one organization, all but one of the top executive committee members reported that their relationships with their subordinates were "relatively good to excellent." When asked how they judged their relationships, most of the executives responded with such statements as: "They do everything that I ask for willingly," and "We talk together frequently and openly." The picture from the middle management men who were the immediate subordinates was different. Apparently, top management was unaware that:

—71 percent of the middle managers did not know where they stood with their superiors; they considered their relationships as ambiguous, and they were not aware of such important facts as how they were being evaluated.

—65 percent of the middle managers did not know what qualities led to success in their organizations.—87 percent felt that conflicts were very seldom coped with; and that when they were, the attempts tended to be inadequate.

—65 percent thought that the most important unsolved problem of the organization was that the top management was unable to help them overcome the intergroup rivalries, lack of cooperation, and poor communications; 53 percent said that if they could alter one aspect of their superior's behavior, it would be to help him see the "dog eat dog" communication problems that existed in middle management.

—59 percent evaluated top management effectiveness as not too good or about average; and 62 percent reported that the development of a cohesive management team was the second most important unsolved problem.

—82 percent of the middle managers wished that the status of their function and job could be increased but doubted if they could communicate this openly to the top management.

Interestingly, in all the cases that I have observed where the president asked for a discussion of any problems that the top and middle management men present thought important, the problems mentioned above were never raised.

Rather, the most frequently mentioned problem (74 percent of the cases) was the overload problem. The executives and managers reported that they were overloaded and that the situation was getting worse. The president's usual reply was that he appreciated their predicament, but "that is life." The few times he asked if the men had any suggestions, he received such replies as "more help," "fewer meetings," "fewer reports," "delay of schedules," and so on. As we will see, few of these suggestions made sense, since the men were asking either for increases in costs or for a decrease in the very controls that the top management used to administer the organization.

## Distrust and Antagonism

Another result of the behavior patterns earlier described is that management tends to keep promotions semisecret and most of the actual reasons for executive changes completely secret. Here is an example from an organization whose board we studied in some detail over a period of two years:

> The executives complained of three practices of the board about which the board members were apparently unaware: (1) the constant alteration of organizational positions and charts, and keeping the most up-to-date versions semiconfidential; (2) shifting top executives without adequate discussion with all executives involved and without clearly communicating the real reasons for the move; and (3) developing new departments with product goals that overlapped and competed with the goals of already existing departments.
>
> The board members admitted these practices but tended not to see them as being incompatible with the interests of the organization. For example, to take the first complaint, they defended their practice with such statements as: "If you tell them everything, all they do is worry, and we get a flood of rumors"; "The changes do not *really* affect them"; and, "It will only cut in on their busy schedule and interrupt their productivity."
>
> The void of clear-cut information from the board was, however, filled in by the executives. Their explanations ranged from such statements as "They must be changing things because they are not happy with the way things are going" to "The unhappiness is so strong they do not tell us." Even the executives who profited from some of these moves reported some concern and bewilderment. For example, three reported instances where they had been promoted over some "old-timers." In all cases they were told to "soft-pedal the promotion aspect" until the old-timers were diplomatically informed. Unfortunately, it took months to inform the latter men, and in some cases it was never done.

There was another practice of the board that produced difficulties in the organization:

> Department heads cited the board's increasing intervention into the detailed administration of a department when its profit picture looked shaky. This practice was, from these subordinates' view, in violation of the stated philosophy of decentralization.
>
> When asked, board members tended to explain this practice by saying that is was done only when they had doubts about the department head's competence, and then it was always in the interests of efficiency. When they were alerted about a department that was not doing well, they believed that the best reaction was to tighten controls, "take a closer and more frequent look," and "make sure the department head is on top of things." They quickly added that they did not tell the man in question they were beginning to doubt his competence for fear of upsetting him. Thus, again

we see how the values of de-emphasizing the expression of negative feelings and the emphasizing of controls influenced the board's behavior.

The department heads, on the other hand, reported different reactions. "Why are they bothered with details? Don't they trust me? If not, why don't they say so?" Such reactions tended to produce more conformity, antagonism, mistrust, and fear of experimenting.

Still another board practice was the "diplomatic" rejection of an executive's idea that was, in the eyes of the board, offbeat, a bit too wild, or not in keeping with the corporate mission. The reasons given by the board for not being open about the evaluation again reflected adherence to the pyramidal values. For example, a board member would say, "We do not want to embarrass them," or "If you really tell them, you might restrict creativity."

This practice tended to have precisely the impact that the superiors wished to *avoid*. The subordinates reacted by asking, "Why don't they give me an opportunity to really explain it?" or "What do they mean when they suggest that the 'timing is not right' or 'funds are not currently available'?"

## Processes Damaged

It is significant that defensive activities like those described are rarely observed during group meetings dealing with minor or relatively routine decisions. These activities become most noticeable when the decision is an important one in terms of dollars or in terms of the impact on the various departments in the organization. *The forces toward ineffectiveness operate most strongly during the important decision-making meetings.* The group and organizational defenses operate most frequently when they can do the most harm to decision-making effectiveness.

Another interesting finding is that the more effective and more committed executives tend to be upset about these facts, whereas the less effective, less committed people tend simply to lament them. They also tend to take on an "I told them so" attitude—one of resignation and noninvolvement in correcting the situation. In short, it is the better executives who are negatively affected.

## WHAT CAN BE DONE?

What can the executive do to change this situation?

I wish that I could answer this question as fully as I should like to. Unfortunately, I cannot. Nevertheless, there are some suggestions I can make.

## Blind Alleys

First, let me state what I believe will *not* work.

Learning about these problems by listening to lectures, reading about them, or exploring them through cases is not adequate; an article or book can pose some issues and get thinking started, but—in this area, at least—it cannot change behavior. Thus, in one study with 60 top executives:

> Lectures were given and cases discussed on this subject for nearly a week. A test at the end of the week showed that the executives rated the lectures very high, liked the cases, and accepted the diagnoses. Yet when they attempted to apply their newfound knowledge outside the learning situation, most were unable to do so. The major problem was that they had not learned how to make these new ideas come to life in their behavior.
>
> As one executive stated, pointing to his head: "I know up here what I should do, but when it comes to a real meeting, I behave in the same old way. It sure is frustrating."[1]

Learning about these problems through a detailed diagnosis of executives' behavior is also not enough. For example:

> I studied a top management group for nearly four months through interviews and tape recordings of their decision-making meetings. Eventually, I fed back the analysis. The executives agreed with the diagnosis as well as with the statement by one executive that he found it depressing. Another executive, however, said he now felt that he had a clearer and more coherent picture of some of the causes of their problems, and he was going to change his behavior. I predicted that he would probably find that he would be unable to change his behavior—and even if he did change, his subordinates, peers, and superiors might resist dealing with him in the new way.
>
> The executive asked, "How can you be so sure that we can't change?" I responded that I knew of no case where managers were able to alter successfully their behavior, their group dynamics, and so forth by simply realizing intellectually that such a change was necessary. The key to success was for them to be able to show these new strategies in their behavior. To my knowledge, behavior of this type, groups with these dynamics, and organizational cultures endowed with these characteristics were very difficult to change. What kind of thin-skinned individuals would they be, how brittle would their groups and their organizations be if they could be altered that easily?
>
> Three of the executives decided that they were going to prove the prediction to be incorrect. They took my report and studied it carefully. In one case the executive asked his subordinates to do the same. Then they tried to alter their behavior. According to their own accounts, they were unable to do so. The only changes they reported were (1) a softening of the selling activities, (2) a reduction of their aggressive persuasion, and (3) a genuine increase in their asking for the subordinates' views.

My subsequent observations and interviews uncovered the fact that the first two changes were mistrusted by the subordinates, who had by now adapted to the old behavior of their superiors. They tended to play it carefully and to be guarded. This hesitation aggravated the executives, who felt that their subordinates were not responding to their new behavior with the enthusiasm that they (the superiors) had expected.

However, *the executives did not deal with this issue openly*. They kept working at trying to be rational, patient, and rewarding. The more irritated they became and the more they showed this irritation in their behavior, the more the subordinates felt that the superiors' "new" behavior was a gimmick.

Eventually, the process of influencing subordinates slowed down so much that the senior men returned to their more controlling styles. The irony was that in most cases the top executives interpreted the subordinates' behavior as proof that they needed to be needled and pushed, while the subordinates interpreted the top managers' behavior as proof that they did not trust their assistants and would never change.

The reason I doubt that these approaches will provide anything but temporary cures is that they do not go far enough. If changes are going to be made in the behavior of an executive, if trust is to be developed, if risk taking is to flourish, he must be placed in a different situation. He should be helped to (a) expose his leadership style so that he and others can take a look at its true impact; (b) deepen his awareness of himself and the dynamics of effective leadership; and (c) strive for these goals under conditions where he is in control of the amount, pace, and depth of learning.

These conditions for learning are difficult to achieve. Ideally, they require the help of a professional consultant. Also, it would be important to get away from the organization—its interruptions, pressures, and daily administrative tensions.

## Value of Questions

The executive can strive to be aware that he is probably programmed with a set of values which cause him to behave in ways that are not always helpful to others and which his subordinates will not discuss frankly even when they believe he is not being helpful. He can also strive to find time to uncover, through careful questioning, his impact on others. Once in a while a session that is focused on the "How am I doing?" question can enlighten the executive and make his colleagues more flexible in dealing with him.

One simple question I have heard several presidents ask their vice presidents with success is: "Tell me what, if anything, I do that tends to prevent (or help) your being the kind of vice-president you wish to be?" These presidents are careful to ask these questions during a time when they seem natural (e.g., performance review sessions), or they work hard ahead of time to create a climate so that such a discussion will not take the subordinate by surprise.

Some presidents feel uncomfortable in raising these questions, and others point out that the vice presidents are also uncomfortable. I can see how both would have such feelings. A chief executive officer may feel that he is showing weakness by asking his subordinates about his impact. The subordinate may or may not feel this way, but he may sense that his chief does, and that is enough to make him uncomfortable.

Yet in two companies I have studied where such questions were asked, superiors and subordinates soon learned that authority which gained strength by a lack of openness was weak and brittle, whereas authority resting on open feedback from below was truly strong and viable.

## Working with the Group

Another step that an executive can take is to vow not to accept group ineffectiveness as part of life. Often I have heard people say, "Groups are no damned good; strong leadership is what is necessary." I agree that many groups are ineffective. I doubt, however, if either of the two leadership patterns described earlier will help the situation. As we have seen, both patterns tend to make the executive group increasingly less effective.

If my data are valid, the search process in executive decision making has become so complicated that group participation is essential. No one man seems to be able to have all the knowledge necessary to make an effective decision. If individual contributions are necessary in group meetings, it is important that a climate be created that does not discourage innovation, risk taking, and honest leveling between managers in their conversations with one another. The value of a group is to maximize individual contributions.

Interestingly, the chief executive officers in these studies are rarely observed making policy decisions in the classic sense, viz., critical selections from several alternatives and determination of future directions to be taken. This does not mean that they shy away from taking responsibility. Quite the contrary. Many report that they enjoy making decisions by themselves. Their big frustration comes from realizing that most of the major decisions they face are extremely complex and require the coordinated, honest inputs of many different executives. They are impatient at the slowness of meetings, the increasingly quantitative nature of the inputs, and, in many cases, their ignorance of what the staff groups did to the decision inputs long before they received them.

The more management deals with complexity by the use of computers and quantitative approaches, the more it will be forced to work
with inputs of many different people, and the more important will be
the group dynamics of decision-making meetings. If anyone doubts this,
let him observe the dry runs subordinates go through to get a presentation ready for the top. He will observe, I believe, that much data are
included and excluded by subordinates on the basis of what they believe
those at the top can hear.

In short, *one of the main tasks of the chief executive is to build and
maintain an effective decision-making network*. I doubt that he has
much choice *except* to spend time in exploring how well his group
functions.

Such explorations could occur during the regular workday. For
example:

> In one organization the president began by periodically asking members
> of his top group, immediately after a decision was made, to think back
> during the meeting and describe when they felt that the group was not
> being as effective as they wished. How could these conditions be altered?
>
> As trust and openness increased, the members began to level with each
> other as to when they were inhibited, irritated, suppressed, confused, and
> withholding information. The president tried to be as encouraging as he
> could, and he especially rewarded people who truly leveled. Soon the
> executives began to think of mechanisms they could build into their group
> functioning so they would be alerted to these group problems and correct
> them early. As one man said, "We have not eliminated all our problems,
> but we are building a competence in our group to deal with them effectively
> if and when they arise."

### Utilizing Feedback

Another useful exercise is for the superior and his group members
to tape-record a decision-making meeting, especially one which is expected to be difficult. At a later date, the group members can gather
and listen to the tape. I believe it is safe to say that simply listening
to the tape is an education in itself. If one can draw from skilled
company or outside help, then useful analyses can be made of group
or individual behavior.

Recently, I experimented with this procedure with an "inside" board
of directors of a company. The directors met once a month and listened
to tape recordings of their monthly board meetings. With my help they
analyzed their behavior, trying to find how they could improve their
individual and group effectiveness. Listening to tapes became a very
involving experience for them. They spent nearly four hours in the
first meeting discussing less than 10 minutes of the tape.

**"Binds" Created.** One of the major gains of these sessions was that the board members became aware of the "binds" they were creating for each other and of the impact they each had on the group's functioning. Thus:

Executive A was frequently heard antagonizing Executive B by saying something that B perceived as "needling." For example, A might seem to be questioning B's competence. "Look here," he would say, "anyone who can do simple arithmetic should realize that. . . ."

Executive B responded by fighting. B's way of fighting back was to utilize his extremely high capacity to verbalize and intellectualize. B's favorite tactic was to show A where he missed five important points and where his logic was faulty.

Executive A became increasingly upset as the "barrage of logic" found its mark. He tended to counteract by (a) remaining silent but manifesting a sense of being flustered and becoming red-faced; and/or (b) insisting that his logic *was* sound even though he did not express it in "highfalutin language" as did B.

Executive B pushed harder (presumably to make A admit he was wrong) by continuing his "barrage of logic" or implying that A could not see his errors because he was upset.

Executive A would respond to this by insisting that he was not upset. "The point you are making is so simple, why, anyone can see it. Why should I be upset?"

Executive B responded by pushing harder and doing more intellectualizing. When Executive A eventually reached his breaking point, he too began to shout and fight.

At this point, Executives C, D, and E could be observed withdrawing until A and B wore each other out.

**Progress Achieved.** As a result of the meetings, the executives reported in interviews, board members experienced fewer binds, less hostility, less frustration, and more constructive work. One member wondered if the group had lost some of its "zip," but the others disagreed. Here is an excerpt from the transcript of one discussion on this point:

*Executive A:*

My feeling is, as I have said, that we have just opened this thing up, and I for one feel that we have benefited a great deal from it. I think I have improved; maybe I am merely reflecting the fact that you [Executive B] have improved. But at least I think there has been improvement in our relationship. I also see signs of not as good a relationship in other places as there might be.

I think on the whole we are much better off today than we were a year ago. I think there is a whole lot less friction today than there was a year ago, but there's still enough of it.

Now we have a much clearer organization setup; if we were to sit down here and name the people, we would probably all name exactly the same people. I don't think there is much question about who should be included and who should not be included; we've got a pretty clear organization.

*Executive B:*

You're talking now about asking the consultant about going on with this week's session?

*Executive A:*

It would be very nice to have the consultant if he can do it; then we should see how we can do it without him, but it'd be better with him.

*Executive B:*

But that's the step, as I understand it, that should be taken at this stage. Is that right?

*Executive A:*

Well, I would certainly favor doing something; I don't know what. I'm not making a specific recommendation; I just don't like to let go of it.

*Executive C:*

What do you think?

*Executive D:*

I'm not as optimistic as A. I wonder if anybody here agrees with me that maybe we haven't made as much progress as we think. I've personally enjoyed these experiences, and I'd like to see them continued.

*Executive A:*

Would you like to venture to say why I think we have made progress and why I might be fooled?

*Executive D:*

Well, I think maybe you are in the worst position to evaluate progress because if the worst possible thing that can happen is for people to no longer fight and struggle, but to say "yes, sir," you might call that progress. That might be the worst thing that could happen, and I sort of sense some degree of resignation—I don't think it's progress. I don't know. I might be all alone in this. What do you think?

*Executive C:*

On one level it is progress. Whether it is institutional progress and whether it produces commensurate institutional benefits is a debatable question. It may in fact do so. I think it's very clear that there is in our meetings and in individual contact less heat, less overt friction, petulance, tension, than certainly was consistently the case. Do you agree?

*Executive D:*

Yes, I think so.

*Executive C:*

It has made us a great deal more aware of the extent and nature of the friction and clearly has made all of us intent on fighting less. There's some benefit to it; but there are some drawbacks.

*Executive A:*

Well, if you and D are right, I would say for that reason we need more of the program.

## Laboratory Training

Another possibility is for the executive to attend a program designed to help increase competence in this area, such as laboratory education and its various offshoots ("T-groups," the "managerial grid," "conflict management labs," and so on[2]). These learning experiences are available at various university and National Training Laboratory executive programs. They can also be tailor-made for the individual organization.

I believe outside programs offer the better way of becoming acquainted with this type of learning. Bear in mind, though, that since typically only one or two executives attend from the same organization, the biggest payoff is for the individual. The inside program provides greater possibilities for payoff to the organization.

At the same time, however, it should also be kept in mind that in-house programs *can* be dangerous to the organization. I would recommend that a thorough study be made ahead of time to ascertain whether or not a laboratory educational experience would be helpful to company executives individually and to the organization.

## Open Discussion

I have never observed a group whose members wanted it to decay. I have never studied a group or an organization that was decaying where there were not some members who were aware that decay was occurring. Accordingly, one key to group and organizational effectiveness is to get this knowledge out into the open and to discuss it thoroughly. The human "motors" of the group and the organization have to be checked periodically, just as does the motor of an automobile. Without proper maintenance, all will fail.

## NOTES AND REFERENCES

1. See my article, "Explorations in Interpersonal Competence II," *Applied Behavioral Science* 1, no. 3 (1965), p. 255.

2. For detailed discussions of such variations, see my article, "T-Groups for Organizational Effectiveness," *Harvard Business Review*, March–April 1964, p. 60; R. R. Blake, J. S. Mouton, L. B. Barnes, and L. E. Greiner, "Breakthrough in Organization Development," *Harvard Business Review*, November–December 1964, p. 135; and Edgar Schein and Warren Bennis, *Personal and Organizational Change through Laboratory Methods* (New York: John Wiley & Sons, 1965).

# 35

# Participation by Subordinates in the Managerial Decision-Making Process

*Robert Tannenbaum*
*and*
*Fred Massarik*

*This article examines three major approaches to dealing with participation in decision making: experiential, conceptual, and experimental. The possible advantages of participation as a management tool are analyzed, as are the psychological conditions necessary for effective participation.—Eds.*

## I. INTRODUCTION

The role of "participation" by individuals or groups in American culture in general and in industrial organizations specifically has been treated by many writers. Its implications for political theory as well as for a theory of human relations in formal organizations are numerous. However, in spite of this academic and extra-academic interest, a clear-cut, operational definition of the concept, or a precise set of hypotheses regarding its dynamics, has not been developed. While to do so will be the object of this paper, the treatment will not be completely operational. The development of appropriate methods of measurement is conceived as a next step that should follow the preliminary one of conceptual clarification undertaken in this paper.

A review of the literature indicates that three major approaches have been taken in dealing with "participation":

SOURCE: From *The Canadian Journal of Economics and Political Science* 16, no. 3 (August 1950), pp. 408–18. Reprinted with permission.

*(1) The Experiential Approach.* This approach is exemplified by writers who in the course of their experience in enterprise work have obtained a "feel" for the role of participation in the decision-making process and have put down their experiences in article or book form.[1] Writings such as these provide a set of insights and hunches whose verification in any systematic fashion has not been attempted. The actual referents from which these formulations are derived often are single sets of observations in a single or in a few enterprises—observations generally made in an uncontrolled fashion.

The experiential approach, operating outside the bounds of scientific method, nonetheless adds to scientific knowledge indirectly by providing the raw material from which hypotheses may be moulded. The precise structure of these hypotheses is not stated neatly by the experiential writers, but rather remains to be formulated.

*(2) The Conceptual, Nonexperimental Approach.* This approach characterizes the writings of authors who are, essentially, academicians with strong theoretical backgrounds. It is typified by writings that deal with "conditions," "functions," and other abstractions, generally of a socio-psychological nature, that attempt to explain the dynamics of participation.[2] The conceptual, nonexperimental approach at its best is the process of theory or hypothesis formulation. Ideally it lays the groundwork for actual testing and experimental work, but much of this type of technical literature so far published on participation lacks the clarity of conceptual definition necessary to make it useful as a basis for experimental work.

*(3) The Experimental Approach.* This approach is found in the writings of authors who have seen fit to apply experimental techniques either to especially constructed social situations involving participation, or else in natural settings in which participational activities prevail.[3] With adequate controls and with a meaningful theoretical structure within which individual findings may be placed, this approach is doubtless the most fruitful. Ideally it indicates what will happen under specified sets of conditions and with what degree of probability. Unfortunately, up to now experimental work on the dynamics of participation in the decision-making process has been sporadic.[4]

The present paper is of the conceptual, nonexperimental type. Participation in the decision-making process is conceived here as an instrument that may be used by the formal leadership of an enterprise in the pursuit of its goals. No attempt will be made to examine it from an ethical standpoint or in terms of its consistency within the frame of a democratic society, although it is by no means assumed that such considerations are less important than the ones set forward here.

## II. DEFINITION OF PARTICIPATION

It is essential, in dealing with participation, to make clear the meaning which is to be attached to the concept. One must specify both who the participators are and in what they are participating. Too frequently in the available literature on the subject the reader must determine these matters for himself since no explicit statements bearing on them are made by the writers.

As already indicated, this paper is primarily concerned with participation as a managerial device. Attention is therefore focused on the subordinates of managers in enterprises as the participators. It is important to note that these subordinates may be either nonmanagers or managers.[5] If they are managers, they are subordinates of superior managers in the formal organization of the enterprise in addition to having subordinates who are responsible to them.

Because of space limitations, consideration of the participation of individuals as union members in specific activities of an enterprise is excluded from the scope of this paper. Suffice it to say here that in those cases where the participation of union members is direct and personal, the benefits to be derived by the enterprise are similar to those derived from participation within the superior-subordinate relationship. However, in those cases (which are the greatest in number) where the participation of the union member is indirect and impersonal, it is doubtful if such is the result. It is our conclusion that most of the statements which follow are relevant to the former cases.[6]

What then is the meaning of participation, and with what type of participation by subordinates are we here concerned? An individual participates in something when he takes a part or share in that thing. Since taking a part or sharing is always involved, participation takes place in a social context. Managerial subordinates in formal enterprises are responsible to their superiors for the performance of designated tasks. In such performance, they are participating in the production of the good or service of the enterprise. They also participate (share), through the receipt of wages or salaries, in the distribution of the total revenue received by the enterprise. These types of participation are common to all enterprises. But there is another type of participation which is much less frequently encountered, although its use as a managerial device has, of recent years, grown rapidly in importance. This type involves participation by subordinates with their superiors in the managerial decision-making process.

Decisions are made by managers in order to organize, direct, or control responsible subordinates to the end that all service contributions be coordinated in the attainment of an enterprise purpose.[7] Since managers are those who accomplish results through subordinates, the latter are always directly and intimately affected by managerial decisions and therefore may have a considerable interest in them. Because of this possible interest, subordinates may have a strong desire, particularly in a nation with deeply ingrained democratic traditions, to participate in the determination of matters affecting them. It is of importance, therefore, to consider the form which such participation might assume.

Decision making involves a conscious choice or selection of one behavior alternative from among a group of two or more behavior alternatives.[8] Three steps are involved in the decision-making process. First, an individual must become aware of as many as possible of those behavior alternatives which are relevant to the decision to be made. Secondly, he must define each of these alternatives, a definition which involves a determination of as many as possible of the consequences related to each alternative under consideration. Thirdly, the individual must exercise a choice between the alternatives, that is, make a decision.

In enterprises, managerial subordinates, as subordinates, can participate in the first two steps of the managerial decision-making process. They cannot participate in the third step. The actual choice between relevant alternatives must be made or accepted by the manager who is responsible to his superior for the decision.[9] However, subordinates can provide and discuss with their manager information with respect both to relevant alternatives and to the consequences attendant upon specific alternatives. In so doing they are participating in the managerial decision-making process.[10]

The participation with which we are here concerned may take place in two different ways. First, it may involve interaction solely between a subordinate and his manager.[11] This would be the case where a worker originates a suggestion which he transmits to his boss. Secondly, it may involve interaction between a group of subordinates and their manager. This would be the case where a manager calls his subordinates together to discuss a common problem or to formulate a recommendation.[12]

## III. POSSIBLE ADVANTAGES OF PARTICIPATION AS A MANAGERIAL DEVICE

It becomes useful to inquire why managers might find it advantageous to use this device. In other words, what are the possible benefits which might accrue to an enterprise whose managers made it possible for subordinates to participate in the decision-making process? In providing an answer to this question, it is first necessary to indicate the criterion which would guide the managerial choice relating to the use of participation.

A manager of an enterprise (profit or nonprofit) who behaves rationally will attempt to make a selection from among alternatives related to any problem which will maximize results (the degree of attainment of a given end) at a given cost or which will attain given results at the lowest cost.[13] This is the criterion of rationality. Guided by this criterion, rational managers will find it advantageous to use participation whenever such use will lead to increased results at a given cost or to the attainment of given results at a lower cost.

There are many advantages which *may* stem from the use of participation as a managerial device. The following are the principal ones:

(1) A higher rate of output and increased quality of product (including reduced spoilage and wastage) as a result of greater personal effort and attention on the part of subordinates.[14]

(2) A reduction in turnover, absenteeism, and tardiness.

(3) A reduction in the number of grievances and more peaceful manager-subordinate and manager-union relations.

(4) A greater readiness to accept change.[15] When changes are arbitrarily introduced from above without explanation, subordinates tend to feel insecure and to take countermeasures aimed at a sabotage of the innovations. But when they have participated in the process leading to the decision, they have had an opportunity to be heard. They know what to expect and why, and they may desire the change. Blind resistance tends to become intelligent adaptation as insecurity is replaced by security.

(5) Greater ease in the management of subordinates.[16] Fewer managers may be necessary, the need for close supervision may be reduced, and less disciplinary action may be called for. Subordinates who have participated in the process leading toward a determination of matters directly affecting them may have a greater sense of responsibility with respect to the performance of their assigned tasks and may be more willing to accept the authority of their superiors. All managers possess a given amount of formal authority delegated to them by their superiors. But formal authority is not necessarily the equivalent of effective authority. The real source of the authority possessed by an individual lies in the acceptance of its exercise by those who are subject to it. It is the subordinates of an individual who determine the authority which he may wield. Formal authority is, in effect, nominal authority. It becomes real only when it is accepted. Thus, to be effective, formal authority must coincide with authority determined by its

acceptance. The latter defines the useful limits of the former.[17] The use of participation as a managerial device may result in a widening of these limits, reducing the amount of resistance to the exercise of formal authority and increasing the positive responses of subordinates to managerial directives.

(6)  The improved quality of managerial decisions. It is seldom, if ever, possible for managers to have knowledge of *all* alternatives and *all* consequences related to the decisions which they must make. Because of the existence of barriers to the upward flow of information in most enterprises, much valuable information possessed by subordinates never reaches their managers. Participation tends to break down the barriers, making the information available to managers. To the extent that such information alters the decisions which managers make, the quality of their decisions may thereby be improved.

These, then, are the principal advantages which *may* stem from the use of participation as a managerial device.[18] The conditions under which it *will* accomplish them—under which participation will lead to motivation—is the concern of the section which follows.

## IV. THE PSYCHOLOGICAL CONDITIONS OF EFFECTIVE PARTICIPATION

All managers of an enterprise are faced with the problem of eliciting services—contributions from their subordinates at a high level of quality and intensity. These service contributions are essential if the formal goals of the enterprise are to be attained. What induces subordinates to contribute their services? What motivates them?

A motivated individual is one who is striving to achieve a goal; his activity is goal-oriented.[19] But it should be stressed that motivation is only *potential* motion towards a goal. Whether or not the goal is reached depends not only upon the strength of the force in the direction of the goal, but also upon other forces (both driving and restraining) in the given situation.[20] To illustrate, a person may be motivated to produce 200 units of an item per day, while the restraining force in the form of machine failure or a quarrel with the next man may lead him to attain an output of only 150 units.

In enterprises, the goals towards which individuals strive may be of two kinds. They may be the formal goals of the enterprise, or they may be goals which are complementary to the formal goals. The latter is the typical case. Individuals may strive for monetary reward, prestige, power, security and the like, or they may strive for certain psychological gratifications through the very act of doing the job (that is, they work because they like their work). The primary reason why they contribute their services is to attain these latter goals. In attaining these desired goals, they make possible the attainment of the formal goals of the enterprise which to them are simply means to their own ends. In this sense, the desired goals and the formal goals are complementary.

In the former case, the goals desired by the individual and the formal goals are the same. The individual contributes his services primarily because such contribution makes possible the attainment of the formal goals of the enterprise which coincide with his own personal goals. To the extent that this coincidence of goals exists, the necessity for managers to provide complementary goals for subordinates is thereby lessened, and related costs are reduced. It is suggested that participation tends to bring about a coincidence of formal and personal goals.[21] It may be that through participation, the subordinate who formerly was moved to contribute his services only because he sought, for example, security and financial rewards, now comes to be moved additionally because he recognizes that the success of the enterprise in turn will enhance his own ability to satisfy his needs.[22]

Whether one conceives of participation as involving separate subordinates with their superiors or subordinates in groups with their superiors, in the final analysis one must not lose sight of the fact that the subordinate is a unique human being with a given personality. This implies that whether or not participation will bring forth the restructuring of his goal pattern (incorporating the formal goals within the scope of the personal goals) will depend upon a set of dynamic psychological conditions, the primary ones of which are outlined below:

(1) The subordinate must be capable of becoming psychologically involved in the participational activities. He must be free from "blockages" which may prevent him from rearranging his particular goal pattern in the light of new experience. He must possess some minimum amount of intelligence so that he may grasp the meaning and implications of the thing being considered. He must be in touch with reality. If he responds to a dream world, any "real" developments, such as opportunities to take part in certain decision-making processes, may not penetrate without gross distortion and as a result miss their point.

(2) The subordinate must favor participational activity. In other words, the person who believes that "the boss knows best" and that the decision making process is none of his business is not likely to become strongly motivated if given an opportunity to participate. It is apparent that for personality types shaped intensely by an authoritarian system, opportunities for participation may be

regarded as signs of weakness and leadership incompetence and on that basis may be rejected unequivocally.[23]

(3) The subordinate must see the relevance to his personal life pattern of the thing being considered. When he realizes that through participation he may affect the course of his future in such a fashion as to increase its positive goal elements and to diminish the negative ones, he will become motivated. For example, a person who can see the relationship between "putting his two bits" into a discussion of a new way of using a stitching machine and the fact that this may mean greater job security and increased pay for himself may be motivated.

(4) The subordinate must be able to express himself to his own satisfaction with respect to the thing being considered. He must be psychologically able to communicate; and, further, he must feel that he is making some sort of contribution. Of course, if he cannot communicate (owing to mental blocks—fear of being conspicuous, etc.), by definition he is not participating. If he does not feel that he is contributing, he may, instead of becoming motivated, come to feel inadequate and frustrated. This presupposes that not only is he articulate, but that he has a certain fund of knowledge on which to draw. Participation may fail if it involves considering matters that are quite outside the scope of experience of the participators.

All of the above conditions must be satisfied to some minimum extent. Beyond this requirement, however, the conditions may be mutually compensating, and a relatively low degree of one (although necessarily above the minimum) may be offset somewhat by an extremely high degree of another. For example, if a subordinate is unusually anxious to take part in participational activity (perhaps for reasons of prestige desires), he may come to be quite involved in the process of restructuring his goal pattern so that it will include some of the formal goals, even though he is not always certain as to whether or not he is really contributing anything worthwhile. Further, the relationships specified by the conditions are essentially dynamic. Opportunities for participation, reluctantly used at first, ultimately may lead to a change of mind and to their enthusiastic acceptance.[24]

It is apparent that individual differences are highly important in considering the effectiveness of participation as a motivational device; however, the "amount of participation opportunities" made possible by the managers is also a variable quantity. Thus, it is necessary to inquire what the limits to opportunities to participate are in terms of maximum results.

Common sense experience indicates that when some subordinates are given too many opportunities for participation, or too much leeway in participating, they may tend to flounder; they may find themselves unable to assimilate effectively the range of "thinking opportunities" with which they are faced.[25] On the other hand, if they are given little or no opportunity to take part in the decision-making process, by definition they will not come to be motivated by participational activity. For each individual, an amount of participation opportunities lying somewhere between these two extremes will result in a maximum amount of motivation. A hypothesis stemming from this formulation is that for effective operation of participation as a motivational device in a group situation, the members of the group must respond similarly to given amounts of participation, for wide divergences of response may bring forth social tensions and lack of team work within the group.

Of course, many factors act together to motivate an individual. Therefore, the usefulness of the conceptualization advanced depends upon the possibility of breaking down the total of motivational forces into those owing to participation and those owing to other factors. Experimental control methods, matching of cases, and similar devices may have to be utilized to make such an analysis possible. Whether or not the increment of motivation owing to participation is worthwhile depends to an important extent upon the level of intensity of motivation that prevailed previous to introduction of the device of participation. No doubt, there are upper limits to intensity of motivation, and, if motivation has been strong all along, the effect of participation may not be very great.

## V. EXTRAPARTICIPATIONAL CONDITIONS FOR EFFECTIVE PARTICIPATION

Beyond the factors governing the relationship between participation and possible resultant motivation, certain conditions "outside" the individual must be considered by the managers in deciding whether or not this particular device is applicable.[26] It would be possible to distinguish a great number of such outside conditions that may determine whether or not the use of participation is feasible in a given situation. Those here indicated are suggestive rather than fully definitive. All are viewed with this question in mind: "Granting that participation may have certain beneficial effects, is it useful in a given instance if the ends of the enterprise are to be achieved?"

To answer this question affirmatively, the following conditions must be met:

(1) *Time Availability.* The final decision must not be of a too urgent nature.[27] If it is necessary to arrive at some sort of emergency decision rapidly, it is obvious that even though participation in the decision-making process may have a beneficial effect in

some areas, slowness of decision may result in thwarting other goals of the enterprise or even may threaten the existence of the enterprise. Military decisions frequently are of this type.

(2) *Rational Economics*. The cost of participation in the decision-making process must not be so high that it will outweigh any positive values directly brought about by it. If it should require outlays which could be used more fruitfully in alternative activities (for example, buying more productive though expensive equipment), then investment in it would be ill-advised.

(3) *Intraplant Strategy.*

　(a) *Subordinate Security.* Giving the subordinates an opportunity to participate in the decision-making process must not bring with it any awareness on their part of unavoidable catastrophic events. For example, a subordinate who is made aware in the participation process that he will lose his job *regardless* of any decisions towards which he might contribute may experience a drop in motivation. Furthermore, to make it possible for the subordinate to be willing to participate, he must be given the feeling that no matter what he says or thinks his status or role in the plant setting will not be affected adversely. This point has been made effectively in the available literature.[28]

　(b) *Manager-Subordinate Stability.* Giving subordinates an opportunity to participate in the decision-making process must not threaten seriously to undermine the formal authority of the managers of the enterprise. For example, in some cases managers may have good reasons to assume that participation may lead nonmanagers to doubt the competence of the formal leadership, or that serious crises would result were it to develop that the subordinates were right while the final managerial decision turned out to be in disagreement with them and incorrect.

(4) *Interplant Strategy.* Providing opportunities for participation must not open channels of communication to competing enterprises. "Leaks" of information to a competitor from subordinates who have participated in a given decision-making process must be avoided if participation is to be applicable.

(5) *Provision for Communication Channels.* For participation to be effective, channels must be provided through which the employee may take part in the decision-making process. These channels must be available continuously and their use must be convenient and practical.[29]

(6) *Education for Participation.* For participation to be effective,

efforts must be made to educate subordinates regarding its function and purpose in the overall functioning of the enterprise.[30]

It must be stressed that the conditions stipulated in this section are dynamic in their own right and may be affected by the very process of participation as well as by other factors.

## VI. EFFECTS OF PARTICIPATION AS A FUNCTION OF TIME

An area of research that still remains relatively unexplored is that relating to the variation of the effects of participation with time. Some experimental studies have examined these effects in terms of increased productivity over a period of several weeks or months and found no appreciable reductions in productivity with time; while other evidence indicates that in some cases participation may have a sort of "shock" effect, leading to a surge of interest and increased motivation, with a subsequent decline.[31] Inadequate attention seems to have been given to this rather crucial question, and the present writers know of no studies that have traced the effects of participation (or other motivational devices) over periods as long as a year. However, on a priori grounds, and on the basis of experiential evidence, it would seem that, after an initial spurt, a plateau of beneficial effects will be attained, which finally will dissolve into a decline, unless additional managerial devices are skillfully employed.

## NOTES AND REFERENCES

1. For example: H. H. Carey, "Consultative Supervision and Management," *Personnel,* March 1942; Alexander R. Heron, *Why Men Work* (Palo Alto, 1948); Eric A. Nicol, "Management through Consultative Supervision," *Personnel Journal,* November 1948; James C. Worthy, "Changing Concepts of the Personnel Function," *Personnel,* November 1948.
2. For example: Douglas McGregor, "Conditions for Effective Leadership in the Industrial Situation," *Journal of Consulting Psychology* 8 (March–April, 1944); Gordon W. Allport, "The Psychology of Participation," *Psychological Review,* May 1945.
3. For the concept of the "natural experiment," see F. Stuart Chapin, *Experimental Designs in Sociological Research* (New York, 1947), and Ernest Greenwood, *Experimental Sociology* (New York, 1945).
4. For a good summary of relevant experimental work, see Ronald Lippitt, "A Program of Experimentation on Group Functioning and Productivity," *Current Trends in Social Psychology* (Pittsburgh, 1948).
5. For definitions of these terms as used here, see Robert Tannenbaum, "The Manager Concept: A Rational Synthesis," *Journal of Business,* October 1949.

6. In connection with this discussion, it should be noted that when participation takes place within the superior-subordinate relationship, managers have primary control over the nature of the activity; when it takes place as a part of the manager-union relationship, they may or may not, depending upon the relative power of the two parties.

7. See Tannenbaum, "The Manager Concept: A Rational Synthesis."

8. This discussion of the decision-making process is based upon Robert Tannenbaum, "Managerial Decision-Making," *Journal of Business,* January 1950.

9. In a democratic group, the choice can be made through a vote participated in by the rank and file. But, in such a case, the leader is organizationally responsible to the rank and file, and the members of the rank and file are not properly, insofar as the decision is concerned, subordinates of the leader.

   Members of a democratic group, making the final choice in matters directly affecting them, may be more highly motivated as a result thereof than managerial subordinates who are granted the right to participate only in the first two steps of the managerial decision-making process. For evidence of the motivational effects of group decision, see Kurt Lewin, "Group Decision and Social Change," *Readings in Social Psychology,* ed. T. M. Newcomb and E. L. Hartley (New York, 1947).

10. It is this type of participation that most writers who deal with human relations in enterprises have in mind when they use the concept. The following examples illustrate this contention: "One of the most important conditions of the subordinate's growth and development centers around his opportunities to express his ideas and to contribute his suggestions before his superiors take action on matters which involve him. Through participation of this kind he becomes more and more aware of his superiors' problems, and he obtains genuine satisfaction in knowing that his opinions and ideas are given consideration in the search for solutions" (D. McGregor, "Conditions for Effective Leadership in the Industrial Situation," p. 60); "I am not suggesting that we take over intact the apparatus of the democratic state. Business cannot be run by the ballot box. . . . We must develop other inventions, adapted to the special circumstances of business, which will give employees at all levels of our organizations a greater sense of personal participation and 'belonging' " (J. Worthy, "Changing Concepts of the Personnel Function," p. 175); "Action initiated by the responsible head to bring his subordinates into the picture on matters of mutual concern is not a sharing of prerogatives of authority. Rather, it is an extension of the opportunity of participation in the development of points of view and the assembly of facts upon which decisions are made" (H. Carey, "Consultative Supervision and Management," p. 288).

11. The concept of interaction as used here is not restricted to direct person-to-person, two-way communication (as in the process of superior-subordinate discussion), but encompasses more indirect forms (such as, for example, written communication) as well.

12. It may be observed that participation in the latter way, where there is communication between participators and where the act of participation

is carried out through the medium of the group (as in cases of "group decision"), may often yield the more useful results. The level of derivable benefits may be higher than if participation had proceeded through channels in which there had been no interparticipator communication. Some factors important in this context are the following: (a) the feeling of "group belongingness" obtained by means of "action together" and (b) the role of norms, set as a result of group discussion, toward which behavior will tend to gravitate.

13. The term *cost* is here used in its highly precise form to refer to whatever must be given or sacrificed to attain an end. See "Price," *Webster's Dictionary of Synonyms*. The term *end* is broadly conceived to embrace whatever factors (monetary or nonmonetary) the managers themselves define as the formal ends of the enterprise.

14. For examples, see Lippitt, "A Program of Experimentation on Group Functioning and Productivity"; John R. P. French, Jr., Arthur Kornhauser, and Alfred Marrow, "Conflict and Cooperation in Industry," *Journal of Social Issues*, February 1946; *Productivity, Supervision and Morale*, Survey Research Center Study no. 6, Ann Arbor, 1948.

15. See, for example, Alex Bavelas, "Some Problems of Organizational Change," *Journal of Social Issues*, Summer 1948; Elliott Jacques, "Interpretive Group Discussion as a Method of Facilitating Social Change," *Human Relations*, August 1948; Lewin, "Group Decision and Social Change."

16. See, for example, L. P. Bradford and R. Lippitt, "Building a Democratic Work Group," *Personnel*, November 1945; O. H. Mowrer, "Authoritarianism vs. 'Self-Government' in the Management of Children's Aggressive (Antisocial) Reactions as a Preparation for Citizenship in a Democracy," *Journal of Social Psychology*, February 1939, pp. 121–26.

17. This concept of effective authority is expanded upon in Tannenbaum, "Managerial Decision Making."

18. These advantages will henceforth be referred to as enterprise advantages.

19. A goal is defined as a result which, when achieved, has the power to reduce the tension of the organism that has caused the organism to seek it.

20. Thus, motion in the direction of goals may be achieved not only by adding forces in the goal direction, but also by reducing forces impeding such motion. See K. Lewin, "Frontiers in Group Dynamics," *Human Relations* 1, no. 1 (1947), pp. 26–27.

21. It must be noted that participation as used in this context is only one device which may lead to additional motivation by bringing about a coincidence of formal and personal goals. For example, some other devices that under certain conditions may result in motivational increases and their derivative benefits to the enterprise are permitting personal discretion to the person to be motivated and stimulation of a sense of pride of workmanship. In the former context, managers in all enterprises must always decide the amount of discretion to permit to subordinates. Many considerations naturally underlie this decision. For present purposes, it is important to emphasize that, in many circumstances, the granting of considerable discretion may lead to substantial increases in motivation.

Several devices may be used concurrently, and the dynamics of the devices themselves are interrelated. For example, use of discretion may bring about an enhanced pride-of-workmanship feeling.

22. It must be recognized that typically goal configurations, rather than single goals, act as motivating agents.

23. For example, see A. H. Maslow, "The Authoritarian Character Structure," *Twentieth Century Psychology*, ed. P. L. Harriman (New York, 1946). For more detailed treatments, see the major works of Erich Fromm and Abram Kardiner.

24. It should be stressed that "life spaces" of individuals (that is, their conceptions of themselves in relation to the totality of a physical and psychological environment) and their readiness for action in the light of these conceptions are never static. Constant change and "restructuring" take place, making for an essentially dynamic patterning of behavior. For alternative definitions of the concept "life space," see Robert W. Leeper, *Lewin's Topological and Vector Psychology* (Eugene, 1943), p. 210.

25. For the belief that "thinking" as a solution for the industrial problem of motivation is usable more effectively on the supervisory level, but less applicable on the "lower levels" of the organizational hierarchy, see Willard Tomlison, "Review of A. R. Heron, *Why Men Work*," *Personnel Journal*, July–August, 1948, p. 122.

26. For analytical purposes, this article differentiates between conditions regarding the dynamics of participation as a psychological process and all conditions outside this psychological participation-to-motivation link. The latter category of conditions is treated under the present heading.

27. See Chester I. Barnard, *Organization and Management* (Cambridge, 1948), p. 48.

28. See McGregor, "Conditions for Effective Leadership in the Industrial Situation," passim.

29. For a rigorous mathematical treatment of channels of communication within groups see Alex Bavelas, "A Mathematical Model for Group Structures," *Applied Anthropology*, Summer 1948, p. 16ff.

30. See French, Kornhauser, and Marrow, "Conflict and Cooperation in Industry," p. 30.

31. For evidence of no decline in the motivational effect of certain participational procedures in an industrial retraining situation after a relatively brief time period subsequent to initiation of participation had elapsed, see, for example, L. Coch and J. R. P. French, "Overcoming Resistance to Change," *Human Relations* 1, no. 4, pp. 522–23. Also Lewin, "Group Decision and Social Change," pp. 338 and 343. For the hypothesis that under certain conditions decline may occur with time, see Heron, *Why Men Work*, p. 180.

*D. Organizational Development*

# 36

# The Human Side
# of Enterprise

### Douglas M. McGregor

*In this, one of the most widely reprinted articles in the management literature, Douglas McGregor introduces the notion that under proper conditions, unimagined resources of creative human energy could become available within organizational settings. Designating the conventional view of managing as Theory X and the social science based approach as Theory Y, McGregor discusses the advantages of decentralization, job enlargement, participation, and performance appraisal.—Eds.*

It has become trite to say that industry has the fundamental know-how to utilize physical science and technology for the material benefit of mankind, and that we must now learn how to utilize the social sciences to make our human organizations truly effective.

To a degree, the social sciences today are in a position like that of the physical sciences with respect to atomic energy in the thirties. We know that past conceptions of the nature of man are inadequate and, in many ways, incorrect. We are becoming quite certain that, under proper conditions, unimagined resources of creative human energy could become available within the organizational setting.

We cannot tell industrial management how to apply this new knowledge in simple, economic ways. We know it will require years of exploration, much costly development research, and a substantial amount of creative imagination on the part of management to discover how to apply this growing knowledge to the organization of human effort in industry.

SOURCE: Reprinted by permission of the publisher from *Management Review,* November 1957, © 1957 by American Management Association, Inc.

## MANAGEMENT'S TASK: THE CONVENTIONAL VIEW

The conventional conception of management's task in harnessing human energy to organizational requirements can be stated broadly in terms of three propositions. In order to avoid the complications introduced by a label, let us call this set of propositions "Theory X":

1. Management is responsible for organizing the elements of productive enterprise—money, materials, equipment, people—in the interest of economic ends.

2. With respect to people, this is a process of directing their efforts, motivating them, controlling their actions, modifying their behavior to fit the needs of the organization.

3. Without this active intervention by management, people would be passive—even resistant—to organizational needs. They must therefore be persuaded, rewarded, punished, controlled—their activities must be directed. This is management's task. We often sum it up by saying that management consists of getting things done through other people.

Behind this conventional theory there are several additional beliefs—less explicit, but widespread:

4. The average man is by nature indolent—he works as little as possible.

5. He lacks ambition, dislikes responsibility, prefers to be led.

6. He is inherently self-centered, indifferent to organizational needs.

7. He is by nature resistant to change.

8. He is gullible, not very bright, the ready dupe of the charlatan and the demagogue.

The human side of economic enterprise today is fashioned from propositions and beliefs such as these. Conventional organization structures and managerial policies, practices, and programs reflect these assumptions.

In accomplishing its task—with these assumptions as guides—management has conceived of a range of possibilities.

At one extreme, management can be "hard" or "strong." The methods for directing behavior involve coercion and threat (usually disguised), close supervision, tight controls over behavior. At the other extreme, management can be "soft" or "weak." The methods for directing behavior involve being permissive, satisfying people's demands, achieving harmony. Then they will be tractable, accept direction.

This range has been fairly completely explored during the past half century, and management has learned some things from the exploration. There are difficulties in the "hard" approach. Force breeds counterforce: restriction of output, antagonism, militant unionism, subtle but effective sabotage of management objectives. This "hard" approach is especially difficult during times of full employment.

There are also difficulties in the "soft" approach. It leads frequently to the abdication of management—to harmony, perhaps, but to indifferent performance. People take advantage of the soft approach. They continually expect more, but they give less and less.

Currently, the popular theme is "firm but fair." This is an attempt to gain the advantages of both the hard and the soft approaches. It is reminiscent of Teddy Roosevelt's "speak softly and carry a big stick."

## IS THE CONVENTIONAL VIEW CORRECT?

The findings which are beginning to emerge from the social sciences challenge this whole set of beliefs about man and human nature and about the task of management. The evidence is far from conclusive, certainly, but it is suggestive. It comes from the laboratory, the clinic, the schoolroom, the home, and even to a limited extent from industry itself.

The social scientist does not deny that human behavior in industrial organization today is approximately what management perceives it to be. He has, in fact, observed it and studied it fairly extensively. But he is pretty sure that this behavior is *not* a consequence of man's inherent nature. It is a consequence rather of the nature of industrial organizations, of management philosophy, policy, and practice. The conventional approach of Theory X is based on mistaken notions of what is cause and what is effect.

Perhaps the best way to indicate why the conventional approach of management is inadequate is to consider the subject of motivation.

## PHYSIOLOGICAL NEEDS

Man is a wanting animal—as soon as one of his needs is satisfied, another appears in its place. This process is unending. It continues from birth to death.

Man's needs are organized in a series of levels—a hierarchy of importance. At the lowest level, but preeminent in importance when they are thwarted, are his *physiological needs*. Man lives for bread alone, when there is no bread. Unless the circumstances are unusual, his needs for love, for status, for recognition are inoperative when his stomach has been empty for a while. But when he eats regularly and adequately, hunger ceases to be an important motivation. The same is true of the other physiological needs of man—for rest, exercise, shelter, protection from the elements.

*A satisfied need is not a motivator of behavior!* This is a fact of profound significance that is regularly ignored in the conventional approach to the management of people. Consider your own need for air: Except as you are deprived of it, it has no appreciable motivating effect upon your behavior.

## SAFETY NEEDS

When the physiological needs are reasonably satisfied, needs at the next higher level begin to dominate man's behavior—to motivate him. These are called *safety* needs. They are needs for protection against danger, threat, deprivation. Some people mistakenly refer to these as needs for security. However, unless man is in a dependent relationship where he fears arbitrary deprivation, he does not demand security. The need is for the "fairest possible break." When he is confident of this, he is more than willing to take risks. But when he feels threatened or dependent, his greatest need is for guarantees, for protection, for security.

The fact needs little emphasis that, since every industrial employee is in a dependent relationship, safety needs may assume considerable importance. Arbitrary management actions, behavior which arouses uncertainty with respect to continued employment or which reflects favoritism or discrimination, unpredictable administration of policy—these can be powerful motivators of the safety needs in the employment relationship *at every level,* from worker to vice president.

## SOCIAL NEEDS

When man's physiological needs are satisfied and he is no longer fearful about his physical welfare, his *social needs* become important motivators of his behavior—needs for belonging, for association, for acceptance by his fellows, for giving and receiving friendship and love.

Management knows today of the existence of these needs, but it often assumes quite wrongly that they represent a threat to the organization. Many studies have demonstrated that the tightly knit, cohesive work group may, under proper conditions, be far more effective than an equal number of separate individuals in achieving organizational goals.

Yet management, fearing group hostility to its own objectives, often goes to considerable lengths to control and direct human efforts in ways that are inimical to the natural "groupiness" of human beings. When man's social needs—and perhaps his safety needs, too—are thus thwarted, he behaves in ways which tend to defeat organizational objectives. He becomes resistant, antagonistic, uncooperative. But this behavior is a consequence, not a cause.

## EGO NEEDS

Above the social needs—in the sense that they do not become motivators until lower needs are reasonably satisfied—are the needs of greatest significance to management and to man himself. They are the *egoistic needs,* and they are of two kinds:

1. Those needs that relate to one's self-esteem—needs for self-confidence, for independence, for achievement, for competence, for knowledge.
2. Those needs that relate to one's reputation—needs for status, for recognition, for appreciation, for the deserved respect of one's fellows.

Unlike the lower needs, these are rarely satisfied; man seeks indefinitely for more satisfaction of these needs once they have become important to him. But they do not appear in any significant way until physiological, safety, and social needs are all reasonably satisfied.

The typical industrial organization offers few opportunities for the satisfaction of these egoistic needs to people at lower levels in the hierarchy. The conventional methods of organizing work, particularly in mass production industries, give little heed to these aspects of human motivation. If the practices of scientific management were deliberately calculated to thwart these needs, they could hardly accomplish this purpose better than they do.

## SELF-FULFILLMENT NEEDS

Finally—a capstone, as it were, on the hierarchy of man's needs—there are what we may call the *needs for self-fulfillment.* These are the needs for realizing one's own potentialities, for continued self-development, for being creative in the broadest sense of that term.

It is clear that the conditions of modern life give only limited opportunity for these relatively weak needs to obtain expression. The deprivation most people experience with respect to other lower level needs diverts their energies into the struggle to satisfy *those* needs, and the needs for self-fulfillment remain dormant.

## MANAGEMENT AND MOTIVATION

We recognize readily enough that a man suffering from a severe dietary deficiency is sick. The deprivation of physiological needs has behavioral consequences. The same is true—although less well recognized—of deprivation of higher level needs. The man whose needs for safety, association, independence, or status are thwarted is sick just as surely as the man who has rickets. And his sickness will have behavioral consequences. We will be mistaken if we attribute his resultant passivity, his hostility, his refusal to accept responsibility to his inherent "human nature." These forms of behavior are *symptoms* of illness—of deprivation of his social and egoistic needs.

The man whose lower level needs are satisfied is not motivated to satisfy those needs any longer. For practical purposes they exist no longer. Management often asks, "Why aren't people more productive? We pay good wages, provide good working conditions, have excellent fringe benefits and steady employment. Yet people do not seem to be willing to put forth more than minimum effort."

The fact that management has provided for these physiological and safety needs has shifted the motivational emphasis to the social and perhaps to the egoistic needs. Unless there are opportunities *at work* to satisfy these higher level needs, people will be deprived; and their behavior will reflect this deprivation. Under such conditions, if management continues to focus its attention on physiological needs, its efforts are bound to be ineffective.

People *will* make insistent demands for more money under these conditions. It becomes more important than ever to buy the material goods and services which can provide limited satisfaction of the thwarted needs. Although money has only limited value in satisfying many higher level needs, it can become the focus of interest if it is the *only* means available.

## THE CARROT-AND-STICK APPROACH

The carrot-and-stick theory of motivation (like Newtonian physical theory) works reasonably well under certain circumstances. The *means* for satisfying man's physiological and (within limits) his safety needs can be provided or withheld by management. Employment itself is such a means, and so are wages, working conditions, and benefits. By these means the individual can be controlled so long as he is struggling for subsistence.

But the carrot-and-stick theory does not work at all once man has reached an adequate subsistence level and is motivated primarily by higher needs. Management cannot provide a man with self-respect, or with the respect of his fellows, or with the satisfaction of needs for self-fulfillment. It can create such conditions that he is encouraged and enabled to seek such satisfactions for *himself*, or it can thwart him by failing to create those conditions.

But this creation of conditions is not "control." It is not a good device for directing behavior. And so management finds itself in an odd position. The high standard of living created by our modern technological know-how provides quite adequately for the satisfaction of physiological and safety needs. The only significant exception is where management practices have not created confidence in a "fair break"—and thus where safety needs are thwarted. But by making possible the satisfaction of low level needs, management has deprived itself of the ability to use as motivators the devices on which conventional theory has taught it to rely—rewards, promises, incentives, or threats and other coercive devices.

The philosophy of management by direction and control—*regardless of whether it is hard or soft*—is inadequate to motivate because the human needs on which this approach relies are today unimportant motivators of behavior. Direction and control are essentially useless in motivating people whose important needs are social and egoistic. Both the hard and the soft approach fail today because they are simply irrelevant to the situation.

People, deprived of opportunities to satisfy at work the needs which are now important to them, behave exactly as we might predict—with indolence, passivity, resistance to change, lack of responsibility, willingness to follow the demagogue, unreasonable demands for economic benefits. It would seem that we are caught in a web of our own weaving.

## A NEW THEORY OF MANAGEMENT

For these and many other reasons, we require a different theory of the task of managing people based on more adequate assumptions about human nature and human motivation. I am going to be so bold as to suggest the broad dimensions of such a theory. Call it "Theory Y," if you will.

1. Management is responsible for organizing the elements of productive enterprise—money, materials, equipment, people—in the interest of economic ends.

2. People are *not* by nature passive or resistant to organizational needs. They have become so as a result of experience in organizations.

3. The motivation, the potential for development, the capacity for assuming responsibility, the readiness to direct behavior toward organizational goals are all present in people. Management does not put them there. It is a responsibility of management to make it possible for people to recognize and develop these human characteristics for themselves.

4. The essential task of management is to arrange organizational conditions and methods of operation so that people can achieve their own goals *best* by directing *their own* efforts toward organizational objectives.

This is a process primarily of creating opportunities, releasing potential, removing obstacles, encouraging growth, providing guidance. It is what Peter Drucker has called "management by objectives" in contrast to "management by control." It does *not* involve the abdication of management, the absence of leadership, the lowering of standards, or the other characteristics usually associated with the "soft" approach under Theory X.

## SOME DIFFICULTIES

It is no more possible to create an organization today which will be a full, effective application of this theory than it was to build an atomic power plant in 1945. There are many formidable obstacles to overcome.

The conditions imposed by conventional organization theory and by the approach of scientific management for the past half century have tied men to limited jobs which do not utilize their capabilities, have discouraged the acceptance of responsibility, have encouraged passivity, have eliminated meaning from work. Man's habits, attitudes, expectations—his whole conception of membership in an industrial organization—have been conditioned by his experience under these circumstances.

People today are accustomed to being directed, manipulated, controlled in industrial organizations and to finding satisfaction for their social, egoistic, and self-fulfillment needs away from the job. This is true of much of management as well as of workers. Genuine "industrial citizenship"—to borrow again a term from Drucker—is a remote and unrealistic idea, the meaning of which has not even been considered by most members of industrial organizations.

Another way of saying this is that Theory X places exclusive reliance upon external control of human behavior, while Theory Y relies heavily on self-control and self-direction. It is worth noting that this difference is the difference between treating people as children and treating them as mature adults. After generations of the former, we cannot expect to shift to the latter overnight.

## STEPS IN THE RIGHT DIRECTION

Before we are overwhelmed by the obstacles, let us remember that the application of theory is always slow. Progress is usually achieved in small steps. Some innovative ideas which are entirely consistent with Theory Y are today being applied with some success.

## Decentralization and Delegation

These are ways of freeing people from the too-close control of conventional organization, giving them a degree of freedom to direct their own activities, to assume responsibility, and, importantly, to satisfy their egoistic needs. In this connection, the flat organization of Sears, Roebuck and Company provides an interesting example. It forces "management by objectives," since it enlarges the number of people reporting to a manager until he cannot direct and control them in the conventional manner.

## Job Enlargement

This concept, pioneered by IBM and Detroit Edison, is quite consistent with Theory Y. It encourages the acceptance of responsibility at the bottom of the organization; it provides opportunities for satisfying social and egoistic needs. In fact, the reorganization of work at the factory level offers one of the more challenging opportunities for innovation consistent with Theory Y.

## Participation and Consultative Management

Under proper conditions, participation and consultative management provide encouragement to people to direct their creative energies toward organizational objectives, give them some voice in decisions that affect them, provide significant opportunities for the satisfaction of social and egoistic needs. The Scanlon Plan is the outstanding embodiment of these ideas in practice.

## Performance Appraisal

Even a cursory examination of conventional programs of performance appraisal within the ranks of management will reveal how completely consistent they are with Theory X. In fact, most such programs tend to treat the individual as though he were a product under inspection on the assembly line.

A few companies—among them General Mills, Ansul Chemical, and General Electric—have been experimenting with approaches which involve the individual in setting "targets" or objectives *for himself* and in a *self*-evaluation of performance semiannually or annually. Of course, the superior plays an important leadership role in this process—one, in fact, which demands substantially more competence than the conventional approach. The role is, however, considerably more congenial to many managers than the role of "judge" or "inspector" which is usually forced upon them. Above all, the individual is encouraged to take a greater responsibility for planning and appraising his own contribution to organizational objectives; and the accompanying effects on egoistic and self-fulfillment needs are substantial.

## APPLYING THE IDEAS

The not infrequent failure of such ideas as these to work as well as expected is often attributable to the fact that a management has "bought the idea" but applied it within the framework of Theory X and its assumptions.

Delegation is not an effective way of exercising management by control. Participation becomes a farce when it is applied as a sales gimmick or a device for kidding people into thinking they are important. Only the management that has confidence in human capacities and is itself directed toward organizational objectives rather than toward the preservation of personal power can grasp the implications of this emerging theory. Such management will find and apply successfully other innovative ideas as we move slowly toward the full implementation of a theory like Y.

## THE HUMAN SIDE OF ENTERPRISE

It is quite possible for us to realize substantial improvements in the effectiveness of industrial organizations during the next decade or two. The social sciences can contribute much to such developments; we are only beginning to grasp the implications of the growing body of knowledge in these fields. But if this conviction is to become a reality instead of a pious hope, we will need to view the process much as we view the process of releasing the energy of the atom for constructive human ends—as a slow, costly, sometimes discouraging approach toward a goal which would seem to many to be quite unrealistic.

The ingenuity and the perseverance of industrial management in the pursuit of economic ends have changed many scientific and technological dreams into commonplace realities. It is now becoming clear that the application of these same talents to the human side of enterprise will not only enhance substantially these materialistic achievements, but will bring us one step closer to "the good society."

# 37

# Organization Development: Objectives, Assumptions, and Strategies

## Wendell French

*In a concise overview of organizational development, the author defines what it is, identifies OD program objectives and basic assumptions, and discusses "action research models," a frequently used strategy in organization development programs.—Eds.*

Organization development refers to a long-range effort to improve an organization's problem solving capabilities and its ability to cope with changes in its external environment with the help of external or internal behavioral-scientist consultants, or change agents, as they are sometimes called. Such efforts are relatively new but are becoming increasingly visible within the United States, England, Japan, Holland, Norway, Sweden, and perhaps in other countries. A few of the growing number of organizations which have embarked on organization development (OD) efforts to some degree are Union Carbide, Esso, TRW Systems, Humble Oil, Weyerhaeuser, and Imperial Chemical Industries Limited. Other kinds of institutions, including public school systems, churches, and hospitals, have also become involved.

Organization development activities appear to have originated about 1957 as an attempt to apply some of the values and insights of laboratory training to total organizations. The late Douglas McGregor, working with Union Carbide, is considered to have been one of the first behavioral scientists to talk systematically about and to implement an organization development program.[1] Other names associated with such early efforts are Herbert Shepard and Robert Blake who, in col-

---

SOURCE: Reprinted from *California Management Review* 12, no. 2, pp. 23–46, by permission of the Regents; © 1969, by The Regents of the University of California.

laboration with the Employee Relations Department of the Esso Company, launched a program of laboratory training (sensitivity training) in the company's various refineries. This program emerged in 1957 after a headquarters human relations research division began to view itself as an internal consulting group offering services to field managers rather than as a research group developing reports for top management.[2]

## OBJECTIVES OF TYPICAL OD PROGRAMS

Although the specific interpersonal and task objectives of organization development programs will vary according to each diagnosis of organization problems, a number of objectives typically emerge. These objectives reflect problems which are very common in organizations:

1. To increase the level of trust and support among organization members.
2. To increase the incidence of confrontation of organization problems, both within groups and among groups, in contrast to "sweeping problems under the rug."
3. To create an environment in which authority of assigned role is augmented by authority based on knowledge and skill.
4. To increase the openness of communications laterally, vertically, and diagonally.
5. To increase the level of personal enthusiasm and satisfaction in the organization.
6. To find synergistic solutions[3] to problems with greater frequency. (Synergistic solutions are creative solutions in which 2 + 2 equals more than 4, and through which all parties gain more through cooperation than through conflict.)
7. To increase the level of self and group responsibility in planning and implementation.[4]

## DIFFICULTIES IN CATEGORIZING

Before describing some of the basic assumptions and strategies of organization development, it would be well to point out that one of the difficulties in writing about such a "movement" is that a wide variety of activities can be and are subsumed under this label. These activities have varied all the way from inappropriate application of some "canned" management development program to highly responsible and skillful joint efforts between behavioral scientists and client systems.

Thus, while labels are useful, they may gloss over a wide range of phenomena. The "human relations movement," for example, has been widely written about as though it were all bad or all good. To illustrate, some of the critics of the movement have accused it of being "soft" and a "hand-maiden of the Establishment," of ignoring the technical and power systems of organizations, and of being too naively participative. Such criticisms were no doubt warranted in some circumstances, but in other situations may not have been at all appropriate. Paradoxically, some of the major insights of the human relations movement, e.g., that the organization can be viewed as a social system and that subordinates have substantial control over productivity have been assimilated by its critics.

In short, the problem is to distinguish between appropriate and inappropriate programs, between effectiveness and ineffectiveness, and between relevancy and irrelevancy. The discussion which follows will attempt to describe the "ideal" circumstances for organization development programs, as well as to point out some pitfalls and common mistakes in organization change efforts.

## RELEVANCY TO DIFFERENT TECHNOLOGIES AND ORGANIZATION SUBUNITS

Research by Joan Woodward[5] suggests that organization development efforts *might be more relevant to certain kinds of technologies and organizational levels and perhaps to certain workforce characteristics, than to others.* For example, OD efforts may be more appropriate for an organization devoted to prototype manufacturing than for an automobile assembly plant. However, experiments in an organization like Texas Instruments suggest that some manufacturing efforts which appear to be inherently mechanistic may lend themselves to a more participative, open management style than is often assumed possible.[6]

However, assuming the constraints of a fairly narrow job structure at the rank-and-file level, organization development efforts may inherently be more productive and relevant at the managerial levels of the organization. Certainly OD efforts are most effective when they start at the top. Research and development units—particularly those involving a high degree of interdependency and joint creativity among group members—also appear to be appropriate for organization development activities, if group members are currently experiencing problems in communicating or interpersonal relationships.

## BASIC ASSUMPTIONS

Some of the basic assumptions about people which underlie organization development programs are similar to "Theory Y" assumptions[7] and will be repeated only briefly here. However some of the assumptions about groups and total systems will be treated more extensively. The following assumptions appear to underlie organization development efforts.[8]

## ABOUT PEOPLE

- Most individuals have drives toward personal growth and development, and these are most likely to be actualized in an environment which is both supportive and challenging.
- Most people desire to make, and are capable of making, a much higher level of contribution to the attainment of organization goals than most organizational environments will permit.

## ABOUT PEOPLE IN GROUPS

- Most people wish to be accepted and to interact cooperatively with at least one small reference group, and usually with more than one group, e.g., the work group, the family group.
- One of the most psychologically relevant reference groups for most people is the work group, including peers and the superior.
- Most people are capable of greatly increasing their effectiveness in helping their reference groups solve problems and in working effectively together.
- For a group to optimize its effectiveness, the formal leader cannot perform all of the leadership functions in all circumstances at all times, and all group members must assist each other with effective leadership and member behavior.

## ABOUT PEOPLE IN ORGANIZATIONAL SYSTEMS

- Organizations tend to be characterized by overlapping, interdependent work groups, and the "linking pin" function of supervisors and others needs to be understood and facilitated.[9]
- What happens in the broader organization affects the small work group and vice versa.
- What happens to one subsystem (social, technological, or administrative) will affect and be influenced by other parts of the system.
- The culture in most organizations tends to suppress the expression of feelings which people have about each other and about where they and their organizations are heading.
- Suppressed feelings adversely affect problem solving, personal growth, and job satisfaction.

- The level of interpersonal trust, support, and cooperation is much lower in most organizations than is either necessary or desirable.
- "Win-lose" strategies between people and groups, while realistic and appropriate in some situations, are not optimal in the long run to the solution of most organizational problems.
- Synergistic solutions can be achieved with a much higher frequency than is actually the case in most organizations.
- Viewing feelings as data important to the organization tends to open up many avenues for improved goal setting, leadership, communications, problem solving, intergroup collaboration, and morale.
- Improved performance stemming from organizational development efforts needs to be sustained by appropriate changes in the appraisal, compensation, training, staffing, and task-specialization subsystem—in short, in the total personnel system.

## VALUE AND BELIEF SYSTEMS OF BEHAVIORAL SCIENTIST-CHANGE AGENTS

While scientific inquiry, ideally, is value-free, the applications of science are not value-free. Applied behavioral scientist-organization development consultants tend to subscribe to a comparable set of values, although we should avoid the trap of assuming that they constitute a completely homogeneous group. They do not.

One value, to which many behavioral scientist-change agents tend to give high priority, is that the needs and aspirations of human beings are the reasons for organized effort in society. They tend, therefore, to be developmental in their outlook and concerned with the long-range opportunities for the personal growth of people in organizations.

A second value is that work and life can become richer and more meaningful, and organized effort more effective and enjoyable, if feelings and sentiments are permitted to be a more legitimate part of the culture. A third value is a commitment to an action role, along with a commitment to research, in an effort to improve the effectiveness of organizations.[10] A fourth value—or perhaps a belief—is that improved competency in interpersonal and intergroup relationship will result in more effective organizations.[11] A fifth value is that behavioral science research and an examination of behavioral science assumptions and values are relevant and important in considering organizational effectiveness. While many change agents are perhaps overly action-oriented in terms of the utilization of their time, nevertheless, as a group they are paying more and more attention to research and to the examination of ideas.[12]

The value placed on research and inquiry raises the question as to whether the assumptions stated earlier are values, theory, or "facts." In my judgment, a substantial body of knowledge, including research on leadership, suggests that there is considerable evidence for these assumptions. However, to conclude that these assumptions are facts, laws, or principles would be to contradict the value placed by behavioral scientists on continuous research and inquiry. Thus, I feel that they should be considered theoretical statements which are based on provisional data.

This also raises the paradox that the belief that people are important tends to result in their being important. The belief that people can grow and develop in terms of personal and organizational competency tends to produce this result. Thus, values and beliefs tend to be self-fulfilling, and the question becomes "What do you choose to want to believe?" While this position can become Pollyannaish in the sense of not seeing the real world, nevertheless, behavioral scientist-change agents, at least this one, tend to place a value on optimism. It is a kind of optimism that says people can do a better job of goal setting and facing up to and solving problems, not an optimism that says the number of problems is diminishing.

It should be added that it is important that the values and beliefs of each behavioral science-change agent be made visible both to himself and to the client. In the first place, neither can learn to adequately trust the other without exposure—a hidden agenda handicaps both trust building and mutual learning. Second, and perhaps more pragmatically, organizational change efforts tend to fail if a prescription is applied unilaterally and without proper diagnosis.

## STRATEGY IN ORGANIZATION DEVELOPMENT: AN ACTION RESEARCH MODEL

A frequent strategy in organization development programs is based on what behavioral scientists refer to as an "action research model." This model involves extensive collaboration between the consultant (whether an external or an internal change agent) and the client group, data gathering, data discussion, and planning. While descriptions of this model vary in detail and terminology from author to author, the dynamics are essentially the same.[13]

Figure 1 summarizes some of the essential phases of the action research model, using an emerging organization development program as an example. The key aspects of the model are *diagnosis, data gathering, feedback to the client group, data discussion and work by the client group, action planning,* and *action.* The sequence tends to be cyclical, with the focus on new or advanced problems as the client

**FIGURE 1**   An Action Research Model for Organization Development

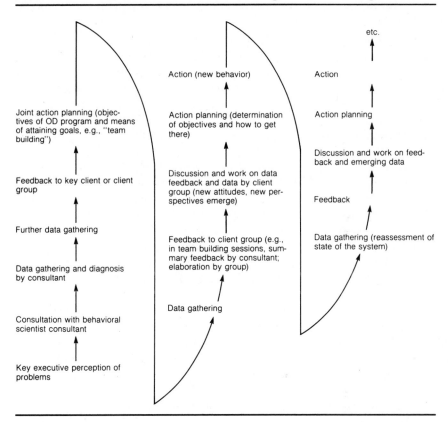

group learns to work more effectively together. Action research should also be considered a process, since, as William Foote Whyte says, it involves ". . . a continuous gathering and analysis of human relations research data and the feeding of the findings into the organization in such a manner as to change behavior."[14] (Feedback we will define as nonjudgmental observations of behavior.)

Ideally, initial objectives and strategies of organization development efforts stem from a careful diagnosis of such matters as interpersonal and intergroup problems, decision-making processes, and communication flow which are currently being experienced by the client organization. As a preliminary step, the behavioral scientist and the key client (the president of a company, the vice president in charge of a division, the works manager or superintendent of a plant, a superintendent of schools, etc.), will make a joint initial assessment of the critical problems which need working on. Subordinates may also be interviewed in order to provide supplemental data. The diagnosis may very well indicate that the central problem is technological or that the key client is not at all willing or ready to examine the organization's problem-solving ability or his own managerial behavior.[15] Either could be a reason for postponing or moving slowly in the direction of organization development activities, although the technological problem may easily be related to deficiencies in interpersonal relationships or decision making. The diagnosis might also indicate the desirability of one or more additional specialists (in engineering, finance, or electronic data processing, for example) to simultaneously work with the organization.

This initial diagnosis, which focuses on the expressed needs of the client, is extremely critical. As discussed earlier, in the absence of a skilled diagnosis, the behavioral scientist-change agent would be imposing a set of assumptions and a set of objectives which may be hopelessly out of joint with either the current problems of the people in the organization or their willingness to learn new modes of behavior. In this regard, it is extremely important that the consultant *hear and understand* what the client is trying to tell him. This requires a high order of skill.[16]

Interviews are frequently used for *data gathering* in OD work for both initial diagnosis and subsequent planning sessions, since personal contact is important for building a cooperative relationship between the consultant and the client group. The interview is also important since the behavioral scientist-consultant is interested in spontaneity and in feelings that are expressed as well as cognitive matters. However, questionnaires are sometimes successfully used in the context of what is sometimes referred to as survey feedback, to supplement interview data.[17]

Data gathering typically goes through several phases. The first phase is related to diagnosing the state of the system and to making plans for organizational change. This phase may utilize a series of interviews between the consultant and the key client, or between a few key executives and the consultant. Subsequent phases focus on problems specific to the top executive team and to subordinate teams. (See Figure 2.)

Typical questions in data gathering or "problem sensing" would include: What problems do you see in your group, including problems between people, that are interfering with getting the job done the way you would like to see it done?; and What problems do you see in the broader organization? Such open-ended questions provide wide latitude on the part of the respondents and encourage a reporting of problems *as the individual sees them.* Such interviewing is usually conducted privately, with a commitment on the part of the consultant that the

**FIGURE 2**   Organization Development Phases in a Hypothetical
Organization

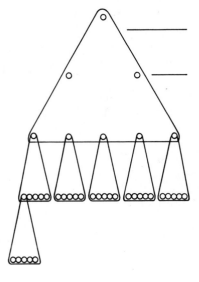

**1st phase.** Data gathering, feedback, and diagnosis—consultant and top executive only.

**2nd phase.** Data gathering, feedback, and revised diagnosis—consultant and two or more key staff or line people.

**3rd phase.** Data gathering and feedback to total top executive team in "team-building" laboratory, with or without key subordinates from level below.

**4th and additional phases.** Data gathering and team-building sessions with 2nd or 3rd level teams.

**Subsequent phases.** Data gathering, feedback, and interface problem-solving sessions across groups.

**Simultaneous phases.** Several managers may attend "stranger" T-groups; courses in the management development program may supplement this learning.

information will be used in such a way as to avoid unduly embarrassing anyone. The intent is to find out what common problems or themes emerge, with the data to be used constructively for both diagnostic and feedback purposes.

Two- or three-day offsite *team-building or group problem-solving sessions* typically become a major focal point in organization development programs. During these meetings the behavioral scientist frequently provides *feedback* to the group in terms of themes which emerged in the problem-sensing interviews.[18] He may also encourage the group to determine which items or themes should have priority in terms of maximum utilization of time. These themes usually provide substantial and meaningful data for the group to begin work on. One-to-one interpersonal matters, both positive and negative, tend to emerge spontaneously as the participants gain confidence from the level of support sensed in the group.

Different consultants will vary in their mode of behavior in such sessions, but will typically serve as *"process" observers and as interpreters of the dynamics of the group interaction* to the degree that the group expresses a readiness for such intervention. They also typically encourage people to take risks, a step at a time, and to experiment with new behavior in the context of the level of support in the group. Thus, the trainer-consultant(s) serves as a stimulant to new behavior but also as a protector. The climate which I try to build, for example is "Let's not tear down any more than we can build back together."[19] Further, the trainer-consultant typically works with the group to assist team members in improving their skills in diagnosing and facilitating group progress.[20]

It should be noted, however, that different groups will have different needs along a task-process continuum. For example, some groups have a need for intensive work on clarifying objectives; others may have the greatest need in the area of personal relationships. Further, the consultant or the chief consultant in a team of consultants involved in an organization development program will play a much broader role than serving as a T-Group or team-building trainer. He will also play an important role in periodic data gathering and diagnosis and in joint long-range planning of the change efforts.[21]

## LABORATORY TRAINING AND ORGANIZATION DEVELOPMENT

Since organization development programs have largely emerged from T-Group experience, theory, and research, and since laboratory training in one form or another tends to be an integral part of most such programs, it is important to focus on laboratory training per se. As stated earlier, OD programs grew out of a perceived need to relate laboratory training to the problems of on-going organizations and a recognition that optimum results could only occur if major parts of the total social system of an organization were involved.

Laboratory training essentially emerged around 1946, largely through a growing recognition by Leland Bradford, Ronald Lippitt, Kenneth Benne, and others, that human relations training which focused on the feelings and concerns of the participants was frequently a much more powerful and viable form of education than the lecture method. Some of the theoretical constructs and insights from which these laboratory training pioneers drew stemmed from earlier research by Lippitt, Kurt Lewin, and Ralph White. The term "T-Group" emerged by 1949 as a shortened label for "Basic Skill Training Group." These terms were used to identify the programs which began to emerge in the newly formed National Training Laboratory in Group Development (now NTL Institute for Applied Behavioral Science).[22] "Sensitivity Training" is also a term frequently applied to such training.

Ordinarily, laboratory training sessions have certain objectives in common. The following list, by two internationally known behavioral scientists,[23] is probably highly consistent with the objectives of most programs:

## SELF-OBJECTIVES

- Increased *awareness* of own feelings and reactions, and own impact on others.
- Increased *awareness* of feelings and reactions of others, and their impact on self.
- Increased *awareness* of dynamics of group action.
- *Changed attitudes* toward self, others, and groups, i.e., more respect for, tolerance for, and faith in self, others, and groups.
- Increased *interpersonal competence,* i.e., skill in handling interpersonal and group relationships toward more productive and satisfying relationships.

## ROLE OBJECTIVES

- Increased *awareness* of own organizational role, organizational dynamics, dynamics of larger social systems, and dynamics of the change process in self, small groups, and organizations.
- *Changed attitudes* toward own role, role of others, and organizational relationships, i.e., more respect for and willingness to deal with others with whom one is interdependent, greater willingness to achieve collaborative relationships with others based on mutual trust.
- Increased *interpersonal competence* in handling organizational role relationships with superiors, peers, and subordinates.

## ORGANIZATIONAL OBJECTIVES

- Increased *awareness* of, *changed attitudes* toward, and increased *interpersonal competence* about specific organizational problems existing in groups or units which are interdependent.
- *Organizational improvement* through the training of relationships of groups rather than isolated individuals.

Over the years, experimentation with different laboratory designs has led to diverse criteria for the selection of laboratory participants. Probably a majority of NTL-IABS human relations laboratories are "stranger groups," i.e., involving participants who come from different organizations and who are not likely to have met earlier. However, as indicated by the organizational objectives above, the incidence of special labs designed to increase the effectiveness of persons already working together appears to be growing. Thus terms like "cousin labs," i.e., labs involving people from the same organization but not the same subunit, and "family labs" or "team-building" sessions, i.e., involving a manager and all of his subordinates, are becoming familiar. Participants in labs designed for organizational members not of the same unit may be selected so as to constitute a heterogeneous grouping by rank ("diagonal slice"). Further, NTL-IABS is now encouraging at least two members from the same organization to attend NTL Management Work Conferences and Key Executive Conferences in order to maximize the impact of the learning in the backhome situation.[24]

In general, experienced trainers recommend that persons with severe emotional illness should not participate in laboratory training, with the exception of programs designed specifically for group therapy. Designers of programs make the assumptions, as Argyris states them,[25] that T-Group participants should have:

1. A relatively strong ego that is not overwhelmed by internal conflicts.
2. Defenses which are sufficiently low to allow the individual to hear what others say to him.
3. The ability to communicate thought and feelings with minimal distortions.

As a result of such screening, the incidence of breakdown during laboratory training is substantially less than that reported for organizations in general.[26] However, since the borderline between "normalcy" and illness is very indistinct, most professionally trained staff members are equipped to diagnose severe problems and to make referrals to psychiatrists and clinical psychologists when appropriate. Further, most are equipped to give adequate support and protection to participants whose ability to assimilate and learn from feedback is low. In addition, group members in T-Group situations tend to be sensitive to the emotional needs of the members and to be supportive when they sense a person experiencing pain. Such support is explicitly fostered in laboratory training.

The duration of laboratory training programs varies widely. "Micro-Labs," designed to give people a brief experience with sensitivity training, may last only one hour. Some labs are designed for a long weekend. Typically, however, basic human relations labs are of two weeks-duration, with participants expected to meet mornings, afternoons, and evenings, with some time off for recreation. While NTL Management Work Conferences for middle managers and Key Executive Conferences run for one week, team-building labs, from my experience, typically are about three days in length. However, the latter are usually only a part of a broader organization development program involving problem sensing and diagnosis, and the planning of action steps and subsequent sessions. In addition, attendance at stranger labs for key managers is frequently a part of the total organization development effort.

Sensitivity training sessions typically start with the trainer making a few comments about his role—that he is there to be of help, that the group will have control of the agenda, that he will deliberately avoid a leadership role, but that he might become involved as both a leader and a member from time to time, etc. The following is an example of what the trainer might say:

> This group will meet for many hours and will serve as a kind of laboratory where each individual can increase his understanding of the forces which influence individual behavior and the performance of groups and organizations. The data for learning will be our own behavior, feelings, and reactions. We begin with no definite structure or organization, no agreed-upon procedures, and no specific agenda. It will be up to us to fill the vacuum created by the lack of these familiar elements and to study our group as we evolve. My role will be to help the group to learn from its own experience, but not to act as a traditional chairman nor to suggest how we should organize, what our procedure should be, or exactly what our agenda will include. With these few comments, I think we are ready to begin in whatever way you feel will be most helpful.[27]

The trainer then lapses into silence. Group discomfort then precipitates a dialogue which, with skilled trainer assistance, is typically an intense but generally highly rewarding experience for group members. What goes on in the group becomes the data for the learning experience.

Interventions by the trainer will vary greatly depending upon the purpose of the lab and the state of learning on the part of the participants. A common intervention, however, is to encourage people to focus on and own up to their own feelings about what is going on in the group, rather than to make judgments about others. In this way, the participants begin to have more insight into their own feelings and to understand how their behavior affects the feelings of others.

While T-Group work tends to be the focal point in human relations laboratories, laboratory training typically includes theory sessions and frequently includes exercises such as role playing or management games.[28] Further, family labs of subunits of organizations will ordinarily devote more time to planning action steps for back on the job than will stranger labs.

Robert J. House has carefully reviewed the research literature on the impact of T-Group training and has concluded that the research shows mixed results. In particular, research on changes as reflected in personality inventories is seen as inconclusive. However, studies which examine the behavior of participants upon returning to the job are generally more positive.[29] House cites six studies, all of which utilized control groups, and concludes:

> All six studies revealed what appear to be important positive effects of T-Group training. Two of the studies report negative effects as well . . . all of the evidence is based on observations of the behavior of the participants in the actual job situations. No reliance is placed on participant response; rather, evidence is collected in his normal work activities.[30]

John P. Campbell and Marvin D. Dunnette,[31] on the other hand, while conceding that the research shows that T-Group training produces *changes in behavior,* point out that the usefulness of such training in terms of *job performance* has yet to be demonstrated. They urge research toward "forging the link between training-induced behavior changes and changes in job-performance effectiveness."[32] As a summary comment they state:

> the assumption that T-Group training has positive utility for organizations must necessarily rest on shaky ground. It has been neither confirmed nor disconfirmed. The authors wish to emphasize . . . that utility for the organization is not necessarily the same as utility for the individual.[33]

At least two major reasons may account for the inconclusiveness of research on the impact of T-Group training on job performance. One reason is simply that little research has been done. The other reason may center around a factor of cultural isolation. To oversimplify, a major part of what one learns in laboratory training, in my opinion, is how to work more effectively with others in group situations, *particularly with others who have developed comparable skills.* Unfortunately, most participants return from T-Group experiences to environments including colleagues and superiors who have not had the same affective (emotional, feeling) experiences, who are not familiar with the terminology and underlying theory, and who may have anxieties (usually unwarranted) about what might happen to them in a T-Group situation.

This cultural distance which laboratory training can produce is one of the reasons why many behavioral scientists are currently encouraging more than one person from the same organization to undergo T-Group training and, ideally, all of the members of a team and their superior to participate in some kind of laboratory training together. The latter assumes that a diagnosis of the organization indicates that the group is ready for such training and assumes such training is reasonably compatible with the broader culture of the total system.

## CONDITIONS AND TECHNIQUES FOR SUCCESSFUL ORGANIZATION DEVELOPMENT PROGRAMS

Theory, research, and experience to date suggest to me that *successful* OD programs tend to evolve in the following way and that they have some of these characteristics (these statements should be considered highly tentative, however):

- There is a strong pressure for improvement from both outside the organization and from within.[34]

- An outside behavioral scientist-consultant is brought in for consultation with the top executives and to diagnose organizational problems.

- A preliminary diagnosis suggests that organization development efforts, designed in response to the expressed needs of the key executives, are warranted.

- A collaborative decision is made between the key client group and the consultant to try to change the culture of the organization, at least at the top initially. The specific goals may be to improve communications, to secure more effective participation from subordinates in problem solving, and to move in the direction of more openness, more feedback, and more support. In short, a decision is made to change the culture to help the company meet its organizational goals and to provide better avenues for initiative, creativity, and self-actualization on the part of organization members.

- Two or more top executives, including the chief executive, go to laboratory training sessions. (Frequently, attendance at labs is one of the facts which precipitates interest in bringing in the outside consultant.)

- Attendance in T-Group program is voluntary. While it is difficult to draw a line between persuasion and coercion, OD consultants and top management should be aware of the dysfunctional consequences of coercion (see the comments on authentic behavior below). While a major emphasis is on team-building laboratories, stranger labs are utilized both to supplement the training going on in the organization and to train managers new to the organization or those who are newly promoted.

- Team-building sessions are held with the top executive group (or at the highest point where the program is started). Ideally, the program is started at the top of the organization, but it can start at levels below the president as long as there is significant support from the chief executive, and preferably from other members of the top power structure as well.

- In a firm large enough to have a personnel executive, the personnel-industrial relations vice president becomes heavily involved at the outset.

- One of two organizational forms emerges to coordinate organization development efforts, either (a) a coordinator reporting to the personnel executive (the personnel executive himself may fill this role), or (b) a coordinator reporting to the chief executive. The management development director is frequently in an ideal position to coordinate OD activities with other management development activities.

- Ultimately, it is essential that the personnel-industrial relations group, including people in salary administration, be an integral part of the organization development program. Since OD groups have such potential for acting as catalysts in rapid organizational change, the temptation is great to see themselves as "good guys" and the other personnel people as "bad guys" or simply ineffective. Any conflicts between a separate organization development group and the personnel and industrial relations groups should be faced and resolved. Such tensions can be the "Achilles heel" for either program. In particular, however, the change agents in the organization development program need the support of the other people who are heavily involved in human resources administration and vice versa; what is done in the OD program needs to be compatible with what is done in selection, promotion, salary administration, appraisal, and vice versa. In terms of systems theory, it would seem imperative that one aspect of the human resources function such as any organization development program must be highly interdependent with the other human resources activities including selection, salary administration, etc. (TRW Systems is an example of an organization which involves top executives plus making the total personnel and industrial relations group an integral part of the OD program.[35])

- Team-building labs, at the request of the various respective executives, with laboratory designs based on careful data gathering and problem diagnosis, are conducted at successively lower levels of the organization with the help of outside consultants, plus the help of internal consultants whose expertise is gradually developed.

- Ideally, as the program matures, both members of the personnel staff and a few line executives are trained to do some organization development work in conjunction with the external and internal professionally trained behavioral scientists. In a sense, then, the external change agent tries to work himself out of a job by developing internal resources.

- The outside consultant(s) and the internal coordinator work very carefully together and periodically check on fears, threats, and anxieties which may be developing as the effort progresses. Issues need to be confronted as they emerge. Not only is the outside change agent needed for his skills, but the organization will need someone to act as a "governor"—to keep the program focused on real problems and to urge authenticity in contrast to gamesmanship. The danger always exists that the organization will begin to punish or reward involvement in T-Group kinds of activities per se, rather than focus on performance.

- The OD consultants constantly work on their own effectiveness in interpersonal relationships and their diagnostic skills so they are not in a position of "do as I say, but not as I do." Further, both consultant and client work together to optimize the consultant's knowledge of the organization's unique and evolving culture structure, and web of interpersonal relationships.

- There needs to be continuous audit of the results, both in terms of checking on the evolution of attitudes about what is going on and in terms of the extent to which problems which were identified at the outset by the key clients are being solved through the program.

- As implied above, the reward system and other personnel systems need to be readjusted to accommodate emerging changes in performance in the organization. Substantially improved performance on the part of individuals and groups is not likely to be sustained if financial and promotional rewards are not forthcoming. In short, management needs to have a "systems" point of view and to think through the interrelationships of the OD effort with the reward and staffing systems and the other aspects of the total human resources subsystem.

In the last analysis, the president and the "line" executives of the organization will evaluate the success of the OD effort in terms of the extent to which it assists the organization in meeting its human and economic objectives. For example, marked improvements on various indices from one plant, one division, one department, etc., will be important indicators of program success. While human resources administration indices are not yet perfected, some of the measuring devices being developed by Likert, Mann, and others show some promise.[36]

## SUMMARY COMMENTS

Organization development efforts have emerged through attempts to apply laboratory training values and assumptions to total systems. Such efforts are organic in the sense that they emerge from and are guided by the problems being experienced by the people in the organization. The key to their viability (in contrast to becoming a passing fad) lies in an authentic focus on problems and concerns of the members of the organization and in their confrontation of issues and problems.

Organization development is based on assumptions and values similar to "Theory Y" assumptions and values but includes additional assumptions about total systems and the nature of the client-consultant relationship. Intervention strategies of the behavioral scientist-change agent tend to be based on an action-research model and tend to be focused more on helping the people in an organization learn to solve problems rather than on prescriptions of how things should be done differently.

Laboratory training (or "sensitivity training") or modifications of T-Group seminars typically are a part of the organizational change efforts, but the extent and format of such training will depend upon the evolving needs of the organization. Team-building seminars involving a superior and subordinates are being utilized more and more as a way of changing social systems rapidly and avoiding the cultural-distance problems which frequently emerge when individuals return from stranger labs. However, stranger labs can play a key role in change efforts when they are used as part of a broader organization development effort.

Research has indicated that sensitivity training generally produces positive results in terms of changed behavior on the job, but has not demonstrated the link between behavior changes and improved performance. Maximum benefits are probably derived from laboratory training when the organizational culture supports and reinforces the use of new skills in ongoing team situations.

Successful organization development efforts require skillful behavioral scientist interventions, a systems view, and top management support and involvement. In addition, changes stemming from organization development must be linked to changes in the total personnel subsystem. The viability of organization development efforts lies in the degree to which they accurately reflect the aspirations and concerns of the participating members.

In conclusion, *successful organization development tends to be a total system effort; a process of planned change—not a program with a temporary quality; and aimed at developing the organization's internal resources for effective change in the future.*

# NOTES AND REFERENCES

This article is largely based on the . . . second edition of my *The Personnel Management Process: Human Resources Administration* (Boston: Houghton Mifflin, 1970), chap. 28.

1. Richard Beckhard, W. Warner Burke, and Fred I. Steele, "The Program for Specialists in Organization Training and Development," mimeographed, NTL Institute for Applied Behavioral Science, December 1967, p. ii; and John Paul Jones, "What's Wrong With Work?" in *What's Wrong with Work?* (New York: National Association of Manufacturers, 1967), p. 8. For a history of NTL Institute for Applied Behavioral Science, with which Douglas McGregor was long associated in addition to his professorial appointment at M.I.T. and which has been a major factor in the history of organization development, see Leland P. Bradford, "Biography of an Institution," *Journal of Applied Behavioral Science* III:2 (1967) pp. 127–43. While we will use the word "program" from time to time, ideally organization development is a "process," not just another new program of temporary quality.

2. Harry D. Kolb, Introduction to *An Action Research Program for Organization Improvement* (Ann Arbor: Foundation for Research in Human Behavior, 1960), p. i.

3. Cattell defines synergy as "the sum total of the energy which a group can command." Daniel Katz and Robert L. Kahn, *The Social Psychology of Organizations* (New York: John Wiley & Sons, 1966), p. 33.

4. For a similar statement of objectives, see "What is OD?" *NTL Institute: News and Reports from NTL Institute for Applied Behavioral Science* II (June 1968), pp. 1–2. Whether OD programs increase the overall level of authority in contrast to redistributing authority is a debatable point. My hypothesis is that both a redistribution and an overall increase occur.

5. Joan Woodward, *Industrial Organization: Theory and Practice* (London: Oxford University Press, 1965).

6. See M. Scott Myers, "Every Employee a Manager," *California Management Review* X (Spring 1968), pp. 9–20.

7. See Douglas McGregor, *The Human Side of Enterprise* (New York: McGraw-Hill, 1960), pp. 47–48.

8. In addition to influence from the writings of McGregor, Likert, Argyris, and others, this discussion has been influenced by "Some Assumptions About Change in Organizations," in notebook "Program for Specialists in Organization Training and Development," NTL Institute for Applied Behavioral Science, 1967; and by staff members who participated in that program.

9. For a discussion of the "linking pin" concept, see Rensis Likert, *New Patterns of Management* (New York: McGraw-Hill, 1961).

10. Warren G. Bennis sees three major approaches to planned organizational change, with the behavioral scientists associated with each all having "a deep concern with applying social science knowledge to create more viable social systems; a commitment to action, as well as to research . . . and a belief that improved interpersonal and group relationships will ultimately lead to better organizational performance." Bennis, "A New Role for the

Behavioral Sciences: Effecting Organizational Change," *Administrative Science Quarterly* VIII (September 1963), pp. 157–58; and Herbert A. Shepard, "An Action Research Model," in *An Action Research Program for Organization Improvement,* pp. 31–35.

11. Bennis, "A New Role for the Behavioral Sciences," p. 158.

12. For a discussion of some of the problems and dilemmas in behavioral science research, see Chris Argyris, "Creating Effective Relationships in Organizations," in Richard N. Adams and Jack J. Preiss, eds., *Human Organization Research* (Homewood, Ill.: Dorsey Press, 1960), pp. 109–23; and Barbara A. Benedict. et al., "The Clinical Experimental Approach to Assessing Organizational Change Efforts," *Journal of Applied Behavioral Science,* (November 1967), pp. 347–80.

13. For further discussion of action research, see Edgar H. Schein and Warren G. Bennis, *Personal and Organizational Change Through Group Methods* (New York: John Wiley & Sons, 1966), pp. 272–74.

14. William Foote Whyte and Edith Lentz Hamilton, *Action Research for Management* (Homewood, Ill.: Richard D. Irwin, 1964), p. 2.

15. Jeremiah J. O'Connell appropriately challenges the notion that there is "one best way" of organizational change and stresses that the consultant should choose his role and intervention strategies on the basis of "the conditions existing when he enters the client system" (*Managing Organization Innovation* [Homewood, Ill.: Richard D. Irwin, 1968], pp. 10–11).

16. For further discussion of organization diagnosis, see Richard Beckhard, "An Organization Improvement Program in a Decentralized Organization," *Journal of Applied Behavioral Science* 1 (January–March 1966), pp. 3–4; "OD as a Process," in *What's Wrong with Work?,* pp. 12–13.

17. For example, see Floyd C. Mann, "Studying and Creating Change," in Timothy W. Costello and Sheldon S. Zalkind, eds., *Psychology in Administration—A Research Orientation* (Englewood Cliffs: Prentice-Hall, 1963), pp. 321–24. See also Delbert C. Miller, "Using Behavioral Science to Solve Organization Problems," *Personnel Administration* XXXI (January–February 1968), pp. 21–29.

18. For a description of feedback procedures used by the Survey Research Center, University of Michigan, see Mann and Likert, "The Need for Research on the Communication of Research Results," in *Human Organization Research,* pp. 57–66.

19. This phrase probably came from a management workshop sponsored by NTL Institute for Applied Behavioral Science.

20. For a description of what goes on in team-building sessions, see Beckhard, "An Organizational Improvement Program," pp. 9–13; and Newton Margulies and Anthony P. Raia, "People in Organizations—A Case for Team Training," *Training and Development Journal* XXII (August 1968), pp. 2–11. For a description of problem-solving sessions involving the total management group (about 70) of a company, see Beckhard, "The Confrontation Meeting," *Harvard Business Review* XLV (March–April 1967), pp. 149–55.

21. For a description of actual organization development programs, see Paul C. Buchanan, "Innovative Organizations—A Study in Organization Development," in *Applying Behavioral Science Research in Industry* (New

York: Industrial Relations Counselors, 1964), pp. 87–107; Sheldon A. Davis, "An Organic Problem-Solving Method of Organizational Change," *Journal of Applied Behavioral Science* III:1 (1967), pp. 3–21; Cyril Sofer, *The Organization from Within* (Chicago: Quadrangle Books, 1961); Alfred J. Marrow, David G. Bowers, and Stanley E. Seashore, *Management by Participation* (New York: Harper & Row, 1967); Robert R. Blake, Jane S. Mouton, Louis B. Barnes, and Larry E. Greiner, "Breakthrough in Organization Development." *Harvard Business Review* XLII (November–December 1964), pp. 133–55; Alton C. Bartlett, "Changing Behavior as a Means to Increased Efficiency," *Journal of Applied Behavioral Science* III:3 (1967), pp. 381–403; Larry E. Greiner, "Antecedents of Planned Organization Change," *ibid.*, III:1 (1967), pp. 51–85; and Robert R. Blake and Jane Mouton, *Corporate Excellence through Grid Organization Development* (Houston, Texas: Gulf Publishing Company, 1968).

22. From Bradford, "Biography of an Institution." See also Kenneth D. Benne, "History of the T-Group in the Laboratory Setting," in Bradford, Jack R. Gibb, and Benne, eds., *T/Group Theory and Laboratory Method* (New York: John Wiley & Sons, 1964), pp. 80–135.

23. Schein and Bennis, p. 37.

24. For further discussion of group composition in laboratory training, see Schein and Bennis, pp. 63–69. NTL-LABS now include the Center for Organization Studies, the Center for the Development of Educational Leadership, the Center for Community Affairs, and the Center for International Training to serve a wide range of client populations and groups.

25. Chris Argyris, "T-Groups for Organizational Effectiveness," *Harvard Business Review* XLII (March–April 1964), pp. 60–74.

26. Based on discussions with NTL staff members. One estimate is that the incidence of "serious stress and mental disturbance" during laboratory training is less than one percent of participants and in almost all cases occurs in persons with a history of prior disturbance (Charles Seashore, "What is Sensitivity Training," *NTL Institute News and Reports* II [April 1968], p. 2).

27. Ibid., p. 1.

28. For a description of what goes on in T-groups, see Schein and Bennis, pp. 10–27; Bradford, Gibb, and Benne, pp. 55–67; Dorothy S. Whitaker, "A Case Study of a T-Group," in Galvin Witaker, ed., *T-Group Training: Group Dynamics in Management Education*, A.T.M. Occasional Papers, (Oxford: Basil Blackwell, 1965), pp. 14–22; Irving R. Weschler and Jerome Reisel, *Inside a Sensitivity Training Group* (Berkeley: University of California, Institute of Industrial Relations, 1959); and William F. Glueck, "Reflections on a T-Group Experience," *Personnel Journal*, XLVII (July 1968), pp. 501–504. For use of cases or exercises based on research results ("instrumented training") see Robert R. Blake and Jane S. Mouton, "The Instrumented Training Laboratory," in Irving R. Weschler and Edgar H. Schein, eds., *Five Issues in Training* (Washington: National Training Laboratories, 1962), pp. 61–76; and W. Warner Burke and Harvey A. Hornstein, "Conceptual vs. Experimental Management Training," *Training and Development Journal* XXI (Dec. 1967), pp. 12–17.

29. Robert J. House, "T-Group Education and Leadership Effectiveness: A Review of the Empiric Literature and a Critical Evaluation." *Personnel Psychology* XX (Spring 1967), pp. 1–32. See also Dorothy Stock, "A Survey of Research on T-Groups," in Bradford, Gibb, and Benne, pp. 395–441.
30. House, *ibid.*, pp. 18–19.
31. John P. Campbell and Marvin D. Dunnette, "Effectiveness of T-Group Experiences in Managerial Training and Development," *Psychological Bulletin*, LXX (August 1968), pp. 73–104.
32. Ibid., p. 100.
33. Ibid., p. 101. See also the essays by Dunnette and Campbell and Chris Argyris in *Industrial Relations* VIII (October 1968), pp. 1–45.
34. On this point, see Larry E. Greiner, "Patterns of Organization Change," *Harvard Business Review* XLV (May–June 1967), pp. 119–30.
35. See Sheldon A. Davis, "An Organic Problem-Solving Method."
36. See Rensis Likert, *The Human Organization: Its Management and Value* (New York: McGraw-Hill, 1967).

# 38

## Criteria of Organizational Effectiveness

### Stanley E. Seashore

*An important objective of organization development is to improve organizational effectiveness. In this article, Seashore argues that achieving effectiveness requires taking into consideration the multiple, conflicting, and changing goals of organizations. A framework is proposed for conceptualizing organizational performance.—Eds.*

## MULTIPLE, CONFLICTING GOALS

The aim of the following discussion is to outline a way of viewing the relationships among the numerous criteria that might be considered in the evaluation of the performance of an organization. To understand such relationships we shall need to make some distinctions between different kinds of criterion measures. We shall need to create some encompassing conceptions that serve to aid the evaluation of performance when some desired measures are not available, or when the number of measures is inconveniently large.

The issues taken up here arise because most organizations have multiple goals rather than a single goal, and goal achievement may not be directly measurable. The formal objectives of the organization may themselves be multiple and, in any case, there are multiple short-run goals and subgoals that need to be examined. The matter would be simple if the various goals were all of similar priority and combinable in some simple additive way; but this is not the situation. The manager making decisions that rest upon multivariate assessments of the performance of his organization has to calculate the weights and

SOURCE: Reprinted by permission from the July 1965 issue of the *Michigan Business Review*, published by the Graduate School of Business Administration, The University of Michigan.

the correlation values that he will apply when estimating the net outcome of a course of action.

A typical example would be the case of a manager who wishes his firm to obtain a substantial profit, and at the same time to grow in size, to insure future profit by product improvements, to avoid financial risk, to pay a substantial annual dividend to his investors, to have satisfied employees, and to have his firm respected in the community. He cannot maximize all of these simultaneously, as increasing one (e.g., dividends or risk avoidance) may imply reduced achievement on another (e.g., growth, product research). He must consider their trade-off value, their contingencies, and the presence of negative correlations among them. To estimate an optimum course of action he has to evaluate the dependability and relevance of the various measures and then estimate the way in which they combine to provide an overall evaluation of performance or a prediction of future change in performance. This task will be easier when we have for his use a theory to describe the performance of organizations. The following suggestions are a step in that direction.

## CRITERIA AND THEIR USES

To begin with we need to make some distinctions among different kinds of criteria and their uses.

1. *Ends vs. means.* Some criteria are close to the formal objectives of the organization in the sense that they represent ends or goals that are valued in themselves; others have value mainly or only because they are thought to be necessary means or conditions for achieving the main goals of the organization. Substantial profit, for example, may be a goal sought by a business organization, while employee satisfaction may be valued because it is thought to be an aid in reaching the goal of substantial profit.

2. *Time reference.* Some criterion measures refer to a past time period (profit for the past year), others to current states (net worth), and still others to anticipated future periods (projected growth). Whatever their time reference, all may be used for drawing inferences about past or future conditions or changes.

3. *Long vs. short run.* Some criterion measures refer to a relatively short period of time, others to a longer period; they may refer to performances that are relatively stable (do not change much in the short run) or relatively unstable (erratic or highly variable in the short run). The usefulness of a criterion measure is limited if the period covered is not appropriate to the usual or potential rate of change in the variable.[1]

4. *"Hard" vs. "soft."* Some criteria are measured by the characteristics of, or number or frequency of, physical objects and events, while others are measured by qualitative observation of behavior or by evaluative questions put to people. Dollar measures, for example, or tons of scrap, or number of grievances, are "hard" measures; while employee satisfaction, motivation to work, cooperation, product quality, customer loyalty, and many others are usually "soft." *The distinction is useful, but it contains a trap,* for we commonly think of the hard variables as being in some way inherently more valid, more reliable, and more relevant to the performance evaluation problem, when this is not necessarily true. Profit rate, for example—a popular hard variable—is a rather vague concept to begin with (accountants dispute about definition and about conventions for measurement) and it is often in the short run unreliable as a performance indicator and thus quite irrelevant to the evaluation problem, even for an organization whose long-run goals include making a profit. Similarly, a soft variable, such as one representing the intentions of key executives to stay with the organization, may be measured with high reliability in some circumstances and may be vital in the assessment of the organization's performance.

5. *Values.* Some variables appear to have a linear value scale (more is always better than less), while others have a curvilinear scale (some optimum is desired; more and less are both to be avoided). The shape of the curves determines in part the trade-off relationship among assessment variables under conditions where simultaneous optimization is not possible. Examples: profit rate is usually linear in value in the sense that more is better than less; maintenance costs, by contrast, are usually curvilinear in value in the sense that either excessively high or low costs may be judged to diminish overall firm performance.

## THE HIERARCHY OF CRITERIA

A full accounting for the performance of an organization requires consideration for (1) achievement of the organization's main goals over a long span of time, (2) performance over shorter periods on each of those criteria that represent ends valued in themselves, and which, jointly, as a set, determine the net ultimate performance, and (3) performance on each of a number of subsidiary criteria that provide an immediate or current indication of the progress toward, or probability of achieving, success on end-result variables. The network of criteria of performance can be viewed as a pyramid shaped hierarchy:

1. *At the top* is the "ultimate criterion"—some conception of the net performance of the organization over a long span of time in achieving its formal objectives, whatever they may be, with optimum use of the organization's environmental resources and opportunities. The ultimate criterion is never measured (except possibly by historians); yet some concept of this kind is the basis for evaluation of lesser criteria of performance.

2. *In the middle* are the penultimate criteria. These are shorter run performance factors or dimensions comprised by the ultimate criterion. They are "output" or "results" criteria: things sought for their own value and having trade-off value[2] in relation to each other. Their sum, in some weighted mixture, determines the ultimate criterion. Typical variables of this class for business organizations are: sales volume, productive efficiency, growth rate, profit rate, and the like. There may be included some "soft" (usually behavioral) variables, such as employee satisfaction or customer satisfaction. In the case of some nonbusiness organizations these penultimate criteria might be predominantly of the behavioral kind, as in the case of a school whose output is judged in terms of learning rates, proportion of students reaching some standard of personal growth or development, etc.

3. *At the bottom* of the hierarchy of assessment criteria are measures of the current organizational functioning according to some theory or some empirical system concerning the conditions associated with high achievement on each of the penultimate criteria.[3] These variables include those descriptive of the organization as a system and also those representing subgoals or means associated with penultimate criteria. The number of criteria in this class is very large (over 200 have been used in some studies without sensing that the limits were being approached), and they are interrelated in a complex network that includes causal, interactional, and modifier types of relationships. Included are some criteria that are not valued at all except for their power to reduce the amount of uncontrolled variance in the network. Among the "hard" criteria at this level, for a business organization, might be such as: scrappage, short-run profit, productivity against standards, meeting of production schedules, machine downtime, ratio of overtime to regular time, product return rate, rate of technological innovation, and the like. Among the "soft" criteria at this level may be such as these: employee morale, credit rating, communication effectiveness, absenteeism, turnover, group cohesiveness, customer loyalty, pride in firm, level of performance motivation, and others.

## CHARACTERISTICS OF BEHAVIORAL CRITERIA

Such a model locates the behavioral criteria—those descriptive of the members (in this context, customers and clients are also "members") of the organization and of their values, attitudes, relationships, and activities—mainly in the lower regions of the network of assessment criteria, distant and perhaps only indirectly related to the ultimate goals by which the organization is eventually judged.

If behavioral criteria appear near the top of the network, it is because they are valued in themselves and have trade-off value in relation to other priority goals of the organization. In general, however, the hard—nonbehavioral—criteria are the preferred ones for most business organizations for the good reason that they are more relevant to the formal objectives of the organization.

The behavioral measures are presumed to have some stable relationships to the various nonbehavioral measures; these relationships may be causal, interactional, or merely one of covariance. It is further presumed that the criteria and their relationships are not entirely unique to each organization, nor transient, but are to some degree stable and to some extent common to all or many organizations. These presumptions appear to have some partial confirmation from analyses performed so far.[4]

We come now to the question of the role of behavioral criteria in the light of this broader conception of the evaluation of organizational performance. It appears that behavioral criteria are not likely, for most business organizations, to have a prominent place in the roster of penultimate criteria although they may and do appear there. Their chief role will arise from their power to improve the prediction of future changes in the preferred "hard" criteria, i.e., their power to give advance signals of impending problems or opportunities.

A second use that they may commonly have is to complement the available hard criteria in such a way as to give the manager a more balanced and more inclusive informational basis for his decisions in the case where the hard variable measures are incomplete or not reliable for short-run evaluation.[5]

In some rare instances, the behavioral criteria have to be used exclusively instead of the preferred hard criteria of organizational performance for the reason that measurements of hard criteria are not available at all or not at reasonable cost.

There are three basic strategies that may be applied in formulating a unique version of this general scheme that may be appropriate for a particular organization.

1. There exist several partially developed general theories concerning the survival requirements of organizations. These

assumed requirements may be defined in performance terms and posited as the roster of penultimate criteria or organizational goals. From this starting point, a set of subsidiary goals and performance criteria may be constructed on empirical grounds, on theoretical grounds, or on some combination of the two.

2. The existing personal values of the owners of a firm, or of the managers as representatives, may be pooled to form an agreed upon roster of penultimate criteria together with their corresponding performance indicators, and from this starting point the set of subsidiary goals and performance criteria can be constructed.

3. Comparative empirical study can be made of the performance characteristics of a set of organizations assumed to share the same ultimate criterion but clearly differing in their overall success as judged by competent observers (for example, such a study might be made of a set of insurance sales agencies, some clearly prospering and others clearly headed for business failure). Using factorial analysis methods and actual performance data to identify the sets of lower-order performance criteria, and using trend and correlational analyses to detect the relationships among these sets of criteria over time, one can, in principle, draw conclusions about the penultimate components of performance that bear upon organizational survival or failure in that particular line of business.

## ALTERNATIVE THEORETICAL APPROACHES

These three approaches can and do produce strikingly different systems for describing the network of criteria to be used in evaluating organizational performance. One of the general theories, for example, proposes that there are nine basic requirements to be met, or problems to be continuously solved, for an organization to achieve its long-run goals; these include such requirements as adequate input of resources, adequate normative integration, adequate means of moderation of organizational strain, adequate coordination among parts of the organization, etc. Theories of this kind are produced mainly by general organizational sociologists and stem from the view that an organization is a living system with intrinsic goals and requirements that may be unlike those of individual members. By contrast, the second mentioned approach stems from the personal values of managers. The resulting networks of criteria are different.[6]

A start has been made at the Institute for Social Research in exploring such alternative strategies. With respect to the first approach, two theoretical models have been tested against empirical data from a set of organizations in a service industry, using executive judgments of unit overall effectiveness as the ultimate criterion. Both models proved to be about equally valid, but of limited utility in explaining variance on the ultimate criterion: each "accounted for" about half of the ultimate criterion variance, with the unexplained portion arising from measurement errors and/or faulty theory. An attempt to apply the wholly empirical approach to the same set of data proved to be a failure in the sense that it was no more powerful in explaining variance on the ultimate criterion than were the simpler, theory based models, and furthermore the resulting roster of performance dimensions was not very satisfactory in common-sense terms.

A third effort is now in progress, using objective data about the performance of a set of insurance sales agencies over a span of 12 years; the early results look very promising on first examination. It appears that there will be identified a roster of about 10 penultimate criteria of agency performance, each independent of the others and of varying weight in relation to ultimate performance, and each associated with a roster of subsidiary criteria of kinds that lend themselves to ready measurement and statistical combination. It remains to be seen whether these criteria are unique to this particular line of business, or have some applicability to other kinds of organizations.

## NOTES AND REFERENCES

1. May firms' current operating and financial statistics, although appropriate for control and accounting purposes, prove to be of little value for performance evaluation for the reason that they are short-period measures of unstable performances. Monthly plant maintenance costs, for example, may be extremely variable (perhaps seasonal) and may be useful as a performance criterion measure only when applied to longer periods of time. In the short run, apart from other considerations, low maintenance costs may or may not be a favorable indicator.
2. By trade-off value we mean only that an amount of one kind of performance may be substituted for an amount of another; for example, an increase in sales volume may be judged to offset a decline in profit rate per sales unit.
3. One large U.S. firm has published what appears to be a carefully considered formulation of its own roster of assessment criteria at this penultimate level. It includes one behavioral category, "employee attitudes," which is further defined in operational terms in a manner compatible with the system outlined here.
4. See "Applying Modern Management Principles to Sales Organizations," Foundation for Research on Human Behavior seminar report, 1963, for an illustration of the similarity across three sales organizations in the relevance of behavioral measures to hard penultimate criteria of organizational performance. Also, "Models of Organization Performance," an unpublished

manuscript by Basil Georgopoulos, Stanley Seashore, and Bernard Indik; and "Relationships Among Criteria of Job Performance," by Stanley Seashore, Bernard Indik, and Basil Georgopoulos, *Journal of Applied Psychology* 44 (1960), pp. 195–202.

5. As an example, a decision to raise prices is likely to rest not only upon estimates of hard performances, past and future, but also upon estimates of political and economic climate, of customer loyalty, of the feasibility of alternatives such as employee collaboration in cost reduction, etc.

6. To illustrate, take the criterion of profit: in one case, profit is likely to be treated as one of a few penultimate criteria (ends valued in their own right), while in the other case profit is relegated to a subsidiary role as one of several alternative means for insuring adequate input of resources. If this seems implausible, note that some organizations—government, educational, and religious organizations, for example—have survived and prospered without profit from their own activities.

# 39

# How to Prevent
# Organizational Dry Rot

*John W. Gardner*

*Organizational renewal is the concern of this essay. The author proposes nine rules to follow to achieve positive renewal or development. Do not be misled by the lighter tone of this article; what it has to say is important food for thought.*—Eds.

Like people and plants, organizations have a life cycle. They have a green and supple youth, a time of flourishing strength, and a gnarled old age. We have all seen organizations that are still going through the diseases of childhood, and others so far gone in the rigidities of age that they ought to be pensioned off and sent to Florida to live out their days.

But organizations differ from people and plants in that their cycle isn't even approximately predictable. An organization may go from youth to old age in two or three decades, or it may last for centuries. More important, it may go through a period of stagnation and then revive. In short, decline is not inevitable. Organizations need not stagnate. They often do, to be sure, but that is because the arts of organizational renewal are not yet widely understood. Organizations can renew themselves continuously. That fact has far-reaching implications for our future.

We know at least some of the rules for organizational renewal. And those rules are relevant for all kinds of organizations—U.S. Steel, Yale University, the U.S. Navy, a government agency, or your local bank.

*The first rule* is that the organization must have an effective program for the recruitment and development of talent. People are the

---

SOURCE: Copyright © 1965 by Harper's Magazine.

ultimate source of renewal. The shortage of able, highly trained, highly motivated men will be a permanent feature of our kind of society; and every organization that wants its share of the short supply is going to have to get out and fight for it. The organization must have the kind of recruitment policy that will bring in a steady flow of able and highly motivated individuals. And it cannot afford to let those men go to seed, or get sidetracked or boxed in. There must be positive, constructive programs of career development. In this respect, local, state, and federal government agencies are particularly deficient, and have been so for many years. Their provisions for the recruitment and development of talent are seriously behind the times.

*The second rule* for the organization capable of continuous renewal is that it must be a hospitable environment for the individual. Organizations that have killed the spark of individuality in their members will have greatly diminished their capacity for change. Individuals who have been made to feel like cogs in the machine will behave like cogs in the machine. They will not produce ideas for change. On the contrary, they will resist such ideas when produced by others.

*The third rule* is that the organization must have built-in provisions for self-criticism. It must have an atmosphere in which uncomfortable questions can be asked. I would lay it down as a basic principle of human organization that the individuals who hold the reins of power in any enterprise cannot trust themselves to be adequately self-critical. For those in power the danger of self-deception is very great, the danger of failing to see the problems or refusing to see them is ever-present. And the only protection is to create an atmosphere in which anyone can speak up. The most enlightened top executives are well aware of this. Of course, I don't need to tell those readers who are below the loftiest level of management that even with enlightened executives a certain amount of prudence is useful. The Turks have a proverb that says, "The man who tells the truth should have one foot in the stirrup."

But it depends on the individual executive. Some welcome criticism, others don't. Louis Armstrong once said, "There are some people that if they don't know, you can't tell 'em."

*The fourth requirement* for the organization that seeks continuous renewal is fluidity of internal structure. Obviously, no complex modern organization can exist without the structural arrangements of divisions, branches, departments, and so forth. I'm not one of those who imagine that the modern world can get away from specialization. Specialization and division of labor are at the heart of modern organization. In this connection I always recall a Marx Brothers movie in which Groucho played a shyster lawyer. When a client commented on the dozens of flies buzzing around his broken-down office, Groucho said,

"We have a working agreement with them. They don't practice law and we don't climb the walls."

But jurisdictional boundaries tend to get set in concrete. Pretty soon, no solution to a problem is seriously considered if there is any danger that it will threaten jurisdictional lines. But those lines aren't sacred. They were established in some past time to achieve certain objectives. Perhaps the objectives are still valid, perhaps not. *Most organizations have a structure that was designed to solve problems that no longer exist.*

*The fifth rule* is that the organization must have an adequate system of internal communication. If I may make a rather reckless generalization, I'd say that renewal is a little like creativity in this respect—that it depends on the existence of a large number of diverse elements in a situation that permits an infinite variety of combinations and recombinations. The enormous potentialities of the human brain are in part explainable in terms of such possibilities for combination and recombination. And such recombination is facilitated by easy communication, impeded by poor communication.

*The sixth rule:* The organization must have some means of combating the process by which men become prisoners of their procedures. The rule book grows fatter as the ideas grow fewer. Thus almost every well-established organization is a coral reef of procedures that were laid down to achieve some long-forgotten objective.

It is in our nature to develop an affection for customary ways of doing things. Some years ago a wholesale firm noted that some of its small shopkeeper customers were losing money because of antiquated merchandising methods. The firm decided that it would be good business to assist the shopkeepers in bringing their methods up-to-date, but soon discovered that many had no desire to modernize. They loved the old, money-losing ways.

Sometimes the organization procedures men devise to advance their purposes serve in the long run to block those purposes. This was apparent in an experience a friend of mine had in Germany in the last days of World War II. He was in Aachen, which had only recently been occupied by the American forces, when he received a message instructing him to proceed to London immediately. He went directly to U.S. Army headquarters, and showed the message to a sergeant in the Adjutant's office.

The sergeant said that the only plane for London within the next few days was leaving from the nearest airfield in 30 minutes. He added that the airfield was 25 minutes away.

It was discouraging news. My friend knew that he could not proceed to London without written orders, and that was a process that took from an hour to a couple of days in a well-established and smoothly functioning headquarters. The present headquarters had been opened the day before, and was in a totally unorganized state.

My friend explained his dilemma to the sergeant and handed over his papers. The sergeant scratched his head and left the room. Four minutes later he returned and said, "Here are your orders, sir."

My friend said he had never been in such an efficient headquarters. The sergeant looked at him with a twinkle in his eye and said, "Sir, it's just lucky for you we weren't organized!"

*The seventh rule:* The organization capable of continuous renewal will have found some means of combating the vested interests that grow up in every human institution. We commonly associate the term "vested interests" with people of wealth and power, but in an organization vested interests exist at every level. The lowest employees have their vested interests, every foreman has his, and every department head has his. Every change threatens someone's privileges, someone's authority, someone's status. What wise managers try to do, of course, is to sell the idea that in the long run everyone's overriding vested interest is in the continuing vitality of the organization itself. If that fails, everyone loses. But it's a hard message to get across.

Nowhere can the operation of vested interests be more clearly seen than in the functioning of university departments. There are exceptions, of course: some departments rise above their vested interests. But the average department holds like grim death to its piece of intellectual terrain. It teaches its neophytes a jealous devotion to the boundaries of the field. It assesses the significance of intellectual questions by the extent to which they can be answered without going outside the sacred territory. Such vested interests effectively block most efforts to reform undergraduate instruction.

*The eighth rule* is that the organization capable of continuous renewal is interested in what it is going to become and not what it has been. When I moved to New London, Connecticut, in 1938 I was astonished at the attitude of New Londoners toward their city's future. Having grown up in California, I was accustomed to cities and towns that looked ahead habitually (often with an almost absurd optimism). I was not prepared for a city that, so far as I could discover, had no view of its future, though it had a clear view of its past.

The need to look to the future is the reason so many corporations today have research and development programs. But an organization cannot guarantee its future by ritualistic spending on research. Its research-and-development program must be an outgrowth of a philosophy of innovation that guides the company in everything it does. The research program, which is a way of looking forward, cannot thrive if the rest of the organization has the habit of looking backward.

*The ninth rule* is obvious but difficult. An organization runs on motivation, on conviction, on morale. Men have to believe that it really makes a difference whether they do well or badly. They have to care. They have to believe that their efforts as individuals will mean something for the whole organization, and will be recognized by the whole organization.

Change is always risky, usually uncomfortable, often painful. It isn't accomplished by apathetic men and women. It requires high motivation to break through the rigidities of the aging organization.

So much for the rules.

One of the ominous facts about growth and decay is that the present success of an organization does not necessarily constitute grounds for optimism. In 1909 it would have been unwise to judge the future of the Central Leather Company by the fact that it ranked seventh in the nation in total assets. It would have been a disastrous long-term investment. A better bet would have been the relatively small Ford Motor Company which had been founded only six years earlier and was about to launch its Model T. As a company it wasn't huge or powerful, but to borrow a phrase from C. P. Snow, it had the future in its bones. (Not many of 1909's top 20 companies did—only 4 of them are in the top 20 today.)

Businessmen are fond of saying that, unlike other executives, they have a clear measure of present performance—the profit-and-loss statement. But the profits of today *may* be traceable to wise decisions made a good many years earlier. And current company officers may be making bad decisions that will spell disaster ten years from now.

I have collected many examples of organizations that experienced crises as a result of their failure to renew themselves. In the great majority, certainly 9 out of 10, the trouble was not difficult to diagnose and there was ample warning of the coming catastrophe. In the case of a manufacturing concern that narrowly averted bankruptcy recently, the conditions that led to trouble were diagnosed by an outside consultant two years before the crisis came. In the case of another well-known organization, a published article outlined every essential difficulty that later led to disaster.

But if warning signals are plentiful, why doesn't the ailing organization take heed? The answer is clear: most ailing organizations have developed a functional blindness to their own defects. They are not suffering because they can't *solve* their problems but because they won't see their problems. They can look straight at their faults and rationalize them as virtues or necessities.

I was discussing these matters with a corporation president recently, and he said, "How do I know that *I* am not one of the blind ones? What do I do to find out? And if I am, what do I do about it?"

There are several ways to proceed. One way is to bring in an outside consultant who is not subject to the conditions that create functional blindness inside the organization.

A more direct approach, but one that is surrounded by subtle difficulties, is for the organization to encourage its internal critics. Every organization, no matter how far deteriorated, has a few stubbornly honest individuals who are not blinded by their own self-interest and have never quite accepted the rationalization and self-deceptions shared by others in the organization. If they are encouraged to speak up they probably will. The head of a government agency said to me recently, "The shrewdest critics of this organization are right under this roof. But it would take a major change of atmosphere to get them to talk."

A somewhat more complicated solution is to bring new blood into at least a few of the key positions in the organization. If the top level of the organization is salted with vigorous individuals too new to be familiar with all the established ways of doing and thinking, they can be a source of fresh insights for the whole organization.

Still another means of getting fresh insights is rotation of personnel between parts of the organization. Not only is the individual broadened by the experience, but he brings a fresh point of view to his new post. After a few years of working together, men are likely to get so used to one another that the stimulus of intellectual conflict drops almost to zero. A fresh combination of individuals enlivens the atmosphere.

In the last analysis, however, everything depends on the wisdom of those who shape the organization's policy. Most policy makers today understand that they must sponsor creative research. But not many of them understand that the spirit of creativity and innovation so necessary in the research program is just as essential to the rest of the organization.

The future of this nation depends on its capacity for self-renewal. And that in turn depends on the vitality of the organizations and individuals that make it up. Americans have always been exceptionally gifted at organizational innovation. In fact, some observers say that this is the true American inventiveness. Thanks to that inventiveness we now stand on the threshold of new solutions to some of the problems that have destroyed the vitality of human institutions since the beginning of time. We have already made progress in discovering how we may keep our institutions vital and creative. We could do even better if we put our minds to it.

# Index to Readings